BETTER TEACHING IN SECONDARY SCHOOLS

BETTER TEACHING IN SECONDARY SCHOOLS

THIRD EDITION

MARVIN D. ALCORN
JAMES S. KINDER
JIM R. SCHUNERT
San Diego State College

HOLT, RINEHART AND WINSTON, INC.
NEW YORK · CHICAGO · SAN FRANCISCO · ATLANTA · DALLAS
MONTREAL · TORONTO · LONDON · SYDNEY

Copyright 1954, © 1964, 1970 by Holt, Rinehart and Winston, Inc.
All rights reserved
Library of Congress Catalog Card Number: 71-88815
ISBN 0-03-076605-2
Printed in the United States of America
123456 038 9876543

PREFACE

The third edition of *Better Teaching in Secondary Schools* is designed to give beginning teachers practical help in solving the complex problems of teaching. Each aspect of the teaching–learning situation is analyzed, from the concrete procedures used in constructing a test or developing a daily lesson plan to the more subtle processes used in motivating students or building classroom morale.

In the classrooms of this nation, teachers are confronted with increasing numbers of students who are rebelling against authority and against established curriculums. In the same classrooms, teachers are faced with the task of meeting the educational needs of students of extreme diversity—diversity in basic skills, academic potentials, and occupational aspirations. In the light of these problems, the authors stress the need for classroom teachers to be concerned with the common, as well as diversified, needs of *all* students, regardless of racial or cultural backgrounds or future goals. Furthermore, it is pointed out that satisfaction of such needs demands a continuing supply of teachers better prepared than ever before.

Better Teaching in Secondary Schools not only re-emphasizes procedures that have been successful in the past, but also introduces teachers to promising current developments in methods and materials of instruction. For example, the book delineates team teaching and automated learning, describes the use of educational games in the classroom, and explains how to use instructional television and the newer techniques of evaluation.

In this text the approach to the problems of the teacher is realistic. Step by step, the teacher is given practical assistance with every phase of teaching, from making an initial class analysis to evaluating and reporting student progress. Although precisely what a teacher and his students do receives major emphasis, classroom procedures are not separated from tested theory or from the subject matter taught. The authors recognize that method, theory, and content are inseparable.

This edition of *Better Teaching in Secondary Schools* emphasizes recommendations that are supported by the most recent findings of research and by the authors' extensive teaching experience in high school and college. Furthermore, the revision rests firmly on its predecessor's widespread use in the classroom. Pertinent suggestions for improvement have come from many users: college professors, high school teachers, and student teachers.

The introductory chapters of the book provide an orientation to teaching. Special attention is given to the opportunities of teaching, to the roles of teachers and their patterns of behavior, and to the techniques employed in studying students, schools, and communities.

In planning for instruction teachers are urged to define their specific objectives in terms of desirable changes in student behavior. The discussion of teaching techniques ranges from standard procedures to latest developments in computer-assisted instruction. Expanded attention is given to motivational techniques and provision for individual differences, including those methods and materials most likely to be effective with the disadvantaged.

In the chapters on classroom management and control, renewed emphasis has been placed on the realistic insights of psychologists and psychiatrists who work closely with classroom teachers.

The chapter on secondary school curriculum introduces the beginning teacher to the current trends, challenges, and problems facing the curriculum builder.

The comprehensive coverage of evaluation has been up-dated to include greater stress on measurement of behavioral objectives.

The concluding section on becoming a professional person highlights new material on the legal rights and responsibilities of teachers. The purposes and procedures of the American Federation of Teachers and the National Education Association are compared and contrasted. The book closes with an optimistic, yet realistic, outlook on the teaching profession.

We are deeply indebted to professional colleagues who made critical analyses of the manuscript and to the editorial staff of the publisher. Further acknowledgment of assistance is made to the various authors and publishers who have allowed us to quote or summarize their materials and to the many school systems that have supplied us with pictures.

San Diego, California
November 1969

M.D.A.
J.S.K.
J.R.S.

TABLE OF CONTENTS

CHAPTER 1 / *Orientation to Teaching as a Profession*

What greater or better gift can we offer the republic than to teach and instruct our youth?—*Cicero*

Cicero's words are as true today as they were 2000 years ago. Teachers still provide valuable and unique professional service to the nation. By guiding students in the acquisition of knowledge and in the development of high ideals and true appreciation of the freedoms and the responsibilities of American citizenship, and by assisting them to develop the skill of clear and critical thinking, teachers contribute significantly to the character of the adults who will determine America's future. To a considerable extent it is true that the destiny of a nation lies in the hands of those who guide its youth. Experienced teachers appreciate the critical importance of that role. But is the opportunity to give service a motive sufficiently strong to keep the nation's schools manned by competent teachers? Are there not other important opportunities in teaching?

TEACHING OFFERS MANY OPPORTUNITIES

The thousands of young men and women who each year enter college classes leading to careers in teaching seldom are fully aware of the many opportunities awaiting them. They have decided to teach for a great variety of reasons and look upon their decision with varying degrees of assurance. Some are absolutely certain they want to teach, others are a bit unsure, and a few gravely doubt the wisdom of their choice. Sometimes doubts are accentuated by the picture of teachers and teaching frequently presented on television, at the theater, and in the public press.

Is the average woman in teaching really a frustrated, unloved old maid? Are men teachers typically undersexed, underpaid, and overworked? Do teachers usually live apart from the community? Are they frequently dominated by administrators, dictated to by parents, and bullied by students? Prospective teachers may well ask such questions even though they usually remember their own high school teachers with favor. Repeated confrontation with the type of story judged newsworthy by the mass communications media may well lead beginners to doubt the validity of their own experience. Therefore, in an effort to give needed balance to the beginner's picture of the teaching profession, the next paragraphs review infrequently published evidence and arguments which support the conclusion that teaching offers many opportunities.

OPPORTUNITY TO GAIN THE RESPECT OF YOUTH AND SHARE THEIR ENTHUSIASM

Teachers have the opportunity to gain the respect and admiration of youth and share in their zest for life. Many veteran teachers agree that among the greatest rewards of teaching are the feelings of appreciation expressed over the years by their students. The beginning teacher who received the following note, quoted verbatim, was well rewarded for his efforts to motivate a "reluctant scholar."

Dear Mr. _____

What I have to say isn't very much. I'm only one out of all the boy in the 5 period class. But I hope you don't hold it agin't me for the way I felt about you at the begining.

I didn't think very much of you. I thought you where just a man who thought he new it all. Well, I was bad to you. But you still was nice to me in more then one way. I don't know how to thank you for what you did for me. But I'll never forget. Your one of the Best men I've known. You see I don't have a father, He died but your just like him in a lot of way's.

Please go on with your teaching, and I hope fore the best fore you.

Your Pal

_____

P.S. Thank's again. Please don't mine the writing or the spelling, Im not so good at it.

Teachers also rank high among their compensations the opportunity to work in an atmosphere charged with the hope and the enthusiasm of youth. In the book and motion picture, *Goodbye, Mr. Chips,* this idea is well illustrated by an admirer who says to the schoolmaster, "I should think you would never grow old in a world where everyone is young." Unfortunately, teachers, like all mortals, grow old in years, but while doing so they retain a remarkable opportunity to remain young in spirit.

OPPORTUNITY TO EARN COMMUNITY RESPECT

Perhaps because they expect to find in teachers attributes they wish their youth to acquire, communities usually are ready to grant teachers respect and social acceptance considerably above that granted most nonteachers of similar age, education, and income. Contrary to a once-popular opinion

PART ONE / *Introduction to Secondary School Teaching*

which maintained that teachers tend to be isolates, research published by the National Education Association in 1967 revealed that less than 5 percent of experienced teachers fail to develop a feeling of acceptance in the social life of the community in which they teach (9:41).[1] Moreover, only 10 percent reported that the prestige of teachers was low in their community (9:42). In the final analysis, social acceptance seldom is automatic. It must be earned by each individual. Nevertheless, teaching clearly offers that opportunity.

OPPORTUNITY FOR SECURITY AND INDEPENDENCE

Teachers, through tenure laws, usually enjoy job security in a given school system but retain the sense of independence and freedom which results from the knowledge that the demand for good teachers is nationwide and likely to remain so for many years.

Research indicates that most teachers—86 percent—intend to remain in the positions they hold and, if given the chance to relive their lives, the majority again would choose to be teachers (9:51). In fact, fewer than 10 percent reported that they probably would choose another profession and less than 2 percent actually planned to make such a change (9:52).

Possession of tenure in a given job and the knowledge that experienced teachers are in short supply combine to give teachers feelings of security and independence enjoyed by few, if any, other occupational groups.

OPPORTUNITY TO EARN A REGULAR INCOME

In an increasing proportion of our nation's schools teaching offers an opportunity, without investment other than that in education, to earn income that is regular, perhaps modest, but no longer meager.

In 1967, the average annual salary for instructional staff ranged from $6000 in the Southeast to $8600 in the Far West (10:10). These averages have been increasing each year. For example, during the decade 1958 to 1968, the national average annual salary of classroom teachers in secondary schools increased 55 percent, from $4900 to $7600. This amounted to a gain of approximately 35 percent in purchasing power (11:16).

When it is realized that the national average annual income for teachers in the early 1940s was $1400, it must be granted that teacher salaries are indeed improving, even though they are not yet equal on an annual basis to those of the best-paid professions (10:11). Furthermore, teaching offers the opportunity to earn salary increments based upon specific schedules of service and advanced study or travel, rather than upon individual bargaining or political maneuvering. Many teachers place a high value on these differences.

[1] Figures in parentheses refer to the Selected Readings at the end of each chapter. The first figure is the number of the reading; the second is the page number in that reading.

OPPORTUNITY FOR VARIETY OF SERVICE WITHIN THE PROFESSION

Education offers many professional roles in addition to teaching. Opportunities vary from administrative and supervisory positions, such as principal, dean, department head, supervisor, and superintendent, to special service positions, such as curriculum coordinator, librarian, audiovisual director, psychometrist, counselor, guidance worker, and researcher. Most require professional preparation as a teacher, teaching experience, and additional college study.

Depending upon the level of responsibility accepted and the size of the district served, salaries in these positions range from about 25 percent above the average for teaching to more than four or five times that amount. Many teachers find added challenge and opportunity within the profession in these administrative, supervisory, and special service roles.

OPPORTUNITY FOR SCHOLARLY LIFE

Teachers have the opportunity to pursue, in depth, a favorite study and to interest young people in its possibilities. In fact, many are first attracted to teaching because of their intense interest in a particular field of study. Teaching not only offers them the opportunity to pursue their major intellectual interest and to inspire others to share the same interest but provides long vacation periods in which teachers may conveniently engage in graduate study.

OPPORTUNITY TO WORK IN AN ATMOSPHERE OF FRIENDSHIP AND CULTURE

Teachers work with professional colleagues who characteristically have stimulating minds and high ideals. They share common intellectual interests, educational background, ethics, and professionalism, all of which form the basis for a pleasant working atmosphere in the typical school. Teaching provides superior associations. It is not likely to attract to its ranks those who would place money above morality. Consequently, of all the professions, teaching is most free of the "fast buck" artist. Because eminence in teaching is gained by working well with colleagues, not by pushing them aside nor taking their livelihood from them, the profession is not likely to attract those who, ignoring human values, accept cutthroat competition as the best avenue to success. Teachers place high value on scholarship, service, and moral character. They are friendly working associates.

OPPORTUNITY TO ENJOY ACADEMIC FREEDOM

High school teachers typically enjoy at least a fair measure of the academic freedom so cherished by the professorial members of the profession. Unlike the situation in which close supervisory control characteristically dominates the worker in many occupations, teachers usually enjoy exceptional freedom of decision in their daily work. The trend of supervision in schools is toward action based on concepts of cooperation, not dictation. The major purpose of this type of supervision is the cooperative improvement of instruction. Teachers thus feel that they work with supervisors and administrators, not for them. These distinctions are important contributors to the pleasant atmosphere in which teachers work.

OPPORTUNITY TO LIVE A FULL LIFE

Teachers have an excellent opportunity to live a life with family and friends, and particularly to enjoy frequent vacations with them. According to research, teachers participate in more community activities, belong to churches in greater numbers, and vote more regularly than the average citizen (9:96–98). Teachers are active in their communities, but they also find time to see the world. During their frequent vacation periods, teachers can be observed in all the outstanding recreational areas of the United States and in almost every land where travel is encouraged. Teachers are inveterate students and travelers.

Finally, it must be emphasized that the stereotype of a teacher as a frustrated old maid is untrue. Research in 1967 revealed that more than half of the teachers in American high schools were men, over 80 percent of whom were married. Likewise, more than half of the women teachers in high schools, 64 percent, were married (9:58). Furthermore, research also showed that marriages involving a teacher tended to be considerably more stable than the national average. Only 9 percent of teachers were divorced, separated, or widowed (9:39), whereas the comparable statistic for all workers in the United States exceeded 20 percent.[2]

Nationwide research points to the conclusion that the typical high school teacher in America is a happily married man who intends to teach until retirement and who would again choose to be a teacher if he were to reselect his lifework.

In the preceding discussion, consideration has been given to opportunities offered by the teaching profession. It must be remembered, however, that such opportunities are neither gifts nor the results of chance. They are products of continuous efforts on the part of the teacher to acquire the knowledges and skills demanded of his profession. Some of these demands are suggested in the following paragraphs.

KNOWLEDGE AND SKILLS REQUIRED IN TEACHING

The mediocre teacher tells. The good teacher explains. The superior demonstrates. The great teacher inspires.—*William Arthur Ward* [3]

[2] U.S. Bureau of the Census, *Statistical Abstract of the United States, 1967.* Washington, D.C.: Government Printing Office, 1967, p. 33.
[3] *Phi Delta Kappan,* 43 (November 1961), 59.

WHAT IS TEACHING?

At the outset, anyone who plans to become a teacher needs to give thoughtful consideration to the question, What *is* teaching? Unfortunately, a clear answer to that question is sometimes clouded by those who confuse fact and fiction.

One fiction is the notion that if a person knows his subject, he is able to teach it. One of the authors once supervised a student teacher whom he chided for lecturing too much to his junior high school students. In reply, the young man said, "What am I supposed to do? After spending four or five years in college accumulating information, now I am not permitted to tell what I know." He clearly demonstrated a common misconception about the nature of teaching. Telling is not teaching. It is the process of giving information.

Another fiction concerning teaching is expressed in the cliché that teachers are born, not made. Although it is true that some candidates for teaching are more richly endowed than others, yet *all must learn how to teach*. No one would think of going to a doctor who lacked the knowledges and skills required of his profession, nor would anyone employ an engineer to build a bridge if he had never learned how to build bridges. Yet teaching, which requires skillful ability to diagnose learning difficulties and skillful engineering to deal with human materials, is apparently considered by those who recommend little or no professional preparation as a job requiring no specialized knowledge or skills.

Closely related to both fictions are a number of fallacies concerning *methods* of teaching. They go something like this: Educationists recommend that prospective teachers study methods *rather than* subject matter; methods courses take up so much of the student's time he receives insufficient preparation in his subjects; and, finally, the propaganda device of labeling all education courses as "methods" courses. In answer to all these fictions, there is abundant evidence that education does not monopolize the program of the prospective teacher. The fact is that of total graduation requirements, *all* education courses, including student teaching, represent a maximum of 18 to 21 percent (1:1463).

In the light of these fictions, a few comments concerning the need for a teacher to know his subject are relevant. Products of higher education with a strong emphasis upon academic education themselves, educators have never discounted for one moment the need for teachers to know the subjects they teach. They do object, however, to a consideration of subject matter mastery as the ultimate end of education. They also object to a number of fictions concerning this so-called mastery.

First of all, no prospective teacher, no matter how many college units he accumulates, is adequately prepared in anything. There are at least two reasons for this. For one, new developments in all areas of knowledge are taking place at such a dizzy pace that every teacher has to study diligently and continuously lest he become a purveyor of irrelevant, if not false, information. Furthermore, there is much truth in the hackneyed expression that the only way to learn a subject is to teach it. As a teacher begins to teach his subject, it takes on new meaning. He develops new insights, motivations, and sense of perspective, as well as a degree of humility. Furthermore, no subject can be taught until it is organized, and that organization must be in terms of the needs and maturity of the students.

Scholarship in teaching is important, but the meaning of the term has not always been made clear. Scholarship is certainly more than the accumulation of thirty-five, fifty, or even sixty units of credit in a particular subject. It is as much a state of mind as anything. To attain it, a person not only must be equipped with the tools of learning but must also have the desire and the intellectual curiosity to broaden his understanding of the world of people, events, and things.

Now that a few superficial notions about teaching have been exposed, let us consider how teachers may continue to grow in the science and art of teaching. At the outset, it is necessary for teachers to analyze and evaluate continuously their beliefs and practices in relation to effective student learning. Because the perceptions, the convictions, and the patterns of behavior of teachers are of such vital importance, opinion polls have often been taken to discover what teachers themselves consider to be their greatest needs.

When teachers in service are asked to evaluate the adequacy of their teacher-preparation programs, their conclusions typically correspond to those of a survey reported in the December 1963 *NEA Journal.* Using "a scientifically selected cross section of the nation's 1.5 million public school teachers," the NEA Research Division found that although "only 27 percent of the teachers felt that they had received too little preparation in their subject field, nearly 41 percent felt that they had received too little preparation in teaching methods."[4]

THE ROLES OF TEACHERS

Because teaching methods have such an important bearing on effective teaching, at least in the judgment of teachers themselves, a study of methodology becomes a prime target of research. One of the first problems facing the researcher is that of developing a classification scheme for describing consistent patterns of teacher behavior. One such scheme,

[4] "Teacher-Opinion Poll on Teacher Preparation," *NEA Journal,* 52 (December 1963), 34.

expressed in terms of *roles* that teachers play, was developed by Kinney [5] and has since been used as a basis for extended study by Fishburn.[6] The following six roles of the teacher have been identified:

1. As a director of learning
2. As a counseling and guidance person
3. As a mediator of the culture
4. As a member of the school community
5. As a link between school and community
6. As a member of a profession

In order to understand what knowledges and skills are required by the profession, the teacher must know what *he must do*—what functions he must perform—in order to fulfill the six roles expected of him. Some of these activities, most of which are discussed at length in other parts of this book, will be indicated in the following paragraphs.

AS A DIRECTOR OF LEARNING

In developing competence as a director of learning, the teacher plans interesting and meaningful learning experiences for his students; develops satisfactory relationships with his students and effective classroom management and control; uses a variety of instructional materials and procedures effectively; provides for individual differences; and appraises, records, and reports student growth and achievement.

AS A COUNSELING AND GUIDANCE PERSON

In discharging his responsibility for counseling and guidance of students, the teacher seeks to know his students and their needs; uses various sources and procedures for studying his students; learns how to interpret and use data concerning his students effectively; works closely with the guidance office, referring special problems to appropriate specialists; and uses group guidance techniques in an effective manner.

AS A MEDIATOR OF THE CULTURE

"Culture is activity of thought and receptiveness to beauty and humane feeling. Scraps of information have nothing to do with it." [7] The teacher is not merely a conveyor of information nor a transmitter of the cultural heritage. Through the use of many media, not books alone, the teacher helps students gain a knowledge of and respect for our democratic institutions—their history, traditions, and processes. By means of varied ex-

---

[5] L. B. Kinney, *Measure of a Good Teacher*. San Francisco: California Teachers Association, 1952.

[6] C. E. Fishburn, "Teacher Role Perception in the Secondary School," *Journal of Teacher Education*, 13 (March 1962), 55–59.

[7] Alfred North Whitehead, *The Aims of Education and Other Essays*. New York: The Macmillan Company, 1929, p. 1.

periences—reading, travel, observation, work experience, participation in school and community groups—students learn to understand and appreciate the moral and spiritual values, the infinite variety, and the problems of their culture. The role of the teacher as a mediator of the culture has been well expressed in these words:

For five and twenty years . . . I have been giving sight to the blind. I have given understanding to some thousands of boys. . . . My boys have learnt the history of mankind so that it has become their adventure; I have had languages taught to make the past live again in their minds and to be windows upon the souls of alien peoples. Science has played its proper part; it has taken my boys into the secret places of matter and out among the nebulae. . . .[8]

AS A MEMBER OF THE SCHOOL COMMUNITY

The new teacher needs to be accepted as a member of the professional family with which he works each day, both for personal and professional reasons. The establishment of harmonious relationships with his coworkers contributes to his own happiness and to his effectiveness as a teacher.

In order to gain acceptance as a member of his school community, the beginning teacher is advised to observe a few simple rules.

1. First of all, he needs to be a good listener and a willing worker. No matter how much he should be tempted to do it, the novice should refrain from giving advice. He still has too much to learn to do that.

2. The well-bred, truly professional teacher is always considerate of the feelings of others. By being temperate in speech, dressing in good taste, and respecting the customs and traditions of the school, the newcomer soon wins acceptance by his co-workers. Although the new teacher may criticize inadequacies, he should be sure to direct these criticisms through proper channels and to the proper people.

3. The new teacher needs to become familiar with the correct procedures for securing the many services the school has to offer. Because the modern school must of necessity be highly organized and staffed by specialists, proper channels of communication have to be followed. In securing supplies and in obtaining the assistance of nonteaching personnel—librarians, custodians, secretaries—the teacher must observe established regulations and procedures. By being considerate and refraining from making excessive demands of them, the teacher soon discovers that nonteaching staff members will go beyond the call of duty in helping him.

4. The beginner needs to be accepted and known by parents as well as by colleagues as a "good teacher" under the prevailing [existing] condi-

[8] H. G. Wells, *The Undying Fire.* New York: The Macmillan Company, 1919, p. 61.

tions before he insists on major curricular revisions. Change is seldom unanimously accepted; however, change is more easily accomplished when the newcomer has earned a praiseworthy reputation within the school and community.[9]

No classroom is an island. Although the classroom teacher seemingly works alone with his students day after day, he is always a part of a professional team. The members of that team stand ready to give assistance to the beginner within their ranks. All he has to do is to learn the rules of the game and play his part as best he can. Newcomers in any situation always lack the status of the more experienced. However, by exercising tact and good judgment, by observing established customs and regulations, and by demonstrating a willingness to carry his fair share of responsibility as a faculty member, the new teacher can soon gain acceptance as a respected member of the school community.

AS A LINK BETWEEN SCHOOL AND COMMUNITY

Another vital role the teacher plays is to help establish a closer bond between the school and the larger community. The process of building better bridges of understanding between school and community poses a number of problems. For instance, one difficulty pertains to the concept of the community itself. A *community* is usually thought of as a geographical area in which the residents are bound together by common interests, ties, and traditions. When one of the authors began teaching in a small rural high school, he was advised to make no disparaging remarks about anyone because the people were all related. Today, the situation is rapidly changing. As large urban centers replace the intimate neighborhoods of an earlier agrarian society, well-defined communities, as originally conceived, cease to exist.

A growing national concern is how to improve the quality of education in city slums or ghettos. About all the inhabitants of these blighted communities have in common is their struggle for survival against terrific odds. Deprived of their rightful benefits as American citizens—adequate schooling, equal employment opportunities, and a decent living environment—slum dwellers are building up an explosive tide of resentment against the power structure that perpetuates their deprivation. A large number of ghetto youth who drop out before they complete high school are becoming self-educated in the fourth R—rioting. Substantial federal aid is now being used to provide better educational opportunities for boys and girls from the prekindergarten level through the high school years. Although this is a good beginning, complete mobilization of all social institutions—home, church, business and industry, and the like—

---

[9] The authors are indebted to Wallace C. Schloerke, Iowa State University, for this paragraph.

is required to meet the needs of disadvantaged youth. Efforts are also being made to provide more parental and community participation by the establishment of more or less autonomous local school districts *within* large cities. The great challenge facing the public schools is to provide good teachers, great teachers, the best we have to teach disadvantaged children. Such teachers will need both dedication to their jobs and special preparation for a difficult assignment. Because they must be "hand-picked" and "tailor-made" to fill such a demanding position, perhaps teachers in the ghettos should receive "combat pay."

Closely related to the problem of identification of communities is the subject of public relations. Probably with some justification, teachers have often been criticized for being unaware of the importance of good relations with the public. They have been content to leave the whole matter in the hands of administrators or public relations experts. The problem is further complicated by the fact that there are many publics, not just one. Because of that fact, there is more reason than ever for teachers to play their role in improving school-public relations. It is true that good teaching, with its product of happy, successful students, is the best avenue to good public relations that a school can have, yet every teacher has his own circle of friends to whom he can act as an interpreter of the school and its program.

As a teacher becomes aware of the close link between the school and community, he conceives of the community as a laboratory for learning or as an extension of the classroom. The criticism that the school program is "a two-by-four curriculum" confined to the two covers of a textbook and the four walls of the classroom, as someone so succinctly said, no longer holds true. By using community resource speakers in the classroom, by taking students on field trips to study community functions and organizations, or by directing surveys of community life to study real problems, the teacher adds a new dimension to learning that takes place in the classroom.

There is a personal reason why the teacher should mingle with the people of the community. As has already been suggested, working with youth is a rewarding experience; yet the teacher needs the additional emotional and intellectual stimulus of association with other adults. Although he associates every day with his professional colleagues, he occasionally needs to get away from shoptalk and the cares of the classroom by meeting, socializing, and working with people from other occupations as well.

The teacher needs to know his community—its composition, values, impact on youth, and its resources for learning. That the out-of-school environment of boys and girls has a direct bearing on what they learn in school no one will deny. As the teacher attempts to assess these environmental influences, he may very well seek answers to such questions as the following: How do students spend their free time? Do they work? If so, what do they do? Or do they merely loaf on the streets? What are the occupations of parents? Do both parents work outside the home? Does the community provide adequate recreational facilities for youth? What character-building agencies are available for teen-age boys and girls? What commercial amusements—motion pictures, materials on news-stands, television programs—are competing for the time and tastes of adolescents? To what social, economic, and moral pressures are students subjected? The school does not operate in a vacuum.

In the development of good citizenship, the improvement of com-munication skills, and the elevation of the cultural levels of students, teachers must have community support. Students themselves cannot operate successfully in two conflicting worlds, one represented by the school and the other by the neighborhood or community.

How does a teacher get to know his community? He may make a tour of it, observing its homes, churches, business and industrial firms, and parks and playgrounds. He may read the local newspapers, noting weekly entertainment guides and the activities of clubs, churches, and other agencies which serve youth. The teacher should attend social and cultural functions and visit libraries, museums, and other cultural centers. He may talk with citizens engaged in various occupations and he may offer his services as a speaker for certain occasions. By becoming an active, inter-ested citizen of the community, the teacher increases his effectiveness in the classroom and strengthens the ties between school and community.

AS A MEMBER OF A PROFESSION

In playing his role as a professional person, the first mark of the teacher is this: *He takes pride in his profession.* He never feels obliged to apolo-gize for his choice of a vocation. Many stories have been related about teachers who try to hide their occupational identity away from home or who apologetically identify themselves by saying, "I am just a teacher." If that is the way teachers feel about their profession, they cannot expect to command much respect for it, either from adults or youth. The truly professional person believes in the worthwhileness, the significance, of teaching as a career; he would not exchange jobs with anyone.

As a member of a profession, the dedicated teacher exhibits a second quality: *He is loyal to his profession.* Not for a moment does he consider teaching as a steppingstone to some other occupation. He is loyal to his professional colleagues, never stooping to petty gossip about them nor exhibiting a contemptuous attitude toward opinions which may differ from his own.

The teacher of integrity works constantly to improve himself as a person and as a member of the profession by maintaining high standards of per-sonal and professional conduct, by continuing to grow professionally (reading, studying, and actively participating in professional organizations), by cultivating an appreciation for the best in our culture, and by continuous self-evaluation.

In conclusion, it might be pointed out that this discussion of the six roles of the teacher has stressed *the importance of interpersonal relations* as much as anything. Studies of personnel failures in business and industry indicate that most employees fail, not because of a lack of necessary knowledge and skills, but because of their inability to work with others. By logical inference, the same thing is true of teaching. Almost without exception, every function of the teacher has a more or less direct bearing on his harmonious relations with others, particularly students.

PATTERNS OF TEACHER BEHAVIOR

Despite widespread usage of the term "role" in the categorization of teacher behavior, some prefer to use different classification schemes.

In lieu of "role," Wallen and Travers recommend the use of "the term *pattern of behavior* . . . an identifying grouping of behaviors which occur in the same teacher . . . ." [10] They propose the following classification of patterns of teaching behavior:

1. Patterns derived from teaching traditions. (Illustration: A teacher teaches as he was taught.)
2. Patterns derived from social learnings in the teacher's background. (Illustration: A teacher reinforces the behavior of pupils so as to develop a middle-class ideology.)
3. Patterns derived from philosophical traditions. (Illustration: A teacher teaches in accordance with the Froebel or Rousseau tradition.)
4. Patterns generated by the teacher's own needs. (Illustration: A teacher adopts a lecture method because he needs to be self-assertive.)
5. Patterns generated by conditions existing in the school and community. (Illustration: A teacher conducts his class in such a way as to produce formal and highly disciplined behavior because this represents the pattern required by the principal.)
6. Patterns derived from scientific research on learning.[11]

In analyzing these patterns of teacher behavior, Wallen and Travers make some thought-provoking generalizations, such as the following:

"The writers consider the teacher's own personality prior to the impact of a teacher education program to be the main determinant of teacher behavior in the classroom." [12]

Wallen and Travers contend that "little has been done to develop teaching methods on the basis of scientific knowledge of learning. Most

---

[10] Norman E. Wallen and Robert M. W. Travers, "Analysis and Investigation of Teaching Methods," *Handbook of Research on Teaching*. A Project of the American Educational Research Association, N. L. Gage, ed. Chicago: Rand McNally & Company, 1963, p. 451.
[11] Wallen and Travers, pp. 452–453.
[12] Wallen and Travers, p. 454.

widely advocated teaching methods are based either on philosophical tradition or on the personal needs of the teacher. . . ." However, they hasten to add "that many learning principles founded on folklore are probably sound and may ultimately be demonstrated to be sound." [13] Thus it seems that until research demonstrates a better way teachers must continue to operate on the basis of the best procedures they know, gained from their own experience and the accumulated experience of other successful teachers. But it should be noted that during the past decade the federal government has increased the availability of funds for educational research to such an extent that teachers may soon be able to base their teaching patterns of behavior on more scientific foundations.

CHARACTERISTICS OF GOOD TEACHERS

What are the qualities of the effective teacher? For over a half century attempts have been made to find the answer to that question, but there are still no criteria upon which common agreement has been reached.[14] Efforts to establish such criteria have been based on three factors: product, expressed in terms of student behavior; process, defined in such terms as the ability of the teacher to maintain effective discipline or rapport with his students; and "presage criteria," based on such factors as intelligence, adjustment, and character of the teacher. All have their limitations. For example, when the product criterion is used, it is impossible to isolate the unique contribution of the school or any one teacher from those of other agencies or to determine how the school affects ultimate behavior.[15]

A recent, comprehensive study, directed by David G. Ryans (past president of AERA), seems to throw the most light on the qualities of a good teacher. He reports the following characteristics appear to be associated with effective teaching: superior intelligence and school achievement; "good emotional adjustment"; favorable attitudes toward pupils and enjoyment of relationships with them; generosity in appraising the motives and behavior of others; strong interests in reading and cultural matters (art, literature, music); "participation in social and community affairs; early experience caring for children and teaching (such as reading to children and taking a class for a teacher)"; family support or identification with teaching; and "strong social service interests." [16, 17]

---

[13] Wallen and Travers, pp. 465–466. The reader is urged to consult the original source for a detailed analysis of the six patterns of teacher behavior, including a provocative discussion of the implications of each one.

[14] Harold E. Mitzel, "Teacher Effectiveness," *Encyclopedia of Educational Research*, 3d ed., Chester W. Harris, ed. New York: The Macmillan Company, 1960, p. 1481.

[15] Mitzel, pp. 1483–1485.

[16] David G. Ryans, "Predictions of Teacher Effectiveness," *Encyclopedia of Educational Research*, 3d ed., Chester W. Harris, ed. New York: The Macmillan Company, 1960, p. 1490.

[17] *Phi Delta Kappan*, 42 (January 1961), 147.

Someone has said that preparation for retirement begins in kindergarten. The same generalization could be made about teaching. The summary of characteristics associated with effective teaching, just indicated above, suggests that the prospective teacher needs to engage in many kinds of significant preprofessional experiences. Working with community-sponsored youth groups, participating in cocurricular activities with peers (especially in a capacity of leadership), and broadening cultural interests are ways in which future teachers may well lay the foundation for their career. Fortunate is the person who begins in his youth to engage in activities which stand him in good stead later as a teacher. The profession has been remiss in failing to identify promising candidates for teaching in the elementary or secondary school and encouraging them to consider teaching as a vocation. In some cases, high school students who show an interest in teaching are provided opportunities for observing and assisting pupils in the elementary school.

STUDENT OPINIONS ABOUT TEACHERS

A number of studies of student opinions of their teachers have been made from time to time. After reviewing a number of these surveys (most of which summarized the opinions of junior or senior high school students), Weintraub concluded that students like teachers who have a sense of humor and who have "warmth, sympathy, understanding, and the ability to teach well." [18]

Using student evaluation of former teachers as a criterion for judging success of teachers, Hall sought the opinions of 1217 undergraduate students at Ohio State University concerning the qualities of their "best" and their "worst" teachers (more high school teachers were chosen by the respondents than any other group). More than 10 percent of the students ranked (in descending order) the following qualities of their "best" teachers: personal interest in students—understanding (46 percent of the students listed this category); sense of humor; fair and objective; no problem with discipline; interesting; respected; likes subject; and well versed. More than 10 percent of the students ranked (in descending order) the following characteristics of their "worst" teachers: favoritism shown—unfair; poor discipline; disinterested in students—won't take time to explain; talks of irrelevant things in class, not respected; and unable to communicate.[19] One of the very important conclusions was as follows: "Perceived effects of teachers were investigated and shown to center around motivation." [20]

This chapter has made a survey of teachers—their opportunities, roles,

[18] Samuel Weintraub, "Pupil Conception of the Teacher: What Research Says to the Reading Teacher," *The Reading Teacher*, 20 (February 1967), 445.
[19] Vernon C. Hall, "Former Student Evaluation as a Criterion for Teacher Success," *Journal of Experimental Education*, 34 (Fall 1965), 1–19.
[20] Hall, p. 6.

patterns of behavior, characteristics, and their students' opinions of them
—and the nature of teaching. The following chapter is concerned with
the characteristics of secondary school students.

SELECTED READINGS

1. American Educational Research Association, *Encyclopedia of Educational Research,* 3d ed., Chester W. Harris, ed. New York: The Macmillan Company, 1960.

2. American Educational Research Association, *Handbook of Research on Teaching,* N. L. Gage, ed. Chicago: Rand McNally & Company, 1963, pp. 448–470.

3. Clark, Leonard H., and Irving S. Starr, *Secondary School Teaching Methods,* 2d ed. New York: The Macmillan Company, 1967, chap. 1.

4. Dahl, John A., and others, *Student, School, and Society.* San Francisco: Chandler Publishing Company, 1964, Part I.

5. Davis, E. Dale, *Focus on Secondary Education.* Chicago: Scott, Foresman and Company, 1966, chap. 12.

6. Faunce, Roland C., and Carroll L. Munshaw, *Teaching and Learning in Secondary Schools.* Belmont, Calif.: Wadsworth Publishing Company, Inc., 1964, chap. 5.

7. Green, J. A., *Fields of Teaching and Educational Services.* New York: Harper & Row, Publishers, 1966.

8. Oliva, Peter F., *The Secondary School Today.* Cleveland: The World Publishing Company, 1967, chap. 2.

9. Research Division, NEA, *The American Public School Teacher, 1965–'66.* Research Report, 1967–R-4. (Published at 5-year intervals; consult the latest report.)

10. Research Division, NEA, *Economic Status of Teachers, 1966–'67.* Research Report, 1967–R-8. (Published annually; consult the latest report.)

11. Research Division, NEA, *Estimates of School Statistics, 1967–'68.* Research Report, 1967–R-19. (Published annually; consult latest report.)

CHAPTER 2 | *Characteristics of Secondary School Students*

In order to establish rapport with their students and thus enhance the effectiveness of their teaching roles, teachers must study the characteristics of students and how those characteristics affect learning. This study should include the generalizations applicable to students as a whole in addition to detailed specifics concerning the personality of each class and of each student. This chapter will discuss the outstanding physical, intellectual, social, and emotional characteristics of students and what those characteristics imply for teachers.

STUDENTS FACE COMPLEX PROBLEMS

Students typically enter the seventh grade as 12-year-olds and complete the twelfth grade at age 18. Thus, they enter secondary school as children and leave as young adults. During that six-year span most students are in adolescence, a stage of development known for its rapid physical growth and its perplexing problems of adjustment. Adolescents are in an in-between status—too young to be accepted as adults, but too old to view themselves as children.

Teachers who understand the nature of adolescents know that typically they are self-centered; yet they seek acceptance by their peers. They wish to be independent of adults; yet they seek security in adult approval. However, when adult values and peer-group values are in conflict, adolescents adopt the values of their own age group. Consequently, each older generation occasionally feels that the younger generation is certainly headed for ruin. Adolescence is accused of being an age of rampant delinquency in which fads of dress, language, art, music, and antisocial behavior are commonplace expressions of rebellion against the traditions of adult society.

Admittedly, these charges are at least partially true; nevertheless, the majority of teen-agers are good citizens. They do their best to solve peaceably the problems associated with their growth, development, and adjustment to society. Teachers must realize that concern with these problems is typical of American youth. The boy who is never quite ready to give an assigned oral report to his English class, and the girl who refuses to shower after exercise in physical education are not likely to be rebelling against either their teachers or the required activities of their classes. The boy, newly anxious to be attractive to the opposite sex, may well be overly conscious of his pimply complexion or his inability to control his changing voice, whereas the girl may be fearful that a shower would spoil her meticulous hairdo.

The experienced teacher, recognizing the basic problems involved, would not seek solutions in the use of physical force or automatic failure; but, depending on his knowledge of the individual students and the educational goals involved, he would try such solutions as a prerecorded speech or a written report in the first case, and perhaps the use of an ample shower cap in the second. In any event, the teacher who understands the problems of youth will be better prepared to help students reach satisfactory educational goals.

STUDENTS ARE INDIVIDUALS

The greatest single fact to note about students is that they are remarkably different. They differ in physical ability, growth rate, health, intelligence, emotional development, social development, home background, interests, abilities, knowledges, skills, work habits, citizenship, and in endless other ways. Students, no matter how they are grouped, are essentially individuals of greatly differing characteristics.

PHYSICAL DEVELOPMENT

No topic is more important nor more perplexing to teen-agers than their physical development. The following discussion first points out the physical stature and physical maturity characteristics of secondary school students and then elaborates on their implications for teachers.

PHYSICAL STATURE In terms of averages, girls at ages 12 and 13 (grades seven and eight) exceed boys in physical stature. At age 12 boys average about 57 inches in height; girls are about an inch taller. The height of approximately two thirds of 12-year-olds lies within 3 inches of the average. However, the shortest boy at this age may be about 4 feet tall, while his classmate of greatest height may be more than 18 inches taller. By the time they are seniors in high school (18 years old), boys average 68 or 69 inches in height, about 5 inches in excess of the average for girls (13:90).

PHYSICAL MATURITY Perhaps of greatest effect upon a student's self-concept during his high school years is his progress toward sexual maturity. According to statistics, about 20 percent of the girls, but practically none of the boys, have entered puberty prior to enrollment in seventh grade at about 12 years of age. At age 14 (in ninth grade), 85 percent of the girls have entered puberty and half of them have attained physical maturity.

The comparable figures for boys at age 14 are approximately 40 percent and 10 percent, respectively. Two years later, when the majority are in the eleventh grade, 90 percent of the girls are physically mature, and only 60 percent of the boys. At age 18, when the average high school student is graduated, practically all have attained physical maturity.

IMPLICATIONS FOR TEACHERS   Teachers realize that physical differences readily accepted by adults are frequently the cause of great concern to adolescents. Most students desperately want to be like their peer group. Many of those who deviate from the norm more than they think desirable worry to the point that it affects their school adjustment. The fat and the thin, the short and the tall, and the late maturing as well as the early maturing—all need the special understanding of their teacher. Some over-compensate, a few withdraw, most just "grin and bear it," but all, none-theless, require sympathetic understanding.

Teachers, through their attitude, leadership, and counseling, can help students realize that it is normal for individuals to develop at different rates. Physical education teachers, in particular, can accomplish much through adjustment of goals and activities to the needs and abilities of individual students. Above all, teachers must remember that students at this age seek acceptance and fear ridicule and rejection.

HEALTH AND HANDICAPS

High school teachers instruct approximately 150 to 200 students each day. Research-based estimates indicate that in an average group of that number:

1. Five to ten will have speech defects requiring attention if therapy has not been provided in the elementary school (1:1333).
2. Three to six are afflicted with hearing loss serious enough to require medical attention (1:997).
3. Twenty to fifty require corrective lenses to achieve "normal" vision.[1]
4. Ten to fifteen suffer from known allergies, such as eczema, asthma, hay fever, and hives (1:1002–1004).
5. One to ten have epilepsy, diabetes, or cardiac disability (1:1003).

IMPLICATIONS FOR TEACHERS   What are the implications of these data? The answer is clear. Teachers are not expected to have the skills of

[1] Howard L. Kingsley and Ralph Garry, *The Nature and Conditions of Learning.* Englewood Cliffs, N.J.: Prentice-Hall, Inc., 1957, p. 184.

doctors or nurses, but they are expected to be alert to the physical and health status of their students so that seating rearrangements can be made, educational goals and activities can be modified for individuals, and ailing students can be referred to the appropriate medical service.

In addition, teachers are expected to be ready to cope with unexpected emergencies. By developing the ability to recognize colds and other contagious illness in early stages, teachers can contribute to reduction in their spread. It is also known that early detection and remedy of sight, speech, and hearing defects can reduce educational retardation common to many physically handicapped. Thus, it is easy to understand why teachers give high priority to careful observation of students and to study of their health records and reports.

INTELLIGENCE

Differences in intelligence among students are subtle and more difficult to determine than physical differences; nevertheless, intellectual differences are just as real and just as extensive. The most commonly used intelligence tests place approximately two thirds of a given age group between intelligence quotients (IQ's) of 84 and 116; approximately 14 percent between 116 and 132; and the same percentage, between 84 and 68. Only 2 percent have IQ's above 132, and 2 percent fall below 68. These percentages will vary somewhat, depending upon the test used and the group measured.

Since a disproportionately large number of those who drop out of school have IQ's below average, high school teachers can expect that the average IQ of their classes will exceed 100. Also, more than one sixth of their students will have IQ's above 116. However, in most schools there will be classes having an IQ average below 100, and in some schools all classes may average below that figure. It is not unusual to find an IQ difference of fifty or more points between the highest and lowest scoring member of a class. This fact poses a difficult problem for educators.

ABILITY GROUPING   One attempted solution has been to assign students to classes on the basis of intelligence quotients. Ordinarily, two or at most three classifications are used. This procedure reduces the ability range in any one class but fails to achieve homogeneity with respect to ability to learn specific subject matter. Teachers of so-called homogeneous classes should keep in mind that their classes, too, are composed of individuals who differ widely.

Research has revealed that trait differences within an individual are so great that persons with like intelligence scores will have other very different attributes. It has been shown that homogeneous grouping with respect to one ability has reduced the range of other abilities only approximately 20 percent (13:284). For example, in typical heterogeneous ninth-grade English classes, students range about six years in attributes such as mental ability, grammar ability, and reading ability—from performance that is typical for seventh graders to that which is average for high school seniors.

If these classes are regrouped into three levels according to mental ability, the range of mental age in each class section can be reduced to two years, but each class section would still retain a range of approximately 4.8 years in grammar performance, in reading, and in other abilities. Similar grouping according to other factors would have similar results. Thus it appears obvious that when a teacher desires homogeneous grouping, he must regroup for each change of activity. Such frequent change is feasible only within the class.

IMPLICATIONS FOR TEACHERS   Other factors being equal, students of higher IQ can be expected to understand directions and explanations more easily, to learn more quickly, to retain their learning for a longer period of time, and to apply what they have learned to new situations more adeptly. With respect to academic learning ability, they are richly blessed.

In addition, students of high IQ, when compared as a group with those of average and low IQ, also show greater originality, greater determination, greater perseverance, and greater interest in intellectual tasks and academic subjects. They demonstrate greater ability to reason, to generalize, to synthesize, and to deal with abstract concepts. Students of superior intellect also tend to be more mature physically, emotionally, and socially. They are not necessarily more talented artistically nor mechanically, but through more intensive effort they seem to develop their special talents more effectively (1:584–585).

Of course, to these research-supported generalizations there are many exceptions. Nevertheless, teachers must reject the old saws of "a strong back and a weak mind," and "easy come, easy go," since they describe the exception, not the rule. (Further discussion of the meaning and interpretation of intelligence quotients is found in Chapter 19.)

ACHIEVEMENT IN SUBJECT MATTER AND BASIC SKILLS

Research has revealed that differences in educational achievement among students at the extremes of any grade level are so great as to be almost unbelievable. For example, with a typical seventh-grade class of thirty to forty students, the lowest achievers in arithmetic, reading, science, history, and English make scores no better than those made by average fourth or fifth graders, while the highest achievers in the same seventh-grade class make scores equal to the ninth- or tenth-grade average. The typical range in achievement within one school grade is six to eight grades.

Project Talent, an extensive study of achievement in secondary schools, revealed that 20 percent of ninth graders were more knowledgeable than the average twelfth grader (11:3–74). This achievement variability persists throughout the secondary school and continues in college. In fact, high school seniors testing in the top 10 percent in any school subject have been found to exceed the median college senior in knowledge of that subject. Conversely, the lowest 10 percent of college seniors have tested lower than the median for high school seniors (13:277).

Another study conducted within a single college tested all students in English, fine arts, social studies, science, and mathematics. It was found that had the graduation list been made up of the highest quarter of the student body on the basis of the test results, the graduating class would have included 15 percent of the freshmen, 19 percent of the sophomores, 21 percent of the juniors, and only 28 percent of the seniors (13:278). Obviously, such extensive achievement differences among students present difficult instructional problems at all school levels.

IMPLICATIONS FOR TEACHERS

Lest teachers become discouraged by these facts of variability among students, they should remember that the distribution of achievement, like that of intelligence, is normal. The middle two thirds of a class are typically not more than one grade level ahead or behind the class average in any single trait. This knowledge is of value to teachers, but has led many to conclude erroneously that by removing the lowest sixth and the highest sixth from a typical class, the remaining group would range only three years on additional traits involved in learning. Research refutes this conclusion by showing that students who are alike in one aspect of a subject may be very different in other aspects of the same subject. This fact was illustrated in the preceding section on intelligence.

Knowing that students in the same school year differ widely in knowledge of subject matter as well as in ability to read, write, speak, spell, and compute, alert teachers include study of these factors as they prepare to teach a class. Armed with this information, teachers compare present performance of students with their past performance and with their estimated potential.

Students who are not working up to capacity can be identified and encouraged to improve, students who are low for their grade can be given remedial help, and high achievers can be commended and encouraged to work on more advanced assignments. The old practice of using identical assignments and activities for all students in a class is then replaced with the more modern practice of modifying both the pace and the procedure to bring about maximum learning in a particular class.

SOCIAL AND EMOTIONAL DEVELOPMENT, INTEREST, AND ADJUSTMENT

Some of the social and emotional characteristics of adolescence were mentioned in an early part of this chapter. Here it will be emphasized that awareness of a student's social and emotional status may be the real key to success in his instruction.

TYPICAL BEHAVIOR   Gesell has described typical behavior of students at various secondary school ages. He states that the seventh grader and eighth grader are noted for their enthusiasm and their intense interest in physical action.[2] Boys will snatch a classmate's possessions just for the joy of chasing and being chased. Gesell also observes that students at that stage of development find it almost impossible to stand in line without considerable jostling and horseplay. They are responsive, however, to appeals to group loyalty; they are proud to be members of a team or club; and in eighth grade they seem to concentrate better and enjoy school more than they did a year earlier.

In the ninth grade, at age 14, "he is quieter within himself, even though . . . more noisy with the group. . . . His contemplation of his own personality is becoming less uneasy, dissatisfied, and defensive, more calm and judicious." [3] It should be noted, however, that while the 14-year-old quite readily criticizes his classmates, he is not yet able to take criticism objectively. In the words of a teen-ager, "He can dish it out, but he can't take it." Teachers, when conducting group evaluations, should keep in mind that adolescents are extremely sensitive to peer opinion.

According to Gesell, the tenth grader sometimes exhibits a hostile attitude toward school and toward teachers. Dropouts are frequent in the sophomore year.[4] In the eleventh and twelfth grades, students show the results of steady growth toward social and emotional maturity. They realize that college, trade school, military service, or work are just over the horizon and they seek to make the most of their remaining school opportunities.

Teachers can also gain clues to effective motivation from research describing adolescent interests in motion pictures, music, television, radio, books, magazines, stories of adventure (boys), stories of romance (girls), famous people, hobbies of collecting, boy-girl relationships, and, above all, from adolescents themselves (1:1105–1109). Of particular importance is the fact that adolescent interests can be broadened and directed. How-

[2] Arnold Gesell *et al., Youth: The Years from Ten to Sixteen.* New York: Harper & Row, Publishers, 1956.
[3] Gesell *et al.,* p. 204.
[4] Gesell *et al.,* pp. 241, 270.

ever, the attention span of junior and senior high school students is likely to be limited. "Adolescents are usually willing to explore new areas, but are unable to sustain concentrated attention if there is not an immediate satisfaction gained from them."[5]

Experienced teachers realize that even though these statements are valid generalizations, individual students also differ greatly in these characteristics. A student's social and emotional development is dependent to a large degree upon his home background and upon the behavior patterns accepted by the adolescent group with which he regularly associates.

DIFFERENCES ASSOCIATED WITH SOCIOECONOMIC LEVELS   It is important for teachers, largely the product of middle-class homes, to realize that almost 60 percent of the nation's school-age youth are from homes of low socioeconomic classification. Between 35 and 40 percent are from middle-class homes, and about 3 percent are children of the upper class (5:174).

Patterns of values, beliefs, and acceptable behavior differ somewhat from home to home within the same social class but, in general, the differences between classes are drastic with respect to work habits, acceptance of responsibility, occupational outlook, the guidance of children, attitude toward money, morality, manners, uncouth language, proper grammar, physical combat, punishment, the arts, music, reading, home study, education, teachers, and schools. There is little wonder that sociologists and teachers look to the home first when seeking causes of social and emotional behaviors of children and youth.

It should also be noted that "the adolescent has not yet learned to compartmentalize his life; an emotional experience in one area is likely to affect all his other relationships. Parental denial of a request or a quarrel with a schoolmate, for example, may cause a young person's school work to suffer."[6] No doubt, all teachers benefit from developing understanding and a degree of tolerance of the differences that exist in American social structure.

SERIOUS PROBLEMS OF ADJUSTMENT   Early identification of pupils who are potential leaders as well as those who have adjustment problems can do much to keep the learning atmosphere of a class at its optimum. Alert teachers are particularly conscious of the fact that a few students have potentially serious behavior problems.

Research indicates that while the incidence of serious maladjustment may vary greatly from community to community and from school to school, it may not be unusual for a teacher to have three or four individ-

---

[5] Roland C. Faunce and Morrel J. Clute, *Teaching and Learning in the Junior High School.* Belmont, Calif.: Wadsworth Publishing Company, Inc., 1961, p. 41.
[6] Lester D. Crow, Harry E. Ritchie, and Alice Crow, *Education in the Secondary School.* New York: American Book Company, 1961, p. 91.

uals with serious adjustment problems among the 150 to 200 students he teaches each day (1:139). About the same number, in some cases the same students, have been brought before the juvenile court prior to the age of 19.

In court cases, and in school misbehavior, boys outnumber girls about 5 to 1. Boys' offenses against the law most frequently are stealing or malicious mischief, whereas girls are cited for "ungovernable behavior, running away, and sex offenses." [7] There is evidence, however, that considerably more than 2 percent of adolescents at one time or another are involved in infractions of law. In a study of 6000 illegal actions including 600 serious infractions, all of which were committed over a five-year period by 114 boys, only 1 percent of the cases resulted in court action (1:366). Exact figures are not available, but there is reason to believe that the incidence of psychological maladjustment among teen-agers is also a serious problem (1:824).

With the seriously maladjusted, the teacher's proper role is that of an important but subsidiary member of a professional team which cooperates in the diagnosis and treatment of problems. In large schools, the psychiatrist, sociologist, psychologist, visiting caseworker, and the special teacher are the professionals who direct the study and treatment of each case. In small schools the school counselor or principal may take the leadership role. In the opinion of experts, "Help to an individual delinquent can come only through individual study and diagnosis followed by treatment carefully prescribed and systematically carried out, utilizing all community resources." [8]

The classroom teacher, even though he has had "a case just like this last year," or has had experience "straightening them out in the Marines," should never take it upon himself to solve such problems singlehanded. His role in each case is to follow the prescription of the personnel professionally prepared for the job. For a community to leave such problems in the undirected hands of a well-meaning classroom teacher is like turning an ailing child over to a witch doctor in spite of the availability of twentieth-century medical care.

TYPICAL DISCIPLINE PROBLEMS The school misbehaviors of seventh- and eighth-grade boys are most often talking, fighting, throwing things, and truancy. The misbehaviors of girls in those grades are most often talking, gum chewing, eating candy, fighting, and immorality. In the senior high school, common difficulties involve noisy conduct, rudeness to faculty and to other students, lying, petty thievery, and damage to property (1:139).

[7] William Kvaraceus, "Delinquency," *Encyclopedia of Educational Research,* 3d ed., Chester W. Harris, ed. New York: The Macmillan Company, 1960, p. 366.
[8] Kvaraceus, p. 368.

According to research conducted by the National Education Association, some misbehaviors occur in the best of schools, but the incidence of serious difficulty seems greatest in schools located in the slum areas of large urban centers. In these schools only 15 percent of the teachers report that their students are "exceptionally well behaved," whereas the corresponding figure in "good" residential areas is 47 percent. In the same study involving a nationwide sample of 4000 teachers, more than two thirds rated student behavior not nearly as bad as pictured by movies, press, and radio; seven teachers out of eight reported that fewer than 5 percent of their students were troublesome, one out of three found fewer than 1 percent of their students in that category, and one in four reported complete absence of troublemakers (1:139).

It is evident that the problem of discipline, even though overrated by mass communications media, still remains a concern of many teachers. In Chapters 12–14, the teacher's role in maintaining discipline is fully discussed. It may be well for beginning teachers to study that section carefully before taking charge of a class.

SPECIAL TALENTS, EXPERIENCES, AND GOALS

The teacher who acquaints himself with his students' special talents, educational experiences, vocational plans, and educational goals finds in that knowledge a remarkable reservoir from which he can draw to keep his classes at peak performance. In almost every class, there are students who have special interests and talents in such subjects as music, drama, speech, mechanics, and athletics. Many will have selected at least tentative vocational and educational goals. Some will have traveled broadly; others will have had interesting work experiences. All these facts can be used by the expert teacher better to motivate learning.

THE ADOLESCENT'S WORKDAY

Teachers should be alert to the fact that competing for the attention and efforts of adolescents are many ideas and activities other than those associated with the academic life of schools. In addition to the school's activity program designed to aid in the social, emotional, physical, artistic, and cultural development of youth, there are also the important developmental programs of church, home, and other community organizations and agencies.

Some teen-agers, typically the products of middle- and upper-class homes, are notorious joiners. They frequently find themselves involved in an impossible schedule of community club activities, church responsibilities, and special lessons or tasks scheduled by the home—all in addition to the leadership roles they assume in the curricular and the cocurricular programs of the school. Other students, more typically the product of homes of less fortunate economic circumstance, have an equally heavy schedule because they are required to work to help support themselves and their sometimes numerous brothers and sisters.

In these days of the twenty-five- to forty-hour workweek for adults, some parents are looking critically at the expanding demands upon adolescents. Without question, proper coordination of the various programs requires a great deal of awareness, cooperation, and a measure of compromise on the part of all, including the classroom teacher.

Knowledge of a student's complete schedule makes it possible for teachers to plan activities and assignments more realistically and effectively. Most teachers accept the principle that each school subject should have a right to its share of a student's time and effort, but none should demand uncompromising and monopolistic control.

SECURING INFORMATION ABOUT A PARTICULAR CLASS

In addition to being scholars in subject matter and experts in the various teaching techniques, teachers need to know the learning-related characteristics of each class and its individual students if the best possible job of teaching that class is to be accomplished. Teachers need to answer such questions as, What proportion of the class is fast moving, average, or slow intellectually? As a group and as individuals, are they eager to learn or are they indifferent or antagonistic to school in general or to this subject in particular? What is the level of their achievement in the subject and in the fundamental skills needed? What clues to class motivation can be gained from the interests, experiences, and special talents represented? Which students have special problems of health, growth, adjustment, or learning? What clues to better instruction can be gained from knowledge of their home and community environment? Which students can be depended upon for cooperation and leadership toward desired ends?

All these questions and many more are important in teaching. The answers are not automatic. They are not granted with successful completion of a college course, nor do they necessarily accompany years of teaching experience, although both can be factors contributing to successful solutions.

Data basic to answers must be secured and studied for each new group of students. The needed information can be obtained in many ways and from various sources, including school records and reports of all types, comments of teachers and school personnel, student essays, interviews, questionnaires, teacher observation, and conferences with parents.

RECORDS AND REPORTS

The keeping of records and reports varies considerably from school to school. However, the files in the offices of the principal or counselor provide such facts as information concerning the academic progress of each student (subjects taken and grades in each), scores on group intelligence tests, reading scores, and results of standardized achievement tests. School files ordinarily include other miscellaneous items of information of value, such as data about the family, health records (serious illnesses, past examination results, and recommendations concerning health problems), and anecdotal reports of significant behavior recorded by observant teachers.

UNOFFICIAL INFORMATION

Fellow teachers and other school personnel often know many valuable bits of information—material that never gets into official records—about students, families, and neighborhoods. Counselors, homeroom teachers, the visiting teacher, former teachers of the students, principals and vice-principals, and other staff members may have gained some keen insights or valuable information pertaining to students.

However, some words of caution need to be given concerning the use of unofficial information about students. Never give or receive such information except for confidential, professional use. Teachers must also screen hearsay evidence carefully to distinguish probable fact from mere gossip or biased opinion. They will particularly have to guard against prejudice toward students with a bad reputation. The student who is branded summarily as a hopeless problem has no chance for redemption, whereas many if not most of the problem cases work out of their difficulties when given proper guidance and opportunity.

INFORMATION FROM STUDENTS

Quite often the most significant data concerning a student are what he says about himself. Autobiographies, informal talks, questionnaires, interest inventories, discussion of hobbies, and open-end questions are all useful devices whereby the student gives information about himself.

The open-end question, for example, can be used to get an expression of attitude or feeling on the part of the student. The student is asked to complete a statement somewhat as follows: "I like class activities that _____" or "I like teachers who _____" or "I can study best when _____." The possibilities are unlimited for exploring student attitudes in this manner. However, best results cannot be obtained unless there is good group morale as well as excellent teacher-student rapport.

Interviews with students should be conducted in private and without encouraging them to reveal information they or their families would not choose to share. For example, to determine parents' occupations usually is acceptable, but to ask about incomes, political preferences, or religious beliefs is unwise. As a matter of principle, the right to privacy and the rules of good taste should be observed in all data-gathering processes.

Inquiries should be restricted to matters that teachers, students, and parents clearly recognize as related to the planning of instruction and the motivation of learning.

OBSERVATION OF STUDENTS

Much can be learned by careful observation of students in many situations—in class discussion, in committee work, during study, in the library, on the school grounds, at school functions, and wherever the student has opportunity to demonstrate behavior in which the teacher is interested. Observation can be used for several purposes: to get the feeling of a class and how it reacts, to determine the effectiveness with which a group studies or carries on school activities, to evaluate instruction, and to gain clues concerning an individual's adjustment and growth.

Specific techniques of observation including use of rating scales, checklists, and anecdotal records are discussed fully in Chapter 16. Here it will merely be pointed out that to furnish reliable evidence, observation must be carefully conducted over an extended period of time. Otherwise the behavior observed might be misleading or unimportant. Therefore teachers should be particularly careful in reaching conclusions based on observation alone. When combined with other information, however, observational evidence frequently can provide the clues that complete the picture.

CONFERENCES WITH PARENTS

In most teaching situations the opportunity to meet parents is limited. Teachers should therefore seize every opportunity to make their acquaintance by meeting them at parent-teacher association functions, open houses, and class programs and demonstrations. In some instances, classroom teachers visit the homes of their students, but as a rule home visits are reserved for the experienced visiting teacher. Successful home visitation requires considerable tact and skill.

ORGANIZING INFORMATION ABOUT STUDENTS

In organizing data about a group of students, teachers should make a general description of the class and keep an individual record of as many students as possible. Summary sheets, graphs, and charts help to give meaning to the data. Detailed class analyses are particularly useful to beginning teachers but many experienced teachers regularly take the time to make them. These teachers are aware of a major finding of educational and psychological research: "The learner, whether animal, child, or adult, moves most efficiently toward a prescribed objective when the process of instruction is best adapted to *him*. This would seem to demand some knowledge of *him* on the part of the teacher." [9] Such analyses, which re-

[9] H. Orville Nordberg, James M. Bradfield, and William C. Odell, *Secondary School Teaching*. New York: The Macmillan Company, 1962, p. 64.

quire the investment of much time and effort, return dividends in increased class achievement.

A SAMPLE CLASS DESCRIPTION

The following section of this chapter contains a sample class description and analysis representative of those regularly completed by student teachers under the supervision of the authors of this text. The expressions and the factual content are largely those of the reports from which the study was abstracted. The students described may seem unique, but almost all are typical of those regularly appearing in the classes of all teachers. It would be of benefit to every student teacher and to most regular teachers to make similar analyses.

My third-period class in ninth-grade science at Central High School enrolls nineteen boys and sixteen girls. Each is identified only by number in this report. Their ages range from 13 to 16 years. From observation it appears that all are well adjusted to school and to their classmates, although school records reveal that four received unsatisfactory citizenship ratings last semester, one for unexcused absences, two for repeated chatter and nonattention, and one for fighting on the school grounds and for general insubordination. One additional student is under direction of the county youth authority and has a history of law violation. On the other hand, seven students, five girls and two boys, received "outstanding" as a rating in citizenship last semester. One of this group is ninth-grade president. Several other students in this class also are active in the cocurricular program of the school. Evidently this class is quite typical in its attitude toward school and study. It contains both positive and negative leadership potential, but most mem-

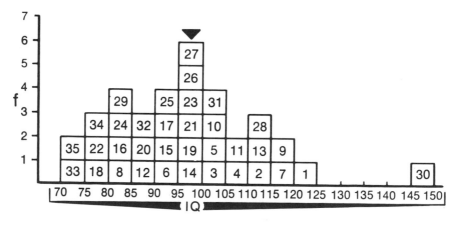

H-N test form "A" administered in ninth grade
H-N test standard deviation: 15
H-N test standard error: 5
▼ class median: 96

Fig. 2-1   *Mental ability of thirty-five students*

bers of the class are solid, "satisfactory" citizens. I have conferred with my cooperating teacher on how best to work with students having problems. He has suggested a follow-up conference regarding student #30.

From observation, study of health records, and examination of the student-questionnaire results it appears that the health of this group is generally good with the exception that one girl regularly complains of headaches and one boy is subject to epileptic seizures. In addition, seven students wear glasses regularly and two others (girls) should be wearing theirs but keep them in their purses. One student has a 30 percent hearing loss and also has an apparent speech defect. Six students are concerned about acne and skin blemishes; two students are at least 20 pounds overweight; one is 6 feet 2 inches tall and concerned about it; and three others are obviously slow in their physical development.

A slow drive through the school neighborhood, during which I noted the size and condition of homes and the general development of the community, was very revealing. One section of homes a few blocks in length borders a park and retains a considerable portion of its earlier elegance; otherwise most of my students live in a rather old and run-down residential area which is losing its battle with the encroachment of multiple dwellings and minor business establishments.

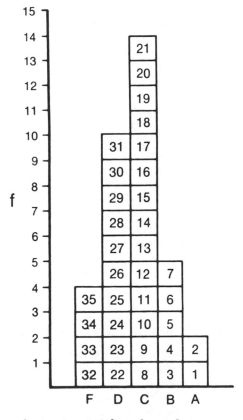

Fig. 2-2 Semester grades in science of thirty-five students

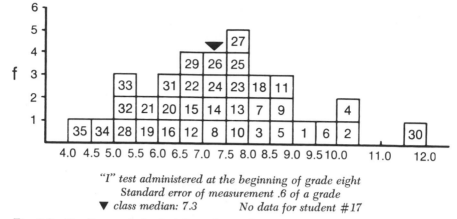

"*I*" *test administered at the beginning of grade eight*
Standard error of measurement .6 of a grade
▼ *class median: 7.3*   *No data for student #17*

Fig. 2-3   *Reading grade level of thirty-five students*

Study of parent occupations—many mothers are working at production-line tasks, and most fathers are in "blue-collar" jobs—confirms the observation that most of the students in this class are of lower to lower-middle socioeconomic background. These factors must be given careful consideration as I try to understand the motivations of each student.

Analysis of test scores in the cumulative files indicates that IQ's of this class range from 72 to 145, with the class median between 95 and 100 (see Figure 2–1). The class does not appear to be well motivated toward science study, for only 20 percent earned A or B grades in the subject last semester (see Figure 2–2). Their standardized achievement scores also indicate generally low achievement. Seventy percent scored below grade level in science background last year. In a reading test also administered last year, they ranged from 4.4 to 11.8 in grade level. The class median at 7.3 was approximately one grade below average (Figure 2–3). I will have to keep these facts in mind as I prepare and select their reading materials in science.

Twelve students say they plan to go to college but most are somewhat indefinite in their choice of education and vocational goals. Eight feel that they might attend trade or business schools; five say they intend to quit school as soon as the law allows; the remainder indicate a tentative preference for blue-collar jobs and the military.

From this survey, it appears that my third-period class is a fairly typical heterogeneous group; however, it is a little below average in academic interest and ability. To get them all interested in science will be a real challenge.

ANALYSIS TO FACILITATE BETTER INSTRUCTION OF INDIVIDUALS

The remainder of this class analysis will be devoted to study of individuals, including those who need special attention as well as those who might make special contributions to the class.

Students who need enrichment materials and activities: Students #1 through #7 all earned A's or B's in science last semester. I plan to get them interested in special projects, including reading, term papers, special reports related to their interests, and to the best of my ability I will encourage them to keep up their good work. A few may become interested in careers in science.

Students #9, #11, and #13 seem to have potential for better work than they have been producing. Perhaps conferences with them could get them to study better. Student #30 might eventually qualify for top-level assignments, but at present he is involved with problems of adjustment.

Students who need remedial materials and activities: Failing students #32 through #35 and D students #22 through #31 can all benefit from planned review, special drill based upon diagnostic tests, and use of interesting applications. They appear to need specific directions in how to study the subject of science. I am preparing a handout of study suggestions and will guide them through the appropriate steps in supervised study at the first opportunity. Student #28 may need special remedial help in reading. In fact, as so many of this class read at an inferior level, I plan to give group instruction to them in science vocabulary and reading skills. From the mass of supplementary reading materials available, I will select those which are easiest to read and assign them specifically to this group. I also will take particular care to see that these students know (and record) exactly what is expected of them in each assignment. They will be tested frequently and given daily drill in selected areas of weakness.

Students who have interests or hobbies that could be used: Students #8 and #29 have interests in camping which I will use during the conservation unit. Student #5 has interest and some talent in art which I plan to encourage by asking her to develop bulletin boards and displays for the class. Student #4 has a hobby of raising tropical fish, student #27 collects rocks, and student #30 is a "bug" on electronics. These students will be asked to report orally to the class and perhaps exhibit their work when the class reaches the related scientific study. Students #33, #22, and #15 have relatives who work in science-related jobs. The students will be asked to inform the class about the requirements and opportunities in work of this type. The uncle of student #19 is an officer in the narcotics detail of the sheriff's department. He sometimes speaks to community groups about his work. Student #19 will be asked to invite him to speak to our class when we study the unit on alcohol and narcotics. Several other students have hobbies which I may be able to use to stimulate interest in science and which I might use as a key to discussion with them.

Students who need special consideration because of physical limitations: Students #17 and #25 seldom wear their glasses although they need them. I will assign these students to seats near the front of the room so that they can see the chalkboard. Number 26, who has a hearing difficulty, will also be given a seat near the front of the room. I must remember to look in his direction more when I speak to the class so that he can use his developing skill of lip reading. In our unit on health, I will ask a dermatologist or the school nurse to speak to our class on the health concerns of adolescents. With their assistance I also expect to develop a list of readings to help students understand these problems.

My greatest concern with the health problems of this class is to be able to do exactly the right thing should #12 have an epileptic seizure. I have conferred with the nurse and she has given me explicit instructions for this case. She also has assured me that if #12 takes his medication regularly a seizure is unlikely. The nurse will be immediately availble should the unusual occur.

Students who need special consideration because of adjustment problems: Student #30 is under direction of the youth authority of this county. The caseworker in charge will confer regularly with me and with his other teachers. I will follow the caseworker's suggestions. So far #30 seems to be getting along well in this class.

Number 35 failed this course last year. He is lowest in reading ability, lowest in intelligence score, and lowest in achievement in this class. He is in a state of rebellion against all teachers and other symbols of authority. His father is unemployed and his mother has a police record as an alcoholic. A social worker is expected to be assigned to this case. Perhaps he can salvage the boy. I will cooperate but I don't feel adequately prepared to do much alone. In the meantime I will be friendly but particularly careful to keep a close check on him because I have been warned that to give him a free hand for even a few minutes may lead to classroom disaster.

Number 28 is an enigma. She is a problem not because she is poorly adjusted, but because she is too well adjusted to academic achievement below her apparent ability. She is extremely well developed and attractive for a girl of her age (and aware of it). She seems to be in a constant whirl of cocurricular and social activities. The upper-class boys as well as the more mature males in her own class all seem much more important to her—and she to them—than the "bugs and mice" of science. She can describe every detail of last night's TV spectacular but can't seem to remember a single fact of science from one moment to the next.

When I took over the class she seemed to get more interested in studying. She even volunteered to do a special report on William Harvey's description of blood flow. To this end I signed three library passes on successive days so she could research the subject. That was two weeks ago, and I am now afraid that William Harvey and science have been outpointed by romanticism. In class she gives no attention to subject matter but loses no opportunity to attract the attention of her admirers. (And I'm afraid she has some designs on me!) The fact that her scholastic rating in all her classes is a straight D doesn't seem to bother her in the least. She meets all suggestions concerning study with a sweet smile, but does the absolute minimum to get by.

Mr. Jones, my cooperating teacher, remarked that last semester he too tried to direct her attention to science study, but to no avail. He added, perhaps in jest, that he no longer looked upon her with dismay, but rather with a degree of envy, since she is obviously so delightfully happy in her own little world. He concluded that it might not be psychologically defensible to upset her dreams with the disturbing facts of science, and after all she and others like her undoubtedly will create lovely, peaceful havens for their hard-driving ulcer-prone science-wise husbands a few years hence. Mr. Jones has a point there, but I'm certain he wasn't serious because we both agree that knowledge of science is important for everybody.

Students who can be depended upon to be positive leaders: Student #2 is president of the ninth grade and very popular. He is the center of a strong group which has a positive influence on this class. When the room gets noisy and I don't notice it—one of my weaknesses that must be remedied—he shushes them successfully.

Student #16 is of below-average ability according to test scores, but she works hard and sets a good example for those around her. In committee work she easily takes the leadership role and elicits productive cooperation from her group. If there were a #16 in all groups my problems in group work would be effectively reduced, if not eliminated.

Student #7 is an all-around athlete. He is active in all major sports and was a regular on the school's championship basketball team this year. He hopes to go to college and become a coach some day. He is respected by all students but is particularly effective in setting an example which helps to keep the rougher boys in line. His willing cooperation makes this an easier class to teach.

Students who need help to become effective members of the group: Observation of the class and the class sociogram both indicate that students #30, #35, and #17 are isolates in this class. I will take no action in the cases of #30 and #35 until I get the advice of experts, but student #17 appears to be a less complicated case. She transferred into this school two weeks ago from a small town in an adjoining state. She told me that she didn't like Central High because it was too big and the students were all "snooty." She customarily sits in the back of the room and talks to no one the entire period. I plan to move her seat next to #16 and ask #16 to be her sponsor. Working with #16's friendly cooperative group should soon convince her that getting acquainted requires little more than friendly reaction and acceptance by both the old and the new. I will soon give her opportunity to tell the class something about her former school and what she likes about Central High.

USING INFORMATION ABOUT STUDENTS

In the process of gathering data about students, teachers need to keep several important considerations in mind. First, such material is for *use,* not for storage in a dead file. Second, the information must be kept strictly *confidential,* to be used for professional purposes only. Unless items are coded or recorded in an anonymous manner, personal data should be kept under lock and key and made available only to authorized persons. Unfortunately some teachers are afflicted with wagging tongues. They are inclined to relieve their tensions by gossiping about their students freely in the cafeteria or some other public place. Such practice is highly unprofessional. Third, teachers need to use information about students *intelligently.* This skill involves collection and organization of data, correct and judicious interpretation of the facts, and wise application to teaching situations. In making intelligent use of information about his students, a teacher must consider especially the data that are significant in his particular class. For example, a low reading score may not be significant in a physical education class whereas health status and physical coordination would be very important. On the other hand, reading skill is quite necessary in a social studies class, where success depends to a great extent on ability to read. Furthermore, in interpreting data, teachers must guard against making hasty generalizations or drawing dogmatic conclusions. Test score interpretation is a skill that involves understanding of the concepts of normal and nonnormal distributions, errors of measurement, and systems of standard scores. A later chapter deals fully with these problems.

Finally, teachers must always remember that each student is a person, not just another name or statistic. Each one has his hopes and fears, his strengths and weaknesses, his advantages and his handicaps, his virtues and his faults, and his own optimum route to learning. The teachers who proceed scientifically to search for those optimum routes are most likely to discover them and thereby receive the top reward in teaching: high student achievement.

SELECTED READINGS

1. American Educational Research Association, *Encyclopedia of Educational Research*, 3d ed., Chester W. Harris, ed. New York: The Macmillan Company, 1960, pp. 24–29, 680–686, 853–855.

2. Association for Supervision and Curriculum Development, NEA, *Youth Education: Problems—Perspectives—Promise*. Prepared by the ASCD 1968 Yearbook Committee. Washington, D.C.: 1968.

3. Bent, Rudyard, and Henry H. Kronenberg, *Principles of Secondary Education*, 5th ed. New York: McGraw-Hill Company, Inc., 1966, chaps. 9 and 5.

4. Blount, Nathan S., and Herbert J. Klausmeier, *Teaching in the Secondary School*, 3d ed. New York: Harper & Row, Publishers, 1968, chap. 2.

5. Burton, William H., *The Guidance of Learning Activities*, 3d ed. New York: Appleton-Century-Crofts, Inc., 1962, chaps. 7, 8, and 10.

6. Callahan, Sterling G., *Successful Teaching in Secondary Schools*. Chicago: Scott, Foresman and Company, 1966, chaps. 1 and 2.

7. Clark, Leonard H., and Irving S. Starr, *Secondary School Teaching Methods*, 2d ed. New York: The Macmillan Company, 1967, chap. 2.

8. Cyphert, Frederick R., and others, *Teaching in the American Secondary School*. New York: McGraw-Hill Book Company, Inc., 1964, Part II and selection 18.

9. Dahl, John A., and others, *Student, School, and Society*. San Francisco: Chandler Publishing Company, 1964, Part I.

10. Faunce, Roland C., and Carroll L. Munshaw, *Teaching and Learning in Secondary Schools*. Belmont, Calif.: Wadsworth Publishing Company, Inc., 1964, chap. 3.

11. Flanagan, J. C., and others, *The American High School Student*. Technical Report to the U.S. Office of Education, Cooperative Research Project No. 635. Pittsburgh: Project Talent Office, University of Pittsburgh, 1964.

12. Lee, Florence Henry, *Principles and Practices of Teaching in Secondary Schools*. New York: David McKay Company, Inc., 1965, chap. 4.

13. Mouly, George J., *Psychology for Effective Teaching*, 2d ed. New York: Holt, Rinehart and Winston, Inc., 1968, chaps. 5–10.

14. Oliva, Peter F., *The Secondary School Today*. Cleveland: The World Publishing Company, 1967, chap. 13.

15. Smith, Frederick R., *Secondary Schools Today*. Boston: Houghton Mifflin Company, 1965, Part III.

CHAPTER 3 / *Preparation for Teaching*

One characteristic of a profession is that it requires an extended period of specialized preparation on the part of the candidate before he is authorized to become a practitioner. This is becoming increasingly true of teaching. Preservice preparation includes a series of graduated steps for admission to teacher education and for advancement toward receipt of a license or credential, culminating in student teaching. Before undertaking this last and most important phase of preparation, the teacher candidate is advised to take careful inventory of his own assets, to reassess the requirements for teaching, and to evaluate his own fitness for the teaching profession.

BEFORE STUDENT TEACHING

"I love to teach as a painter loves to paint, as a musician loves to play, as a singer loves to sing, as a strong man rejoices to run a race."—*William Lyon Phelps*

AN INVENTORY BEFORE STUDENT TEACHING

As the prospective teacher approaches the most important phase of his professional preparation, observation of and work with students in the classroom, he may very well take further stock of his motives for becoming a teacher. It is important that the teacher candidate ask himself what satisfactions he wants from life. Teachers have listed a number of reasons for choosing their career: among them, interest in teaching a particular subject (especially true of men), the desire to be of service, security and permanency of employment, and good working conditions. One study concludes that teachers have less need or desire than the general public for "prestige, income, and professional recognition."[1] In the beginning

---

[1] Earl W. Anderson and Elfreda M. Rusher, "Staff—Characteristics," *Encyclopedia of Educational Research*, 3d ed., Chester W. Harris, ed. New York: The Macmillan Company, 1960, p. 1359.

chapter, basic satisfactions of teaching, as well as the several roles of the teacher, were summarized. The prospective teacher is advised to give thoughtful consideration to these things. By all means, he should recognize that teaching is more than a bread-and-butter occupation. It is the fine art of helping boys and girls grow toward maturity.

The prospective teacher must give thoughtful consideration to his *commitment to teaching*. Although it has already been noted that teacher satisfaction is relatively high in the profession, 17.3 percent of the men teaching in secondary schools certainly or probably would not reenter teaching.[2] These teachers fail to achieve the satisfactions teaching has to offer and probably render a double disservice to the profession: They fail to give students the help to which they are entitled and they discourage promising high school candidates from considering teaching as a career. One perceptive high school senior made the comment about a very poor teacher: "I had thought of becoming a teacher, but, if he is representative of the profession, I think I shall decide on some other occupation."

The prospective teacher needs to become informed about *professional requirements* as early as possible and to work diligently toward their fulfillment. Such requirements usually include a program of general education, specialization in one or more teaching fields, courses in professional education, and laboratory experiences with boys and girls. Each requirement is designed to contribute to an important aspect of teacher preparation, a fact that is not always clearly recognized by the neophyte in the profession. No doubt very few teachers have completed their professional preparation without later regretting that they did not spend more time and effort on some neglected phase of the program.

DIRECTED OBSERVATION

Probably directed observation of classroom learning activities is second only to student teaching as a means of preparing the teacher candidate for the assumption of full-time responsibilities in teaching. There is an increasing tendency to introduce "laboratory experiences prior to student teaching." [3] Observation of and work with pupils in the classroom before actual student teaching has a number of advantages. First of all, the teacher candidate can get a better idea of whether or not his choice of teaching as a vocation has been a wise one. Sometimes vocational choices are made on a nebulous, unrealistic basis. The demonstrated insights and actual performance of the prospective teacher in observing and assisting pupils with their learning may also be used as a criterion for the predic-

[2] Research Division of the National Education Association, *The American Public School Teacher, 1965–'66*, NEA Research Report, 1967-R-4, p. 51.
[3] Laurence D. Haskew, "Teacher Education—Organization and Administration," *Encyclopedia of Educational Research*, 3d ed., Chester W. Harris, ed. New York: The Macmillan Company, 1960, p. 1459.

tion of future success. Finally, these laboratory experiences serve as a valuable introduction to student teaching itself.

In order to profit most from his experience in directed observation, the observer must make his observations intelligently and systematically. First of all, it is advisable to take careful notes as a basis for future study and discussion with the teacher conducting the class. What should the beginning observer watch for? The most fruitful study of any teaching situation is a study of the learners themselves—their varied social, emotional, and intellectual reactions; their differences and similarities in abilities, achievement, and home backgrounds; and their fluctuation in behavior in different situations. The observer needs to be aware of the physical environment—its comfort, attractiveness, cleanliness, and evidences of cooperative housekeeping. The observer should note the routine organization of the classroom—time schedules, student traffic, and distribution and storage of materials. By all means, the observer should carefully consider the procedures used in classroom management and control—standards maintained, responsibilities of teacher and students respectively, rapport between the teacher and the class, and general classroom atmosphere.

Usually the student teacher has a few days of observation, followed by a period of assisting and presenting parts of the lesson, before assuming full responsibility for teaching the class. By making the most of these opportunities, he should be able to make a smooth transition from an observer to a full-fledged teacher.

Observation, even the most informal type implied in this discussion, presents a number of problems. Many variables must be kept in mind: individual behaviors, different situations (classroom, playground, and so on), sampling, objectivity, and the competence of the observer. As a newcomer to the profession, the prospective teacher must be aware of his own limitations. Occasionally a beginning observer may be unduly critical of classroom procedures or situations that he does not fully comprehend because of his own immaturity and inexperience. Consequently, he must avoid jumping to unwarranted conclusions. It has already been suggested that observations should be recorded. This should be done with as much objectivity as possible, primarily by the omission of biased interpretations from the record. The observer should have an adequate sampling in order to give his observations more reliability. It is obviously illogical to draw any final conclusions about a student on the basis of only one or two examples of his conduct. Furthermore, because the student is quite often a different person in the formal classroom from what he is in other settings, a study of student behavior under varied conditions is advisable.

STUDENT TEACHING

As the prospective teacher enters the final and most important phase of his professional preparation—student teaching—he must become fully aware of the purposes and functions of the experience. Briefly stated, student teaching marks the transition from student to teacher. And what a transition that is! One day the candidate for teaching is a student; the next day he is a teacher. After spending fifteen or sixteen years as a student, the prospective teacher may understandably have difficulty in making a sudden adjustment to the many roles of the teacher. When he takes his place *behind* the teacher's desk, he finds himself giving instructions and sometimes orders, and, much to his surprise, he finds students complying with his requests.

As the first shock of strangeness and self-consciousness wears off, the student teacher will need to get his bearings. For one thing, the amassing of units and grade points, which may have been a major concern in his academic life, should no longer seem so important to him. The student teacher must also realize that student teaching is not designed primarily for his convenience nor as a laboratory in which his students are the guinea pigs. The welfare of students, their learning, always has priority. Only by careful preparation and by conscientious performance daily in the classroom can the student teacher justify his continued presence as a guest of the school in which he teaches. The student teacher must also realize that he is not fully prepared as a teacher when he has completed his student teaching assignments. At best, student teaching is only a partial, even unrealistic, introduction to full-time teaching. Because he is frequently assigned to a limited number of classes often more or less carefully selected and to a superior cooperating teacher whose presence is felt in the classroom, the student teacher is sheltered from many problems he will ultimately face when he is entirely on his own. Some student teachers who have had no problems develop a cocksure, "I have it made" attitude, largely because of their good fortune rather than their teaching skill. Beginners can always benefit from the advice of experience.

The following major section of this chapter is addressed specifically to the beginning student teacher. The advice offered comes directly from three professors with many years of teaching in high schools and indirectly from the more than one thousand student teachers they have supervised in junior and senior high schools during the last twenty years. Careful consideration of suggestions based on their experience should help to accelerate a beginner's progress toward successful teaching.

It is thoroughly normal behavior for a student teacher to approach his first actual teaching with some degree of perturbation. No doubt you are wondering what successes lie ahead. What failures? What will your response be to the challenges of teaching? Will you be strong or weak in discipline? Will students respect you? Will they learn? Will supervisors be sympathetic and helpful? These questions and many more, according to research, trouble those who enter this most important phase of professional preparation.[4] Unfortunately there is no crystal ball to supply immediate answers.

Nor is there any set of prescriptions that can guarantee success to all. The best advice at this stage is to avoid dwelling on advance fears. There is a job to be done, and, once action begins, preliminary tensions will be replaced with the satisfactions of growth accomplished. Be assured that many co-workers are vitally interested in your problems and can do much to help you solve them. It is of utmost importance that you learn to work harmoniously with these persons, recognize their value, and come to earn their cooperation. Who are your co-workers? What can be expected of them? How can their respect and cooperation be earned?

KNOW YOUR SUPERVISORS [5]

A cooperating teacher at your assigned school, together with supervisors from the college, will observe and direct your teaching with one purpose in mind: they want you to succeed. They will help you plan your work, suggest a variety of activities and source materials, and constructively evaluate your teaching techniques. In periodic conferences they will strive to help you improve such factors as the quality of your voice, the appropriateness of your dress, the efficiency of your classroom organization, your rapport with students, and the overall effectiveness of your teaching methods. At the conclusion of your student teaching experience, they will write recommendations that should help you get a teaching position. They can be important contributors to your success. To help you receive full benefit from supervisory assistance, several points must be emphasized.

THE COOPERATING TEACHER IS YOUR SPONSOR IN THE SCHOOL   The cooperating teacher is the main source of information concerning the customs, regulations, and services of the school. He will help clarify your precise position in the school's social structure. Determine through him at the beginning of the term your duties and privileges as a junior member of the faculty. Get his approval before you request the special help of school staff, such as the nurse, counselor, principal, secretary, or custodian. In

[4] John U. Michaelis, "Teacher Education—Student Teaching and Internship," *Encyclopedia of Educational Research*, 3d ed., Chester W. Harris, ed. New York: The Macmillan Company, 1960, p. 1478.
[5] The term *supervisors* includes college faculty members who have supervisory responsibilities related to student teaching, as well as cooperating teachers who are the certificated instructors of the classes taught by student teachers.

like manner, do not ask faculty members, other than your supervisor, to contribute to your classes unless your cooperating teacher gives complete approval. Avoid the error of one student teacher who, within his first week, aroused the ire of an entire faculty by officiously seeking guest speakers, models of art, bulletin displays, and other products of faculty effort. Your cooperating teacher can usually provide the help you will need. If supplementary assistance is advisable, he will know where, when, and how to request it. Furthermore, your cooperating teacher is legally responsible for the progress of the class he has turned over to you. Therefore, all your teaching must be subject to his approval. Check your plans with him before you teach.

SUPERVISORS ARE YOUR FRIENDS Discuss your problems frankly with them. Relate your successes; admit your failures. Avoid alibis or rationalizations. Making excuses may save your ego temporarily, but the cost will be loss of opportunity to improve. Certain ethical and personal considerations should govern the relationship between a student teacher and his supervisors. Eight suggestions follow.

1. *Be prudent.* No one admires a talebearer. If a disturbing situation should arise between you and one of your supervisors, discuss the problem directly with him; if that does not seem feasible, take the matter to the director of student teaching. Do not spread your problems of teaching among your friends. Your supervisors and the director of student teaching are responsible persons. They alone are professionally prepared to help solve the problems that may perplex you. It would be poor policy to risk deterioration of supervisory relationships by broadcasting the problems that are solvable professionally.

2. *Be loyal.* If one of your students should criticize a regular staff member of the school, do not fall into the trap of agreement, either overt or implied. For example, a student, for motives of his own, may tell you he prefers your teaching to that of the cooperating teacher. Such a statement may be music to your ears and therapy for your entire personality, but by all means you should resist rigorously any temptation to be a receptive listener. One student who comments in this manner may be blunderingly sincere; another may be attempting only to gain personal advantage. In either case the basic impropriety of such remarks should be recognized and dealt with promptly. At no time should you or your students get the idea that you are in any sort of competition with your cooperating teacher. The two of you form a professional team that can operate effectively only when loyalty on the part of each is automatic.

3. *Accept responsibility.* Take over full teaching responsibility as soon as your cooperating teacher recommends it. Be regular in attendance and be on time. If an emergency should arise to prevent your attendance at a class or a conference, inform your supervisors as soon as it is humanly

possible. Messages of this nature are usually handled by the school secretary. There is almost no adequate reason to excuse your failure to inform the cooperating teacher prior to an enforced absence or tardiness.

4. *Give attention to details.* Have your lesson plans carefully prepared in advance so that your cooperating teacher can inspect them and discuss anticipated problems with you. Keep up-to-date in recording and reporting. Have attendance reports ready when they are needed in the central office. Give immediate attention to all tasks assigned by your supervisors. Neglected minutiae have a way of developing into full-fledged problems.

5. *Show initiative.* Avoid becoming a mental parasite, existing only on the ideas of others. Give continuous thought to your work so that you will not appear at planning sessions empty-handed and devoid of ideas. Professional periodicals and books in your college library are rich in ideas for better teaching.

6. *Seek advice and follow it.* Do not merely shop around until you find an opinion that agrees with your own. Supervisors take pride in observing the successful application of their suggestions, and are thus stimulated to share their rich knowledge and experience. On the other hand, they are not entirely immune to discouragement or impatience when their advice is ignored.

7. *Be a good listener.* Too many student teachers fall short of their potential as teachers because they have not learned to listen. Do not become a person who is so busy planning his response or searching for excuses that he is deaf to the suggestions of his supervisor. To be a good listener requires effort and practice as well as basic courtesy.

8. *Be absolutely honest in self-evaluation.* Be frank and honest with yourself and with your supervisors. Only then will real communication be possible. Anything less than absolute honesty in continuous self-evaluation and in periodic supervisory conferences will very seriously retard the progress that should be yours.

SUPERVISORS DIFFER   Supervisors—all successful teachers—occasionally differ among themselves concerning specific teaching practices. Student teachers should realize that differences of opinion among supervisors are the normal result of varying backgrounds of education and experience. Avoid making an issue of them. For example, most student teachers will be given teaching responsibility after a week or two of observation whereas a few may be plunged into full responsibility at once. Still others may be denied teaching privileges for a month or more. Some supervisors will demand extensive daily lesson plans; others may be satisfied with bare outlines or nothing. Do not be disturbed by such inconsistencies. Treat them with tact. Throughout your entire career you will encounter an abundance of conflicting opinions. The sooner you learn to live with them, the better. A guiding principle might well be to adapt supervisory advice to the specific requirements of the school in which you do your student teaching, but also keep in mind that the experience gained must be broad enough to prepare you for success in one of the many different schools that soon may offer you a teaching contract.

KNOW THE SCHOOL'S ADMINISTRATORS

The administrative head of the school is the principal. He is directly responsible for providing effective leadership of the school and of its entire educational program, including the classes taught by student teachers. To student teachers he usually appears to be a rather mysterious person hidden away in a remote office. However, even though he may not see you regularly, he knows you are in the school and feels some responsibility for your success. Because he undoubtedly examined your papers when he helped select your cooperating teacher he probably knows more about you than you suspect. Through conferences with supervisors most principals keep informed concerning the progress of the student teachers in their building. Some principals briefly visit classes taught by student teachers, although such visits are seldom made during the first weeks of student teaching.

The principal will expect you to adapt quickly to the requirements of your position and become a cooperative and creative member of the school community. He will expect not only that you do a good job of instruction but also that you carry your share of the extra duties of teaching. Many schools provide manuals that contain the school regulations as well as specific suggestions to guide the orientation of new teachers. If such a manual exists at your school, study it carefully.

A principal is a good person to know. Not only is he a man rich in educational experience; he also specializes in understanding human relations. Furthermore, he is chiefly responsible for the selection of his staff and through his friends can effectively recommend teachers for positions in other schools.

Quite obviously, the principal is an important person in the school community. Student teachers should not stand in awe of him. Neither should they rush to his office in an ill-concealed attempt to win attention. In some schools, the principal makes a practice of inviting each student teacher into his office for a friendly conference. In others, he can be seen only when the student teacher requests an appointment. Your cooperating teacher can advise you of the custom in your school. If you are given the opportunity of an interview with the principal, put your best foot forward. It is likely that he will direct the conversation; however, if he can be drawn out, he can undoubtedly contribute much to your knowledge of such topics as the qualities that contribute to the success of a beginning teacher, the relative supply and demand of teachers in neighboring areas, or the desirability of administration as a career in education.

Answer his questions honestly, but avoid introducing any discussion of grievances or personalities. He is interested in your personality and potential as a teacher and not in your ability to analyze critically the internal relationships of his staff.

One or more vice-principals (or a dean of boys and a dean of girls) complete the administrative staff of most large schools. The duties of vice-principals usually include the accounting of student attendance and the enforcement of discipline. Customarily, it is to the vice-principal that rebellious, truant, or tardy students are sent. You and your cooperating teacher should discuss your proper role in dealing with attendance or discipline problems. Be sure you understand the policies and procedures accepted at your school before you take charge of the class.

As head of the school, the principal will do all that is possible to provide a pleasant working atmosphere. You can contribute to that goal by observing certain rules of operation:

1. Complete reports accurately and on time. The administrative staff learns to know you through your reports of attendance, marks, and so on. The impression the reports make is important.

2. Keep a strict accounting of books and supplies. The materials of instruction are costly. You are expected to use them sensibly and keep accurate records of books issued to students.

3. Enforce and follow the regulations of the school. If a regulation forbids smoking on the school grounds, you will be expected to follow the regulation yourself and to assist in its observance by your students. Some students will take immediate advantage of new teachers who fail to learn or to observe the school's regulations.

4. Keep the principal informed of field trips and other changes in the regular schedule of your classes. Clearance in the principal's office is usually required for all field trips and other deviations from the regular class schedule (this will usually be done through your supervisor).

5. Avoid disturbing the classes of other teachers. Their work is just as important as yours. They have every right to be free from disturbances caused by the irresponsibility of neighboring classes. For instance, do not permit your students to be noisy or to roam the halls; you are responsible for their conduct during the entire class period.

6. Follow a strict code of professional ethics in all your relationships. Many of the problems of beginning teachers arise from the fact that they have been unaware of the proper procedure to follow. Study the codes adopted by your school and the leading professional organizations in education. They will be helpful.

KNOW THE TEACHING STAFF

The reception you will receive from the regular teaching staff will be governed by your own attitudes and actions. If you are courteous, professional, and not overly aggressive, you will soon earn acceptance as an important junior member of their society. Be sure, however, to remember continually that you are in their midst to receive advice, not to give it. You lack prestige on two counts: you are a learner and a newcomer. Keep in mind that, like the owl, you can gain a reputation for wisdom by being silent. You will be wise to remain comparatively silent when the occasional informal gatherings develop into gripe sessions or turn toward the discussion of personalities. You might temporarily gain satisfying attention and apparent status by freely volunteering your opinions concerning topics such as the comparative uselessness of college courses, the awesome gap between educational theory and practice, the relative demerits of campus leaders, the entertaining peculiarities of your associates, or the inadequacy of the instruction received by your students from their former teachers. At best, the status gained by such idle talk would be a transitory illusion. If you should be tempted to seek such attention, remember that the successful student teacher follows a professional code of ethics. He works through his cooperating teacher in all relations with the school staff, says nothing in the absence of his supervisor that he could not say without embarrassment in his presence, and acknowledges the maxim that "he who would build himself up does not attempt to tear others down."

Your cooperating teacher has to cooperate with other teachers in many ways. As you assume increasing responsibility for the class assigned to you, you will need to work closely with other teachers. For instance, the type and quality of control you set up in your class will be influenced by the control other teachers exercise in their classes. The behavior of students in your class will, in turn, be reflected in other classes. Each teacher has to learn to work within the framework of patterns to which students have been accustomed. The noise in your classroom may disturb the class next door. When you assign homework, be sure that you do not make excessive demands which conflict with the assignments of other teachers. Whenever you take your class on field trips during the school day and those trips cut across other periods, you are interfering with some other teacher's work. If you rearrange the seats in your classroom and then leave them in disorder for the next class, you are not being thoughtful. Neither is it thoughtful to monopolize bulletin board space or to leave a room with chalkboards unerased. Untidy desks and paper-strewn floors also testify to a teacher's carelessness. Thoughtless actions lead to misunderstandings, and accumulated misunderstandings can easily destroy harmonious relationships among members of a teaching staff. No student teacher can afford to be careless. Thoughtfulness pays in terms of improved staff relationships.

KNOW THE NONTEACHING STAFF

The school's specialized personnel includes the nurse, the librarian, the counselors, the cafeteria manager, the secretaries and clerks, and the custodians. All these people are able and willing to help you unless you ignore them. Never become deluded with the notion that you are better than some of the staff members because you have had greater educational advantages than they. They can teach you much if you are teachable. The principal's secretary knows the inner workings of the school much better than you do and can help you avoid mistakes. She can make school resources more accessible to you, pave the way to better relationships with other staff members for you, and speak a good word for you to the principal. The custodian is also a valuable person to know. Quite often he is a respected citizen in the school community and a friend of long standing to students as well as to faculty members. Be considerate of him in keeping your room neat and clean and by respecting his work schedule. He is a busy man, but he can always find time to give a bit of friendly advice to the beginner or to lend a helping hand when it is needed. Each of the other persons in specialized services can also contribute to your success. Confer with your cooperating teacher concerning how they might best be approached.

KNOW YOURSELF AS A TEACHER

Now that you are entering the most important phase of your professional preparation, you should take another inventory of your qualifications for teaching. Many factors are vital to success. Student teaching is intended to provide opportunity for improvement. No one is perfect. Have you identified the specifics in which your needs are greatest?

CHECK YOUR MASTERY OF BASIC SKILLS AND SUBJECT MATTER   Do you qualify as a teacher in the mastery of skills and subject matter? Your communications skill, study habits, and ability and willingness to plan and to organize your work—all these are important. Regardless of your teaching field, students and their parents expect you to know your subject and to speak, write, and spell with the skill of a teacher.

ASSESS YOUR ABILITY TO WORK WITH PEOPLE   "Unsatisfactory response to supervision" is a recurring comment of supervisors of student teachers. Although no supervisor expects you to be a "yes" man without initiative or will, he does expect to see evidence of gracious and responsive acceptance of wise counsel. How do you react to constructive criticism? Supervisors sometimes state, "Any suggestion I make to John seems to bounce back in my face," or "When I try to help Helen, she immediately goes on the defensive and begins to rationalize," or "I might help Bill if he ever came to see me." Supervisors are your friends. It is not their purpose to destroy your self-esteem, but to help you become an effective teacher. Criticisms are given in a spirit of kindly helpfulness. When you master the art of working with others, most of your problems in teaching will vanish.

DEVOTE ADEQUATE TIME TO STUDENT TEACHING   How much time are you willing to give to your teaching? Some student teachers fail to do themselves justice by attempting to do too much besides their teaching. If you can take seventeen hours of college work, hold a job for forty hours a week, become a social lion on campus, and, at the same time, do a creditable job of student teaching, you are indeed a most unusual person. When you enter a profession, you dedicate yourself to the skillful performance of the services of that profession. Student teachers with "so little time" often say, "I must work," "I must finish in June," or "I must" do this and that. Most professions would not tolerate the halfhearted performance that a few student teachers exhibit during their internship. Although you are not expected to be a social recluse, your professional activities must come first. Whenever you spend too much time on other things during student teaching, certain important functions suffer—adequate planning or preparation, keeping appointments with supervisors, making necessary reports on time, and maintaining vitality, enthusiasm, and even temper in the classroom. If you are too busy to do a satisfactory job of student teaching, you are too busy. Your alternatives are to reduce your load or drop your teaching.

REEXAMINE YOUR PERSONALITY   How would you assess your personality and its effect on others? Do you possess integrity, sincerity, a sense of responsibility, forcefulness and conviction, sympathy and understanding, and a keen sense of values? How do you rate on warmth, tact, voice, attractiveness, sense of humor, manners, neatness, and friendliness?

Perhaps through introspection, you should reexamine your personality for teaching. Beware of becoming one of the following:

1. The "sophisticated scholar." He is overly critical of all—except himself.
2. The "born teacher." His mind is closed to suggestion. He has known since birth exactly how best to teach.
3. The "reformer." He scoffs at the abilities of his teaching colleagues. He entered teaching only to save it as a profession.
4. The "pseudoeducationist." He is so convinced of the importance of method that he neglects to learn all he can about the learner and the content.
5. The "pseudopsychologist." He is so convinced of the importance of the learner that he neglects to learn all he can about method and content.
6. The "pseudoacademician." He is so convinced of the importance of content that he neglects to learn all he can about method and learner.

The personality pictures listed above are not as easy to improve as is knowledge of subject matter, but insofar as they are learned characteristics, they can be changed through effort and training. Many student teachers make that effort successfully.

DEVELOP THE HABITS YOU EXPECT TO POSSESS AS A REGULAR TEACHER
What habits are you developing? The habits you display as a student are
likely to be the ones you exhibit as a full-time teacher on your first job.
As a teacher, you are expected to encourage habits of promptness and
regularity of attendance in your students. For example, have you checked
your own college class attendance habits lately? This is but one illustration.

Occasionally, a supervisor finds it necessary to remind a student teacher
that he is expected to dress in a manner more appropriate to teaching
and to exhibit more exemplary habits of personal cleanliness. The woman
who dresses in the style of evening wear, and the man who appears ready
for a picnic are both out of place in the business office of education, the
classroom. Laboratory jackets, gym clothing, and other uniforms as well
as dress shirts should be laundered regularly. Cleanliness of hands and
fingernails, frequent haircuts and shaves, or hairdos and facials are all
details that should be taken care of automatically. It should never be
necessary for a grown man or woman to suffer the embarrassment of being
told that his mode of dress or degree of cleanliness fails to meet professional standards. However, approximately 10 percent of student teachers
have failed in one or more of these particulars. You can avoid possible
embarrassment for yourself and for your supervisors by giving daily
attention to grooming.

All in all, you need to see yourself always as a teacher and a leader of
young Americans. You share with home and church a large measure of
responsibility for the learning, the attitudes, and the actions of tomorrow's
adults. Recognize the importance of your job. Dress to look like a leader
in this important profession. Abandon mannerisms peculiar to the college
campus and be proud of your selection of teaching as an occupation. Then
you will have made a long stride toward success in the eyes of your students and those of your future professional colleagues.

KNOW WHAT TEACHERS DO

"I thought I was hired to teach school" is sometimes the plaint of the
first-year teacher. In looking ahead to the time not far away when you
will be a regular, full-time teacher, you need to realize that you will be
expected to do more than teach your classes. There will be supervisory
duties (on the playground, in the lunchroom and the halls, at assemblies
and athletic events); cocurricular activities to sponsor; parent-teacher
and staff meetings to attend; and community campaigns to sponsor. The
inefficient teacher who can never get his classwork done or the isolate
who frets about the extra things to do is likely to be an unhappy person.
But the person who enjoys working with parents, students, and fellow
teachers in various cooperative endeavors will find these experiences outside class valuable roads to professional growth. Whether or not you

derive much benefit from these activities will depend to a great degree upon your mental acceptance or rejection of them.

KNOW SCHOOL RESOURCES AND REGULATIONS

Learn all you can about school policies and regulations governing such items as the following: health and safety (what to do in case of a fire drill or a student injury); care of the building and other school property; conduct of students and faculty on the school premises (for example, smoking); use and conservation of supplies; attendance of students and staff members; faculty committees; school activities and organizations; school calendar; daily and assembly schedules; use of library and textbooks; detention and referral discipline; homework; marking and reporting student progress; and changing location of classes or transporting students from the school grounds. A faculty handbook is often used to supply much information concerning policies and regulations dealing with these matters. However, your cooperating teacher is always your primary source of information in clarification of school policy.

While you are learning the school's regulations, get acquainted with the school plant. Visit administrative offices, the cafeteria, shops, laboratories, gymnasium, nurse's office, library, attendance office, and guidance or counselor's office for your particular grade level. Learn what functions these centers perform or what services they render.

Find out what audio-visual equipment and materials are available, how they are procured, and what regulations govern their use. Obtain the same type of information about the library, science laboratories, or shops if they are facilities to be used by your class.

Learn to accept any physical limitations graciously. In many communities the school population has outstripped school buildings and equipment. If there are policies or regulations with which you do not agree, remember that you are professionally obligated to support them until they are changed by democratic means.

In getting to know your school, you have been urged to learn to know your co-workers, your own assets in relation to the teaching situation, and the policies and regulations of the school, as well as its resources. You will probably not learn everything suggested in the preceding paragraphs during the short time you serve as a student teacher. Yet the better informed you are, the more likely you are to succeed. It should be obvious by now that teaching involves much more than a mastery of one or two subject matter areas in college classes. A great body of knowledge is to be learned and many competencies are to be gained by direct apprenticeship on the job.

If you are not thoroughly acquainted with the community in which you are to do student teaching, you should make a brief community study to supplement the intensive class study you should complete in the manner illustrated in Chapter 2. You then will be ready to review your knowledge of how students learn.

REFRESH YOUR KNOWLEDGE OF HOW STUDENTS LEARN

If student teachers are to guide the learning of students most effectively, they will not only know their subject and their students but keep clearly in mind the guidelines to efficient learning offered by educational psychology. A brief overview follows; however, serious students will recognize the need for a more complete refresher that can be provided better by restudy of a textbook in educational psychology.

LEARNING REQUIRES EFFORT

Psychologists recognize learning as an active process involving attention and effort on the part of the learner. Teachers may work themselves to near exhaustion in an effort to deliver learning to students the way merchants deliver products to customers; yet teachers will fail unless students themselves put forth effort. In fact, research has verified that too much guidance can impede the learner (8:313). Learning, therefore, is not a package that can be wrapped up and delivered. It is more like a do-it-yourself project that can benefit from expert guidance, when needed, but that can reach completion only through the continued intent and effort of the worker. Consequently, one of the greatest concerns of teachers is the problem of developing and maintaining interest and effort on the part of their students.

SUCCESS SUSTAINS EFFORT   Research demonstrates that students will work harder, longer, and more successfully when they know the goal of their efforts, when they understand the reasons for seeking the goal, when they believe that the goal can be reached, when they want to reach the goal, and when they are promptly informed of the degree of success resulting from their efforts. Of great importance in teaching is "the desirability of insuring frequent and regular experiences of success—or reinforcement—throughout all phases of learning, but particularly in the earlier, and generally more difficult phases." [6]

Furthermore, if interest and effort are to be maintained, teachers need to organize learning into realistic tasks that can be achieved successfully by each learner.

Just as a child can sometimes be induced to eat when presented with a small portion of food, after refusing to start on a larger portion, so a student can more often be stimulated to work on a reasonable partial assignment than by assignment of the whole task all at once.[7]

[6] Melvin H. Marx, "Motivation," *Encyclopedia of Educational Research*, 3d ed., Chester W. Harris, ed. New York: The Macmillan Company, 1960, p. 896.
[7] Marx, p. 898.

On the other hand, learning experiences should not be so cut and dried as to stifle initiative and curiosity. Research in the United States and in Russia indicates that "an effective teacher . . . will be able to hold student interest by maintaining some degree of suspense as to outcomes of problems and by allowing the student to work through to discoveries for himself." [8]

Educational psychologists tend to agree that "learning experiences are peculiarly satisfactory and mastery and retention are promoted when students are encouraged to discover for themselves important relationships and principles." [9] In addition, educational psychologists seem to agree that "students enjoy learning when they learn about things which are relevant to their past or present circumstance, problems, or difficulties, when learning is meaningful, significant, and timely in terms of their own concerns." [10]

Likewise, "students find learning experiences more satisfying when they participate in defining what they are trying to learn and in judging their success in learning it." [11] Many teachers make regular use of this knowledge to increase the success of their instruction.

EXTRINSIC INCENTIVES SHOULD BE USED WITH CAUTION The entire problem of pupil motivation is taken up in a later chapter of this text. Only a few highlights will be pointed out for review here. It is important to note that, according to the research-supported opinion of experts, "progressive loss of interest in academic learning activities . . . may be inhibited by carefully planned . . . [use] of a variety of incentives and rewards." [12] Researchers seem to agree that extrinsic incentives, such as competition, rewards, praise, and reproof, can be effective supplementary instructional tools when used selectively by an expert teacher. However, dependence upon their use must be limited.[13] At least one authority adds the specific precaution that even though organized competition and rivalry in the classroom can serve as strong incentives, they are not generally regarded as first-rate teaching procedures. Such incentives sometimes lead to undesirable social attitudes, and frequently fail to develop interest in learning that persists after removal of the incentives.[14] Specifically, it has been found that:

1. Extrinsic incentives are most useful in the earliest stages of learning when the learning itself has not yet developed to the stage of providing its own satisfaction.

[8] Marx, p. 898.
[9] Eugene McCreary, "Pawns or Players?" *Phi Delta Kappan,* 49 (November 1967), 142.
[10] McCreary, p. 141.
[11] McCreary, p. 141.
[12] Marx, p. 898.
[13] Marx, p. 898.
[14] Howard L. Kingsley and Ralph Garry, *The Nature and Conditions of Learning.* Englewood Cliffs, N.J.: Prentice-Hall, Inc., 1957, p. 273.

2. To be most effective, extrinsic incentives should be attainable by a large proportion, if not by all, of the class. Goals that are out of reach fail to motivate.

3. Extrinsic incentives should be used cautiously and with the understanding that they are temporary substitutes for the real thing: recognition of value in the learning itself.[15]

In this connection teachers should note that "pupils experience special satisfactions when their work gains the recognition of others, especially their peers. Such recognition does not have to be achieved in purely competitive activities." [16] It can also be attained when the teacher plans opportunities for each student to earn group approval by participation in such activities as class discussion, dramatic productions, role playing, and the display of individual or group projects. In fact, many educators accept the principle that "pupils enjoy learning experiences most [and thereby increase their learning] when they are provided frequent opportunities to express themselves." [17]

EARLY STAGES OF LEARNING ARE CRITICAL Psychological research has identified a number of principles associated with the acquisition of knowledge and skills.

1. Learning tasks are accomplished more effectively when drill and practice periods are spaced rather than massed. Short sessions spread over several days are to be preferred to a single long session. Longer practice and drill lessons should be interspersed with rest periods or change-of-pace activities to avoid the deleterious effects of fatigue and boredom.

2. Instructional emphasis should be on the correct performance, not on the incorrect. Teacher demonstration of error may introduce desirable humor into a lesson, but as a teaching technique it rates low. A corollary of this principle is that the crucial elements of a performance should receive attention, not the noncrucial. For instance, when speed is the predominant factor of successful performance, speed should be emphasized even in the initial learning. When speed and accuracy are both important, emphasis should be on both.

3. Students should not be expected to work on several similar new learnings simultaneously. Similar but nonidentical tasks interfere in the early stages of learning.

4. Research strongly indicates that when a student has not yet identified the correct response in a learning situation, it is of paramount importance to reinforce that response as soon as it occurs, for "even a few seconds delay . . . may mean the difference between maximal learning

[15] Marx, p. 898.
[16] McCreary, p. 142.
[17] McCreary, p. 141.

and no learning whatever." [18] The teaching-machine industry is based upon this principle. However, in the absence of machine assistance, teachers can at least partially satisfy the learning principle by giving close supervision to practice periods, by supplying answers for out-of-class problems and encouraging immediate scoring and correction by students, and by returning all teacher-scored papers promptly. Estes summarizes this point succinctly:

In any educational context, it is important to emphasize that what becomes strengthened during practice is the behavior that actually occurs, not necessarily the behavior that is the goal of the educator. If the learner has hit upon an inferior mode of response, continued practice (without correction) will simply strengthen it. . . .[19]

RETENTION OF LEARNING CAN BE STRENGTHENED   The teacher's responsibility does not end when student learning has once reached a satisfactory level. The fact is that both older and newer learning interfere with the retention of unreinforced learning. Loss is greatest in the first few days, whereas over a period of a few months more than 50 percent is frequently forgotten. One researcher found that when two reinforcement periods were employed, learning loss in sixty days was less than that which occurred in one day when no reinforcement was used (8:302). Thus it is clearly the teacher's responsibility to provide a program of reinforcement:

1. *Teachers should provide review spaced at increasing intervals.* The first review might best be placed the day following the learning, the second review, a week later, and the third, several weeks later. As a review technique, rereading is seldom as beneficial as "skimming a related source for new ideas, working through a quiz, thinking through the implications of the material, or using the knowledge as a steppingstone to more advanced learning in the field." [20] Mouly also points out that "effective review is more than just bringing the material back to the original level: it involves reorganization . . . to bring about new understandings, new insights, and new relationships that are more functional as well as more permanent than the original learning." [21]

2. *Teachers should encourage overlearning up to about 50 percent.* Overlearning is not a substitute for review, but serves to reduce the likelihood that learning will drop below the threshold of recall before the first review takes place. Overlearning is important, but not as important as review.

[18] William K. Estes, "Learning," *Encyclopedia of Educational Research*, 3d ed., Chester W. Harris, ed. New York: The Macmillan Company, 1960, p. 758.
[19] Estes, p. 762.
[20] George J. Mouly, *Psychology for Effective Teaching*. New York: Holt, Rinehart and Winston, Inc., 1960, p. 303.
[21] Mouly, p. 302.

3. *Teachers should make the learning meaningful to the student.* Understanding is basic to learning and to retention. Students understand best that which is related to their own experience—past, present, and future. Experienced teachers follow this principle regularly.

4. *Teachers should encourage students to accept retention as one goal of learning.* It has been shown that goals which are clearly identified are more likely to be attained. Consciousness of the importance of remembering will improve performance in remembering. One successful technique is to point out at the time of learning the specific instances in the future when the student will be called upon to put the learning to use. Frequent tests can partially serve this purpose.

TRANSFER OF LEARNING CAN BE INCREASED   The teacher's task is only partially completed when he has facilitated the acquisition and retention of learning. He must also give consideration to maximizing the likelihood that his students will be able to use their learning wherever and whenever it might be applied. This third aspect of learning is termed *transfer.* Like the acquisition and retention of learning, transfer depends not only upon the quality of the learner, but also upon the quality of the instruction. Research amply demonstrates that "the amount of transfer induced can be increased by the method of teaching used." [22] Placing instructional emphasis upon the aspects of the subject that are expected to be transferred; encouraging generalization on the part of students; providing extensive practice in applications—all are procedures that have been found to increase the transfer of learning. It has also been shown that no particular school subject or group of subjects is outstandingly superior to any other subject or group of subjects in its contribution to a student's intellectual performance, although each subject can make contributions to improved performance in specific tasks when taught with that purpose clearly emphasized. Thus a teacher of foreign language who wishes to encourage increased understanding of English will place special emphasis upon generalization and practice in that aspect of his course. The teacher of junior high school mathematics who wishes to increase his students' future use of ratio and proportion will emphasize generalization and practice in the application of that subject to appropriate problems in geometry, physics, chemistry, art, music, homemaking, personal purchasing, and the like. In the same manner, the teacher of physical education who wishes to increase his students' application of sportsmanlike conduct and sense of fair play will place instructional emphasis upon generalization and application of those qualities not only to participation in and observation of athletic contests, but also to daily living in the school and in the community.

[22] J. M. Stephens, "Transfer of Learning," *Encyclopedia of Educational Research,* 3d ed., Chester W. Harris, ed. New York: The Macmillan Company, 1960, p. 1542.

Teachers of all subjects should realize that the transfer of learning is a major goal of instruction, not a concomitant outcome that develops automatically. The extent to which students succeed in transfer is dependent to a large degree upon the character of the learning experiences provided. Successful teachers plan their lessons carefully to facilitate efficiency in acquisition of learning, promote greater retention of learning, and encourage wide transfer of learning.

SELECTED READINGS

1. American Educational Research Association, *Encyclopedia of Educational Research,* 3d ed., Chester W. Harris, ed. New York: The Macmillan Company, 1960, pp. 1473–1480.

2. Batchelder, Howard T., Maurice McGlasson, and Raleigh Schorling, *Student Teaching in Secondary Schools,* 4th ed. New York: McGraw-Hill Book Company, Inc., 1964, chap. 1.

3. Byers, Loretta, and Elizabeth Irish, *Success in Student Teaching.* Boston: D. C. Heath and Company, 1965.

4. Callahan, Sterling G., *Successful Teaching in Secondary Schools.* Chicago: Scott, Foresman and Company, 1966, chap. 16.

5. Clark, Leonard H., and Irving S. Starr, *Secondary School Teaching Methods,* 2d ed. New York: The Macmillan Company, 1967, chap. 19.

6. Faunce, Roland C., and Carroll L. Munshaw, *Teaching and Learning in Secondary Schools.* Belmont, Calif.: Wadsworth Publishing Company, Inc., 1964, chap. 3.

7. Lee, Florence Henry, *Principles and Practices of Teaching in Secondary Schools.* New York: David McKay Company, Inc., 1965, chap. 3.

8. Mouly, George J., *Psychology for Effective Teaching,* 2d ed. New York: Holt, Rinehart and Winston, Inc., 1968, chaps. 12–14.

9. Perrodin, Alex F., ed., *The Student Teacher's Reader: A Collection of Readings.* Chicago: Rand McNally & Company, 1966, chaps. 1–4.

10. Tanruther, Edgar M., *Clinical Experiences in Teaching for the Student Teacher or Intern.* New York: Dodd, Mead & Company, Inc., 1967, chaps. 1, 2.

PART TWO / *Planning*

CHAPTER 4 / *Planning for Instruction*

Planning is the foundation for good teaching. Neither ingenuity nor experience can serve as a substitute for thorough planning. Schools were created by society to provide an environment for effective and economical learning, and they—and those who work in them—are parts of society's "total plan."

Instructional planning consists of a composite of professional skills that have to be learned, beginning in the preservice or preparation period of a teacher's career. The major portion of this book deals with the development of these skills—setting up meaningful objectives, using appropriate learning activities, selecting the best materials or resources, maintaining a wholesome classroom environment for learning, and evaluating student progress.

CHANGES IN EDUCATIONAL THEORY AND PRACTICE

Not only must the teacher develop the necessary skills of instructional planning, but he must keep informed of changes that occur in educational theory and practice. Tyler, who has concisely summarized some significant changes that have occurred during the first fifty years of this century, indicates these aspects of the curriculum that have been affected: the formulation of objectives and the selection and organization of learning experiences. First, the *nature* of objectives has changed from formal discipline to behavioral objectives. Second, the *sources* of objectives have changed from determination by subject matter specialists alone to the inclusion of four other forces: the psychology of learning, the demands of society, social and educational philosophy, and studies of the learner. And, third, the *range* of objectives has changed with the current problem of establishing priorities among a great diversity of goals becoming acute. Significant changes have also occurred in the selection of learning experiences. Notions about the *nature* of learning experiences have changed from a focus on recitation and the teacher to learning experiences of students; the *range* of learning experiences has expanded from verbal exercises to varied learning activities; and the *selection* of learning experiences has been designed to provide for individual differences or diversity in a system of mass education. Least attention has been given to the organization of learning experiences. More consideration has been given to the "ordering of content" than to changes in student behavior. Consequently, the integration of student experiences within the framework of separate subjects continues to be a persistent problem.[1]

Changes in educational theory and practice during the second half of this century promise to be more dramatic than those of the first fifty years. Some comparatively new developments are already affecting the role of the teacher in instructional planning: increasing stress on behavioral objectives; an interdisciplinary approach to the study of formerly discrete subjects; emphasis on "discovery" by the learner—on process rather than on content alone; and flexibility in planning as an imperative (due to such factors as team teaching and application of the technological revolution to education).

Specifically, what are some of the tangible rewards that the teacher may expect from carefully planning his instruction? First of all, continuous and thoughtful planning by the teacher gives purpose and direction to everything that takes place in the classroom. Aimless rambling, fruitless activity, and disciplinary incidents are reduced to a minimum. Wise selection and organization of varied and appropriate learning materials and activities are most likely to ensure the achievement of worthwhile objectives.

Another outcome of thorough planning by the teacher is the development of an atmosphere of confidence and security in the classroom. Students gain confidence in his leadership. The teacher, in turn, is freed of subject matter anxieties and nagging details of classroom management and control that stem from poor organization. Good organization is virtually synonymous with good teaching.

Still another advantage of careful planning of instruction is that it eventually becomes a timesaver. The teacher who systematically accumulates and organizes a file of supplementary references, curriculum guides, resource units, and audio-visual materials is able to enrich future learning experiences with a minimum of time and effort. Furthermore, although it is imperative for the beginning teacher to learn to build and to use complete written plans, he may well develop a pattern or habit of thinking

[1] Ralph W. Tyler, "The Curriculum—Then and Now," *Proceedings, 1956 Invitational Conference on Testing Problems.* Princeton, N.J.: Educational Testing Service, 1956, pp. 79–94. Also published in *Testing Problems in Perspective* by the American Council on Education, 1966.

that will later enable him to substitute mental plans for written ones. A first-year teacher summarized this last point in these words:

Even though I do not write all my plans, as I did in student teaching, I mentally go through all the steps of planning. What are my specific objectives? What materials and resources do I need? What learning activities are likely to be best in achieving my objectives? How much time should be devoted to each? And (after the lesson has been taught) how successful was the class period today? How can I determine how well my students have achieved today's goals?

At this point, the authors must add that no teacher can ever completely abandon the use of written plans.

From an administrative standpoint, written plans are important for two reasons: to make supervision more effective and to facilitate the work of substitute teachers. Because supervisory visits can be made only at irregular intervals, written plans provide a record of the continuity of classroom learning experience that would not otherwise be evident. This assumes, of course, that the plans are adequate and that the teacher makes incisive postanalyses of each day's work. Some principals consider written plans so important that they require new teachers to prepare both unit and daily plans as evidence of adequate preparation. Another value of written plans is to facilitate the work of substitute teachers. When the regular teacher is forced to be absent on short notice, his plans should enable a substitute teacher to carry on the work of the class as usual. As supervisory aids in student teaching, written plans are indispensable.

PRINCIPLES OF EFFECTIVE PLANNING

The right decision at the right moment is the essence of good teaching—*Goodlad* [2]

Planning is an individual matter. The composition of a class, the nature of the subject, the goals to be achieved, and the personality and background of the teacher account for inevitable variations in planning, but certain basic principles are applicable to every classroom situation.

Proper planning facilitates learning. To be sure, people learn from experience, both organized and unorganized. It is, of course, also true that education takes place both inside and outside the school. However, the increasing complexity of the world, the expansion of culture, and the forces of miseducation bidding for the attention of everyone constitute a real challenge to the modern school. Never before has the school been required to teach so much to so many. There is no time for unplanned,

[2] John I. Goodlad, "The Teacher Selects, Plans, Organizes," *Learning and the Teacher,* 1959 Yearbook. Washington, D.C.: The Association for Supervision and Curriculum Development, 1959, p. 39.

aimless teaching. The teacher must know where he is going, how to get there, and when he has arrived. Superior planning is required to facilitate the quality of learning needed in our day.

Effective instructional planning provides opportunities for students to practice desired behavior. The statement "Learning is an active process" has been parroted so often as to become almost devoid of meaning, yet no one learns except through his own activity. But just any kind of activity is not sufficient. For example, it is not enough for the student to talk, to read, and to write about good citizenship. Learning activities must go beyond those of a purely verbal nature. The student must apply his knowledge to real life situations in order to think, to feel, and to act as a good citizen should, both in school and in later adult life.

Effective instructional planning provides for continuity in learning. This principle may be difficult to apply for the beginning teacher whose major concern is often, "What am I going to do today?" He may be justified in making short-range assignments based on a well-organized textbook as he faces for the first time five or six classes a day with two or three different preparations. Nevertheless, as he gains experience, the new teacher will need to develop plans of a higher order. As a first step toward continuity, he will relate today's lesson to those of yesterday and tomorrow. A second step, if the nature of the subject and the situation warrant it, is the development of long-range or unit plans. As the new teacher becomes more aware of the total school program and the educational problems of his students, his plans should attain a higher level of development. Helping students to bridge the gap between the logical organization of subject matter and the way they learn, to maintain continuity in their educational experiences as they go from one school level to the next, and to make a smooth transition from school to life on the outside will be reflected in the plans of the teacher who gains insight through experience. Although some of the problems related to continuity involve the school as a whole, or even more than one school level, the individual classroom teacher still has an important role to play. The teacher can help the transfer student, from the elementary or another school, feel more at home in a strange environment. He can help the student who leaves school to work or who goes to college to be more adequately prepared. The classroom teacher can help the student bridge the gap between school and life by showing the relevance of history to current affairs, by relating scientific laws to problems of everyday living, or by cultivating a taste for better art, literature, and music that will enrich the student's leisure hours forever after.

Effective instructional planning provides for correlation of knowledge and skills derived from the various subjects offered in school. Like continuity, this is another principle of good planning that the beginning teacher may not be ready to put into effect. Again expediency comes before desirability. However, as the teacher grows more sure of himself, his subject, and his students, he can lift his eyes above his immediate concerns and catch a vision of a higher level of planning. The secondary school curriculum, traditionally organized on the basis of discrete subject matter lines, has made it difficult for the student to integrate his knowledge. Anecdotes from the classroom are replete with accounts of students who consider a teacher unfair if he requires good written compositions except in an English class or if he insists on effective speaking except in a speech class. Upon the classroom teacher, who is himself a specialist in one or two subjects, falls the task of helping each student put together the jigsaw puzzle of his fragmented school experiences. Present reactionary forces would not only perpetuate fragmentation of subject matter, extending it downward into the elementary school, but would also divorce development of the student's intellectual life from all other aspects of his personality development.

Effective instructional planning takes into consideration the readiness of the student to learn. Readiness is dependent upon such factors as maturity, previous experiences, and motivation. To function with maximum efficiency as an individual, the student must mature or develop all aspects of his personality—emotional, intellectual, moral, social, and physiological—on a unified front. In providing incentives to stimulate students to pursue schoolwork with vigor and enthusiasm, the teacher is primarily concerned with strengthening drives that lead to sustained activity toward worthy goals. That is motivation at its best.

Effective instructional planning recognizes individual differences in student interests, needs, and abilities. Because our nation is committed to the ideal of equal educational opportunity for all youth of secondary school age, a heavy responsibility falls upon the shoulders of the classroom teacher. The public school has a twofold task: to provide mass or quantity education and, at the same time, to educate for quality. The schools also have the dual responsibility of educating for uniformity (providing students with a common heritage) and educating for diversity (capitalizing upon the unique contribution of each individual). Despite present efforts to solve the problem of diversity by grouping students subject by subject on the bases of aptitude, intelligence, and achievement, other variables that determine a student's success or failure in school are often disregarded. To mention a few of these significant differences, students obviously differ with respect to sex; personality (interests, emotional adjustments, relations with others); past experience; family backgrounds (socioeconomic status, national or ethnic origin, parental values and expectations for their children); and the neighborhoods from which they come. Providing for individual differences is discussed at length in Chapter 8.

Effective instructional planning enables the student to participate as much as possible in planning his own educational experiences. As already suggested, the key to learning is involvement by the student. If all he learns to do in school is to follow instructions of the teacher, then he is ill equipped to assume responsibility as a citizen in a self-governing society. However, despite the advantages often claimed for more coopera- tive planning in the classroom, the activities of the typical secondary school class are still largely planned and directed by the teacher alone. There will be further discussion of cooperative planning in this chapter.

Above all, effective instructional planning must provide for educational experiences that are meaningful and satisfying to the learner. Students will soon forget most of the facts that the teacher attempts to teach them, but they are likely to learn attitudes of likes or dislikes for a subject, the school, or even society itself, that will persist for the rest of their lives.

PROBLEMS IN INSTRUCTIONAL PLANNING

Never before have we had so little time in which to do so much—Franklin D. Roosevelt

The problem of the selection and organization of instructional activities and materials has become more difficult with the expansion of available materials and teaching aids; the broadening of educational objectives, to meet the needs of all students, not just the college-bound; and the in- creasing heterogeneity of the school population.[3]

"Educational shortages" is a common topic in educational circles. Probably the greatest shortage of the average classroom teacher is *time*. With more students of greater diversity to teach, with more to be taught, and with more duties outside the classroom and in the community, when does the teacher find time to plan his work adequately? The following verse no doubt expresses the feelings of many teachers in today's crowded schools:

SOUNDS LIKE FRIDAY

By Ann Coyle

Some people say a teacher is made out of steel,
Their mind can think, but their body can't feel.
Iron and steel and hickory tea,
Frowns and gripes from nine to three.
You teach six full hours, and what do you get?
Another day older and deeper in debt.

[3] William G. Brink, "Secondary Education—Programs," *Encyclopedia of Educational Research*, 3d ed., Chester W. Harris, ed. New York: The Macmillan Company, 1960, p. 1265.

You pay your dues in this and that,
Then for 29 more days your billfold's flat.
I was born one morning, when it was cloudy and cool,
I picked up my register and headed for school.
I wrote 84 names on the homeroom roll
And the principal said, "Well, bless my soul!
You teach six hours and what'd you get?
Cuts and bruises and dirt and sweat."
I got 84 kids and 42 seats,
Sixty-one talking while 23 sleep.
I can hardly get 'em all through the door,
And if I don't watch out they'll be sending me more.
I taught six full hours, my day is made,
But I still have 300 papers to grade.
You teach six full hours and what do you get?
Another day older and deeper in debt.
I'll go to St. Peter but I can't stay,
I gotta come back for the PTA.[4]

In planning his work, the busy teacher has several alternatives. He may attempt to teach without plans or use the same plans year after year.

Neither of these alternatives satisfies the professional person. It is obvious that an effective teacher must be a highly organized person who is able to budget time wisely, think clearly, and act decisively. The experienced teacher can utilize more mental planning in lieu of the detailed written plans needed in preservice teaching. As said before, some written plans are always necessary. Equipped with curriculum guides or courses of study and textbooks, the teacher still needs to prepare an outline of suggested objectives, materials, activities, and evaluative techniques for each course. Resource units, prepared on a cooperative basis in summer workshops, constitute one of the best sources for unit or long-range planning. But in addition to making use of ready-made materials, the teacher needs to be freed periodically from the pressures of a daily teaching schedule in order to keep abreast of new developments in subject matter areas, to become acquainted with more up-to-date materials, to explore the research and experimentation dealing with better methods, and to pause for reflection.

Another problem in instructional planning at the secondary level is the fact that the teacher may be lacking in a sense of perspective. Educated essentially as a subject matter specialist, he can easily lose sight of the fact that such subject matter is a means to an end, not an end in itself. He would do well to keep in mind a shrewd observation attributed to the philosopher Whitehead that, as bare facts, knowledge keeps no better

[4] Reprinted from *San Diego Teachers Association Bulletin*, November–December 1956.

than fish. Unless the teacher is able to relate the subject to the student and to the way he learns, little or no learning is likely to occur. Either extreme is to be avoided: undue preoccupation with adult-centered demands or with the passing fancies of immature youth. On one hand, the teacher needs to be aware of the relationship of all subjects to the total objectives of the school; but on the other, he must be sensitive to past successes and failures, present undertakings, and future aspirations of his students. The teacher must place his planning endeavors in proper perspective to find the best answers to the right questions: Is his planning to be based upon the content and formal organization of the various subject matter disciplines or upon personal-social goals expressed in terms of improved student behavior? Is his planning to be based upon facts to be learned or upon problems of everyday living to be solved? This implies more than a narrow utilitarian view of education, for growth in appreciation and enjoyment of art, music, and literature is as important in everyday living as the development of vocational skills. Concisely stated, the chief task of the teacher is to utilize the cultural heritage, now organized in terms of separate subjects in the secondary school, to help youth achieve their present developmental tasks and, at the same time, develop an awareness of important future needs and ways to satisfy them.

Another problem in planning instruction is that of maintaining a balance between uniformity and flexibility. The need for thorough preplanning has already been stressed. But to preplan does not mean to predetermine everything that happens in the classroom. There are unpredictable variables in every teaching-learning situation. Consequently, the skillful teacher is able to change his plans, "to play it by ear," when deviations from his plans are necessary. Furthermore, if students are to be involved in planning at all, there must be enough flexibility to permit it. However, in order to avoid undesirable gaps or duplications in a student's learning experiences, it has been necessary for schools to establish guidelines in the form of courses of study or curriculum guides for teachers to follow. Once the teacher has assessed the broad limitations of the framework in which he operates, he is free to incorporate valuable student suggestions or to deviate from his own preconceived plans. A resolution to take advantage of the freedom he has is probably the most important decision the teacher makes. This freedom is often lost by overdependence upon a single textbook, resulting in a monotonous routine and a loss of creativity, flexibility, and proper attention to individual differences by the teacher. The accumulated cultural heritage has now reached a point where textbooks may represent a hopeless number of pages to be covered. Unless a teacher exercises selectivity with respect to content, he is caught in a treadmill of assign-study-recite-test procedures with no time for the inclusion of rich and varied supplementary instructional activities and materials. How often practice teachers have been told by their supervisors in American history, for example, that they may not use pertinent films because there is no time for them!

THE KINDS OF PLANNING THAT TEACHERS DO

If a man write little, he had need have a great memory—*Francis Bacon*

Planning is an art, a "skill in performance acquired by experience, study, or observation" ("art" as defined in *Webster's New Collegiate Dictionary*). In mastering the art of planning, the teacher needs to learn how to develop long-range course and unit plans, daily plans, and cooperative plans that are all interrelated. Logically, the teacher develops them in this order: first, the course plan; second, unit plans; and third, daily plans. Cooperative planning, the highest and most difficult level, would not be used by all teachers. In practice, beginning teachers probably more often develop a term or semester calendar and go directly into preparation of daily plans.

COURSE PLANNING

Reduced to its simplest terms, course planning involves the following steps: (1) making an analysis of a particular subject to be taught; (2) listing general objectives to be achieved; (3) developing a tentative outline of content to be covered during a semester, term, or school year; and (4) setting up a tentative time allotment by days and weeks for each topic or problem in the content outline. Stated in another way, the teacher has to decide *what* is to be learned, *why* it is to be learned, the *order* in which learning experiences should take place, and the *time* to be devoted to each learning experience.

In planning course outlines, the teacher plays a major role. However, a number of factors or conditions preclude planning as a solitary, independent teacher activity. First of all, instructional planning takes place within a framework of rules and suggestions as set forth in state school codes, state and local district courses of study or curriculum guides, other school district regulations, and operational schedules. Another vital element in planning is the human factor. Classroom teachers are becoming more and more involved with their colleagues, with interested laymen, and with their students in continuous, cooperative improvement of the total school program. Also the development of the team approach to teaching has further promoted the human relations factor in instructional planning. In fact, teaching itself is primarily an enterprise in human relations. Ability to work with others—administrators, fellow teachers, students, parents—is the first hallmark of a good teacher.

Other factors that affect course planning are instructional resources and physical facilities. Availability of text and other printed materials, audio-visual materials and services, and rich community resources is obviously a most important factor in course planning. Likewise, adequacy of physical facilities is an important element in the learning environment.

One of the first steps the teacher takes, however, in course planning is to examine the curriculum guide or course of study for his school. By way of example, the following excerpt from "A Digest of the Secondary School Curriculum" is included:

SCIENCE PROBLEMS 1–2 (two-semester course—grades 11 and 12—no prerequisites).[5]

This is an elective course designed primarily for those who need to fulfill the high school graduation requirements. It is not intended for students who have completed biology or chemistry. It may be elected by those who have had only General Science 1–2 or Basic Biology 1–2 and wish to continue the study of science to include more of the physical sciences.

Areas of emphasis and time allotments:

The Nature of Science	1–2 weeks
Matter and Energy	3–4 weeks
The Atmosphere	2–3 weeks
The Hydrosphere	3–4 weeks
The Lithosphere (optional)	2–3 weeks
Plants and Animals	4–5 weeks
The Human Body	4–5 weeks
Energy and Machines	2–3 weeks
Heat Energy	2–3 weeks
Wave Energy	3–4 weeks
Electrical Energy	1–2 weeks
Electronics	1–2 weeks
Nuclear Energy	1–2 weeks
The Earth in Space (optional)	1–2 weeks
Astronomy and Astronautics	2–3 weeks

Basic Text:
Herron and Palmer, *Matter, Life, and Energy,* 1965
Supplementary Texts:
Brooks and Tracy, *Modern Physical Science,* 1957/1962/1965
Smith and Lisonbee, *Your Biology,* 1958/1962
Fitzpatrick, *et al., Living Things,* 1962
Osborn, *et al., Science in Everyday Life,* 1958
Herron and Palmer, *Study Guide and Laboratory Activities for Matter, Life, and Energy,* 1965
Teachers' Guides:
Guide for Teaching Science Problems 1–2, 1966 (300-page manual) *
Handbook of Science Laboratory Practices and Safety, 1966

* (Includes General Objectives, General Teaching Procedures, Supplies and Equipment, 15 units, maps and charts, worksheets, and laboratory exercises.)

[5] "A Digest of the Secondary School Curriculum," p. 130, 1966 revision, Science Problems 1–2. San Diego, Calif.: San Diego City Schools. Used by special permission of the San Diego City Schools.

PROCEDURES IN COURSE PLANNING

Once the teacher has been given his course assignments and has been made aware of the curricular framework within which he is to operate, he is ready to attack the practical problem of course organization. As already suggested, he has to make decisions about objectives, scope, sequence, and time allotments.

The first decision involves objectives. The use of content, such as the textbook, for example, as a starting point is a mistake. It leads to an over-emphasis upon subject matter to be learned rather than to desirable behavioral changes to be achieved. In contrast to daily plans, the objectives of course outlines are more general in nature. They should, however, be socially significant, be acceptable to both teacher and students, and be achievable.

The following objectives would be appropriate for a course outline:

English: Students will improve written composition skills.
American history: Students will develop a better understanding of their national heritage.
Physical education: Students will improve in bodily vigor and coordination.
Music: Students will learn to appreciate better music.

These objectives may imply desirable changes in student behavior (thinking, feeling, doing). However, for a daily lesson plan, they must be more precisely defined in terms of observable student behavior. Examples are given in Chapter 6. Desirable changes in skills, understandings, appreciations, and attitudes constitute the general objectives of course outlines.

SELECTING SUBJECT MATTER

In selecting course content, the teacher uses all the resources available —curriculum guides, resource units, other teachers, textbooks, audiovisual materials, and his own ideas. The selection of content or subject matter in course planning is closely related to the type of organization used. Such organization may be based on a discrete subject such as American history; a broad subject matter area, general science; or on significant problems. In terms of structure, the teacher may use a single textbook, a topical outline, or a series of units as the basis for organization. Use of the table of contents of a single textbook is likely to be least adequate. This approach tends to stifle teacher creativity and imagination; to neglect differences in interests, backgrounds, and abilities of students in today's classrooms; and to make a class too dependent on the generalizations and interpretations of a single authority.

By all means, the user of any textbook must be aware of its limitations. First of all, it represents a highly condensed, logical organization of a designated body of knowledge. And, second, it is the product of scholarly, mature minds. As such, it serves as a convenient reference and guide in the field of study but fails to provide the bridge to student experiences or methods of learning. Improperly used, the textbook may impede learning. Student memorization of technical terms, formulas, or generalizations developed by experts may be mistaken by the teacher for genuine understanding. Amusing boners that appear in examinations and the tendency on the part of students to preface remarks with "the book says" furnish evidence of the misuse of textbooks. Although modern textbooks have been greatly improved in readability, format, content, and authorship, the danger of misuse or of overdependence on them is ever present. A more complete discussion of textbooks follows in Chapter 9.

The traditional topical outline, still in common use, is especially adapted to organized subjects of a specialized type. The scope of the course, sequence of topics, inclusion of subtopics, and time allotments are relatively easy to set up and to follow. Although the topical outline represents a better approach to course planning than the use of a table of contents of a single textbook, it still has some of the inherent weaknesses of the textbook approach.

A third approach to long-range planning is the unit plan. Wherever its use is appropriate, especially in general education courses, as well as some specialized education courses, the unit plan is superior to either the single textbook or the exclusive topical outline approach to course planning.

UNIT PLANNING

The unit plan of organizing instruction was developed to overcome the limitations of the isolated, daily assignment with its tendency to fragment learning. The unit concept in instructional planning is an outgrowth of several movements. One of these has been changes in psychological conceptions about learning. Traditional acceptance of formal discipline—a theory that the mind is composed of separate faculties (such as memory and reason, for example) which can be strengthened like muscles through exercise—has been challenged since the turn of this century. The experiments of Thorndike and others, who found no evidence of so-called "faculties" nor superiority of any particular subjects as mind trainers, did much to discredit faculty psychology. The gestalt psychologists added another dimension to the psychological picture by concluding from their experiments that the "organism always reacts as a whole." [6] The testing movement of the 1920s made educators sharply aware of the individual differences among students. These developments have revolutionized the teaching process. No longer can a strictly academic curriculum be justified

[6] Carter V. Good, ed., *Dictionary of Education*, 2d ed. New York: McGraw-Hill Book Company, Inc., 1959, p. 427.

for all students on the basis of being "good training for the mind." No longer can a classroom fare of limited instructional materials and of exclusively verbal activities meet the needs of all youth now in school. The unit plan is an effective means of providing the variety and flexibility needed in today's classroom.

Another movement that lends support to the unit method of planning has been changes in educational philosophy. It has come to be recognized that the American ideal of education for all youth can never be realized in an institution restricted to the sole function of preparing students for college. Furthermore, if the unique qualities of each individual are to be cultivated, it has become obvious that a school program which meets the needs of students of varying interests, needs, and abilities must be provided. Another belief gaining widespread acceptance, at least in theory, is that democratic citizenship can be achieved only by the assumption of the responsibilities of such citizenship while the youth are in school.

Other factors contributing to the unitary concept of planning are changes in the nature of objectives from learning isolated facts to improving student behavior, changes in evaluation procedures from stress on oral examination or recitation to many evidences of growth, growing dissatisfaction with the fragmentation of learning in the secondary school, and increasing recognition of the unitary nature of human development. Thus the unit method of planning instruction is an attempt to ensure that integrated development of all aspects of the student's personality, not the dead storage of isolated facts, becomes the focal point of secondary schooling. A more complete discussion of the unit method follows in Chapter 5.

DAILY PLANNING

There will always be a need for daily planning of instruction. Even when the learning experiences of a class are all organized on a unit basis, it is within the daily class period that many of the unit activities—planning, working, evaluating—must necessarily occur. Unfortunately, despite the apparent advantages of the unitary approach to learning, instructional planning based almost entirely on discrete, daily assignments is still quite common, more so than the theoretical treatment of the subject in methods books would lead one to believe. That teachers often use day-by-day planning rather than more unified long-range planning is probably due to a number of reasons. One is the time element. It takes much less time and thought to assign a chapter in a textbook each day than to organize a comprehensive unit, incorporating a variety of materials and activities and extending over several weeks. Another problem may be the difficulty of understanding the unit concept. The teacher who merely considers a unit as more chapters in a book or a larger block of subject matter to be learned is likely to find so-called unit planning busywork. When the teacher does not organize instruction on a unit basis, the daily plan becomes more important than ever. In some cases the nature of the class or of the subject matter itself may make the unit type of organization impractical (for example, orchestra or band, advanced courses in science or mathematics). Highly specialized courses with a definite sequence of facts or skills to be learned, without clearly defined subproblems or centers of interests, may be better structured in terms of semester outlines. Still other courses may be set up on the basis of individual project work (such as art or industrial arts) so that the class as a whole does not work on problems or projects as a group. Thus it becomes evident that daily lesson planning is here to stay, not only as a vehicle for implementation of unit plans but also as a means of ensuring effective organization of learning activities where unit planning is inappropriate. Further discussion of daily planning is included in Chapter 6.

COOPERATIVE PLANNING

Cooperative or teacher-student planning has been a subject of increasing concern during recent years. However, it is a subject that is more often discussed than practiced, for most schools still use teacher-dominated methods of instruction.[7] Although proof is lacking that academic achievement is greater in classes where students participate in planning than in those where they do not, available evidence does indicate that teaching methods "which provide for adaptation to individual differences, encourage student initiative, and stimulate individual and group participation are superior to those methods which do not."[8]

VALUES OF COOPERATIVE PLANNING

So far, the claims made for cooperative planning by its advocates are unsupported by research. Nevertheless, simple logic, as well as the experience of a good many teachers, lends support to the contention that a number of values are to be derived from teacher-student planning of learning experiences in the classroom.

In the first place, students who share in planning their own learning activities are likely to be more highly motivated. It is a normal human reaction to take pride in a venture one has helped to plan and to feel responsible for its success. Also, whenever a student neglects his responsibility in a cooperatively planned enterprise, he may face not only the displeasure of his teacher but of his peers as well (5:126).

Another product of cooperative planning is most likely to be the establishment of stronger rapport between teacher and students, as well as among students themselves. As an authoritarian atmosphere disappears,

[7] G. Max Wingo, "Methods of Teaching," *Encyclopedia of Educational Research,* 3d ed., Chester W. Harris, ed. New York: The Macmillan Company, 1960, p. 851.
[8] Wingo, p. 853.

a spirit of unity and cooperation is nourished. Unwholesome competition, even antagonism in some cases, is replaced by a "we" feeling. In analyzing the findings of social psychology, McNeil cites a number of advantages of the "nondirective school" (not to be confused with laissez-faire) over the "directive school." Tensions, aggressions, and hostilities are lessened. Students like one another. There is an increase in class cohesiveness and satisfaction. Better solutions to problems are proposed.[9]

The most important values of teacher-student planning are those that contribute to the development of more effective citizenship in our society. Development of a sense of responsibility, ability to work with others, and opportunities to make decisions—these are the priceless fruits of successful cooperative planning. When students experience twelve, fourteen, or even sixteen years of schooling in classes where they are permitted to make no important decisions, are they entirely at fault if they later exhibit apathy or indifference toward the obligations of adult citizenship? Teachers may set up and enforce regulations to ensure acceptable social behavior in the classroom, but students who obey these laws are deprived of valuable experience in decision making. They have little opportunity to grow in moral stature. Students must have opportunities to make important decisions, with the possibility of making mistakes and suffering the consequences, and have some freedom in acting upon the insights they have gained. Cooperative planning offers students experience in learning to work with others. Teacher-student planning at its best makes students both willing and able to discharge their obligations as responsible persons in a world marked by ever-increasing interdependence.

PRECAUTIONS IN COOPERATIVE PLANNING

To be convinced of the values of cooperative planning is not enough to ensure beneficial results, for there is no one road to its achievement. In fact, such planning requires far greater skill and understanding than does a more autocratic approach to teaching. At the outset, the teacher must be aware of certain pitfalls and take precautions to avoid the dangers of chaos and frustration.

The first thing the teacher should do is to take inventory of his own assets and liabilities. He must know his students well, be thoroughly prepared in his subject, and possess leadership in organizing and directing the learning activities of youth. If he lacks experience in teacher-student planning, the teacher is advised to proceed cautiously.

A second important consideration is the composition of the class. Degree of maturity, level of ability, interests, past experiences in cooperative endeavors, and potential leadership are the assets of group members

[9] John McNeil, "Toward Appreciation of Teaching Method," *Phi Delta Kappan,* 39 (March 1958), 295–301.

that must be assessed before the teacher plunges too deeply into cooperative planning. Quite often teachers tend to underestimate the abilities of their students. Rapport between the teacher and his students is a most important factor in determining how successful the teacher is likely to be in stimulating willingness on the part of students to assume responsibility. Obviously, it is unwise to place too much self-direction in the hands of an unstable group where control is still an acute problem.

Possible school limitations on cooperative planning must also be considered. Administrative policies, school philosophy, supervisory approval, emotional support of one's colleagues, parental understanding, class size, time limitations, and availability of resources are factors that affect the degree of cooperative planning that may be employed in the classroom.

The nature of the subject matter may also be a limiting factor. Highly specialized subjects, such as algebra or chemistry, which are organized on the basis of a definite sequence of concepts to be learned offer only limited opportunities for student decisions.

IMPLEMENTATION OF COOPERATIVE PLANNING

No doubt many teachers would like to incorporate more student participation in planning classroom activities but are not certain how to begin. At this point, it is well to remember that cooperative planning may take place on either a group or an individual basis. For a teacher to discuss with one student how to do an individualized assignment involves no risks with respect to group control and requires no particular skill in group procedures. What the situation does require of the teacher is an awareness of individual student needs, time, and knowledge of the infinite variety of learning materials and activities the subject for study has to offer. Cooperative planning on a group basis is another matter. The inexperienced teacher is advised to proceed gradually in the implementation of full cooperative planning by the class as a whole. Some practical steps to be taken are suggested in the discussion which follows.

Certain practices in giving students limited responsibility for classroom procedures are not new. They have been used by many teachers for a long time. A common practice is to utilize student monitors or helpers in taking care of heat, light, and ventilation for physical comfort; in distributing and collecting materials; in checking attendance; in acting as custodians of equipment; in serving as shop foremen; and in assisting as squad leaders. Giving students a choice of two or more alternatives—such as the day for a test, the time needed for the next assignment, the date when notebooks are due—is a minor step toward more student decision making.

Opportunities for group decisions frequently present themselves in the course of normal class activities. The following example illustrates the point:

Each Thursday the world history class studied current events. Class procedures had been traditional, with the teacher conducting discussion on the articles read by the students in an assigned current events paper. One Wednesday the teacher asked the class if it would like to have a debate on an article on American foreign policy. Class members indicated considerable interest in the proposal. A student was then asked to take charge of the class and to secure volunteers to serve as chairman, debaters, and judges. Having had no responsibility for class procedures in the past, the class responded slowly at first. However, volunteers were eventually secured and the debate was organized and took place as scheduled. At its conclusion, many students demonstrated eagerness to discuss the issues further from the floor and there was enthusiastic consensus in favor of more debates.

Other class situations offer golden opportunities for more student assumption of responsibility. Discussion of common problems—class behavior, homework assignments, improvement of marks—is an excellent way to solve problems with greater satisfaction to all concerned. Some classes elect their own officers who call the class to order, make announcements, read the school bulletin, take care of homeroom business, and relieve the teacher of handling minor administrative details. Class officers may even be in charge of learning activities.

An eighth-grade speech teacher and her class developed a constitution and bylaws under which a class president served as chairman in charge of all class activities and a secretary kept a record of class business and acted as parliamentarian. Class officers served for one week with no one eligible for reelection until all students had had an opportunity to hold office. To ensure worthwhile activities in speech and to protect the class from possible chaos, it was agreed that the teacher should introduce each new unit and should have veto power. The plan worked so well that the teacher never exercised her veto power. It was gratifying to observe how well the students took care of the usual problems which arise in speech classes, such as the monopoly of class time by a few individuals, several students talking at one time, and some students refusing to give their speeches. Not only did the students solve the usual problems as well as the teacher might have solved them; but also absorbed two students from other classes, one from shop and one from band, who had been suspended for disciplinary reasons, and secured their participation as cooperative citizens.

A further step to the gradual development of student responsibility is the selection of committees to perform special services for the class. For example, a committee might develop a bulletin board related to the unit, assume responsibility for making the room more attractive, secure additional information for the class from a library research project, interview a prominent citizen, or visit the city council in session. In each case, the committee not only profits from a valuable experience but also renders a service to the class. The development of an inclination to help others is both a necessary condition and an important product in cooperative planning.

In helping students to learn how to work with others, the teacher may begin on a modest scale by having students work in pairs, using student preferences as a major guide in initial pairings. These pairs may check one another's work in spelling, homework assignments in mathematics, memorization of lines in literature; review for a test; share information on a particular problem; or help each other when one has mastered some problem and the other has not.[10] Pairing is especially helpful in the orientation of new students to class.

As the teacher anticipates more and more involvement in the cooperative approach to planning, he must build upon sound foundations of both external and internal conditions that are vital to success. He should consider, first of all, the external factors that have already been mentioned, such as administrative policies, emotional support of colleagues, and parental understanding. Internal factors involve especially a spirit of class unity and a willingness on the part of students to assume more responsibility for their own learning. Even a minor factor, such as students' knowing one another's names, is important. Of course, the teacher should learn the names of his students as soon as possible. Many opportunities should be provided for students to talk, work, and play together. If a student seems isolated from the group, other members need to be encouraged to lend a helping hand. In the beginning, willingness on the part of students to become involved in planning may pose a major problem. When students have been told for years what to do, how to do it, and when to do it, they will need assurance at first that their advice is actually being sought. Some gradual steps toward more student involvement have been suggested above. What does the teacher do next?

ADVANCED STAGES OF COOPERATIVE PLANNING

Full participation by a class in cooperative planning implies making important decisions in all aspects of the teaching-learning process: (1) choice of purposes or objectives, (2) selection and use of learning materials and activities, and (3) evaluation of learning experiences.

As the teacher reviews the various stages of the teaching-learning process, he must give careful consideration to the extent to which students may participate in each phase of the process and to the kinds of decisions they may make. There is, for example, some disagreement over student participation in the choice of unit objectives. Some say it is the sole responsibility of the teacher to set up unit objectives; others maintain that students should participate fully in their selection. At any rate, by

[10] J. Galen Saylor and William M. Alexander, *Curriculum Planning for Modern Schools.* New York: Holt, Rinehart and Winston, Inc., 1966, pp. 472–473.

means of thorough discussion, the teacher should clarify objectives and attempt to show their relevance to student needs and concerns. Otherwise, motivation is likely to remain at a low level with an attendant loss in significant learning. It is in the selection and development of learning resources and activities that the students have the most opportunity to participate in planning. The discussion approach is a good one to use. For example, in a laboratory situation such factors as safety, proper use and care of equipment, and such class procedures as getting started, working effectively, and cleaning up are always appropriate subjects for discussion. In planning a field trip or excursion, the teacher and his class need to clarify such routine procedures as permits from parents, transportation, and proper conduct; to discuss what to look for on the trip; and to plan for follow-up activities upon completion of the excursion. When the class as a whole is organized into committees to develop a project much discussion and planning are necessary. The point is well illustrated in the educational film, *Broader Concept of Method*, which is briefly summarized here:

During a class discussion of damage to city parks, a student raised a question about what might be done to improve conditions in their own school lunchroom. Eventually, it was decided to make improvement of the school lunchroom a class project. As a result of a discussion led by the teacher, five subproblems were identified and made the basis for committee assignments. Each student was asked to make a first, second, and third choice of committee and assigned accordingly. The next step was to develop a "work plan" for the committees. Again under the guidance of the teacher, it was determined that each committee had to decide *what* information was needed, *how* to get the information, and *who* was to get it. During both organization and work periods, the teacher circulated among the groups, giving assistance as needed. Finally, the chairmen of the committees made reports on their findings and recommendations to the class and the principal (who came as a special guest). At the conclusion of the reports, the principal indicated that he and the lunchroom manager were ready to help carry out the recommendations of the class.[11]

Evaluation, the final phase of the teaching-learning process, is also well adapted to the discussion approach. At the beginning of a unit, the teacher and his students may discuss criteria for evaluating their work, such as the requirements for effective speaking in a speech class, the necessary steps in preparing and serving a meal in a homemaking class, or the different processes in developing a project in industrial arts. At the conclusion of a unit, the teacher and his students may use the same criteria to judge not only the finished product but also day-by-day procedures in work periods. Thus, students may participate in evaluating the effective-

[11] *Broader Concept of Method: Part II—Teacher and Pupils Planning and Working Together,* film, 19 min. New York: McGraw-Hill Book Company, Inc.

ness of the unit as a whole as well as their own progress toward the achievement of unit goals. However, one aspect of evaluation is the sole responsibility of the teacher: securing, interpreting, and weighing the relative importance of various types of data as a basis for translating student growth into a final mark or grade for the course.

By way of summary of the discussion on ways of implementing cooperative planning, the authors cite the following eight categories or areas that have been developed through school experimentation, reported by Miel and associates:

1. Planning the use of time for a day or for a longer period, with suggested sequences of activities for work periods, free time, or special events.
2. Planning for the care and improvement of the classroom—housekeeping, seating, or making the room more attractive.
3. Planning proper conduct in terms of people and specific situations—attending assemblies, working in laboratories, or settling misunderstandings.
4. Planning subjects and methods by suggesting topics or problems, discussing how to proceed, and locating resources.
5. Planning products and productions—developing a room mural, making Christmas cards, cultivating a school garden, planning a party, or organizing an exhibit.
6. Planning service projects—making the playground safer, beautifying the community, sending parcels overseas, making Thanksgiving donations, or acting as teachers' aides in elementary schools.
7. Planning solutions to all-school problems—taking care of lavatories, making better use of the cafeteria, or making better use of community recreational facilities.
8. Evaluating group work. The emphasis is always on "how *we* are doing." [12]

GUIDELINES TO COOPERATIVE PLANNING

By way of conclusion, it is appropriate to summarize a few important guidelines for success in teacher-student planning. Some of these may be evident in the foregoing discussion on how to implement cooperative planning; others may not.

The first consideration in cooperative planning is that it must be *honest*. Neither permitting students to do as they please nor inveigling them into accepting a teacher's preconceived plans is genuine teacher-student planning. The first is pernicious permissiveness and the second is sheer hypocrisy. Choices that students make must be honest choices. When a teacher decides to share more responsibility with his students, he must be emotionally prepared to accept certain conditions. For instance, the teacher must accept the fact that cooperative planning takes time. If the

[12] Adapted from Alice Miel and associates, *Cooperative Procedures in Learning*. New York: Teachers College Press, Columbia University, 1952, pp. 277, 302–343. Used by permission of the publisher.

object of the teacher is to cover ground or the pages in a voluminous textbook, he is advised to abandon the idea of cooperative planning. In sharing decisions with a class, the teacher must be willing to surrender some of his own control of the situation at the risk of some confusion or even disorder. Above all, the teacher must have faith in his students and their ability and willingness to assume responsibility. Usually, students will justify the confidence of a teacher who has faith in them. As a further safeguard to honesty in cooperative planning, the teacher must clarify, at the outset, the boundaries within which students may exercise freedom of choice. However, there are professional responsibilities that teachers may not renounce. They are employed by school districts to *guide* the learning experiences of students and to make curricular decisions that cannot be left to inexperienced adolescents.

Another important guideline for cooperative planning is the *necessity for thorough planning by the teacher in advance.* Cooperative planning is no substitute for preplanning on the part of the teacher. Indeed, cooperative planning demands more thought and preparation by the teacher than do autocratic procedures. In order to give effective guidance to students who may be immature and inexperienced in cooperative procedures, the teacher must have the ability to offer many alternative suggestions, know his materials and resources well in order to assist students in their research, possess skill in capitalizing on student questions and suggestions, and discern the infinite possibilities for the achievement of unit objectives. Thus, it can readily be observed that a teacher who is committed to cooperative planning needs thorough knowledge, organizational ability, good judgment, and imagination.

If cooperative planning is to succeed, *the respective roles of teacher and students must be clarified.* As a general guideline, Wiles suggests that it is the task of the teacher "to provide enough direction to give the pupils a sense of security, but not enough to discourage initiative." [13] Democracy is not a gift; it has to be learned and earned. Because that is so, the democratic process of sharing responsibility with a class requires careful guidance by the teacher. Some failures are to be expected. However, if there is too much disorder, chaos, or failure in group processes, those involved develop feelings of insecurity and dissatisfaction. The teacher has to exercise discrimination in deciding when to keep hands off and when to rescue a class from its own inept operation. The respective areas of responsibility of both teacher and students must be clearly defined at the outset. When students have been assigned responsibility, the teacher not only provides the necessary freedom for students to exercise that responsibility but also provides necessary guidance as needed in defining

[13] Kimball Wiles, *Teaching for Better Schools,* 2d ed. Englewood Cliffs, N.J.: Prentice-Hall, Inc., 1959, p. 109.

problems, in developing leadership, in learning how to work together, and in reporting findings effectively to the class. The teacher must also remember that he has definite obligations to the school, to parents, and to the community that he cannot delegate to others. Although students may participate in assisting with class routine, in setting up their own rules of conduct, in planning learning activities, and in evaluating their own progress, the teacher is ultimately responsible for reporting student growth in terms of valid marks or grades, for keeping accurate records of attendance, and for maintaining an acceptable learning situation in the classroom.

Finally, it is logical to assume that cooperative planning, properly conceived and executed, should result in a number of permanent values for the student:

1. *He learns to make intelligent choices.* This involves accumulating and weighing evidence, developing value judgments, and acting upon the basis of his own decisions. He learns to do all these things only by experience.

2. *He learns to work with others.* Developing respect for the rights and abilities of others, acquiring social skills, and knowing how to lead and how to follow are learned only through practice.[14]

3. *He learns to assume responsibility*, to stand on his own feet, and to live with decisions that he and his own peers have made. He learns all this in the only way possible—by being responsible.

4. Finally, *he learns to evaluate his own actions*, to weigh the positive and negative results of his choices, and to develop a system of values by which to live. He becomes a responsible, moral individual by assuming responsibility for his own decisions and actions.

COOPERATIVE TEACHING

In addition to cooperative planning with their students, teachers are beginning to plan more classroom activities with their fellow teachers in some form of cooperative or team teaching arrangement. Although teachers have worked with others in the development of curricular resources (curriculum guides and resource units, for example), they have ordinarily worked more or less alone in teaching their classes. Now there is evidence that the use of team teaching is increasing. In 1956, 4 percent of large secondary schools reported the use of team teaching; by 1961, the proportion had increased to 30 percent.[15]

In January 1966 the Research Division of the NEA sent a questionnaire "to a stratified sample of public school systems enrolling 300 or more

[14] Leland P. Bradford, "Developing Potentialities through Class Groups," *Teachers College Record,* 61 (May 1960), 443–450.

[15] Project on the Instructional Program of the Public Schools, *The Principals Look at the Schools.* Washington, D.C.: National Education Association, 1962, p. 18.

pupils" to gather information about school programs and practices.[16] The schools were divided into three classes, based on total enrollments, both elementary and secondary: large schools, 25,000 or more pupils; medium-sized schools, 3,000 to 24,999 pupils; and small schools, 300 to 2,999 pupils. Of the secondary schools reporting team teaching, "9 percent of the small systems, 37 percent of the medium-sized systems, and 63 percent of the large systems reported having team teaching programs . . . ."[17]

It is also predicted that some form of cooperative planning and teaching will most likely continue to increase for a number of reasons: (1) the complex problem of working with disadvantaged youth demands some form of cooperative teaching and (2) many new developments —nongraded classes, instructional television, programmed learning, computer-assisted instruction—lend themselves logically to cooperative planning.[18]

It seems obvious that future teachers will need to develop a high order of skill in instructional planning and to cultivate the art of working closely with fellow teachers.

SELECTED READINGS

1. Batchelder, Howard T., Maurice McGlasson, and Raleigh Schorling, *Student Teaching in Secondary Schools,* 4th ed. New York: McGraw-Hill Book Company, Inc., 1964.

2. Burton, William H., *The Guidance of Learning Activities,* 3d ed. New York: Appleton-Century-Crofts, Inc., Division of Meredith Corporation, 1962, chap. 9.

3. Callahan, Sterling, *Successful Teaching in Secondary Schools.* Chicago: Scott, Foresman and Company, 1966, chap. 3.

4. Carter, William L., Carl W. Hansen, and Margaret G. McKim, *Learning to Teach in the Secondary School.* New York: The Macmillan Company, 1962, chap. 6.

5. Clark, Leonard H., and Irving S. Starr, *Secondary School Teaching Methods,* 2d ed. New York: The Macmillan Company, 1967, chap. 5.

6. Haskew, Laurence D., and Jonathan C. McLendon, *This Is Teaching,* rev. ed. Chicago: Scott, Foresman and Company, 1962, chap. 9.

7. McKean, Robert C., *Principles and Methods in Secondary Education.* Columbus: Charles E. Merrill Books, Inc., 1962, chap. 5.

8. Tanruther, Edgar M., *Clinical Experiences in Teaching for the Student Teacher or Intern.* New York: Dodd, Mead & Company, 1967, chap. 4.

[16] Research Division, NEA, *Research Bulletin,* 45, no. 4 (December 1967), 103.
[17] Research Division, NEA, p. 115.
[18] Marian Pope Franklin, ed., *School Organization: Theory and Practice.* Chicago: Rand McNally & Company, 1967, pp. 278–280. This book of selected readings covers a number of recent developments, including team teaching.

CHAPTER 5 / *Unit Planning*

It has already been suggested that a persistent problem in secondary education is that of providing greater unity and coherence in the educational experiences of boys and girls. A number of factors—the quantitative interpretation of education in terms of Carnegie units, the specialized subject matter emphasis in teacher training, and college entrance requirements—have conspired to make integration of learning difficult. Unit planning for instruction is an attempt to offset some of the disadvantages of a fragmented curriculum and to broaden the range of learning materials and activities in the classroom, even within the present framework of separate subjects. In the discussion that follows, clarification of the definition of a unit, values and limitations of unit planning, and suggestions for the development and implementation of unit plans will be considered.

THE UNIT DEFINED

The unit may be simply defined as a means of organizing instructional activities and materials into larger, related, unified patterns of learning in order to achieve significant educational objectives. According to Burton, "The important thing is to provide a combination of subject matter and processes which will have real meaning for the learner, which will aid him in continuously integrating his learning" (3:328).

One of four definitions of a unit in the *Dictionary of Education* describes the unit as "an organization of various activities, experiences, and types of learning around a central problem or purpose, developed cooperatively by a group of pupils under teacher leadership. . . ."[1] The

---

[1] Carter V. Good, ed., *Dictionary of Education*. New York: McGraw-Hill Book Company, Inc., 1959, p. 587.

86

definitions above imply that a unit includes these characteristics: a comprehensive coverage of a theme or problem; a time allotment of more than one class period; cooperative planning; a variety of learning activities and materials; and achievement of significant objectives. It should be noted that neither a chapter in a textbook nor a larger block of subject matter necessarily constitutes a unit. The authors contend that cooperative planning is not always a necessary element in unit planning. Teachers everywhere still prepare unit plans unassisted and teach them without consulting the class concerning what is to be done or how. The nature of the subject, the ability of the class, and the competence of the teacher determine how much cooperative planning is practicable.

The fact that there are more than two dozen types or kinds of units can create considerable confusion in the mind of a beginning teacher who wishes to engage in unit planning.[2] Consequently, some clarification and simplification of the problem are in order at this point.

TYPES OF UNITS

Due to a difference in function, a distinction needs to be made between "experience units" and "subject matter units." In some instances, a third type, the "process unit," is introduced to add still more confusion to the concept of unit planning. The authors contend that, except for semantic reasons, an unnecessary dichotomy is set up when so-called experience units are contrasted with subject matter units. Differences are a matter of degree, not kind, for the student cannot learn without experience or without subject matter or content. By the same token, violent controversies that sometimes rage in academic circles over the relative merits of methods and subject matter are pointless because both are inseparable and necessary aspects of the teaching process.

Their differences in function make unnecessary a distinction between a teaching unit and a resource unit. In structure they are similar, but each serves a different function. The teaching unit is prepared by the classroom teacher for use in a particular class. (For example, a teaching unit might be one on "conservation" for use in Social Studies 9 in Fremont High School during the fall semester of 1969.) The resource unit (often prepared by a group of teachers during a summer workshop) is a comprehensive compilation of suggested objectives, topics or problems related to a unifying theme, activities and materials, evaluative techniques, and references. The teaching unit, prepared by the teacher alone or in cooperation with his class, is for use by the teacher and his students. The resource unit is prepared by and for teachers. Including more suggestions than any one teacher could possibly use, the resource unit provides the raw materials for teaching units. It is a time-saver for the busy classroom

[2] Good, pp. 587–588.

teacher. Product of a cooperative effort, the resource unit not only saves time and effort for the individual teacher but also represents the rich and varied contributions of a professional team. (*Note:* Sometimes a teacher working alone may develop a resource unit, but the advantages of cooperative thinking are lost.) As yet, there are many areas of the curriculum for which resource units are not available.

VALUES OF UNIT PLANNING

It has already been suggested that less time and thought are required to develop daily plans than to construct comprehensive unit plans. But there are values in the integrated approach to planning that can never be achieved by planning on a day-by-day basis alone.

In contrast to a segmented, piecemeal approach to planning, which so often characterizes the daily assignment from a single textbook, unit planning is likely to ensure more integrated, meaningful learning experiences for students. All the elements of a theme or problem are explored with a continuity that is maintained over a period of days or weeks.

Unit planning incorporates a great variety of learning activities, such as reading, writing, speaking, listening, dramatizing, experimenting, cooperative planning, researching, and reporting. Furthermore, unit planning makes use of many different kinds of learning aids, such as audio-visual materials, electronic devices and laboratory equipment, and community resources.

Unit planning makes possible more adequate provision for individual differences within the classroom. Because of the rich and varied materials and activities a well-developed unit has to offer, more opportunities for student choices, greater appeal to diversified interests, and better use of a variety of talents are assured.

There is also greater likelihood that each student will achieve some measure of success when activities are not limited to those of a verbal type, as is so often true of academic courses in the secondary school. The heterogeneity of the secondary school population today should impress upon every teacher the fact that no two classes nor any two students have the same learning experiences or achieve identical outcomes.

Better integration of content from different subjects is possible within the framework of unit organization for instruction. This is especially true of general education subjects, those required of all students, where the block-time schedule of two or more consecutive periods under one teacher is used.

Better continuity in learning can be achieved in unit teaching. The teacher and his students are able to attack problems requiring an extended period of research and to pursue their study until possible solutions are found.

Classroom procedures are less likely to be dominated by the teacher under unit planning than under assign-study-recite procedures based upon a single textbook.

Although it is true that the extent of student participation in planning is dependent upon several variables, already discussed in the preceding chapter, the unit plan provides more opportunities for the development of student initiative and responsibility than is possible under more limited and formalized types of plans. For example, where different groups or individuals are responsible for investigating different aspects of a problem, a number of desirable outcomes are possible—a better solution to the problem, more opportunities for sharing ideas, and a better use of student talent.

Unit planning is based upon sound psychological principles of learning. As already stated, the unit emphasizes learning by wholes, the continuity of learning, and the integration of student learning experiences. With more student involvement made possible by the unit approach to teaching, a higher degree of motivation is likely to occur.

LIMITATIONS OF UNIT PLANNING

Not all subjects or courses are equally adaptable to unit planning. As a rule, the nonspecialized general education courses required of all students lend themselves more readily to unit organization and cooperative planning than do more highly specialized courses. The following types of classes or subjects might more appropriately use some other type of instructional plan: subjects requiring mastery of a definite sequence of concepts or problems as a prerequisite for more advanced study (for example, specialized courses in mathematics or science); classes in which students devote most of their time to individual projects (for example, classes in art or industrial arts); classes devoted to achievement of specific skills (for example, classes in shorthand or typing); and courses in which most of class time is spent in practice or rehearsal (such as band or choral groups). Even such a general education course as English often includes discrete elements that may not be related to a particular unit. For instance a typical daily time budget in an English class may look something like this: ten minutes, pretest on a formal spelling word list; twenty minutes, composition papers returned and errors analyzed; and twenty minutes, reading and discussion of short poems in a literature text. Although the teacher may teach two units alternately in this case (for example, a unit on poetry and a unit on usage of pronouns), there would still probably be some discrete elements that would not be related to either unit. The point is this: not every learning activity in the classroom has to fit within the framework of a particular unit for study.

Some teachers now encounter increasing difficulty in using unit plans. Short class periods, large classes, a high degree of departmentalization, prescriptive courses of study, agitation for more specific subject titles (such as "history" or "geography" instead of the term "social studies"), mandatory use of uniform textbooks and pressure for statewide examinations for all students—all these make unit planning more difficult.

Because unit planning implies the use of more teacher-student planning, when feasible, more varied activities, and comprehensive coverage of a theme or problem, some teachers view unit planning with misgivings. They are apprehensive of the confusion and disorder that may result when a number of individuals or small groups concurrently work on a variety of activities. Discipline problems may be serious. However, careful preparation and organization, as well as a realistic appraisal of the limitations and conditions related to cooperative planning and group work, discussed in the preceding chapter, should offer proper safeguards for an orderly, productive learning situation.

Inasmuch as unit teaching seeks to achieve greater breadth of understanding in terms of the interrelationship of all subjects, the teacher may feel insecure because of inadequate preparation in some specialized subjects. Greater breadth in preservice teacher education, continuous inservice preparation, and placement of more responsibility upon students for their own learning offer a partial solution to the problem. Teachers have to realize that they cannot be the fount of all knowledge; neither can they learn during their undergraduate years in college all they are expected to know. What teacher has not learned that the best way to learn a subject is to teach it? Furthermore, the *team* approach to teaching (with different team members specializing in different subjects) could provide another solution to the problem of subject matter mastery.

There are a number of minor difficulties that a teacher may encounter in unit teaching. Occasionally, it may be difficult to sustain interest in a single theme, topic, or problem for a relatively long period of time. This is especially true of immature or slow-learning students. The obvious solution is to plan shorter units. A related problem may be the tendency to overextend the unit, to drag out the work after objectives have been achieved. Sometimes it may seem inappropriate to include drill or remedial lessons on fundamental skills as needed and still maintain continuity in the unit. Unit development has to take place within the framework of daily periods of short duration, hence the teacher must organize each period in such a way as to maintain continuous progress toward long-range unit goals, but he can still include remedial work as needed without destroying continuity of the unit.

PRINCIPAL PARTS OF THE UNIT
AND THEIR FUNCTIONS

Basically, the unit, or any other complete instructional plan, consists of four minimum essentials: objectives or expected outcomes, activities or learning experiences, materials, and evaluation. Each of these divisions of the teaching-learning process provides the answer to an important question. Objectives indicate *why* any activity, lesson, or unit should be undertaken at all. They provide the answer to a petulant query that has often been voiced by students: "Why do we have to study this stuff?" Activities answer the question *how*. They include all the things that the teacher and students *do* to achieve the objectives. Materials provide the answer to the question *what*. They consist of all aids or means (printed and audio-visual materials, apparatus, equipment) for implementation of the activities. Evaluation is an attempt to answer the question *how much* or *how well*. It consists of the criteria and the procedures used by the teacher and his class to determine to what extent the objectives have been achieved.

An examination of printed units usually reveals a more elaborate structure than that suggested by the four minimum essentials listed above. In fact, if all possible items in unit structure were included, an outline of the major divisions would consist of the following titles:

    I. Setting and overview
   II. Outline of topics or problems
  III. Objectives
      A. General
      B. Specific
  IV. Activities
      A. Initiatory or introductory
      B. Developmental
      C. Culminating
   V. Materials
  VI. Correlation with other subjects
 VII. Evaluation
VIII. Bibliography
      A. Student
      B. Teacher

For further clarification, each of the above items in the detailed unit structure is briefly described in the following paragraphs.

SETTING AND OVERVIEW

The *setting* includes such items as unit title, subject and grade level (for example, English 9), and approximate time limit of the unit. The unit title should be concise, descriptive, and interesting. It should also suggest the unifying principle around which the unit is organized. Note the different unifying principles in the following examples.

    Problem (physiology): "How does diet affect one's health?"
                (or Diet in relation to health)

Project (ind. arts):	"How can an automobile owner get more service from his car?" (or Automotive maintenance)
Project (homemaking):	"How can a housewife prepare an attractive, balanced meal?" (or Preparation of balanced meals)
Topic (social studies):	"How did the people of Europe settle the New World?" (or The colonization of North America)
Activity (physical ed.):	"How does tennis contribute to better use of leisure time?" (or Tennis for recreation)
Generalization (science):	"Water is important for human survival" (or Water and human survival)

As mentioned before, the teacher may take a position from one extreme to another, from a stress on student experience to a major emphasis upon subject matter to be learned. Emphases will vary according to "the level of maturity, the experiential background, the purposes, needs, and interests of the learner" (3:329). However, the most effective planning makes student experience the focal point of teaching and uses subject matter as the means to an end, namely, the improvement of the quality of student experience.

The *overview* broadly outlines the purpose and content of the unit, relating it to the preceding units and to the course as a whole. An example appears in a unit outline later in this chapter.

OUTLINE OF TOPICS OR PROBLEMS

To give structure or body to the unit in terms of a definite scope and sequence of activities and materials, some teachers find it helpful to include a content outline of topics (history), problems (science), or activities (physical education.)

OBJECTIVES AND EXPECTED OUTCOMES

Unit objectives must have value for the student and for the society that supports the schools. The student must feel that activities to achieve unit goals have personal value for him; society must require that such activities help to perpetuate it. Objectives are both general and specific. They range from the general objectives of secondary education to the specific objectives of the classroom. Differences in types of objectives may be illustrated as follows:

An example from English:
Objective of secondary education: Students are expected to develop skill in the fundamental processes (also applicable to other subjects).

General objective in English: Students are expected to improve their reading skills.

Specific objective in English: Students will demonstrate the use of various clues in reading a book effectively (such as using the table of contents, noting illustrations, scanning headings).

An example in music:

Objective of secondary education: Students are expected to learn how to use leisure time wisely.

General objective in music: Students are expected to learn to appreciate better music.

Specific objective in music: Students will be able to identify similarities between given selections of popular music and their classical counterparts.

A further analysis of objectives appears later in this chapter under the topic "Unit Objectives."

ACTIVITIES

Initiatory or *introductory* activities get the unit under way. They may serve several purposes: to determine what the student already knows about the proposed unit; to relate student interests, backgrounds, and abilities to the new unit; and to motivate the class to pursue the study of the unit with enthusiasm. *Developmental* activities are the heart of the unit. These activities need to be extensive and varied, for they constitute about everything the teacher and the class do to achieve the objectives of the unit. *Culminating* activities are designed to summarize, to review, and to reemphasize the central, unifying theme or problem of the unit. The following activities are typical: an exhibit of students' work (art), a tournament (physical education), a series of committee reports (social science), or a tea honoring mothers (homemaking).

MATERIALS

It has already been assumed that subject matter and learning activities are inseparable. Materials (printed and audio-visual materials, apparatus, equipment), constitute the substance of the learning activities. The teacher is responsible for acquainting his students with the rich and varied sources of information and for teaching them how to locate and use accurate, relevant data in solving their problems.

CORRELATION WITH OTHER SUBJECTS

Because the secondary school curriculum is so highly fragmented, the teacher must make a conscious effort at all times to integrate student knowledge in the various subjects. A short anecdote, which could be duplicated countless times, illustrates the point:

A mechanical drawing teacher was giving a test. When a student asked, "Does spelling count?" he was told that it would. The student protested on the grounds that spelling should count only in English classes.

EVALUATION

The unit cycle is completed with evaluation. When all evaluation data are in, everyone concerned should know how well unit objectives have been achieved. There are several approaches to evaluation. First of all, the teacher and the class may cooperatively evaluate the successes and failures experienced in the development of the unit as a guide to future operations. As another phase of evaluation, the teacher may evaluate his own teaching of the unit. Certainly no unit evaluation is complete until the teacher has gathered all available data concerning the progress of each student and has translated it into a mark or grade to be used in progress reports to parents and as part of the cumulative record of the student. Final marks or grades are part of the student's permanent record; hence each member of a class has a right to know in advance what criteria and procedures will be used by the teacher in evaluating his work for each unit.

BIBLIOGRAPHY

A list of selected references, sometimes one for students and another for the teacher, is included at the end of the unit to supplement the materials suggested in the body of the unit. Appendices may be added that include charts and graphs, word lists, suggested class organization, and other miscellaneous items.

UNIT DESIGN

Although a teacher may know that any instructional plan, reduced to its most basic elements, consists of but four parts—objectives, activities, materials, and evaluation—he may still have difficulty in organizing these into a coherent, unified sequence. The structure of a unit plan, as well as a daily plan, may be set up according to either of two formats—an outline form or a columnar or parallel form. The outline form, the one longest in use, is illustrated as follows:

UNIT: THE SHORT STORY

I. *Setting:* English 10, Mt. Miguel High School.
   Teacher—Mrs. J. M.   *Dates*—October 8 through October 17.
II. *Overview:* The short story is a work of fiction characterized by a single theme treated with dramatic intensity. Any short story will have a setting,

made up of scene and time, one or more characters, and a plot. As the unit progresses, we shall read several short stories written by well-known authors, attempt to analyze their characteristics and the elements that make them short stories, and try to write a short story of our own. Throughout the unit we shall be attempting to arrive at some criteria by which the worth and effectiveness of any short story can be evaluated.

III. *Topics to be covered:*
  A. In *English Grammar and Composition* by Warriner and Griffith (Chapter 14, pp. 323–340):
    1. "Finding Suitable Incidents."
    2. "Deciding the Purpose."
    3. "Deciding the Characters."
    4. "Importance of Scene and Time."
    5. "Organization of the Story."
  B. In *Adventures in Appreciation* by Cook *et al.*:
    1. "Reward" by Jean C. Becket (pp. 152–159).
    2. "Windwagon Smith" by Wilbur Schramm (pp. 113–127).
    3. "Revolt of Mother" by May E. Wilkins Freeman (pp. 59–69).
  C. Other Short Stories:
    1. "The Necklace" by de Maupassant.
    2. "The Celebrated Sassage Factory" by Charles Dickens.

IV. *Objectives:*
  A. General: Students should be able:
    1. To develop an understanding of the short story as a literary term and type.
    2. To develop an appreciation for well-written short stories.
    3. To develop an understanding of the techniques necessary for writing a good short story.
  B. Specific: Students should be able:
    1. To define and identify terms related to the short story as follows: plot, character, time, setting, mood, theme, and purpose.
    2. To show enthusiasm in describing the style and interpreting the message of "Reward" by Becket and "Windwagon Smith."
    3. To show a desire to write narrative prose in the best style possible.
    4. To exhibit growth in intelligent self-criticism of narratives for suitability and purpose.
    5. To apply the criteria of purpose to "The Necklace."
    6. To show gratification over ability of the author to delineate characters in "Revolt of Mother."
    7. To develop criteria for the interpretation and evaluation of the short story.
    8. To apply these evaluative criteria to stories they read as well as to original work.

V. *Activities:*
  A. Discuss "Reward" to cover questions on understanding of plot and character.

    B. Write a paragraph on what might have happened if Joe had remained in Ware's Landing.

    C. Read "Windwagon Smith."

       1. Be able to apply theme to what we know of the "American ideal" of progress.

       2. Explain "exaggeration" as a literary term and find examples of it in the story.

       3. Be able to discuss types of characters, mood, incidents of the story.

    D. Read orally "The Celebrated Sassage Factory" as an example of a subject for writing.

    E. Read and discuss Chapter 14, pp. 323–327, on purpose and suitability of incident in narrative writing.

    F. Write a brief narrative from personal experience.

    G. Listen to a recording of "The Necklace," discuss story as to purpose and characterization and relate it to personal experiences.

    H. Read aloud randomly selected samples of narrative writing and get oral criticism of purpose and effectiveness.

    I. Write, in class, a vivid description of some person, read to class, and secure class criticism as to effectiveness of characterization.

    J. Read and discuss "Revolt of Mother" as to effectiveness of characterization and significance of theme for family life of students. Compare characterization with that of "The Necklace."

    K. Read and discuss Chapter 14, pp. 335–340, on title, first draft, and revision of first draft of short story.

    L. Review orally and outline on chalkboard the principles for writing a short story.

    M. Write an original short story.

    N. Show filmstrip-recording of "Interpretation and Evaluation of the Short Story," summarizing principles and having students apply them to stories read and to stories written by themselves.

VI. *Materials:*

    A. Stories in *Adventures in Appreciation* (as listed above).

    B. Chapter 14 in *English Grammar and Composition.*

    C. Recording of "The Necklace."

    D. Filmstrip-recording of "Interpretation and Evaluation of the Short Story."

    E. Story of "The Celebrated Sassage Factory" (from *Tell Me a Story* by Charles Laughton).

    F. Original work of students.

VII. *Evaluation:*

    A. Participation in class discussion.

    B. Performance on written work.

    C. Performance on tests (quizzes, unit test).

VIII. *Bibliography:*

    A. Cook, Luella B., *et al.*, *Adventures in Appreciation.* New York: Harcourt, Brace & World, Inc., 1952.

    B. Laughton, Charles, *Tell Me a Story: An Anthology.* New York: McGraw-Hill Book Company, Inc., 1957.

C. Warriner, John E., and Francis Griffith, *English Grammar and Composition.* New York: Harcourt, Brace & World, Inc., 1958.[3]

The newest and most functional design for a unit is the columnar or parallel type, illustrated by the two following examples:

UNIT: GIRLS' BASKETBALL [4]

I. *Subject and Grade:* Girls' Physical Education (Grade 12).

School: Hoover High School *Teacher:* Catherine Fogarty.

Time: Four weeks (Feb. 14–March 14).

II. *Overview:* Basketball is a team sport played by two teams of six members each. In achieving the main objective of the game, the teacher is concerned with teaching two types of skills: offensive and defensive. The game is a noncontact, "action" sport that requires the student to develop ball-manipulatory skills, body movement control, a working knowledge of the game rules, and cooperative teamwork.

The first two weeks of instruction include basic ball-handling skills and efficient court locomotor movements. The following four weeks, presented in this unit, concentrate on individual team strategy, rules, and officiating techniques.

Unlike any former basketball the students may have played in earlier grades, this unit deals particularly with defensive zone guarding. The stress is on "un-learning" familiar methods and on the acquisition of new defensive positioning with relationship to the ball.

The last week of the unit is devoted to tournament play in which students apply their newly acquired skills in winning for their team.

III. *General Objectives:*
- A. *Developing Physical Fitness:* Agility, power, speed, stamina, and co-ordination are factors that contribute to total fitness.
- B. *Increasing Movement Skills:* Simple basic foundation experiences in body control (running, jumping, landing, stopping, throwing, catching) are used to develop skills of speed, power, balance, rhythm, accuracy, and timing—all of which are used in the game of basketball.
- C. *Socializing the Student:* In team sports, the individual is a group member engaged in a united effort of contribution and cooperation. Citizenship qualities of fair play, self-control, and consideration for others are all very important.
- D. *Fostering Better Use of Leisure Time:* Stress is placed on the carry-over value of basketball as a recreational skill, as a constructive use of leisure time, and as a means of promoting good health.

[3] This material reprinted by permission of Robin Briscoe.
[4] This material is reprinted by permission of Catherine Fogarty.

IV. *Specific Objectives, Activities, and Facilities:*

SPECIFIC OBJECTIVES	ACTIVITIES	FACILITIES & EQUIPMENT
1. Students will be able to show progressive development in physical fitness—in strength, endurance, flexibility, balance, power, coordination, and agility.	1. Daily exercises that concentrate on major parts of the body and daily running to develop cardiorespiratory endurance.	1. Courts and unobstructed running areas
2. Students will demonstrate development of body mechanics that are used in basketball.	2. Conditioning exercises; mimetic and practice drills, lay-up footwork and stationary pivot drills, dynamic guarding agility exercises.	2. Courts, balls
3. Students will demonstrate ability to catch and pass accurately while on the move.	3. Practice drills that stress passing ahead, aiming, absorbing shock, and meeting the ball—Fig. B drills and shuttle drills.	3. Courts, instruction cards, balls
4. Students will furnish evidence of strategy and game sense for both offensive and defensive positions.	4. Present box zone—relate to meaningful image (house). Demonstrate on court. Use chalk talk and bulletin board display. Complete work sheet. Stress importance of rovers.	4. Marked court, balls, and pinnies (pinafores), chalkboard
5. Students will exhibit ability to combine skills smoothly.	5. Use Give-and-Go play. Demonstrate and drill. Study Bulletin Board. Use Hand-off and Cut-in play (same as Give-Go).	5. Courts, balls, and instructional cards
6. Students will demonstrate principles of aim and more accuracy in shooting skills.	6. *Aids* on where to aim. Demonstrate and discuss. 30-second shooting tests. Lay-up drills.	6. Markings on backboards, team score cards, stopwatch

SPECIFIC OBJECTIVES	ACTIVITIES	FACILITIES & EQUIPMENT
7. Students will show a mastery of at least one offensive shooting skill and an awareness of other possibilities.	7. Demonstrate advantages of three basic shots in basketball.	7. Posted visual aids
8. Students will evidence good body mechanics through principles of weight shift, force application, and rebound strategy.	8. Dribble drills: stopping and starting quickly, bouncing the ball for different reasons, and using proper hand and finger action.	8. Courts, balls
9. Students will display a working knowledge of the rules of basketball.	9. Daily questions and study aid on bulletin board. Game situation rule violations cited. Dramatization of rules by class members.	9. Daily situation posted on bulletin board, court, balls, and pinnies
10. Students will show development in officiating skills.	10. Demonstrate good officiating positioning—leading and trailing official. Officiate in tournaments.	10. Visual diagrams and whistles
11. Students will manifest enjoyment of the recreational values in basketball and the development of a cooperative team spirit.	11. Daily tournament play.	11. Courts, balls, pinnies
12. Students will have an opportunity to show growth in leadership and responsibility.	12. Students will be assigned as game officials and team captains—the latter to assign players' positions; lead warm-ups and drills; aid in skill tests.	12. Drill cards and score cards signed by captains

V. *Evaluation and Grading Procedures:*

CRITERIA	PROCEDURES OR TECHNIQUES	SCORING	WEIGHT
Performance on skill tests.	30-second shooting test, speed dribble test, and wall pass test.	Average of tests in Z-scores.	25%
Form, sportsmanship, knowledge of rules and officiating, game play, and quick grasp of new skills.	Objective rating charts used by the teacher.	Scored as check, plus, or minus.	25%
Knowledge of rules, strategy, and skills.	Full period, teacher-made test of knowledge.	Z-score.	25%
Cardiovascular endurance test.	440 Fitness Running Test.	Z-score.	25%

UNIT: EAST ASIA[5]

I. *Subject:* 9th-Grade World History.   *Teacher:* P. Stanbro.

School: Pacific Beach Junior High.   *Time:* Two weeks (April 15–30).

II. *Overview:* About one third of the earth's population lives in East Asia. We are the minority. It is our responsibility to learn as much about this area and its people as we can so that we can contribute our share to a better understanding among all peoples of the world. This unit is a meager attempt to make a start toward that desired understanding.

III. *General objectives:* Students will develop an awareness of the importance of East Asia and its overwhelming population and gain a desire to learn more about this area and its peoples. In addition, they will learn to understand and to appreciate some of the values and problems of the people of East Asia and the relationship of these values and problems to the United States, historically, today, and in the future.

[5] This material is reprinted with the permission of Philip Stanbro.

IV. *Specific objectives, activities, and materials:*

SPECIFIC OBJECTIVES	ACTIVITIES AND MATERIALS
1. Students will be able to locate on the map and to describe physical (topographic and climatic) features, and outline the major effects of these features on distribution of population.	1. Read text (pp. 359–364). Study question 4, p. 376. Label outline map. Use overlays on OHP to demonstrate interrelation of climate, topography, and mineral location to population distribution and agriculture.
2. Students will be able to trace the basic history of China from 1900 to Mao Tse-tung's rise to power.	2. Read text (pp. 358–359). Preview, show, and discuss the film *Mao Tse-tung,* to clarify the order of events in history. Write answer to question 3, p. 376.
3. Students will be able to locate and describe the importance of the 7 key political regions in China, including their main cities.	3. Show the film *Canton: Oriental City.* Complete outline map. Write answer to question 5, p. 376. Selected students will name regions and class will discuss why they are important— also make a location analysis.
4. Students will be able to locate and to describe importance and political status of the outlying regions of China.	4. Read text, pp. 367–372. Label outline map. Selected students will describe outlying regions. Class will discuss their importance and make a locational analysis.
5. Students will be able to list several important features and values of the traditional Chinese culture and indicate their present place in the communist system.	5. View and discuss the filmstrip *Confucianism and Taoism.* Read text, pp. 272–274. Write answer to question 7, p. 376. Discuss conflict between communism and traditional family and religious values.
6. Students will be able to list several important potentials and problems of the economy and international politics of China.	6. Read text, pp. 374–376. See and discuss the filmstrip *Living in China and Korea.* Discuss contemporary problems of China. (Stress relation to the United States.)

SPECIFIC OBJECTIVES	ACTIVITIES AND MATERIALS
7. Students will be able to describe briefly the major events of political significance in Korea from 1890 to 1960 and the country's present political and economic status.	7. Read text, pp. 377–379. Write answers to questions 2, 4, and 5, p. 379. Develop outline map. Discuss events leading to Korean conflict and its effects on present-day Korea.
8. Students will be able to locate and describe the major physical features of Japan and discuss their effects on the Japanese economy and population.	8. Read text, pp. 379–384. Write answers to questions 5, 6, and 7, p. 389. Show the film *Japan*. Discuss interrelationship between physical environment and man in Japan.
9. Students will be able to describe the present-day importance of Japan in the world in terms of her history and technology.	9. Read text, pp. 384–389. Write answers to questions 7, 9, and 11, p. 389. View and discuss the film *Japan: An Historical Overview*. Discuss methodology and results of technology in Japan.
10. Students will be able to describe important traditional cultural values of the Japanese and changes in recent years.	10. Show the film *Japanese Village Life*. Write answer to question 10, p. 389. Use large, color study prints of Japanese family life to stimulate discussion and for comparison with life in the United States.

V. *Evaluation:* Observation of class response to determine student weaknesses and special interests; outline maps; answers to written questions ($\nu-$, ν, $\nu+$): 25%; comprehensive unit test: 75%.

VI. *Resources: Text:* Jones and Murphy, *Geography and World Affairs;* Wheeler, Kostbade, and Thoman, *Regional Geography of the World;* Norton Ginsberg (ed.), *The Pattern of Asia;* and *Guide for Teaching World Geography 1–2*, San Diego City Schools, 1965. Films and filmstrips (*see* body of unit).

It should be noted that three major divisions (sometimes four when an outline of topics or problems is included) appear in the columnar structures while the remainder of the unit is in outline form. That this type of structure is more functional than the older outline type can be seen at a glance. Parts that are inseparable in the instructional process—objectives, materials, activities—are closely related in the unit structure. Because *evaluation* appears as a separate category it is not to be assumed that evaluation occurs only at the end of the unit. It is continuous with each evaluative activity included under the same category with other activities. However, for marking purposes it is necessary to have defined quite clearly both criteria and procedures, as well as the relative weights assigned to each.

It should also be noted that these illustrations of the columnar type of unit show but one of a number of variations which may be used. For example, the columnar design may be reduced to two categories:

Activities and Materials | *Expected Outcomes* (or *Specific Objectives*)

Or an expansion of the columnar type of unit might include these:

Topics or *Problems* | *Materials* or *Resources* | *Activities* | *Expected Outcomes*

Suffice it to say, the important thing is to include at least the minimum essentials of the teaching-learning process in a plan that has unity, coherence, and continuity.

UNIT PREPARATION AND IMPLEMENTATION

The first step a teacher takes in unit planning is to make a tentative list of the units he expects to teach in a given course or subject. A choice of units will need to be made within the framework of a curriculum that has been developed cooperatively by many professional people. This framework usually appears in the form of a course of study or curriculum (or teachers') guide.

How much freedom a teacher has in planning his work, aside from general school policies, is dependent upon the breadth and flexibility of the curriculum guide. Traditional courses of study differed considerably from modern teachers' guides. The former were highly prescriptive, stressed subject matter to be learned, were infrequently revised, and were usually prepared by experts in subject fields. In contrast, modern curriculum guides offer many suggestions for achieving unit goals and permit considerable freedom of choice by the teacher on how to achieve them. Present-day guides also stress expected outcomes in terms of desirable changes in student behavior, using subject matter as a means to that end; they are subject to continuous revision; and they incorporate the contributions of many groups (psychologists, sociologists, specialists in subject fields, and educators) in their preparation, with classroom teachers occupying a prominent role.

Although modern curriculum guides, provided at both state and local levels, allow considerable freedom for the teacher, they have been designed to establish a framework within which the teacher should operate in order to ensure proper scope, sequence, and continuity for the school program as a whole. In recognition of the problem of providing for individual differences, makers of curriculum guides are further refining them to the extent that, in some cases, they are adapted to different levels of ability.

After a teacher has made a tentative choice of units for a given course, the next step is to set up a tentative time budget for each unit, subject to such revisions as may become necessary in the course of the term or semester.

Before proceeding very far in actual construction of unit plans, the teacher will need to know a number of things. Above all, he will need to know the type of students with whom he will work. Then he will need to know what instructional materials are available for implementation of the proposed units.

After the teacher has made a tentative selection of units to be developed during a term or semester, with a time allotment for each, usually his next step is to take an inventory of such available resources as physical facilities, instructional materials, and community resources. A detailed analysis of instructional materials follows in Chapters 7 through 11.

As soon as enrollments have been completed, the teacher will need *to get information about his students.* Several sources may be used—school records, the students themselves (interviews, autobiographies), parents, other professional personnel (teachers, counselors), personal observations, and the community—as discussed in Chapter 2. Armed with a knowledge of available resources and the types of students he will teach, the teacher is then ready to settle down to the business of unit construction.

UNIT OBJECTIVES

Unit construction begins with the selection of objectives. They give direction to everything the teacher and his students do. Lest unit objectives become merely window dressing, the teacher must regard them as functional, practical aspects of the total plan. The new teacher has to develop certain perceptions in order to recognize expected outcomes as the foundation of unit structure.

OBJECTIVES IN HISTORICAL PERSPECTIVE

Sometimes educational objectives are taken for granted. But it must be remembered that objectives expressed in terms of social and personal goals are less than sixty years old. At the turn of this century, it was assumed that the secondary school would perform such functions as preparing the student for college or training his mind. It was nearly twenty years before purposes or objectives as we know them were stated. Educational psychologists began to raise serious doubts about the claims of faculty psychology. Sociologists began to stress the needs of society. Educational philosophers believed that the needs of children and youth should be given priority in teaching. At first, educational objectives were based upon analyses of the activities of adults. Later, objectives were stated in terms of meeting the needs of students in school. Educators themselves were often split into two camps: the "essentialists," who subscribed to preparation for adult life, and the "progressives," who stressed the interests and needs of children and youth. Since 1950, an attempt has been made to harmonize these two approaches to the derivation of educational objectives. Today, many factors are considered necessary in the selection of objectives. Most important are analyses of students, contemporary society, and the learning process. Other considerations include expert opinion; *local* tradition, courses, personalities, and vested interests; and accrediting agencies (1:358–359, 573).

OBJECTIVES: THEORETICAL OR PRACTICAL?

The relationship of objectives to assigned learning activities determines the effectiveness of learning. It is at this point that the sharpest cleavage between theory and practice probably exists. Certainly no teacher in his preservice experience today has not had impressed upon him the importance of objectives. Yet how often the relationship between stated objectives and what takes place in the classroom is purely incidental! Objectives serve for ornament, not for use. Why is this so? There are probably several reasons.

The nonfunctional nature of educational objectives may actually be the product of preservice preparation of teachers. Repeated exposure to classical statements of objectives (the seven "Cardinal Principles of Secondary Education," the "Ten Imperative Needs of Youth" of secondary school age, and so on) can lead to familiarity or even contempt. This is especially true when the teacher in training is exposed to much theory without concurrent practical experience in the classroom. Vague, general statements of expected outcomes that sometimes appear in a teacher's plans lend further support to the useless character of objectives. Plans that include too many objectives too broadly stated are another deterrent to commitment to stated objectives. Despite repeated efforts to involve the total college faculty in the program of teacher education, students in training are often confused by conflicting purposes. In academic courses, stress may be placed upon mastery of subject matter; in professional courses, meeting the needs of students may be the point of emphasis. Furthermore, it is quite possible that the prospective teacher may never become aware of the fact that the purposes of the high school, as well as the type of students to be served, are by no means identical with those of the college.

In spite of the confusion about objectives, prospective teachers will find the "Cardinal Principles" or the "Ten Imperative Needs of Youth" reliable starting points for all secondary school learning experiences.

CRITERIA FOR OBJECTIVES

This discussion clearly indicates the need for definite criteria for judging the value of stated objectives if they are to be functional.

First of all, expected outcomes must represent goals that are understood and accepted by the teacher and his students. It is a mistake to assume that teacher and student goals are identical. Frequently they are not. Teacher-imposed objectives are likely to be primarily concerned with remote social goals and preparation for adult life, whereas students are concerned with their own immediate problems and needs. A major difficulty in teaching is how to reconcile the goals of the teacher with those of his students and to secure genuine motivation for learning. In some way, the demands of adult society must be reconciled with the here-and-now concerns of youth. When unit goals have finally been formulated, they should represent statements that students either have helped formulate or have accepted as being personally worthwhile.

OBJECTIVES MUST BE ACHIEVABLE

It is futile for the teacher to set up idealistic, unattainable goals. The maturity and experience of the class, available resources and feasible learning activities, the complexity of the topic or problem under consideration, and the competence of the teacher—all these factors determine whether or not a given set of objectives is achievable. It is a mistake to gear instruction below the maturity and achievement level of the students or to set the level of instruction beyond their attainment. The subject of social studies offers a good example. On the one hand, it is no longer considered advisable to limit classroom experiences of pupils in lower grades to a study of the local environment. Increasing opportunities for travel and rapid developments in communication, especially television, have expanded the horizons of even first graders to include not only the world but outer space. On the other hand, a group of immature junior high school students may be wrestling with a problem that confounds the experts. For example, what conclusions might a teacher and his class reach with respect to a protective tariff, American foreign policy, and membership in the United Nations in relation to national interest? Aside from being controversial, the end result of such discussions may very well be a superficial grasp of a complex problem, or, what is worse, misunderstanding between the teacher and the parents of his students.

OBJECTIVES MUST PROVIDE FOR DIVERSITY

Committed to the task of educating all boys and girls of secondary school age, our schools must meet the needs of students who exhibit great diversity of interests, abilities, and backgrounds. As the new teacher gains enough experience to engage in a higher level of instructional planning, his first consideration should be to provide for individual differences. The practice of grouping students according to ability and achievement into so-called homogeneous groups is becoming quite common. However, the teacher needs to remember that many classes are still grouped on a heterogeneous basis, that there is no such thing as a truly homogeneous group, and, finally, that there is conflicting evidence concerning the effectiveness of so-called homogeneous grouping. Consequently, the teacher in the classroom can never escape responsibility for individualizing instruction in order to meet the needs of all his students. Such provision for individual differences must be included in both daily and unit planning.

OBJECTIVES MUST BE BOTH PERSONAL AND SOCIAL

Any nation that establishes and supports schools has a right to demand that education be socially useful. The schools are obligated to develop good citizens, as defined by the state. At the same time, a state such as ours demands the highest development of the unique qualities of each individual citizen. Thus, a precise balance between education for uniformity and education for diversity must be maintained. Psychologically, educational objectives must become personal goals for the student. Otherwise no real learning occurs.

OBJECTIVES MUST BE SUSCEPTIBLE TO EVALUATION

As a teacher lists his unit objectives, he should consider the kind of evidence he will need to evaluate student achievement in each one. Of course, both formal means (such as tests) and informal means (such as teacher observations) may be used to gather data for evaluation. In listing objectives, the teacher may very well visualize unit development in its entirety: setting up goals, selecting appropriate materials and activities to achieve expected outcomes, and choosing procedures whereby he and his students may evaluate their achievement of unit objectives. A more thorough discussion of the evaluation of objectives follows in Chapter 16.

SPECIFIC OBJECTIVES MUST BE STATED IN BEHAVIORAL TERMS

It has already been stated that there is a nice distinction between *general* and *specific* objectives. The former are properly stated as broad, general goals of education or of a specific subject. On the other hand, *specific* objectives of *a daily lesson plan*, for example, must be stated in terms of *student behavior* that is identifiable or observable. Behavioral objectives have to be stated precisely enough for a teacher to be able to specify exactly what educational experiences are necessary for their achievement.

Furthermore, such objectives will suggest appropriate evaluation procedures to determine to what extent they have been achieved. Note the
following examples:

General Objective (Speech): Students will learn the principles of
effective speech.

Specific Objective (Speech): Students will demonstrate effective voice
placement.

General Objective (Industrial Arts): Students will learn to appreciate
good craftsmanship.

Specific Objective (Industrial Arts): Given a blueprint, a student will
be able to interpret it well enough to develop a satisfactory project.

OBJECTIVES NEED TO BE PROPERLY STATED

Objectives should be stated in grammatically consistent terms. Note the
following examples:

Students should be able to_____.

To develop an appreciation of_____.

Helping the student develop skills in_____

Objectives should not be confused with activities. Note the following
activities that are mistakenly stated as objectives:

To make a speech on the responsibilities of the citizen

To write an autobiography

To demonstrate the broad jump

To rehearse for a music festival

In the above examples, the stress is on *what* is to be done, not on *why*
it should be done.

Above all, objectives need to be stated in terms of desirable changes in
student behavior—thinking, feeling, or doing. If behavioral changes are
to result in continuous growth toward maturity, students must be able to
satisfy basic developmental needs. Some of these are the need to develop
independence in thought and action, the need to satisfy intellectual
curiosity, and the need to gain social acceptance. The teacher has a
responsibility not only for helping students satisfy present needs, but
also for making them aware of more remote needs to be met. Once objectives have been stated in terms of desirable changes in behavior in
relation to student needs, opportunities must be provided for practicing
the desired behaviors by means of appropriate learning materials and
activities in the classroom.

UNIT MATERIALS AND ACTIVITIES

The heart of a unit consists of the learning activities and materials. Most
of the teacher's time and effort in preplanning units needs to be devoted

to the selection of the best activities and resources available because nine tenths of class time will be spent upon implementing or executing the unit.

INTRODUCING THE UNIT

Heywood's familiar proverb, "Of a good beginning cometh a good end," has particular relevance to the introductory stage of unit development. First of all, it is important to get the class vitally interested. Like a good advertising manager, the teacher needs to whet the appetites of his customers. In order to do that, he must know both his customers and his product. The launching of a new unit is like the beginning of any other important enterprise. A certain amount of inertia, sometimes resistance, has to be overcome at the outset. Consequently, an appetizing sample or preview of what is to come is always in order in getting a new unit underway. Either extreme is to be avoided in the introduction of a unit: a presentation that overwhelms students in terms of difficulty or an introduction that presents no challenge to the class. A second necessary step in the introductory stage is provision for proper orientation to the unit. Clarification of objectives, definitions of problems, location of resource materials, selection and organization of appropriate activities, and the establishment of scope and sequence of events with a tentative timetable for each task—all need to be done quite early in unit development.

In arousing student interest, the teacher may use any number of approaches. *An appeal to direct experience* is one good way to stimulate class interest. Many a lagging discussion has been revived by a simple question, such as, "How many saw the television program about ————?" or "Did you hear the youth concert last Saturday night?" One new science teacher became quite adept at *personalizing problems* for a group of eighth-grade students of average ability or below. In getting students to understand the stratosphere, he began like this:

Teacher:	"Bill, could you fly in the stratosphere in an open cockpit plane?"
Bill:	"No."
Teacher:	"Why not?"
Bill:	"I would freeze to death."
Teacher:	"Right. What else might happen to you?"
Bill:	"I wouldn't have enough air to breathe."

A primary key to interest is student *involvement*. Sometimes students can be encouraged to share valuable experiences, hobbies, or collections that are related to the unit. Cooperative development of bulletin boards, exhibits, or centers of interest in the classroom also serves to motivate students to attack a new unit with enthusiasm. If the teacher has shown an interest in student activities, the class is more likely to respond to regular class assignments. Other approaches to a new unit that may be used are excursions, resource persons, motion pictures or recordings, or well-chosen selections read to the class.

Research indicates that socioeconomic status, aptitude, and personal needs and values are important factors in the determination of student interests.[6] Different levels of maturity and varied backgrounds of experience also influence the effectiveness of any given approach to unit development as far as the members of a class are concerned.

In the final analysis, the teacher is the key factor in arousing student interest in a new unit. He needs to be imaginative, alive, and sensitive to the concerns of youth. In addition to his personal qualities, the teacher needs a cultural background of depth and breadth to share with his students.

Not only is the introductory phase of the unit a time to stimulate interest and to arouse curiosity; it is also the place where the direction, or course of action, of the entire unit is established. Some teachers provide the class with duplicated assignment guides or work plans as the last step before actual work is begun on a new unit. It is also helpful to have each student develop a brief, flexible work plan of his own. Such a plan might include proposed activities, committee assignments, readings to be done, and things to be made (6:138–139).

UNIT DEVELOPMENTAL MATERIALS AND ACTIVITIES

Later chapters will, of course, include more complete discussions of various materials and methods of instruction that the teacher may use. However, as the teacher considers the next stage of unit development, some guidelines for selection of materials and activities need to be indicated at this point.

Just before listing tentative learning activities and materials, the teacher may wish to include an outline of topics or problems to be covered. This provides a skeleton or framework around which learning experiences may be organized.

The first criterion of well-selected unit activities and materials is *variety*. Variety adds spice to the classroom. "A major difficulty in our educational efforts seems to be the progressive loss of interest by students in academic learning activities."[7] The pedantic teacher without imagination who relies on a single source of materials or on the same deadly routine repeated day in and day out is likely to have a dull class on his hands. Since no two students have identical experiences or the same interests or tastes, variety ensures more motivation for more students more of the time. If all students enrolled in today's schools who exhibit

[6] Donald E. Super, "Interests," *Encyclopedia of Educational Research*, 3d ed., Chester W. Harris, ed. New York: The Macmillan Company, 1960, pp. 729–730.
[7] Melvin H. Marx, "Motivation," *Encyclopedia of Educational Research*, 3d ed., Chester W. Harris, ed. New York: The Macmillan Company, 1960, p. 898.

such great diversity of talents and abilities are to learn, variety in teaching procedures and materials becomes imperative. This point was stressed under the discussion of objectives. Slow learners need more concrete learning materials, simpler concepts, easier reading materials, and more frequent reviews. On the other hand, gifted students need more complex problems, more opportunity for individual research, and more breadth and depth of content to challenge them.

So often learning experiences in the classroom are limited almost exclusively to those of a verbal nature. The following excerpt from a unit illustrates the use of a variety of types of learning experience:

UNIT: THE ELIZABETHAN AGE

Activities (covering the subunit on Shakespeare's *Macbeth*):

1. In class, read and record Shakespeare's *Macbeth*, Inglis, pp. 136–199. Structure of the play and the characterization of Macbeth and Lady Macbeth should be discussed after each act.
2. Listen to the recording of *Macbeth* by the Old Vic company and compare with tape recording of students' interpretation.
3. See the following films: *English Inns* (to show how they were used as theaters); *Memories of Shakespeare* (to learn more about Shakespeare the man); and *Elizabethan Literature* (for a summary of literary types and of information about great writers of the period).
4. Outside class, students are to read a second Shakespearean play, choosing one of the following: *Hamlet, Romeo and Juliet, Julius Caesar, Twelfth Night,* or *The Tempest.*
5. The class will divide into groups, according to the play read outside class, and conduct a panel discussion on the respective plays, following the study guide for Shakespearean plays (provided by the teacher). Selected passages are also to be read to the class.
6. Car pools are to be arranged for those who wish to see Laurence Olivier's version of *Henry V*, to be shown free on November 18 at Russ Auditorium.
7. Students will also be encouraged to see the film version of *Romeo and Juliet*, sponsored by the University of California Extension, to be shown on December 1.
8. *Macbeth* will be televised on Sunday, November 20. Students should not miss this.[8]

Every student must learn in the way that is most appropriate to him— by observing, demonstrating, speaking, listening, writing, drawing, experimenting, thinking, and feeling. Consequently, provision for a variety of learning experiences in the classroom is imperative.

The raw materials of a unit may be classified according to four levels of abstraction: symbolic, pictorial, manipulative, and related to reality. These abstractions range from concrete sensory experiences to printed

[8] Used with the permission of Joan Knight.

materials, scientific formulas, or musical scores.[9] How far a student can delve into the mysteries of abstractions depends on his academic aptitude. How far a student should pursue these abstractions is another matter. Some educators are insisting that all students should pursue an academic program of solid subjects because it has been discovered that students of lower ability can learn more than was once believed if they are skillfully taught. However, the question as to what is best for students who may be underprivileged culturally, economically, intellectually, and emotionally has not yet been satisfactorily answered.

In selecting the most effective learning activities for a unit, the teacher needs to *stress action toward desirable goals* as a second criterion. *What students do determines what they learn.* They may talk or read about good health, appreciation of better music, or how to build a boat; but, unless they practice good health, listen to good music, or actually build a boat, learning is likely to be a superficial thing. Mere verbalization about or contemplation of real experience has, no doubt, accounted for disappointing results in formal education. It is unfortunate that the word "activity" has a bad connotation for some people. Properly defined and understood, activity is relevant to learning in three ways: Learning is an active process. No one learns except by his own activity. Second, learning activity may vary from an abstract process (solving a problem in mathematics) to a simple skill (sawing a board in a straight line). Finally, no learning activity can be divorced from content or subject matter.

As a third criterion for the use of better unit activities and materials, the teacher should *build upon as much firsthand experience as possible.* Although limitation of time and space make it necessary to depend upon much vicarious experience and symbolic material in the classroom, there is no substitute for direct experience as the foundation for all abstract learning and as a means of making learning more vivid and permanent. Something vital is missing from the classroom when students read about papermaking without visiting the nearby paper mill; when students discuss flowers and draw pictures of them from a book without picking and identifying the parts of the flowers growing on the school grounds; or when students talk about Indian culture without visiting the local museum housing an excellent collection of Indian artifacts. In progressing from concrete materials to effective use of symbolization, the student has to be guided through a series of gradual steps from the reality level (field trips, interviews, and so on), to the use of manipulative materials (exhibits, bulletin boards, specimens, models), to the use of pictorial materials, and finally to the abstract level or use of symbolic materials.[10]

[9] Fred P. Barnes, "Using the Materials of Learning," *NEA Journal,* 50 (September 1961), 54–56.
[10] Barnes, pp. 54–56.

CULMINATING ACTIVITIES OF THE UNIT

Culminating activities have already been discussed briefly. A unit may or may not include this phase of development as a separate category. When activities are included that present the highlights of the unit (by means of reports, exhibits, or assembly program), they should not rehash the entire unit, interrupt the continuity from one unit to another, include unit tests, nor be dragged in as an afterthought after the unit has already served its purpose (3:368). The teacher does well in encouraging students to share interesting discoveries or significant products of research with their classmates, but he should protect the class from the boredom occasioned by a series of uninspired oral reports. If reports are given, they should be informative, interesting, and varied in type of presentation.

UNIT EVALUATION

Evaluation has already been mentioned briefly and is discussed thoroughly in Chapters 16 through 19; hence only a few principles or guidelines will be stressed here. Although "evaluation" appears as the last heading in unit structure, this does not mean that evaluation occurs only at the conclusion of a unit. Evaluation is *continuous*. This is important for two reasons: By securing evidence of student progress continuously, the teacher is more able to make readjustments in learning activities as needed and to provide for a higher degree of student motivation (1:896, 857). Evaluation should employ a variety of data-gathering instruments. This recognizes both the diversity of unit goals and the different ways in which students may make progress toward those goals. Traditionally, oral and written tests have been the chief instruments for measuring student progress while achievement in subject matter has been the major goal. In addition to using written tests (oral testing has largely disappeared with formal recitations) to secure a more comprehensive picture of student development, teachers now use observations, sociograms, behavioral checklists, anecdotal records, and interest inventories.

The criteria and procedures for evaluation need to be stated in terms that are *definite, clear,* and *acceptable* (to the student and to the school). In some classes, where much of the activity consists of work on individual projects, it is not uncommon for the teacher to assign "A," "B," and so on to finished products in what appears to be a capricious fashion. Before work on a unit begins, students have a right to know what criteria and procedures are to be used in evaluating their work. If the procedure is based almost exclusively on teacher judgment, then students must clearly understand what criteria the teacher will use and the approximate weight assigned to each criterion. Such specificity in evaluation is illustrated in the following excerpt from a unit plan:

Evaluation:

1. A test (50 percent objective, 50 percent essay) on the Elizabethan theater and *Macbeth* (weight—50 percent).
2. Students' panel discussion of Shakespearean play read outside class (weight —20 percent).
3. Grade on the compositions: "The Passionate Teen-ager to His Love" and "The Girl's Reply" (weight—10 percent).
4. Short papers written in class, based on one of the following series of questions:
   a. What is the theme of the second Shakespearean play you read? How does it affect you personally? Does it sharpen your insights into human motives and desires? Discuss, citing pertinent passages from the play.
   b. How does Shakespeare reveal the character of the hero or heroine in the second play you read? What are the ways a playwright can reveal character? Which of these ways or devices does Shakespeare use? Does this character seem real to you? Why or why not? (weight—20 percent).[11]

In conclusion, it needs to be reemphasized that the primary purpose of evaluation in the classroom is the improvement of learning and instruction. When both teacher and students are informed concerning progress toward accepted goals, the students are more highly motivated, and the teacher is better able to provide remedial instruction where needed, as well as correct his own limitations as a teacher.

Daily planning, the third and final aspect of instructional planning to be considered, is discussed in the following chapter.

[11] Reprinted by permission of Joan Knight.

SELECTED READINGS

1. American Educational Research Association, *Encyclopedia of Educational Research,* 3d ed., Chester W. Harris, ed. New York: The Macmillan Company, 1960.

2. Blount, Nathan S., and Herbert J. Klausmeier, *Teaching in the Secondary School,* 3d ed. New York: Harper & Row, Publishers, 1968, chaps. 6 and 7.

3. Burton, William H., *The Guidance of Learning Activities,* 3d ed. New York: Appleton-Century-Crofts, Inc., Division of Meredith Corporation, 1962, chaps. 13–15.

4. Callahan, Sterling, *Successful Teaching in Secondary Schools.* Chicago: Scott, Foresman and Company, 1966, chaps. 4–7.

5. Carter, William L., Carl W. Hansen, and Margaret G. McKim, *Learning to Teach in the Secondary School.* New York: The Macmillan Company, 1962.

6. Clark, Leonard H., and Irving S. Starr, *Secondary School Teaching Methods,* 2d ed. New York: The Macmillan Company, 1967, chap. 6, Appendix.

7. McKean, Robert, *Principles and Methods in Secondary Education*. Columbus, Ohio: Charles E. Merrill Books, Inc., 1962, chap. 5.

8. Oliva, Peter F., *The Secondary School Today*. Cleveland: The World Publishing Company, 1967, chaps. 7, 8.

9. Rivlin, Harry N., *Teaching Adolescents in Secondary Schools*, 2d ed. New York: Appleton-Century-Crofts, Inc., Division of Meredith Corporation, 1961, chap. 4.

10. The Yearbook Committee, "Individualizing Instruction," *Sixty-first Yearbook of the National Society for the Study of Education, Part I*. Chicago: University of Chicago Press, 1962.

CHAPTER 6 / *Daily Planning*

Our time is all today—*James Montgomery*

All aspects of a teacher's preplanning, including course outlines and unit plans, culminate in the daily plan. If the daily plan is sound and well executed, the teacher is usually assured of a "good day." Without an adequate plan, the teacher courts disaster. The discussion in this chapter covers basic elements, structure, successful implementation, and evaluation of a daily plan. Although the presentation, together with examples, is directed to those who teach in typical classroom situations (one teacher responsible for a given group of students daily for a specified period of time for a five-day week), suggestions are also applicable to such innovative developments as team teaching and flexible scheduling. It makes little difference whether a teacher works with others or alone; whether he works with an individual student, a small group, or a large group; or whether his schedule fluctuates every day of the week. He still must plan thoroughly for his personal contribution to the total operation. If a teacher has never learned how to develop a good lesson plan or chooses to do only enough to "get by," he is likely to be subject to embarrassment by his more professional colleagues.

Because the unit concept is not always clearly understood, and some supervisors do not practice unit teaching themselves, it is often advisable for new teachers to begin by developing well-organized daily plans before attempting to develop the more difficult unit plan.

As a prerequisite to effective daily planning, the teacher needs to know his students, as was discussed at length in Chapter 2; his subject and its potential contribution to the goals of education; his best sources of materials; the activities that are most appropriate; and the physical facilities of the school. Flexible arrangement of classroom furniture can be helpful in the development of a desirable atmosphere for learning. Because of large classes and immovable furniture in some schools, the most appropriate learning activities are sometimes difficult to achieve. Inasmuch as secondary school teachers often have to share classrooms with other teachers, use of chalkboards and bulletin boards becomes a problem. In selecting learning activities and materials, the teacher needs to be governed by such criteria as their contribution to objectives, economy (in terms of cost, time, and energy expended), and usability (in relation to the maturity, ability, and backgrounds of the students).

Like the unit plan, the daily plan consists of four minimum essentials: objectives, materials, activities, and evaluation. In structure, too, the daily plan may be similar, either in outline or columnar (parallel) form. Columnar structure may vary in categories as long as the minimum essentials are included. For example, the columnar portion of the daily plan may look like this:

APPROXIMATE TIME	EXPECTED OUTCOMES	ACTIVITIES	MATERIALS
			(TEACHER AND STUDENTS)

or this:

TIME LIMITS	SPECIFIC OBJECTIVES	ACTIVITIES AND MATERIALS		EVALUATION
		TEACHER	STUDENTS	

or this:

TIME	ACTIVITIES (TEACHER AND STUDENTS)	RESOURCES

Because they are learning how to plan for instruction and are usually teaching under close supervision, new teachers are advised to develop complete *written* plans. They may find it a time-saver to construct a format similar to that of lesson plans shown later, duplicate it, and fill in the content for each daily plan as needed.

DEVELOPMENT OF THE LESSON PLAN

Now that the minimum essentials and structural organization of the daily lesson plan have been briefly outlined, a more thorough analysis of each step the teacher takes in developing a lesson is needed.

Assuming that the teacher has already developed his course outline, based on the school's curriculum guide, and prepared his first tentative unit, he should think about specific objectives that should be achieved. Today, this brings up the subject of *behavioral* objectives, which often needs clarification.

ORIGIN AND NATURE OF BEHAVIORAL OBJECTIVES

Why is there so much current stress on behavioral objectives? There are at least three sources of dissatisfaction with the old nonbehavioral objectives. First of all, test makers insist on more precise statements of student behavior in order to develop valid instruments for measuring it. In the second place, until they can define objectives in terms of precise student behavior, members of teaching teams are unable to agree on what learning experiences are of most worth. Finally, the programmers for programmed texts or teaching machines, and, more important in the future, the developers of programs for computer-assisted instruction (CAI) must depend entirely upon behavioral objectives.

The history of the development of behavioral objectives is brief but turbulent. Roughly between 1918 and 1925, objectives were stated in very specific behavioral terms, such as "the ability to spell 'believe'" or "to add 2 and 3." As a result, objectives in any given subject were so numerous that the system fell of its own weight. After 1930, the pendulum swung to the opposite extreme—objectives were stated in broad terms of generalized behavior. Hence, they were not "clearly enough defined to have meaning for the teacher." [1]

When the American Psychological Association met in Boston in 1948, an informal gathering of college examiners marked the first of a series of meetings for the purpose of classifying educational objectives and defining them in more precise behavioral terms in order to facilitate communication among examiners and to stimulate research in testing and curriculum building. After eight years, a special committee made a report in 1956 on the *cognitive domain* of educational objectives (2). Eight years later, in 1964, a second handbook on the *affective domain* was published (5). Educational objectives were placed in three classes or "domains": *cognitive, affective,* and *psychomotor*.[2, 3] The three "domains" were defined as follows:

1. *Cognitive:* Objectives which emphasize remembering or reproducing something which has presumably been learned, as well as objectives which involve the solving of some intellective task for which the individual has to determine the essential problem and then reorder given material or combine it with ideas, methods, or procedures previously learned. Cognitive objectives vary from simple recall of material learned to highly original and creative ways of combining and synthesizing new ideas and materials. We found that the largest proportion of educational objectives fell into this domain.

2. *Affective:* Objectives which emphasize a feeling tone, an emotion, or a

---

[1] Ralph W. Tyler, "The Curriculum—Then and Now," *Proceedings, Invitational Conference on Testing Problems.* Princeton, N.J.: Educational Testing Service, 1956, pp. 79–94. Also published in *Testing Problems in Perspective* by the American Council on Education, 1966.

[2] Benjamin S. Bloom, ed., *Taxonomy of Educational Objectives: Handbook I, Cognitive Domain.* New York: David McKay Company, Inc., 1956, p. 7.

[3] David R. Krathwohl, Benjamin S. Bloom, and Bertram B. Masia, *Taxonomy of Educational Objectives: Handbook II, Affective Domain.* New York: David McKay Company, Inc., 1964, pp. 6–7. The extract is used by permission of David McKay Company, Inc.

degree of acceptance or rejection. Affective objectives vary from simple attention to selected phenomena to complex but internally consistent qualities of character and conscience. We found a large number of such objectives in the literature expressed as interests, attitudes, appreciations, values, and emotional sets or biases.

3. *Psychomotor:* Objectives which emphasize some muscular or motor skill, some manipulation of material and objects, or some act which requires a neuro-muscular coordination. We found few such objectives in the literature. When found, they were most frequently related to handwriting and speech and to physical education, trade, and technical courses.[4]

The Cognitive Domain Taxonomy (or Classification) has been organized so that it contains six major classes (with subcategories under each, with one exception); the Affective Domain Taxonomy has been organized so that it contains five major classes (with subcategories under each). An attempt was made to arrange a hierarchy of classes under each taxonomy, ranging from the simple to the complex. The authors of the taxonomies point out that hierarchies within the classes may very well overlap; also, the cognitive and affective domains may be closely intertwined.

Below are listed the six major classes of educational objectives under the Cognitive Domain with an appropriate example of each.

COGNITIVE DOMAIN [5]

1.00 Knowledge
    Example: Students will be able to define technical terms related to a given field of study.

2.00 Comprehension
    Example: Students will be able to define and give original examples of figures of speech (metaphor, simile, etc.).

3.00 Application
    Example: Students will be able to apply scientific principles to new situations.

4.00 Analysis
    Example: Students will be able to detect and cite logical fallacies in modern advertising.

5.00 Synthesis
    Example: Students will be able to create a verse, a story, or a musical composition.

6.00 Evaluation
    Example: Students will be able to apply given criteria in judging a speech, a work of art, or a poem.

(*Note:* The examples have been supplied by the authors of this text.)

[4] Krathwohl *et al.*, pp. 6–7.
[5] Bloom, Appendix, pp. 201–207. Used by permission of David McKay Company, Inc.

Below are listed the five major classes of educational objectives under the Affective Domain with an appropriate example of each:

AFFECTIVE DOMAIN [6]

1.00   Receiving (Attending)
       Example: Students will show an awareness of esthetic factors in dress, furnishings, or building design (Art).
2.00   Responding
       Example: Students will show enjoyment of self-expression in a given subject.
3.00   Valuing
       Example: Students will exhibit "a continuous desire to develop the ability to speak and to write effectively." [7]
4.00   Organization (of Values)
       Example: Students will express judgments about people of other races or cultures in terms of their behavior as individuals. [8]
5.00   Characterization by a Value or Value Complex
       Example: Students will show a pattern of an open mind by changing their minds "when new facts or insights demonstrate the need for revision of opinions formerly held." [9]

(*Note:* Unless otherwise indicated the examples are supplied by the authors of this text.)

(Although examples are often chosen from specific subject areas, the classification scheme from both the Cognitive and Affective Domains is equally applicable to all subject areas.)

In a handbook *Preparing Instructional Objectives* (originally published under the title *Preparing Objectives for Programmed Instruction*), Mager further refined the Cognitive Domain Taxonomy (the handbook on the Affective Domain had not yet been published) by making *all* his examples behavioral. [10] Then he went two steps further by (1) stating what *conditions* were to be imposed "upon the learner when he is demonstrating his mastery of the objective" [11] and (2) indicating "the cri-

---

[6] Krathwohl *et al.*, Appendix A, pp. 176–185.
[7] Krathwohl *et al.*, p. 159.
[8] Krathwohl *et al.*, p. 181.
[9] Krathwohl *et al.*, p. 167.
[10] The authors of the two original handbooks of the *Taxonomy of Educational Objectives* chose their examples from educational literature, revising some objectives to make them more behavioral, but admittedly included some examples that are not behavioral. However, the reader will find it profitable to consult the two handbooks in order to study illustrations of appropriate examination questions or problems that relate to the categories of both domains and to enjoy the stimulus of a provocative discussion.
[11] Robert F. Mager, *Preparing Instructional Objectives*. Palo Alto, Calif.: Fearon Publishers, Inc., 1962, p. 26.

terion of acceptable performance." [12] Examples of statements of *condition* follow.

Given a list of _____.
Given a standard set of tools _____.
Without the aid of a slide rule _____.[13]

The following are examples of statements of *criteria* of acceptable performance:

The student must be able to reply in grammatically correct French to 95% of the French questions that are put to him during an examination.[14]

The student must be able to use the chemical balance well enough to weigh materials accurately to the nearest whole number.[15]

For other examples of good behavioral objectives that include both conditions and criteria of acceptable performance, the reader may consult the January 1967 issue of the *Phi Delta Kappan*. One such example is the following: "Given 20 sentences containing a variety of mistakes in capitalization, the student is able, with at least 90 percent accuracy, to identify and rewrite correctly each word that has a mistake in capitalization." [16]

The teacher of the 1970s may very well wonder why the authors of this book have made such an issue of behavioral objectives. This is still a comparatively new approach to the statement of expected outcomes of classroom instruction, but teachers of the future will come to realize, no doubt, the values of behavioral objectives. After decades of busywork in writing ambiguous, meaningless objectives, teachers should experience deep satisfaction in being able to facilitate learning, to use more clear-cut bases for evaluating student achievement (a decided source of student satisfaction as well), and to expedite professional communication through the use of behavioral objectives.

INTRODUCTION TO THE DAILY LESSON

The beginning of a lesson sets the tone for the entire class period. Motivation, provision for continuity, clearly defined goals, effective organization—all must be established at the outset.

To stimulate interest, the teacher may use any number of approaches, such as raising provocative questions, telling an interesting anecdote, giving a brief demonstration, asking students to share some of their experiences. These are but a few of the ways to introduce a lesson effec-

[12] Mager, p. 44.
[13] Mager, p. 26.
[14] Mager, p. 50.
[15] Mager, p. 51.
[16] Thorwald Ebensen, "Writing Instructional Objectives," *Phi Delta Kappan*, 48 (January 1967), 247.

tively. At the other extreme, the unimaginative teacher begins by attempting to conduct a formal recitation over "the next ten pages" assigned in the textbook. Without an "icebreaker" to precede the body of the lesson, the net result is likely to be an unresponsive class and a frustrated teacher. The teacher who is overly concerned about teaching students a mass of irrelevant facts may well heed the advice of Archibald MacLeish, who made the shrewd observation that the teaching of English "always stands with a foot in the text and a foot in the world. . . . The greatest poem, removed from the ground of our being, is an irrelevance. The ground of our being without the poem is a desert." [17]

TIMING THE LESSON

Because the typical school day is cut up into segments or class periods of less than one hour each, a teacher has to make the most of the time he has with each group of students. Lesson plan structure, illustrated before, includes a column for approximate time limits for each activity. Although such limits must always remain flexible, they do help in the conservation of valuable time.

Poor timing can result in a number of problems. Some teachers fail to get the class underway promptly or allow five minutes or so at the end of the period as an unorganized, socializing activity. Such practice is a breeder of discipline problems and a waste of the students' time. Beginning teachers often experience the embarrassment of completing a lesson fifteen or twenty minutes before the end of the class period. Being panicky, talking too much and too fast, and failing to stimulate student questions or responses, the novice races through his lesson. One new teacher who taught five lessons in one day expressed the fear that he was going to finish the course during the first week. One solution to the problem of using class time profitably is for the teacher to plan more than he thinks the class will be able to do for the day. It is also advisable for the teacher to have one or two spare lessons tucked away in his desk for use when, because of poor class attendance, for example, a deviation from the scheduled lesson is better. At the other extreme of poor timing is the teacher who progresses at such a leisurely pace or pursues so many sidelines that the final bell rings with most of the important aspects of the lesson not completed. Teachers often remark, "My students ask so many questions, I am unable to cover any ground." When students are interested enough to ask relevant questions, any teacher should be delighted, not frustrated. On the other hand, a teacher does have to guard against being sidetracked by peripheral questions, futile debate, or even delaying tactics. Then, too, the teacher is the only one who has the necessary back-

[17] Archibald MacLeish, "What Is English?" *Saturday Review*, December 9, 1961, p. 14. Copyright Saturday Review, Inc., 1961.

ground to enable him to determine how much emphasis to give to each aspect of a course for a given term or semester. Thus, any well-organized beginning teacher needs to have a time budget for the daily lesson and to glance at it occasionally if necessary, to decide how closely he should adhere to this schedule. Through experience, most teachers develop a time sense that makes a formal schedule unnecessary.

To conclude a lesson just as the dismissal bell rings is an art not all teachers are able to achieve. Consequently, it is advisable to plan a flexible ending. A teacher should have in reserve a number of alternative activities of short duration, such as recordings, short selected readings, or critiques of classwork. It is futile to assign a five-minute study period or to attempt to begin work on an activity of extended duration when little time remains. The flexible ending is, however, designed to achieve expected outcomes of the daily lesson, not to kill time.

LESSON ACTIVITIES AND MATERIALS

Like the unit plan, the very heart of a lesson plan consists of learning activities and materials, the "how" and the "what" for the achievement of objectives. It is best to keep lesson plan structure as simple as possible for ready reference. Usually a single sheet of 8½- by 11-inch loose-leaf notebook paper will suffice. However, most lesson plans are not complete unless they include material on additional cards or pages. By way of elaboration on this point, a *discussion* should always be based on a few key questions prepared in advance. Questions made up on the spur of the moment are often poorly worded and lacking in significance. Furthermore, if the teacher is not sure of his subject matter, he should jot down important facts to refresh his memory. A *demonstration* should include an outline of step-by-step procedures, to ensure completeness and continuity of the presentation, and suggestions for follow-up with the class. At the outset, before the demonstration begins, it is well to list the materials needed. *Audio-visual presentations* should include teacher preparation, class preparation, effective presentation, and follow-up activities. Unless all these suggestions are included on supplementary notes (preferably on 3- by 5-inch cards) attached to the basic lesson plan, the lesson for the day is likely to be inadequate.

THE ASSIGNMENT

The assignment, whether for a day or on a long-range basis, is a critical phase of the teaching-learning process. A common source of teacher irritation is an inadequately prepared assignment or one that students have not done at all. How often a well-planned discussion fails miserably because the class has not studied the assignment or has read it without understanding!

A generation ago, school periods were lengthened in the hope that assignments might be prepared in class under the direct supervision of the teacher. But teachers have failed to budget class time well, often using the study period for lecture. Then, too, the school day is so short and there is so much to do, it has become necessary to have students make considerable preparation outside the class period. This brings up the subject of homework, discussed at length in another section of this chapter.

An effective assignment is one designed to achieve at least two objectives: to contribute to the achievement of specific objectives of the lesson plan and to motivate students to learn with a minimum of coercion. Why are these goals not always realized? The teacher would do well to make a careful analysis of his assignments. Do they provide a challenge for bright students or constitute mere busywork? To assign an able student more problems of the type he has already mastered is a test of endurance, not learning. Are assigned tasks beyond the capabilities of slow learners? Are assignments so vague or permissive as not to be taken seriously? Is stress placed upon the memorization of unrelated facts or upon mastery of significant concepts or ideas? Too often, not enough time and thought are given to the assignment. Such an assignment as "Take the next ten pages in the text" is a typical example. *"It would be difficult to devise an educational practice so grossly ineffective, so certainly calculated to interfere with learning, as a page assignment to a single text followed by a formal verbal quiz."* [18] Because the teacher is responsible for the assignment, he is the only one who can correct its inadequacies.

What are the characteristics of a good assignment? At least four questions need to be answered for the student: What is to be done? How is it to be done? Why is it to be done? When is it due? Sometimes the question is raised, When is the best time to make an assignment? The best assignments develop naturally from ongoing class activities. Logically, an assignment should be given just before work on it is begun. Certainly the worst time to make an assignment is at the time the bell rings ending the class period. Teachers frequently make assignments orally. It is recommended that short assignments also be written on the chalkboard and that long assignments be duplicated for each member of the class.

Because it is often difficult to relate formally organized subject matter to the here-and-now concerns of youth, the alert teacher seizes every opportunity to relate the subject to current issues or problems of general interest. Whenever possible, assignments are made with reference to previous experiences, interests, and everyday concerns of boys and girls. In addition to general information about his class, both as individuals and as a group, the teacher also needs to know what information and attitudes

[18] William H. Burton, *The Guidance of Learning Activities,* 3d ed. New York: Appleton-Century-Crofts, Inc., Division of Meredith Corporation, 1962, p. 290. Reprinted by permission of the publisher.

students have with respect to the particular subject for study. Such information may be secured by means of pretests, class discussions, personal interviews, autobiographies, questionnaires, and checklists. Inasmuch as a wide range of individual differences exists within any class, even when students are homogeneously grouped, individualized assignments are always necessary. This has sometimes been accomplished by means of a minimum, basic assignment for the class as a whole with enrichment materials provided for average and bright students. The teacher who provides such "extra-credit" assignments, especially for gifted students, must make sure that they are not just more of the same. Enriched assignments should provide greater depth and breadth of understanding. Perhaps a better approach to differentiated assignments is provision for a variety of learning activities and materials so that students have several avenues, not just one, for achieving expected outcomes.

Even a single assignment in a heterogeneous class can be differentiated in terms of the *level* of understanding expected of students of different ability. For example, suppose a class in English, which is analyzing exercises in the correct use of verbs, comes across this sentence: "The boys had (gone, went) downtown." The very slow learner may be able to make the correct choice of "gone" only because he has been habituated to the correct usage until it sounds right to him. A more able student should be able to decide that "gone" is correct because the past participle must be used with the helping verb "had." The college-bound student may be expected to go a step further in analyzing the sentence by indicating that the tense or time is past perfect, or action having been completed in the past.

Sometimes students do not know how to deal with an assignment. It is now common practice for teachers to provide study guides, to conduct lessons on how to study or read a book, to provide orientation on effective use of the library, and to use other aids to promote better study habits.

The following is an example of a study guide used in poetry:

A STUDY GUIDE FOR POETRY

1. What is the poet trying to do?
   a. To express a thought?
   b. To convey a mood?
   c. To sing a song?
   d. To rid himself of an emotion?
   e. To grasp and communicate an experience?
2. How is he going about it?
   a. What does the poem mean?
   b. What is its meter?
   c. What elements of harmony and melody appear in the poem (pauses, changes of speed, rhyme scheme, special devices—alliteration, onomatopoeia, and so on)?

      d. What is the poem's discoverable symbolism?

      e. What is the poem's prevailing tone (gay, melancholy, bitter, and so forth)?

      f. What memorable images are there (appeals to the senses)?

3. Was the poem worth doing?
   a. Is it fresh or tired?
   b. Is it too trival or too solemn?
   c. Is it too obscure?

4. What is the psychological significance of the poem? (Or what kind of person was the poet?)
   a. As reflected in the poem itself?
   b. As having indirectly made the poem possible?
   c. As having more directly predisposed the poet to write it? (For example, what moved, angered, or soured him? What does he believe in? Does his poetry reflect an obsession or a persistent preoccupation?)

5. What is the personal significance of the poem (that is, to me as a reader)?
   a. Can I be specific about the nature of my pleasure or distaste?
   b. Can I justify my pleasure or displeasure in terms of what there is in the poem, corroborated, of course, by my own emotional and intellectual experience?
   c. Can I put my finger on any irrelevant reasons why I like or do not like the poem (my beliefs, temperament, and so on)? [19]

To ensure better motivation and more effective learning, teachers today are making more use of student assistance in setting up projects, planning attacks on problems, and organizing discussions of vital issues (for example, panels, symposiums). Research indicates that most assignments are still teacher-dominated, however, with only one type of assignment typically made. Yet students dislike both laissez-faire and authoritative assignments and prefer those made on the basis of teacher-student planing (1:855–856). Older types of assignments stressed chapters, pages, and topics in textbooks, given with little or no consideration for student interests, needs, and abilities. Newer types of assignments are based on units, varied activities and materials, problems, and projects, with an emphasis on student motivation and involvement. There is a discernible trend to allow some students to work on self-assigned, planned-with-teacher learning experiences on an independent basis.

By way of summary, *a good assignment* is based on the following criteria:

1. Specific objectives are clearly stated.
2. Subject matter is related to student interests, needs, and abilities.
3. Outcomes that serve the purposes of our society are included.
4. Study guides and other useful aids are provided.
5. A great variety of learning activities and materials is included to provide for individual differences.

[19] Reprinted by permission of Joan Knight.

6. Guidance toward satisfactory completion of units of work, covering substantial periods of time, is assured.
7. Considerable time, thought, and energy go into the preparation of the assignment.
8. Students are involved in the development of assignments.
9. Either measurable or observable evidence of student achievement is provided each day.[20]

HOMEWORK

Assignments naturally bring up the subject of homework. Today there are increasing demands for more of it. Conant recommends a minimum of fifteen hours of homework a week for academically talented students in grades nine to twelve.[21] Illogical comparisons of American education with education in other cultures, and charges that our youth are soft, sometimes delinquent, and often nonintellectual have appeared in the press, resulting in agitation for more homework. Ironically enough, despite the tendency to increase leisure time for adults, there is insistent pressure to lengthen the school day and the school year and to increase homework for youth. Some voices, like that of anthropologist Margaret Mead, have been raised in protest against pressures which would rob children of their childhood and youth.[22]

Crash programs in education have been based on unexamined and unproved assumptions. Widespread acceptance of increased homework, grouping, and mass instruction by schools, to name a few current trends, have been made on the basis of little research or without reference to known findings of research. What does research have to say about homework? First of all, opinions and practices ranging from no homework to excessive amounts differ widely. Variations occur "among schools, among classes in the same school, and among individuals in the same class." [23] It thus appears that uniformity in homework assignments is neither desirable nor practicable. A more serious question is raised concerning the effectiveness of home study assignments, for increased student achievement is the only justification for them. What relationship between homework and scholastic success is indicated by experimental studies? *The results are inconclusive.*[24] Before becoming zealots of homework assignments, teachers and administrators are advised not only to study the findings of research but also to consider the problems related to home study assign-

[20] Burton, pp. 295–296. An adaptation and condensation.
[21] James B. Conant, *The American High School Today.* New York: McGraw-Hill Book Company, Inc., 1959, p. 57.
[22] Margaret Mead, "Are We Squeezing Out Adolescence?" *National Parent–Teacher,* 40 (September 1960), 4–6.
[23] Ruth M. Strang, "Homework and Guided Study," *Encyclopedia of Educational Research,* 3d ed., Chester W. Harris, ed. New York: The Macmillan Company, 1960, p. 677.
[24] Strang, p. 678.

ments. If and when such assignments are made, certain conditions need to be set up to realize maximum values from them.

HOMEWORK ASSIGNMENTS—PROBLEMS AND RECOMMENDATIONS

The first problem of homework is one of definition. Some teachers who keep students after school to do assigned work or assign book reports to be prepared outside class maintain that they require no homework.[25]

Sometimes students have parental help with homework or they copy the work of their peers. There is evidence that the incidence of copying increases as students progress to higher levels, with most of them experiencing no guilty feelings about the practice.[26] This brings up the problem of evaluation of homework. Obviously, the teacher who spends hours of drudgery each week in reading and scoring homework assignments is merely accumulating unreliable evidence of student progress. Whenever possible, homework assignments should be checked by students themselves. If the teacher desires evidence of completion of homework, he may quickly check written exercises, without grading them, or give a short quiz over the assignment. For grading purposes the best evidence of achievement is secured by a comprehensive test on the material, prepared and scored by the teacher.

Although the claim is not easily documented, it has often been contended that the pressure of excessive homework has been detrimental to health. Even in Russia, where everyone seems to have so much zeal for education, doctors have warned that the intense pressures of the educational system are proving detrimental to children. Certainly, home study assignments have often been a source of conflict between parents and their children. Another home problem is the difficulty of providing satisfactory conditions for study. Although research is inconclusive concerning the effect of distractions on learning and modern youth may be able to make reasonably adequate adaptations to distraction, students themselves express a preference for study conditions that provide "privacy, quiet, interest in the subject, freedom from worries and competing interests, absence of distracting radio and television programs, effective teaching, and well-spaced and clearly understood assignments."[27] The preceding statement not only indicates student preference but also suggests guidelines for making effective homework assignments. It is obvious that few, if any, students study under these ideal conditions.

On the basis of considerable accumulated experience and limited research, it does become evident that certain conditions for home study are necessary for effective learning. First of all, administrative regulation of

[25] Lloyd McCleary, "Homework," *Educational Leadership,* 17 (January 1960), 217–218.
[26] Strang, p. 678.
[27] Strang, p. 678.

assignments made by various teachers is imperative. Assignments that make excessive demands of the student on certain nights, over weekends, during holidays, or in competition with other activities of youth must be avoided. One solution to the problem is provision for long-range assignments, which allow the student some flexibility in budgeting his time. Another important consideration is the type of home study assignment made. Individualized assignments that allow the student some freedom of choice, assignments that the student can do without the teacher's assistance, and assignments that have personal values for the student are much more likely to be successful than assignments that violate these criteria. Assignments that stimulate student initiative and creativity are always in order. On the other hand, blanket assignments, with the same tasks assigned to fast and to slow learners, are often done inadequately or not at all. The ideal solution to the problems related to homework would seem to be to have students complete all their preparation at school. An era of lengthened periods and supervised study attempted to eliminate home study problems. But interest in supervised study has declined and research on the effectiveness of such study is not in agreement.[28] Perhaps an increase in the number of school periods, as proposed by Conant (if it does not revive the large, ineffective study halls of the past), may make it possible for students to complete their assignments under better study conditions, under better supervision, and with more adequate facilities.

With the advent of a more individualized approach to learning, via programmed instruction or computer-assisted instruction, for example, the student will need to do his "homework" where facilities are available.

USE OF THE SCHOOL LIBRARY

Assignments often involve use of the library. If such assignments are to be effective, the teacher must work closely with the librarian. When the teacher informs the librarian in advance of topics assigned and materials needed for research papers, the librarian is able to make such materials readily available. Assignments of materials that are not in the library, or that are in limited supply, or that are frequently used by other teachers can be avoided. There is no better place to practice the Golden Rule than in the use of the library. The most materials made accessible to the greatest number of students is the goal. Another fact to be kept in mind by every teacher is that there are students at every grade level who do not know how to use the library. No other person is better qualified than the school librarian to assist in teaching library skills.[29] The teacher should also make use of the resources of public libraries to supplement the facilities of the school.

[28] Strang, p. 679.
[29] Mary Peacock Douglas, "School Library—Classroom Partner," *NEA Journal,* 50 (September 1961), 51–53.

EVALUATION IN LESSON PLANNING

Lesson plan structure, as indicated previously, encourages the teacher to anticipate how he is going to evaluate student progress on each specific objective listed. Also, it is obvious that evaluative activities of the unit, such as tests, will appear in the activities of daily plans. Another type of evaluation especially helpful for student teachers or new teachers, who are usually teaching under close supervision, is the postanalysis of the daily lesson plan. It serves two purposes: It enables the teacher to analyze his successes and failures at the end of each lesson and it helps the supervisor to assess the ability of the teacher to analyze his own teaching. As soon as possible after a lesson has been taught, the teacher should take about fifteen minutes to jot down informally answers to such questions as these:

1. What did I do particularly well today? What could I have done better?
2. How well am I taking care of classroom routine and management?
3. What is the status of classroom morale? Are there any potential discipline problems? Do I need help with critical problems?
4. Are all students working to capacity?
5. Am I providing a sufficient variety of activities and materials to keep the class interesting? Or do I depend too much on a single activity based on a single source?
6. Do I make provision for individual differences in student interests, needs, and abilities? Do I challenge the gifted and enable slow learners to taste success?
7. Was class tempo good or was it too fast or too slow?
8. Am I gearing instruction to the level of the class (for example, vocabulary or concepts), neither talking down to students nor going beyond their level of comprehension?
9. Am I providing opportunities for students to apply what they learn?
10. What steps can I take to remedy student failure in achievement or in self-control?
11. How do I react to supervision? How can I profit most from supervisory assistance?

SAMPLE LESSON PLANS

Now that all aspects of the lesson plan have been thoroughly discussed, the reader may find it helpful to study the two following examples of lesson plans developed and used by graduate students in their preservice preparation for teaching.

Lesson Plan One [30]

Class: 6th Period Girls' P.E. (Grade 12)   *Date:* 3/1

School: Hoover H.S.   *Teacher:* C. Fogarty

Unit: Basketball   *Lesson:* Inside and Outside
                                                   Offensive Screens.

Facility: Ouside Courts   *Equipment:* 5 balls, 14 pinnies,
         and Girls' Gym.   4 whistles.

Reminders: Tournament next Friday.

TIME	LESSON OBJECTIVES	ACTIVITIES	CLASS ORGANIZATION
5 min.	1. Students will demonstrate good posture during roll check.	1. Roll check — admit slips—announcements.	1. Established.
10 min.	2. Students will be able to discuss rules and identify playing positions.	2. Discuss rules (see bulletin board), good guarding, and forward strategy.	2. Roll call formation.
8 min.	3. Students will show continuous development in physical fitness.	3. Physical fitness exercises (teaching cards—with stick figures and diagrams).	3. Open squad formation (teacher behind group).
10 min.	4. Students will show awareness of different types of offensive strategy through preplanned plays and thought problems.	4. Teach screen plays (cards — diagrams—and instructions). (a) Student demonstration (inside and outside screens) omit —no time (b) Drills	4. Same court assignments as in games. Diagram shows positions of players.
6 min.	5. Through self-evaluation students will show improvement in shooting skills.	5. Shooting tests (scores of 5 teams recorded by captains on prepared score cards.)	5. Same court assignments as in games.
?	6. Students will continue to show satisfaction in this type of recreation and team play.	6. Games	6. Team positions (indicated on charts) — 3 students assigned as officials— teams 2 and 5 wear pinnies.

[30] Reprinted by permission of Catherine Fogarty.

Postanalysis (on back of Lesson Plan):

Screen demonstrations went well today—will go over outside screen tomorrow. Several students asked questions. On the whole, the class seemed very much interested. The learning atmosphere was good.

Student cooperation was excellent. I felt the students really enjoyed today's lesson—I did, too!

Routine procedures for the collection of equipment at the end of the period must be given more attention in the future! Monitors must be reminded to do an efficient job.

Lesson Plan Two

Hoover High School   *Date:* March 31
American Government I (Grade 12)   *Teacher:* Maryann Roulier

Unit: California State Government

Reminders: Distribute federal census cards; send Bill for projector.

Specific Objectives:	*Proposed Evaluation:*
1. Students will be able to relate administrative departments to the structure of government.	1. Panel presentation and class response (rating by teacher).
2. Students will be able to enumerate the more important departments and agencies of government and describe their functions.	2. Performance on work sheets.
	3. Unit test.

TIME	ACTIVITIES	MATERIALS
8:00	Flag salute and bulletin—Jeff. Complete roll while panel organizes.	
8:10	Panel presentation: Departments and agencies of government. Class participation.	Text: Chapters 7 & 8 (pp. 86–117). Work sheets 14 and 15, Part II, 12–16.
8:25	Summarize and evaluate panel presentation.	
8:35	Introduce film and project it for class with follow-up discussion. (Supplementary notes and questions.)	Film: *Trial by Jury.*

Assignment: Review Chapters 3–8, inc., and work sheets for test on Friday. Work sheets are also due.

Postanalysis: The panel selected the most important departments for consideration and covered each one very well. Again, the reports were not stimulating and I doubt if the class, as a whole, benefited. In the future, panels should be given controversial topics, resolutions, or problems for discussion. We had little time for questions or a summary because of excessive administrative details.

Unfortunately, time ran out before the film could be finished. Tomorrow, I shall recap important conclusions when I summarize the film with the class. I think the film is good for illustrating the jury process. Next time I use it, I shall devote the entire period to it.[31]

Neither one of these two plans is flawless but both present practical, workable plans that were used with success by two new teachers.

QUESTIONS AND ANSWERS ON LESSON PLANS

Beginning teachers often raise specific questions about requirements for lesson plans. Some of these questions with suggested answers follow.

How long should a lesson plan be? Long enough and complete enough to be of definite help, yet not so detailed as to be confusing. Usually a single page will suffice for the basic plan. The written plan should serve as a simple, ready reference that can be easily read and that will, at the same time, preserve the continuity of the lesson without unnecessary duplication or undesirable omissions. One beginning teacher wrote three or four pages in longhand each day. As a result, he had difficulty using such a plan for ready reference. However, the one-page plan often needs to be supplemented. A discussion period should include well-worded key questions, prepared in advance. If the teacher is not sure of his material, he may also need to jot down pertinent information that answers the questions. Often it is advisable for the teacher to outline on separate notes or cards the steps of a demonstration. It is sometimes advisable for a teacher to compose a short lecture and review it a number of times so that he can give it effectively without marring his presentation with "uhs" and "wys."

What form of lesson plan is best? There is no one best form. The authors have illustrated types that can be adapted to various subjects. A teacher will usually find a lesson plan structure he has developed himself more useful than commercially prepared plans.

How much in advance should daily plans be prepared? New teachers or student teachers, who are under close supervision, are advised to prepare plans about a week in advance, so that supervisors can give helpful suggestions before the lessons are taught. No doubt the new teacher will be allowed considerable freedom in his planning, but he should avail himself of as much supervisory assistance as possible in order to avoid costly mistakes.

Should a daily plan be rigidly followed? Never. It is neither possible nor desirable to follow plans without deviation. Unexpected changes in schedules often occur. Sometimes half of the class may be absent because of illness or conflicting activities, thus necessitating a complete shift in plans. Inflexible, teacher-made plans leave no opportunity for students to participate in planning. Studies of teacher behavior have also indicated

[31] Reprinted by permission of Maryann Roulier.

a lack of responsiveness to student questions and answers. Sensible use of daily plans enables the teacher to make adaptations freely and, at the same time, provides him with the security and organization needed for a well-taught lesson. Beginning teachers often find it helpful to provide a time budget for each activity. This prevents unprofitable deviations, assures a better distribution of class time, provides for more variety, saves time for more important matters, and makes it more likely that planned activities will be completed on schedule.

How can a teacher avoid busywork in planning? Daily plans are for use, not to impress supervisors. A new teacher in physical education was asked for his daily plan. After considerable searching, he found it under a pile of other papers in the third drawer of his desk. Unnecessary duplication should be avoided. It has already been suggested that the teacher should develop his own format with appropriate headings that remain unchanged and duplicate this as a basis for all his plans. In some cases, the same activity, such as a series of speeches in a speech class or a project in an art class, may be continued for a number of days. Obviously, a complete new plan for each day is unnecessary. The first basic plan may be used for a number of days with only minor revisions, such as reminders, special assignments, remedial activities, and daily postevaluations.

Note the following example of a *weekly* plan in Industrial Arts:

Weekly Plan

School: Central High School   *Date:* January 4–8.

Class: IA (Metal Shop)—Grades 11–12   *Teacher:* John Doe

Unit: Welding

Monday, January 4

(*See* complete *Daily Lesson Plan* for today.)

It is assumed that a lecture-demonstration which will cover most of the period provides the foundation for work on individual projects for the rest of the week.

Specific Objectives: Same as Monday   Tuesday, January 5
Reminders:
Major Activity: Students work on individual projects under teacher superivsion.
Special Instruction: (a) *Individuals*—based on observation and evaluation by
                              the teacher.
                         (b) *Small group* instruction (as needed).
Postanalysis: (On back of plan or on a separate sheet or card.)

Same abbreviated plan as on Tuesday, January 5.	Wednesday, January 6 Thursday, January 7 Friday, January 8

Are daily plans always part of a larger unit? Not always. As previously suggested, not all subjects lend themselves readily to effective unit planning. Also, many teachers find it advisable to include remedial work on fundamental skills, to review concepts that may not even be a part of the course, or to incorporate special lessons of a timely nature that may bear no relation to the unit being studied.

By way of summary, to be sure that the lesson plan includes all of the necessary items, the teacher would do well to refer to the following checklist:

1. Orientation: Does the introduction clarify objectives and provide motivation for the day's activities?

2. Discussion: Are key questions listed? Are appropriate illustrations and important facts included?

3. Demonstration: Are the principal steps outlined?

4. Laboratory procedures: Are activities well organized (distribution and collection of materials, work plan, cleanup)?

5. Audio-visual presentation: Are all the necessary steps for preparation, presentation, and follow-up included?

6. Committee work: Are committees well organized in terms of selection, carefully defined problems, work plans, and methods of presenting findings?

7. Activities in general: Is a variety provided to meet individual differences in needs, interests, and abilities of students?

8. Materials: Is there variety? Are the best materials provided to achieve objectives? Is each item listed specifically (for example, the text, pages, and exercises assigned; film, title, and description, and so on)?

9. Assignment: Is the assignment complete, answering the questions why, what, how, and when? Are there modifications to fit the capabilities of fast and slow learners and to appeal to a diversity of interests and backgrounds?

10. Timing: Does the time budget provide for a complete and balanced coverage of the topic or problem for the day?

11. Application: Are opportunities provided for students to practice newly acquired skills, to utilize new knowledge, or to strengthen new insights and appreciations?

12. Evaluation: Are appropriate activities included to determine how well students are achieving expected outcomes? Is a postanalysis included that describes the impressions of the teacher concerning the achievement and behavior of his students and his own performance?

A FINAL WORD ON PLANNING

Three chapters have been devoted to three phases of instructional planning—long range, cooperative, and daily. Plans should always be tentative. The teacher should use them, but never become a slave to them. However, any plans should be done thoroughly and well in advance of their use in the classroom. While each classroom teacher is responsible for his own planning, no teacher today works alone. The classroom of yesterday may have been an academic island, unrelated to other school subjects and activities, poorly articulated with the school above or below, and isolated from community life on the outside. This is no longer the case. The modern teacher has to develop greater skill in working with many people—fellow teachers, administrators, students, parents, and resource persons of the community. Curriculum committees of the past were composed of the "experts." Today, every teacher is involved in planning the total school program. Whereas curriculum committees were at one time composed of teachers of a given subject matter area, now teachers work with teachers of other subjects and other school levels, as well as interested and informed laymen. More and more teachers are also working together as teams at the classroom level. The development of skill in planning, both on an individual and a cooperative basis, is a prerequisite to successes in teaching.

SELECTED READINGS

1. American Educational Research Association, *Encyclopedia of Educational Research*, 3d ed., Chester W. Harris, ed. New York: The Macmillan Company, 1960, pp. 677–79.

2. Bloom, Benjamin S., ed., *Taxonomy of Educational Objectives: Handbook I, Cognitive Domain*. New York: David McKay Company, Inc., 1956.

3. Blount, Nathan S., and Herbert J. Klausmeier, *Teaching in the Secondary School*, 3d ed. New York: Harper & Row, Publishers, 1968, chap. 6.

4. Clark, Leonard H., and Irving S. Starr, *Secondary School Teaching Methods*, 2d ed. New York: The Macmillan Company, 1967, chap. 5.

5. Krathwohl, David R., Benjamin S. Bloom, and Bertram B. Masia, *Taxonomy of Educational Objectives: Handbook II, Affective Domain*. New York: David McKay Company, Inc., 1964.

6. Mager, Robert F., *Preparing Instructional Objectives*. Palo Alto, Calif.: Fearon Publishers, Inc., 1962.

7. Oliva, Peter F., *The Secondary School Today*. Cleveland: The World Publishing Company, 1967, chap. 9.

8. Perrodin, Alex F., ed., *The Student Teacher's Reader: A Collection of Readings*. Chicago: Rand McNally & Company, 1966, chap. 8.

9. Saylor, J. Galen, and William M. Alexander, *Curriculum Planning for Modern Schools*. New York: Holt, Rinehart and Winston, Inc., 1966, chap. 13.

10. Tanruther, Edgar M., *Clinical Experiences in Teaching for the Student Teacher or Intern*. New York: Dodd, Mead & Company, Inc., 1967, chap. 4.

PART THREE / *Methods and Materials of Instruction*

CHAPTER 7 / *Teaching Methods: Basic Instructional Procedures*

Modern high school populations are so diverse that it is next to impossible to generalize about them. Somewhat like the celebrated Chinese proverb, a high school population needs a thousand words to describe it.

To take a class as he finds it, to study it, to provide helpful learning experiences, and to direct the growth of the students are the tasks of the teacher. As never before, society is clamoring for quality teaching. In many quarters the schools are under attack and are accused of doing an inferior job. They are beset by legions of problems that stem from conditions inside and outside the schools.

There are so many students to be taught so many things in so short a time. The teacher knows that some of the students are indifferent, even negativistic, about school; yet these pupils must be taught something. This kind of teaching calls for skill in dealing with students, ability to apply teaching and learning techniques that will accomplish optimum results, and patience in guiding development. The discerning adjustment of the student to his changing world must be nurtured.

Since the beginning of time, man has sought ways of communicating the accumulated knowledge and skills of one generation to another. Some of these methods have been spectacularly successful in certain time periods, or with certain groups of people, or for certain purposes. The teacher of today can call upon a great variety of methods to assist in guiding the learning of students.

Some of these methods are traditional and some are modern; others are still in the experimental stage. Some methods have outlived their usefulness, and have been or should be discarded. A threadbare example is the regurgitation method of memorizing isolated facts, and of repeating inane questions and answers. There are, however, occasions on which both memorization and the question-and-answer method may appropriately be used in the learning formula. But, in the main, modern learning theory calls for understandings, appreciations, positive skills, the development of judgment, independence in study, and the ability to analyze and to select a mode of action, to discriminate, and to create. Again, the connection between method and the aims of education is close.

Self-instructional techniques are much in the limelight today; also, experimentation with large and small groups is equally noticeable. It is through constant experimentation of this type that quality instruction emerges.

Someone has said that method is a teaching hypothesis. Certainly, it changes with experience and research. Change is gradual from where one is to where he wishes to go. Pupil behavior, too, changes gradually. There are hundreds of ways of handling the learning process. The teacher begins by using the one from his education and experience that seems logical to him, and with which he feels at home. But certain situations seem to call for new approaches. These should be tried little by little and with a critical but open mind.

THE DEVELOPMENT OF COMMUNICATION SKILLS

The ability to do high school work—all learning for that matter—depends chiefly on the four communication skills: reading, writing, speaking, and listening. These same skills play a significant role throughout life. They help an individual in his career and in many of the enjoyments he gets from the cultural arts. Even the fullest and wisest use of leisure time will often be based on one or more of these skills. Ideas from other people come to us through reading, a skill that must be carried out with reasonable rapidity and with understanding. We must be able to attach meaning to words and sounds that come to us through the sense of hearing. Then we convey our ideas through effective writing, and through clear, understandable, and often persuasive speech. Regardless of the methods used in instruction, good communication skills are basic.

READING

Evidence is quite clear that reading skills among high school students are erratic, substandard, and uniformly disappointing. All national surveys and studies verify this conclusion. Far too many students have had their reading experience begin in frustration and end in failure. Reading retardation is high. Many high school students are unable to read above the third- or fourth-grade level. The reading problem is noticeable early in the school experience but it becomes critical in the junior high school. For example, Krugman says that "in city-wide group testing in New York City schools, the third graders in a large low economic district had a median IQ ten points lower than that of all third graders throughout the city. The median IQ of sixth graders from the same area was seventeen points lower than that of eighth graders, twenty points lower than the median IQ for the entire city. City-wide reading tests showed similar results. The low economic children were retarded one year in reading in the third grade, almost two years in the sixth grade, and more than two and a half years in the eighth grade." [1] Another study of 30,000 Negro and white children in grades four to twelve found that "the white pupils at all grade levels attained a higher level of vocabulary and comprehension proficiency than did the Negroes. The most serious and startling finding was that at no time were Negro pupils reading on grade level and that as grade levels increased, these pupils fell one to five years behind." [2] Another report from a midwestern metropolis found that "mean achievement scores favored the higher income groups increasingly from grade to grade, and that the lowest scores of the lower income children consistently occurred in the reading portions of tests." Arithmetic and other work study skills were less affected.[3]

Many educators consider the biggest failure of the schools of today to lie in ineffective reading performance; consequently crash or panic programs have sprung up about the country. The relationship between poor reading skills and predictive or potential dropouts is so clear that most alert school systems are seriously tackling the problem with either short- or long-term procedures. It is not surprising that Brickell, as he surveyed innovative instructional programs in New York State in 1961, found a great number of various types of reading clinics and programs in the public and private elementary and secondary schools.[4]

READING AND THE POTENTIAL DROPOUT   The United States has become painfully aware of the school dropout problem. National surveys and major research findings warrant brief summary: [5]

1. Dropouts, as a class, are not uneducable. The United States Department of Labor has published data showing that 70 percent of the dropouts surveyed had IQ's of 90 or above. In New York State it was reported

---

[1] Morris Krugman, "Educating the Disadvantaged Child," *NEA Journal,* 50 (April 1961), 23.

[2] Joan M. Karp and Irving Sigel, "Psychoeducational Appraisal of Disadvantaged Children," *Review of Educational Research,* 35 (December 1965), 404.

[3] Edith H. Grotberg, "Learning Disabilities and Remediation in Disadvantaged Children," *Review of Educational Research,* 35 (December 1965), 416.

[4] Henry M. Brickell, *Commissioner's 1961 Catalog of Educational Change.* Albany: New York State Education Department, October 1961.

[5] Daniel Schreiber, ed., *The School Dropout.* Washington, D.C.: Project: School Dropouts, NEA, 1964; National Committee for Children and Youth, *Social Dynamite.* Report of the Conference on Unemployed, Out-of-School Youth in Urban Areas. Washington, D.C.: 1961; Research Division and Department of Classroom Teachers, NEA, "High-School Dropouts," Discussion Pamphlet No. 3, Washington, D.C.: 1959; John K. Norton, *Changing Demands on Education and Their Implications.* Washington, D.C.: National Committee for Support of the Public Schools, 1963; Goodwin Watson, *No Room at the Bottom.* Washington, D.C.: Project: Educational Implications of Automation, NEA, 1963.

that 13 percent of these unfortunates had IQ's of 110 or above. Even the very high-ability group, 130 or more, is found among the "leavers." These data would seem to indicate that school failure and dropout are not just a matter of low intellectual ability.

2. Underprivileged groups suffer a high percentage of dropouts. Children from the lower socioeconomic and minority groups swell the statistics. The environment in the homes of these people quite naturally shows a paucity of cultural materials, books, pictures, maps, toys. Reading plays no part in the leisure or work world at this level. Both the schools and the homes in these areas usually have different social goals; yet it is noticeable today that because of contemporary socioeconomic patterns the "poor readers" actually stay in junior and senior high school longer than they formerly did. But dropouts are not confined to the slum and ghetto areas. They are found among the children in rural areas, small towns, and suburban communities.

3. School retardation is characteristic of the dropout. Nine out of ten of them have lost a year or more somewhere along the line.

4. The term "functional illiterate" has been used to describe these youth. Reading, this most important educational tool, has never been mastered. Also, reading and other verbal experiences go hand in hand. Consequently, failure is evident in almost the entire school program— social studies, languages, sciences; for example, the youngster who cannot read well is likely to do very poorly in word analysis problems in mathematics. Fully three fourths of all slow learners do better in the nonverbal school subjects. Another often noted characteristic is the fact that slow learners—potential dropouts—almost invariably score higher on nonverbal sections of standardized tests. It will be recalled that contemporary intelligence tests rely heavily on verbal content.

SCHOOL PATTERNS

There are many subproblems in each of the communication skills. In reading, for example, students must read textbooks, novels, newspapers, science books, and poetry. They must also grasp meaning from mathematics symbols, charts, tables, graphs, maps, footnotes, and legends. Meaning must also be forthcoming from chapters, paragraphs, passages, sentences, and words.

Several false assumptions have been made about reading: that the elementary school has sole responsibility for teaching reading; that the school is at fault when all students do not learn to read well; that nonreaders are incapable of learning and should be eliminated from school; and that reading is a purely mechanical skill unrelated to experience.

Even when the elementary school has done a good job of developing basic reading skills, secondary school teachers still must teach their students to understand the new words and concepts as they encounter new subject matter. Different kinds of reading ability are required in interpreting a literary selection, a mathematics problem, an issue in social studies, or a blueprint in shop. Each subject sets its own reading demands, and the teachers must help the student to cope with them. Scanning, skimming, analytical interpretation, noting differences between facts and opinion, drawing conclusions, and improving vocabulary are aspects of these demands. It is not too much to expect every content teacher to become a reading teacher in his field so that students can read and study the textbook used in the course. Reading should be looked upon and approached as an interdisciplinary skill. Books, pamphlets, periodicals, and the like have many difficulty levels. Only as students understand what they read will they be able to assimilate.

When a student is unable to read, an analysis of his problem is not as simple as finding his IQ. Causes of reading difficulty are often complex and difficult to identify. Junior and senior high schools are so aware of existing reading problems that nearly all are introducing some kind of remedial plans, formal or informal, to help alleviate the problem. Brickell has described scores of programs in New York State.[6] The range includes individualized assistance, classes made up of students from several age groups, large and small group instruction, cooperative or team effort, motivation techniques of many kinds, enrichment effort for both gifted and slow learners, extensive library assignments and assistance, clinical approaches scheduled for either school or nonschool hours, reading laboratories, vacation reading classes or seminars, personal counseling, and basic curricular adjustments. Other districts, notably Melbourne, Florida,[7] feel that the nongraded high school with its "phasing" instead of "grading" structure can do much toward a practical solution of the school reading problem. Other districts are tackling the problem according to their own perceptions, but the involvement of the average secondary school is indicative of the urgency and extensiveness of the problem. Stress is being placed on the readiness to read. Some educators would like to see distinctive national curriculum study groups work up materials, sequences, and procedures along the lines developed by various committees, such as the Physical Science Study Committee (PSSC), the School Mathematics Study Group (SMSG), the Biological Science Curriculum Study (BSCS), the Chemical Education Materials Study (CHEM), and the Chemical Bond Approach Project (CBAP).[8] Great satisfaction frequently stems from these extended and enriched programs.

[6] Brickell, pp. 33–200.
[7] B. Frank Brown, "An Answer to Dropouts: The Nongraded High School," *The Atlantic Monthly*, November 1964, pp. 88–90.
[8] See Nelson B. Henry, ed., "Development in and through Reading," *Sixtieth Yearbook of the National Society for the Study of Education, Part I.* Chicago: University of Chicago Press, 1961.

There are at least three types of programs currently in use. The first is for slow learners whose native ability is a handicap. These youth need individual coaching and guidance so that they can use what potential they have. Another type is aimed at boys and girls who for some reason have just not learned as society has expected. The preceding paragraphs have described ways of dealing with this group, most of whose members are decidedly educable; in fact, the literature provides evidence of tremendous gains in standard reading scores by many pupils at this level. Underachievers can become, or at least approach, normal achievers, but they need motivation, guidance, technical help, and reading materials that stimulate their interests—trade books, supplementary paperbacks, high adventure, fiction, or whatnot. Taba and Elkins [9] have shown that large numbers of students who could scarcely read and those who did not care to read can be given new interest in and new attitudes toward reading. "Motivation" is an overworked word but it has great applicability here. The third type of program is aimed at improving and exploiting the reading skills of pupils who have already reached an acceptable level.

To students the word "remedial" has bad connotations, but remedial reading, clinical or developmental, can pay good dividends. Programs are no longer stuffy; many have novelty, innovation, and intrinsic merit. The characteristics of a good developmental reading program have been described by Weiss:

1. Reading instruction must aim at individual students, taking into account their different backgrounds, abilities, and interests.

2. Flexibility of instruction depends upon the availability of a wide range of reading material of all kinds and on all sorts of subjects. In an effective program much of the initiative passes to the student, and the teacher's role changes to that of a guide, a "listener," a resource person, a critic.

3. Reading instruction means paying attention not only to the basic skills of reading, but also to the general end which education should serve: the widening of the student's intellectual, emotional, and moral horizons.

4. Reading instruction is completely successful only when the student has acquired the habit of active continuous reading and can read with ease in all of the subject areas which, by necessity or choice, he faces.

5. The reading program is not the product of one teacher, but demands the involvement of the entire faculty and administration in a whole-hearted and single-minded concentration on drawing the best possible work out of each student.[10]

It has been emphasized that reading is more than a mechanical process of word recognition and correct pronunciation. Unless words provide for

[9] Hilda Taba and Deborah Elkins, *Teaching Strategies for the Culturally Disadvantaged.* Chicago: Rand McNally & Company, 1966.

[10] M. Jerry Weiss, *Reading in the Secondary Schools.* New York: The Odyssey Press, Inc., 1961, p. 10. Used by permission.

understanding or stimulate pictures in the mind, reading becomes a useless exercise dealing with meaningless symbols and abstractions. The foundation of understanding and comprehension must rest on concrete experience, either direct or vicarious. How this foundation is to be built raises some central problems.

MAKE A PRACTICAL BEGINNING   At the outset, it is necessary to find out the reading abilities of the students. This can be done from reading scores in the school records, from oral reading, and from simple reading tests administered in class. The teacher might also begin by thinking of himself as a reading teacher; providing varied experiences for the students; locating simple reading materials for the slow learners; securing clinical help if needed; providing the students with varied lists of reading material which will be of interest to them; and giving words meaning through association with a variety of multisensory materials. For example, how does one understand what the human heart is and does? For this understanding he reads, looks at films, handles models, looks at diagrams, and then organizes the facts.

BEYOND THE MECHANICS OF READING   Even after a student has learned to read, the responsibility of the teacher does not end. He now begins to teach discrimination in reading. In the first place, the student must be taught to separate the wheat from the chaff. This involves developing a taste for better reading material and learning the skill of scanning so that the reader may judge whether or not a selection is worth careful reading. Improving taste in reading involves a slow and subtle process. The beginning is made at the student's own level of appreciation. The wise teacher never expresses surprise or scorn at what the student likes. Gradually the student raises his appreciation as he continues to read, and as he is exposed to more worthwhile material. He must be given help in his reading selections. The more poorly he reads, the less likely he will be to select reading material that is suitable. Above all, every reading experience should be a meaningful one, and hopefully, enjoyable, too. Finally, improvement in reading should be a cooperative undertaking that involves parents and other teachers. Their encouragement and support are essential. An overexposure to reading material that is beyond the student's comprehension or an overanalysis of what has been read will nullify the procedures just suggested for improving interest in reading and taste for better material.

Often students who read reasonably well develop lopsided reading tastes. They get into a habit of reading one kind of material only, and even grow to disdain anything else. A boy, for example, reads extensively, but always adventure stories; he may even narrow this adventure to westerns, pirates, war, or sea stories. Teachers have tried many techniques to secure a better balance in reading selections. Reading lists should provide variety. Records might be maintained, even posted, to show what is being read; the librarian is asked to exhibit books and book covers to call attention to materials of many types.

The next step in fostering discrimination is to help students distinguish between fact and falsehood. There is often a naïve tendency to believe that anything which appears in print is true. Normally a serious limitation of using a single textbook becomes obvious. Not only does one book fail to meet the needs of students with varying degrees of reading ability; it encourages too much dependence on what "the book says." Through an analysis of propaganda techniques, a comparison of conflicting viewpoints, and a study of exaggerated claims often made in advertisements, students can be taught to be wary in their reading. As a part of this general point, they need to learn the value of investigating the reliability of the sources of their reading.

WRITING

No one can deny that writing is a communication skill that should be taught in school. It has a great deal of bearing on the ability to do well in school, it is needed in most vocations, and it is part of everyday living. Many adults write very poorly, and for that reason find writing a painful experience. Many procrastinate over the simplest of writing chores, such as personal letters, requests, inquiries, newspaper notices and advertisements, invitations, and similar bit pieces.

Corporations, distributors, and purveyors recognize these facts. They never state in an advertisement that the reader should write in for information, or even formulate an order: "Simply fill in the attached blank." This is the only way to get the replies, even if the readers really want the goods or services advertised. Suggestions that groups write their congressman on an issue are usually accompanied by a sample letter (of course, the specimen letter presents the point of view being advocated). Ofttimes clubs find it difficult to locate a member who will serve as secretary—the usual excuse is, "I can't write" or "I can't take notes." Instead of letters the telephone and the telegraph frequently become the means of communication.

TEACHING THE WRITING SKILLS   Most of what was written in the paragraphs above about reading can be repeated almost verbatim about writing. Change the nouns and the ideas remain much the same.

High school students should write abundantly, and in most classes. It is unfair to saddle on English teachers alone the burden of developing the habits and skills of writing. Probably students do not write enough today, but artificial pressure writing has been tried, and it has failed. In many quarters there has been an overemphasis on singling out errors, too many unkind remarks about faulty unity, emphasis, or coherence.

At the same time, the rewards for good composition have been few.

Some teachers appreciate writing skill and pass along a friendly note of encouragement, but most teachers merely mark the errors and hand the paper back to the student.

Here again the individual differences in students are vast. In class after class, a teacher sees students who contribute well to discussions, who volunteer to give reports, or who organize committees, but who cannot write a good test paper or a term report. And there are those who are just the opposite.

Motivation means as much in developing writing skills as in reading or study skills. It has been truly said that teachers in assigning written work should bear in mind that students must have something to say, must have a purpose in writing it, and must have a desire to improve their writing. Creating the conditions for acceptance, and hopefully desire, is a necessity. It is not just more composition that is needed, but more purpose. Actually, too much emphasis on composition may be harmful; certainly a truism if a pedantic following of rules and construction is the basic pattern. Student exploration of guidelines for writing, self-evolved if possible, is often a good starting place. Suggestions for achieving these conditions include such matters as orientation, followed by time spent on analyzing why a certain magazine article or story was written, truthfulness, omissions, and other clues. Student effort should be discussed in a helpful manner, and revisions made if warranted or new compositions started. Personal conferences between teacher and student or a small group of students are highly beneficial. More purpose and more content are likely to grow from cooperation, or an integration of related subject matter such as in the social studies, literature, and science.

One of the most individual aspects of stimulating an interest in writing is to develop in the student a habit of writing, and the ability to recognize things to write about.

Miss J. successfully uses an occasional writing round robin. A student takes a sheet of paper and writes one sentence on it. The paper is handed to another student who reads the sentence, then adds a second sentence. The paper passes to every member of the class, who makes a contribution. It is a potpourri to be sure, but it accomplishes a purpose.

Mrs. N. teaches in a school that has a policy of assigning twenty minutes of each junior high school English period to formal spelling. Mrs. N. got permission to substitute a twenty-minute daily writing exercise. Students were told about the scheme and were asked to write for twenty minutes on any subject or any idea that came to mind. In the beginning some students could not get going; they were given individual help. Each day at the end of the period, Mrs. N. reminded the pupils that there would be another writing period tomorrow, and that perhaps they would like to think of something to write about. From time to time, she set up large action pictures (rodeo, a canoe shooting the rapids, a ship in a heavy gale) on the chalkrail. On such occasions the students usually were asked to suggest action verbs and to write them on the board. The teacher did not use the time to correct papers or fill out office reports. She moved about the room. In effect, she became a supervising writing teacher.

Among the techniques used by Mr. W. was that of occasionally playing a symphonic or orchestral record. Once it was Ferde Grofé's "Grand Canyon Suite," at another time Moussorgsky's "Pictures at an Exhibition." At still another time it was Tschaikovsky's "Overture of 1812," and at still another time a Strauss waltz. Mr. W.'s purpose was to create a mood. After each record, and the writing that followed it, he told the class the story of the selection and stressed the fact that the composer had written a great piece of descriptive literature but used a musical score instead of lines of prose. This occasional feature of Mr. W.'s composition class became quite popular.

Mrs. W., junior high English, suggested to Mr. C., industrial arts, that she would like his help with a group of boys who had no interest in writing. The boys (and two girls) were at the time working on a six-week unit in photography. Mr. C. tried to show the students that the camera (Kodak Instamatic and color Polaroid) would enable them to do more than just take pictures; they could actually communicate visually. As the students became more adept at seeing things they had never seen before—sadness, happiness, anger, drama, and various behavior patterns—Mrs. W. quietly edged into the picture and slowly led the students to write about their pictures, what they saw, their frustrations, successes. Vocabularies expanded with such words as mood, dominance, contrast, infinity, image, microcosm, macrocosm, exposure, and other words that would never have been learned out of context. Now students had something of interest to write about. Both Mr. C. and Mrs. W. felt great satisfaction.

SPEAKING

No activity in which students engage in school is more important to their future happiness or success than speaking. On the job, in the home, in all their relations with others, they must express themselves well in order to be understood and to be accepted by their fellows. To teach students the ability to communicate ideas effectively is a job that cannot be delegated to speech and English teachers alone. It is humiliating to meet students from other countries who can speak three or four languages fluently while the products of American schools are unable to speak one language —their own—well.

ENCOURAGING CORRECT SPEECH   In class the students should be provided as much opportunity as possible to engage in discussion, to relate good stories, to report, and to serve as chairmen of groups. The authors have observed many adults, suddenly cast into roles of minor leadership, who were embarrassed by being unable to present a simple motion properly. Everyone enjoys a good story, yet how few tell one effectively. Students may well be encouraged to read good stories and to practice the art of telling them to their classmates. They need to be encouraged to take pride in correct, colorful, effective speech. The importance of vocabulary building, of using the exact word to express one's meaning, and the avoidance of such stereotyped words as "fine" or "nice" to describe something can very well be stressed in every class. The use of clean speech, the avoidance of slang, and the correction of lazy speech habits are taught by precept and example.

Voice is often a deterrent to effective speaking. Because no one knows exactly how his voice sounds to others, playbacks of voice recordings for each member of the class constitute the first step in the improvement of voice quality. In some instances, clinical help may be needed. Teachers themselves would do well to remember King Lear's eulogy of Cordelia: "Her voice was ever soft, gentle, and low, an excellent thing in woman." Men, too, need good voices. A raspy, raucous, strident, whiny voice is not a model to be imitated.

ORAL READING   The amount of oral reading by pupils has decreased in today's high schools. Some teachers disagree with this change, but the psychological and physiological changes taking place in teen-age boys and girls justify it. Whenever there is oral reading, it should be voluntary. It should be done informally; that is, the reader remains at his seat or, if standing to recite is customary, he stands, but he does not go to the front of the room to read.

Choral and responsive reading are widely used as oral reading activities. These are to be found more frequently in speech or drama classes than in regular English classes. When students cooperate well in group reading, an alert teacher can accomplish about everything that could be accomplished in solo reading. The tape recorder is also commonly used in connection with choral reading work. The occasional use of a recording of an expert, such as Charles Laughton or Charlton Heston, reading well-known literary pieces can be beneficial. Some teachers prefer to have printed copies of the readings in the hands of the students so that they can follow along with their eyes. Others prefer to have them concentrate completely on the listening.

TEACHERS' SPEECH   Although this discussion on speaking has stressed what students do, a bit of advice to teachers concerning their own speech is in order. Rough and tough language is never proper. Firm measures are required at times, to be sure, but reversion to a lower cultural level is never justified.

Another misconception that a few teachers entertain is that the use of slang leads to popularity with adolescents. A judicious use of the right kind of slang can contribute color and force to speech. For example, a good way to express a man's depressed state is to say that he is "down and out." On the other hand, an excessive use of slang or colloquial speech cheapens language. Too much use of slang suggests intellectual bankruptcy, inability to express oneself, and a lack of refinement. Students look with suspicion on the teacher who attempts to speak their jargon; they consider such usage by an adult an invasion of the fraternity of youth.

LISTENING

As indicated in the introduction to the section "Auditory Instructional Materials" in Chapter 10, listening is a significant factor in communication. It has always played an important part in the educational pattern of schools, yet in most instances, it is an act that has been little studied. It has been assumed that, if told to do so, all students can and do listen. It is only within recent years that much attention has been given to the act of listening. This new emphasis seems to parallel the development of the newer mass media, and the development of extensive equipment has sharpened school sensitivity to the learning problems involved. Just as reading and written communication received a great impetus from the invention of the printing press, oral communication and listening have received a similar boost from modern electronics.

LISTENING OBJECTIVES   Many secondary school students do not read well, nor do they listen well. The ability to grasp meaning from auditory stimuli is as difficult and as important as the ability to grasp meaning from visual stimuli. The task of the teacher is to try to develop both skills in students, and to keep their use balanced and in focus.

It is now generally accepted that discriminative listening to informative speech can be taught. For a general communications course, schools have accepted such objectives as these:

1. To develop a respect for listening as a learning skill
2. To eliminate bad listening habits already formed
3. To develop the basic skills, concepts, and attitudes essential to good listening habits.
4. To increase markedly student experience in listening to informative speech
5. To coordinate specific listening assignments with related assignments in speaking, reading, and writing

Are these goals behavioral?

Although all teachers can and should be concerned with developing good listening habits in students, the more active promotion of the listening objectives fall to the speech, English, music, and foreign language teachers. It is not difficult to develop a respect for listening as a medium of learning when students become aware of the fact that listening can be measured, improved, and remeasured. It is possible to chart improvement in listening habits, and research has demonstrated that grade point averages in numerous school subjects can be improved by promoting better listening. When a student becomes aware of his listening pattern, he begins self-evaluation. He may ask himself: Why am I a poor listener? How can I become a better listener? How will this help me get better grades?

Techniques for improving listening habits include:

1. Finding a central idea or ideas in the communication he is hearing, relating the contributory or embellishing ideas to the central one. Someone has said that the listener should try to "see" the central idea.
2. Trying to anticipate what the speaker will say next. This keeps the listener alert.
3. Trying to distinguish between the essential points and the details.
4. Trying to distinguish between facts and opinions.
5. Trying to separate relevant and irrelevant ideas.
6. Trying to distinguish between information and persuasion but not debating with the message.
7. Trying to relate the message to contextual clues—the announced theme, time, place, background, and other data.
8. Trying to develop a feeling of immediacy or urgency. The speaker is not going to repeat.
9. Trying to obtain a good physical vantage point for listening—not too far away, not among distractions.
10. Trying to evaluate what has been said. The evaluation may serve as a brief mental summary.

GROUP DISCUSSION

TEACHER-PUPIL INTERACTIONS

In order to understand what takes place in the classroom it is necessary to remember that at least three "bodies" are involved—teacher, students (individuals), group (students). Each has its own peculiar characteristics. The teacher's goal is to promote behavioral changes in the cognitive, affective, and psychomotor domains of learning. This means that the teacher should be primarily concerned with "how" to bring these objectives about, not with "what." During the interactions of teacher-student-group, each influences the others. The teacher brings a personality, attitudes, social outlook, biases, emotions, personal health, and many other factors to the schoolroom. Students bring an even larger number of factors. And when the students as individuals become a class they have additional characteristics.

Amidon and Flanders,[11] after an extensive study of classroom behaviors,

[11] Edmund J. Amidon and Ned A. Flanders, *The Role of the Teacher in the Classroom.* Minneapolis: Paul S. Amidon and Associates, 1963, pp. 12 ff. Used by permission.

developed a sophisticated analysis of the interactions that take place. Table 7.1 summarizes these interactions. An analysis of Table 7.1 is enlightening. Seven of the ten categories are either directly or indirectly teacher-centered. The authors noted:

Two-thirds of the time spent in a classroom, someone was talking. Two-thirds of the time someone is talking, it is the teacher—for the teacher talks more than all of the students combined. Two-thirds of the time that the teacher is talking, he

Table 7.1 Summary of Categories for Interaction Analysis

Teacher Talk	Indirect Influence	1. *Accepts Feeling:* accepting and clarifying the feeling tone of the students in a nonthreatening manner. Feelings may be positive or negative. Predicting and recalling feelings are included.
		2. *Praises or Encourages:* praising or encouraging student action or behavior. Jokes that release tension, not at the expense of another individual, nodding head or saying "uhhuh" or "go on" are included.
		3. *Accepts or Uses Ideas* of *Students:* clarifying, building, or developing ideas or suggestions by a student. As teacher brings more of his own ideas into play, shift to category 5.
	Direct Influence	4. *Asks Questions:* asking a question about content or procedure with the intent that a student answer.
		5. *Lectures:* giving facts or opinions about content or procedure; expressing his own ideas; asking rhetorical questions.
		6. *Gives Directions:* giving directions, commands, or orders with which a student is expected to comply.
		7. *Criticizes or Justifies Authority:* making statements intended to change student behavior from nonacceptable to acceptable pattern; reproving someone; stating why he is doing what he is doing, extreme self-reference.
Student Talk		8. *Student Talk-Response:* students talking in response to teacher. Teacher initiates the contact or solicits student statement.
		9. *Student Talk-Initiation:* talk by students, which they initiate. If "calling on" student is only to indicate who may talk next, observer must decide whether student wanted to talk. If he did, use this category.
		10. *Silence or Confusion:* pauses, short periods of silence, periods of confusion in which communication cannot be understood by observer.

is lecturing, giving instructions, or criticizing the behavior of students. One-third of the time he is asking questions, reacting to student ideas, or giving praise.[12]

These remarks, although they may seem harsh or exaggerated, are borne out by an alarming booklet published by the ASCD that summarizes the findings of 102 observers of American junior high schools.[13] A few quotations from this study will show how debilitating the atmosphere is in many classrooms.

The data . . . seemed to cast the junior high school classroom as a miniature lecture hall inhabited by a central figure of authority and his helpless captives. . . . It does seem almost indisputably evident that the typical eighth-grade situation is teacher-dominated, with pupils psychologically absent a large portion of the time. . . . There are abundant examples of both physical and psychological wandering (by pupils) and a great variety of random activity: twisting hair, biting nails, cracking knuckles, thumbing through books and papers, and the like. . . . The classrooms observed reflected clearly these kinds of instructional practices rather strikingly: (a) lecture-demonstration, (b) read-recitation, and (c) correct-explain-practice. These patterns of instruction were predominantly under the explicit direction of the teacher . . . students seemed to receive few pushes to substantiate, show causality, or project the possibilities of further application. . . .[14]

After several months of study and work in secondary schools, Sprague and Shirts go a step beyond method and question the "system" when they say:

The main trouble with schooling in America is that the system is designed to support information flow from adults to kids, to produce learn*eds*, not learn*ers*. Given the rate of change in most important aspects of life, such a system will produce carriers of an obsolete culture, instead of viable, renewing individuals.[15]

Although these remarks stress the verbal nature of learning, there are nonverbal aspects as well. Most of the nonverbal aspects fall in the psychomotor domain, and are primary in certain subject areas, while quite secondary in others. In cases where the demonstration is a primary method, or in remedial work, the nonverbal is important. Amidon and Flanders state that all types of students learned better from working with the indirect teacher than the direct. They also concluded that teachers who had the flexibility to shift from direct to indirect and vice versa were more successful. Furthermore, such shifts were easier for teachers who were es-

---

[12] Amidon and Flanders, p. 57.
[13] John H. Lounsbury and Jean V. Marani, *The Junior High School We Saw: One Day in the Eighth Grade.* Washington, D.C.: Association for Supervision and Curriculum Development, NEA, 1964.
[14] Lounsbury and Marani, pp. 54–55.
[15] Hall T. Sprague and Garry Shirts, "Exploring Classroom Uses of Simulations." La Jolla, Calif.: Western Behavioral Sciences Institute, October 1966, p. 21 (litho).

sentially categorized by the "indirect influence" position.[16] Soar suggests that teachers with satisfactory personality traits and those who use "integrative" rather than "dominative" teaching methods are more successful. As a result of a study with the *Minnesota Multiphasic Personality Inventory,* Soar concludes that the "socially skilled" teachers ("people who are primarily comfortable with other people and with themselves—confident, self-assured, and skillful in establishing harmonious working and social relationships with other people") relied "less on individual seat work—assignments in workbooks, individual reading, written work of various sorts—and employed more activities which involved interaction between pupils."[17] This would seem to indicate that pupil-pupil interaction is exceedingly important in methods to be employed.

THE LECTURE METHOD IN THE SECONDARY SCHOOL

In spite of the fact that secondary school teachers are constantly admonished not to lecture to their students, the technique is widely used. This method of teaching has been grossly abused by many teachers and their students have suffered; but, correctly used, it is functional.

At the outset it should be pointed out that there is a difference between formal lecturing and informal lecturing or "teacher talks." The short informal lecture can be used to good advantage in introducing a unit, summarizing a problem for study, providing information difficult for students to find, supplying motivation, or sharing one's own cultural experiences with the class.

The lecture method in high school can be used to explain a problem in which students are interested, to illustrate a process by a lecture demonstration, to illustrate a point by creating a word picture, or to tell a good story. Recounting the story of William Tell, relating Galileo's experience with his telescope, reviewing Irving Stone's *The Agony and the Ecstasy,* explaining the forces of aerodynamics in space conquest, or describing the emerging needs for broader world markets are merely some of the forms of the lecture. To be effective, teachers need to understand its various forms and uses.

HOW TO MAKE THE LECTURE EFFECTIVE   The teacher talk or informal lecture can be made more effective by giving attention to the following suggestions:

1. Lectures for secondary school students should usually be short. One of fifteen or twenty minutes is possibly the maximum; in most cases five or ten minutes may be better. Teachers must recognize that attention

[16] Amidon and Flanders, p. 57.
[17] Robert Soar, "The Effect of Teachers' Classroom Methods and Personality on Pupil Learning," in Alex F. Perrodin, *The Student Teacher's Reader.* Chicago: Rand McNally & Company, 1966, p. 334.

spans are relatively short. Although instruction by television depends chiefly on lecture, it is also highly spiced with demonstration and visual cuing. Time intervals tend to be longer, but variety is the key. Straight lecturing must still be for short periods.

2. The approach to the lecture should be informal. The language should be clear and simple, not stilted. The purpose is to inform, to enrich, to motivate.

3. Lectures should be tailored to people, and in the high school the teachers must not forget that the audience is one of adolescent boys and girls. Lecturing teachers are inclined to use words beyond the students' working vocabularies.

4. Lectures should be related to students' backgrounds, knowledges, skills, and interests. If they are not, the students are soon "lost." This point was emphasized in discussing the potential dropout.

5. Lectures should not rehash textbooks or other material the students have read, or should read for themselves. The lecture should present new and fresh ideas not readily available to the students.

6. Lecturers should avoid reminiscences or discourses on trivial personal incidents.

7. Lectures should be planned and organized so that they do not digress. In the main, the teacher should announce his purpose at the beginning of the lecture. Its development should then stick to the theme. The exact purpose of the talk must not be forgotten as it develops. Some lectures are like the classic report on Columbus and his discovery of America, "He didn't know where he was going when he started, he didn't know where he was when he got there, and when he returned he didn't know where he had been."

8. Talks should be replete with verbal illustrations. Illustrations can accent abstract ideas.

9. Frequently, lectures are improved if supplemented by simple visual aids, such as specimens, flat pictures, or chalkboard sketches.

10. Many students, especially in the advanced classes, will be going to college. They should be told that lecturing is customary at the college level, and that some practice in learning from this technique while they are still in high school will help them later.

11. The relatively long lecture should include a summarization at its close.

12. The teacher should give the class instruction in taking simple notes and in organizing verbal material. Students should learn to review these notes and to make them part of their cultural growth.

Lecturing, a difficult but useful method of teaching, involves more than verbal fluency. It is a method in itself, but it also supplements practically all other teaching devices, such as demonstration, role playing, the introduction of film lessons, and group discussion. It is not merely a case of all or none; it is pervasive. Teachers will sense when their talks are effective and when they are not.

College teachers, ministers, and public lecturers often supplement their lectures with mimeographed copies of the material they have covered. This may not be a practical suggestion for the high school teacher, but modifications of the idea are worth consideration. These modifications would include mimeographed outlines, summaries, follow-up questions, or projects.

Research bearing on the lecture as a secondary school teaching method is inconsistent. Some researchers have found it notably effective, especially with older students, but other investigators have found other methods of greater value. Method must relate to the educational objectives sought by the school; thus, if the objective is to transfer knowledge or information about a topic, then the lecture method is satisfactory; but if the objective is problem solving or the building of attitudes of inquiry, other methods are preferable (1:280, 851).

ILLUSTRATIONS: VERBAL AND VISUAL

It has already been pointed out that illustrations can accent or underscore abstract lecture ideas. Audiences of all ages become more interested when the speaker clarifies and enlivens his talk with anecdotes, verbal illustrations, witticisms, apt stories, examples, and even pertinent reminiscences. However, injudicious illustrations cheapen the talk or render it valueless. Slang is very much a case in point.

Visual illustration, like verbal, is used to clarify, to render ideas concrete and meaningful. Good teachers try to make their talks more effective by introducing various forms of visualization. An old Chinese proverb says, "One picture is worth a thousand words." This overworked generalization has a point: a few well-placed visual illustrations will often save a great deal of telling, add variety, and stimulate interest.

AUDIO-VISUAL MATERIALS AS A PART OF METHOD

Film, radio, television, and magnetic tape recordings loom large in any discussion of large group instruction. Although these techniques and materials may be successfully used with small groups, and even with individuals, they play their most useful role in communication with large groups. Today's schools make extensive use of these materials, whether the school organization is conventional or whether it uses some form of team teaching. In the following chapter it will be noted that team teaching plans make provision for 40 percent of a student's time to be spent in large group instruction. Specific techniques for the use of many instructional materials are presented in Chapters 9 through 11.

THE ORAL RECITATION

One still finds much secondary school teaching making use of the traditional method, which is commonly dependent upon the "assign-study-recite-test" procedure. This is not a stimulating mode of instruction. Essentially, this method values information simply for the sake of information and rests squarely upon memorization as a technique. It emphasizes specifics—definition, classification, chronology—rather than meaningful wholes. Rote recall rather than understanding or true knowledge is fostered. This type of instruction does not produce the changes in student behavior that the schools are trying to bring about. Then, too, this kind of instruction fails to foster retention of learning.

Under the traditional recitation plan, the teacher is largely a drillmaster. The drill method rests on the assignment of a certain number of pages of a text to be read, problems to be solved, or exercises to be completed. The work is usually completed at home or in a study hall. A question-and-answer period the following day covers the material assigned.

Although many students apparently accept this method of schoolwork, it is doubtful if any really enjoy it. The method is inflexible; pupil interest is usually disregarded. The method is unacceptable to teachers educated in the rationale of modern education, except where the primary purpose is overlearning by means of drill.

The use of the question in group discussion is quite a different thing from questioning in recitation.

QUESTIONS AND QUESTIONING

Although the traditional teaching formula—assign, study, recite, test—has fallen into disrepute, the use of questions is another matter. It is part of the instructional method, to be sure, but it is more than that. It is a useful art or tool and, in the hands of a skillful teacher, serves numerous useful learning purposes. Good questions stimulate thought and encourage students to questions themselves, other students, and the teacher; they act as a sounding board against which the correctness or acceptability of ideas may be tested; they promote the aims of the lesson in a concise manner; and they encourage discussion.

THE NATURE OF QUESTIONS Good questions will have some of these characteristics:

They should be worded in clear, concise, and suitable terms to fit the abilities and ages of the pupils.

They should avoid vague, general queries. As far as ambiguity is concerned, the most common type of faulty question begins with, "What about . . . ?" Such a vague query as "Are there any questions?" also fails to elicit a response. Make the question specific, as in this example, "What causes the earth to rotate on its axis?"

Questions should be asked in a quiet, encouraging manner. Avoid firing questions like pistol shots or conducting a third degree. Students need to be at ease and free from tension.

Key questions should be well worded and thought out in advance; however, there should be flexibility to deviate from preplanned discussion to allow for unexpected and timely questions by students.

Questions should elicit complete responses except in unison drill, not just "yes" or "no." Ask a few significant questions during a discussion period rather than innumerable, minute ones that usually capitalize on the memorization of isolated facts. This is why it was suggested in the chapter on lesson planning that a few key questions be included in daily plans.

Questions should be varied in type. Questions may be asked to elicit simple recall, comparison and contrast, choice of alternatives, classification, illustration or example, or to present a relationship. Other types may ask the students to describe, explain, outline, or organize ideas in any of several ways.

THE APPROACH TO GOOD QUESTIONING   The conditions under which questions are asked should be kept consciously in mind:

There should be an even distribution of questions among the members of the class. Solicit volunteers, call on others.

The conditions under which questions are asked should be varied. Use panels, debates, and other devices. At times student chairmen may conduct the discussion. A pretest may serve as a basis for a good follow-up question period.

Students should be encouraged to direct their remarks to the class. Students should answer each other insofar as possible.

Many questions should be framed so as to relate to current happenings. This is especially important in such a subject as history, for example.

Grade books should not be marked as students recite.

Students should have time to think about what they are going to say before answering a question. The answer may seem simple to the teacher because he has already formulated it, but the student has to have time to organize his thinking. A rewording of the question may be in order, although this is often overdone.

Students should be encouraged to ask questions of the teacher and of other members of the class, but they should be discouraged from making insignificant or irrelevant queries.

Students should show each other common courtesies. Only one speaks at a time, and he should not be rudely interrupted. He should be allowed to have his say.

Students have a right to have their questions answered if they are germane to the discussion. Do not put questions off. If you do not know the answer, it is usually best to admit it. There may be students who have the answer; if so, bring them to your assistance.

Teachers should permit students to question their point of view. There is also a difference between factual and point of view considerations. The teacher must learn to distinguish between the honest questioner and the heckler or time waster.

It is not inappropriate to show sincere appreciation of good student responses. Commend without embarrassing. Give students as much credit as possible for honest responses, even though the responses may need to be supplemented. In cases of incorrect or ungrammatical, poorly constructed replies, use tact in making corrections. When a shy student makes his first contribution, it is better to overlook any deficiency in expression. Sometimes corrections in English for the group as a whole can be made without identifying any one person.

DISCUSSIONS

To discuss, says Webster, is to consider, examine, or investigate the various sides of a question, topic, or problem. A great deal of contemporary secondary school teaching is of this type, especially in literature, social studies, health, speech, and certain aspects of science. The discussion method ranges all the way from a narrow question-and-answer technique to a nondirective approach with the teacher playing a laissez-faire role. Ruja defines the method as an

interchange of questions and answers [*sic*] among students primarily with the instructor playing a role . . . of moderator. The instructor roughly defines the area of discussion and supplies information when directly asked for it or when it illustrates a point already made or . . . poses a question relevant to the topic under consideration. . . . Mostly the activity of the instructor consists in reflecting the content and feelings of students' comments, relating these to one another and to the central topic, and promoting orderly sequences of discussion.[18]

The problem for the beginning teacher is how best to sharpen the discussion technique in order to make it effective in motivating high school students. The discussion technique is an essential part of the democratic process. It assumes that the class is less teacher-centered, whereas the older recitation assumed the opposite. Discussion connotes a give-and-take between teacher and students, and among students themselves. It assumes a willingness to share points of view, to hold an open mind, to weigh evidence. Textbooks, visual media, and all forms of instructional

[18] Harry Ruja, "Outcomes of Lecture and Discussion Procedures in Three College Courses," *Journal of Experimental Education*, 22 (June 1954), 385–394.

materials are used and weighed as the teacher guides the class through the content of his field.

Although discussion is used here in the sense of the primary technique, it will nearly always be supplemented with other techniques. Which ones used will depend upon the maturity of the students, the subject matter, and the objectives sought. These goals range from the more remote ones more or less fixed by the school system and society on to the more immediate ones, which may be set by the teacher or by the teacher and students in a cooperative understanding. The methods used in achieving the former may be thought of as general methods and those used in achieving the latter as specific or course methods, but the two are not discrete; they become one and the same. Then, too, there is no one technique or method, whether in asking questions, lecturing, or whatnot; there are many. Teachers must select from among several appropriate approaches.

A good discussion has the following characteristics:

1. It has *purpose.*
2. It is based on *important information.* Although the primary purpose of the discussion may be to share ideas and opinions, it must issue from factual sources rather than "pooled ignorance."
3. It *draws in every student.*
4. It is founded on *mutual respect* for different opinions and *consideration* for one another's rights.
5. It deals with a topic, problem, or subject that has *significance* for students and for society.
6. It should lead to some *conclusions.*

INTRODUCING THE DISCUSSION   Discussions may be initiated in a number of ways. The most common procedure is, of course, by means of questioning on the part of the teacher. Other methods that provoke a good response are a panel, symposium, buzz session, debate, sociodrama, report, or demonstration.

In laying the foundation for a successful discussion, the teacher needs to take a number of precautions. First of all, *he must be prepared* and make sure that *the class is prepared.* Are the students ready? Have they prepared for the discussion? A warm-up period is often a good idea to get the attention of all the students and to create an interest in the topic. Is everyone comfortable? Is the seating arrangement conducive to discussion? A circle, semicircle, or some other face-to-face arrangement is preferable to a face-to-back arrangement.

CONDUCTING THE DISCUSSION   Actually, conducting an effective lesson through discussion follows the general pattern for lessons of all types. The essential elements are teacher preparation, student preparation and involvement, and possible follow-up, such as research or experimentation.

First of all, *the teacher must be prepared.* This assumes thorough understanding of the content to be covered, and careful planning of the specific topic to be covered. The teacher's understanding assumes a depth of knowledge beyond the two covers of the text. Discussions have a way of ramifying, and the teacher must not depend upon a day-by-day understanding of the material. Such a situation invites disaster because bright students will push a teacher over the brink of limited knowledge. These statements are not a negation of the need for constant day-to-day class preparation. This kind of preparation renews and reorients the teacher to his objectives, content, and most appropriate teaching method.

Student preparation is as important as teacher preparation. Unless students have sufficient background related to the discussion topic or problem, little can be accomplished. Also, there is need for specific information about the problem being discussed. A discussion of the United Arab Republic, the Suez Canal, or Israel, if it is to do more than air superficial opinion, must rest on a political, geographical, and economic understanding as well as knowledge of contemporaneous happenings.

Insofar as the actual discussion itself goes, responsibility is shared by teacher and students, although not on an equal basis. Much of the responsibility may be delegated to students. Although the teacher is seated as a member of the class while a student chairman assumes leadership, in the final analysis the teacher is in charge. The responsibility for worthwhile work belongs to the teacher and cannot be delegated. He is paid for this leadership.

The teacher keeps the discussion from rambling. A clear statement of the problem is imperative. This may call for the exploration of possible interpretations, definitions, and delimitations. A statement of the problem written on the chalkboard helps to prevent rambling. At times the group may wish to develop and place on the chalkboard an outline of the topic. Significant points as they develop may be listed by the teacher or class recorder. For this purpose an overhead projector is often more useful than a chalkboard because the recorder may make entries without leaving the discussion circle. Furthermore, such reports may be saved from day to day for further reference. The teacher evaluates tangential remarks and decides on their relevancy. He decides to what extent the original statement of the problem should be revised—how much new evidence so to speak, will be admitted.

The teacher is responsible for summaries and conclusions. As discussions draw to a close, students should know that the group raised various issues, accepted certain evidence, and rejected other evidence. At times teachers will ask students to write individual summaries for their notebooks; at other times the class recorder may ditto a brief summary to be passed out to the class.

The teacher fosters broad student participation. Some students will be inclined to sit back and let others do the work, and still other students will tend to monopolize the discussion. In both cases the firm hand of the teacher must lead. Shy students should be brought into the discussion possibly by such commonplace remarks as, "Bill, what does this point mean to you?" Dorothy, would you like to speak to this point?" "Oscar, have you some personal information on this problem of interest to the class?" At the same time the fluent, extroverted, enthusiastic student must learn to listen, to share the time with others, to adapt to the situation.

The teacher must recognize individual differences among the participants. Some have unusual ability and verbal fluency, others are limited. Some come from homes where discussion is the rule; others have little or no home participation, nor are cultural topics ever subjects of conversation.

Discussion lessons, like most other lessons, *lead naturally into follow-up activities.* It is unfortunate that bells have to terminate most lessons. Students will usually be reluctant to abandon lively, stimulating discussions. The teacher may wish to suggest that an individual student, or the group, check out some of the leads developed in the class. These activities may well take the students to the library, the audio-visual department, the community, or other sources. Reporting back to the class is a natural activity.

Greater involvement may also come out of the class discussions, involvements for the group as a whole as well as for individuals. Forms of the involvement may be a field trip, a program to be given in the school assembly, or an invitation to certain other classes to join in a cooperative effort of a designated type. Individuals also may come upon ideas so appealing that they develop into a science fair project, a story or a poem that is entered in a national students' competition, or even an enduring career motive.

Student involvement in class discussion may provide for leaders, recorders, evaluators, observers, and resource persons. In such a structuring the teacher delegates most of the responsibility for the discussion to designated or elected class members. In such instances the teacher becomes the chief resource person or an observer. All of these roles assume considerable understanding and responsibility. Students usually welcome this leadership and attempt to carry out their assignments with integrity.

EVALUATING THE DISCUSSION   There are many ways of evaluating a discussion—formal and informal. For his own benefit the teacher may wish to draw up a flow chart either before or after discussion. The prediscussion chart idea might begin with an attempt to illustrate Ruja's interpretation of a group discussion (p. 159) or possibly that implied in the quotation from Sprague and Shirts (p. 153). A postdiscussion chart hopefully is a simon-pure illustration of what has actually taken place—interchanges back and forth among students, leaders, and teacher. This postdiscussion flow chart may very well be prepared by a student who, with a little experience, may become very adept at analysis. Such a chart, enlarged on the chalkboard or shown on an overhead projector for the entire class to see and discuss, may provide a stimulus for livelier and vitalized future discussions.

Several other types of appraisal include group listening to a tape recording of the discussion, and a teacher postdiscussion evaluation against a set of criteria such as these: Did the group accomplish what it set out to do? Did the group stick to the topic? Were the members of the class objective? Was there a shortage of facts and valid evidence? Did everyone participate? Did any "eager beavers" monopolize the class? Will this class experience lead to greater maturity in further discussions?

Now that the lecture and the group discussion techniques have been presented, a comparison of the two may add another dimension to insight. Research has shown no basis for the elimination of either in secondary school practices. Class size, degree of formality, the opportunity to interrupt and ask questions, and the rate of presentation are important variables in both cases. A thorough search of all the literature in connection with the two methods led Stovall to write that

the lecture is equal or superior to group discussion if the criterion is acquisition of information, but discussion produces better results in terms of retention of this type of learning. Discussion has been found to be more effective than lecture as a means of stimulating critical thinking and in aiding students to attain a deeper understanding of subject matter, which is reflected in the ability to make applications of knowledge newly acquired, to interpret, and to draw inferences. Likewise, discussion has a greater effect on attitudes and is more conducive to the development of desirable interpersonal relationships in the classroom.[19]

BUZZ SESSION

Frequently, classes are too large for effective discussion, and teachers may wish to subdivide the class into smaller groups. One method is to approach discussions through the use of temporary small groups. Buzz groups are frequently so small and time is so short that they have been referred to as "Discussion 66," meaning six persons in a group meeting for six minutes, although a buzz session may last for a half hour. The purpose of these groups is exploratory. They are "boosters." Hopefully, they set the groundwork to get a discussion started.

A teacher who is planning to make use of buzz sessions should plan with care. In starting a buzz group, the teacher lights a fuse that can blow up in his face if improperly handled, or he may open doors that would

[19] Thomas F. Stovall, "Lecture vs. Discussion," *Phi Delta Kappan*, 39 (March 1958), 256.

otherwise remain tightly closed. Preplanning and timing are important ingredients in success with the technique. Specific factors include the following:

1. Both students and teacher should have a clear idea of the purpose of the work they are to do and how they are to accomplish it. They do no research; hence they merely arrive at a consensus.

2. Buzz sessions must be timely. They may be announced at the beginning, middle, or near the close of a class period. There is a strategic time in nearly every instance. The purpose is to allow more people to express an opinion on an issue that many members of the group wish to speak about, for example, problems of school policy, grading, class events, and serious controversial subjects.

3. Buzz groups must be small so that all members will have a chance to be heard, but not so small that there is a dearth of ideas and resources. The size may range from three to six.

4. Choosing the members of a buzz group must be simple. The groups are temporary, and their findings are accepted only as a consensus. Groups may be formed alphabetically, by seating proximity, by passing out numbered cards, or by similar arrangements.

5. Buzz sessions are usually short. Students are told that they will have so many minutes to buzz. Experience will help the teacher to judge what is a reasonable limit; if the time is too short, students will be frustrated; if unduly long, they dawdle and become noisy and disinterested. If the teacher sets a five-minute limit for buzzing, but finds that at the end of the time all are working earnestly, he can announce a time extension.

6. Very little organization is needed by the groups, probably only a chairman and a recorder. It is risky to allow the groups to make their own selections. Usually, it is better for the teacher to do it. There are several sides to this matter of selection.

7. Groups are asked to report back to the entire assembled class on the action of the group. This is usually done by the recorder, but it could be done by any member of the group. Group reports may be written on the chalkboard or delivered orally. Sometimes, the group reporters are instructed to get together later and summarize their findings.

PANEL AND SYMPOSIUM

Panels and symposiums may be used in either large or small classes, or in groups smaller than those considered to be of class size. The purpose is to provide an opportunity for a few well-prepared students to discuss pertinent topics. In the panel discussion, four to eight students are selected for the discussion. There is usually a free exchange of ideas among the members of the panel. The presentations are considered impromptu, but the participants are well informed, and should be students with divergent points of view. A panel implies that opposing points of view will be expressed.

A good panel technique places large responsibility on a chairman, who may be selected by the teacher, the class, or the panel members. He acts much as a good chairman of any discussion meeting. He states the topic for consideration, introduces the panel members, and makes a statement or two concerning the topic. It is his responsibility to bring all the members of the panel into action, yet to control the discussion so that the time is not monopolized by a few. Another duty of the chairman is to recognize contributions from the floor. Finally, he summarizes the talks, closes the discussion, and dismisses the panel.

A symposium is slightly different from a panel. It requires members to prepare and present a set speech (statement) of facts or opinions regarding the topic. This is followed by discussion from the floor. The chairman has the same duties as the panel chairman.

Panels and symposiums accomplish approximately the same results. They increase discussion opportunities, and they are appropriate techniques for introduction of new materials, for enrichment as a unit progresses, for culmination of a unit of work, and for motivation.

DEBATE

The debate is a traditional way of promoting discussion in classes. Unfortunately, the debate is usually formal and is limited in participation to two or four of the better students in the class. Attempts have been made to modify the debate by introducing the British style or House of Commons procedure. Two students take affirmative or negative positions and present short arguments of five to eight minutes. A shorter talk is then given by a second member on each side. This debate is followed by open debate from the floor, but these talks must be in affirmative-negative sequence. The goal is to balance the arguments and to make partisanship objective. The main speakers on each side more or less marshal their adherents and set the trend for the speaking sequence.

COMMITTEE

In order to divide classes into smaller groups, teachers often arrange for working committees. These committees may be brought into existence for short-term assignments of a day or two, or they may be given a working schedule of two or three weeks, as, for example, in unit teaching. The use of committees was discussed in Chapter 4 in relation to cooperative planning. The discussion is brought up again here briefly to fix it in mind as one of several techniques for effective instruction of small groups.

DRAMATIZATION

Various forms of dramatization are employed by teachers at all school levels from kindergarten to college. Naturally, some forms and some content are better suited to certain maturity levels than to others. Youth enjoy the dramatic form, and, although some individuals are shy, most of them enjoy both being participants and being members of an audience. Dramatization adds realism, zest, and interest to classwork on many occasions. It tends to promote cooperation and group unity. If kept within reasonable bounds, this technique or methodology can be signally effective.

The chief forms of dramatization used by secondary school teachers are extemporaneous dramatization, role playing, pantomime, and puppetry.

Extemporaneous dramatization and role playing are much the same. There is an informal, impromptu characterization or creation of a role. This action depends on knowledges and interpretations rather than on memorized lines and actions. Historical incidents and social organization lend themselves to role playing. Teachers of English and speech accept dramatization as a natural concomitant, but the activity must fit into the course objectives or it becomes artificial and time wasting. Dramatization or role playing can be just as effectively employed in foreign language classes, or in courses stressing job application, consumer buying, and family living.

Role playing, although simple, must follow certain rules to be effective: situations must be set up with care; roles must be assigned thoughtfully; members of the class who become the audience should understand what the actors will be trying to accomplish and should show proper behavior; actors should be allowed a few minutes for consultation and strategy; the presentation should then be made; and an evaluation of the action by the entire group should follow immediately. The discussion should be frank but not punitive; it should evaluate the portrayal of the incident and not the dramatic merits of the performance. Often scenes can be repeated with profit by changing the actors in the several roles.

Puppetry is a specialized form of dramatization that has many values, but it is often time consuming and difficult to dissociate from entertainment. The use of puppets and marionettes is a highly creative activity that calls for skill and understanding.

High school teachers have found puppetry useful in subjects as home economics, social studies, foreign languages, health, and English. Many educational television programs make extensive use of puppets in serious presentation for children and adults.

Other forms of dramatics can be successfully used at times. Among these forms are pantomimes, mimicry, mock conventions, simulations (a sophisticated form of role playing), skits, and sociodramas. The authors do not make a noticeable distinction between the sociodrama and role playing. "The sociodrama is merely a form of role playing designed to give a better understanding of human relations." [20]

[20] Carter V. Good, ed., *Dictionary of Education*. New York: McGraw-Hill Book Company, Inc., 1959, p. 510.

DEMONSTRATION

A simple way to define demonstration is to point out that it is the learning of a skill through guided performance. But the demonstration is more than a simple act of showing a process or a skill. Although it employs concrete materials and involves a performance, it also presents facts and principles.

The demonstration is useful for teachers and students alike. It may be used in almost any field, and it serves well in the introduction, development, and culmination of units. Teachers tend to use the technique more in the first two stages of a unit, but students probably use it more at the culmination of a unit. For example, students demonstrate skill with typewriters, with science equipment, with sewing machines, or with the horizontal bars in the gymnasium. There are some demonstrations that students can do better than teachers.

EFFECTIVE DEMONSTRATIONS MUST BE PLANNED   The principles of a good demonstration are essentially the same as the principles of any good lesson presentation—preparation, presentation, and follow-up.

Tips for a good demonstration:

Prepare well in advance by practicing the act, by readying all equipment and supplies, by being sure the demonstration will work, and by building confidence.
Prepare the learner in advance in what to look for. Give needed background and purpose.
Be sure everyone can see clearly.
Keep the directions simple; vary the tempo to suit the class.
Check frequently during the performance to know that each step is being followed. Explain and perform simultaneously.
Summarize the entire demonstration. Repeat, if necessary, but ask questions.
Follow up with individual or group tryouts immediately if possible.

Students appreciate good demonstrations, and successful performance builds confidence in the teacher. A junior high school science teacher demonstrated how a volcano erupts. A plaster of paris mound with hollow crater was made in advance on a plywood board. Then in class, with the room semidarkened, the chemicals in the cone were ignited. The eruption occurred on schedule: slow action, rapid action, decreased action. Ash fell at the base of the volcano for a radius of 15 inches. The discussion after the demonstration was spirited, to say the least. Both student motivation and teacher confidence were enhanced by the experience.

Science demonstrations may involve elaborate equipment with many materials. Physical education classes, too, may involve sports or gymnasium equipment. Demonstrations in other subject areas have almost unlimited possibilities, some involving no equipment, or only a few inexpensive, easily collected materials. Mathematics demonstrations may call for templates, measuring forms, cardboard, pieces of wire, crayon, string, and other simple supplies. A student demonstration once used a yardstick, a chalkboard eraser, a clothespin, and a piece of string to show the effects of friction and centrifugal force in driving a car.

Demonstrations vary somewhat in their concreteness, yet even the more abstract ones are basically concrete. In demonstrating how *pi* (π) is derived and computed, the teacher might use a bicycle wheel, a cutout on a feltboard, or a drawing on the chalkboard. In the follow-up, problems are solved or applications are made. How do foreign language students achieve correct pronunciation? They listen to oral demonstrations with full explanation; then they practice.

REMEDIAL TEACHING

For a variety of reasons a few students or an entire class may fail or show predictive failure of the mastery of a unit of work. A failure may be due to a complex of factors, such as a deep-seated background of inadequacy, especially in fundamental skills, a splurge of school social activities, epidemics with more than normal absences, the presence of numerous substitute teachers, poor pacing of the learning schedule, or other causes. Evaluation shows whether there is a need for further work on a given unit. Remedial teaching—reteaching—assumes that normal instruction can proceed once weaknesses have been corrected.

Teachers need to know a great deal about their students; only in this way can they be of most assistance. By observation, by continuous evaluation, by the employment of diagnostic procedures, and by feedback from the students, teachers know which students need remedial help. To locate these students most efficiently, teachers employ a variety of evaluative devices and techniques. These range from teacher-constructed subject tests to standardized achievement tests.

Once the need for remedial help is noted, either for individuals or for groups, a chief concern is with the techniques to be employed. Reteaching may actually be more difficult than original teaching. It should be more specific, direct, and concentrated; actually it is more effective per time unit spent. Techniques may involve coaching, tutoring, or group review and restudy.

Usually, both teacher and students approach remedial work with a negative attitude. Unless the teacher is psychologically and professionally equipped to persuade the students of the value of the work, it will be mechanical and lackadaisical. It means extra time and effort. The teacher's task is to search for motivation as well as effective techniques of correcting the deficiencies.

Two main difficulties are discernible. At times, the trouble is basic and indicates a lack of background understanding. This calls for the development of corrective skills and fundamentals that were supposed to have been previously mastered. Corrective actions along these lines are likely to be long-term measures, and are employed so that they parallel the normal course of study while the regular work goes right ahead. Whether the students are slow learners or gifted has a bearing on the procedures.

The second difficulty is traceable to a topic or unit deficiency. For some reason the class, or certain individuals, simply failed to grasp the work, but the failure is apparently not due to any deep-seated background deficiency. The teacher usually reviews or reteaches in more concentrated form the topic that has caused the trouble. Review here means a new view, a fresh look with an attempt to produce new understanding through reinterpretation and new association. In this instance, work on the next topic of study is delayed until the group achieves a satisfactory mastery level. The time necessary to make the needed adjustments is variable— part of a class period, a few days, or the teacher may feel that the class can move ahead and that the necessary understandings be incorporated in the next unit.

Among the problems that arise in reteaching is what to do for those students who already understand the content. Provision must be made so that they can enrich themselves, move ahead with new studies, or study the subject in greater depth. Possibly there is not much difference in the values of these schemes, but the teacher may find it difficult to convince the students of their merit. At times some teachers are able to deploy the class in such a manner that those who have mastered the work assist those who have not. Such a scheme is one of the hallmarks of a master teacher.

DRILL AND PRACTICE

Although modern educational practice tends to decry drill and repetition, they are still characteristic of practically every school. But ideas about drill have changed. Research shows that spaced, meaningful, and varied drill can be valuable instruction. Just any kind of drill or practice is no longer acceptable. In fact, a golfer, for example, may become even less proficient by practicing his errors. In the schoolroom a student may fail to learn to play a trumpet or to master factoring because he lacks motivation or understanding. Knowledge is seldom retained after one exposure, and skills are not learned in a single trial. Even the professionals on the concert stage or the athletic field, for example, practice, practice, practice. But for anyone to profit from this practice certain conditions need to be met.

Drill, practice, or memory work must be meaningful. It must serve a purpose that students understand and accept. Why should they learn to spell words they never use? Why should students be required to memorize lines of poetry that represent the teacher's choice? Why should students be required to memorize isolated facts or dates that have no significance to them? Why should laws, principles, or rules be learned? If these instances can be made meaningful, they are learned in less time and retained longer. In most instances an endemically related curriculum has more meaning and motivation than one that is not so related.

Drill needs to be spaced as indicated above. By and large, classroom drill tends to be spaced, but students, like golfers, may grow stale through overpractice. Boredom and fatigue cannot produce good results.

The intensity of drill has much to do with its effect on learning. Drill that is vigorous, has mild emotional overtones, and receives heightened attention tends to be effective. This sort of drill is more easily accomplished in independent study than in group study.

Practice must produce correct responses that must be made satisfying in some way.

Procedures to perfect skills and factual learning should be not only interesting but economical of time. Games and contests often have a legitimate use in making drill interesting. Simulation, even in professional education, is receiving considerable attention currently. The use of games and simulated devices is discussed in connection with motivation.

Both individual and group concert exercises have their merits; the first to check accuracy of individual performance, and the latter to produce a feeling of unity. Learning a foreign language, for example, calls for a great deal of drill and practice. In the past much of the drill was of the concert type. Today, the emphasis is on individual practice made effective by language laboratories and other new techniques.

REVIEW

Drill and review are not the same, although the connotations are much the same. Review does not emphasize practice or repetition, but *re-view*, a new view, a new look. Review is a fresh look, or a refresher look at what has been accomplished.

Reviews are chiefly of two types: those occurring daily and those occurring at the culmination of units of work. Daily reviews involve smaller segments of knowledge or skill. The daily review is necessitated largely by the fact that conventional school organization segments learning into fifty-minute periods. Before beginning a new day's work, teachers feel that they need to "heat up" what has gone before. Such a review puts the new work into perspective. The teacher may initiate reviews by asking:

Would you like to review what we did yesterday in class?
What conclusions did we reach yesterday?

To bring ourselves up-to-date, what have we found out since we started studying this topic?

Review may also come at the end of the hour, or it may come at any appropriate time during the period. At the end of the hour, review tends to tie together the strands developed and traced during the hour. Without such a review students frequently leave class feeling frustrated, asking themselves, "What is it all about?" The teacher may begin the review by remarking:

The hour is nearly over; let us see if we can arrive at any conclusions. Will you summarize what we did today?
How did the lesson today relate to that of yesterday (or the last few days)?
Are there any questions about what we did today?
How do you think this lesson relates to the one for tomorrow?

Unit completion review stresses the long view. It may be likened to the ascent of a mountain. Once at the top, a pause is made to look back over the route traveled. This is a time to retrace some of the trials of the trip, to appraise some of the procedures, and to get the picture as a whole. This may have been done segment by segment on the way up, but now it is the overall view that is needed. A review of this type may call for a part of a class period, a full period, or more. It may call for new outside study to fill in gaps that appear. The traditional review for a test is usually dull. Unless new approaches or motivations can be arranged, very little is likely to be accomplished.

MOTIVATION

Teachers employ many incentives to promote positive learning. They recognize that many of their students can be approached through such avenues as the need to explore, to manipulate, to achieve, to know; they recognize, too, the influences of peer groups, general social forces, family, physical environment, variety and modernity of learning materials, and the impact of the personality of the teacher. Motivational procedures vary with the maturity, background, interests, and aspirations of the students. For example, procedures for the kindergarten and senior high school differ in kind and degree; those for the college-bound and the potential dropout, too, differ widely. Students who fall at the extremes in ability will most likely respond differently to motivational effort. A student who can perceive satisfying rewards in self-imposed tasks and disciplines is motivated accordingly, but a less able student will depend largely on more concrete motivational forms.

Motivation is an inner drive and implies an emotion or desire of some sort that energizes the will and causes it to act. An *intrinsic* form of motivation is one originating or existing within the student that causes him to respond, whereas an *extrinsic* one originates outside the student. Simplified, teacher-created incentives are essentially extrinsic, but the student supplies intrinsic motivation. Concepts of motivation undergo change in time, for example, the motivational techniques of the past tended to be extrinsic, but, hopefully, modern ones tend to be intrinsic. However, many good teachers in the past used intrinsic techniques and some of today's teachers still depend on an assortment of external aids— rewards and punishments. These latter devices are questionable, to say the least. Man seems to learn best when he aspires to learn.

Motivation is a conditioning factor; hence acts that are satisfying are reenacted and reinforced—quite different from passive practice or repetition. The youth who practices his tennis strokes because of intrinsic motivation is a different learner from the one who practices merely because of some extrinsic reward or punishment. Two conditions are most important for purposeful learning: student involvement or participation, and learning activities that are relevant and meaningful to the student.

Self-involvement is imperative. It is generally believed that this involvement must be overt; however, recent research tends to validate covert involvement as just as effective as overt in some instances, for example, reaction to an instructional film.

The American Educational Research Association emphasizes that "too much motivation, like too little, can be a dangerous thing" (1:896) and cites some undesirable consequences:

1. There may be "anxiety and overstimulation of ambition without adequate reward."
2. "Errors may be accentuated."
3. Undesirable habits (for example, cheating) may be fostered.
4. "The breadth and scope of learning may be seriously limited."
5. Loss of economy can result if there is engagement in more activity than is necessary.
6. Physical health may be jeopardized.

SOME TECHNIQUES FOR MOTIVATING STUDENTS How can you arouse genuine interest in the work of a class? Normally, a student is interested when he considers an activity important; obviously, if he truly believes an activity to be important he does not need artificial stimulation. Here are some suggestions that may assist in class motivation:

1. Set up a definite *purpose* for each class period. Students must feel that the work is worth doing. Use group goals to supplement individual goals. Follow through on all assignments. If they are not important, do not make them. Course content and objectives should be subject to constant examination. Is the content challenging? Is it socially significant? Is it suited to the maturity level of the students?

2. Use a *variety* of learning activities, methods, and materials. Think about ways of introducing purposeful variety into classwork. Talk to other teachers. Read the professional journals. Introduce concrete learning materials (films, resource speakers, field trips, projects). Consider surprise, suspense, and curiosity in connection with method.

3. Encourage wider student *participation*. Get all students involved. Involvement may be only a matter of degree, but all the students belong to the class.

4. Place more *responsibility* on students for their own learning. Well-placed responsibility inflates the ego. Find ways of quietly encouraging better students to feel that they have some responsibility for group progress. Let the students share in the planning.

5. Keep students *informed of their progress*. Hand back papers promptly. No one likes to work in the dark. Encourage students to learn to evaluate their own work. The cybernetic principle of feedback is most applicable here. Feedback in its multiple forms promotes rapport between teacher and student, and enables the latter to establish controls over his own tasks, skills, feelings, and knowledges.

6. *Relate schoolwork to the world* in which we live. Tie principles and theories to contemporary developments if appropriate.

7. Set up learning situations where every student may experience some degree of *success*. Success is a prime motivator. "Nothing fails like failure." Commend if possible.

8. Establish *an environment* that is attractive and comfortable. This has been stressed at several places in this book.

9. Show *enthusiasm* for the subject you teach. Convince your students that your subject is important. They may have entered the class with a prejudice against it. Subtly correct their bias, not by preachment, but by positive action.

10. *Individualize* assignments and tasks. Motivation is largely an individual matter. Try to fit the work to the needs and capabilities of each.

11. *Build both group and individual esprit de corps.* A team spirit is helpful, but it need not rest solely on competition.

12. *Do not overlook home influences.* Parents are first-line allies. They should be kept informed of the progress and difficulties of their children at all times. In this area feedback is most important.

13. Keep in mind that as a motivational force *peer group approval* is more effective than teacher-imposed pressure.

14. Recognize the fact that *proper motivation is closely related to creativity*. Teachers in the arts are aware of this. Science teachers know that "Science Fair" projects possess high motivation and that this motivation closely relates to creativity.

SOME MOTIVATIONAL SITUATIONS Besides the specific suggestions for building incentives numerous situational conditions add much to teachers' efforts to stimulate students. Sometimes critics want to label motivational approaches and contrived situations as "frills," something that tags them as inferior to so-called real learning. The point will not be debated except to say that the proliferation of devices and techniques has been enormous in the last decade or so, and there appears to be no diminution in the near future.

EDUCATIONAL GAMES AND SIMULATIONS   Since 1960 much attention has been devoted to the development of educational games and devices that simulate experience. These contrivances provide both a method and a realistic motivation in certain curricula in which it has been difficult to apply other motivational approaches, particularly in social studies, guidance, vocational opportunities and community problems. Most of the simulated devices provide for participants (students) to assume designated roles and to act out a part. In many cases there are no "correct answers" but participants are encouraged to employ all their concepts in discussing a problem. Teachers provide the needed introduction of the problem (stage-setting), materials, and follow-up. Professional teachers' manuals are available for the panoply of researched and published devices.

Simulated experience devices provide

1. highly stimulating and realistic motivation;
2. opportunities for participants to work their way through designated problems without fear of reproof, criticism, or failure; the teacher's role is diminished;
3. applications suitable for use both at junior and senior high levels, and for students who are slow, average, or bright;
4. opportunities for intuitive thinking and an analytical approach to problems;
5. rather realistic opportunities for decision making, often based on a multiplicity of complex factors;
6. opportunities for students to see the results of their actions when applied to a significant situation;
7. springboards for valuable discussion of problems and topics;
8. avenues leading to enrichment, involvement, and applications of many learning skills;
9. more integration and interrelations between the various topics and units in a given field of study; also, wide opportunities for transfer of ideas and skills; and
10. opportunities for students to cope with situations that may lead to personal growth and self-confidence.

Obviously these benefits do not come about automatically. Teachers must prepare classes for the use of the simulation. The device is not used in isolation; it must relate to known objectives and units of study. Like most motivating techniques, simulations must be followed up intelligently.

Educators who are not convinced of the value of these simulated approaches point out that research has not established that learning is greater than that which occurs in the use of conventional methods. Some feel that the situations are artificial and that some of the games are vulnerable to abuse. Finally, some contend that the so-called involvement is largely excited classroom activity merely for the sake of activity.

Much of the impetus for research and development of these devices has been made possible through grants-in-aid by the United States Office of Education with funds provided by the National Defense Education Act (NDEA) and the Elementary and Secondary Education Act (ESEA). Other financing has come through some of the national foundations and universities. Noteworthy work has been done at Johns Hopkins University in cooperation with the Baltimore Public Schools, Northwestern University with Inter-Nation Simulations (INS), Systems Development Corporation (PLANS), and Western Behavioral Science Institute in cooperation with certain high schools in San Diego County (SIMILE— not an acronym but a comparison or similarity).

Project SIMILE has researched several simulation devices but its chief interest has been in developing NAPOLI and CRISIS. NAPOLI (NAtional POLItics) is a simulation in which participants serve as members of a legislature, representing one of two political parties and one of eight geographical regions. NAPOLI combines aspects of both houses of the United States Congress, illustrating the legislative process and the representative nature of democracy rather than the exact procedure of either house. The goal of each participant is to be reelected at the end of the simulation by working toward the passage or defeat of eleven bills before the House. As he appraises the legislation each participant experiences conflicts between his party, his constituency, and his personal views. Through speeches, negotiation, and logrolling he is also subject to pressures from other members of the legislature.[21]

The simulation CRISIS is structured so that participants form teams of three to six members to manage the affairs of six fictional countries. The teams are briefed on the conditions of their countries as to military positions, social and political problems, finances, and so on. In order to accomplish their national goals the teams may form international alliances, create world police forces, sponsor fact-finding commissions, and even go to summit conferences. As the simulation progresses, participants become deeply involved in the affairs and decision making of their fictional nation.

---

[21] *NAPOLI: Teacher's Guide.* La Jolla, Calif.: Western Behavioral Science Institute, 1966, p. 4.

The directors of Project SIMILE state that they believe simulations are important because they are conventional enough in appearance and superficial effect to gain acceptance into the public school system, but at the same time they excite students about learning, help them to learn how to learn (by provoking inquiry), provide experimental tools for learning, and influence the classroom climate so that subsequent sessions allow for more relevant learning activities (12:21).

AUDIO-VISUAL   The "new media" instructional materials provide both dynamic motivation and instructional methodology. Modern schools are equipped with expensive equipment for the use of teachers. Students of today, almost without exception, accept audio-visual materials and communication media as part of their world. Their preferences for these media are marked. Chapter 10 discusses the values in detail. Briefly, they provide the following:
1. New scope and depth to the motivational repertoire
2. Understandings based on concrete materials and ideas
3. Appeal for all the senses
4. Adaptability for all ages and abilities
5. Illustration, clarification, and understandings
6. Helpfulness in the learning and perfecting of skills
7. Stimulation for further study

Audio-visual materials are not subject areas. They are instructional materials and techniques that can be applied to practically any discipline. Their scope will be discussed in later chapters.

THE LABORATORY SITUATION   In Chapters 10 and 11 the laboratory is discussed as an instructional technique. Here we merely emphasize its function as a motivational device, as a "discovery-inquiry" approach to learning.

Students often find incentives in laboratory situations that are lacking in other instructional approaches. Students entering high school may be especially intrigued. Many of the new departmental curricula employ a laboratory approach; examples are found in mathematics, biology, physical science, chemistry, and foreign languages.

Like all motivational approaches, the laboratory design has limitations: time may be wasted; the study may become mechanical and passive; there are limited opportunities for verbal expression; and it is difficult to apply the approach to all curriculum areas.

TRIPS, FIELD RESEARCH, RESOURCE PERSONS, COMMUNITY STUDY   Here again these materials and resources are discussed fully in Chapter 10, but as motivational resource activities they should not be overlooked here. Implementation in these areas has not been spelled out as have simulations; hence each teacher must study and experiment with applications. Some suggestions on utilization of these resources will be found in Chapter 10.

THE SCHOOL LIBRARY   Another important resource for motivation is the library. As a general rule, librarians are highly trained people who are eager to encourage students to use their materials. As a motivational source, the library may possibly have greater applicability to those with well developed reading skills. Slow learners, however, find reading fascinating when materials suitable to their maturity level are made available to them.

MISCELLANEOUS SITUATIONS   There is no end to motivational approaches to learning. Imagination and industry on the part of the teacher are the only limits. During the last few years Title III of the Elementary and Secondary School Act has stimulated many innovations in education, some of which are basic motivational techniques and approaches. During 1967 some $208 million was budgeted for this purpose.[22]

TEACHER MOTIVATION   It is not difficult to understand that teachers who are themselves highly motivated are likely to do a better job of motivating their students. The teacher who "loves his work" does not depend primarily on external rewards, such as those furnished by the administration, students, parents, or pressure groups; he experiences satisfaction and enjoyment from watching students grow and master their tasks. Such a teacher does not rely on authoritative allocation of values. He is inspired and motivated from within.

Research indicates that students prefer teachers who are friendly, considerate, and fair, know their subject and how to teach it, are enthusiastic about their subject and can make it interesting, are businesslike, and can maintain good classroom control. In short, students are placing their stamp of approval on teachers who are intrinsically motivated.[23]

WHAT WOULD YOU DO?   It may be well to try to recall some personal classroom experiences at this point. If the recall can get down to specifics the exercise will have value. Let us begin by listing a dozen units or topics of learning that all have studied at one time or another: factoring; Shakespeare (life and times as well as the reading of a certain play); the causes of World War I; tariff (late nineteenth and early twentieth centuries); development of a free public school system; Bismarck and German expansion; nationalism in Europe; communicable diseases; the nitrogen cycle; diet; the vitamin complex; and volcanic explosion. The list is only illustrative.

How did your teacher motivate his students to study these topics?
How successful was the attempt?

---

[22] *Scholastic Teacher*, December 7, 1967, p. 9.
[23] American Educational Research Association, *Encyclopedia of Educational Research*, 3d ed., Chester W. Harris, ed. New York: The Macmillan Company, 1960, pp. 481–491; N. L. Gage, ed., *Handbook of Research on Teaching*. Chicago: Rand McNally & Company, 1963, pp. 566–570.

Can you suggest additional approaches without researching the topic?
What should be the focus of attention in trying to motivate such topics?
How much provision can or should be made for individual differences?

The following examples illustrate how a few teachers have tried to provide motivation:

Mr. A. began his study of "Skin Disorders" in health education by bringing to class a large number of advertisements clipped from local papers dealing with acne, blackheads, psoriasis, itching, and skin discoloration. The discussion soon extended to similar radio and TV advertising. Mr. A. then asked the students to turn in unsigned lists of personal skin problems.

Miss H. showed her ninth-grade French class a film that depicted a French home in which there were three teen-age youths.

A study of our town was started by the social studies teacher, who showed a film on Colonial Williamsburg.

Most of the students in a drama class had never seen a play other than a few school productions. As a group the class attended a matinee performance of *South Wind* at a local theater.

"The first day of the unit the students walked into an environment which was definitely Japanese. In front of the room was a wall map of Japan. But the best materials were on the table in front of the room, some of the many products made in Japan" (8:447).

"I have a large coil which, as you can see, is insulated wire wound together. I am going to connect the two ends of the coil to this current-measuring instrument called a galvanometer. Here is a friend we have already studied, a bar magnet. Watch what happens to the needle of the galvanometer when I push the north pole of the magnet inside the coil of wire [needle moves to the left]. Now watch when I pull the magnet out this way [needle moves to the right]. Now I am going to go through the same operations once more. You ask me questions that will help you to decide why the galvanometer reacted the way it did" (8:447).

During the study of "Westward Expansion," the teacher brought to the class a hearty, elderly gentleman who talked about cattle branding, big drives, fencing, and the life of cowboys. The speaker brought with him a collection of branding irons used in the United States and Mexico, pictures of brands, spurs, and some barbed wire.

The senior English teacher had the print shop print up a dummy front page of a newspaper with a 4-inch headline—DICTATOR SLAIN. As the class entered Mr. W. sat at his desk presumably reading the paper, but the front page of the paper was facing the class.

Mr. C. introduced the study of *Macbeth* by showing the class a set of 2-by-2-inch slides he had made over several years. The slides showed the characters of *Macbeth* in costume taken at the time of a dress rehearsal of the play by a local group a few years earlier.

Upon entering the classroom a junior high school English class noticed on the teacher's desk a small tree (about 3 feet tall) bare of leaves. Instead of leaves there were 2-inch strips of paper clipped to the twigs. The papers contained a variety of words and short phrases. Immediately a wild chorus of voices asked, "What is it?" The teacher answered, "It is a word tree."

The Problems of Democracy class of Mr. V. had developed an attitude of indifference and lethargy probably because three of the boys in the class were going into the army soon and were merely marking time at school. Their behavior had infected the rest of the class. Mr. V. brought to class a tape recording (Dr. Meyer) of brainwashing in a Korean prison camp.

With the help of selected students, Mrs. J. used a press camera and took fourteen shots of making a buttonhole. The pictures were enlarged to size 10 by 14 inches and mounted. This project seemed to give the sewing class a boost.

To introduce a unit on poetry, the senior English teacher showed a set he had made of lantern slides of animals. He accompanied each picture with a tape recording of an appropriate poem by Ogden Nash, Rainer Rilke, or William Blake, and background music from Camille Saint-Saëns.

To introduce his junior high school class to the study of the novel, Mr. K. selected *The Lance of Kanana* by Harry W. French (Abd El Ardavan). To start things off, Mr. K. brought to his class a Muslim turban and a sheik's white robe. These were fitted on one of the boys before the class. Next, two short films were shown—*Desert Nomads* and *Mohammedan World*.

The junior high social studies class began the unit on soil erosion by listening to the record *Grand Canyon Suite* (Capitol 33⅓, Ferde Grofé) and two days later saw *The Grand Canyon*, a film produced by Walt Disney.

In connection with the study of Central Europe, the teacher used a large wall map of the Austro-Hungarian Empire at its height. Over this he placed an amber cellophane map of present-day Austria drawn to the same scale.

The day before the President was to address Congress, the P.O.D. teacher asked his class members to draw up a list of topics they thought would be mentioned in the speech. A summary of the list was placed on the chalkboard with a "Please Do Not Erase" beside it. The following day the class listened to the President on the radio. Then another list of what the President actually talked about was placed beside the original one.

The teacher introduced the unit "Exploring Music" by playing a 15-inch tape recording he made with ten musical interludes, varying in scope from classical to modern, from sacred to secular, from opera to jazz. Examples of the selections included Verdi's *Rigoletto, Winchester Cathedral, Dance of the Sugar Plum Fairy, and Silent Night.*

A Michigan high school typing teacher placed a large map of the United States on a side wall. A route from Michigan to Florida was outlined with a felt pen. Members of the typing class were to travel along this route each day at the rate of 100 miles for each correct-word-per-minute of typing beyond the speed attained at the time the project was started. For example, a student whose typing rate increased from 35 to 60 words a minute made a net increase of 25 words, which, when multiplied by 100, gave him a distance of 2500 miles on the map. Map tacks and colored labels indicated progress of the trip. The labels were moved each day in accordance with the student's speed of improvement. The project lasted twelve weeks.

A junior high school science teacher introduced the study of volcanoes by staging an explosion in the class. The teacher took a piece of 4-by-4-foot plywood and built up on it a thin volcano shell about 12 inches high. A small amount of magnesium powder had been placed in the hollow, to which a fuse from the outside led. With the window shades partly drawn for dramatic effect, the fuse was lighted. The top of the volcano was blown off and settled around the base on the plywood foundation. (*Note:* Such a demonstration must be very carefully staged and rehearsed.)

SELECTED READINGS

1. American Educational Reesarch Association, *Encyclopedia of Educational Research*, 3d ed., Chester W. Harris, ed. New York: The Macmillan Company, 1960.

2. Carlson, Elliott, "Games in the Classroom," *Saturday Review*, 50 (April 15, 1967), 62–64, 82.

3. Cherryholmes, Cleo, "Development in Simulation of International Relations in High School Teaching," *Phi Delta Kappan*, 46 (January 1965), 227–231.

4. Early, Margaret, ed., *et al*, "Perspectives in Reading No. 2," *Reading Instruction in Secondary Schools*. Newark, Del.: International Reading Association, 1964.

5. Getzels, J. W., "Creative Thinking, Problem-Solving, and Instruction," in *Theories of Learning and Instruction*, Ernest R. Hilgard, ed. *The Sixty-third Yearbook of the National Society for the Study of Education, Part I.* Chicago: University of Chicago Press, 1964, pp. 240–267.

6. Harris, Albert J., ed., *Readings on Reading Instruction*. New York: David McKay Company, Inc., 1963.

7. Hunkins, E. P., "Using Questions to Foster Pupil Thinking," *Education*, 87 (October 1966), 83–87.

8. Klausmeier, Herbert J., and William Godwin, *Learning and Human Abilities*, 2d ed. New York: Harper & Row, Publishers, 1966.

9. Miller, Richard I., *Perspectives on Educational Change*. New York: Appleton-Century-Crofts, Inc., Division of Meredith Corporation, 1967.

10. Pulliam, Lloyd, "The Lecture—Are We Reviving Discredited Teaching Methods?" *Phi Delta Kappan*, 44 (May 1963), 382–385.

11. Sears, Pauline S., and Ernest R. Hilgard, "The Teacher's Role in the Motivation of the Learner," in *Theories of Learning and Instruction*, Ernest R. Hilgard, ed., *The Sixty-third Yearbook of the National Society for the Study of Education, Part I.* Chicago: University of Chicago Press, 1964, pp. 182–209.

12. Sprague, Hall T., and R. Garry Shirts, "Exploring Classroom Uses of Simulation, Project SIMILE." La Jolla, Calif.: Western Behavioral Science Institute, 1966, 22 pp. (Mimeo.)

13. "Teaching Science without Lectures," *Educational Technology*, 7 (January 15, 1967), 16–18.

14. Watson, Goodwin, ed., *No Room at the Bottom—Automation and the Reluctant Learner*. Washington, D.C.: National Education Association, 1963, "Motivation to Learn," pp. 18–29; "Motivation to Achieve," pp. 63–75.

15. Wrightstone, J. Wayne, "What Research Says to the Teacher," *Class Organization for Instruction*, Bulletin 13. Washington, D.C.: National Education Association, 1961.

Cooperative planning by teachers is a characteristic of professional maturity, whether in matters of instructional procedures as in team teaching or in discussing policies of welfare and professionalism. (Courtesy Pittsburgh [Pennsylvania] Public Schools.)

Youth want to be heard. Small discussion groups provided by contemporary schools offer unequaled opportunities for dialogue on issues ranging from the morality of King Arthur's knights to today's illicit use of drugs. In small groups students advance and defend ideas. (Courtesy Glenbrook South High School [Glenview, Illinois], photo by Ed Baker and J. F. Borowski.)

Although the relationship between creativity and intelligence may be unclear, the response of a student to a freely chosen individual project is limited only by his imagination and effort. Listlessness and indifference disappear. (Courtesy West Junior High School [Warren, Ohio].)

Some hands go up, some do not—a familiar scene in many classrooms. Modern teachers are becoming increasingly aware of newer approaches to materials and procedures that provide for a more individualistic style of learning. (Courtesy Raytheon Education Company.)

CHAPTER 8

Teaching Procedures: Individualized and Varied Instructional Procedures

The discussion thus far has been related to activities involved in the instruction of large and small groups. These groups are made up of individuals, and it is with and about these individuals that we are concerned. A democratic society accepts the adage that the chain is no stronger than its individual links.

To the schools come all the pupils. This is a broad statement because it includes the gifted, the slow, and the average insofar as scholastic abilities are involved; it also includes the shy and the aggressive; the balanced and the maladjusted; those who have a high degree of self-concern and those with concern for others; those who enjoy ideas and those who enjoy people and things; those who have natural artistic talents and those who do not. Teachers have always been concerned with individuals, whether their instruction is organized around large classes, small classes, or a single student. The question is how they can best give optimum service.

People must react individually in order to learn. They can profit from the shared experience of others, but in order really to learn, persons must in some way make these experiences their own. To learn, they repeat or interpret the experience. Learning is unique in many ways; it cannot be forced upon a person, except in a minor sort of way. Each person's learning pattern is his own.

In recent years there has been a resurgence of individualized work in the secondary school. The climate today favors extending capable students more than was done a few years ago; also, slower students are provided with greater assistance with their scholastic and personal problems. Various plans are being tried; their applications and values vary widely. Teachers will do well to evaluate these plans and select those that seem appropriate.

MEANS INVOLVED IN INDIVIDUAL INSTRUCTION

In order to accomplish individual study and learning, teachers provide varied activities. All the means involved in individual instruction have some merit, but some have more than others. We shall discuss the ones most commonly used.

INDIVIDUAL PROJECTS AND PROBLEMS

Project work allows much leeway for students to pursue interests in depth if they have the initiative, ability, skills, and persistence. All students have these traits but in different degrees. Consequently, the teacher recognizes that student projects will vary in comprehensiveness and creativity.

SELECTING A PROJECT   Teachers guide and direct students in the selection of projects, but they are careful not to dictate. Student selections are made after listening to the teacher's talks on significant topics, reading, observing demonstrations, examining community problems, discussing national problems, talking with peers, viewing films and television programs, and the like. For some students, the teacher may have to prepare a list of projects from which selections are to be made. The hope is that this will be rare.

Project approaches in learning are appropriate for both group and individual instruction. The chief ingredient in project teaching is motivation, for students need sufficient interest in a given activity to initiate, plan, execute, and evaluate it. Many students have enough drive and inquisitiveness to have one or more projects or problems they would like to tackle in a concerted manner. For those who have not, the teacher's job is to arouse them and to guide them into an activity they will find interesting and worthwhile.

These are the main questions in deciding what projects to choose: Is the activity of value to the student? Is it appropriate for the student in terms of time and talent? Are there sufficient resources—facilities, equipment, personnel—to achieve a solution? Is the project pertinent to the course?

COMPLETION AND EVALUATION   Although students will require assistance from the teacher, each will work out the project largely by himself. He will need to read, to explore, to investigate, and to create as the project progresses. Such activities help him to gain the knowledge, insight, skill, and appreciation that are parts of his education.

At the outset the student should know that his project will require real effort on his part. He will not be able to ride along on the ideas and efforts of others. He should work out his plan and submit it to the teacher for approval. This plan will entail objectives; procedures or plan of attack; materials needed; and limitations, difficulties, or possible obstacles that can be foreseen.

Many people have the idea that the project is a useful technique only with superior students. This is not true. Slower students profit enormously from project work, but they require more assistance from the teacher, more encouragement, a longer time in which to accomplish their objectives, and simpler problems. A successful individual study project may stimulate the student as no other activity can. Success is a precious coin, and all students need a certain amount of it. The student who all through school has been the last to be chosen by his peers in games or class activities, and the first to be eliminated in competition, needs the feel of success. The project may bring this feeling. Experience has shown that successfully completed projects develop confidence.

Usually, projects are judged by the teacher, but it is also important to have the student, and possibly other students, judge what has been accomplished. In an art or shop class the project is visible and of course is seen by everyone. In social studies, science, foreign language, or literature this may not be so. In most instances, therefore, the work accomplished should be brought to the attention of the class. Even in making a presentation of his project, the pupil learns.

SUPERVISED STUDY

Study is almost always an individual matter, although there are occasions when two or more students study together to solve problems, to improve pronunciation skills, to create tangible devices, or to plan activities.

Supervised study is usually considered a part of regularly organized class periods in which students work individually at their tasks. Teachers, as a result of their own initiative, or in accordance with school policy, may use a part of each class period—a quarter, a half, or more—for directed or supervised study. The remainder of the period, and it may be at the beginning or at the end of the hour, is used for such conventional class work as discussion, review, teacher talks, or film study. Such occasions have real advantages because the student can call upon the teacher for assistance when it is most needed. The teacher, on the other hand, has an opportunity to see the student react as he works alone on his problems. The teacher is observer, helper, and guide. Such study or work periods may take place in the classroom, in the library, in the laboratory, in the community, or in whatever setting may be appropriate. During a study period the teacher has to be alert, judicious, and resourceful. On the spur of the moment he must often decide how much help to give a student or where to send him for additional assistance. The teacher must be sensitive to the welfare of all the students and see that the rights of all are protected. He must decide how much interchange of ideas is best for the pupils, whether there shall be quietness, or how much movement about the classroom should be permitted.

Supervised study is not a time for the teacher to catch up on some personal reading or letter writing, or on correcting student papers. He must be on call by all students. Usually, he moves among the class, ready to give assistance. Less closely supervised work is carried over to free periods or for work at home. Supervision in the laboratory depends upon student maturity and the nature of the work. The laboratory will be discussed as a separate topic later.

WORK-STUDY SKILLS

Secondary school teachers know very well that they cannot assume their students have learned how to work and study. Because for want of these skills many students fail; the procedures and habits of study must be learned in high school. The junior high school, in particular, is concerned with improving the work-study skills of the pupils.

Study skills are more than just the ability to read with comprehension. Also involved is the ability to take notes, to write a paper, to do reference work, to make written and oral reports, to skim and to read carefully, to get ideas from the spoken word, and to plan and outline. But study skills involve recall and association of knowledge as well as acquisition. Weakness in any of these often spells inefficient and unsuccessful work.

EVERY TEACHER IS INVOLVED   The promotion of good work-study habits and skills is the business of every teacher. Some schools have tried initiating general how-to-study courses, but these have met with indifferent success. Such courses are popular with neither teachers nor students. There is a specificity about how to study, a uniqueness about studying each course. Although the ability to read with reasonable speed and understanding is a general one, there are also specific reading skills in every subject. For example, reading and analyzing a mathematical problem involves different skills from those used in reading and interpreting a poem. This understanding has led to a belief among teachers that work-study skills should be thought of as interdisciplinary.

Much of the goal of teaching students how to study can be accomplished in making assignments. Teachers know that it is pointless to make such remarks as "Study well," "Do this carefully," and the like. Better results are achieved, first, by making sure that every student knows what the assignment is, its length, purpose, and whether it involves just reading, written work, or problem solutions. To accompany and direct reading assignments, teachers furnish students mimeographed study guides, lists of questions, outlines, exercises to be followed, or problems to be solved. Sometimes the work is written on the chalkboard, but this is a wasteful activity for the teacher, and for the students, too, if it is to be copied, and if the directions are more than simple page notations.

PUPIL EFFORT   Again, it is the pupil who must finally do the job. If he expects to learn, no teacher can do it for him. He must be so motivated that he desires to read, to learn new vocabulary, to know more about a topic, or to experiment further. Concentration is particularly an individual matter. Good study skills are basic and important, as are the habits and attitudes of work.

Teachers have been prone to assume that every child has a desire to learn, to excel in schoolwork. Instructors have expected that the home would nurture this desire to learn. Today's teachers go beyond this assumption. They try to show students why they should work, why effort is important to them. This they do, not by mere admonition, but by precept, by specific acts, and by creating a learning environment.

HOMEWORK   Homework is essentially individual work, and the teacher assumes that the student possesses proper work-study skills to do it by himself.

Homework has become an issue in some communities with teachers and parents taking sides—sometimes one way and sometimes another. Many relevant questions soon arise when homework is considered: How much work is reasonable? Should it be the same for all students? How should it be evaluated? Should students with out-of-school jobs and chores be excused?

Teachers should become familiar with the policy of the school, as well as the abilities and maturity levels of the students. Regardless of the policy of the school, the teacher should be aware of the problems related to homework assignments.

In the first place, when a teacher assigns homework without knowing what other teachers expect of a student, as is usually the case, demands upon the student's time can easily become excessive. Furthermore, it is well to realize that a student may engage in activities other than classwork in school which he considers important, for example, private music lessons. (Homework was also discussed in Chapter 6. A review of this section will be helpful.)

WORK-STUDY SKILLS NEED MOTIVATION   The idea that good work-study skills are geared to motivation has been implied in the foregoing paragraphs. Unless the interest and the will to study are present, the teacher faces a losing battle in teaching efficient work-study skills and in building effective habits.

Wiles has said, "a motivated student is one with a purpose"; and "Motivation is closely associated with the values that a pupil holds" (23:208–209). Purpose is many-headed, and is developed in various ways and under various conditions. Motivation in association with attitudes and skills is learned, and there is much teachers can do to bring it about. This is what the psychologists call the "law of effect." Teachers do have difficulty in providing "continuing reinforcement." Motivation and all other behavior patterns must bring satisfaction to the student. The subject of motivation was discussed in the preceding chapter. At this time our objective is merely to point out that the relationship between work-study skills and incentive exists and is very vital.

INVESTIGATION AND REPORT

In independent work much emphasis is placed on locating and collecting data, on organizing material, and on reporting it.

LIBRARY   The emphasis on individual study places a new value on the library as a research center. Mahar has pointed out that more and more class library units are being developed, and that libraries are being used less and less as mass study halls.[1] As gifted students are given more encouragement, as more project assignments are made, and as the science interest continues, the library becomes increasingly important. It will be more fully discussed later in the chapter.

New types of instructional materials, such as prerecorded tapes, discs, and programmed devices, should be housed in the book library or the audio-visual center. In some instances, a school has a valuable collection of foreign language tapes. These may quite appropriately be catalogued and housed in a library or audio-visual center, or even in the expanded facilities of the language laboratory. Teaching machines and programmed materials must be housed somewhere—in the library, the A-V center, or in a separate laboratory. Also, there must be space for their use, probably for group instructional use, but more likely for individual study.

FIELD INVESTIGATION   Without question today's students do more research and investigation than did students of a decade or two ago. Reading and research go beyond textbooks, even beyond the library, as students search for primary data in order to document their answers to dynamic questions and problems. Singly or in committee groups, students probe the community for the raw data it holds.

REPORTING   Sharing the results of study and investigation has a new emphasis in the high school of today. Lackadaisical oral reports before a class are passé. Even book reports go far beyond telling the story. They resemble researched literary criticisms. Reports are made in writing and orally. Oral reports may be made individually or may be a part of a panel or a seminar. It is not unusual to tape reports so that they can be used by other classes or individuals. Taped reports may also be kept for use in later years.

---

[1] Mary Helen Mahar, "Promising Practices in Secondary School Libraries," *National Association of Secondary School Principals Bulletin,* 43 (November 1959), 13–19.

THE LABORATORY IN INDIVIDUAL STUDY

The laboratory is becoming less of a facility where large classes of students work on common assignments performing experiments by recipes. Much of this sort of activity is performed by the teacher as demonstration. But laboratories are places for depth study, investigation, analysis, and research by bright students, and students with real, identified problems and projects. There is much about science that can be read, but there is also that which must be tested, measured, manipulated, and perceived.

Group work will also be found in the science laboratory, the industrial arts shop, and the music and art studios. A much more permissive climate prevails in these situations than in most discussion classrooms. The teacher allows as much freedom as the situation will permit. But when one or more students interfere with the work of others, waste time in aimless wandering, endanger the safety of fellow students, or create chaos, their freedom will have to be restricted for the good of the group. The laboratory instructor will likely circulate about the room to give help wherever needed.

Workshop and laboratory sessions for nonscience and nonshop classes are becoming increasingly popular with high schools. It is realized that learning is more than reading and talking. Today, there are English laboratories, mathematics laboratories, economic laboratories, and so on. Indeed, any classroom can be arranged for a laboratory type of activity. The laboratory feature calls for "space freedom," along with movable chairs, tables, counters, racks, closets, electrical connections, darkening facilities, library units, exhibit cases, tackboards, filing cases, and similar features.

Procedures or methods are more important than the physical features because learning focuses on individuals, committees, small groups, or average-sized classes. All students may be on a common task, or they may be working on numerous projects or assignments. In the workshop or laboratory organization, a clear understanding by students of their goals is important.

IMPROVISING   Few schools are fortunate enough to have the variety of facilities and fixtures that modern-day organization and teaching method favor. The situation at its best was outlined above. But, if teachers do not have such ideal conditions, they can, if they wish, improvise. Students are extremely cooperative and, together with the teacher, can work wonders. With the teacher's desk, a worktable, and a few side chairs, many new groupings are possible. By making shelves from plain boards and construction blocks, files from orange crates or apple boxes, tack space from a wall covered with monk's cloth or burlap, the teacher can create a working area with a new atmosphere.

In some instances, schools, even with average or better science laboratory facilities, have found that some of their gifted students need more equipment and assistance than the school is able to provide. At times cooperative arrangements have been made with large industrial concerns in the community for a few students to go to the industrial laboratories on released time to pursue their advanced work.

PROGRAMMED INSTRUCTIONAL MATERIALS, COMPUTERIZATION, AND OTHER MATERIALS AND TECHNIQUES DESIGNED FOR INDIVIDUAL INSTRUCTION

PROGRAMMED INSTRUCTIONAL MATERIALS

In the last analysis most instructional materials are designed for individual use. Books, although used individually, are mass media. They are bought in great numbers and passed from one class or one individual to another. Workbooks, small outline maps, pamphlets, and many similar items are classified as consumable media. Programmed lesson materials (see Chapter 11) are sometimes bound as books, but in other instances they are provided as sheets, rolls, or strips for use in a teaching machine. Some of the programmed materials are consumed; others are not. Nontextbooks on the shelves of the library act as programmed, nonconsumed learning materials. They are used by one student at a time to help solve an individual problem.

It is quite likely that the profession will see a great deal more of teaching machines and programmed learning in the years ahead. These programs base one of their chief claims on the fact that they are geared for individual instruction. The need may be for remedial assistance, for drill (reinforcement), or for advanced work in a subject or area. In the first two instances, the teacher's time is saved, and in the last, gifted high school students may be forging ahead with work ordinarily done in the first year or two of college. This is notably true in the sciences, mathematics, and foreign languages. Thousands and thousands of copies of the programmed book *English 2600* have been sold to college students over the country, not because it is a required text, but because it permits a sharpening of language skills by the individual on his own time.

Workbooks, boon or bane? Without passing on the merits of these instructional materials, it is pointed out here that they fit the program of individualized instruction. They are simple, programmed materials providing drill and thus are an aid for busy teachers. They are usually expendable, and for this reason are not as generally used as the textbook.

COMPUTERIZATION IN EDUCATION

Technological tentacles reach the schoolroom as well as the office and the factory. Elsewhere the so-called new media will be discussed in some depth; however, it seems appropriate at this point to mention the effect of the modern computer on instructional methods. Computers do many things when programmed or told to do so. Electronic computers vary from key-punched cards or paper tapes to coded and documented magnetic tape, drums, and discs that can record, organize, sort, store, retrieve, and transmit information of any sort.

Uses in the schools range from administrative, secretarial, and library to instruction in the classroom. A number of high schools and universities are already gearing some of their instruction into computer operation. Computers used in this manner are highly sophisticated teaching machines. Into computers data can be fed that describe complete work-study orders and understandings for units of instruction. The student can obtain a print-out of his skills and understandings at daily, weekly, or other intervals. Such a print-out can tell both teacher and student what has already been done, and what needs to be done. Instruction can be individualized in an almost unheard-of manner. An instructional aid of this kind calls for a new kind of imagination and skill on the part of teachers. Current developments in CAI (computer-assisted instruction) have been summarized as follows:

The computer can provide lessons tailored to individual needs so that a student can regulate the rate of inculcation, as it were, in terms of his own ability to progress. The imparting of knowledge can be done in writing, through still pictures, moving pictures, voice, or combinations of these. Responses can be made by pressing buttons, operating typewriter keyboards, by voice, or by using other alternatives. One of the fascinating possibilities is that both students and teachers can be supplied with a record of progress at any point in the curriculum. . . .[2]

ORGANIZATION RELATED TO METHOD OF HANDLING INDIVIDUAL DIFFERENCES

Every teacher knows that great differences exist in individuals in traits and behavior, but surprisingly little in the way of realistic adaptations is done about it. Such a statement needs no documentation; however, some discussion is needed to show the scope, nature, and the general logistics of the topic. The range of individual uniqueness is as great as the number of people involved.

The Declaration of Independence affirms, "All men are created equal," that is, they have certain inalienable rights; but no assumption is made that all persons are the same in such matters as sex, color, genetics, ethnic background, social or economic position, or physical measurement. However, a nation built on the principles of freedom and equality of opportunity for all has tried to fashion a school system to fit this credo. Too

[2] John R. Stark, "Educational Technology: A Communications Problem," *Phi Delta Kappan*, 48 (January 1967), 196.

often the matter has rested principally on lip service, but in some instances genuine and even realistic attempts have been made to implement the principles. To assume that students are equally literate is a fallacy. Some find pleasure in theoretical discussion; others do not. Some enjoy science; others prefer the arts. Some are disturbed when questions and problems do not fall into neat and precise arrangements; others enjoy putting unorganized ideas into logical order. These individuals are challenged by the need for classification and identification.

As culture increases and society becomes more complex, such differences present many new problems. Society attempts to hold more and more of its school-age youth until graduation. There is now *more to be learned by more students.* And, the interests, aptitudes, dispositions, attitudes, aspirations, and home backgrounds vary enormously. All these variations come to school with the students.

Schools, however, cannot solve all the problems inherent in group and individual differences. Merely going to school does not create or guarantee equal opportunity. In addition to the broad generalized differences in race, color, creed, mental ability, and socioeconomic factors, there are those of subtler nature—security, social antagonisms, emotional balance, interests, health, and so on and on. Even siblings and twins differ much from one another. Individual difference means as many different things as those who use the phrase attribute to it.

MEETING THE PROBLEM OF INDIVIDUAL DIFFERENCES

Schools on the average have not been unaware of these problems. Prescriptions as to how best to deal with them vary considerably. The following outline sketches in some of the schemes. A casual glance at the history of education will reveal many more.

School Attempts to Care for Individual Differences
I. School Organization
    1. Heterogeneous grouping: Variations in content and teaching method
    2. Homogeneous grouping
       a. Enrichment coupled with evaluated achievement grouping
       b. Special classes—languages, arts, basic skills, emotionally disturbed, etc.
    3. Acceleration
       a. Grade skipping
       b. Irregular promotions
    4. Special schools
       a. Academic—science, language, for example, Boston, Philadelphia, and the Bronx High School of Science
       b. Vocational—business, industrial arts, agriculture

      c. Continuation

      d. Work-study (analogous to Antioch College plan)

      e. Exceptional children

    5. Nongraded: "Phasing" vs. "grading"

  II. Personnel

    1. Gifted teachers for accelerated; retarded; delinquent

    2. Tutors

    3. Counselors

    4. Paraprofessionals

  III. Methods and teaching techniques

    1. Team teaching

    2. Flexible scheduling

    3. Special equipment; electronic and otherwise

    4. Special facilities; laboratories, shops, studios

    5. Learning resource centers

    6. Variable-sized classes

    7. Multiple classes

    8. Shared services

    9. Student (peer) assistance

As subject content of the curriculum varies, so will methods and resources as imaginative uses appear. At one time the focus of attention was on the average student, but today the two extremes—gifted or talented and slow or disadvantaged—receive more attention. It must also be mentioned that curriculum change is in metamorphosis as much from governmental override and assistance as from within the profession. Such programs as HEADSTART, (federal assistance for preschool education), FOLLOW THROUGH (federal assistance for special groups of children who have started in the HEADSTART program), PACE (Projects to Advance Creativity in Education), VISTA (Volunteers in Service to America), TESL (Teaching English as a Second Language), PCP (Personalized Curriculum Project), and other operations and programs have either a direct or an indirect bearing on the formal school curriculum.

As pointed out earlier, the dropout problem is receiving careful attention. According to the best available data, about 70 percent of the youth finish twelve years of education. For those who drop out gainful employment is often difficult to find. How can the schools, through curriculum, methods, facilities, and staff, reduce the percentage of dropouts? And of those who do drop out, how can they be educated so that they are employable? A recent newspaper account of a certain Job Corps training center stated that some of the boys had never had a hammer and nails in their hands. Then there are the able dropouts—how can they be salvaged? Many of the solutions to these questions lie beyond the reach of the schools; nevertheless, they must do what they can to alleviatae the problem. Halfway measures, such as "social promotions" or desegregation, are not enough. Someone has said that meeting individual difference "is not a technique; it is a way of life."

Without administrative adjustment teachers with heterogeneous classes will wish to try such suggestions as these:

Use a laboratory situation. In a laboratory situation students work as individuals or as groups on various problems and with various instructional materials while the teacher acts as consultant. Not only is it possible to ensure variety in problems and projects and in the use of resources; it is possible to make adjustments in time and in remedial work as needed.

Use more than one textbook. It is important to select reading references that vary in difficulty, as well as in appeal and in point of view.

Form subgroups within the class. The teacher may help one group while another group works alone. Groups should be flexible so that the composition of the one being given instruction may vary as needed.

Make assignments of different levels of difficulty. In a class that has to meet the general education needs of all students and the specialized needs of a few, differentiated assignments become a necessity. However, in any subject there should be not only basic requirements that are common to all, but also more advanced work for those who have the interest and ability to pursue the subject at higher levels. It should be pointed out that an assignment common to all does not necessarily mean that everyone must do the same thing in order to meet the requirements of the assignment.

Use more group activity. Groups should be so organized that there will be several centers of interest, requiring various skills and resources for their development.

Use a variety of evaluation procedures. No matter how wide a range of activities and resources is used in the class to take care of individual differences, the efforts of the teacher will be defeated if all evaluation is based on tests that measure mastery of subject matter, with everyone expected to attain the same standard. In physical education, for example, evaluation that is based on skill in performance alone is inadequate in the appraisal of the total objectives of the course.

All these procedures have been used by experienced teachers with some degree of success in providing for individual differences in the classroom. In the discussion that follows, special consideration will be given to two groups of students, the slow and the gifted.

TEAM TEACHING

At first glance team teaching may seem to be strictly an administrative procedure but it is not. Appearing late in the 1950s, a plan called *team teaching* has had a spectacular growth. In the early 1960s it was a center of controversy. Although still not accepted by all educators, the concepts and procedures of team teaching, cooperative teaching, or team planning —whatever it is called—have been responsible for a reexamination of both the departmentalized high school organization and the self-contained classroom of the elementary school. At the very least, team teaching has provided a fresh approach to some current organizational problems.

Team teaching aims at a reorganization of teachers, students, and schedules; reassignment of curriculum and class schedules; change in staffing patterns; and more extensive use of technological aids. Is it possible to develop more fully the intellectual capacities of students through such reorganizations? Can fluidity and flexibility in school organization assist educators in providing the type of education that society seems to demand? How can a better knowledge of individual differences, a better utilization of teachers, an improved understanding of ability groupings, a willingness to experiment with radically new ideas in class size, and the like, contribute to educational effectiveness?

TEAM TEACHING IN PRACTICE   By definition, team teaching implies that two or more teachers assume the responsibility of working together for all or a significant part of the instruction of a designated group of students. The arrangement may be so complete that the entire school program follows the team plan; on the other hand, team teaching may be limited to one subject or to a group of related subjects as in a core. The plan is applicable to both the elementary and the secondary school. In one form, for example, only the English teachers for the seventh grade are involved because all teach exactly the same content; in another school the plan might group all departments in three divisions—humanities (English, social studies, foreign languages), science (sciences, mathematics), and arts and physical education (physical education, home economics, music, art). Faculties and departments in a school may be completely organized into teams or the arrangement may cover only a segment of the school. Anderson uses a picturesque metaphor to describe the structure in this manner; "Many of the so-called team teaching projects, especially in the secondary schools, are in effect voluntary federations of sovereign teachers—the participants have, metaphorically speaking, touched fingers without interlocking arms." [3]

Team teaching embodies in many ways all the desirable features attributed to departmental organization: like-minded students are grouped together, subgroups are easily arranged, teachers follow their special academic interests and education, and classrooms can be provided with

[3] Robert H. Anderson, *Teaching in a World of Change.* New York: Harcourt, Brace & World, Inc., 1966, p. 84.

appropriate equipment and furnishings. The plan allows every subject to be taught by a specialist, yet preserves the interrelations of content and learning. Hopefully, too, it makes optimum use of all the skills and knowledges of every staff member of a school. But, as is pointed out by all authorities, the team idea must be accepted as cooperative: there must be integral involvement of all the teachers. A paper team organization is not enough; teachers must plan together, instruct together, evaluate together. These efforts should include those of all the personnel of the team—teachers, assistants, interns, paraprofessionals, and anyone else involved.

The team teaching is based on the following hypotheses:

The best teachers in a school are shared by more students. This statement approaches Alfred North Whitehead's remark that students need an "exposure to greatness."

Teachers are provided with a schedule that allows time for better preparation and planning. Aides are usually provided to take care of typing, mimeographing, proctoring, arranging for equipment, and the like.

Teachers get more help from the nonteaching branches of the school: test service, school office, guidance, audio-visual services, and the library.

Teachers should have, and can have, more exact knowledge of their students.

The best teachers in any system are entitled to recognition.

Teachers can grow and keep abreast of increasing knowledge.

Teachers do not plan and work in isolation. The team approach minimizes repetitious effort.

Teachers make better use of teaching techniques and technological devices.

New teachers are more quickly and easily oriented and assimilated.

Students are given new responsibility for their progress.

Students develop better study habits.

Special student needs are more easily diagnosed, and remedial assistance is more easily planned.

Flexibility permits groupings and regroupings of students.

The plan provides for flexible class size.

Resource people from outside the school are more easily used.

It can be quickly seen that in practice both formal and informal team plans have emerged. Anderson [4] summarizes them in this manner:

[4] Anderson, p. 88.

TYPES OF COOPERATIVE TEACHING
Informal

Simple, voluntary collaboration without structure or assumption of permanence.
Division of responsibility to simplify workload or preparation.

Interchange of pupils for specific grouping purposes.
Combining of classes for specific experiences.

Informal team structure with voluntary membership and relative ease of withdrawal ("cheese wedges").[*]
Older teacher working with an apprentice or younger teacher (relationship temporary).

Formal

Formalized team structure with leadership designated on a continuing or rotating basis; leader primarily a chairman, peer status emphasized ("pie tin").[†]
Teacher or teachers assisted by teacher aide on a continuing basis.

Formalized team structure on hierarchical basis, leader in assumed permanent role and with salary supplement or equivalent remuneration ("pyramid").[‡]
Formalized hierarchical structure with several levels of responsibility above that of teacher.

[*] "Cheese Wedge"   [†] "Pie Tin"   [‡] "Pyramid"

T = Teacher   T = Teacher   TL = Team Leader
                                          ST = Senior Teacher/
                                                 specialist
                                          T = Teacher

Teaching teams vary in size and makeup according to the school situation. Usually, a team has a *team leader*. A team of two or more teachers assumes joint responsibility for instructing a group, but one member of the team is designated leader or coordinator. This person serves as chairman of the planning sessions and exercises varying degrees of leadership.

Team leaders are mature, experienced teachers, and frequently are given extra compensation. A *team teacher* is simply a fully qualified teacher who is a member of a teaching team. A *student teacher* or *intern teacher* is usually a senior college student from a teacher-education program who is assigned to a team to observe and assist under supervision from the team leader. A *teacher aide* is a noncertified person who works with the team in a part-time capacity doing clerical, library, or other routine tasks. Numerous other arrangements for teaching teams may include technical assistants, audio-visual and language laboratory specialists, for example, so that teams consist of professional and paraprofessional personnel.

Team teaching schedules require that student time be divided into blocks: large group instruction, small group instruction, and individual study, with time allotments of 40 percent, 20 percent, and 40 percent, respectively, advocated by the originators of the plan.

Team teaching makes significant allowance for independent study, a condition that is emphasized at every turn in today's education, but one that is often difficult to manage. The facts of individual differences have been known for a long time, but it has been difficult to provide for the variety of interests and capabilities that exist. Usually the provision for individual differences relies heavily on assigned homework. There is little provision for that which is creative or truly independent. The new organization of instruction attempts to assist students to assume more responsibility for their own education. Independent learning activities make use of reading, writing, viewing, listening, doing, working with automated teaching devices, experimenting in laboratories, and engaging in many other significant activities. There will be opportunities for studying in depth. Independent study should make provision for both horizontal and vertical growth and enrichment. As teachers guide independent study, more of it can be expected of the older and more mature students. In fact, some students may spend as much as 40 percent of their time in independent study.

Large groups, possibly 100 or more, are feasible, even desirable, and, if professionally understood and planned, do not result in what one critic calls "bargain-basement" education. Large groups can be formed to introduce units, add new common knowledge, summarize, and test. Techniques employed in large group teaching are lecturing, film and television presentation, and the use of resource speakers. Technological equipment is more efficiently used. Large group instruction can be high-quality instruction and at the same time conserve a certain amount of staff time for behind-the-scenes planning and preparation. This time is not to be consumed by administrative detail.

Small groups are usually likened to seminar arrangements—groups of fifteen or fewer. The number in a so-called small group might realistically be that which can engage in effective discussion for a reasonable period of time. These groupings are very flexible and the need for them frequently grows out of problems or ideas first brought up in large group meetings. New time modules employed in most team teaching situations— 15-, 20-, or 30-minute blocks instead of the conventional 45- or 55-minute periods—lend effectiveness to seminar groupings. In these groups students spend a great deal of time in developing communication skills, in critical thinking, in advancing and defending ideas, and in interpersonal relations. Teachers usually conceive of their role as that of a *guide* rather than a "giver of knowledge." Often teachers find it more difficult to guide than to lecture or quiz.

Individual, large, and small group instruction all call for varied school facilities, such as seminar rooms, large lecture rooms, and small study and work areas, such as booths and cubicles. New schools are being built with provisions for such facilities. Movable partitions promote the space fluidity required by this type of organization. Existing buildings present problems, but not insurmountable ones. In fact, some excellent programs are found in some of the older buildings. At times a few partitions can be removed at small cost. There are, of course, some large areas—auditoriums, cafeterias, or even well-lighted woodworking shops—that need not be tiered to be used effectively. Seminar-sized areas present little difficulty. Individual study areas may be screened off from laboratories, offices, workrooms, shops, or closets. Only a few minor changes will make much open library space available as individual study carrels or booths. Imagination and cooperation by administration and staff are the chief ingredients.

TEAM TEACHING: EVALUATION   Some critics feel that students do not have the maturity that, theoretically at least, the plan demands. Others affirm that costs are too high and that quality is lowered by any kind of large grouping. But most teachers agree that this iconoclastic development has subjected conventional practices to much-needed scrutiny.

Some educators believe that team teaching offers an environment that appeals to prospective teachers. Many in-service teachers feel that it breaks a lockstep and provides professional challenges not found in conventional plans. They are also of the opinion that their skills and specialized knowledge can be used more fully. Research provides no clear-cut answer to the quality of student grades, but heavy claims are made for greater motivation and learning in depth. Parents, if properly advised of the features of the scheme, generally favor it. Alexander says:

Team teaching like other innovations, past and present, succeeds only to the extent that the following conditions are met:
1. The broad implications of the change are realized and met.
2. Teachers are reeducated on the job prior to and during the change.
3. Evaluation changes proceed along with the innovations.

4. Shortcomings are remedied as soon as they are discovered.
5. Appropriate facilities are obtained.
6. The financial implications are considered so that the new procedures are reasonable in their demands for added expenditures.
7. Adequate, honest, easily understood information about the changes is provided to lay and professional groups.[5]

NONGRADED SCHOOLS

Among the many plans evolved to care for individual differences better is the nongraded school. Over a period of many years various educators have become disenchanted with the so-called lockstep in school organization whereby students are promoted chiefly by age and time spent rather than by achievement. Over the last two decades a plan has evolved that allows individuals and small groups to work together regularly and systematically according to their levels of accomplishment, their objectives and goals, and their capacities. This plan is presently known as the nongraded, the ungraded, or the gradeless school. In 1955 Goodlad [6] identified sixteen schools with some sort of ungraded organization, and estimated that possibly 1 percent of the schools in the nation had at least the elements of an ungraded plan. Ten years later an NEA survey showed a tremendous growth in the number of such schools.[7] Practically all the programs were experimental and as a whole touched only one or a few schools in a district, but they were found in 57.9 percent of the elementary schools and in 3.4 percent of the secondary schools.

Insofar as the secondary schools are concerned, the nongraded plan is essentially one that stresses independent study. Achievement in a subject area rather than intelligence scores or age is the key to progress. The plan thus makes possible an accurate classification of students followed by frequent reclassification. In this way students move forward as rapidly as they can, and on an individual basis. Students with teacher assistance set their own goals in terms of standards compatible with their abilities. Miller has defined the characteristics of this school organization: "The nongraded school is one without grade failure and/or retention, in the conventional sense; it has individualized instruction with the purpose of permitting youngsters to progress as they—individually—show competence to do so; and it permits sufficient flexibility in the instructional program to make instructional adjustments both in terms of intrapersonal variability (differences within an individual) and in terms of interpersonal variability (differences among individuals)." [8]

[5] William M. Alexander, *The Secondary School Curriculum: Readings.* New York: Holt, Rinehart and Winston, 1967, p. 264.
[6] John Goodlad, "Ungrading the Elementary Grades," *NEA Journal,* 44 (March 1955), 170–171.
[7] Research Division, NEA, "Nongraded Schools," NEA Research Memo, May 1965.
[8] Richard I. Miller, *The Nongraded School.* New York: Harper & Row, Publishers, 1967, p. 131.

Some high schools that have claimed notable success with the non-graded idea include those in Melbourne (Florida); Bassett (California); Nova, Broward County (Florida); Chippewa Valley, Mt. Clemens (Michigan); Middletown (Rhode Island); Hurricane (Utah); Lakewood, Jefferson County (Colorado); Newton (Massachusetts); and Borrego (California). This is a representative list only; it should be stressed that ungrading may be only partial in some instances.

In the Melbourne High School the students find themselves in fluid learning situations. "Temporary learning situations, *ad hoc* arrangements" called *phases* replace the grade organization. Students move forward at any time they are ready. A student may, for example, remain in a lower phase indefinitely, whereas another may progress rapidly into higher phases. "These phases are learning dimensions designed to group students in relation to their knowledge of skills: low, minimal, medium, high, superior." [9] The Melbourne five regular phases are:

PHASE 1   Subjects are designed for students who need special assistance in small classes.
PHASE 2   Subjects are designed for students who need more emphasis on the basic skills.
PHASE 3   Material is designed for students with average ability in the subject matter.
PHASE 4   Subject matter is designed for capable students desiring education in depth.
PHASE 5   Challenging courses are available to students with exceptional ability who are willing to assume responsibility for their own learning and go far beyond the normal high school level.[10]

The nongraded plan at the Middletown (Rhode Island) High School is somewhat different. In this six-year school students do not fail, neither are they promoted, but progress at their own pace. Rollins says:

It is expected that the so-called "average" pupil will complete the curriculum in six calendar years, and that the "academically talented" pupil will complete some areas of the curriculum in less than six calendar years, going on to advanced work in the areas he has completed, or exploring another field of interest. It is expected, also, that some pupils will not complete the curriculum in the six calendar years allotted to it. Minimum specific achievement levels in each of the subject fields are required for graduation from the Middletown High School.[11]

Curriculum content in each subject area at Middletown is broken down into sequential concepts and skills that range from easy to complex. In

[9] B. Frank Brown, *The Ungraded High School*. Englewood Cliffs, N.J.: Prentice-Hall, Inc., 1963, p. 50.
[10] Brown, p. 50.
[11] Sidney P. Rollins, "The Middletown Project: The Development of a Nongraded Secondary School," in William M. Alexander, *The Changing Secondary School Curriculum: Readings*. New York: Holt, Rinehart and Winston, Inc., 1967, p. 329.

English, for example, the 111 stages range from "taking part in conversation" (1), "listening for information" (2), "obtaining the main idea from a paragraph or a story" (25), "listening to evaluate truths, half-truths, and falsehoods" (49), "appreciating the historical novel for literary form and content" (63), "writing the paragraph with reasoning, such as syllogistic, inductive, deductive, and critical" (103), up to "writing the full length research paper with footnotes, preface, and bibliography" (111).[12] Similar sequences have been worked out, published, and are available to students and staff for the different curriculum areas.

Within the framework of the nongraded organization, several high schools employ team teaching, mass media techniques, and even extensive computerization. The computers are used chiefly in guidance, in remedial work, and in providing students with individual instructional tasks.

In an attempt to evaluate the gradeless school, McLoughlin gives only faint praise: "Research, then, finds little to impede or impel practitioners interested in nongrading. Under either organization (graded or ungraded) children's adjustment and achievement appear to remain remarkably constant . . . Taken at face value, current research on the nongraded school seems to say that its contribution to the academic, social, and emotional development of children is marginal." [13] McLoughlin's criticisms are actually not directed at the *truly* nongraded school, but at the pseudonongraded one. Undoubtedly many so-called nongraded schools are not nongraded. They are merely "homogeneous groupings and semi-departmentalizations of instruction" designed for "administrative expediencies developed to make the *graded* school work."

THE EDUCATION OF EXCEPTIONAL CHILDREN

The remainder of this chapter will be organized around three groups of students—slow learners, the disadvantaged, and the gifted. In the preceding chapter, dropouts were briefly discussed. Although the dropouts come from the normal groups as well as from the exceptional, they are in the main chiefly from the slow learners and the disadvantaged.

SLOW LEARNERS

Teachers have always been concerned about slow-learning students who have at times been referred to as the "students in the back row." They are often terminal students. Many of the people one meets in everyday life may very well have been slow learners in school.

---

[12] Rollins, p. 330.
[13] William P. McLoughlin, "The Phantom Nongraded School," *Phi Delta Kappan*, 49 (January 1968), 249.

Teachers, too, may have been slow learners at one time in one or more subjects. Some teachers will readily admit that as far as statistics, economics, or science, for example, are concerned they were pretty slow. Others may say that they got through by the "skin of their teeth." Or they may say that had it not been for a sympathetic and understanding teacher who reduced the complexities of the subject to their simplest terms, failure might have resulted.

How, then, shall we approach slow-learning pupils? Some practical suggestions for teachers include these:

1. *Try to find out why the student does not learn.* The reasons may be manifold. It is a common fallacy to conclude that all slow learners are stupid. Slow learning may or may not be due to low general aptitude.

2. *Stress concrete learning materials.* Wide use should be made of field trips, pictures, demonstrations, firsthand experience.

3. *Use shorter units*, that stress personal needs, immediate values, and practical applications. Short-term goals are helpful.

4. *Make assignments clear and definite.* Discuss the assignment in class. Have it repeated. Talk about *how* it is to be done.

5. *Help the slow learner to succeed.* "Nothing succeeds like success." Provide activities he can master and give him competition he can challenge. This may very well be his own record.

6. *Try to overcome communications barriers.* These students may not understand what the teacher tells them. Their vocabulary and knowledge of symbolization are limited. Do not hesitate to provide generous oral interpretation of the textbook.

7. *Accept even naïve questions or replies with grace and patience.*

8. *Convince the students that the subject is important and that they can learn it.* Improved attitudes and encouragement on the part of the students are likely to follow.

9. *Use every opportunity to provide enrichment in content.* Enrichment is usually lacking in the home environment, and may be a significant factor in the slow learning.

10. Try to find time to *give a little individual attention* to these students, or at least provide small group contacts. These students often feel lost in the crowd and frequently fear to reveal their ignorance to their peers.

11. *Consider modification of the content in basic courses.* This is not to be construed as a lowering of standards but merely an adaptation to individual differences.

THE DISADVANTAGED

Children variously tabbed as disadvantaged, underprivileged, or in need of compensatory programs can be found almost anywhere. However, they are most likely to be found in slum areas of the metropolitan districts.

Their presence is closely tied to inner-city deterioration, interstate migration, metropolitan sprawl, and socioeconomic decline.

Social changes have brought increased social problems. A wealth of new opportunities and benefits have accrued to American citizens during the last century but in recent decades it has become painfully clear that the growth of urban culture has spread unevenly. The harsh fact is that millions of children and adults are impoverished and disheartened, and that many are hostile. They have been unable to adjust to changing work patterns, varying family relationships, rural-urban migration, a crowding of human traffic, and a host of other conditions.

Although it is true that it is increasingly rare for children to avoid school altogether, large numbers of them profit little from it. In some cases the schools are poor, but the primary factor appears to be lack of motivation. At least 10 percent of the population has completed less than six years of schooling.[15] This means millions who, if not actually illiterate, are so lacking in skills that they fall into the unskilled category. At best, employment for this group is precarious. Low earning capacity and high unemployment go hand in hand. Many become the hard-core unemployed and drift onto state and national welfare rolls, where they remain for the rest of their lives.

CHARACTERISTICS OF THE DISADVANTAGED   Elinor F. McCloskey of the National Regional Education Laboratory at Portland (Oregon)[16] has attempted to synthesize the major extant studies that deal with disadvantaged children. She lists and documents the following seven generalizations:

1. Disadvantaged pupils have immense potentials.
2. Poverty is an overriding condition of disadvantaged children.
3. In cities, disadvantaged children tend to reside in overcrowded slum neighborhoods.
4. Disadvantaged children have relatively impoverished self-concepts.
5. Disadvantaged children actually believe they are inadequate.
6. Generally, disadvantaged pupils do learn less and their learning skills are poorly developed.
7. Disadvantaged children have not developed sufficient cognitive and reasoning skills essential for typical rates and dimensions of school progress.[17]

Housing conditions are nearly always bad for the impoverished and contribute to low morale. Stability of residence, too, is nearly always low,

[15] John K. Norton, *Changing Demands on Education and Their Fiscal Implications.* Washington, D.C.: The National Committee for Support of the Public Schools, 1963, p. 47.
[16] Elinor F. McCloskey, *Urban Disadvantaged Pupils: A Synthesis of 99 Research Reports.* Portland, Ore.: Northwest Regional Educational Laboratory, 1967.
[17] McCloskey, pp. 3–7.

and overcrowding is usually present. Family life is marked by numerous disadvantages, such as broken homes, unemployment, below-average health and medical attention, and usually parental communications that tend to be arbitrary and authoritarian. Discipline is marked by physical controls.

Many children, particularly those of minority groups, tend to be hostile or withdrawn.[18] Very few of them have been conditioned either to seek or to value the rewards of schooling. Formal school routines constrict their natural tendencies toward physical activity. Often they see little connection between the goals they have set and attendance at school. Lack of a strong positive home attitude toward school is usually reflected in the children. On the other hand, some studies have found that parents and associates of children from the lower social classes place great faith in the benefits of education.[19]

Stress has been placed on the urban problem; however, dropouts and the disadvantaged are not confined to city areas. The problem exists in small towns and on the farms, but it has not been so widely publicized, except for an occasional flurry of interest in Appalachia.[20] The rural-to-urban migration of both white and Negro minority groups continues. For many of these people, the move to the city is expected to open up a small utopia. What actually happens is all too well known. Many relatives of these migrants do not move. Nor does their status improve noticeably. The children of many disadvantaged rural families drop out of school and join the ranks of the unemployed (general unemployment in the United States varies around 6 percent, but for the school dropout the rate is about 20 percent). The lot of the tenant farmer is no less enviable than that of his urban cousin.

For all these disadvantaged people, environmental influences are more significant than heredity.[21] School, home, church, neighborhood, and place of employment provide most of the understandings of social conditions as well as some of the keys to change. Here, of course, we are essentially concerned with the school.

THE SCHOOL AND THE DISADVANTAGED   If we can judge by what is written in the journals and the press, said at conferences (school and government), heard on radio and television, and bandied about in general conversation, educators are conscious of the problems of underprivileged. This may be a belated awareness, but there is evidence to show that the educators are facing up to the situation. The public, too, senses the prob-

---

[18] McCloskey, p. 37.
[19] See summaries in McCloskey, pp. 36–37.
[20] Peter Schrag, "Appalachia: Again the Forgotten Land," *Saturday Review*, 51 (January 27, 1968), 14–18.
[21] Goodwin Watson, *No Room at the Bottom.* Washington, D.C.: National Education Association, 1963, p. 7.

lems and sees them as adjuncts of unemployment, automation, civil strife, feelings of insecurity, and general rising living costs.

To the educators most of the problems appear to revolve around finances, properly trained personnel, and motivation. How can schools prepare and present a school program that is realistically sound and appealing both to youth and to their parents? What can be done to change apathy into ambition to achieve? Children who have found school a baffling, confusing, and, at times, a humiliating experience, will need school programs of radically new design. For these the school experience has been one of a cumulative series of failures.

At the junior and senior high school levels, subject matter and the practical aspects of life, as youth sees them, go in different directions. To many youths the conventional curriculum does not seem to prepare them for the kind of life they expect to live. It is inescapable that both teachers and nonachieving students find each other a disappointment. Watson pointedly describes the situation in this manner:

Those children are unusually fortunate who had many teachers they admired, loved, and wanted to please. Most children have known few such teachers. Motivation to stay in school is weakest among those pupils who have frequently had to contend with teachers they disliked. Often the dislike has been mutual, and both teacher and pupil have vied in effort to make life uncomfortable for the other. The vicious circle of attack-resentment-counterattack brings mounting hatred. Each longs to escape the endless, frustrating struggle with the other.[22]

Deutsch speculates that disciplinary efforts in slum schools engage as much as 80 percent of some teachers' time, and that this percentage is seldom less than 50.[23]

It is little wonder that many applicants for teaching positions see these divergent social-behavioral norms as a type of blackboard jungle, and refuse to teach in slum areas. In spite of intensive recruitment efforts, large city school districts find it most difficult to staff schools in these areas adequately. This often leads to a situation in which the least expert and the least experienced teachers are assigned to areas with the most complex social problems. In consequence, there is a turnover in the teaching staff. The situation is worsened when the administration uses uncertified and substitute teachers to staff the schools.

It is becoming increasingly clear that many of the teachers assigned to disadvantaged areas have not had any realistic preparation for the tasks they will face. Numerous writers stress the fact that a majority of the

[22] Watson, p. 13.
[23] Martin Deutsch, "The Disadvantaged Child and the Learning Process," *Education in Depressed Areas,* A. Harry Passow, ed. New York: Bureau of Publications, Teachers College, Columbia University, 1963.

teachers have a set of middle-class values they try to apply to all types of students but these preconceptions often impede effective communication between teacher and student. Strom suggests a preservice teacher education program in these broad terms: "Were the future teachers in any academic major to receive some training in urban sociology, psychology of motivation, culture pattern and personality, human development and the teaching of reading, our circumstance within the slum might be markedly improved in terms of instructional quality, pupil progress, home-school relations, and teacher morale and tenure." [24]

Special teacher training programs may well go beyond the curriculum. They might very well provide some sort of special incentive plans to identify, recruit, and place these teachers. Scholarships coupled with later special compensation commensurate with school placement have been recommended. Programs of this sort would attract teachers committed to serving disadvantaged youth. They would develop an interest in and a rapport with the underprivileged that would include a faith in the ability of these children.

Not only preservice education needs close scrutiny but in-service as well. Special classes, workshops, conferences, and bulletins need to stress the concepts and recommendations noted above. An involvement in neighborhood life and an ingenuity in devising and adapting new teaching materials must not be overlooked. The assistance of paraprofessional aides (parents and young people from the neighborhood) should be sought. Also needed is the cooperation of representatives of outside civic and social organizations, such as youth agencies, churches, police, welfare agencies, the Urban League, administrators of national groups and programs, including HEADSTART, FOLLOW THROUGH, VISTA, and others. Some sort of rapport needs to be built up between teachers and parents. This has been one of the major goals in the HEADSTART programs.

In numerous ways instructional methodology must provide greater motivational emphases for students in both curricular and extracurricular activities. Their involvement in learning should make students participators instead of spectators. Pupil-centeredness should come before subject-centeredness. Teachers too frequently acknowledge the differences in the social, physical, and motivational postures of youth but take the same instructional approach to all.

Earlier in this chapter attention was directed to the matter of individual differences. Disadvantaged youth need a generous share of this type of understanding and treatment. Nongraded school arrangements that stress subject matter sequences instead of grade level designations are recommended for youth who need to work at their own level of competency

[24] Robert D. Strom, *Teaching in the Slum School.* Columbus, Ohio: Charles E. Merrill Books, Inc., 1965, p. 33.

and without number-letter grade labels. Programmed instructional materials (not necessarily machines) will permit each learner to work at his own rate and on tasks that provide satisfaction from mastery. To repeat an old shibboleth, "Nothing succeeds like success!"

A massive national effort has been directed toward the better educational development of children who are slow learners, disadvantaged, dropouts, or behavioral deviates. Federal funds are being advanced directly to schools to apply to school problems. Other funds aid in an auxiliary manner—funds that support such programs as HEADSTART, FOLLOW THROUGH, VISTA, the Job Corps, the Neighborhood Youth Corps, as well as numerous studies, surveys, and clinics handled through the Office of Economic Opportunity.

GIFTED LEARNERS

Interest in developing the gifted student continues to grow. Present-day scientific, political, and cultural developments emphasize the need to identify gifted students early and to give them some sort of special treatment.

It has been estimated that at least half of all gifted children never realize their full potentialities. This is an appalling loss. Over the years school programs have tended to neglect the gifted while concerning themselves with the slow learner. They have assumed that the gifted will shift for himself and will learn anyway. No one knows how much potential leadership has been lost because gifted students have been permitted to loaf day in and day out, doing assignments that never challenged them.

It has been common practice to identify gifted students on the basis of achievement and intelligence tests (labeling as "gifted" those who have an IQ above 120 or 130, for example). There seems to be little doubt that ability to do academic work or work of increasing complexity in other fields is related to scores on mental tests. However, of late years there has been definite objection to such a narrow definition of the "gifted student," especially in terms of ability to do academic work or to make a good score on a verbal mental test. Although a certain degree of intelligence, as measured by tests of mental ability, is necessary to success in any field, the IQ is not always the most significant factor in successful achievement. Often a student of average intelligence will outstrip a classmate who is rated higher in innate ability. Teachers should look for various kinds of aptitudes among their students.

Klausmeier and Goodwin distinguish between gifted and talented in this way: the former student is "consistently superior in most academic subjects, or promises to be," whereas the latter is "superior in only one field such as music, art, foreign language, or mathematics" (12:502).

MEETING THE NEEDS OF GIFTED STUDENTS   Freehill has suggested that teaching procedures for the gifted should provide:

1. *A program organized around unit topics, projects, or study themes.*

2. *Lessons organized around a problem or a purpose.* It is proper that in some of these, the severe arrangements of formal logic will give way to psychological organizations more truly characteristic of unsolved problems.

3. *Encouragement of side issues that develop incidental and concomitant learning.*

4. *Special emphasis on the tools of workshop learning.* These include reading skills, individual study, finding materials, observing, graphing, reporting, orderly disagreeing, and appraising opposite viewpoints.

5. *Informal classrooms with reference works more frequently used as texts.*

6. *Increasing awareness of the learning process on the part of the learner.* Effort is expended toward ensuring his participation in focusing and systematizing his work.

7. *Student involvement in planning or at least awareness of what the expected learnings are.*

8. *Participation in periodic evaluation.* Gifted students in the regular classroom should be encouraged to serve in discussions, as the person who says, "This is where we are," "This is the issue on which we disagree," or "Perhaps this will help."

9. *Student summaries that require rearrangements and conclusions as differentiated from reiterations and repetitions.*[25]

Other suggestions in caring for needs of the gifted are:

1. Encourage gifted students to *participate widely in the learning activities* by giving demonstrations, making special reports, preparing displays, and tutoring slower students.

2. Urge gifted students to *engage in service projects* for the class, school, community (serving on committees, making surveys, conducting interviews, writing or speaking for special occasions, engaging in work experience projects). These students can make a valuable contribution and at the same time can help counteract a tendency to use unusual ability for selfish ends alone.

3. Encourage *participation in extraclass activities.* There is no better opportunity in school for the development of leadership than that found in participation in student activities.

4. Enlist the *aid of the parents.* A gifted child is often either exploited or ignored by his parents.

The word "underachievers" has come into prominence lately. Such persons are assumed to be bright students who are not living up to their full

[25] Maurice F. Freehill, *Gifted Children.* New York: The Macmillan Company, 1961, pp. 156–157.

potential academically. The extent of underachieving is not fully known, but observation, personal experience, and measurement by standardized tests indicate it to be great. The *Encyclopedia of Educational Research* suggests some causes of underachievement: keeping the gifted in classes with students of lesser ability (competition with average learners is not challenging); lack of enrichment programs; inflexible and undifferentiated teaching methods; and lack of proper encouragement. To these causes one might add inadequate identification and the fact that the potential fast achiever has often not developed good work-study habits early in his educational career. There is also the possibility of emotional imbalance arising at various times in the lives of these students. Such disturbances can be triggered by a variety of causes, and may even produce traumatic effects. Key words in working with the gifted are innovation, acceleration, enrichment, individualization, and motivation.

SPECIAL CLASSES AND SCHOOLS FOR THE GIFTED Some metropolitan school districts have found it practical to set aside schools for high achievers. This is not possible in small districts. They can, however, identify their talented students and make provisions for special classes for all or part of their instructional programs. This is possible both at elementary and secondary school levels. Often the enrichment or acceleration for these students is in the special fields of art, music, and drama, but similar work is being done in the "solid subjects." Special classes for the gifted are common.

Some teachers enjoy working with gifted students; other feel more secure with heterogeneous groups. Teachers selected for work with gifted groups usually volunteer, and even among volunteers selections should be carefully made. These teachers, commonly referred to as master teachers, can be expected to turn out a quality product.

There is a relationship between giftedness and creativity. Until lately both have been given little more than lip service by the schools. The public and school administrators give much attention to numerous other types of pupil growth. There seems to be very little time to teach creativity, but if schools are committed to the concept of the development of the "whole person," why is there no obligation to develop creativity wherever possible? The answer may lie in the fact that creativity is misunderstood. It is confused with the esoteric and the narrowly individualistic.

Miel says: ". . . the quality of creativity has been shown if the individual has made something *new to himself* that is satisfying and in that sense useful to him, if he has related things that were previously unrelated in *his* experience, and if the product is 'surprising' (that is, new) to *him*." She then adds the following statement, "We wish to emphasize that the process of making something new must at some point be a deliberate one in order to be labeled creative."[26]

This point of view is also held by Margaret Mead:

To the extent that a person makes, invents, thinks of something that is new to him, he may be said to have performed a creative act. From this point of view the child who rediscovers in the twentieth century that the sum of the square of the hypotenuse of a right-angled triangle equals the sum of the squares of the other two sides is performing as creative an act as did Pythagoras, although the implication of the discovery for cultural tradition is zero, since this proposition is already a part of geometry.[27]

CHARACTERISTICS OF CREATIVITY   Creative persons are intelligent, but there is no one-to-one relationship between creativity and intelligence. The most intelligent persons as measured by prevailing tests are not necessarily the most creative; nevertheless, a certain amount of intelligence is required for true creativity. Many of the facets of high intelligence are marks of creative people. Creative persons understand rather easily without much formal drill and, in fact, are bored by the drill type of assignment. They like new ideas. These traits are also held by persons of high intelligence.

Creative persons are original. This is not just a tautology. They make responses and do things in a novel way, at least in ways that are infrequently seen. Tests have shown that those who are more facile in suggesting new ideas also tend to come up with better and more adaptive ones.

Many of the great creative figures of history showed their originality early in life, for example, Leonardo da Vinci, Sir Francis Galton, and Wolfgang Mozart. Many schoolchildren show creative tendencies quite early. In some, it seems to fade later for no definite reason. There are many pupils who start their own neighborhood papers, or who draw, explore, tinker, or venture into paths new to them.

Creative persons seem to have intuitive perception. Without teaching, they seem to possess inferential knowledge and perception. They seem to be more sensitive to deeper meanings and their implications than noncreative persons.

Esthetic interests mark creative persons. These interests are closely tied to intuitive perception, and the works of creative persons have a freshness often observed in dramatics, visual arts, music, writing, and speaking. Such students are said to be talented.

[26] From *Creativity in Teaching*, ed. Alice Miel. © 1961 by Wadsworth Publishing Company, Inc., Belmont, Calif., pp. 6–7.
[27] Margaret Mead, "Creativity in Cross-Cultural Perspective," as quoted in Byron G. Massialas, and Jack Zevin, *Creative Encounters in the Classroom*. New York: John Wiley & Sons, Inc., 1967, p. 12.

Creative students are prone to show more disturbances of stress and tension than other students. People do not understand them, so it is said. Because creative persons are keyed as they are, they chafe and rebel easily; they are impatient. They feel the need for independence, and conformity creates tension and turmoil.

The characteristics of the gifted and the creative are numerous, but the following list is representative:

1. They are perceptive and inquiring.
2. They have a wide range of interests and abilities.
3. They tend to be critical of persons, facts, arguments, claims.
4. They prefer abstractions, generalizations, and concepts.
5. They accept responsibility and take the initiative. They enjoy planning and innovation.
6. They prefer to work independently.
7. They learn quickly and easily; motivation is not a problem.
8. Their concentration is marked, as is their attention span.
9. They accumulate a large vocabulary at an early age.
10. Most of them have tremendous energy.
11. They have a sense of humor; their jokes are of a high order.
12. They possess a sense of social and ethical values.
13. Emotional imbalance is not uncommon.
14. They tend to show evidence of creative talent early in life.

HOW TO IDENTIFY AND ENCOURAGE CREATIVITY   Before teachers can assist creative students, three points need to be posited: teachers must know what to look for, they must want to find it, and they must know what to do about it.

Immediately one thinks of "brainstorming" as a possible way to develop a number and variety of ideas in a short time. Ideas, all kinds, wild or conventional, are presented, with no attempt to evaluate them at the time. Such a technique stimulates imagination and creativity and can be applied to almost any problem or subject. This spontaneous free-wheeling technique of free association of ideas without preset conditions, which has proved fruitful in many instances with children and adults, is becoming increasingly used as a point of departure in high-level conferences and "retreats" for executives.

But do teachers wish to locate their creative students? They have grave responsibilities and heavy schedules. Do they really want to know these students? Teachers, however, are the most altruistic people in the world. Regardless of the effort involved, they *do want to know*. And the opportunity to work with some of the creative individuals is among the most rewarding in the profession.

What can teachers do when the creative students have been identified? They can provide stimulating experiences and an atmosphere in which these students can express their talents. Encouragement and guidance are the kind of assistance that creative students need most. With the exception of an art teacher, a drama teacher, or a composition teacher, imagination has had few sponsors. A review of page 208 will help summarize the provisions schools have made for these youths. Robert E. Samples, director of the Instructional Materials Development, Earth Science Curriculum Project, has recently written an indictment of the school and society for their failure to understand "Kari" (the symbolic creative student):

The school's compartmental treatment of intellectualism is a microcosm of society's pattern. Words, numbers, and activities are separated by fences labeled LANGUAGE, MATH, and GYM. . . . She appears strange to the conformity-cloistered society around her . . . her resistance is interpreted as immaturity and stubbornness that must be overcome. . . . The teachers *say* they will serve the individual, but in action they homogenize individuals into anonymous, ineffective groups. . . . We need the Karis, all of them, but how can they be saved? [28]

To these remarks we might add those of Jules Henry of Columbia University: "We must conserve culture while changing it, we must always be *more* sure of surviving than adapting . . . . *Homo sapiens* has wanted acquiescence, not originality, from his offspring . . . . Creative intellect is mysterious, devious, and irritating." [29]

INDIVIDUALIZED INSTRUCTION: RECAPITULATION Lloyd Trump has emphatically stated that the "magic number of twenty-five students to one teacher" does not represent the most productive means of utilizing a teacher's time. He suggests that the schools of the future form three distinct groupings of students—large classes, small classes, and independent (individual) study arrangements. Under this scheme a student's time might be divided 40 percent, 20 percent, and 40 percent, respectively, for the three groupings.[30]

In connection with independent study, the National Association of Secondary School Principals (NASSP) emphasizes the desirability of differentiated assignments, rooms of various shapes and sizes, and a flexible time schedule that practically eliminates class-period bells. There would be space for students to study independently, with study cubicles in the ratio of 1 to 4 students. There would also be a new laboratory space

[28] Robert E. Samples, "Kari's Handicap—The Impediment of Creativity," *Saturday Review*, July 15, 1967, pp. 56–57, 74. Copyright Saturday Review, Inc.
[29] Jules Henry, "American Schoolrooms: Learning the Nightmare," *Columbia University Forum*, 6 (Spring 1963), 24–30.
[30] Trump was formerly director of the NASSP Commission on the Experimental Study of the Utilization of the Staff in the Secondary Schools. His latest book was written with Dorsey Baynham as collaborator. J. Lloyd Trump and Dorsey Baynham, *Guide to Better Schools: Focus on Change*. Chicago: Rand, McNally & Company, 1961.

arrangement to fit the concept of independent study accommodating science, mathematics, English, social studies, and foreign language laboratories. Similar spaces, called "areas" or "centers," would be arranged for the practical arts, fine arts, and health, physical education, recreation. The scheme also places a new emphasis on the library and the audio-visual center. Rooms and spaces would be arranged around two centers: an "instructional materials center for teachers" and a "learning resources center for students." [31]

Teachers in the future will in all likelihood find school buildings that have been more functionally designed than present ones. They will have been constructed with more flexibility and more adaptability to the curriculum. Classrooms will not be uniform in size—they will be adapted for large classes where Cultural Heritage, for example, will be offered by use of mass media, but there will be areas for small groups to work, and even carrels and cubicles for individuals.

When one attempts to divide instructional method into categories and to say that this method is reserved for large classes, that for small classes, and another for independent study, one soon realizes the illogicalness of these arbitrary separations. Yet, in order to emphasize that teaching is basically related to the three points listed on page 140, the separation is made. As presently constituted, no school relies solely on one or another. In the past, some schools have tried complete organization around such plans as unit methods, project methods, and platoon systems.

The authors of this text are aware that the unit plan or the laboratory-workshop method, although emphasizing independent study, is being utilized successfully with large and small groups. In fact, the ingenuity to modify and adapt plans to local conditions is one of the notable achievements of secondary educators.

QUALITY TEACHING: A SYNTHESIS OF METHOD

At the beginning of Chapter 7, it was made clear that good teaching may result from any one or more of a great number of methods. Teachers need to keep before them constantly the thought that learning needs to be related to students' needs and experiences. It is well to point out that the needs of society must also be kept in mind, but the schools must be wary of jumping in with untested curricula and methods at each new wave of developing educational theory.

Everywhere teachers with even a spark of professional spirit wish to do the best possible job of teaching. They see in it a challenge. They are willing to experiment and to try new approaches in their teaching. They expect the psychologists and research workers to help them with hypotheses and evaluations. The teacher who seeks quality in his work is

[31] Trump & Baynham, pp. 23-45 *passim.*

constantly experimenting with new methods, tools, and evaluations. Every experience adds something. Teachers are quick to see whether students are responding to their instructional activities and procedures. Nor do they have to wait until the end of a term to know in a general way the pupils' successes. The question and answer periods, the requests for assistance or the absence of such requests, the written exercise handed in from time to time—even the facial expressions—tell the teacher that methodology is correct or needs a change. It may be a simple matter of reinforcement, or it may be the deeper matter of stimulating challenge. Nevertheless, the alert teacher reads the signs and reacts accordingly. The experienced teacher knows that it is not so much what he puts in a student as what he gets out. Quality teaching is the result of a continued search for greater insight and constant effort to improve skills and procedures. It is achieved, if ever, by study, by evaluation, by experimentation, and by revision of goals, theory, and techniques in the light of new data (23:282).

SELECTED READINGS

1. American Educational Research Association, *Encyclopedia of Educational Research*, 3d ed., Chester W. Harris, ed. New York: The Macmillan Company, 1960.

2. Amidon, Edmund, and Elizabeth Hunter, *Improving Teaching*. New York: Holt, Rinehart and Winston, Inc., 1966.

3. Blount, Nathan S., and Herbert J. Klausmeier, *Teaching in the Secondary School*, 3d ed. New York: Harper & Row, Publishers, 1968.

4. Brown, B. Frank, *The Nongraded High School*. Englewood Cliffs, N.J.: Prentice-Hall, Inc., 1963.

5. Clark, Leonard H., and Irving S. Starr, *Secondary School Teaching Methods*, 2d ed. New York: The Macmillan Company, 1967, chaps. 9–11.

6. Franklin, Marian P., *School Organization: Theory and Practice*. Chicago: Rand McNally & Company, 1967, pp. 400–489. Excellent review of literature on team teaching, nongraded schools, multigraded schools, and homogeneous vs. heterogeneous grouping.

7. Gentile, J. Ronald, "The First Generation of Computer-Assisted Instructional Systems: An Evaluative Review," *A.-V. Communication Review*, 15 (Spring 1967), 23–53.

8. Gilchrist, Robert S., "Promising Practices in Education," *Phi Delta Kappan*, 42 (February 1960), 208–211.

9. Gold, Milton J., *Education of the Intellectually Gifted*. Columbus, Ohio: Charles E. Merrill Books, Inc., 1965.

10.   Kemp, C. Gratton, *Perspectives on the Group Process.* Boston: Houghton Mifflin Company, 1964.

11.   Kerber, August, and Barbara Bommerito, *The Schools and the Urban Crisis.* New York: Holt, Rinehart and Winston, Inc., 1966.

12.   Klausmeier, Herbert J., and William Goodwin, *Learning and Human Abilities,* 2d ed. New York: Harper & Row, Publishers, 1966, chap. 6.

13.   McCloskey, Elinor F., *Urban Disadvantaged Pupils: A Synthesis of 99 Research Reports.* Portland, Ore.: Northwest Regional Educational Laboratory, 1967.

14.   Medill, Bair, and Richard G. Woodward, *Team Teaching in Action.* Boston: Houghton Mifflin Company, 1964.

15.   Miller, Richard L., *The Nongraded School.* New York: Harper & Row, Publishers, 1967.

16.   Reissman, Frank, "Teachers of the Poor: A Five-Point Plan," *Journal of Teacher Education,* 18 (Fall 1967), 326–336.

17.   Shaplin, Judson T., and Henry F. Olds, Jr., eds., *Team Teaching.* New York: Harper & Row, Publishers, 1964.

18.   Smiley, Marjorie, "Research and Its Implications," *Improving English Skills of Culturally Different Youth,* Arno Jewett, ed., U.S. Office of Education Bulletin no. 5, 1964. Washington, D.C.: Government Printing Office, 1964.

19.   Strom, Robert D., *Teaching in the Slum School.* Columbus, Ohio: Charles E. Merrill Books, Inc., 1965.

20.   Suppes, Patrick, "The Uses of Computers in Education," *Scientific American,* 215 (September 1966), 207–220.

21.   Taylor, Calvin W., and Frank E. Williams, eds., "Instructional Media and Creativity," *Proceedings of the Sixth Utah Creativity Conference.* New York: John Wiley & Sons, Inc., 1966.

22.   Wightman, M. A., "Secret of Discovery," *American Biology Teacher,* 28 (October 1966), 609.

23.   Wiles, Kimball, *Teaching for Better Schools,* 2d ed. Englewood Cliffs, N.J.: Prentice-Hall, Inc., 1959.

CHAPTER 9

Instructional Materials, Including Printed Materials

A visit to most modern secondary or elementary schools will demonstrate clearly that teachers use a multitude of instructional materials. A casual visitor to a science classroom might see a variety, including models, specimens, charts, diagrams, chalkboard illustrations, as well as projection equipment for slides and films and opaque materials. In the social studies classroom, similar evidence of the use of a variety of instructional materials is apparent. A mathematics classroom might have a large number of so-called teaching machines, wooden-paper-string models, and templates. Trips to such other classrooms as industrial arts, fine arts, health education, English, and home economics would reveal much the same picture. Details would differ because certain curricular areas employ specialized techniques and materials. The foreign languages, for example, by their very nature lean heavily on such audio devices as record players, magnetic tape recorders, and microphones; perhaps all these materials are provided in an integrated pattern such as a language laboratory. This is not to say that teachers of the language arts do not make use of visual-graphic-dimensional materials. Furthermore, numerous instructional materials and techniques will not be evident to the casual visitor unless he happens to be present exactly at the time of their use. These aids are represented by demonstrations, dramatizations, use of resource persons, field trips, surveys, off-campus interviews, and many similar devices or techniques.

There is a constantly growing array of instructional materials. At one time teachers had to rely almost solely on a single textbook, a chalkboard, and possibly an out-of-date political map. How fortunate is the modern teacher! How fortunate is the modern student! The authors of one textbook portray the old and the new in this way:

Contrast the picture of the physical environment of the Latin grammar school of colonial times with that of the modern secondary school. That the latter houses thousands of dollars' worth of instructional materials is a phenomenon which has occurred neither by accident nor the imprudent use of money. Appropriate equipment and materials are necessary aids to efficient learning. At the present time dramatic events are taking place in schools across the nation through the extended use of varied instructional materials, particularly television and teaching machines. The curricula and methodology of tomorrow's schools promise to be shaped considerably by the extent to which these innovations prove successful; it behooves the teacher to know what will be expected of him in using both new and established instructional materials.[1]

The employment of modern tools is not confined to schools. In some respects education lags behind such professional and occupational areas as medicine, communications, advertising, industry, the armed services, agriculture, and others. Americans are proud to point to their accomplishments in these areas. Much of this progress is due to the heavy dependence on modern technology. Are we as rightly proud of our schools as we are of our medicine and our industrial output?

PROBLEMS IN SCHOOL EFFECTIVENESS

It is generally accepted that the audio-graphic communications media are effective with people of all ages. Experience tends to show that people generally remember

10 percent of what they READ
20 percent of what they HEAR
30 percent of what they SEE
50 percent of what they HEAR and SEE
70 percent of what they SAY
90 percent of what they SAY as they DO a thing [2]

If education is to keep pace with the ever-increasing world of knowledge, with new technology, with the population explosion, with new ideas, and with new skills, an educational pattern must be developed that provides effectiveness in both depth and breadth.

[1] H. O. Nordberg *et al.*, *Secondary School Teaching*. New York: The Macmillan Company, 1962, p. 108.
[2] These figures on the relative importance of various senses to learning and retention are only approximations and must be taken as such. They were developed at the University of Texas, Industrial Education Department, about 1950 by the late P. J. Phillips. On November 27, 1963, Charles Cyrus, Training Specialist, University of Texas, wrote the Bureau of Naval Personnel, Department of Navy, Washington, D.C., as follows: ". . . the percentages included in our sheet 'Some Training Principles, TIM–151 (11–55),' appeared in a passout sheet used in 'Methods of Teaching' classes and other instructing situations . . . . Our classes are not organized in such a manner that we can experiment and check with controlled groups, but our experiences in teaching give us no reason to question the apparent reasonableness of these percentages."

By its very nature formal school experience tends to be removed from life, to be patterned and structured. To the extent that the school can capture more and more life experiences and substitute reality for artificiality, the school is a more effective agent of society. Yet the school must not depend upon narrow direct experience solely. To do so builds on the status quo and fails to capitalize upon our racial and cultural heritage, not to mention the challenge to probe into uncharted horizons.

The field trip is generally regarded as being an effective means of promoting acquisition and retention of facts, conditioning attitudes, stimulating attention and interest, and illustrating and clarifying details and processes about things and places. The students who can experience more of our contemporary culture firsthand are very fortunate. Students study the Nile, the Congo, the Orient, the Louvre, the opera, the culture of Scandinavia, the booming of suburbia, but for the most part vicariously. Events from history—the first Continental Congress, the birth of the French Republic, World Wars I and II, westward expansion in the United States—must be studied in the same manner. Teachers are constantly striving for techniques and materials that will enable them to present their courses more realistically and meaningfully. To do this they employ the whole audio-visual repertoire.

The novelist Thomas Wolfe expressed the viewpoint of modern educators quite well when he wrote: "The world is full of people who think they know what they really do not know." And he went on to discuss knowledge thus: "It is finding out something for oneself with pain, with joy, with exultancy, with labor, and with all the little ticking, breathing movements of our lives, until it is ours as that only is ours which is rooted in the structure of our lives." [3] The underlying thought here harks back to the criticisms expressed by such noted educators as Comenius, Rousseau, Pestalozzi, Froebel, Herbart, and Dewey. As a matter of fact, as library study will verify, this underlying, nagging thought of the school's inefficiency has been a common bond of many renowned schoolmen.

VERBALISM

Too frequently the poorly understood word "symbolization" passes for mastery. "Verbalism" is the term usually applied when pupils have only a vague or even a wildly incorrect knowledge of the words they use, or when the words are known in a limited use instead of in their complete meaning. One child referred to caviar as surgeon eggs. Why such a boner?

Verbal counterfeiting occurs most frequently in conceptualization and generalization. Pupils read or listen to concepts formulated into words. Soon they are able to use the same words apparently without error but

[3] Thomas Wolfe, *The Web and the Rock*. New York: Harper & Row, Publishers, 1930, p. 380.

without understanding the concept. For them it has been borrowed instead of derived. Teachers, quite generally, exaggerate the pupil's ability to acquire and understand concepts.

Teaching in generalities is common. Some teachers simply do not know how to illustrate to clarify meaning, and some appear to believe that to do so is juvenile and unacademic. Apt and meaningful illustrations and examples, verbal and pictorial, should be generously used. The material presented in most textbooks needs such supplementation. Correct thinking, to reiterate, must be built upon definite knowledge, clear concepts. Many instances have been reported of how badly pupils garble the Pledge of Allegiance or the Lord's Prayer when requested to write it and to discuss its real meaning. There is an inclination to think that such instances are "cute." Or we treat indulgently the high school student who defined a complex sentence as "a thought with one independent clause and one despondent one."

In response to Polonius' question, "What do you read my lord?" Hamlet answered: "Words, words, words." [4] Then there is Humpty Dumpty, who confused Alice by saying, "When I use a word, it means just what I choose it to mean, neither more nor less." Poor Alice thought the words should have definite meanings.

In high school we expect the students to read and to understand material such as: "The public school [English] still tries to pump more character into the boys than most of them will ever have occasion to use, while slipping them a romantic humanism that undermines this character and heckles its theology at every turn." [5]

How does one grow from hazy word understanding to true knowledge? Terminology is often a hindrance to understanding for many pupils. The commonest of teaching platitudes, "study this carefully" or "you have not studied your lesson," are of no avail. The problem is not one of more time to be spent, more reading to be done, or more homework to be assigned, but one of concept formation. Someone has said that "the verbal cram is worse than worthless, it is injurious."

The abstract study of parallel lines in geometry must in some way be tied up with the parallelism of the planks of the floor, railroad tracks and ties, corn rows, streets, bookshelves, and all incidents of parallelism, concrete or abstract, wherever found. Laboratory work ordinarily clears up many misinterpretations and misconceptions. Home economics students, for example, are not baffled by their problems. Perceptual foundations and experiences are a definite part of the laboratory procedure.

Verbalism is insidious. Fluent speech is acceptable coin for understanding in most classrooms. It is easy enough for pupils to say that to divide

---

[4] *Hamlet*, Act II, sc. ii.
[5] Wilfred Sheed, "School as a One-Sex Society," *Saturday Review*, 51 (January 20, 1968), 29. Copyright Saturday Review, Inc. 1968.

a fraction by a fraction, one must invert and multiply. They can easily be taught this rule, but they should also know why this rule is a rule. Students quickly learn that the circumference of a circle is πd, but have they also learned that there is a ratio involved here, and that π is a constant? Teachers know that experiments in the psychological laboratory have shown conclusively that meaningful material is more easily learned than nonsense material, and that retention is greater.

THE VALUES OF INSTRUCTIONAL MATERIALS

Modern instructional materials are not fads and frills. Some critics are quick to apply this opprobrious statement, but it is patently unjustified. Audio-visual materials are frequently misused. Teachers show movies instead of using instructional films, often in an auditorium or a cafeteria instead of in the regularly assigned classroom, laboratory, or shop. Many illustrative pictures and models have been employed merely because they are interesting. At times a plethora of aids is used. Pictures have been passed around the class in random fashion. Realia and exhibit materials have been used promiscuously under the impression that they will make the lesson objectives concrete. Often materials have been used that have no relation to the objectives to be accomplished. A trip just for the sake of a trip or to pacify students' longing to get away from the classroom is a trip without justification. Materials have been used without proper preparation by teacher and students. At other times, there has been no follow-up of their use.

It is well to keep in mind these simple criteria when discussing the potential effectiveness of instructional materials: they must be *properly prepared;* they must be *wisely selected;* and they must be *intelligently used.* The first two of these criteria are essentially administrative in character, whereas the third—as well as the second to some extent—is teacher-oriented. Any learning material, be it a textbook, pamphlet, map, or film, cannot help but add significantly to the learning situation if it meets these criteria.

SPECIFIC VALUES OF CONCRETE INSTRUCTIONAL MATERIALS

It is difficult to enumerate all the benefits to be had from a wise use of varied instructional materials without seeming to present a panacea for all the problems of learning. But some of these benefits are enumerated here because they have not been fully understood and accepted by all educators. Audio-visual materials as used in this instance do not include textbooks, readings, and lectures, or what one might term conventional learning materials. This should in no way be interpreted to mean that the authors repudiate conventional learning materials and methods. The values of concrete instructional materials are as follows:

1. They illustrate and clarify nonverbal symbols and images, quantitative relationships, complex relationships, abstract concepts, spatial relations, and specific details.
2. They facilitate attitude and behavior changes.
3. They show inaccessible processes, materials, events, things, and changes in time, speed, and space.
4. They promote greater acquisition and longer retention of factual knowledge.
5. They provide increased interest in learning.
6. They provide objectivity for the study of a delicate or controversial subject.
7. They stimulate interest in voluntary reading.
8. They allow all members of a group the opportunity to share a joint experience.
9. They get and hold attention.
10. They reinforce verbal messages.
11. They bring experts and a variety of resources to the classroom.
12. They provide for a direct interaction of students with the realities of their social and physical environment.
13. They provide integrated experiences that vary from concrete to abstract.
14. They are valuable for all age and ability groups.

All lesson planning employs four major categories: objectives, learning activities, learning materials, and evaluation. In other words, *what activities* will students pursue involving *what materials* to *achieve what objectives* and with *what evidence* of attainment of goals?

For generations educators have been using varied learning activities, each generation rearranging and reevaluating these activities to suit its philosophy. For example, at one period in our educational history reciting was given major consideration. Although not abandoned today, it has a smaller role. Teachers should remember Margaret Mead's remark, "No one will live all his life in the world into which he was born, and no one will die in the world in which he worked in his maturity." [6]

What learning materials are used with different learning activities? Perceptive teachers use every invented or developed material now known, and man's inventive genius will constantly add new ones. Supervisors of student teachers constantly look for originality and regularly discuss new techniques and methods with their student teachers and with other supervisors. Teachers are not dismayed when an occasional critic speaks of these materials and techniques as gimmicks or as hardware. They could be, but they need not be.

[6] Bureau of Educational Research and Service, The Ohio State University, *Newsletter*, December 1960, p. 2.

The term *audio-visual materials* is used in most books in the field of instructional materials and has become standardized in education, industry, and the military; moreover, the public understands it. Although the authors use the term in this text from time to time, in the main they speak of learning or instructional or curricular materials. Such terminology is broader and permits the inclusion of all aids.

Learning is a complex business. No one method nor instructional material will achieve modern educational objectives. Direct experience goes hand in hand with vicarious and abstract experience. Looking at pictures alone is far from adequate. Explanation and analysis are as much needed today as ever before. Not only must Johnny read; he must read more and be able to evaluate what he reads.

But what are *good* instructional materials? Intelligent, well-prepared teachers know what they are; however, the following criteria may be of some value since they apply equally well to all materials—printed pages, lectures, motion pictures, prerecorded magnetic tapes, machine-programmed lessons, physical maps, mock-ups, or puppets:

Appropriateness—related to curriculum, units of study, daily lessons; suitable for particular age or grade level
Freedom from bias, prejudice, distortion, antisocial attitudes, untruthfulness
Recency—up-to-date, reflecting current thought, original or revised
Availability—obtainable when needed
Appeal—esthetic, attention holding
Technical quality—simplicity, workability
Cost—within school budget limitations

Teachers who wish more specific assistance with problems of utilization should take advantage of the many special courses in methods and materials offered in all teacher-education institutions. In addition to formal courses, there are often workshops and conferences. Specialized books and magazines are also helpful. Nevertheless, the discussion of instructional materials would fall short of a reasonable target if it did not point up some ways to use them. Accordingly, the remainder of this chapter and the two following chapters will describe instructional materials and their use.

PRINTED MATERIALS

TEXTBOOKS

Although modern secondary school teachers use a wide variety of teaching materials, the textbook is still the primary tool for a vast majority of them. Over the years it has been practically revered by students, teachers, and the public. As late as 1962, textbooks came first in a ranking of materials and resources most helpful in a teaching program. A report by the NEA Project on Instruction found that 1442 principals *unanimously* agreed that "the textbook was the resource listed by both elementary and secondary principals as the one most useful for a teaching program (1960–61). *What the publishers printed for school use was indicated as a strong determinant of what the students had studied.* The textbook not only kept its preeminence from 1956 to 1961, but gained slightly in importance if compared with the other resources" (4:9; italics in source.)

This dependence on textbooks (usually a single text) started years ago when books were scarce and costly. Teachers were poorly prepared for their tasks and the textbook saved many from failure. However, the profession became aware of the slavish use of printed materials about the turn of the twentieth century, and since then much effort has been expended to improve the selection of textbooks. Studies and researches by individuals, committees, and commissions have followed. In 1931 the National Society for the Study of Education devoted Part II of the thirtieth yearbook to a code of ethics on textbook selection and adoption. Some assistance in the solution of the problem was given by the development of textbook rating scales during the thirties and forties. These scales have helped to objectify textbook selection, but they are mechanical and have not accomplished a great deal. Much more has been achieved by curriculum groups in local areas using specific criteria developed by the group and its consultants for the selection of books in a given curricular field (2).

A significant study of the use of textbooks was made by a group of scholars at the University of Illinois, who not only surveyed the dependence placed on texts by teachers but went on to offer helpful suggestions for the improvement of texts and ways to vitalize their use in the classroom. The opening statement of the report highlights the problem:

At the center of the present-day educational scene in America is the textbook. It takes a dominant place in the typical school from the first grade to the college. Only the teacher—and perhaps a blackboard and writing materials—[is] found as universally as the textbook in our classrooms (2:3).

Some light is shed on the reasons for this dependence on textbooks when one notes the heavy schedules of teachers. Assigned classes, counseling, administrative and clerical routine, and committee work leave little time for planning and preparation. A comprehensive time study of a large group of teachers revealed that on the average only one quarter of an hour per day was devoted to daily preparation. This was coupled with some out-of-school preparation, but the total was less than forty minutes.[7] This time factor alone undoubtedly accounts for the fact that teachers fall back heavily on textbooks as "assistant teachers."

Conditions in the modern, efficient high school are actually somewhat improved. Teachers are busy and time is limited, true enough, but there are ameliorating circumstances. Reading materials continue to be important and significant learning resources, but they are not slavishly followed; neither are they accepted unquestioned. The preparation of today's teachers qualifies them for a more professional and intelligent understanding of books and their use. In the first place, the range and variety of books have been multiplied. In many schools, several texts are used in a course instead of one. Paperbacks take their place along with the hard-covered books. Adequate libraries take the pressure from single assigned texts as the teacher draws heavily on supplementary references, encyclopedias, almanacs, dictionaries, source books, workbooks, magazines, pamphlets, brochures, and even comic book materials.

VALUES OF TEXTBOOKS

There can be no question that textbooks are being improved constantly. Critical feedback from schools and teachers is a potent factor. Authors and publishers spend more time and effort to provide books of better quality. Competition is strong. Within recent years textbooks have become more scientific in conception and construction. Studies constantly being made of quality, quantity, and kind of content are being translated into textbooks at all levels and in all curricular areas. It is also noteworthy that a majority of the textbooks for today's elementary and secondary schools are written by practicing elementary and secondary school teachers, or in collaboration with college and university specialists.

Furthermore, present-day textbooks actually blend with, or at least integrate with, many of the newer instructional media, such as films, filmstrips, records, and prerecorded tapes. These materials tend to reinforce each other, and frequently allow teachers to make varied approaches to their curricular problems. An example is almost any standard textbook in science, home economics, social studies, or foreign language. The book itself is artistic in design with generous margins, adequate spacing, large and clear type, and meaningful and relevant illustrations. A majority of the texts provide some of these illustrations in color. Pictures of color spectra, mineral-bearing rocks, national costumes, fauna and flora, festivals, ceremonies, art, landscapes, and legions of other illustrations are frequently in full color. Color adds a realism that is much needed. Chapter "closings" employ many teaching aids and suggestions, such as

[7] *A Cooperative Study for the Better Use of Teacher Competencies*, 2d report. Mt. Pleasant, Mich.: Central Michigan College, 1955, pp. 29, 33–34. See also p. 432 of this text.

library references, film and flimstrip references, project activities, questions for discussion, songs, dramatizations, construction activities, study helps, and review devices. These related learning materials and aids are varied and ingenious.

A number of the larger publishing companies now produce and distribute numerous audio-visual materials that are author-integrated with their textbooks. One publisher produces books integrated with sound motion pictures; another produces books and audio materials; another, books and filmstrips; and so the procession goes. And, just as publishers desire to reinforce their books with audio-visual materials, at least one audio-visual producer supplements his motion pictures with printed readers, and another is augmenting his films with preprogrammed lessons for use in teaching machines.

Books are written so that learning is facilitated. Content is organized, systematized, and sequentially arranged so that greater economy may prevail. Books should be intelligently read and often reread because everyone forgets a great deal. They are a convenient ready reference for review and restudy, but most students are not aggressively enthusiastic about textbooks. Some prefer other competing mass communication media, such as television, the theater, the motion picture; and others may prefer the more challenging and meaty books of the nontext type. Claims have been made that textbooks actually dampen and shrivel reading desires and habits.

The needs of students will determine what and how many learning materials are to be used. The chances are that the teacher will have a textbook for each class taught. He may have the option of using several texts. At any rate, the teacher must determine the needs of his students because these needs vary from community to community and from class to class. It is a matter of interest to turn back to page 222 and reread the quotation from the NEA report, especially the italicized sentence. This, in a professional report, states blandly that what the publishers printed was a strong determinant of what is studied. A vicious implication overrides this statement. The curriculum may become a matter of what authors and publishers present. Textbooks must not be allowed to become planned courses even though they may be well organized and well written. Some textbooks provide too much material, at least on some topics; others too little. The teacher must make intelligent adaptations. He supplements with radio, television, films, tapes, paperbacks, source books, and other materials as needs dictate.

HOW TO USE TEXTBOOKS

Teachers can and should encourage students to:

1. Read assignments rapidly for a once-over pattern. This overview will show the "flavor" of the assignment. In this survey, note should be made

of topics treated; graphs, maps, and other devices included; illustrations shown; and, above all, the reasons for the assignment. This becomes essentially a skimming process.

2. Follow the skimming of the assignment by a closer reading for the meaning of words, sentences, paragraphs, graphs, and tables. This is the dictionary meaning of the verb "study." At this time the text may raise numerous questions in the student's mind. It may stimulate thinking. It may present new data, and lead the student to go beyond the text to find answers to questions and problems that seem to be insufficiently answered.

3. Take notes on what has been read. Not all teachers agree that this is a useful activity, but some note taking may be valuable. If it is done, students should be encouraged to do it perceptively, not mechanically. The best plan is to use an outline consisting of questions. Notes should be carefully taken and never allowed to become a jumble of disorganized, disconnected words, phrases, or sentences. At this point, the teacher should do an educational job concerning the care of books—personal, school texts, or library materials. Underscoring, writing in margins, and otherwise marking or cuing is not allowable unless the book is personally owned; even then there is a question of value.

4. Try to recall the main ideas in the assignment after it has been read. This includes not only the topics but some of the salient facts.

5. Review notes at the completion of a unit of work or before an examination. This review should attempt to coordinate notes, text, class discussions, laboratory experiments, and other learning activities.

6. Reread text, when needed for clarification of vague or uncertain concepts, facts, or other knowledges. This is also a good time to evaluate what has been read. Did the author stick to facts or did he present personal opinions? Is there any evidence of bias? Did he attempt to generalize from isolated cases?

7. Understand and know how to use table of contents, index, glossaries, reference lists, and illustrations. Teachers frequently skip the preface to a text. Such an omission is unfortunate because students should know that the preface often provides useful keys to understanding various parts of the book, their relationships, why the book was written, and author's motivations.

Teachers and supervisory personnel also have a responsibility to:

1. Provide a wide variety of reading materials, including multiple texts, auxiliary reading materials, reference books, and library materials.
2. Encourage students to probe all reading materials for facts, answers and solutions for their problems, leads, and intellectual stimulation.
3. Encourage students to evaluate and discriminate as they read. Critical thinking will help sift fact from fiction.

4. Plan instructional units of study, projects, and problems instead of assigned pages, chapters, word or question lists in single texts.
5. Remember that words are symbols for real and concrete experiences. Help students build worthwhile experiential backgrounds.
6. Correlate text with nontext learning materials.

Beginning teachers will, in all likelihood, have little or no opportunity to voice opinions on the matter of texts. They should, however, know how to use text materials as well as know procedures for textbook selection. All teachers should thoroughly acquaint themselves with the texts available in their respective fields even though they may not have an opportunity to select them. The R.R. Bowker Company annually publishes a book that lists under the heading of school subjects all the textbooks of some 150 publishing houses. The books are indexed by author, title, and subject. They are also classified as to elementary, junior high, and senior high school adaptability, but the books are not rated or annotated.[8]

WORKBOOKS

There exists a wide variety of workbooks, drill pads, exercise books, manuals, and other practice devices related to the English language, foreign languages, science, mathematics, and commercial subjects. Whether or not to use workbooks is debatable. As the name implies, the work or practice book provides work for the student to do—drill and practice with skills, problems to be solved, questions to be answered, tests to be taken, remedial work to be followed, words to be mastered, or experiments to be performed.

The workbook idea and its proliferation of materials grew out of the limitations of textbooks, the paucity of practice materials, and the complete absorption of the teacher's time with a multiplicity of tasks.

Research provides no clear-cut answer to the question of the educational value of workbooks. At least the degree of value is undetermined. Some teachers in some subject areas get good results with them; in other instances the materials are so used as to degenerate into busywork, petty exercises, and filling in blanks. The purpose here is merely to call attention to these instructional materials so that beginning teachers will be aware of their values and limitations.

Some of the workbooks now available have been well planned and carefully written. Often they integrate with or accompany basic texts so well that busy teachers feel them to be educationally valuable for students. They enable students to practice skills at a rate consistent with individual abilities. For some students these workbooks achieve acknowledged

---

[8] *Textbooks in Print.* New York: R. R. Bowker Company, published annually in April; another worthwhile source is American Textbook Publishers Institute, New York.

motivation and practice in self-direction and independent study. The recently developed "scrambled" books are in reality workbooks prepared for individualized study. This type of book is closely related to the programmed learning materials prepared for use in the so-called teaching machines.[9] Large group instruction (lecture-discussion type) needs some sort of semi-individualized bolstering. Supplementation, review, and opportunity to reconstruct are imperative. This assistance the workbook can give.

On the other side of the coin one finds instances of slavish adherence to the workbook—students merely following mechanical directions in the laboratory or classroom. Most workbooks call for no originality of thought. Often there is an overemphasis on nonessential outcomes. Some workbooks, manuals, and practice pads have no apparent correlation with textbooks or courses of study, and often the materials are not well graded.

TEACHERS' GUIDES

Teachers' guides bear about the same relation to teachers that students' workbooks bear to students. They are guides or syllabi written by authors to accompany their books. Following the text closely, they offer assistance to busy teachers, but they are essentially crutches, even "ponies." If teachers get any professional assistance from them, however, they undoubtedly serve a useful purpose. On the other hand, it must be said that teachers are capable and that they should prepare their own guides, syllabi, and teaching plans. Some teachers welcome these aids; others disdain their use.

About three fourths of all instructional motion pictures have accompanying teachers' guides, sometimes called study guides. These guides serve two purposes: they act as a standardized lesson plan, and they substitute for a preview before the film is shown. It is pretty generally understood that the second purpose is a makeshift one; the actual preview is preferable. Headings in these guides are usually organized as "Suggestions for Effective Use of the Film," "Suggested Discussion Questions," "Follow-up Projects," "Technical or Foreign Words or Phrases," and "Suggested Reading References." In some cases the teachers' guide will provide a complete scripting of the film. Many of these guides are quite simple, being no more than two folded pages punched for easy filing.

Teachers' guides as discussed here should not be confused with courses of study, units of study, or other curricular guides.

REFERENCE AND SUPPLEMENTARY PRINTED MATERIALS

LIBRARY   The modern secondary school is replete with reference and supplementary books in spite of the fact that one occasionally hears of

---

[9] For a good example of a "scrambled book" see Joseph C. Blumenthal, *English 3200.* New York: Harcourt, Brace & World, Inc., 1962.

a "library gap." Books are housed in different classrooms and in a central library. Professionally trained librarians are usually found on school staffs.

Nevertheless, the power of the school library as a learning center has hardly been touched. The American Library Association has campaigned vigorously for standards and upgrading, but there is still much to be accomplished. Since 1964 great sums of federal money have been appropriated for school libraries and materials so as to promote the upgrading. Public libraries as well as school libraries wage a never-ending fight to obtain the necessary funds so that they can fulfill their function in the educational framework.

Everyone is aware of the knowledge explosion as well as the scientific and population explosions. Every minute more than 2000 pages of books, reports, and newspapers are printed; in the scientific field alone some 30,000 journals publish some 600,000 new papers each year. The task of trying to keep abreast of this vast and complex development even in one area of specialization is overwhelming.

The position of the school library is best described by Eleanor E. Ahlers, formerly president of library services for Washington State and president of the American Association of School Librarians:

A school library today, both elementary and secondary, must be a centrally organized collection, readily accessible, of many kinds of materials that, used together, enrich and support the educational program of the school of which it is an integral part. The librarian, supported by an increasing amount of a wide variety of resources and working with classroom teachers, can help children and young people solve problems, develop inquiring minds and rational powers, think and read critically, be creative, study independently, make wise decisions and accept social responsibility.[10]

In the past and in the minds of many librarians today, the design of the school library was that of a storehouse or reservoir of knowledge. In this framework the librarian's role was to buy, catalogue, and check out books, and to teach pupils how to find materials. But present-day library leadership sees the librarian's role as does Ahlers. This role obligates the librarian to:

1. Have an understanding of children and youth and to know something of their reading interests, habits, and abilities.
2. Be able to foster independent reading habits.
3. Take responsibility for helping students and teachers find and use the most appropriate materials in the solution of their problems.
4. Work with curriculum groups to suggest best materials for specific courses of study.

[10] Eleanor E. Ahlers, "Library Service: A Changing Concept," *Educational Leadership,* 23 (March 1966), 542–453.

5. Meet and plan with department heads, team groups, and individual teachers in furnishing optimum learning materials.
6. Teach students how to use the library.
7. Provide an inviting atmosphere for student study, browsing, and check-out of materials.
8. Assist the faculty in professional growth by providing new books, magazines, courses of study, curriculum units, and a collection of sample textbooks.
9. Provide (if at all possible) a preparation center and some assistance for students to work on reports and projects; this center may also serve as a faculty preparation center if another is not available.

Library or Instructional Materials Center. The library stereotype is a place for housing reading media—chiefly books. More than one school librarian in the past has refused to order or to take display pamphlets or brochures because they did not "look nice on the shelves." Today a great many libraries not only have books, magazines, and other reading matter but also provide films, slides, records, tapes, microfilms, charts, maps, and auto-instructional devices—in fact, any material that properly belongs in a learning resources center.

This multiplication of the library function has evoked considerable discussion as to whether some of it is properly within the scope of the library or whether some other area, perhaps the audio-visual, should not administer some part. At first glance the library and the audio-visual center seem to compete with each other as well as duplicate some personnel, materials, services, and expenditures. No definitive answer to this division has been found. Possibly the best approach to a solution comes if we look at the functions served. The library emphasizes books and materials per se; the audio-visual seeks to improve instruction both in communication and through the enrichment of materials. One, so it seems, is support-oriented; the other, classroom-oriented. Regardless of the posture, the goal of each is to provide the optimum in learning opportunities.

Possibly terms that are becoming increasingly common, "Learning Resources Center" or "Instructional Materials Center," should replace "Library" and "Audio-Visual." The coordination implied by the newer labels avoids a splintering of funds and efforts and seems appropriate for a future that promises greater use of technology, an ever-increasing explosion of learning materials, and even a new outlook on the psychology of learning. The few colleges and universities that have already started along this road have a Dean of Learning Resources who coordinates the conventional library, audio-visual services, educational television, language laboratories, auto-instructional laboratories, campus press, museum, and the production of nonbook materials by ditto, mimeograph, and lithograph processes.

Internal Functioning. Modern libraries try to maintain proper balance in subject areas. They also balance historical and contemporary materials and events, fiction and nonfiction, reference and collateral materials, hard-cover books and paper-bound pamphlets, and magazines and newspapers. As mentioned earlier, it is difficult to keep abreast of the new materials that become available each year. In the area of paperbacks (not pamphlets) alone, more than 35,000 are now in print, and at least 5000 of these are considered appropriate for school use. More and more libraries are adding these to their collections.[11]

It has been charged that the formal classroom work of today kills enjoyment in reading and that a majority of students never read after completing high school except for some desultory reading of magazines and newspapers. If this is true it is not the fault of most librarians, who work assiduously for the opposite result. Library rooms or suites are attractive and comfortable. Many devices are used to motivate students to come to the library, to check out books, and to read. A list of such devices is long, but it will include

Open book shelves
Newspaper and magazine racks
Nonglare lighting
Display and bulletin boards of new books, colorful jackets, advertisements, reviews, clippings
Special holiday book features
Easy check-out of books, and in some cases, magazines, phonograph records, study prints, and other items
Friendly and helpful staff assistance

By and large, high schools no longer give students isolated lessons in the use of the library. Such instruction is handled in most instances by the regular subject teachers as the need arises. The thinking here is that library utilization, much like reading skills, should be interdisciplinary in character. Naturally, this instruction involves a high degree of cooperation between teachers and library staff. There are, of course, still a great many orientation courses in library use. These are usually offered for freshmen and are taught by librarians or English teachers.

Some schools have sufficient library materials so that specific subject matter may, on request of the teacher, be sent directly to the classroom for long-term use. As units of work follow one another, new collections of related books and pamphlets are deposited in the classrooms. Teachers can best fulfill their responsibilities for directing study habits under such circumstances.

These collections become subcenters or satellite libraries. This de-

---

[11] Robert H. Anderson, *Teaching in a World of Change.* New York: Harcourt, Brace & World, Inc., 1966, pp. 163–164.

centralization provides easy access to often-used references, and undoubtedly results in more extensive reading and inquiry. The books in the satellite collection are selected by teachers for particular purposes. They not only fulfill the fact-finding goal but, even more important, provide avenues for inquiry and interpretation. Such collections should be comprehensive enough to provide depth and range for reading in the area involved. Classroom libraries usually allow more flexible loan patterns than does the central library. Students may very well be placed in charge of the collections, possibly on a rotating basis.

Many school districts have cooperative relations with the local public library. An arrangement of this kind can have mutual advantages, especially in smaller districts.

Federal Library Assistance. Beginning with the NDEA of 1958, schools have been receiving federal funds under numerous government acts authorizing assistance in providing learning materials—reading media, audio-visual aids—in addition to funds for buildings and facilities, including workshops for teachers and librarians. Possibly the greatest assistance came through ESEA of 1965, Titles II and III. From 1966 millions of federal dollars have annually been available for the purchase of books, A-V materials, library training, conferences, field visits, special aid for rural districts; Title I has provided additional funds to local agencies for strengthening the educational program in low-income areas. Books and other media are now being purchased on a wide scale, and children may check out for home use several books, study prints, and even filmstrips.

Future Outlook. Slowly, but seemingly grudgingly, study halls have disappeared in high schools. Libraries have largely taken their place, for in libraries the student finds a richer learning environment. We shall probably see more integration and coordination of *all* learning resources, but with specialization still within the general framework.

As indicated in an earlier chapter, computers and data retrieval systems are increasing, for the flood of material is so great that easy access and quick retrieval are imperative. College, university, and foundation libraries are taking the lead in the acquisition of these systems and secondary schools may follow. In fact, such a prediction was made publicly at a library conference held at the Massachusetts Institute of Technology in 1965. Not only may high school students be locating books and documents in their own library through computers; they may even have access to the college and university libraries "through touch-tone telephones, teletypewriter keyboards, television-like displays, and quickly made copies. . . . The information traffic will be controlled by means of a time-shared computer utility on the campus in much the same way that today's verbal communications are handled by the campus telephone exchange." [12]

[12] Sara Jaffarian, "The Library-Centered School," in Robert H. Anderson, *Teaching in a World of Change.* New York: Harcourt, Brace & World, Inc., 1966, p. 164.

The explosion of materials may also accelerate the use of microfilm in any of its various forms. At present, high schools have little need for this development, but the future may change this.

ENCYCLOPEDIAS   There are more than thirty encyclopedias currently available. Although they overlap in content, they vary considerably in approach. Some are aimed at mature interests and reading levels; others are directed at youth. These sets are relatively expensive, costing from one to three hundred dollars. Many of the publishers bring out accompanying yearbooks that keep the sets up-to-date.

Because encyclopedias are expensive, schools should select with care. Chief criteria to be kept in mind are kinds of information needed by the particular school, organization of content in the books, accuracy and reliability, book architecture, and currency. Beginning teachers should be informed about these materials, their use, sources, and manner in which they are selected locally.

DICTIONARIES   Unlike encyclopedias, dictionaries are comparatively inexpensive. It is a common practice to provide each classroom with at least one unabridged edition or a smaller hand volume.

In addition to English dictionaries, schools often provide others, such as those in the foreign languages, biographies, familiar quotations, synonyms and antonyms, and thesauri.

ATLASES AND WORLD ALMANACS   Both of these reference sources will be found in the larger high schools. Usually both will be housed in the central library instead of the classrooms. The world almanac, usually paperbound, is essentially an annual publication and is a handy reference for thousands of facts on diverse topics.

COLLATERAL BOOKS   The *Dictionary of Education* defines collateral reading as "(1) Reading material related to the main topic or theme being studied as distinguished from the textual or basic material of the assignment, (2) reading related to a subject that supports and enriches or broadens the experience of the reader" (3:443).

Textbooks are of necessity much condensed and often encyclopedic in nature. It is, therefore, desirable in most instances to supplement the text with other reading opportunities. At times, the general reference type of materials described there will be adequate, but in many instances extended reading will need to be of a different type.

Teachers and librarians put heavy reliance on the reading of collateral books of the nontext or trade book type. These books cover more thoroughly and in more unified fashion such subjects as specific sciences, travel, adventure, biography, history, and fiction.

Assigned or suggested collateral reading serves several positive purposes. In any high school class there is a wide difference in aptitudes, interests, and backgrounds among the students. Collateral reading allows students to explore some of their individual interests. Textual content is extended and new viewpoints are introduced. Supplementary reading often brings freshness to assignments, as well as a wider range and greater depth. Students working on projects or developing individual reports profit from this type of reading.

Recreational reading is a concern of all teachers. Selecting suitable reading materials to fit individual needs is a never-ending activity. Teachers and librarians are constantly on the alert to locate fresh subjects with varied reading difficulty levels. Only as students find content of suitable interest and difficulty do they get fun from reading. Only then can the printed page really compete with television and the motion picture.

CURRENT MATERIALS

There are many classroom situations for which no textbooks exist; the instructional materials may be too new to be organized into book form, the field too limited or local, the study area too specialized, and so on. Underprivileged students often need learning materials for obvious reasons. Students in experimental programs have similar needs. Individually or in groups teachers attempt to organize current materials to meet their needs. The phrase "current materials" is used here in a loose sense and includes newspapers, periodicals, radio and television broadcasts, resource persons, government reports, advertising matter, field trips, and miscellaneous "fugitive" materials as well as those specifically prepared.

It has been found that the judicious use of current materials, especially in the social studies, science, career studies, and English as a second language, leads to better student understanding, promotes resourcefulness and discovery, lessens the emphasis on purely verbal learning, and in general results in better student acceptance. However, the other side of the coin shows that teachers in most school systems have not been given the time in their schedules to use current materials properly. In fact, this very point has been one of the grievances behind several recent strikes by teachers (see Chapter 20).

In Ecclesiastes we learn "Of the making of many books there is no end. . . ." If this is true of hard-cover books, what can we say of pamphlets, brochures, newspapers, magazines, tracts, comics, and the miscellany of other printed materials?

PAMPHLETS AND BROCHURES   Materials in this classification have three main sources of origin—free or sponsored materials, materials created by the schools themselves, and materials produced by professional sources.

Free, sponsored, or low-cost pamphlets are legion. Literally hundreds of American (and some foreign) manufacturers and commercial groups publish thousands of pamphlets each year. Some are designed for general consumption; others are prepared specifically for the schools. And the reports from these firms indicate that pupils and teachers are requesting free materials in a mighty stream. Some may be thrown away, but many have educational value and find a place in the current materials curriculum files.

Selection of these materials by teachers and librarians becomes a burdensome task. Obviously, the business establishments are not so much interested in the education of the youth as they are in placing their name and their product in a favorable light. Advertising is at times overt; at others, hidden. Propaganda designed to change ideas is even more dangerous than just the sale of products. Teachers considering free materials will do well to study them with great care. Since the use of free and free-loan materials has become a matter of grave concern, schools considering their use should adopt a policy statement to guide both teachers and administrative officials. Several organizations have drawn up criteria to help in the more intelligent selection and use of such materials. For example, the American Association of School Administrators has offered these criteria:

1. Define clearly the relation that such materials must bear to the basic purposes and objectives of the schools.
2. Provide specific guidelines upon which rules for selection and use can be based.
3. Give assurances to teachers concerning the limits within which they have official backing in the selection and use of materials.
4. Delegate responsibility to appropriate administrative officials or other school personnel for selection and handling of materials.
5. Provide some means of maintaining community confidence in the schools and of safeguarding against unwarranted pressures.
6. Make available necessary funds so that teachers are not forced to use free materials as substitutes for superior materials that could be purchased.

And the same association suggests that materials be checked for such biases as the following:

1. Convictions presented as facts
2. One point of view stressed in an obviously two-sided issue
3. Emphasis on what is wrong, rather than what is right
4. "Theme of presentation deals with matters of basic concern to others than the producer of the item—usually others in competition or in conflict with the producing agency" [13]

[13] American Association of School Administrators, *Choosing Free Materials for Use in the Schools*. Washington, D.C.: National Education Association, 1955; see also criteria developed by the Instructional Materials Committee of the California School

Pamphlets produced by professional or semiprofessional organizations, agencies, and groups are also widely used. It can reasonably be assumed that bias and propaganda are absent from these materials, or at least that they are at such a minimum as not to be objectionable. Materials considered here are usually purchased by the school district. Pamphlets supplement standard texts and have the advantage of timeliness. They can be revised easily and frequently at little expense. In this manner the latest events and trends can be made available. Also, it is possible to tailor content to fit specific class and individual needs. These materials fit short units of study, introductory lessons, review or summarizing lessons, or nearly any lesson type. Students tend to take a favorable attitude toward them.

In some states, statutes prohibit the expenditure of public funds for unbound books. This is a problem that time is correcting. An increasing percentage of the schoolbook fund is going into the purchase of pamphlet materials. There is an increasing number of quality paperbacks being published each year, and many schools use them to supplement other texts. Libraries are also adding paperbacks to their collections. The revolution in paperbacks has met with great public favor. Their use in schools both as texts and reference sources has the approval of parents and students. The paperback is economical and problems of currency are less difficult than with the hardback book.

MAGAZINES AND NEWSPAPERS Approximately 1900 daily and 9000 weekly newspapers are printed in the United States with a circulation of nearly 65 million. Some 7000 magazines are published with an output of 400 million copies, and of this output five of the leading magazines account for nearly 32 million copies (5:1;10:3).

Although newspapers are one of the greatest sources of information, they are poorly read by both adults and youth. Studies show that neither have habits of discrimination. Sports and comics are widely read, but editorials are read by less than one fifth of the readers.

Teachers should find a way to encourage discriminative reading, regular study habits, and the use of the newspaper as a source of ideas about current topics. It has been suggested that newspapers be made an integral part of classroom instruction, and that they be readily available to students in all schools. Although the newspaper may be most appropriate for use in the social studies, it carries items of value to practically every teacher in the school. Foreign language teachers know the value of foreign newspapers. Most of the larger magazines print foreign language editions

Supervisors Association, Allen Risdon, chairman, published in Sacramento by the California State Teachers Association, 1954; and Association for Supervision and Curriculum Development, *Using Free Materials in the Classroom*. Washington, D.C.: National Education Association, 1953.

of all issues. Because these have great value in the schools, they are often given to language classes along with the English editions.

Magazines range all the way from the trashy to the scholarly and sophisticated. Students are more at home with magazines than with newspapers. This is due both to content and to structure. Magazine pictures and illustrations, for example, are more striking than those of the newspapers and communicate more effectively.

This discussion of magazines and newspapers has been slanted to publications intended for the general public. There are several magazines and newspapers aimed solely at classroom use. Normally, these are less colorful, less expensive, and less appealing; nevertheless, they fill a useful place and justify their existence. This kind of publication is found more often in classrooms than are general publications. A few of these publications for the secondary school are:

American Education Publications, 1250 Fairwood Ave., Columbus, Ohio, 43216: *Current Events, Every Week, Our Times, Current Science, Read Magazine*

Civic Education Service, 1733 K St. N.W., Washington, D.C., 20006: *Junior Review, Weekly News Review, American Observer*

Scholastic Magazines, 33 W. 42 St., New York, N.Y., 10036: *Junior Scholastic, Senior Scholastic, World Week, Practical English, Literary Cavalcade, Co-ed.*

COMIC BOOKS   Probably no learning material is so controversial as the comic book or comic strip (the cartoon falls into another category). Even to consider the comic book as a learning material is debatable; yet more than a million of these books are printed annually, read avidly, traded, hoarded. The negative attitude of adults toward comics has somewhat abated by the time the child has reached junior high school, and neither teachers nor parents are so militant. There are, however, still antisocial and antimoral aspects that should not be overlooked.

On the positive side, the picture story holds a great educational potential. Students like this medium of communication, and it may become the beginning of rewarding reading habits. There is reason to believe that the quality of comic books is improving. Teachers are finding more and more ways to exploit and capitalize on the medium, many using comic materials regularly in bulletin board displays, either alone or in conjunction with other materials. Still others have used comics as a springboard for written and spoken exercises and for motivation of creative activity in art. Coupled with the cartoon, the comic picture or series has been used in teaching grammatical structure, foreign languages, safety, driver education, science, guidance principles, consumer education, salesmanship, and other topics.

CREATING READING MATERIALS

It is erroneous to think that the creation of reading materials is an activity for the elementary school only. Junior and senior high school teachers have found this a useful learning project in certain situations. Four of the many reasons for such an activity are mentioned here.

1. Students who have written something worthwhile should share it with others, as is done when a good short story or poem is published in a newspaper or magazine. But it may be more valuable to have multiple copies made and used in a standard curricular manner. The material becomes more important, is more likely to be permanent, and is more adaptable to learning purposes.

2. Students need the experience of serious writing. Writing is more real when it is likely to serve more than a mere "exercise need." Material for reproduction and circulation must be carefully and near-professionally produced. This means factual accuracy, careful analysis, originality in presentation, and clarity of expression.

3. Often there is a paucity of material on a subject being studied. If students, singly or as a group, produce something of value, it should be retained as valuable source material for other students who will study the same topic. Such a situation is easily conceivable in the study of a community—industries, ethnic groups, cultural agencies, finances, or other aspects of community life.

4. The motivational value inherent in a project that will probably be used by other students, either at the time or later, is significant.

Who creates these materials at the local level? The introduction above has been entirely from the standpoint of the student, probably the most important production source. But the materials may be produced by teachers, or by committees of teachers and supervisors, as a curriculum unit, for example. There are some study guides of such outstanding worth that they could well be reproduced and made available to other teachers. This has unusual motivational value for teachers. As a matter of fact, a high school might well have as an annual project the publication of a yearbook, anthology, or collection of faculty writings of the year. This would in fact be "our best" for the year—poems, stories, dramas, outlines, study guides, histories, surveys, bibliographies, interviews, reports on foreign trips and study, and other writings.

How will locally produced reading materials be reproduced for use by others? There are many ways. Which one is employed will probably depend upon funds available, facilities, and the permanency sought for the publication. In some cases, extra copies may be unnecessary. A bound typewritten copy is placed on the classroom library shelf or housed in the main library. One college for years has followed a plan of binding in manila folders all its research papers of quality and storing them in the library. They are available for graduate students year after year in much the same way that dissertations are available. Some critics fear the presence of these papers will encourage "cribbing." Of course this may occur, but probably these papers are no more of a temptation than other printed documents in the library.

Important stories, poems, correspondence with foreign students, or other compositions may be printed in the school paper. This is commonplace, but it needs some buildup; otherwise, students may wish to fill the pages of the paper with trivia.

REPRODUCING MATERIALS   To provide multiple copies of materials, schools usually use the liquid duplicator, stencil duplicator, offset press, or letterpress techniques. Each has advantages and limitations. Teachers should know these advantages and limitations and the local production facilities. It is assumed here that all teachers know how to make "ditto" and "mimeo" copy.

Liquid duplicators, often called hectographs, are of two types. The spirit or liquid type, a direct process, is probably the most commonly used throughout the country. It is inexpensive and easy to operate. As many as 300 good copies can be made from one master. Copies will fade and are often messy to prepare, but they are cheap. The gelatin process is similar to the so-called spirit process, but is not in as common use.[14]

The stencil or mimeograph process is also a very common one, and the machine is also easy to operate. Copy lasts almost indefinitely, and a master will reproduce 500 copies with short-run stencils, or as many as 10,000 with special stencils.[15]

Offset printing as represented by the multilith or multigraph is an even more satisfactory reproduction method. Offset printing produces more professional-appearing copy and thousands of copies can be made from a master. Also, photographs can be incorporated into the copy. One disadvantage is that the equipment is expensive and the preparation of masters and plates is more technical than that in the preceding processes. The offset press is more likely to be found in the district school office than in building offices.

Letterpress is expensive and must be done commercially or in the school print shop. School printing is limited. Only a very unusual local publication is likely to be reproduced by letterpress. However, ambitious projects, usually those produced at the supervisory or administrative level for wide distribution, will be set in letterpress type.

[14] Anyone unfamiliar with the operation of this equipment might like to review the motion picture *Duplicating by the Spirit Method,* 15 min., color, produced by Bailey Films, Inc. This film shows step-by-step processes.

[15] *Mimeographing Techniques,* film, 17 min., color, produced by Bailey Films, Inc., explains the process.

A word of caution regarding the use of copyrighted material should be added. There is an increasing liberality in the matter of reproducing copyrighted material for educational use, but there are limits. At this moment the copyright law is being rewritten. Teachers who plan more than a routine reproduction of a small amount of copyrighted material should request the owner of the copyrighted material for permission to use it.

A MATERIALS FILE

A majority of the contents of a materials file will be "print" or "graphic" in type. It is a cliché that a good craftsman must know how to use the tools of his trade. It might also be added that he must have the tools. This applies with equal force to teachers. In the case of teachers, many of the tools are provided by the school districts simply as a matter of course, including textbooks, reference books, maps, globes, projectors, recorders, radios, and many other materials. The provision of these teaching tools is in varying degree. Some schools supply them in abundance; others skimp. Some districts provide what they call "basic" materials and "basic" becomes a matter of definition.

Regardless of district, teachers always feel the need for more and more specific learning materials. These needs go far beyond what is provided. Therefore, teachers make collections of their own, invent devices, reshape what they have, and give their ingenuity full rein.

It is in the area of "fugitive" materials that student teachers and beginning teachers feel at a disadvantage. They simply have not been "in the business" long enough to have collected materials to supplement what is provided. Prospective teachers will be well advised to begin a materials file just as soon as they are admitted to a teacher-education program.

Intelligent long-range planning in this field will pay good dividends. By the time a prospective teacher reaches the stage of student teaching, he should have a sizable materials file. This file, collection, or accumulation could include flat pictures, clippings, poems, bibliographies, lists of field trips, booklets or sources of free and inexpensive materials, charts, graphs, diagrams, sketches, drawings, maps, bulletin board designs and ideas, facsimiles, and other two-dimensional materials. The materials file might just as well include such three-dimensional materials as models, specimens, artifacts, or small hand tools. The industrial arts teacher, for example, will quite naturally have both types.

When materials have been collected, or as they are collected, they must be organized or catalogued in some meaningful manner. Unorganized materials are little better than no materials. There are hosts of possible classifications. The commonest one is by subject matter, topic, or area. The prospective teacher might wish to give some thought to classification by instructional concepts or values with subject matter classifications in subdivisions. Instead of "social studies" with subdivisions of United Nations, UNESCO, U.S. Senate, Supreme Court, these subdivisions might well follow "value" or "goal" headings such as room environment, contemporary problems, individual study, committee study, oral reports, or motivation.

Storage often becomes a problem. It is the last step in the ongoing clip-collect-file-store formula. Each individual must solve this problem in his own way. Schoolrooms are being built with facilities that include built-in drawers and cabinet space for flat and three-dimensional materials. Filing cabinets help with the storage of mounted pictures, clippings, and lists. But, before one has a classroom, one can utilize pressed-board filing drawers, collapsible file boxes and folders, vertical file boxes, orange crates, or other available storage areas.

SELECTED READINGS

1. Bergeson, Clarence O., "Relationship of Library Science and Audiovisual Instruction," *Audiovisual Instruction*, 12 (February 1967), 100–103.

2. Cronbach, Lee J., ed., *Text Materials in Modern Education*. Urbana: University of Illinois Press, 1955.

3. *Dictionary of Education*, 2d ed. New York: McGraw-Hill Book Company, Inc., 1959.

4. *Guidelines for Textbook Selections*. Washington, D.C.: National Education Association, 1963.

5. Kinder, James S., *Audio-Visual Materials and Techniques*, 2d ed. New York: American Book Company, 1959, chap. 1–2.

6. Kinder, James S., *Using Audio-Visual Materials in Education*. New York: American Book Company, 1965, chaps. 1–2, 8.

7. Madden, Charles F., "Person to Person Teaching," *Saturday Review*, 47 (July 18, 1964), 50–51, 60.

8. Murray, Thomas R., and Sherwin G. Swartout, *Integrated Teaching Materials*. New York: David McKay Company, Inc., 1960, chaps. 1–6.

9. *New Teaching Aids for the American Classroom*. Part I: "The Classroom of Tomorrow"; research papers by Ralph W. Tyler, "Social Trends and Problems of Tomorrow's Schools"; Ray M. Hall, "The Nature of Tomorrow's Classroom"; and William E. Spaulding, "Old and New Teaching Aids." Stanford, Calif.: The Institute for Communication Research, 1960.

10. Wigren, Harold E., "A Symposium—Don't Touch! This is Copyrighted!" *Educational Leadership*, 26 (December 1968), 254–257.

11. Wittich, Walter A., and Charles F. Schuller, *Audiovisual Materials: Their Nature and Use*, 4th ed. New York: Harper & Row, Publishers, 1967, chaps. 1–2.

CHAPTER 10 / *Instructional Materials: Conventional Audio-Visual Types*

In addition to the printed learning materials discussed in the preceding chapter, there are almost endless numbers of other learning materials, many of which will be treated in the present and following chapter. For convenience, these materials are separated into those that are rather commonplace, and those that are usually considered to be new. Widely varying uses, innovations, research, and new modifications and extensions of older devices constantly provide new dimensions. A relatively old device may lie dormant for years, only to spring into dynamic prominence as research and technology push ahead.

Teachers need to remind themselves that materials which have become commonplace or which are inexpensive or near at hand are not necessarily obsolete. Often the newer media have more glamour and publicity but do not necessarily replace other tried devices. Usually, the newer devices provide teachers with a greater range of tools with which to do the instructional job demanded by modern developments. Programmed learning materials, for example, do not replace films or field trips; they simply add depth to the teachers' instructional repertoire.

FLAT PICTURES

Pictures do not in and of themselves possess any mystical powers to teach; yet they have one of the greatest potentials of all types of learning materials. Young and old, dull and bright like pictures; their appeal is universal. Children become acquainted with them long before they start to school, and adults continue to "look at" or "read" pictures long after they have completed formal schooling; in fact, as long as they live. Pictures are among the cheapest and most readily available of all learning materials. Many of them are free. Teachers and students gather pictures from magazines, newspapers, advertisements, pamphlets, posters, circulars, and an endless number of sources. But, like all other learning materials, their values vary and their selection and use should be given careful consideration.

Pictures serve many purposes in the learning process. They motivate and vitalize learning and they clarify vague ideas. Abstractions nearly always need clarification, and concrete imagery should be used with them wherever possible. Even knowledge of concrete things, skills, and processes is often vague or limited. Pictures can assist in providing more complete and meaningful ideation.

TYPES OF PICTURES

Flat pictures consist of study prints, photographs, textbook illustrations, and unprojected pictures of all kinds. They are all much the same, although study prints usually are pictures that are more carefully selected, mounted, and curriculum-oriented.

Photographs are either made from original negatives or copied from existing pictures. Usually photographic copies are more interesting than the clippings or newspaper pictures they are taken from because they have more warmth, definition, and detail. If needed in quantity, photographic pictures are usually mounted and sometimes laminated and are expected to serve teachers and students over a long period of time. Many school districts have photographers and equipment and provide this service for teachers, but, on the whole, only a small percentage of the teachers of a district ever get much photographic assistance.

A junior high school social studies teacher felt that he needed pictures of world architecture as found in his city. None of the study prints in the local audio-visual collection told the story. He needed tailor-made materials. With the aid of the school photographer, twenty-six examples of local architecture, representing types from the classic Greek and Roman to the severely functional modern, were photographed. The photographs, enlarged to 11- by 14-inch size, and mounted, along with the other more standard types of learning materials, provided much of the content for the unit "The Emergence of Modern Architecture."

Instead of preparing this study print set as 11- by 14-inch mounted pictures, it would have been just as easy, probably easier, to have made the same content available as a set of 2- by 2-inch color slides. Moreover, if properly prepared, both types of pictures could have been made from the same negatives. More will be said about slide production later in this chapter.

PREPARATION AND USE

Some of the purposes that flat pictures serve have already been pointed out. How can they be most effectively used? A rather common use is the introduction of new units of study. They orient the thinking, they set the stage for new subject matter, and they involve nearly every subject or experience unit in the curriculum.

Flat pictures could do much to motivate a class in American literature preparing to study the short stories of Bret Harte. Pictures of the author, frontier buildings and settlements, signs or posted billboards, dance halls, derringers, costumes, snow drifts, leafless trees, cowboys and miners, and a lonely editor setting hand type by the dim light of a kerosene lamp establish the mood. Additional motivation could be provided by artists' sketches of some of the characters from "The Outcasts of Poker Flat" and "The Luck of Roaring Camp," such as Mr. Oakhurst, Kentuck, the Duchess, and Yerba Bill, or of a grave at the foot of a tree with this epitaph:

BENEATH THIS TREE

LIES THE BODY

OF

JOHN OAKHURST

WHO STRUCK A STREAK OF BAD LUCK

ON THE 23D OF NOVEMBER 1850

AND

HANDED IN HIS CHECKS

ON THE 7TH DECEMBER 1850

Pictures used to introduce units need to be seen and discussed by all members of the class. They may later be exhibited on bulletin boards for study and reference.

One can hardly study pictures without enriching his experience. The nature and extent of this enrichment depend upon the amount of knowledge already possessed, the type of pictures, the manner in which the pictures are employed, and the objectives sought. Pictures do add new dimensions to learning.

Often a single picture will suffice for the objective in mind. One picture of an early cave painting found in southern France may arouse imagination, and it may actually be better than a dozen pictures. If, on the other hand, the unit to be studied is Iran, one picture obviously would not suffice. In introducing the symphonic orchestra, one picture would tell a great deal about the instruments involved, placement (location) of instruments, position of conductor and musicians, and possibly other facts. Additional pictures could very well detail the various instruments, the types of music stands, and even the meanings of the conductor's gestures.

Techniques for using pictures are manifold, but time, place, and purpose will determine which adds most to the learning process. In some instances, the teacher may prefer to arrange a display on a bulletin board and in some way incorporate it into the lesson structure.

Although unprojected pictures are being considered, attention must be called to the use of illustrations in the opaque and overhead projectors. In the former, pictures are projected without processing or preparation; in the latter, they must be transferred to a transparent medium. A projected picture may be copied on the chalkboard or on butcher paper for later use so that repeated projection is unnecessary.

PROJECTED PICTURES

In the preceding discussion, attention was given to flat pictures. Here it is directed to projected pictures, which are of two general types, still and motion.

TYPES OF PROJECTED PICTURES

Practically every high school in the nation is equipped, more or less adequately, to use most types of projected materials. The motion picture, slide, filmstrip, opaque projector, overhead projector, stereoprojector, microprojector, and tachistoscope will be considered here. Only the first is a motion device, although attempts are being made to put motion or animation in slides, filmstrips, and transparencies. These attempts depend upon polarization and are still in their infancy. They are too expensive to buy and too difficult to produce locally to justify more than an experimental use in the high school. For industry that is another matter.

PSYCHOLOGICAL AND EDUCATIONAL ADVANTAGES

As a learning material the projected picture has several advantages over the unprojected. Its use with large classes is obvious: it removes the "front row" feature of the unprojected picture. Projected pictures have a certain amount of novelty, which arouses and maintains positive student attention. To a large extent, extraneous factors that dilute and dissipate attention are eliminated, and all members of a group become engaged in one unifying activity. Minds will wander, but "woolgathering" is reduced. Novelty, of course, is not the only advantage of projected pictures; if it were, their advantage would be largely one of fostering interest.

Contrary to opinions held by some teachers, projection materials are relatively inexpensive because they may be reused many times. Thus the cost per student may become a fraction of a cent. The cost of many other learning materials, verbal and nonverbal, may be appreciably higher. Actually, good projected materials are within the budget range of every school.

In the main, the thought and understanding that go into the preparation of most filmstrips and motion pictures are worthy of mention. They are not made overnight. Producers know that they are working for a professional market and that the general acceptance of their product depends upon its quality. These materials are actually planned in curriculum terms. Of course, this is not to say that there are no poor-quality filmstrips and motion pictures, but their number is decreasing. More and more teachers and administrators have adopted this rule concerning instructional materials: "Properly prepared, wisely selected, and intelligently used."

The major psychological and professional advantage of projected pictures lies in the type of material they are. These materials visualize their topics—idea, fact, skill, process, attitude—and make them concrete and comprehensible for students. Projected materials must enable the teacher to be more proficient than he would be otherwise. School districts buy materials, not to be modern, not to be spectacular, but to enable their teachers to do a better job of instruction.

SLIDES AND FILMSTRIPS

Slides and filmstrips are much alike. One is a series of related pictures arranged in fixed sequence; the sequence of the other falls to the discretion of the teacher. There are advantages for each. It might be pointed out that the use of the filmstrip is increasing much faster than that of the slide. Whether this is occasioned by convenience or by merit cannot be determined at this time.

Slides are available in several sizes but only the 3¼- by 4-inch and the 2- by 2-inch slides will be mentioned here. The former is older, but still has pronounced usefulness in connection with handmade teaching materials. It may be made with India ink, pencils, crayons; typed; photographed on sensitive glass (positive transparency); or reproduced by a diazo or related process. The 2- by 2-inch photographic slide is available commercially, usually in sets, for a great variety of subjects. It may also be easily photographed by teacher or students to document or illustrate curriculum work. Projection is simple and inexpensive. There is a tendency to use one or only a few slides of the 3¼- by 4-inch type in a class session; more of the 2- by 2-inch size are ordinarily used. This is probably due to the fact that most of the smaller slides are bought as sets and used simply because they are there.

As filmstrip and slide materials are available in great quantity and for almost all school subjects, wise selection becomes imperative. Some materials are of most use in introducing study units, whereas others fit developmental, drill, appreciation, and review lessons. In general, slides and filmstrips are most used with large groups, but they can be adapted to small group or individual work. Many schools now making provision for more individual work have fitted out screening carrels or have sectioned off areas with a low light level where students can study slides, filmstrips, or even motion pictures much as they study books. With motion pictures or with record players, earphones are employed so that the sound does not bother nearby students. Filmstrips are as easily checked out from the library as a book, and projectors can be operated after a short period of instruction and practice.

MOTION PICTURES

The motion picture possesses practically all the advantages of other projected materials plus the big factor of motion. Motion pictures are seldom produced on subjects that are static, although animation techniques make it possible to show static subjects with great concreteness. A law in physics, for example, needs demonstration to clarify its application, and the motion picture can do this; yet the law itself is a purely verbal description of a phenomenon. Interaction and dynamic relationships among people allow the motion picture to do a superb job. What is shyness? How do totalitarian regimes operate in daily life? How does courtesy affect friends and acquaintances? How do mores shape the lives of primitive peoples? What were the events leading up to the bombardment of Fort Sumter? How did the "blue laws" of colonial New England shape the character of the citizens? Historical films can re-create and document understandings of time relationships, causes, and effects of man's aspirations, crises, and progress. They bridge the gaps of time and space.

A great many teachers and students think that the motion picture is on a much higher plane than the filmstrip or slide as a learning material. Such an opinion has no factual basis. They are two separate types of materials and one does not supplant the other. It is true that the filmstrip is a simpler and more compact device, but its values are significant. With the motion picture, as with the filmstrip, proper preparation, wise selection, and intelligent use are the teachers' guidelines.

By and large, when educational motion pictures are discussed, one is thinking in terms of the 16mm. There are, however, other sizes, particularly the 8mm. Although the 8mm. width is not a new invention, there has been a recent upsurge in experimentation with it for classroom use. Both film and projector manufacturers are forging new designs. Whereas years ago the 8mm. film was entirely silent and more or less limited to home use, present 8mm. film is essentially designed for school use (other uses still hold) and allows both silent and sound techniques. Sounding employs two devices—magnetic striping and optical sound-on-film. Naturally, different cameras and different projectors are involved.

The 8mm. film is a profitable one. Research and development have worked their way to the small end of the funnel so that we now have a categorization like this:

Image size—Standard 8; Super 8; Format M
Audio—Magnetic sound; optical sound
Loading—Cartridge load; reel load

Further standardization is sorely needed. One film processor reported in mid-1967 that in one year the 8mm. business grew more rapidly than any other film design, and that in the one-year period the ratio of Standard 8 to Super 8 had changed from 95–5 percent to 50–50 percent. Optical sound and magnetic sound are about equally divided as are cartridge and reel loading. Most commercially available 8mm. educational films are, however, cartridge-loaded.

Eight millimeter film appears to offer a simple and practical way for teachers and students to make their own motion pictures. Costs are relatively low and the automation of cameras and projectors has removed the necessity for special technical skills. Teachers College, Columbia University, has pioneered in the use of the 8mm. film for educational purposes. Each year commercial producers add hundreds of titles to the growing inventory of available films.

Many of the 8mm. films have been placed in a new classification known as "single-concept" films. These films run from thirty or forty seconds to four or five minutes and, as the title suggests, hold strictly to a single idea or concept. The mass of facts even in one subject area has increased so fast in a single generation that hundreds of target films may be preferable to a few long ones. These target films are usually designed for a particular teaching need that commercial films either do not fill or are prohibitively expensive.

Someone has said that the 8mm. film will do for the educational film what the paperback book did for publishing. A Canadian educator has set down a blueprint for the future of 8mm. development:

. . . we want a sound projector as portable as a typewriter, the price of which is to be under a hundred dollars; we want foolproof cartridge loading that will allow for individual operation, unaided, by a five-year-old child; we want thousands of single-concept films, silent and sound, in three- to ten-minute continuous loops, and we will personally supervise the visual treatment in accordance with our own professional experience and objectives, these clips to cost no less than cheaper textbooks, no more than the best reference books.[1]

OPAQUE PROJECTIONS

Although opaque projections are treated here along with filmstrips and motion pictures, they are quite different. The opaque projector is a machine that enlarges and projects images from a given medium by reflected light. In all the materials discussed the projection light goes through a translucent material, but in this instance projection is from an opaque medium. Opaque projection requires a dark room; indeed, the darker the better. But the big advantage of opaque projection is apparent: materials need no processing in order to be projected. Flat pictures of any kind, colored or monochrome, charts, graphs, sketches, postcards, cartoons, book illustrations are all ready to be projected as they are. Size

[1] Mark Slade, "Eight Millimeter: The Eighth Lively Art," *Audiovisual Screen and Audiovisual Guide,* 41 (October 1962), 599; also in Florence Henry Lee, *Principles and Practices of Teaching in Secondary Schools: A Book of Readings.* New York: David McKay Company, Inc., 1965, p. 233.

is the only consideration. Aside from the projector itself (a capital equipment item) there is no cost. Even small three-dimensional objects may be projected—for example, a farthing may be enlarged so that every member of a class can see it at the same time. Even the details of milling, date, color, wear, and texture can be noted, and if another known coin is placed alongside it, comparisons are easily made.

OVERHEAD PROJECTIONS

The overhead projector is somewhat newer than the other instructional tools being discussed, but its use is increasing rapidly. Many teachers consider it indispensable in such subjects as mathematics, science, social studies, foreign language, English, business education, and health education. It has many advantages: it gives a bright picture in a fully lighted room; it is operated from the front of the class by the instructor, who faces the class at all times; the teacher can use a pencil to point out features appearing in a picture without leaving his position at the machine; materials to be projected may be prepared in advance by a variety of techniques, or they may be placed on the projector impromptu. Thus, the points made in a lesson may be summarized in concrete form for all the members of the class to see. In this instance, the overhead becomes a "whiteboard" replacing the blackboard, and is actually easier and cleaner to use.

OTHER TYPES OF PROJECTIONS

Stereoprojectors, microprojectors, and tachistoscopes, although standard types of projection apparatus, are specialized and have limited use. Modern stereo materials and projectors are expensive and are chiefly limited to clinics, laboratories, graduate seminars, and analytical study. Microprojectors are especially useful in the biological sciences. Either wet or dry microscopic slides can be shown to an entire class at one time, obviating the need for microscopes for each member of the class. Also, in group projection the teacher knows that each member of the class sees the significant aspects of each slide. The tachistoscope is a still projector equipped with a shutterlike mechanism for flash recognition exposures. It can be used to increase attention span, rate of perception, and accuracy and speed of recognition. This apparatus, too, is specialized and will be operated chiefly by reading or other remedial clinicians. The preservice teacher will rarely, if ever, be called upon to use any of these specialized machines, but it is well to know of their existence and capabilities.

UTILIZATION OF PROJECTED PICTURES

A great deal has already been said about the use of projection apparatus and learning materials. Some more specific principles of use and examples will be of value to the beginning teacher.

A teacher of American history in the eleventh grade had just completed a unit on the War of 1812. He felt that a good review was in order, but that the review would be meaningless if it were a rehash of previous lessons. Accordingly, he selected a filmstrip entitled *The War of 1812* to provide understandings, relationships, and sequence. The filmstrip was shown in the regular classroom equipped with venetian blinds, which provided a semidarkened room. The projector was operated by a student; the instructor stood in the side aisle by the chalkboard and display area. A brief introduction set the stage, and as each frame was projected a few words were said, or, in some cases, students were brought into the discussion. Twice the screen pictures were tied to special reports that had earlier been made in class by students. And twice the instructor went briefly to a large wall map to note spatial relationships introduced in the picture. The teacher set the tempo and balanced the time so that each facet of the topic got its share of attention.

Instead of *The War of 1812* the teacher above could have selected any one or more filmstrips from a dozen titles available to him. For an introductory lesson or for a developmental lesson, undoubtedly the selection would have been different.

During a short period of unstructured discussion about the flag and loyalty that followed the usual Pledge of Allegiance, a junior high school teacher on the first day of the fall term decided that a series of short discussions or programs about the flag would be in order. Accordingly, he prepared a series of lantern slides. On the next day two typed slides were used: 1. PLEDGE: from Old French, *plege, pleige*, and Medieval Latin, *plebium, plevium*. Today's meaning: a promise or agreement by which one binds oneself to do something; a promise. 2. ALLEGIANCE: from Middle English, *allegeaunce* and Old French, *lige, liege*. Today's meaning: devotion or loyalty to that which is entitled to obedience or service and respect.

On succeeding days one hand-drawn and lettered slide was used to illustrate the evolution of the American flag from that of June 14, 1777, with thirteen stars to the present fifty-star flag with thirteen stripes.

A general science teacher began a unit on levers with the slide illustrated in Figure 10-1.

The art class of Miss B_____ used five sets of commercially prepared 2- by 2-inch slides in the study of Japanese art. These sets were arranged to follow time developments of periods of artistic growth. Each set contained from twenty to thirty-seven slides.

Some years ago the head of the English department of an eastern high school developed the idea of using 2- by 2-inch slides in his English literature courses. Using a camera that cost less than fifty dollars, he photographed in color costumes worn by different characters as various Elizabethan plays were given at the high school, a nearby university, and

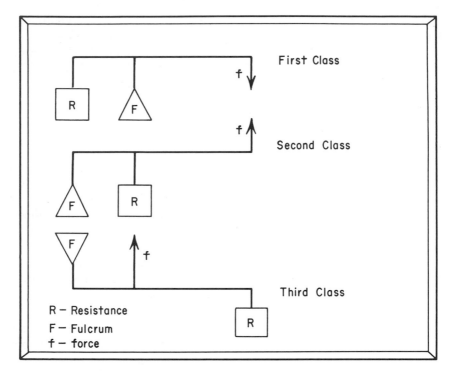

Fig. 10-1   *This handmade slide was done with India ink on clear glass. The edge was bound with regular slide binding tape.*

at the town playhouse. Over a period of several years, he gathered slides of a significant number of Shakespeare's plays. The shooting was accomplished during rehearsals. Then, with a copy lens, the teacher reproduced old frontispieces of each play to be taught. Nevertheless, the main emphasis was on the dramatic quality of the plays, which had a greater meaning for the students than before.

A physical education teacher in a large midwestern high school was required to teach several classes of first aid. Students sat through these classes with varying degrees of indifference as the teacher presented the advice of Red Cross handbooks and manuals, gave demonstrations, discussed lifesaving and economic losses, and provided an occasional Red Cross guest speaker. Using a 35mm. camera, the instructor produced seventy-two slides covering lifesaving and first aid techniques. Cases were simulated but with plausible reality. For example, three slides showed convincingly the differences between first-, second-, and third-degree burns. Skeptics of this application of the slide technique might try explaining the differences among the three types of burns without color pictures.

Use of the motion picture is now common and in the main most effective. The principles of use given later for all projected materials should make needless specific examples of the uses of the motion picture.

Overhead projectors rely to a large extent upon impromptu use or upon teacher-produced materials on a transparency medium. Any good manual gives the details of preparation. Difficult and expensive photographic techniques are no longer a necessity. Standard equipment is now available to make copies of any printed, photographed, hand-drawn, or written material. These transparencies may be made in a matter of seconds with dry, nonchemical materials and in a fully lighted room. As a matter of fact, they may be made in front of the class as needed and projected at once.

Principles of the use of projected pictures are much the same as those for other learning materials—textbooks, maps, models, or records. The particular medium involved naturally calls for adaptations and modifications.

THE TEACHER MUST PREPARE IN ADVANCE   Considering the daily lesson he is teaching, the teacher decides in advance the types of learning materials that will best help accomplish his established objectives. Next comes the selection of appropriate pictures and verbal materials. This process of selection is highly important because there are so many from which to choose. These materials are precise learning media and must fit the objectives of the unit of study. They must be integrated into lesson plans, and at this point consideration should be given to correlation with laboratory, library, creative work, discussion, and composition. Method and material are inseparable. Selection of picture materials goes hand in hand with preview.

THE CLASS MUST BE PREPARED   A class properly prepared for a learning experience profits maximally from it. Proper preparation of students for the use of visual materials shows them why they are doing a particular task, what to look for, and how to relate visual content to previous classwork, thus building a readiness for the experience to follow. Students usually learn more from a film, for example, if they are told in advance that they will be tested on its contents. Tests are not always germane; hence students should be told of other uses to which the material will be put. Unusual words, phrases, references, or locations found in the film should also be pointed out in advance.

THE EQUIPMENT MUST BE MADE READY IN ADVANCE OF PRESENTATION   Whenever equipment is used, whether in laboratory, demonstration, or in film presentation, the teacher must be sure that everything is in working order. Mechanical failure or delay wastes time, destroys confidence and accomplishes little. If student operators are used, they must be scheduled ahead of time.

THE PRESENTATION IS THE CULMINATION OF THE PREPARATION The presentation is made under the best circumstances possible and should proceed according to plan. With filmstrips and slides, there will likely be discussion, reading of captions, or reference to maps. Films are much more likely to be projected without interruption; yet they, too, may at times be used profitably with interruption. If so, the machine is stopped, and the lights may or may not be switched on, depending upon the extent of the interruption.

EFFECTIVE FOLLOW-UP IS ESSENTIAL Seldom does good usage stop with merely showing the material. Something must follow to clarify facts, to provide concept generalization, to tie material to established objectives, to clinch benefits. Follow-up activities vary with maturity of students, subjects, teachers' objectives, and other factors. Among follow-up activities are discussions, reports, tests, creative work, and construction projects. At times these activities may be voluntary; at other times, assigned. Involvement of students is a must.

One of the chief points of this discussion of principles of use is that these materials must be taught. They teach a few things by themselves, but not enough. Hanging a chart in front of a classroom is not going to accomplish much. It must become an integral part of planned instruction— *it must be taught.*

Keep these axioms in mind in using projected pictures:

Materials should be built into the warp and woof of lessons.
Teacher preparation is absolutely essential.
Pupil readiness is equally essential.
Follow-up activities are always appropriate.
Schedules of the right material at the right time in the right place are necessary.
Involvement of students should take place at every step.
Materials should be reshown or replayed as needed.
Discussion after looking and listening tends to set values in students' minds.
Supplementation with all sorts of related learning materials and activities helps give maximum results.

WHAT RESEARCH HAS TO SAY

The volume of research on the use of projected pictures is second only to that in the use of television. By and large it is overwhelmingly favorable. The director of secondary education in Mount Vernon, New York, says:

Learning is more efficient when subject matter can be presented in several forms than when only one is possible. For example, hearing and seeing reinforce reading to increase learning. Studying a globe adds to the meaning of a text book, and viewing a film adds even more (6:238).

An NEA research bulletin states:

In an experiment in ninth-grade science, for example, the classes that used regular teaching methods with a textbook and films learned 20 percent more facts than the control classes which used the same teaching methods and textbook but no films. This immediate improvement, of course, is valuable. But the really significant fact is that after six weeks the film groups retained 38 percent more information than the control group (12:10–11).

In the matter of use, research shows that the effectiveness of a film may be nearly doubled when the presentation is properly handled. Note the following graph (8:18):

Effect of Three Methods of Film Use on Learning (Wittich and Fowlkes)

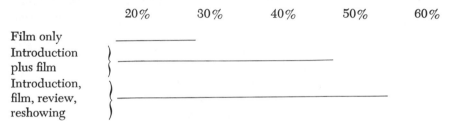

| | 20% | 30% | 40% | 50% | 60% |

Film only
Introduction plus film
Introduction, film, review, reshowing

Other researches show that many films and filmstrips can be repeated for a class with profit. At times the repetition may follow during the same class period; at other times, at a later period. McTavish has reported a research in teaching science to the effect that the second, third, and fourth showings of films produced percentage gains of 35.0, 7.4, and 1.1, respectively. Only factual knowledge was tested. Other investigators report similar results. It would seem that a second showing can be quite important, but that additional showings tend to lead to diminishing returns (8:18).

Instructional materials should be used in the regular classroom. Classes should not be shifted to an auditorium or a special room. Students learn best in their regularly accustomed learning environment. This conclusion is undoubtedly the opinion of many experienced teachers, and is also the finding of controlled researches by Krasker, Knowlton, Tilton, and Stoddard (8:18).

A word of caution is also found in the research on the concentration or density of concepts in films. This relates closely to the research on values to be obtained from repeated showings.

A research study was carried out on how much a film should attempt to teach within a specified time. The variable here, the number of facts, was called the concept density. It was found that most teaching films have too high a concept density, and reduction in the teaching load of a film improves its effectiveness. On the other hand, there is a limit to how little a film should attempt to teach. Oversimplification is a possibility also. The experiment confirms, however, the well-known fact that most audio-visual materials attempt to cover too much ground. In any case, the concept density should be adjusted to the level of the class using the film. Part of this adjustment would, of course, have to be made individually for members of any class by the teacher who knows the class (12: 22–23).

Requests by teachers for students to take notes is almost a stereotyped procedure in the use of films, outside readings, field trips, panel discussions, and the appearance of resource speakers. Insofar as the motion picture is concerned, this procedure cannot be recommended. Experiments have shown that "students who took notes during a film showing learned and retained appreciably less than those who did not take notes. Apparently a motion-picture film is such a condensed, fast-moving body of content that students who took notes missed some important material while they were not looking at the screen" (12:21).

In the matter of values of color over those of monochrome, research provides no definitive answer. About all that can be said is that if color will add to understanding and to artistic appreciation, it should be used. In many instances it adds reality and vividness, as it does in films about people, flora, fauna, art. "In the realm of nature," says one writer, "color and meaning are virtually synonymous." In this modern age, students have come to expect color in communications media—films, television, books, and magazines. Poor color can be distracting, but present-day film can be said to have "natural color" quality. Black-and-white films, like silent films, belong to yesterday, although in some instances they may still have value.

Among the many studies of film grammar some have been directed toward the values of "cues" and "prompts"—pop-in labels, moving arrows, and the like. These devices are effective in emphasizing important points; however, at times these very points seem to be learned at the expense of others in the film.

Graphs in film, like graphs in printed material, require special training for effective use. Types of graphs should be closely related to the kinds of data represented.

A teacher's announcement at the beginning of a film that a test will be given later invariably produces noticeable results. This forced motivation appears to activate viewers toward organizing the content for conscious recall. Research, however, has established the fact that under certain conditions there is demonstrable *covert* learning. Thus, viewers can *think* the material without taking notes, speaking, or otherwise reacting *overtly.*

The preceding paragraphs are intended only to direct attention to the fact that the use of these materials has been carefully studied in laboratory and classroom. The professional literature abounds in researches that illustrate the benefits of audio-visual techniques. The references at the close of this chapter are recommended for further study.

OBSTACLES TO BETTER USE

There are also numerous obstacles to more effective use. Most of these obstacles have administrative origins. Yet in many instances teachers can, if they are willing, offset or minimize them. In the case of projected materials, often-encountered difficulties are inability to darken classrooms properly and to improve the acoustics. Unsatisfactory room conditions plague effective teaching in many ways. Along with physical obstacles is the lack of a suitable place for previewing and studying materials before they are used in the classroom.

Many school buildings are inadequately stocked with equipment. Scheduling becomes a problem, and in some cases only the aggressive teachers get the equipment. Others tend to give up after a few turn-downs. The same difficulty obtains in getting films, maps, and other materials from the central materials center when needed. In some schools, where there is a tendency to schedule "movie days," some misconceptions are involved. First, there is no point in showing "movies"; only educational films should be shown. Next, films should not be scheduled for a stereotyped or mechanical showing because of a calendar. Films should be shown whenever they contribute to the educational goals sought by the teacher; they may be more appropriate on Tuesday instead of Thursday or on Monday instead of Friday. Much of this improper use stems from an inadequate amount of equipment in the building. Even the catalogues are so vague that teachers have difficulty finding materials. Delivery is at times not dependable. Often there is no stand-by equipment in case of breakdown. All this adds up to discouragement and disillusion.

But better audio-visual usage is steadily gaining. School budgets make increasing provision for materials and equipment. Special assistance from the federal government has brought millions of dollars worth of equipment to the schools since the passage of the National Defense Education Act (NDEA) of 1958. Now school buildings are being planned with an eye to a new emphasis on the "new media" in teaching. New instructional organization, such as team teaching, tends to promote better usage. The noticeable upsurge in the use of audio-visual materials steadily minimizes and eliminates many of the obstacles and abuses referred to.

AUDITORY INSTRUCTIONAL MATERIALS

The audio experience is one of the most thrilling man encounters. Some say that it exceeds the visual experience in depth of esthetic emotion. An impairment of either the visual or auditory sense is a severe handicap to any individual.

Audio communication involves two reciprocal acts, speaking and listening. Although the ability to utter sounds is general to the animal kingdom, intelligible language is limited to man. Listening or hearing, too, is a general ability, but when coupled with attention or the ability to concentrate, it has narrow limitations. Training and developing speaking competence has been a part of the school curriculum for years, but listening had received short shrift until about the mid-twentieth century. Even now, listening—hearing, understanding, and remembering—is taught incidentally in most schools, whereas reading, writing, and speaking are given large time blocks. It is commonly understood that adult communication skills consist of about 45 percent listening, 30 percent speaking, 16 percent reading, and 9 percent writing. A Greek philosopher once remarked, "We have two ears and one mouth that we may listen the more and talk the less."

TYPES OF AUDITORY INSTRUCTIONAL MATERIALS

The production of sound, the recording of sound, and the reception of auditory stimuli are phenomenally successful commercial ventures. The equipment used by schools consists of microphones, public address systems, radios, tape recorders, phonographs, earphones, and listening posts. The materials consist of disc records and magnetic tapes. Through the use of these materials and equipment, sound can be conveyed, amplified, and recorded. Other sound instruments and materials serve visual as well as auditory purposes—for example, sound motion pictures, sound filmstrips, videotape, and television. By putting together several pieces of equipment, the school may develop a sound laboratory or a sound system.

USES AND PURPOSES

Practically all high school teachers find that audio devices and techniques have values in teaching. The uses to which these devices and related teaching methods are put are manifold. The following are some of those of most value to high school teachers.

ENRICHMENT   Recorded sound adds a new dimension to culture. Nothing can replace the advantage of hearing great composers play or sing their own compositions, or world renowned orchestras brilliantly perform the orchestrations of the best composers. Through recordings the world becomes a stage where everyone may hear operatic stars, actors, poets, scientists, statesmen, and leaders from all fields.

PRESERVATION   Contemporary sounds need never be lost. They can be preserved for all time. Who has not wished that he could hear the voice of George Washington, Alexander Hamilton, Benjamin Franklin, Daniel

Webster, Abraham Lincoln, or, going farther back, that of Cicero or Demosthenes? Future generations will be able to hear today's world leaders. Although Edison invented the phonograph in 1877, it has only been since 1900 that the sound of history has been recorded "live." Invention of the magnetic wire recorder and later the magnetic tape recorder did much to simplify sound recording.

RECORDING OF CONTEMPORARY EVENTS   All manner of current events can be recorded for later use. Some of these recorded events may have transient value only, as, for example, the early morning recording of news items from the news fronts of the world to be used later in the day in history and social studies classes. Other recordings, such as the President's message to Congress, a session of the United Nations, a court trial, or a conference, may have long-range values. Many school libraries have audio copies of the abdication speech of Edward VIII, President Roosevelt's speech to Congress requesting a Declaration of War against Japan, General MacArthur's speech before Congress, and the Joseph McCarthy hearings.

PATTERN FOR REMEDIAL PRACTICE   Teachers of speech, music, and foreign language make signal uses of audio devices. It is almost imperative that these teachers have available to them sound instruments if they are to be expected to accomplish maximum results.

In remedial work repetition of a sample or pattern is almost axiomatic, but the repetition needs to be matched against the pattern. This is the basis of correct pronunciation whether in English or a foreign language. The requirement is the same for voice development in speech or singing. With the handicapped, techniques may require that the student watch his vocal cords in a mirror, sense the muscle contractions kinesthetically, or employ one or more of a dozen techniques.

Coupled with remedial work is "spot" recording of an analytical nature. A member of the football coaching staff may sit in the stands and, with tape recorder and microphone, analyze an entire game. This can be a penetrating account of the plays seen by a specialist removed from the emotions and immediate actions on the bench. A later playback for staff or players will provoke lively discussion.

The audio-lingual approach is much in favor in foreign language instruction. It requires repetition and continuous practice. The tape recorder is indispensable.

CAPTURE OF NATURAL SOUNDS   Sounds of birds, animals, the sea, the hurricane, the jungle, eruption of a volcano or a geyser, or any other nature sounds can be brought into the classroom anywhere at any time.

CAPTURE OF SOUNDS OF INDUSTRY AND URBAN LIFE   The rhythmic sound of electronic computers and the hum of industry are equally important, and just as easily brought to the classroom. The thud of paced traffic on a freeway, the sound of screeching brakes, or the thumping of a railroad car are a part of modern life.

REPORTING AND RECORDING   Tape recorders enable teachers and students to broaden their means of reporting and recording researches, committee findings, interviews, projects, inquiries, and similar activities. Students in a junior high school social studies class developed individual projects in connection with a unit on Western Europe. Among the projects were political maps, product maps, papier-mâché relief maps, models of castles, scrapbooks of pictures, sketches, and an assortment of papers and pamphlets. Each student made a brief explanation of his project to the class. A table microphone and a tape recorder recorded the oral presentation and the questions raised by members of the class.

To what extent can teachers use this equipment for reporting and recording? How can most effective use be made of the techniques?

"VOICESPONDENTS" AND "TAPE PALS"   The magnetic tape can be to voice communication what letters are to written communication. Pen pals with students in foreign countries are common enough. Somewhat less common are "voicespondents," or an exchange of tapes between, for instance, a junior high school English class in San Francisco and a similar class in the rural Midwest. High school seniors might wish to exchange tapes with their counterparts in Germany, Japan, or any other foreign country. Topics of world concern might well evoke lively interest.

Practically any device or method that creates interest, quickens anticipation, arouses curiosity, or provides similar valuable stimulation finds a place in the instructional repertory. Auditory instructional materials and equipment can often do just that. The topic of listening, important to the use of audio materials, was discussed in Chapter 7 in connection with *communication skills*.

GRAPHIC INSTRUCTIONAL MATERIALS

"Graphics" is a word of Greek origin used to refer to the art of expressing ideas by lines, pictures, charts, or diagrams. As used here the term is general enough to include charts, diagrams, graphs, sketches, cartoons, maps, engravings, and related media. By means of graphics man has added another dimension to communication. Graphics enable us to present ideas and facts in condensed and summarized form in a vivid and concise manner. Usually, graphic presentation means concrete presentation, but this is not always true; some graphics become noticeably abstract.

It is difficult to conceive of modern communication without graphics.

They are widely employed in education, business, industry, government, and advertising. If there is need to catch attention, to present facts succinctly and quickly, or to sell an idea, graphics may be advantageously used.

Someone once defined graphics as "visual shorthand"; undoubtedly they are considered the spark plugs of reporting and selling by business, industry, and the government. Research and innovations have reached a point where it is almost possible to refer to the science of graphics. It might be said that graphics are an essential part of the science of communication, because communication has been very simply defined as "anything that conveys meaning, that carries a message from one person to another."

The five factors that give graphics such importance in the schools have already been implied. Specifically they are communication, concreteness, creativity, motivation, and economy. Little need be said about these facts other than to remark that graphics in and of themselves may not be concrete. To be concrete, ideas and data put in graphic form must be consciously simplified; otherwise the communication may be complex and baffling. Students should be taught how to read graphics. Kinder has remarked, "The teacher who cannot read graphics suffers from a form of illiteracy; the teacher who cannot produce graphics lacks one kind of ability to communicate" (9:379). Of course, commercially produced graphics may be purchased, but those produced by teachers and students predominate.

COMMON TYPES

Practically every teacher in the secondary schools has used these materials at one time or another. In some curriculum areas they are so important that they are used constantly. Diagrammatic drawings in industrial arts are used to show flow of electricity, engine structure, stresses and strains, magnetism, and the workings of many kinds of machinery. Schematic drawings are likewise useful in botany, physics, chemistry, astronomy, and general science. Social studies teachers use them to show relationships among social agencies, institutions, and individuals. Attempts to illustrate the theory of probability in mathematics, for example, will in all likelihood call for some sort of diagrammatic device. Uses in many other subject areas are equally evident.

CHARTS AND GRAPHS Possibly the commonest types of graphics are charts and graphs. Practically every teacher in the secondary school uses them at one time or another, although quite naturally they are more important in certain curricular areas. Textbooks make abundant use of them to illustrate and clarify purely verbal content. Teachers, too, use them for like reasons either by presenting large predrawn sheets or by turning to the chalkboard to illustrate impromptu. Students often use them in oral presentations and reports.

The teacher who feels the need for help in constructing or understanding the various types of charts and graphs should consult any good audiovisual text, or a specialized book on graphics. Many methods texts, as well as courses, give this topic comprehensive treatment.

POSTERS   Posters are used to produce room environment; to promote an event, issue, or campaign; to assist in teaching an idea or a process; and to remind students of something that they may forget. Posters must tell their message quickly because they are read at a glance, and seldom if ever studied intently. Therefore they must be simple, carry a single idea, be concise, and use wording set in banner type with bold titles that tend toward "sloganizing."

Most students enjoy making posters, although older students may try to excuse themselves on the grounds of lack of artistic ability. Posters may be purchased but this is done infrequently because the poster is designed for so specific a purpose that it must ordinarily be made to order. However, in the realm of free and inexpensive or sponsored materials there are posters galore. They may promote some of the school objectives, such as proper diet and nutrition, as do the posters from the dairy council and the meat institute. Other posters may promote safety, continuous savings, or the benefits of exercise. Nevertheless, one must beware of free posters because many of them are designed to promote vested interests. On the use of sponsored materials, schools must maintain a policy that protects students from propaganda but at the same time does not overlook materials that enhance socially approved educational objectives.

Art ability is unquestionably an asset in the preparation of charts, graphs, and posters, yet teachers with little developed art skill can make effective graphics. Measured and ruled lines and geometric forms can be effective although they are likely to be formal. Freehand drawing seems best, but even without this skill, stick figure drawing is so simple that anyone can master it with little practice. Stick figures are rudimentary unadorned drawings of objects and figures. A few conventionalized lines will easily show human figures in such actions as standing, sitting, running, marching, or listening.

CARTOONS   Cartoons are another form of graphics. These interpretive pictures employ bold satire, exaggeration, and caricature to catch and hold attention in order to convey a message. Cartoons tend to be abstract and adult in their communication, and may therefore have to be interpreted; yet they are commonly employed by textbook authors, journalists, reporters, and others with a message. A cartoon can carry associated ideas better than dozens of words. A few thought-provoking cartoons and a few questions about them can interest most classes. Students like to post cartoons on bulletin boards, and if they are appropriate and germane to the subject, they can be valuable. Students also like to use them in poster construction, particularly in such matters as advertising a school dance or a picnic, in promoting a courtesy or cleanup campaign, or in discussions of school policy in the student newspaper.

No one should belittle or underestimate the value of cartoons. The beginning teacher should learn to use them, and whenever possible exploit their uniqueness to make instruction more effective.

MAPS AND GLOBES   The map and globe are very specialized forms of graphics and are so unlike charts, graphs, diagrams, and sketches that their meaning and use must be specifically taught. This instruction begins in the elementary school and more advanced understanding is added in the junior and senior high school. A preponderance of the use of this form of graphics is tied to the area of the social studies. Without these aids the interrelationships of man, his environment, and his culture would at best be hazy. Very few high school students will be carefully drawing maps, a rather common practice in bygone years. Instead they will work with illustrations in books, references, periodicals, large commercial wall maps, and globes. Modern developments in space science have added new dimensions in the understanding, use, and nature of maps and globes.

FREE AND INEXPENSIVE MATERIALS

The extensive use of so-called free and inexpensive or sponsored materials, mentioned in Chapter 9, seems to have had its inception during the depression. Schools are no longer on relief, and they can be and are being financed in a businesslike manner. Curricular, as well as all other types of materials, supplies, and equipment, should be handled by solid budget support. To rely to any extent upon sponsored instructional materials is an admission that teaching materials are of little importance in the learning process. Just as the "laborer is worthy of his hire," so, too, are instructional materials worthy of their price. If schools use sponsored materials, it cannot be too strongly urged that they adopt a policy statement to guide both teachers and administrative officials as to what materials may be used, under what conditions, and to what extent.

It was also pointed out in Chapter 9 that the American Association of School Administrators, in cooperation with principals, classroom teachers, and supervisors, has developed guidelines for a school policy concerning sponsored materials. Teachers who do turn to the sources of free or inexpensive materials may expect to find a vast quantity of mainly unevaluated learning resources. It is not an exaggeration to say that a moderate amount of correspondence would procure a truckload of pamphlets, brochures, outlines, charts, graphs, calendars, pictures, slides, filmstrips, samples, specimens, models, kits, and numerous other items. Some of this material may have real value, depending, of course, on the manner in which it is handled by the teacher. Entire learning units, in general science or health, for example, might be built on these materials.

It has been pointed out by educators that some teachers have been guilty of encouraging students to become beggars through letters requesting materials. Cases exist of pupils actually asking corporations to write term papers for them, or asking them to send packets of materials to save the writers from semester failure. Such are the lengths to which the "something for nothing" idea has spread.

COMMUNITY RESOURCES AS LEARNING MATERIALS

I would have the world to be the book my young gentlemen should study with most attention. Many strange humors, many sects, many judgments, opinions, laws, and customs teach us to judge rightly of our own actions, to correct our faults, and to inform our understanding, which is no trivial lesson.—*Montaigne*

"Have you a compass?" the teacher asked the clerk in the variety store. "Well," answered the clerk, "we have compasses for drawing circles, but none for going places."—*Edward G. Olsen*

FIELD TRIP

The term *field trip* applies to true-to-life activity engaged in by a school group that leaves the classroom and goes out to the actual source of information for learning purposes. The objectives of most field trips are to gather information firsthand about objects, places, people, or processes; to enrich, extend, validate, or vitalize information from printed or other sources; or to try to uncover entirely new data. Whether this activity is called field trip, journey, excursion, or study trip is of no consequence. It is, however, not to be confused with nonstudy trips, such as athletic events, forensic or musical contests, school hikes, picnics, sight-seeing excursions, and the like.

Field trips may not be "real-life experiencing," but their dimensions are *near real life*. Learning is concrete, sensory, and basic. Students see and observe things, places, people, and processes in life settings; they see objects in true size and in all their natural complexity; they hear natural sounds. As the poet says, "Life is real, life is earnest . . . ."

CRITERIA FOR FIELD TRIPS   Before planning any field trip, the teacher should ask himself such questions as the following:

Will the learning value from this trip justify the expense, time, and general inconvenience it may occasion?

Does the trip coordinate closely with the study going on in the classroom?

Is this trip practical from such standpoints as time involved, transportation costs, safety, and similar factors?

Could the same learning values be accomplished by use of films, models, resource persons, or other means?

Will this trip tend to promote good school-community relationships?

Will this trip be essentially an observational one or will students possibly be permitted limited participation in the processes or events studied?

Does the trip have generalized learning values?

Are there any unusual legal liabilities involved?

PLANNING A FIELD TRIP   There are five important steps in planning and executing an effective field trip.

1. *Teacher preparation.* The teacher should:
   Consult the authorities of the area to be visited.
   Visit the area; go over details.
   Arrange for transportation.
   Check on safety, restroom facilities, and so on.
   Obtain approval from school authorities.
   Notify parents; obtain consent; if this is in order, issue invitations for selected parents to accompany class on trip.
   Schedule the trip on the school calendar.
   Make arrangements with other teachers regarding absences.
2. *Class preparation for the trip.* Teachers and students should:
   Discuss the reason for the trip.
   Write questions to be answered; list things to be checked.
   Work out ways to document the trip, such as taking notes, taking pictures, recording sounds, sketching, interviewing, writing.
   Plan pretrip reading, study, film previewing.
   Discuss behavior standards for the group.
   Discuss appropriate dress.
   Plan for and appoint committees as needed.
3. *"At the site."* Students should:
   Arrive on time at scheduled meeting place.
   Stay with assigned groups or guides.
   Show an active interest.
   Procure samples, specimens, booklets, and so on, to take back to the school with permission of hosts.
   Be courteous at all times.
   See that lunch scraps and papers are neatly disposed of if lunches are carried.
   Check to see that no belongings are left behind.
4. *The follow-up.* The members of the group should:
   Review the objectives of the trip.
   Discuss individual and committee findings.

Discuss unexpected problems. Why did they arise?

Draft a thank-you letter to the hosts.

Display any specimens brought back along with any pictures taken or sketches made on the trip.

Discuss the benefits of such a trip for future classes.

Test the sentiment for other field trips.

Share the fruits of the trip with other classes through student reports, newspaper accounts, and so on.

5. *Evaluation.* The teacher should:

Prepare a written evaluation of the trip to be filed with the school principal, and/or the instructional materials center. (This report may be written by teacher or students, preferably by both.)

Answer for himself the questions, Was the trip worthwhile? Was it worth what it cost in time, money, and extra effort?

EXTENDED FIELD TRIPS

The discussion above has been based on a relatively short trip—one of a class period, a half day, or at most a full day. There are, of course, many longer trips that are extremely valuable. These trips require even greater care in planning, are usually more expensive, and are hedged with more limitations, but the values may be proportionately higher. Such trips take students from their local environment to other cities, counties, states, or even to other countries. These trips may see city students visiting the country, and rural students visiting the city. Here are a few samples of extended field trips:

A Spanish class spends a week in Mazatlán, Mexico.

A French class spends a week in Quebec, Canada.

A social studies class goes to the coalfields of southwestern Pennsylvania.

A social studies class spends a week with sharecroppers and tenant farmers.

A class goes to New York City to gather firsthand data regarding urban life and problems, the United Nations, transportation, the stock market.

A science class studies firsthand archaeology and Indian culture in New Mexico or Arizona.

A science class researches field geography in the Death Valley area.

A foreign language class enrolls in a week's seminar in Monterrey, Mexico.

A culturally minded group tours the countries of Europe or other foreign countries.

The most valuable extended field trips are those that focus on a specific topic or a single community. Thus the study of the coal mines is localized to a particular county or a particular town. Students on trips of this sort should not try to cover too much ground, but should cover more intensively a few problems or questions. These long trips should be built on contacts with people; their objective is definitely not sight-seeing, nor are they recommended for the idly curious. The type of trips discussed here are for serious students who have well-defined interests, and who have already acquired some understanding of the subject involved.

In the case of trips to other countries, the problems, understandings, and results are multiplied. Often there has been no prior foreign travel or study by most of the members of the group; hence more generalized culture tours may be in order. Even so, the field trip must be more penetrating than a family sight-seeing tour. Sometimes the problems of foreign study tours are staggering. They involve finances, passports and visas, border crossings, insurance, health risks, clothing, baggage, codes of behavior, and many others. Students and teachers must keep in mind that as visitors and learners, they are welcome; as critics or "do-gooders" they may not be.

RESOURCE PERSONS

By definition resource persons are not professionally connected with the school, but come to the school, usually without pay, to share knowledge or skill with students. It goes without saying that such persons should be unbiased, and should be able to show, present, or discuss their specialty with reasonable lucidity.

Many teachers have the mistaken impression that resource persons are valuable for and limited to the elementary school. This is far from true. Consider the many specialists available in most communities in practically every cultural, professional, vocational, industrial, and governmental field. Often the so-called average person has much to offer for a specific problem or occasion; for example, a resident who was born and reared in another country, a missionary, a soldier, a gourmet, or a senior citizen.

Resource people can often contribute new and vital ideas that enrich and motivate learning. Students develop more respect for out-of-school people; at the same time they may develop a keener appreciation of the community. In reverse, the resource person carries back to his job and the community a new understanding of the school program.

Resource persons may be invited to the school by the teacher, by individual students, or by a committee of the class. The teacher should, however, clear all invitations with the central office.

It is well to plan carefully. Select a person who knows his subject and presents it well in language that high school students understand. Give him guidance in his presentation by providing a list of questions to answer or an outline of topics that you should like to have covered. When a speaker has been secured some time in advance, verify the date a day or two before he is to appear. Needless to say, a visiting speaker should be accorded a courteous hearing. The class should be well enough prepared so that intelligent questions may be expected. A follow-up thank-you letter is in order and may most appropriately be written by the members of the class.

RESOURCES OF AN ACTIVITY OR MATERIAL NATURE

For furthering its educational program the school can conceivably draw upon activities of people, organizations, institutions, industries, and the things and places of the local environment. Increasingly, schools are viewing their communities as learning laboratories. Students are going beyond classroom walls for study and research that are real and concrete. Teachers have found this study practically self-motivating.

Students who use their community as a study laboratory tend to become more sensitive to local needs and to local problems. By its very nature, this study causes students to use scientific study techniques in the collection of data, classification, analysis, and presentation. As students study their communities, they stand to become more sensitive to value patterns and to learn to work together more cooperatively.

The literature concerning the interaction of school and community is extensive. In addition to the large number of magazine articles, several societies and associations have made community study the theme for yearbooks; there have also been numerous studies for degrees at the master's and doctoral levels.

The tendency of these studies is to group community activities into three levels: observational, participatory, and contributory.

Doubtless, most of the activities are observational in type, and remain pretty much the field trip sort. There are, however, increasing numbers of more serious studies and surveys that move into the contributory level, where there are both general and narrowly intensive surveys. These surveys, which need to be properly planned and supervised, depend upon experience and maturity both of teachers and students. To study intensively the problem of racial discrimination in a community, for example, calls for rare insights and judgment. Perhaps more appropriate for beginning teachers would be studies of a less demanding nature and studies that would be less likely to become involved in controversy. Examples are housing; city trash and garbage removal; sanitation, such as eradication of mosquito breeding places; part-time employment possibilities for high school boys and girls. A useful project for a rural area might be a complete register of all purebred or registered livestock, poultry, and pets in the school district.

To be of real value, studies of this nature must arise from the curriculum. They cannot be imposed just for the sake of a study or problem. After completion, community studies should be properly organized for presentation to the entire class and to those who cooperated in the study as well as to any interested adult groups. Throughout studies of this type, the processes of democratic group planning should be evident.

SOME SPECIFIC SCHOOL-COMMUNITY PROJECTS   Many communities sponsor what is called Business-Industry-Education Day under the guidance of the local chamber of commerce. The object of B-I-E Day is to acquaint teachers firsthand with the materials and resources of the community. On this day business and industry hold open house for the teachers of the community. The day chosen is usually one that is a legal holiday for the schools but not for business, such as Veterans Day or Lincoln's Birthday.

Career Days are somewhat like B-I-E Days in reverse. In this instance representatives from business and industry visit schools for the purpose of meeting with teachers and selected students in order to inform them about working conditions and requirements in their fields. The emphasis is upon vocational selection, or upon choice of a college or a professional school for post–high school education.

A participatory effort is represented by the "earn-to-learn" curricular project. This type of project takes many forms in different communities and is suitable for high school and college levels. It is a sort of on-the-job training and is frequently associated with the commercial or industrial departments. This form of experience and study has serious limitations, but through it some students are enabled to find a niche in the work world, or to gain a valuable overview before beginning their careers.

Another type of project is exemplified by one developed in San Diego County in southern California.[2] In this project there is a pooling of suitable resource material from industry so that these materials may be produced and distributed to the schools of the county. The project is sponsored by business and an NDEA grant. The materials involve graphic and photographic pictures from business, industry, and agriculture. They are carefully selected, graded for maturity level, reproduced in uniform sizes, and distributed as study prints. Some of the study print sets have accompanying filmstrips. Similar developments include the production and distribution of three-dimensional models, kits, motion pictures, and specimens. In addition to providing products, the project offers programs and assists research.

This sharing of materials by business is akin to the free or sponsored materials programs described earlier. There is, however, a big difference. In this instance, many businesses cooperate in a pooled project, and the materials distributed to the schools are worked over by educators so that they are educationally sound, and they have been lifted from the realm of propaganda or company salesmanship.

CAMPING

In various sections of the country, schools provide limited camping experiences for students. These experiences may be at the elementary or

[2] San Diego Community Educational Resources Project.

secondary level; they may be weekly winter trips woven into the school curriculum, or they may be summer activities. In any event youngsters learn to live together, to share, and to accept responsibility. A large part of the experience is focused on the urgent business of living—cooking, making beds, cleaning up, keeping warm, and making friends.

Camping as considered here is not an activity just for the underprivileged; it is an enterprise for all students, and is considered an integral part of the total educational development. It features a blending of talents of teachers, camp counselors, and camp staff. Educationally, students have organized time for such activities as reading, discussion, listening to resource persons, and engaging in serious nature study. Other activities involve athletics, hikes, crafts, dramatics, art, motion pictures, and the like.

The value of this activity in the school program is indicated by the remark that "Camping is a straight line to reality."

MISCELLANEOUS INSTRUCTIONAL MATERIALS: SPECIAL BOARDS

Many of the cheaper, less formal and older, but less spectacular instructional materials are often quite as significant as those just discussed. As a matter of fact, most teachers, good teachers, would feel greatly handicapped if they were denied some of these older, simpler instructional materials. To a certain extent, they are taken for granted, but they would be sorely missed if unavailable. Teachers and students use them over and over, probably daily, without much thought as to their importance in the learning program.

The miscellany of materials to follow is grouped in two categories: special boards characterized by the key word *display* and three-dimensional materials characterized by the term *manipulation*.

CHALKBOARDS

The origin of the chalkboard is obscure. Modern teachers take the chalkboard for granted, but would feel lost without it. Place the average teacher in a classroom without a chalkboard, and he will request one before the end of the first day. Yet many principals are of the opinion that the chalkboard is one of the most ineptly used instructional materials. Most of the uses are not only impromptu, but they are often slovenly and clumsy. An educator once remarked that for a quick, informal evaluation of a teacher, the appearance of the chalkboard is about as good as any single criterion.

VALUES   The chalkboard offers so many values for different subjects, different teachers, and different methods that it is difficult to do more than sample them. Some of the more outstanding ones are:

It is both a group and an individual device.

It fits the tempo of any presentation.

No special talent is required for its use.

Teachers of practically all subject content as well as all grade levels use chalkboards.

Pupils' errors can be quickly and easily corrected for all to see.

It is possibly the cheapest of all instructional materials.

It is eminently convenient.

The chalkboard encourages note-taking.

Chalkboard impact is heightened through the use of heavy and light crayon strokes, colored crayons, "black light," and spotlights.

Neatness, orderliness, and graphic skills add new values.

Where certain forms or designs are used repeatedly, as in music, stenography, bookkeeping, logarithms, and the like, permanent rulings save time.

LIMITATIONS

Much time can be wasted at chalkboards by both teachers and students.

Most chalkboards detract from the attractiveness of classrooms.

The desirability of using the chalkboard for assigned work, except for short lists of questions, words, exercises, or problems, may be questioned.

Other forms of duplication are usually better for study guides, tests, and longer exercises.

Hygienic questions may be raised at times.

Students may not be able to see chalkboard materials well without changing seat locations.

Misspelled words, poor handwriting, and slovenly use lower the effectiveness of the device.

Modern facilities and equipment, such as the slide projector, the opaque projector, the overhead projector, and the mimeograph, often serve instructional needs better than the chalkboard.

"DOS" AND "DON'TS" The following are some suggestions for improving the use of the chalkboard: Do not erase with fingers. Do not talk to the class with face to the board; take at least a 45-degree turn. Use a pointer for reference. If the classroom is shared with other teachers, leave the chalkboard neatly erased. Erase materials from the board when classes change. Old materials on the chalkboard have a certain amount of distraction for students.

Five simple methods which can add to effective chalkboard use:

Stick figure drawings. A little practice will enable any teacher to make such drawings. (See Fig. 10.2.)

Proportional squares. By this method (often called grid), a picture to be

Fig. 10-2

copied is ruled off into squares; the chalkboard is then marked off into larger squares. Last, square by square the picture is drawn on the board freehand.

Template. Plywood or cardboard templates or patterns are made of symbols or forms used repeatedly. Forms are traced on the chalkboard whenever needed. A template has rather limited use, but is helpful in geography, science, or wherever a simple form, such as a parallelogram, is used over and over.

Pattern or pounce. Holes are punched in a sheet of paper or fabric to follow the outline of a design or picture, a dusty chalk eraser is patted over perforated pattern held against the board, and chalk dots are connected freehand. Patterns may be stored and reused indefinitely.

Opaque projection. Maps or drawings may be easily transferred from books or loose sheets to chalkboards by using the opaque projector. Enlargement may be made to any size. This technique may be used for holiday decoration as well as for instructional purposes.

FELTBOARDS

Feltboards are inexpensive if bought but they can easily be made by the "do-it-yourself" teacher. These boards are constructed of any lightweight, flat-surfaced material such as plywood or heavy cardboard. The board is covered with any sort of felt, flannel, or duvetyn. Cutouts of similar material adhering to the surface create effective displays.

Feltboards have many uses for imaginative teachers, who have found them helpful in language arts, science, industrial arts, health, home economics, physical education, music, social studies, driver education, foreign language, English, and other subjects. They are used in secondary schools chiefly in drill work, poster or bulletin board display, to accent charts and graphs, and to add variety to many common learning devices. Almost any teacher of any subject may find that a feltboard can be used as a communications device.

If one stops to recall the many uses made of feltboards on television, the teacher may be reminded of the versatility of this simple device.

A substitute material for feltboards called "hook and loop" is capable of supporting three-dimensional objects of noticeable weight, such as pliers, screwdrivers, hammers, scissors, rock specimens, and so on. Ordinary felt or flannel will sustain only light weights, such as cutouts of paper, fabric, or light cardboard.

MAGNETIC BOARDS

High school teachers often find magnetic boards of value in their teaching. Magnets adhere to any steel-base surface. A plate of painted thin sheet metal can make an attractive display board. Instructional materials equipped with magnetic holders adhere easily to the boards and can be moved about at will. Small magnets can be glued to a variety of forms, such as cardboards or small three-dimensional objects to use on the boards. In principle, the magnetic board is similar to the feltboard except that magnetism holds in the one case and friction in the other.

Physical education teachers frequently make use of magnetic boards to mark the boundaries of playing field models, and to indicate the position of players in devising plays. In like manner, home economics teachers might use magnetic boards in the discussion of furniture placement, step-saving remodeling, and table and place settings. Paper cutout parts of a whole, as, for example, bone parts of the skull, might be put together in jigsaw fashion to emphasize name, location, and relative size. Business education teachers could use similar techniques in studying display styles and designs. A teacher of journalism may make effective use of a magnetic board of newspaper size to discuss layout, placement of headlines, lead articles, and advertising blocks.

Magnetic boards may also serve as chalkboards, thus adding a dual purpose to the display area of a classroom. Such a board can also serve as a bulletin board because student papers, notices, and other graphic materials may be held in place by small magnets without defacing the board or marring the papers.

ELECTRIC BOARDS

The electric board is in effect a programmed learning device by which students learn to associate certain facts, principles, skills, or combinations. These boards make a strong appeal to students who like to test their wits against the machine. The principle of the electric board, simple or complex, is to match programmed information so that an electrical contact will ring a buzzer or light a small bulb.

Electric boards are used to generate interest at the beginning of a new unit of study, to drill, to review, and to test. Electric boards can be outlined as maps with many sorts of subdivisions and data that may be matched with the visual clues. The programmed data may be changed from time to time to circumvent position memorization. Students, as well as the teacher, may do the programming. Even the wiring of the device may be changed periodically to forestall memorization.

Following are some uses of electric boards:

Mathematics—nomenclature, arithmetic terms, geometrical figures, combinations
Chemistry—symbols, atomic weights, valences
Foreign language—vocabulary, grammar, easy translations
Geography—place and economic geography
History—dates, locations, leaders, epochs, movements
Commercial subjects—shorthand symbols

Health—rules, diet, proper foods
Industrial arts—tools, equipment, formulas

The more elaborate the wiring, the more flexibility the board will have. The usual board is constructed to care for pairs of matched items only, but boards may be constructed in any high school shop that will match three, four, five, or more sets of items before a circuit is completed.

THREE-DIMENSIONAL MATERIALS

The key word for miscellaneous three-dimensional instructional materials is *manipulation.* The materials include models, mockups, objects, specimens, samples, artifacts, exhibits, dioramas, kits, and loan boxes. Some may be as simple as a pebble; others may be as complicated as a turbine or a plastic model of the human body.

Learning from actual things is as old as the human race. The uneducated depend in great measure upon such everyday experiences. They rely on size, color, shape, texture, odor, and similar characteristics. In the learning process, man wishes to get his hands on the object, or to experience it directly through the sense organs.

The poem "The Blind Men and the Elephant," by John Godfrey Saxe, illustrates how six blind men each sensed by touch six parts of an elephant and how each man thought he understood the elephant—to one it was like a wall, and to others a spear, rope, snake, tree, or fan. Each man was partly right, but all were wrong because their sensory experiencing was too limited. In the classroom, great care must be exercised to prevent generalization from partially observed or experienced stimuli.

OBJECTS, SPECIMENS, AND MODELS

Realia and artifacts of many types collected from a variety of sources should be mounted if necessary, labeled, the source and date of acquisition noted, evaluated, and suitably stored. They provide learning experiences as genuine as other learning materials. A flower that can be examined by every member of the class not only is an excellent way to show pistil, stamen, and calyx, but will also add meaning to the illustration found in the text. A rock specimen, a piece of coal, a shell, soil samples, a seed, dried leaves, insects preserved in formaldehyde or embedded in plastic—all these specimens taken from their natural setting can be found in most classrooms. They can be examined and studied as the need arises.

Do you remember the model of the steam engine displayed in your high school physics class? or in your health education class the model of the man with removable internal organs? Such realistic reproductions make lasting impressions. Models (miniature reproductions) or large-scale representations, such as a plaster of paris paramecium, are widely used in teaching. Their construction is being constantly improved by the use of plastics, glass, and synthetic materials. Many models include all the features of the real object, often contain moving parts that operate, and sometimes have cutaway sections to show inner workings that are not observable in the original. Models may be classified into three main types: solid models used chiefly for recognition of external features; cross-section or cutaway models valuable to show internal structure; and working models that actually demonstrate the operation of the original. Good working models often use contrasting colors for parts so that students can follow actions or processes. This is quite common in models employing gear boxes, cables, and electric circuits.

In many instances, models are of more value to students than real objects. They can be handled, used and reused as needed, and likely to be more available to students. Although the more complex models will have to be purchased from school funds, teachers and students may build many of the models that they use. Cones, pyramids, and the like are easily constructed from cardboard for use in mathematics classes. A model of a city, made of cardboard or papier-mâché, can be used to demonstrate anything from safety education to housing conditions. Thin plywood or balsa offers opportunities in the construction of stage sets for use in drama classes.

MOCKUPS

A mockup is defined as a "contrived or simulated three-dimensional device that imitates certain aspects of the real thing." Mockups may be as simple as a clock dial made from a paper plate or as complicated as a turbine or a synthetic city water supply with settling beds, aeration devices, and reservoirs. Driver-training laboratories may contain car mockups that look like stubby automobiles.

With models or mockups, students must be aware of the fact that the model may be the same size as the original or larger or smaller; however, most models are smaller. It must also be kept in mind that the model may have been removed from context. There may even be a noticeable simplification, a very important point in connection with models of the human body or its organs. A model of the Grand Canyon can show contour, coloring, and proportional dimensions, but it may not show such conditions as sky, sun, and climate. Photographs and motion pictures used with models and mockups help to relate the simulation to reality.

EXHIBITS

Exhibits prepared by students will create pride in workmanship and accomplishment. Exhibits are frequently arranged for special occasions such as Education Week, but they have a value if prepared only for class or building display. Commercial displays and exhibits are usually more complex and involve materials not readily available to students, such as mineral displays, working parts of machine objects, or the exhibits from museums.

DIORAMAS

The *Dictionary of Education* defines a diorama as "a three-dimensional representation composed of various symbolic and real materials such as pictures and specimens; it frequently utilizes both transmitted and reflected light to produce a natural scenic effect."

Both professional and pupil-made dioramas have a place among instructional materials, particularly at the junior high level. Professionally made dioramas are expensive and their range of subject matter is extremely limited. Over the years many school systems have, however, accumulated a fair collection of these objects. Some audio-visual centers employ a staff artist who occasionally finds time to construct something very special, for example, a midwestern farm scene or an Argentine rancho.

LOAN BOXES AND KITS

Loan boxes and kits are inexpensive materials that should be more popular than they are. Kinder defines the loan box as "a collection of related items appropriately boxed for loan to a school," and the kit as "a collection of pertinent materials gathered into a unit" (8:478).

Both loan boxes and kits are usually circulated from an instructional materials center. Health kits, first-aid kits, and tool kits are familiar. Why not similar integrated collections in science, art, home economics, and other areas? The value lies chiefly in the fact that varied materials are brought together in one place. Such a collection is a real time-saver, and sometimes the items might be difficult for a teacher to bring together without great effort, for example, marine-life kits for schools removed from the coast.

Some industries and commercial concerns offer schools loan boxes and kits of their products. These can be effective teaching devices. Among the kits of this type available to schools are those from the Bituminous Coal Institute, the telephone company, the petroleum industry, and companies that manufacture small tools and shop equipment. The boxes and kits discussed here are much the same as the exhibit materials treated above.

EDUCATIONAL GAMES AND SIMULATIONS

In Chapter 7 educational games and simulations were fully discussed. Only brief reference to them need be made here. Materials in this category vary from idea-patterns to three-dimensional devices. When properly presented the manipulation of ideas can be as thrilling to students as the manipulation of mechanical devices. These games simulate life outside the school and help to make learning real. They help students to understand the forces at work in life and provide practice in meeting them. These devices are not toys for play; they are very serious. Actually, they have been adapted to classroom use from exercises developed by military strategists for use in war games, for business executives for use in management training, for school administrators for use with administrative problems, and for government officials in training for diplomatic service.[3]

Chapter 10 has summarized in brief form approximately an entire course in instructional materials. All the conventional materials and techniques taught in such a course are described, including their values and uses. Space consideration has limited the inclusion of examples from classroom practice. Each teacher will be able to think of many additional uses for the materials. The teacher need only ask himself, "How can I employ motion pictures, maps, recordings, or charts to make my teaching more meaningful to my students?"

Chapter 11 will continue the discussion of materials and techniques, their values and uses, with the newer media, such as television, teaching machines, language laboratories, and computers.

SELECTED READINGS

1. Blount, Nathan S., and Herbert J. Klausmeier, *Teaching in the Secondary School*, 3d ed. New York: Harper & Row, Publishers, 1968, chap. 10.

2. Brown, James W., Richard B. Lewis and Fred P. Harcleroad, *A-V Instruction: Materials and Methods*, 3d ed. New York: McGraw-Hill Book Company, Inc., 1964.

3. Coleman, James S., "Games—New Tools for Learning," *Scholastic Teacher*, (November 9, 1967), p. 9.

4. Dale, Edgar, *Audiovisual Methods in Teaching*, 3d ed. New York: Holt, Rinehart and Winston, Inc., 1969.

5. Donoghue, Mildred R., ed., *Foreign Languages and the Schools: A Book of Readings*. Dubuque, Iowa: William C. Brown Company, Publishers, chaps. 11–13, 1967.

6. Harris, Raymond P., *American Education: Facts, Fancies, Folklore*. New York: Random House, Inc., 1961.

7. Hirsch, Werner Z. *et al.*, eds., *Inventing Education for the Future*. San Francisco: Chandler Publishing Company, 1967.

8. Kinder, James S., *Audio-Visual Materials and Techniques*, 2d ed. New York: American Book Company, 1959.

[3] Many of the simulations available for classroom use, sources, and costs for the social studies, mathematics, English, and general education are listed in *Scholastic Teacher*, 91 (November 9, 1967), 12–13.

9. Kinder, James S., *Using Audio-Visual Materials in Education.* New York: American Book Company, 1965.

10. Lee, Florence Henry, *Principles and Practices of Teaching in Secondary Schools: A Book of Readings.* New York: David McKay Company, Inc., 1965.

11. Trump, J. Lloyd, and Delmas F. Miller, *Secondary School Curriculum Improvement,* Boston: Allyn and Bacon, Inc., 1968.

12. Wendt, Paul R., "Audio-Visual Instruction," *What Research Says to the Teacher,* Bulletin no. 14. Washington, D.C.: Department of Classroom Teachers, American Education Research Association, 1957, 1961.

13. Wittich, Walter A., and Charles F. Schuller, *Audio-Visual Materials: Their Nature and Use,* 4th ed. New York: Harper & Row, Publishers, 1967.

Group projects lift learning experiences above the sterile verbalization of the formal classroom environment. (Courtesy Ketchikan [Alaska] Public Schools, photo by Chuen Mak.)

Resource persons often contribute new and vital ideas which enrich and motivate learning, and can provide, as in this case, a better basis for international understanding. (Courtesy Syosset [New York] Public Schools.)

A number of high schools are experimenting with computer-assisted instruction in various forms. In some instances the equipment is based on the school campus, in others, as shown above, cooperative arrangements are made to share the equipment of a nearby college or university. In this photo, students from Hillcrest High School, Salt Lake City, travel once a week to the University of Utah where a regular high school teacher instructs them in computer science. (Courtesy Utah State Board of Education, photo by Ron Davis, instructor.)

An art teacher in the North St. Paul (Minnesota) Schools using an overhead projector to discuss balance and form with her students illustrates one of the fastest growing audiovisual techniques being used in the classroom. (Courtesy 3-M Company.)

CHAPTER 11

Newer Instructional Materials and Devices

Although the National Defense Education Act of 1958 mentioned such audio-visual materials as motion pictures, television, radio, and foreign language laboratories by name, it also referred to all these devices as the "newer instructional media." The term has caught on and is widely used today, chiefly, however, to refer to television, language laboratories, teaching machines, computers, and programmed learning.

COMMERCIAL TELEVISION

THE SOCIAL SIGNIFICANCE OF TELEVISION

In less than two decades, fifty million homes have been equipped with one or more television receivers. The growth of the use of television has been phenomenal. The expansion of the use of radio, motion pictures, automobiles, or electrical appliances for the home cannot match it.

The impact of this new medium of mass communication is a matter of both scorn and approbation. In some quarters it is intellectually fashionable to deride television, to accuse it of mediocrity, to blame it for a large share of the growth of social violence and juvenile delinquency, and to charge that the medium has sold out to advertisers. Some truth may be attached to these charges, but it is not possible to document any of them completely. Although television is censured for mediocrity, the same accusation is hurled against the theater, films, books, and politics; even against the educational system itself.

Some critics who find fault with television should bear in mind that individuals have many and varied specialized tastes and interests. No single program will satisfy all viewers, as no single book, play, concert, or automobile satisfies everyone.

The total American public is made up of many publics. Each day millions of viewers exercise their prerogatives and make thousands of program selections reflecting the discrimination that comes to a viewer because of his education, family, friends, vocation, and personal temperament.

Probably no one should be too concerned about public tastes. There is reason to believe that tastes are on the upswing if viewed in perspective. Since the impact of television was first felt, the population has increased 20 percent, but at the same time the publication of books has shot up 100 percent, and that of juvenile books 200 percent; library circulation has increased 50 percent; the number of museums, 80 percent; production of classical records, 50 percent; and the number of symphony orchestras has doubled. During this same period college enrollments expanded 46 percent. Television cannot be given the credit for any of these statistics; neither can it be shown to have been a millstone about the neck of cultural growth.

Unquestionably, the public has been exposed to ideas and materials that it would never have experienced so directly without television. A few examples may be of interest: tours of foreign cities and countries—Hong Kong, Copenhagen, Vienna, Japan, Venezuela; political activities—UN debates, Congressional committee investigations, and debates by presidential candidates; contemporary news affairs—the coronation of sovereigns, the inaugurations of Presidents, and the visits of foreign dignitaries; revolution and strife around the world—disturbances in Africa and the anti-American demonstrations in Egypt and Cuba; national and international sports—hockey, golf, and the Olympic Games; art and music—the Boston or New York symphonies, Britain's Royal Ballet, or Russia's Moiseyev Dancers; and science and discovery—improvement in hospital care, the development of new drugs, and the globe- and moon-girdling trips of the American astronauts.

Television is not limited to the United States. It is highly developed in many European and Eastern countries, and is fast becoming a reality even in the so-called underdeveloped nations. In few if any is it as commercially oriented as in the United States; foreign countries tend to view it as a public responsibility not unlike the schools, the postal service, and the telephone and telegraph. In some countries, where it is essentially a government propaganda medium, it is subsidized and guarded by the state. Many foreign countries zealously promote it as an educational channel that ranks alongside their schools.[1]

Japan, long recognized as one of the world's foremost nations educationally and industrially, has probably the world's most extensive educational television. Its programs run the gamut of total teaching, major

---

[1] In 1967 the London Centre for Educational Television Overseas (CETO) published a report on the increasing use of ETV in both developed and developing nations of the world. This comprehensive report is available free from The Studio, CETO, Nuffield Lodge, Regent's Park, London NW 1.

resource teaching, supplemental teaching, and instructional observation. All this is supported nationally and is a part of the work of the national network (NHK).

NHK devotes most of its schedule to educational programming—approximately 70 percent may be classified as formal or informal education. At the present time, 94 separate relay stations interconnect with key open-broadcast circuits to provide the most complete educational television coverage in the world. Ninety percent of all primary schools, 81 percent of all intermediate schools, and 72 percent of all high schools participate in a broadcast schedule of 10½ hours per day (16.463).

Recently Mexico has made a spectacular plunge into educational TV. The Ministry of Education has put into operation a plan to supplement secondary education and, theoretically at least, to make high school education available to practically every Mexican citizen. Broadcasts are made Monday through Saturday from 8 A.M. to 12:30 P.M. for grades seven to eight. Students attend supervised "teleaulas," which are designated rooms throughout the nation staffed by a teacher, or students can take courses in their own homes if they are too far removed from a school teleaula. Students in these programs qualify to take examinations that lead to advancement; however, students must be registered and must provide themselves with designated books.

Commercial television, although often banal in many ways, has aided ETV. Millions of home viewers are more ready to accept television as an educational medium than they might have been otherwise. The volume and variety of commercial programs including documentaries, specials, and coverage of great events have led parents to envision wide school applications.

EDUCATIONAL TELEVISION

Almost any television program could be educational, at least for some people somewhere. But commercial television, in spite of the "public interest" clause in Federal Communications Commission regulations, is essentially an entertainment and mass-information vehicle. Schools can and do use commercial television, but for instructional purposes the medium is served best through *educational television.*

Television can be open- or closed-circuit. Both types are employed for educational purposes. The former is familiar as the type seen in our homes; the signal is put on the air by a broadcasting station and is picked up by any receiver in the broadcast area that can be tuned to the channel used. Closed-circuit television is not broadcast on the air. The signal goes only to receivers that are connected to the transmitter by wire or cable. For this reason, no FCC licensing is necessary. Closed-circuit television is widely used in colleges, universities, and public schools where the area to be reached is compact, or where there is need to broadcast several programs simultaneously. This, for example, is the case in the Washington County schools of Maryland, where as many as six programs may be broadcast at one time.

Educational television, like commercial broadcasting, uses either live or recorded programs. Live programs are seen and heard at the instant they are picked up by the television camera, whereas the recorded or delayed program is prerecorded on film (kinescope) or on tape (videotape). Recorded programs necessitate additional equipment, some of which is rather expensive, but prerecording (in general use today) allows the program director a great deal of latitude and flexibility. The equipment consists of 2-inch, 1-inch, or even ¼-inch videotape recorders. Some stations both videotape and kinescope their programs. Ultimate use and the type of equipment available determine the system used.

One of the chief drawbacks of television utilization has been the fact that teachers have had to plan teaching schedules to mesh with TV schedules. This, too, was a problem in earlier days in the use of radio. Magnetic tape solved the problem for the latter. Now, small videotape recorders are solving the TV problem so that programs may be prerecorded, stored, catalogued, and used at will. Lessons may be repeated, shown at off-hours to absentees, evaluated by teachers' committees, or used in various ways.

GROWTH AND STATUS OF EDUCATIONAL TELEVISION

On April 14, 1952, the FCC announced the reservation of 242 television channels for educational allocation and later extended the number to 258 and then to 273. Some of these channels were VHF (very high-frequency) but most of them were UHF (ultra high-frequency) bands. The latter bands have been difficult to use, but technological advancements have overcome this limitation. In 1953, KUHT, University of Houston, made its appearance as the first truly educational TV station. (An educational station is defined as one that is licensed as a nonprofit organization and is organized primarily to serve the educational needs of a community.)

Educational station broadcasting was ten years old in 1961, and in its first decade the number of stations grew to 63, of which 44 were VHF and 19 UHF. Today, there are approximately 200 such stations.

Commercial stations are established for profit and are chiefly supported by revenues from advertising. Educational stations are supported by taxation, public subscription, and grants from foundations and industry. About one third of the educational stations are owned by colleges and universities, one third by city or county school systems, and one third by civic-minded community groups. Educational and commercial stations exist side by side. Because support is different and different types of programs are broadcast, there is no conflict.

In 1967 Congress passed and the President signed the Public Broadcast Act, which emphasized the government's belief in the importance of educational television and radio. The law provides for a federal corporation to carry out financial assistance and program distribution as well as to encourage new and already established stations. It should be noted that the law specifically mentions both TV and radio. This could very well be a renaissance for educational radio, said by some to be the "Hidden Medium," but at this writing very little has been done to implement the new legislation except to appoint the corporation board. Federal monies are not available. *Newsweek* magazine (February 26, 1968) commented, "From the promise of great oaks, only little acorns have grown in the field of public television."

Educational television, on the other hand, has expanded rapidly. Alabama, Florida, Oregon, South Carolina, and New York are examples of a few of the states that have established their own networks. The legislatures of twenty-five have authorized ETV commissions. Interstate networks will soon be a reality.

Still another project of far-reaching potential is the Research Council of the Great Cities Program for School Improvement. This project, which involves sixteen so-called great cities—Baltimore, Boston, Buffalo, Chicago, Cleveland, Detroit, Los Angeles, Memphis, Milwaukee, New York, Philadelphia, Pittsburgh, St. Louis, San Diego, San Francisco, and Washington, D.C.—is financed by a grant from the United States Office of Education, ESEA, Title III. These cities enroll about 10 percent of the nation's school population. One section of the council's project has been focused on ETV. The 1967 report[2] is exceedingly comprehensive in matters of status, involvement, costs, and types of equipment. Systems in use in these cities include closed circuit, open circuit, and so-called narrowcasting (ITFS, Instructional Television Fixed Service, and the 2500 MHz, megahertz). ITFS and 2500 MHz are short-distance, straight-line on-the-air broadcasting. This system has been found very useful for school districts that have reasonably level terrain.

In spite of researches and visible developments, there seems to be reluctance to accept the medium in some quarters. There exists a well-known and frequently mentioned "gap between potential and performance." Some critics claim that ETV has not completely justified the faith that its advocates have placed in it. Yet its use seems to be steadily increasing. Other than in a few isolated instances (usually as a result of

---

[2] *School Television—Great Cities: 1967*. Chicago: The Fund for Media Research, 1967.

financial troubles), ETV has not been abandoned.[3] The biggest handicap to an even wider use of ETV seems to lie in a residual prejudice in some teachers, notably those at the high school level.

CLOSED-CIRCUIT TELEVISION (CCTV)

The discussion thus far has been aimed rather pointedly at open-circuit broadcasting, but many of the implications apply to closed-circuit use. Probably no one knows how many such systems there are in the United States. The number is doubtless about 400 if the count includes colleges, universities, city and county schools, hospitals and medical schools, and those used in scientific research. These facilities vary from a single camera with one or more receivers to elaborate studios that connect a great many elementary and secondary schools by cable. An example is found in Washington County, Maryland, where the system reaches out from Hagerstown to each of the fifty schools in the county. Six programs can be carried simultaneously and TV instruction is given daily for all grade levels and in many subjects. Except for a few high school students who get one and a half hours, no student receives more than one hour of television instruction a day.

City school systems using CCTV are numerous and their number is steadily growing. They are to be found in small school districts as well as in populous centers. Arrangements are often made with the telephone company to place school cables from building to building on telephone poles. In other instances a wire service is leased. On college campuses, television cables are usually laid underground from building to building.

Closed-circuit television can serve quite specific purposes. It may be used for outright instructional purposes or it may be confined to enrichment or special demonstration. All age groups from kindergarten to postgraduate have been taught by television. Although some subjects lend themselves more naturally to the medium, there is possibly not a single subject that has not at some time been presented on television.

Preservice and in-service education programs have found ETV, especially CCTV, helpful in observations, demonstrations, and interviews. The observation of classroom procedures may be available to a large number of viewers without disturbing the class being observed. The effectiveness of teacher supervision can be increased significantly. A case in point here is the recently released results of an NDEA experiment at Fontana, California.[4]

---

[3] The scope of the development of the medium is succinctly set forth in "Teaching: The Viability of Video," *Time*, 90 (October 20, 1967), 50.

[4] *Use of Closed Circuit Television to Improve Teacher Effectiveness*, a research report conducted by the Fontana School District and supported by a grant from the United States Office of Education, Department of Health, Education and Welfare. Proposal 269, Grant no. 704062.00, 77 pp. September 1959–June 1961.

So far this discussion has used the abbreviation *ETV* almost exclusively. Another abbreviation, *ITV* (instructional television), might have been used just as well in most instances. The distinction between *educational* and *instructional* is actually of very little importance because both applications are educational. Instructional television seems to describe programs prepared solely for the purpose of instructing, for direct class use, and often for credit of some sort. *Educational television,* a more generic term, applies to a broader interpretation of what is educational. For example, some programs presented over commercial stations may be educational.

TELEVISION TEACHING: ALL OR NONE?

Some critics of ETV seem to have the idea that students get either all or none of their instruction via television when a program is inaugurated. The practice followed by Hagerstown, Maryland, noted above, is typical. Even where television is widely used, students do not get all their course work, nor all of their work in any one course, by this medium. The following discussion will show how four types of ETV fit into this scheme in terms of use.

TOTAL TELEVISION TEACHING   There are some instances in which the total instruction is carried by the television medium. These instances are usually out-of-school adult programs and are for short duration. They are commonly listed as noncredit courses, for example, a course in Spanish offered over an educational or a commercial station. In this instance, the only help the student gets in addition to the telecast is from a textbook, a recommended set of recordings for listening drill, and possibly a syllabus.

The nearest approach to total television teaching in America is quite likely that found in the remote island of Samoa. Here, 2300 miles from Hawaii, unusual literacy problems are due to a lack of educational facilities and trained personnel, a backward economy, and a low ethnic literacy. The United States government has established a three-channel, island-wide television system. Practically the entire educational experience is provided by this facility, but the programs are prepared by curriculum experts, both native and mainland. Through workshops, conferences, and special courses classroom teachers throughout the island are given maximum assistance in the use of the medium.

The Chicago City Junior College has many courses taught entirely (or almost entirely) by television. It is estimated that the average Chicago City Junior College two-year student takes about one semester of his total work by television.

MAJOR RESOURCE TEACHING   Probably most television teaching today is of resource value. Regular teachers and television teachers share the teaching responsibilities. Television makes possible the assistance of experts and of outstanding facilities so often denied the individual school. After major telecasts, classroom teachers follow up with laboratory experiments, discussions, library work, creative projects, or remedial exercises.

SUPPLEMENTARY TELEVISION TEACHING   Television can supplement what normally takes place in the classroom. A report from the National Education Association says:

Here television follows a course of study in a broad way but adds to it the kinds of fruitful experiences which individual teachers find difficult if not impossible to provide. A series may present visits on film to local industries or institutions. It may feature interviews and demonstrations by outstanding authorities or local officials. Performances by musical, ballet, or dramatic groups may be used to enhance appreciation or to motivate student interest. This type of instructional television is in widespread use from the Bay Region of California to New York City.[5]

Multimedia utilization has become so comprehensive that TV has been called the "A-V synthesis." Wittich and Schuller tell, for example, how a program entitled "Pacifica Oceania" made use of recorded music, environmental sounds, charts, and diagrams, in addition to an impressive list of participating resource persons—authors, museum curators, linguists, and a geophysicist (16:470).

INSTRUCTIONAL OBSERVATION   Instructional observation is a limited and specialized form of television in which a TV camera and a small closed-circuit system are used to enable a class to view close-up demonstrations, dissections, the setting of gems, or other minute operations. A microscope slide or a science demonstration can be enlarged so that every person in a large lecture hall gets an intimate view.

TELEVISION TEACHING—SHARED TEACHING

The teacher who uses television must realize that he is a part of a team, that he shares his instructional efforts with one or more colleagues. No longer does he have complete autonomy in his classroom. To some extent the teacher who uses television in his teaching has less responsibility for purveying content and more for managing learning situations with more time for individual and group learning activities. His counseling role in the learning situation is increased. If he knows his students as he should, he now arranges appropriate learning situations for them—by individual or group—to investigate, practice, read, discuss, or to work with teaching

[5] *And TV, Too!* Washington, D.C.: Department of Audiovisual Instruction and Department of Classroom Teachers, NEA, 1961.

machines, tape recorders, motion pictures, and other devices. He may incorporate field trips, the building of models, or other activities as he diagnoses the needs of his students.

On the other hand, the teacher who actually appears before the television camera must prepare each presentation with great care. He must know his subject content and he must make an effective presentation of it. He must effectively use various visuals, and he is given assistance so that he can do this. One obstacle to more effective conventional teaching lies in the fact that teachers have neither the time nor the facilities to accomplish maximum results.

Each teacher has a role to play, and the roles are complementary. Each gives up something of the age-old role, but this is replaced by a new-found satisfaction in outright effectiveness in a world in which ideas increase geometrically.

STEPS IN CLASSROOM USE

In the immediate years ahead, many beginning teachers will enter school systems that employ television in some form; many others will not. As a part of his professional education, every teacher should realize the strengths and weaknesses of the medium and should know some of the basic principles of use.

The steps in television use are not unlike those in the use of films, recordings, resource persons, or other good instructional materials: teacher preparation, student preparation, reception, and follow-up.

It goes without saying that teachers must be prepared for television lessons as well as for any other type of lesson. This preparation includes content understanding, specific objectives of lessons, emotional *rapprochement,* and best reception conditions. Study guides are as useful in TV teaching as elsewhere. Usually they suggest how to prepare for a telecast and give much pertinent information. Teachers should never turn on telecasts simply because they are tired or have nothing planned for the hour. Schools that regularly use TV usually furnish their teachers with numerous invaluable teaching aids. In many school systems these materials are prepared by a curriculum-coordinating committee.

Pupil preparation is as important as teacher preparation. Students must first be conditioned to the fact that the viewing is a learning experience and not just a pastime. The teacher is a key person in this conditioning process—he provides the difference between a negative, laissez-faire, or positive attitude toward this type of learning. Students must know the purpose of the particular lesson, what to look for, generalizations to be sought, assignments to be copied, or workbooks or texts to be followed.

Meaningful telecast viewing can take place if teacher and students are properly prepared for the experience. Students should also be given instruction in *how to look.* They will then probably be thinking ahead about what activities will follow. Needless to say, work—books or papers—that might act as a distraction should be cleared away. For this period, the particular subject has the floor and should have undivided attention.

The reception of the telecast should take place under the best physical conditions possible. Every school that proposes to use TV should recognize this and make arrangements so that each room has the requisite number of receivers. The sets should be placed at the proper height and in the proper location. Provision should also be made for light and acoustic control; desks and chairs should be arranged; distracting fragments on the chalkboard should be erased; and the teacher should have a place in the room that does not detract from the reception.

In nearly all instances, there are follow-up activities that follow rather naturally from telecast lessons. These activities run the gamut of learning activities. If the preparation for the telecast has been well done, follow-up activities are logical and will be expected by the students. They will feel responsible for doing more than just viewing the lesson.

The culmination of the ideally taught television lesson brings together the studio teacher and the classroom teacher to evaluate the effectiveness of their work. As they evaluate and plan improvements, the preparation for the next phase of the work gets under way.

Alabama has one of the best-developed state ETV programs in the nation. With seven transmitting stations now in operation and two under construction, nearly all Alabama schools are covered. In a bulletin on television use in the schools, the State Department of Education says. "ETV lessons are team effort; they work successfully only when the instructor and you, the classroom teacher, work in concert with mutual understanding. Therefore, there should be effective communication between the two of you." [6]

One of the major faults of ITV today is "overloading." Lessons are supersaturated. This, too, has been a criticism of many educational films. Less easily corrected is the fact that the medium is essentially vicarious, as well as its failure to provide for individual differences. The teaching format is chiefly a "dole" method that allows little firsthand experiencing, usually more productive of significant behavioral changes. There is still too much telling and lecturing.

Many ITV staffs are searching for practical ways to implement the findings from research in human behavior so as to design effective television learning. Unsolved problems still exist in how to use the medium to stimulate inquiry and problem solving, how to provide continuing motivation, how to stimulate creativeness among students, and how to achieve some sort of feedback.

---

[6] *ITV Tips for Teachers*. Montgomery: Alabama State Department of Education and Alabama Educational Television Commission, n.d., p. 10.

MIDWEST AIRBORNE TELEVISION INSTRUCTION

A bold experiment in ETV, known as the Midwest Program of Airborne Television Instruction, was organized around 1960. This project provided for the telecasting of signals from airplanes on established courses five miles above the earth instead of from fixed transmitting stations. Coverage was wide; actually it reached all or parts of six states. Although expensive, the project achieved considerable success. It is now being phased out largely because of costs and the development of new equipment and services.

This pioneer experiment dramatized ETV. It showed the feasibility of reaching several million students at one time from an "in-the-air" station. Predating satellite broadcasting, this project has some similarity to it.

LOOKING AHEAD

Research has shown that students can learn as well as and frequently better by television than by conventional methods, and possibly much better with new studies and techniques in the years ahead. The potential of television integrates the teaching arts, the graphic arts, and the electronic communication process. Television seems to demand more and in turn produces more. A national committee of teachers has summarized it succinctly in this way:

As stated before, television has no magic in itself; but well-planned lessons, in the hands of the skilled teacher, can bring rich, valuable experiences to the classroom. The television teacher, in utilizing television, should look upon it as a helping hand, an assistant who throws open the walls of his classroom, making it as broad as the world itself.[7]

A lunar television facility with hemisphere coverage may not be too many years in the future. Satellite coverage was launched in 1962 with telecasts to and from Europe. In that year Congress passed the Communications Satellite Act authorizing the establishment of a private corporation, Comsat, to handle the nation's interests in this new area of communications. Soon afterward "Telstar" was in the air.[8] Since that date great strides have been made in coverage, in the use of solar light power, in color, in stability of video, and in provision for two-way communications. Weather is no problem for satellite beaming.

An example of what can be achieved took place on February 5, 1967, when an international auction via "Early Bird" satellite was held. The auction of a painting by Picasso was used as a benefit for the restoration of art at Florence, Italy. The television program showed individuals and

[7] *And TV, Too,* p. 37.
[8] M. Virginia Biggy, "Implications of Satellites for Education," *Audiovisual Instruction,* 12 (November 1967), 921–922.

groups at Paris, London, New York, Fort Worth-Dallas, and Los Angeles placing bids. All could be seen and heard as though it took place in a single auction room.

Once a satellite is in orbit its path can be fixed (controlling its coverage as domestic or international), and it is possible to arrange channels with specialized broadcasting, such as news, politics, sports, entertainment, and so on, simultaneously.

Will ITV cost some teachers their jobs? Logic says not. Instead of being unemployed, the teacher, especially the teacher of the self-contained classroom, will have a modified role. A bit of sound advice has been given by Shane: "Let us demonize neither change nor machinery; let us recognize reality. *We cannot change the history of education's collision with the future, but we can conceptualize and build better programs of instruction as we digest the meaning of new opportunities and responsibilities.*" [9]

THE LANGUAGE LABORATORY

Today's interest in foreign language teaching is almost revolutionary. It is uncertain as to just when the new interest began but enrollments in classes studying foreign languages have steadily grown. Just a few years ago many educators and citizens generally looked upon the nation's ignorance of other languages as a disgrace. In 1958, Congress passed the National Defense Education Act authorizing financial assistance to schools for the acquisition of laboratory and other special equipment and materials needed in the teaching of foreign languages. Thus their study was placed alongside science and mathematics for special consideration. The available funds have been used to provide schools with installations ranging from a simple listening corner with a single playback machine to fully equipped electronic laboratories.

WHAT IS A LANGUAGE LABORATORY?

A language laboratory is essentially a place where a student may practice a language just as a music student practices a piano or another instrument. Gene C. Fusco, specialist in school and community relations in the United States Office of Education, says: "In its complete form the language lab is an electronic installation consisting of a booth, headset, microphone, recording facilities for each student, and a monitoring set-up for the teacher. Visual facilities may include a projection screen, a motion picture machine, and slide-, filmstrip-, and overhead-projectors." [10]

---

[9] Harold G. Shane, "Future Shock and the Curriculum," *Phi Delta Kappan,* 49 (October 1967), 70.

[10] Gene C. Fusco, *Technology in the Classroom Challenges to the School Administrator.* Reprint, *School Life,* March–May 1960, p. 4. Washington, D.C.: United States Department of Health, Education, and Welfare, Office of Education.

USE OF A LABORATORY

In the aural-lingual method of teaching a language, the chief elements of the learning process are varied and intensive repetition. Meaningful drill and immediate correction of errors are provided. It is of prime importance not only to be able to hear oneself unhampered by other voices, but also to be able to receive criticism of one's pronunciation from the teacher, and to progress at one's own rate of learning. Language learning was once dull, wasteful, even boring. Students sat through a recitation period with the opportunity to speak only once or twice or only by concert recitation. Much time was spent listening to recitations that were stumbling, halting, and erroneous.

High school students in foreign languages generally have for their use a well-equipped laboratory much like that described by Fusco. The laboratory is shared by all language students in a building.

Foreign language teaching is a good example of the use of multimedia instructional materials. The equipment includes all the commonly used audio-visual devices, plus ITV and teaching machines. Coordinated textbooks have been written so that they are integrated with lab practice. In fact, it might well be said that foreign language teaching is an integrated text-film-tape-workbook-manual method.

The language laboratory as described here is limited to one curricular area. All teachers, however, should have a general understanding of its worth in teaching effectiveness. A new application of the laboratory and its techniques has arisen in connection with the teaching of English as a second language. In the main this application is with younger children and adults beyond high school age.

TEACHING MACHINES AND PROGRAMMED LEARNING

The whole area of programmed learning or self-instruction is popularly associated with the "teaching machine." This term, somewhat of a misnomer, has caught on and will probably stay with us. Some professional educators say that "teaching machine" is more than a misnomer—that it is actually misleading. A person does not truly learn from a machine; he learns from instructional material in the machine. Most educators prefer such terms as "self-instructional devices," "autoinstructional devices," and "programmed instruction." Terms such as these can serve as an umbrella for teaching machines, scrambled books, tutor texts, paper sheets, rolls, and folds.

The notion that Johnny might in some mysterious way learn from a machine has captured the fancy of many people. Books, pamphlets, and articles dealing with some aspect of programmed instruction have appeared in great profusion. Both educators and the general public are interested, and articles frequently appear in metropolitan newspapers, national weekly magazines, library magazines, and in publications aimed specifically for military personnel, engineers, research scientists, personnel managers, training directors, and others.

Many colleges and universities are pursuing extensive automatic tutor research. Actual use with large or small numbers can be found in many elementary schools, secondary schools, industrial training programs, and military centers around the country.

THE BACKGROUND OF PROGRAMMED LEARNING

How did it all start? Like most modern developments the basic idea of programmed learning is very old. Some say it started with Socrates, who at the conclusion of a demonstration said to a friend:

So a man who does not know has in himself true opinions on a subject without having knowledge. At the present these opinions, being newly aroused, have a dream-like quality. But if the same questions are put to him on many occasions and in different ways, you can see that in the end he will have a knowledge on the subject as accurate as anybody's. This knowledge will not come from teaching but from questioning.[11]

A half century ago, Edward L. Thorndike foresaw what contemporary psychologists would devise for the scientifically designed programmed book. He maintained that texts often stated the habits to be formed by students but gave the students no exercises in forming them. This he felt held for books in grammar, sociology, economics, and philosophy as well as arithmetic and foreign languages. He contended that students should be helped just enough at each stage of growth to lead them to help themselves and that proper ingenuity on the part of authors and publishers should overcome conventional textbook faults.

If by a miracle of mechanical ingenuity, a book could be so arranged that only to him who had done what was directed on page one would page two become visible, and so on, much that now requires personal instruction could be managed by print. Books to be given out in loose sheets, a page or so at a time, and books arranged so that the student only suffers if he misuses them, should be worked out in many subjects . . . a textbook can do much more than be on the one hand a mere statement of the results of reasoning such as ordinary geography or German grammar is, or on the other hand a mere statement of problems, such as the ordinary arithmetic or German reader is.

On the whole, the improvement of printed directions, statement of facts, exercise books and the like is as important as the improvement of the powers of teachers themselves to diagnose the condition of pupils and to guide their activities by personal means. Great economies are possible by printed aids, and per-

[11] Printed in "Not from Teaching but from Questioning," *Carnegie Corporation Quarterly*, 9 (October 1961), 1–8.

sonal comment and questions should be saved to do what only it can do. A human being should not be wasted in doing what forty sheets of paper or two phonographs can do. Just because personal teaching is precious and can do what books and apparatus can not, it should be saved for its peculiar work.[12]

The actual construction of contraptions or so-called teaching machines has been traced back to 1866, when a spelling machine was produced. In 1873, a logic machine was supposed "to generate solutions to logical problems represented symbolically." In the 1920s, Sydney L. Pressey of Ohio State University attempted to mechanize testing and to some extent teaching with devices that were supplementary to regular classroom teaching.

SOME CAUSES OF THE PRESENT POPULARIZATION

The popularization of teaching machines has come, however, in the late 1950s through the researches in learning and the design of a practical machine by B. F. Skinner of Harvard. Machines could have been built hundreds of years ago, but their function today rests upon the development of a new technology.

A considerable segment of American society views present teaching methods as inefficient and wasteful. It is generally agreed that the world is experiencing a population and a knowledge explosion of unprecedented proportions. Many people maintain that there exists an acknowledged struggle in the world merely to maintain present literacy levels, or, as Alice remarked, we must run as fast as we can to stay where we are. Concurrent with this dual explosion there exists a deficit in the number of qualified teachers and a dearth of classrooms. Costs are rising and there is concern over society's ability to meet the education bill even if teachers and classrooms are found.

CHARACTERISTICS OF PROGRAMMED MATERIALS

Programmed instruction takes many forms but the forms are characteristically much the same.

The word "program" is important. It denotes a planned learning pattern. The material to be learned is presented to the learner sequentially. This presentation takes place bit by bit in such a way that the learner must respond to each stimulus before he goes further. Actually, the learner progresses in small lucid steps so arranged by the programmer that the learner arrives at the desired outcome with a minimum of errors. Each step is repeated and practiced so that the learner thoroughly understands it before he goes to the next step. The student always knows whether he is right or wrong. There is a low level of difficulty at each

[12] Edward L. Thorndike, *Education*. New York: The Macmillan Company, 1912. Used by permission of Macmillan. pp. 165–167.

step or "frame." Only the material that is pertinent and for which the student is logically and psychologically ready is presented. The student moves slowly from simple ideas to more complex ones and to generalizations. Ideas are repeated several times in new form or in different contexts so that the desired responses are reinforced.

Rewards come to the students in the knowledge that they understand what they are doing, and they immediately see every response that they make as right or wrong. There are no delays of hours or even days. This immediate feedback overcomes one of the greatest difficulties in conventional group instruction.

Each student proceeds at his own rate of progress. Contrary to what some skeptics have thought, students do not dawdle their time away. As a matter of fact, they accomplish much more with self-instructional learning than they do under conventional procedures. Edgar Dale, in reviewing *Teaching Machines and Programmed Learning: A Source Book,* edited by Lumsdaine and Glaser, says: "If we merely want to teach more, teach it faster, and use better what we have learned, there is little doubt that programmed teaching will help offer us significant help." [13]

One junior high school teacher who attempted to program his mathematics classes with scrambled book exercises gave up after two months. His comment, "I can't keep up. They (the students) chew it up faster than I can put it together." He had never had this happen before with conventional teaching methods.

Automatic tutoring functions somewhat like a private human tutor. The machine or book, as the case may be, holds the student at a given task until he is able to make a correct response repeatedly. If the student has trouble with an item, the automatic device, like the tutor, coaches him by suggesting, hinting, and cuing until the correct response is made. There is always immediate feedback; the student knows whether he is right or wrong.

Some critics of programmed instruction have feared that students will be encouraged to cheat. This has not been the case. Errors must be corrected as they are made, and they cannot be hidden. Frequent tests also show the necessity for mastery of the content covered. Most of the machines have ingenious devices built into the equipment to prevent cheating.

PROGRAMMING

The art of planning material for use in a book or a machine is called *programming*, and the planned material is *programmed instructional* material.

---

[13] "Teaching Machines and Language Laboratories," *Theory and Practice* (Ohio State University), 1 (February 1962), 58.

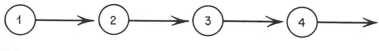

Fig. 11-1

There are two schools of thought as to the best way to plan instructional materials; undoubtedly others will arise. One group advocates a method variously called *linear, fixed-sequence, straight-line,* or *extrinsic programming.* The plan is shown in Figure 11-1.

In this diagram each circle represents a frame, and the arrow represents the response. The frames or steps represent small units of content. These are presented to the student in sequence, but only after he has made a correct response to the previous stimulus. The student responds on the basis of what he already knows or with the help of various cues or suggestions he may or may not need. Each step must be completed, and the student cannot skip around. In the main, the student *constructs* his answers and fills in blanks, writes or types his answers, or manipulates dials on a machine to record his answers. Individual differences are cared for as the student works at his individual rate of speed.

The second school of thought concerning programs uses a scheme called *nonlinear, branching,* or *intrinsic.* Material is presented in small sequential steps or in larger units as desired. The learner usually has a choice of possible answers. After selecting one, he turns to the designated page and checks his response. If correct, he goes to a new exercise; if incorrect, he is told why he is wrong, and is asked to return to the original step, to reread it, and try again. This scrambling with multiple-choice responses permits more flexibility and allows more leeway for meeting individual differences. The branching program is shown in Figure 11-2.

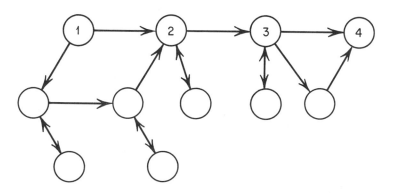

Fig. 11-2

Numerous formats have been devised for printed programmed devices: the programmed textbook, the scrambled textbook, the cut-back page booklet, and the tab-type page. Only the first two will be described here.

The programmed textbook has two types of pages, the information-question page and the answer page, which follows it immediately. As a result, each page is arranged in a series of bands or panels. The learner moves through the pages in succession to the end of the book or section and then returns to page one for the second band or panel.

With the scrambled book the reader finds that pages are not read consecutively. The first page, for example, asks a question, and the reader selects an answer, which then directs the reader to a page that answers the question correctly. From here the reader returns to the original page or goes to another, as directed.

MACHINE DEVICES

Many educators and most of the general public refer to instruction through the use of programmed materials as education by machine teaching. Quite obviously the machine does not teach; it is merely a conveyor of teaching or programmed materials. It puts the learner in contact with the author of the instructional materials. It might even be said to be a laborsaving device that by its novelty helps to motivate the student. It does not need to be monitored, it is patient, and it is practically cheat-proof.

Since the idea of teaching machines occurred to the educational world in 1958 or 1959, there has been a proliferation of devices on the market. More than one hundred companies have made teaching machine models costing anywhere from a few dollars to several thousand, the latter being sophisticated computer-operated devices or elaborate electronic classroom systems.

SIMULATED MACHINE DEVICES

A great many devices on the market can scarcely be called machines; nor are they books. These devices are frequently of the pencil-paper variety. There are also some devices halfway between.

Among these latter devices, often costing only a few cents, are punch-boards, pull-tabs, pluck cards, sliding masks, paper scanners, and chemical cards.

Educational Testing Service has experimented with a variety of self-correcting exercises in the form of tests. Some of these exercises are produced to serve as homework assignments. They are very cleverly programmed materials arranged as blocks of information, as for example, a set of challenging questions to follow a poem. Item writing is the big factor here. The exercise may be actually designed to teach a method of dealing with poems, not merely an examination of understanding. The technique would be used with many difficult poems. As a homework assignment, the program would follow a class discussion of the poem. Students would test themselves on the poem but at the same time would acquire some skill in determining the meaning of the next poem to be studied in class.

The programmed questions are printed sheets. A cardboard or a sheet of paper covers the correct answer until the student has made his response. The sample exercise on "Spring and Fall" shows how it works. (This is an abbreviated illustration and omits the answer key to the test to be given the following day by the classroom teacher.)

SPRING AND FALL

By Gerard Manley Hopkins

Margaret, are you grieving
2   Over Goldengrove unleaving?
Leaves, like the things of man, you
4   With your fresh thoughts care for, can you?
Ah! as the heart grows older
6   It will come to such sights colder
By and by, nor spare a sigh
8   Though worlds of wanwood leafmeal lie;
And yet you *will* weep *and* know why.

10   Now no matter, child, the name:
Sorrow's springs are the same.
12   Nor mouth had, no nor mind, expressed
What heart heard of, ghost guessed:
14   It is the blight man was born for,
It is Margaret you mourn for.[14]

DIRECTIONS: With a sheet of paper, cover everything below the item on which you are working. Read the item, look back at the poem, and write the number of the best answer in the (   ) at the end of the item. Then move the sheet of paper below the next item. The number in parentheses is the intended answer for the preceding item. If your answer was not the same, put a circle around these parentheses. If you disagree and want to discuss the item, add a question mark or an exclamation point.

1. About how old is the person addressed? 1—Six 2—Eighteen 3—Thirty 4—Fifty (   )

(1)   2. What is Goldengrove? 1—Some English flower, like golden-

[14] Gerard Manley Hopkins, "Spring and Fall." Used by permission of Oxford University Press.

rod   2—A particular plant to which she has given this name   3—A patch of woods in autumn   4—A person named Goldengrove   ( )

(3)   3. In line 2 "unleaving" means: 1—not leaving (i.e., staying) 2—failing to produce leaves   3—unfolding leaves from buds   4—shedding leaves   ( )

(4)   4. The *opposite* of "the things of man" in line 3 is: 1—the things of woman   2—the things of children   3—the things of nature   4—the ideas of man   ( )

(3)   5. In line 3 "leaves" are: 1—addressed by the question, "Can you?   2—the subject of "care for"   3—the subject of "can you"   4—the object of "care for"   ( )

(4)   6. In line 7 "nor spare a sigh" means: 1—not be sparing of sighs (i.e., give many of them)   2—not give as much as a sigh   3—not express sorrow openly   4—not permit anyone to sigh   ( )

(2)   7. In line 8 "worlds" means   1—large quantities   2—imaginary worlds   3—planets like our world   4—little worlds (round balls) formed by wanwood   ( )

(1)   8. Which of the following is most like "leafmeal" in line 8? 1—Oatmeal   2—Bone meal   3—Piecemeal   4—Lastmeal   ( )

(3)   Now re-study the items you answered incorrectly.

Test on "Spring and Fall"

DIRECTIONS: Encircle "Yes" if the sentence is a reasonable interpretation of any part of the poem. Encircle "No" if it is not.

Yes No   1. Margaret, are you sad because your lover has deserted you?
Yes No   2. Can't you think of anything but men?
Yes No   3. As you grow older, you will be less moved by sights like this.
Yes No   4. You will not grieve, no matter how many leaves fall.
Yes No   5. But now you keep on weeping and want to know why you weep.
Yes No   6. You have to rake up the leaves that fall on your lawn.
Yes No   7. If you do not know my name, it makes no difference.

. . . .

Yes No 14. The falling leaves told your heart that you, too, must die.
Yes No 15. In the title, "Fall" stands for "immortality." [15]

Why don't students cheat? Some may, but it is soon evident that it does not pay. No credit is allowed for the score on the homework. Only the test taken in class the following day is scored, and no point covered in the homework exercise ever reappears on the text except in new form.

[15] Paul B. Diederich, "Self-Correcting Homework in English," *Proceedings, 1959 Invitational Conference on Teaching Problems.* Princeton, N.J.: Educational Testing Service, 1960, pp. 80–82, *passim.* Used by permission.

Cheating on the homework is pointless and memorization of right answers is impossible. The program is still in the experimental stage.

WRITING PROGRAMS

Who should write the programs? There is no absolute answer, but it seems pretty certain that the time factor alone will rule out any more than token preparations by classroom teachers. Earlier in this discussion a junior high school teacher pretty well summed up the case: "I can't keep up. They (students) chew it up faster than I can put it together."

It seems therefore that most of the programmed materials will have to be written by specialists at program writing, or at least by teaching teams who can pool time and resources for the job. This sort of writing demands special talents and insights.

The broad general requirements for writing a program are thorough knowledge of subject; a large amount of time; patience; students on whom to try out the preliminary drafts; and an above-average understanding of the learning process.

Program writers, like textbook writers, carry a heavy educational responsibility. Because the range of content in any given area is so tremendous, both must be highly skilled at selectivity. The burden of selection seems to be heavier for the programmer. A student going through a program has to remember more—both important and relatively insignificant ideas, even details—before he can proceed. In the textbook, not so much detailed retention is demanded in order to proceed. It is probably a disadvantage of the textbook that it does not require sharply defined responses (they are usually covert), and there is no feedback. On the other hand, the book may be read, reread, outlined, underscored, scanned, or read in straight-line fashion. Some books may even be read irregularly, but with a purpose, usually supplied by the teacher.

IMPLICATIONS FOR EDUCATION

Research shows rather explicitly that students can learn effectively through the use of these individualized techniques. Much of the research has been done in the psychological laboratories over the country; yet there is also a volume of research reported with normal students, with exceptional students, and with out-of-school adults, such as persons in industry or the military services.

In schools, it would seem that teaching machines and programmed materials can perform a valuable service in remedial work, drill and practice, enrichment, and even total teaching. Teachers can be freed from repetitive drill routine to provide time for more creative work. Programmed teaching materials can supplement, complement, and augment the teacher. Hilgard has said, "By relieving the teacher of much of the routine, the teaching machine and program permit other opportunities greater play. If much of the *science* of teaching is taken over by the machine, the *art* of teaching will again come into its own . . . " (6:21).

Pressey believes that

enthusiastic programmers will soon give up trying to replace most textbooks and other core materials with thousands of "frames" viewed seriatim. Drill and rote learning may be so handled. But the larger usefulness of auto-instruction will be found in co-ordination with, not replacement of, other materials and methods. However, the programmers' efforts may bring improvement in these other materials. . . . The efficiency may be embarrassing! A student may deserve five hours of credit though taught in a class meeting only two hours; he may finish a semester course in the first six weeks, and as an outcome finish a four-year college course in three years, or twelve years of public-school work in ten! [16]

No serious person believes that teaching machines will replace teachers. Rather, they can take much of the drudgery out of teaching. The teacher is still essential in any school. The machine may very well multiply his effectiveness. The teacher can become a "teaching engineer" concerned with the teaching process and with students. With less routine work, more time for guidance functions is likewise available.

Organization in schools using teaching machines will be different from conventional organization. Teachers will tend to work more as teams using classrooms of varying sizes. Students may, at certain periods, work in classrooms at machines; they may also work alone with a machine in a conference room or even a cubicle. A teacher may or may not be present, and students may be working on the same content or on different content. Work with motion pictures, television, and other curricular materials and devices will be integrated as needed. Multimedia research shows great values in so doing.

Conventional textbooks will not be eliminated; they will simply take on a changed function. Textbooks will serve for what they are, storehouses of information. The programmed device may assume more of the teaching function.

Most programmed instructional materials, whether used in books or machines, are verbal. Poor readers are at a disadvantage. The limited use of visual symbols other than print has been the subject of some experimentation.

TO USE OR NOT TO USE

Many teachers, both new and experienced, throughout the country will be using autoinstructional devices in one way or another; many others will not. But every teacher should be aware of their potentialities. The literature is replete with articles hailing these devices with gusto, suggesting that they are as revolutionary educationally as were the printing press,

[16] "Teaching Machines and Language Laboratories," p. 37.

the motion picture, or television. In fact *Time* magazine has said ". . . [programmed learning] promises the first real innovation in teaching since the invention of movable type in the fifteenth century." [17] Other articles view the devices with skepticism, saying that they are contraptions, a passing fad. As a matter of fact, the tempo of original growth has slowed considerably. Like TV, there is still a gap between promise and performance.

There are still many unresolved problems about teaching machines. Can they really produce more effective learning? Are they challenging for normal students, for gifted students? How can they be fitted into contemporary school organization? Are they valuable in the same degree for all types of learning and all types of content? Will machines used over a period of time become boring to students? Do they really care for individual differences? Are they economical in terms of adaptability and usability? Are they truly educational parameters? What is known of retention from machine learning? Can students make generalizations or transfer from machine learning as well as from conventional learning?

COMPUTER-ASSISTED INSTRUCTION (CAI)

In Chapter 8 brief mention was made of the growing use of computers in education as curriculum innovation and method. In many ways computerized instruction is an adaptation or extension of teaching machines, television, radio, telephone, and other communications media. If simple teaching machines with programmed learning material (chiefly linear) can assist in teaching, how much more valuable will be digital computers that include manifold branching techniques and their possibilities for decision making.

Giant researches backed by billions of dollars are currently under way to validate the educational values of computers. Behind these researches is a complex of the resources of electronics firms, publishers, the federal government, foundations, and avant-garde educators. For some the end product will be huge sales of expensive equipment (hardware), learning programs (software), and for some, hopefully, a more effective and efficient instructional effort.

PURPOSES TO BE SERVED

Computers have already shown great potential in data processing, information retrieval, research, management, and teaching. How long it will take to bring the potential into full reality and how to find the means of financing the operation are questionable.

Much of the enthusiasm for CAI has been occasioned by the need for a

[17] *Time,* March 21, 1961, p. 36.

means of handling individual differences. Education is much interested in any program, method, or device that will allow students to proceed at their own rates of growth under given conditions. Some of the accumulated research also tends to show significant motivational value tied into the computer innovation. However, Wodtke and others [18] are not impressed by this claimed motivation. They attribute it to the Hawthorne Effect and claim that it will wear off in time.

A common claim for CAI is that subject matter can be taught faster and at eventual cost savings. Hansen says: "One of the most consistent findings with CAI tutorial applications is the marked saving in instructional time along with no loss in post-instructional achievement test performance." [19]

An interesting auxiliary use of the computer is being tested at a western university extension center. Instead of going to the campus in the evening for instruction, students remain at their homes and work with computer and telephone. The class begins with a face-to-face meeting to get acquainted and to get instructions. Members of the class are supplied with a microphone, receiver, and a push-button telephone with slots for punched plastic telephone cards. The service includes two-way communication, to which all the students can listen. Even group discussion is possible. Each class session is taped, the tapes being available to the students. This unique type of class administration, which appeals to busy adults, eliminates long trips to the campus and parking problems.

Already a number of high schools and universities are gearing instruction into computer operation. These computers are highly sophisticated and are able to handle both linear and branching data.[20] Data can be fed into them that describe complete work-study orders and understandings for units of instruction. This complicated programming can be so thorough that none of the behavioral objectives—cognitive, affective, or psychomotor—are lost sight of. The student can obtain a print-out of his skills and understandings at daily, weekly, or other intervals. Such a print-out can tell both teacher and student what has already been done, what needs to be done, and the steps to be taken. Instruction can be individualized in an almost unheard-of manner. An instructional aid of this kind calls for a new kind of imagination and skill on the part of teachers.

[18] K. H. Wodtke, "Relationships among Attitude, Achievement, and Aptitude Measures and Performance in Computer-Assisted Instruction," in *Experimentation with Computer-Assisted Instruction in Technical Education*. Semiannual Report by H. E. Mitzel. University Park: Computer-Assisted Instruction Laboratory, Pennsylvania State University, 1965, p. 124.

[19] Duncan N. Hansen, "Computer Assisted Instruction," *Review of Educational Research*, 36 (December 1966), 596.

[20] See Figs. 11-1 and 11-2 and accompanying text.

Aside from testing—construction, administration, and analysis—present utilization of computers is limited largely to drill, practice, and different forms of remedial work. This means that most of the present uses are centered around the basic skills. Computer-assisted instruction now functions in terms of stored programs prepared by professional programmers or teachers and serves as supplementary, complementary, or optional materials. Research is currently concerned with expansion of the computer function from skill work to concept formulation. The future for this sort of assistance, at all grade levels, seems bright.

Patrick Suppes (see the references at the close of this chapter) is carrying on an extensive experimentation at Stanford University involving instruction in the elementary grades. Fifth-grade children, for example, are taught reading and arithmetic by programmed computers located miles away at computer centers. Programs are sent to selected schools by microwave, coaxial cable, or telephone lines. In the classroom pupils listen to computer instructions and then print out their responses on electronic typewriters. The computer makes evaluations of responses on the spot for the pupils and provides teachers with detailed analyses.

One of the most significant purposes served by CAI deals with diagnosis of students and feedback to teachers. Detailed item analysis is possible. In addition, the computer can store an infinite number of bits of data about students and their past performances.

For libraries, data storage and retrieval are hardly more than in the discussion stage, yet the potentialities are there and need only to be tapped. The advance will come from the large state, university, foundation, and corporation libraries with research emphases, but in time urban school libraries, too, will employ computers for assisting students and teachers to find needed data. With proper computerization, for example, a history teacher might call upon the librarian for assistance with a given unit and get a list of text and reference books, films, filmstrips, slides, and other available resources. This will be a "punch-the-button" operation.

LIMITATIONS OF CAI

Critics of CAI raise many objections. First, they are indignant that huge sums are being spent on hardware whereas little or no support is given to the vital matter of how students learn. Also, among the objections noted, beyond costs, is the concern about who will write the learning programs. Gentile says that "it is ridiculous to ask classroom teachers to program their courses. Even if programming were as easy as writing a book, it would be out of the question to expect classroom teachers to have the time or capability of writing a good program. How many teachers write books? Program writing will ultimately be left to professional programers and their subject-matter consultants." [21]

[21] J. Ronald Gentile, "The First Generation of Computer-Assisted Instructional Systems: An Evaluative Review," *AV Communication Review*, 15 (Spring 1967), 31.

Many teachers have a negative attitude toward programmed instruction. Teachers fail to see how they can be creative in what they regard as a dehumanized environment. They do not wish to work "behind the scenes," or to see the instructional function fragmented. Many object to the predicted threat of becoming "teaching engineers" in a school system operated by a maximum use of clerks, technicians, and administrators.

The foremost—or at least the most often mentioned—drawback of extensive school use of computers is cost, both capital outlay and maintenance. The proponents of CAI counter with plans for rental or lease instead of outright purchase of equipment, which they claim can be used twenty-four hours a day. For example, during school hours the computer would be used for instruction, but at night the same machine would be available for administrative purposes, such as payrolls, attendance records, cost accounts, and similar duties. The equipment might also be subleased to nearby industrial and commercial firms for designated weekend use.

MULTIMEDIA APPROACH TO INSTRUCTION

Teaching is a multiphase business. Each teacher has many pupils who have different and varied needs.

Learning materials play an important part in meeting these needs, but they must be selected with a sagacity that includes an understanding of the learner, the materials and what they can do, and the needs of the social order. Printed materials can accomplish certain objectives. The film, filmstrip, record, map, and similar media accomplish still other objectives. The teacher must decide which instructional media best meet the needs of his students. Possibly it is not a question of an instructional material or a method; it may very well be that several materials and methods should be used in a combination so that they reinforce each other. Each material or method has its own unique characteristics, but if coordinated with other instructional materials, it may assume larger significance.

A social studies teacher may be trying to show the relationship of federal spending to local economy. A field trip to a number of federal projects is taken. A film on the old Civilian Conservation Corps or the more modern Peace Corps is shown. Resource persons are interviewed. The textbook and supplementary pamphlets are read. Maps are consulted. Any one of these media is useful in extending the concept being developed, but in combination, each material takes on new significance.

It has been repeatedly remarked that the various instructional materials are not to be used willy-nilly; they must be used with a purpose and they must be wisely selected. The reservoir of instructional materials is large. There has been a great deal of research bearing on each instructional material but much more is needed to show clearly what each can do: the techniques of use, the limitations. Even some of the oldest techniques can still stand researching.

A PROPOSED ELECTRONIC AUDIO-VISUAL EDUCATION SYSTEM (EAVES)

Instructional materials are so numerous and their distribution in a school system is so complex that conventional A-V centers are undergoing considerable change. A project evaluator for the San Diego Area Instructional Television Authority [22] has suggested that the production and distribution of these learning materials be named EAVES. In such a framework all the conventional audio-visual materials, open-circuit television, closed-circuit television, videotape recording (studio and on-site), computer-tutor programming, and data-phone scheduling would be synthesized.

Other proposals include the "automated classroom" and the "systems" approach.

Telemation is a new term that means an *automated classroom*. A number of experimental centers have set aside especially equipped classrooms that provide the teacher with multiple viewing screens and several sound outlets. Motion pictures, still projections, and television images may occupy the screens simultaneously or in rapid succession. A console with teleprompter allows the instructor to read a lecture and, using electronic cuing devices on the script, to make pictures and sound appear mysteriously from nowhere. All equipment is out of sight. Some of the installations have built-in student response systems at each seat.

Systems, another term often heard, has recently been expanded into *Total Instructional Systems.* This may best be explained by simply quoting a definition:

An "instructional system" refers to recent efforts being made by a few institutions, through clearly delineated, predetermined procedures, to develop, field test, and devise instructional systems capable of changing student behavior with a high degree of success without the presence of a trained instructor. In other words, these instructional systems are "totally" responsible for all instruction imparted in the subject area and for affecting student behavior; thus, the term "total instructional system." [23]

In viewing "Changing Directions in American Education," one writer feels that the "tools" for an upsurge in quality education have now been developed, that technological developments are ahead of the materials and programs. The "tools" as seen by this author are:

[22] De Graff Stanley, "The Consumer as Producer," *Incidental Papers,* App. C, January, 1968, mimeo.
[23] Arnold M. Gallegos, " 'Total Instructional Systems'—A New Learning Opportunity," *Educational Technology,* 7 (July 15, 1967), 1.

1. Centralized tape libraries from which local systems could select, for example, an entire course of instruction, or specialized lectures prepared by the greatest teachers in specific fields
2. Closed-circuit TV systems for a school district or region and individual video-tape players—the see-and-hear devices—to enable each classroom to utilize the course materials that can be made available to every school
3. Electronic teaching machines that have been particularly successful in language instruction
4. Programmed learning systems for detailed, repetitive instruction
5. Scanning devices in each classroom that would be linked to the library and records office to free teachers from many routine functions
6. Computer centers for grading examinations for a school, or an entire school district, relieving teachers of a time-consuming chore
7. Computers for cataloguing and retrieving information
8. A flexible open-circuit educational TV network to bring a variety of current-events type of instruction to classrooms.[24]

In recent years it has seemed, at least to some educators, that the profession has been in a rush to mechanize its operations. Other educators have pointed out that there is a discernible gap between technological development and actual practice. This leaves many teachers in a quandary. An educator and innovator who has given much thought to the use of equipment provides a reasonable statement:

The "mechanizing of education" has been taken literally in the sense of doing by machine what was formerly done by people. Some of the so-called computer-based teaching machines are designed simply to duplicate the behavior of teachers. . . . What is needed . . . is an analysis of the functions to be served, followed by the design of appropriate equipment. Nothing we know about the learning process calls for elaborate instrumentation.[25]

Although Skinner's remarks are directed at the so-called computer-based teaching machines, they may appropriately be generalized to cover all the newer technological developments. *Justification for the use and continued development of elaborate educational instrumentation lies in experimental research.*

ARRANGED ROOM ENVIRONMENT

Each of the three words in the section heading is important to effective learning. The first, "arranged," suggests adjustments, a proper order, or a manner best suited to a purpose. "Room," of course, refers to space. "Environment," according to Webster, refers to the surroundings, spe-

[24] John L. Burns, "Our Era of Opportunity," *Saturday Review*, 50 (January 14, 1967), 38–39.
[25] B. F. Skinner, "Reflections on a Decade of Teaching Machines," *Teachers College Record*, 65 (November 1963), 168.

cifically, "the aggregate of all the external conditions and influences affecting the life and development of an organism," and we might add "the behavior of the organism." Winston Churchill in a speech in 1944 made the statement that "We shape our dwellings and afterwards our dwellings shape us." The implication for an educative environment is clear.

In Chapter 12 it is pointed out that there is a distinct relationship between environment and discipline. There is an equally distinct relationship between environment and learning. It is difficult to show that pupil X will learn y amount in a dismal environment, but z amount in a cheerful environment. But testimony based on observation and experience validates it. Edgar Dale says school environment can be "educative, miseducative, or mal-educative." [26] The child who starts to school at age 6 has a functional vocabulary of some 2500 words. Where did he get this vocabulary? Was it not from his environment? This vocabulary may be larger or smaller, depending upon many things, but surely on the quality of the environment.

In industry, it has been found that job output can be increased by creating a proper environment. Safety can likewise be increased. Restaurant owners are confident that environment in the way of decor, cheerfulness, and esthetics brings customers back, and may even lead to larger orders, with increased cheerfulness in paying the bills.

It is not difficult to accept the thesis that drab, unsightly, or uncomfortable surroundings may underlie tensions and negative behavior. Poor lighting, poor ventilation, and high noise level exact a toll from morale.

The school environmental influence is often more psychological than physical, yet for some unaccountable reason unacceptable physical conditions are more likely to be corrected than unacceptable psychological conditions.

CREATING AN ENVIRONMENT

An environment favorable to learning can be created in almost any school by an industrious and imaginative teacher. Surroundings conducive to a desire to learn, to cooperate, and to diminish interpersonal problems can be established. An air of mutuality can replace an air of distrust.

Students are captive audiences. They must live in the same room an hour or more each day for every school day of the year. It is not too much to expect an unusual effort to make the classroom an attractive place in which to live. An environment that is stimulating and exciting can bring out the best in the students. It is no wonder that modern school architecture and modern educational theory are concerned with providing an interesting and challenging atmosphere.

Time dimensions are important. The schools of a past era were often

[26] Edgar Dale, *Newsletter*, May 1961.

most uninspiring. Compulsive factors dominated education, but times change. Many beginning teachers will be assigned to modern buildings that are attractive in design, flexible in arrangement, and varied and complete in terms of equipment. These buildings are designed so that teaching methods are not frozen by spatial and physical factors. But other beginning teachers will be located in older school buildings, for buildings are built for a lifetime of thirty, fifty, or more years. Ingenuity becomes imperative for these teachers. They must try to make bare, colorless, and dull surroundings come alive. Chalkboards can be kept neat and uncluttered. If bulletin boards or tack areas are available, they can become the nuclei of display areas that add color and interest. Travel posters will add a modern touch. A book shelf may contain new and interesting books, or a corner may be set aside for some specific use—space exploration, tomorrow's transportation, understanding of our neighbors in other lands, and so on. Book jackets and a judiciously placed map, air age or political, will help update a room. Corrugated colored paperboard may cover unsightly walls or cluttered surfaces. Hangings and displays may be placed almost anywhere.

Good art is not the sole prerogative of the art department. Art is appropriate in any classroom. The mathematics teacher may borrow drawings and designs that correlate highly with his subject. Good reprints of the works of some of the art masters are always in order. But let us not hang two or three tired lithoprints of Galahad or Lafayette on the walls for students to "stare through" from September to June.

Does the community have a museum? Does it have an established and well-supplied audio-visual center? If so, it is the source of many objects, specimens, artifacts, pictures, prints, and facsimiles. Could you use a band of flags representing the nations of Asia, Africa, Latin America, or the members of the United Nations? In addition to the museum, other sources to consider are newspapers, water districts, chambers of commerce, industrial plants, ship companies, and a list that grows too long to enumerate further.

Not all these efforts are made just for the sake of appearances. Arranging and rearranging the environment of the classroom help initiate new units of study in an interesting manner. Reality can be created, or at least simulated, and a common background experience provided for the students. Environment can help unify and integrate ideas. Other purposes may also be served, depending upon time, place, and conditions. Much of this assumes, and rightly so, that the environment of the classroom will change periodically. Subject emphases change, seasons change, and the environment might appropriately match these or other changes.

TEACHERS HAVE ASSISTANCE

The teacher need not feel that all these changes fall solely upon his shoulders; yet he does carry the responsibility. Certainly, students in every class should assist in the rearrangements decided upon. These changes provide unique opportunities for various types of learning, and students have a built-in readiness for making innovations. Junior high school students in particular enjoy this type of activity.

The custodial and the entire school staff, too, can be of great assistance. Courtesy pays great dividends in these areas. Custodians can be extremely helpful in making illustrative materials, in finding supplies, in rearranging furniture, in making displays, in doing minor paint jobs, or in distributing equipment. The ability to win friends and influence people is as important here as in any other area of interpersonal relationships. Finally, keep in mind that the parents and the parent-teacher organizations are also interested in the learning environment.

THE QUALITY OF TEACHING MATERIALS

The older schools tended to rely heavily, but certainly not exclusively, on printed, textbook type of instructional materials. Mark Hopkins used more than a log to make education meaningful. He purchased a new device, a model of a man, which cost him $600, and this he used in speeches and in teaching throughout western Massachusetts. Drama and art forms played a significant part in Greek and Roman education. Cicero, Seneca, and Quintilian advocated visual forms and the latter developed the now commonplace alphabet block. Marionettes, frescoes, and stained glass windows contributed their part to the education of the Middle Ages. Field trips and object teaching were stressed by almost every reform-minded teacher of the realism period. Maps were engraved for inclusion in books as early as 1478. Charts and pictures are often credited to Comenius, and such educators as Rousseau, Pestalozzi, and Froebel gave substantial substance to what might be called the modern audio-visual method.

COMPROMISE BETWEEN THE IDEAL AND THE POSSIBLE

Teaching materials, whether books or nontextbook types, are not perfect, but the quality is rising. Textbooks have evolved from the rustic hornbook to the sophisticated and attractive volumes of today. Educational motion pictures have grown from the dull, silent, slow-moving flammable celluloids of the twenties to the nonflammable, sound-color films of today. Other materials have improved in like manner. And as technology strides forward, the equipment used to present these materials improves.

Textbooks are usually selected by a committee of classroom teachers, curriculum specialists, and possibly administrators. Textbook committees examine and evaluate many books before adoptions are made of basic texts, supplementary texts, and workbooks. Films and other nonprinted instructional materials are usually selected in similar manner.

Often the selection is admittedly not ideal, but it is the best available at the time. It is hoped that a producer, publisher, or an author will improve on what is currently available, but students cannot wait. They must have learning materials, so a compromise is made, provided, of course, there is nothing harmful or misleading in the material.

Librarians and audio-visual directors should be broadly trained people in matters of curriculum and instructional methodology, as well as in their areas of specialization. They should therefore assist in the selection of all instructional materials.

Continued research of instructional materials and their use is needed. Materials used in today's schools are good, but they can be better. There are still books as well as films that are dull, repetitive, inartistic, generalizing, and incomplete. Possibly no single instrument is adequate in itself. The cross-media approach helps correct this shortcoming. A symphony of instructional materials produces more acceptable results than a single instrument.

This chapter has completed the discussion of instructional materials. Beginning teachers need to be informed about both the older and the newer ones. Some of the materials are still experimental; others are being modified. The early emphasis on teaching machines, for example, is being transferred to other forms, but the basic principles of programmed learning have not changed. Educational television has not had the expected impact. However, it is a robust medium and its future is bright. Audiovisuals per se, have changed, but their values grow more pronounced each day.

SELECTED READINGS

1. *Audiovisual Instruction,* "Instructional Television," entire issue. vol. 12 (November 1967).

2. Erickson, Carlton W. H., *Fundamentals of Teaching with Audiovisual Technology.* New York: The Macmillan Company, 1965.

3. Fry, Edward F., *Teaching Machines and Programmed Learning.* New York: McGraw-Hill Book Company, Inc., 1963.

4. Guba, Egon G., and Clinton A. Snyder, "Instructional Television and the Classroom Teacher," *AV Communication Review,* 13 (Spring 1965), 5–27.

5. Hayes, Alfred S., *Language Laboratory Facilities.* Washington, D.C.: U.S. Office of Education, Bulletin 1963, no. 37, OE–21024, 1963.

6. Hilgard, Ernest L., "What Support from the Psychology of Learning?" *NEA Journal,* 50 (November 1961), 20–21.

7. Hook, Sidney, and Charles F. Madden, "There Is More than One Way to Teach," *Saturday Review,* 47 (July 18, 1964), 48–51.

8. Kinder, James S., *Using Audio-Visual Materials in Education.* New York: American Book Company, 1965.

9. *Phi Delta Kappan,* "A Special Issue on Programmed Instruction," 44 (March 1963), 241–302.

10. Shane, Harold G., "Future Shock and the Curriculum," *Phi Delta Kappan,* 49 (October 1967), 67–70.

11. Skinner, B. F., *The Technology of Teaching.* New York: Appleton-Century-Crofts, Inc., Division of Meredith Corporation, 1968.

12. Smith, Karl U., and Margaret F. Smith, *Cybernetic Principles of Learning and Educational Design.* New York: Holt, Rinehart and Winston, Inc., 1966.

13. Suppes, Patrick, "The Computer and Excellence," *Saturday Review,* 50 (January 14, 1967), 46–52.

14. Trow, William C., *Teacher and Technology: New Designs for Learning.* Appleton-Century-Crofts, Inc., Division of Meredith Corporation, 1963.

15. Van Til, William, "Supervising Computerized Instruction," *Educational Leadership,* 26 (December 1968), 41–45.

16. Wittich, Walter A., and Charles F. Schuller, *Audiovisual Materials: Their Nature and Use,* 4th ed. New York: Harper & Row, Publishers, 1967.

17. Woodring, Paul, "The Schools Educate Themselves," *Saturday Review,* 47 (August 29, 1964), 153–155, 185.

PART FOUR | *Providing Classroom Control*

CHAPTER 12

An Analysis of Classroom Management and Control

There, in his noisy mansion, skilled to rule,
The village master taught his little school.—*Oliver Goldsmith*

THE IMPORTANCE OF GOOD DISCIPLINE

"No single problem is such a challenge and causes so much teacher heartache, frustration, and failure as the problem of discipline" (7:1). Beginning teachers, especially, view the problem of discipline with apprehension because they realize that their success or failure at the outset will depend largely on their ability to maintain an effective learning environment in the classroom. Administrators are concerned about the ability of new teachers to control their classes because they realize that unless an orderly classroom atmosphere is achieved, very little learning is likely to occur and school problems will be multiplied. Students themselves lose respect for teachers who are unable to maintain good discipline.

It has often been said that good discipline is synonymous with good teaching. Certainly the teacher who is able to keep his students vitally interested and personally involved in constructive learning activities is likely to have few, if any, disciplinary problems.

Wherever large numbers of boys and girls are brought together to be educated, some form of grouping becomes necessary. Each group constitutes a society of its own. As in any other social group, some degree of law and order has to be maintained or the group disintegrates. The teacher, as instructional leader in the classroom, has a twofold responsibility: to help each student develop his abilities to the maximum and to promote cooperative group living.

DISCIPLINE: A COMPLEX PROBLEM

The subject of *discipline* may be a source of confusion to both teacher and parent. The term itself is objectionable to some people because it carries with it an unpleasant connotation. However, because it is a word in common usage and one that seems to have no adequate synonym, "discipline" must continue to be used. At the outset, there is confusion over definition, for Oliva discovered at least twenty-five different meanings of the word (7:5–6). For instance, discipline may be defined as self-control, external control, obedience to authority, the degree of order established in a class, a rigorous course of study, a device used to maintain order, or as a synonym for punishment. Common dictionary definitions of "discipline" include such meanings as instruction to ensure proper conduct, orderly conduct, subjection to rules of conduct, a system of rules regulating conduct, and punishment. *The Dictionary of Education* incorporates such additional concepts as the subordination of immediate impulses for ultimate ideals or purposes and persistent self-direction in the face of difficulty.[1] Sheviakov and Redl believe that teachers ordinarily think of discipline in three different ways: the degree of order established in a group, the means by which order is achieved, and punishment.[2]

As far as the school is concerned, the present tendency is to think of discipline problems largely in terms of "the thoughtless and irresponsible acts of young people who are not maladjusted but are just uneducated and unsocialized."[3] This point of view will serve as a basis for much of the later discussion of techniques for good classroom management and control.

However, certain categories of boys and girls in the classroom demand special consideration.

First of all, there are youth "who have unusual difficulty in maintaining satisfactory interpersonal relationships" (2:137). Deviant behavior may be reflected in either of two extreme forms: an "acting-out response" (characteristic of socially maladjusted deviates) and/or a "pattern of withdrawal behavior" (typical of emotionally disturbed deviates). In some cases, an individual may embody both types of these behavior problems (2:137). The function of the classroom teacher is to be on the alert for danger signals and to secure the advice and aid of experts (counselors, psychologists, and the like) when extreme deviant behavior is evident.

Another group of children which deserves special consideration is the *disadvantaged*. Serious attention to their educational needs is a comparatively recent development. Although they have constituted a signif-

---

[1] Carter V. Good, *Dictionary of Education*. New York: McGraw-Hill Book Company, Inc., 1959, p. 176.

[2] George V. Sheviakov and Fritz Redl, *Discipline for Today's Children and Youth*. New revision by Sybil K. Richardson. Washington, D.C.: Association for Supervision and Curriculum Development, 1956, pp. 2–3.

[3] Asahel D. Woodruff, "Discipline," *Encyclopedia of Educational Research*, 3d ed., Chester W. Harris, ed. New York: The Macmillan Company, 1960, p. 382.

icant group in our society, their educational deprivation (due to such factors as attendance at inferior schools and early school leaving) has not been of major concern. Now a change, hopefully a revolution, is taking place. To solve the educational problems of these children, almost everyone would agree that two courses of action are necessary. In the first place, basic causes of their disadvantaged status (inferior schools, low family income, substandard housing) must be corrected. Until the slums or ghettos of large cities are abolished, some consider the picture dark for either good teaching or good discipline. Interviews with successful Harlem teachers and reports from their supervisors and students led Trubowitz to maintain that "The successful ghetto teacher clearly defines limits and shows his respect and liking for children by insisting that they maintain standards." [4] In conclusion, he states that ghetto teachers must be "truly familiar with the lives of ghetto children . . . their experiences, their interests, their feelings, their needs, their strengths and weaknesses. . . ." [5]

Until removal of the socioeconomic factors responsible for the spawning of disadvantaged populations can be achieved, a second, more immediately pressing need is evident—provision of an adequate number of teachers who are well qualified to teach the disadvantaged. Unfortunately, such teachers are now in short supply. The typical middle-class teacher in the typical school with its middle-class orientation, curriculum, and values has difficulty accepting disadvantaged children as "normal" children whose primary need is to overcome their educational deficiencies. However, some teachers who feel unqualified to deal with the problems of these children will be facing them in their classes for some time to come. Perhaps their first task is to find out all they can about these children. Although there is no such thing as a typical disadvantaged child, there are factors common to most of them: They are children of poverty; they are usually "educationally retarded"; they have low aspirations and self-esteem; and they are likely to be from a minority group. [6, 7]

Although the teacher may find many excellent books and articles about the disadvantaged, he will probably be disappointed if he is looking for suggestions on appropriate classroom management and control techniques. Suggestions that are made usually represent either of two different viewpoints. Some teachers contend that since disadvantaged children come from a disorganized environment, they need a well-structured

---

[4] Sidney Trubowitz, "How To Teach in a Ghetto School," *Today's Education*—NEA *Journal,* 57 (October 1968), 26.

[5] Trubowitz, p. 29.

[6] Elinor F. McCloskey, *Urban Disadvantaged Youth.* A Synthesis of 99 Research Reports. Portland, Ore.: The Northwest Regional Laboratory (February 1967).

[7] American Educational Research Association, "Educational Programs: Adolescence," *Review of Educational Research,* 36 (October 1966), 465–466.

classroom situation. Limits of acceptable behavior are clearly defined and rigidly enforced. Such an environment provides these children with a feeling of security. Taba and Elkins reflect a different point of view when they describe the kind of teacher that the disadvantaged children need: "First of all, students need to see that the teacher cares, that she is a human being who is interested in them personally and cares about what happens to them." [8]

Another problem in dealing with the concept of discipline is the lack of research on the subject. This is apparently true for two reasons: difficulties in delimiting the concept and managing so many variables (2:381). There is, nevertheless, a great deal of good advice to be found in the literature on the subject. Years of accumulated, practical experience of teachers and administrators provide a rich source of helpful suggestions for the beginning teacher. Some see little hope of helping new teachers develop skill in classroom management and control, maintaining that no two situations are identical. Although there is a certain element of truth in this contention, many types of discipline problems have been recurring with monotonous regularity ever since boys and girls began going to school. Furthermore, it has been found that certain practices usually work whereas others frequently do not. The prospective teacher who has opportunities to observe the *expertise* of successful teachers in classroom management and control may gain a knowledge of procedures that should be helpful to him later. By reflecting on such observations, the beginning teacher may be saved from costly mistakes in dealing with his own students.

Historically, the concept of school discipline has undergone a revolution in our society. In colonial times, discipline was severe, with an emphasis on unquestioned obedience to authority and vindictive punishment. New knowledge of the forces of nature and the dynamics of personality, plus acceptance of a more humanitarian philosophy, has brought about a remarkable transition in disciplinary theory and practice. Unreasonable punishment eventually gave way to attempts to reform the offender, later to the prevention of misbehavior, and finally to stress on self-control. The modern concept of discipline has focused on recognition of individual differences in behavior, as well as on fluctuations in the behavior of each individual. The literature frequently reflects the view that individuals often need help in coping with the problems of the world around them.[9] Teachers have always realized the importance of helping students with their school subjects. What they have not always clearly recognized is the fact that students also need help with their personal and social development. The development of a superb intellect in a weak and sickly

[8] Hilda Taba and Deborah Elkins, *Teaching Strategies for the Culturally Disadvantaged.* Chicago: Rand McNally & Company, 1966, p. 265.
[9] Woodruff, p. 383.

physical body, governed by the values of a moral moron, can only result in personal failure for the individual concerned and in waste to society. As the pendulum has swung from one extreme to another, from authoritarian control to self-control, there is a countertrend today which reflects the belief that both home and school have gone too far in the direction of permissiveness.

The present-day note in discipline is reflected from a number of sources. An editorial in the December 1959 issue of the *Phi Delta Kappan* cites a case of a 12-year-old boy who had killed his brother but maintained, "It wasn't my fault." The editor then makes the observation that the boy is right "if we accept the orthodox sociological thesis that practically everyone and everything are responsible for the actions of the delinquent except the delinquent himself. . . . There are haunting and crippling paradoxes in both the humanitarian admonition—'to understand all is to forgive all'—and the Freudian theory—'man is largely the creature of his subconscious drives.'" [10] An even more extreme reflection of this anomalous position is found in the words of a senior judge in New York who said, "The philosophy of responsibility has been replaced by the philosophy of excuse." [11]

In somewhat the same vein, Harold Taylor attacks the problem from the standpoint of the home. He points out that parents have made such a genuine effort to *understand* their children, to stake "everything on a warm and affectionate relationship" with their children, that youth have become independent and self-sufficient in a quasi-adult society of their own. As a result, the strongest force parents are able to exert is to produce feelings of guilt in their children. Consequently, "there is no longer a clear-cut authority-freedom issue for the adolescent, but instead there are ambivalent feelings of obligation, responsibility, and guilt." [12]

Further evidence of a reaction against the "philosophy of excuse" is a new approach to psychiatry by Glasser, called *Reality Therapy*, which "depends upon what might be called a psychiatric version of the three R's, namely, *reality, responsibility, and right-and-wrong*." [13]

The first R, *reality*, begins with the premise that "all patients have a common characteristic: *they all deny the reality of the world around them. . . .* Therapy will be successful when they are able to give up denying the world and recognize not only that reality exists but that they must fulfill their needs within its framework." [14]

---

[10] Stanley Elam, Editorial, "Responsibilities, Revolutions, and Reservations," *Phi Delta Kappan*, 41 (December 1959), 89.

[11] Elam, p. 89.

[12] Harold Taylor, "The Understood Child," *Saturday Review*, 44 (May 20, 1961), 47–49, 66. Copyright Saturday Review, Inc., 1961.

[13] William Glasser, *Reality Therapy: A New Approach to Psychiatry*. New York: Harper & Row, Publishers, Inc., 1965, p. xii.

[14] Glasser, p. 6.

"Responsibility . . . is here defined as the ability to fulfill one's needs, and to do so *in a way that does not deprive others of the ability to fulfill their needs.*" [15] Instead of probing into the past or unconscious of a patient, in order to find out *why* he behaves as he does, the Reality Therapist insists that the patient become fully aware of his present behavior and that he also judge the quality of that behavior—in other words, the patient is asked to face reality and accept the moral responsibility for his own actions.[16] "Right, good, or moral" is defined as follows: "*When a man acts in such a way that he gives and receives love, and feels worthwhile to himself and others, his behavior is right and moral.*" [17]

In teaching classes on Reality Therapy to teachers, Glasser comes to such conclusions as these: "The teachers develop a new confidence in their own ability to understand their children. They learn new techniques to help children fulfill their needs, techniques which always require them to give of themselves and become more involved with their students. At the same time they learn the necessity of employing firm discipline, never in a punitive sense, but to show that they care about their students." [18]

DILEMMAS OF DISCIPLINE

To the new teacher probably nothing is more confusing about discipline than the conflicting points of view and discrepancies between theory and practice that he so often encounters. The classroom teacher must understand these paradoxes in discipline, learn to live with them, and formulate his own philosophy of discipline.

One of the common areas of conflict is found between the so-called guidance point of view and the teaching point of view. It has been known for some time that mental hygienists and guidance specialists consider withdrawal type of behavior most serious, whereas classroom teachers are most concerned with aggressive types of behavior. Guidance workers have devoted more of their attention to underlying causes of misbehavior and to individual adjustment problems. On the other hand, the classroom teacher has had to take large assortments of individuals with varied interests, backgrounds, and abilities and attempt to weld them into cohesive groups in pursuit of common goals. No doubt differences in viewpoints between full-time counselors and classroom teachers are largely due to *differences in situations.* Teachers have been forced through necessity to do that which is expedient and to treat surface behavior rather than search for underlying causes. The counselor who works with students on an individual, face-to-face basis has quite a different

---

[15] Glasser, p. 13.
[16] Glasser, pp. 55–56.
[17] Glasser, p. 57.
[18] Glasser, p. 158.

situation from that of the classroom teacher who is always working with groups.

Another problem that has created confusion about discipline is one of a semantic nature. As one writer has stated, "We should stop equating permissiveness (absence of discipline) with democratic discipline, and realistic adult control and guidance with authoritarianism." In the same article, the author of that statement points out a number of "distortions of democratic discipline," such as the notion that democratic discipline implies freedom from external restraints or that teachers may abdicate responsibility for making final decisions.[19]

Another dilemma of discipline arises from a conflict of *needs*. Which shall have priority, the needs of the individual or the needs of the group? Certainly the individual must have freedom to develop self-control, to achieve maturity as a unique person who is able to think for himself. On the other hand, unless each one learns to respect the rights of others and to conform to certain rules of group living or social control, no stable society, either adolescent or adult, can ever be achieved.

Another paradox in discipline stems from disagreement over *techniques*. Should the teacher stress directive or nondirective control? Is direct modification of behavior through external control better than permitting students much freedom to experiment or learn by trial and error? Is it better for the teacher to correct surface behavior, to demand immediate conformity in the interest of group welfare, or to delay action while he seeks more evidence of causes and permits the offender to suffer the natural consequences of his own acts? Somewhere between the extremes of imposed discipline and permissive control is a sensible middle ground not always easy to determine.

Conflicting *philosophies* constitute a major source of confusion in discipline. The cultural conflict between the philosophy of excuse and the philosophy of responsibility has already been discussed. Likewise, the irreconcilable positions of authoritarianism and extreme permissiveness have been suggested. Social philosophy also has a bearing on school discipline. The widening rift between liberals and conservatives in this country and the worldwide cold war between democracy and communism are conducive to a climate of fear, suspicion, and insecurity. The school is inevitably affected. Censorship of books, the harsher discipline, more and more legislative prescription of school programs, and the increasing peril of dealing with controversial issues reflect the tenor of the present time. Students in school face a very practical problem of making adjustments to the conflicting philosophies and practices encountered from class to class within the same school. As far as the teaching profession itself is

[19] David P. Ausubel, "A New Look at Classroom Discipline," *Phi Delta Kappan,* 43 (October 1961), 25–30.

concerned, not only is there widespread disagreement over theory and practice in discipline, but there are also sharp discrepancies between stated beliefs and actual classroom procedures. Perhaps some teachers are inclined to talk a better line than they are willing to follow.

The problem of conflicting *values* has already been mentioned. To complicate matters, there is always the problem of reconciling the middle-class values of teachers with the values of students who come from lower-class homes. Furthermore, the "generation gap" between adult values and those of an adolescent subculture is apparently becoming wider.

The last area of confusion in discipline to be discussed here is that relating to the *stage of development* of the student. Not only must teacher expectations be geared to the level of maturity of the learner, appropriate procedures must also be used in each case. New teachers, especially, need to avoid several false assumptions: that high school students are as mature as college students, that all students at a given grade level have achieved the same level of maturity, or that all students without exception are capable of achieving complete self-direction. Once these realities are recognized, the teacher has to ascertain ways to adapt control procedures to all the variations in maturity level with which he must cope.

SCHOOL SOURCES OF BEHAVIOR PROBLEMS

The number and kinds of behavior problems with which the teacher of adolescents has to contend are legion. Even though the classroom teacher often has to deal with problems on the basis of expediency rather than on the basis of case studies or an analysis of underlying causes, there is still an advantage in knowing why boys and girls behave as they do. No one would deny that it is far better to remove causes of misbehavior than merely to treat symptoms. Yet detection of basic causes of behavior problems is no easy matter, for it is now recognized that causes of any particular type of misbehavior may stem from many and varied sources. As each student seeks to develop self-direction, he is always influenced by three kinds of environment: physical, cultural, and interpersonal relationships.[20] Oliva has indentified the following sources of behavior problems: the student himself, the student's peer group, the teacher and the school, the home and the community, and the larger social order (7:19–37). In the discussion that follows, factors influencing student behavior will be further explored and suggestions for positive action will be made, beginning with the school as a source of discipline problems.

PHYSICAL ENVIRONMENT

The physical environment of the school is an important factor in influencing the behavior of boys and girls. Dingy, crowded, unattractive school

[20] Woodruff, p. 382.

buildings are conducive to confusion and disorder. On the other hand, a physical environment that is comfortable, attractive, and orderly is likely to bring out the best in student behavior. Maintenance of proper temperature, ventilation, and lighting in the classroom is important, not only from the standpoint of good discipline but also in protecting the physical health of students. Some older classrooms that are poorly arranged and drably decorated pose the problem of attractiveness. However, a teacher can, with the help of his students, brighten the dullest room with flower arrangements, attractive bulletin boards, and centers of interests (science corner, exhibits, and a book nook). In addition to maintaining a comfortable, attractive, tidy classroom, the teacher must by all means provide an orderly working atmosphere in which learning can take place effectively. More will be said about this later under the subject of class organization and management.

THE CURRICULUM

Whenever a teacher has a class that is unresponsive and bored, seeking its satisfactions in rowdy behavior or listless daydreaming, he has a right to be concerned. In seeking the source of the trouble, he may find it originates with the *curriculum.* Unfortunately, as the formal school program is now organized, it fails to meet the needs of many boys and girls who represent such great diversity in interests, abilities, and backgrounds. Traditionally, the secondary school curriculum has been academic and bookish. Learning has been based on the accumulated heritage of mankind as recorded in books, with a singular neglect of the experiences and problems of everyday living.

A half century ago, when only a selected segment of the population (largely academic in character) of secondary school age attended school, the problem of student adjustment to the curriculum was not so acute as it is today. Now, with virtually all boys and girls between the ages of 14 and 17 in school, a strictly academic program falls far short of meeting the personal and social needs of many students, to say nothing of failing to meet the needs of a society experiencing the most rapid socioeconomic changes in history.

For disadvantaged youth especially, the traditional curriculum is sterile. It is most likely to be devoid of relevance or meaning for boys and girls who suffer almost every kind of deprivation—lack of opportunity (social, educational, vocational), basic human rights, or hope for the future.[21]

There is no simple solution to the problem. In some cases, a complete overhauling of the content of certain subjects is long overdue. Perhaps in some cases, specific subjects need to be eliminated entirely. Tradition is apparently a potent factor in the retention of outmoded, nonfunctional

[21] McCloskey, p. 9.

items in the school program. Where changes have been made in existing courses, sometimes the most important goal of education has been neglected: improved behavior of boys and girls. Where there is no immediate relief from the dissatisfaction of students with the curriculum, the teacher will need to exercise the utmost imagination and ingenuity to interest some students in the work to be done. Not only the curriculum but the methods used by the teacher are important. Monotonous routines and inappropriate instructional procedures soon lead to behavior problems.

ADMINISTRATION AND SCHOOL REGULATIONS

Administration plays a critical role in the achievement of satisfactory school discipline. Administrators expect teachers to take care of their own control problems within the classroom. This is a reasonable expectation, but when a teacher encounters a problem with which he is unable to cope, he is entitled to the full backing and support of the administration. Whenever a principal fails to give teachers the help they deserve, control problems multiply and school morale deteriorates rapidly.

Another possible source of discipline problems arising within the school is the policies and regulations that govern achievement and behavior of its students. The conflict that often arises between home and school because of different values has already been indicated. Regulations, as well as their means of enforcement, which are either too severe or too lax may also lead to control problems. Administrators who frequently resort to physical punishment, especially for older children, soon reap a harvest of rebellion and aggressive behavior. When rules that are just and reasonable have been made, they must be enforced fairly and consistently. Enforcement of school regulations—such as regular attendance, proper conduct in halls and on the playground, and respect for public property—is the responsibility of all school personnel, not just administrators. Promotional policies that encourage just "getting by" on the one hand or result in a high incidence of failure on the other are another potential source of discipline problems. Excessive stress on examinations or competition for school marks not only creates a climate conducive to behavior problems but also may be a threat to the mental health of many students.

INTERPERSONAL RELATIONSHIPS

How well teachers are able to work in harmony with fellow teachers, administrators, parents, and students is a vital factor in the promotion of desirable student behavior. When faculties are split into hostile, competing camps, students are forced to develop divided loyalties. They become confused and insecure. If teachers and administrators lack confidence in and respect for one another, students lose confidence in the leadership of the adults who are supposedly helping them achieve maturity. On the other hand, when the personnel of a school work together in harmony, student respect for faculty leadership, strong school spirit, and a high level of achievement in both citizenship and scholarship are encouraged.

Another type of relationship which needs to be strengthened, especially at the secondary school level, is that between teachers and parents. The improvement of student behavior is most likely to occur when parents and teachers are working together as a team. Very often students who are out of step with school policies and practices will strengthen their position by taking advantage of a cleavage between parents and teachers. The student who has to choose between loyalty to his teachers and loyalty to his parents is in an unenviable position. Of course, the most important interpersonal relationships for teachers are those that exist between them and their students.

THE TEACHER

Of all the influences in a school that provoke misbehavior or stimulate good behavior on the part of students, the most pervasive is that of the teachers. Personality, character, attitudes, and observable actions are all factors that determine the effectiveness of teacher relationships, both with students and with colleagues. Some persons attract; others repel. Because successful teaching depends so much on satisfactory interpersonal relationships, it behooves all teachers to cultivate those personal traits which attract others. It is now generally agreed that personality can be changed.

PERSONALITY OF THE TEACHER Some teachers exhibit vivacity; they sparkle. Others present a demeanor of gravity and stability; they inspire confidence. Still others may demonstrate qualities of kindness, sympathy, and understanding; they radiate warmth. All of these may be good teachers. In developing his personality, the teacher must first of all capitalize on his own assets and not attempt to become a poor facsimile of someone else.

First impressions are not always lasting ones, but they are important. Physical attractiveness, cleanliness, and good manners are important factors in the creation of a good first impression. However, in order to wear well, the teacher must be able to demonstrate consistently exemplary professional attitudes and evidence of strength of character. More will be said about this later in the chapter.

Voice quality is an important consideration in teaching. Unfortunately, most teachers do not know how their own voices sound to others. It is surprising how often supervisors of teachers rate voice as "unsatisfactory." As a first step to improvement, a person may listen to a tape recording of his own voice. The experience may prove to be disconcerting but helpful.

A well-integrated personality is mandatory for successful teaching. Not only is a well-adjusted personality important in the maintenance of harmonious relationships with others; it is a necessary condition for safeguarding one's own mental health. Teaching is basically a problem of human engineering. It is especially important for the teacher to accept himself (in his role as a teacher) and others. In no other profession is the commandment "Love thy neighbor as thyself" more relevant. Furthermore, the well-adjusted person is able to face reality, to accept constructive criticism without resentment, to admit failure without rationalizing, and to recognize the need for continuous self-improvement.

In evaluating the qualities of teachers, Redl considers "a *sense of humor* . . . the most vital characteristic of the skillful handler of discipline problems or tough group situations" and *false dignity* as "the one personality trait most injurious to successful discipline. . . ." (10:303).

A professor of psychiatry made an observation that is especially relevant for teachers: "It has been the assumption of education that learning would make men wise, mature, and creative. It is my unhappy conviction that learning alone achieves none of these goals, but more frequently is a mask for immaturity, neurosis, and a lack of wisdom." [22] In helping adolescents achieve the difficult task of growing up, the teacher must first of all be a mature person himself.

TEACHER ATTITUDES   How a teacher feels about his job, his colleagues, and his students has a direct bearing on student behavior. As a member of an honored profession, the teacher should exhibit pride in that fact and continuously strive to be a credit to his profession. Many stories have been related about teachers who try to hide their occupational identity away from home or who apologetically identify themselves by saying, "I am just a teacher." If that is the way teachers feel about their profession, they cannot expect to command much respect for it, either from adults or from youth. The importance of cooperative attitudes and harmonious relationships within the profession has already been indicated earlier in this chapter.

Although the attitudes a teacher has toward his profession and his colleagues may not have the most significant bearing on classroom control, his attitudes toward his students will ultimately determine his success or failure in improving their behavior. The following classroom situations illustrate the point.

One new teacher whose relationships with his students were deteriorating rapidly finally admitted that he disliked his students. Another teacher made this remark to a student teacher who asked permission to observe his class: "I don't know why you came to visit me. I hate kids."

[22] Lawrence S. Kubie, "Are We Educating for Maturity?" *NEA Journal,* 48 (January 1959), 58–63.

However, upon being invited to remain, the student teacher did observe the class. A report on the observation later revealed the fact that much of the class hour was spent in a series of unpleasant incidents in which the teacher was pitted against the students. Still another teacher demonstrated a mistaken attitude about his relationships with 'students when he remarked, "It's the best class I have because the kids are afraid of me."

Students usually try to live up to a teacher's expectations. If a teacher expects the worst of his students, they seldom disappoint him. On the other hand, if he believes in them and shows confidence in their ability to become good citizens, students usually justify that faith.

It is unfortunate that a few persons enter teaching who bring only reproach on the profession. To illustrate the point, caricatures of some of these types follow (with no intention of discrediting the many good teachers who teach the subjects that are used in the illustration). Mr. Biceps of the physical education department is loud, rough, and tough. In order to impress his charges with his red-blooded manliness, he bellows at his boys, punctuating his remarks with an occasional bit of profanity. In social studies, Miss Frustration enters her classroom grimly, expecting trouble from the brats. The artists in teacher-baiting soon get into action and another unhappy hour takes place. In science, Mr. Monotony drones on wearily while his bored students doze or watch the clock. In seventh-grade music, Mr. O. F. Key smiles weakly and murmurs repeatedly, "We are waiting for C_____ to help us with 'The Blackbird Song.'" Mrs. Drudge, who has taught English for twenty-nine years, seldom notices her students when she meets them on the street because of her preoccupation with the litter of ungraded themes on her desk. The teacher who catches a glimpse of his own image in these caricatures is advised to change either his attitudes or his occupation. An unhappy, maladjusted teacher creates a miserable existence for himself and his students. Needless to say, the vice-principal's office is filled with the disciplinary referrals from such unhappy classroom situations.

THE CHARACTER OF THE TEACHER   In praising a new teacher, a supervisor climaxed his remarks with "He has character." Physical attractiveness, good grooming, and neatness in appearance are certainly not to be discounted in the art of influencing people but, in the long run, what a person *is* determines whether or not he will continue to draw others to him. Fairness, integrity, and consideration are not a veneer a teacher can apply at will as he enters the classroom. The "chiseler," whether he cheats in driving a car or in taking a test; the "little Caesar," who takes out his aggressions on a captive audience of students; or the parasite, who takes refuge in tenure laws, will sooner or later reveal his true self. Teachers talk much, but their actions are always more impressive than their words.

CULTURAL SOURCES OF BEHAVIOR PROBLEMS

Of all the factors influencing student behavior, the cultural or societal influence is the most pervasive and, at the same time, most difficult to change.

FAMILY LIFE   A shift from an agrarian to an industrial society has brought about changes with which our social institutions have been unable to cope. The most significant change resulting from the industrial age has been the dislocation of *family life*. The self-sufficient family of the past has been replaced by a modern version that has lost more and more of its former functions to other social agencies. Modern industry has replaced the family as the center of economic life. Commercial entertainment has taken recreation out of the home. Schools have absorbed many educational functions that formerly belonged to the family. The authoritarian role of the father has all but disappeared. With both parents frequently away from home, children are left to their own devices (sometimes referred to as "door-key kids" [23]) or in the care of friends and relatives.

PROBLEMS OF ADOLESCENCE   Dramatic changes in the role of the family have created problems in the education of youth. Lacking the guidance and support of their parents and being unable to identify themselves with the economic life of an industrial society, adolescents are often confused and even resentful. Adult reaction to these bewildered youth is often one of disapproval, or even fear.[24, 25] The problem for adults, especially parents and teachers, is obvious. The values of adult society and of teen-age peer culture are frequently in conflict, and youth tend to show less respect for teachers and the learning they represent.

Although there is some disagreement about whether or not there is a distinct "adolescent society" from which modern young people derive most of their values,[26] the influence of peers cannot be denied. Sherif cites such findings as the following: "The greater frequency and intensity of age-mate association in adolescence (well documented in earlier research) and the rise of distinctive values that adults do not fully share (further documented by research during the period) are symptomatic of the turn

[23] Harold J. McNally, "What Shall We Teach—and How?" *The National Elementary Principal*, May 1957, pp. 6–11.

[24] Donald McNassor, "The Changing Character of Adolescents," *California Journal of Secondary Education*, 31 (March 1956), 128–133.

[25] George Z. F. Bereday, Brian Holmes, and Joseph A. Lauwerys, Editors' Introduction, *The Secondary School Curriculum: The Yearbook of Education, 1958*. London: Evans Brothers, Limited, 1958.

[26] Louis M. Smith and Paul F. Kleine, "The Adolescent and His Society," *Review of Educational Research*, 26 (October 1966), 424–427.

toward peers as a major reference set for self-evaluation, emulation, and approval." [27] A number of studies indicate that peers have more influence than parents on students' decisions about courses students take and what clothes to wear.[28]

Of special interest to teachers is the influence that peers may have on academic achievement. Although some studies find that the "leading crowd" stresses the importance of the athletic boy and the popular girl at the expense of "good grades," others conclude that it cannot be assumed that "youth values invariably depress academic or other socially desirable interests." [29]

MOBILITY AND URBANIZATION   Two trends that make adjustment to our society more difficult for youth are *mobility* of population and increasing *urbanization*. The roots of a migrant population (gaining a livelihood from the fields or the factories) are often shallow. Sorokin has referred to our civilization as "a cut-flower civilization." Cut off from close circles of relatives and friends, both parents and their children lose the supporting and stabilizing influence of such intimate relationships. These migrants of the twentieth century never feel that they quite belong to any community or its institutions. There is no loneliness greater than that experienced by a stranger on a crowded city street or in the halls of a big school. What is the role of the school in dealing with these newcomers, some of whom enter the school almost every week of the year? Every teacher has a responsibility to make a special effort to help them get acquainted, feel at home, and become a part of the group. Making use of the special contributions new students may be able to bring to the class, arranging for students to orient each newcomer to the work of the class, and showing personal friendliness and interest in their welfare are some of the things teachers can do to help the strangers in their classrooms. Even more tragic is the plight of the disadvantaged children who are often locked in the urban slums or ghettos.

VALUES   Conflicting values between home and school have already been noted as a source of behavior problems. The teacher, who usually subscribes to the values of the middle class, may find it difficult to understand, or even tolerate, the behavior of other social groups. Dealing with pampered, overprotected, upper-class children on the one hand and uncouth, neglected, lower-class children on the other is a real challenge for the teacher. He has to become as adaptive as the chameleon. Such actions as fighting, swearing, and smoking may be considered normal behavior in lower-class families but cannot be tolerated by teachers. Thus

---

[27] Carolyn W. Sherif, "Adolescence: Motivational, Attitudinal, and Personality Factors," *Review of Educational Research*, 26 (October 1966), 438.
[28] Smith and Kleine, p. 427.
[29] Sherif, pp. 445–446.

an inevitable conflict arises between the home and the school, with the adolescent caught in the middle. Only by a slow, patient process can youth be educated to accept the values of a society that may be quite different from their own.

The problem of improving the behavior of youth becomes more complex because their world appears to be in a perpetual state of crisis. International tensions and the prospect of atomic warfare, probable interruption of normal life by military service, and inadequate economic opportunities are but a few of the social problems that create anxiety in youth today.

There is evidence that the common core of accepted values in American culture has been shrinking. When adults are often confused about what is acceptable or unacceptable behavior, there is little wonder that young people are likewise confused. As boys and girls read about political scandals, game fixing by athletic heroes, sharp business practices, and corruption in high places, they no doubt find it difficult to reconcile such actions with the high ideals promulgated by the school.

In his relationship with teachers and other adults, the fact that he is treated with fairness and understanding is most important to the adolescent. Despite commitment to the principle of equality of educational opportunity, there is abundant evidence that society has fallen short of attaining its ideal. The extent of discrimination against minority groups is too well known to require elaboration here. That the school may discriminate against children of lower-class families is probably not always so clearly recognized.[30] However, every decade marks definite steps forward in meeting the needs of the underprivileged and those who have been subject to discrimination.

DEALING WITH CULTURALLY INDUCED PROBLEMS

What can the teacher do about the anxieties and resentments created by the ills of our society? Obviously, the problem is not one for which the school alone is responsible. The home and the total community have a most significant role to play. Despite the magnitude of the problem, however, every teacher can do something to help young people satisfy their needs and make adjustments to the demands of contemporary society.

Although no teacher can remove the undesirable cultural conditions surrounding some children and youth, he can provide a happy school environment, an island of security in a sea of trouble.

As far as the school as a whole is concerned, a number of things can be done to reconcile the needs and aspirations of youth with the demands of adult society. Orientation to military service, to the vocations, to school and community life, and to the critical problems of our day are necessities

[30] August Hollingshead, *Elmtown's Youth.* New York: John Wiley & Sons, Inc., 1949.

in the education of boys and girls. Students should be able to examine controversial issues and their own prejudices in the light of available facts and differing points of view. At the same time they must develop the social attributes of good manners and cooperative relationships.

STUDENT NEEDS IN RELATION
TO BEHAVIOR PROBLEMS

Failure to achieve satisfaction of basic needs is a frequent source of rebellion and misbehavior on the part of adolescents. Teachers have to be constantly aware of these needs in order to help students satisfy them in acceptable ways. A primary need of everyone, child and adult, is for *affection.* The warped personality resulting from rejection by the home is almost sure to become a problem in school. Another basic human need is for *security.* Failure, lack of acceptance, and subjection to controls that are too permissive or arbitrarily repressive undermine the security of adolescents in their efforts to achieve maturity. *Success* is another basic need. Students who fail in school are fit subjects for discipline cases. Nothing fails like failure. Schoolwork must be within the capacity of slow learners but difficult enough to challenge gifted students. Classroom procedures must also be adapted to the ability and maturity levels of students.

Acceptance and recognition are necessary ingredients in the achievement of maturity. Probably nothing is more important to the adolescent than acceptance by his peers. To be one of the crowd sometimes becomes almost an obsession. Equally important, although not always so obvious, is the need for acceptance by adults, especially parents and teachers. Other qualities very noticeable in boys and girls in their teens are *curiosity, hero worship,* and *a venturesome spirit.* The wise teacher can use all the needs of youth to an advantage. Boys and girls, especially of junior high school age, need *freedom of movement.* When they are imprisoned in their seats too long, pent up energy eventually dissipates itself in disorder (7:21–24). This list of adolescent needs is by no means complete, but it suggests some very basic ones that cannot be ignored.

PRINCIPLES OF EFFECTIVE CLASS LEADERSHIP

Before launching a discussion of specific techniques for effective classroom management and control, the authors would like to suggest some important principles or guidelines a teacher should keep in mind. Eventually every teacher develops his own philosophy of control. Out of this philosophy are derived certain principles that govern specific acts in the guidance of student behavior. If the principles are sound, the choice of control procedures is likely to be wise.

As a first principle, it should be remembered that the ultimate goal of all teacher control is to enable students to achieve *self-control*. Failure here means that students never mature nor develop the necessary skills of citizenship in a self-governing society like our own. But it must also be remembered that self-direction is not inherited. It must be learned. Furthermore, there is no formula for the achievement of self-discipline overnight. It takes time. Until students have learned to respect the rights and needs of others, the teacher has a legal and moral responsibility to provide whatever external controls are necessary to protect group welfare. The teacher always ensures that there is sufficient control to produce desirable changes in behavior. Adequate teacher support is necessary for individual security and for a happy, orderly group climate.

A second principle of good discipline, which has been implied above, concerns *group welfare*. Teachers often face the dilemma of deciding what is best for the individual or for the group. Redl would apply the *Law of Marginal Antisepsis* from two standpoints. On the one hand, a technique that is right for solving an individual's problems or for bringing about "surface behavioral changes" must be harmless as far as the effect upon the group or on "long-range attitude changes" is concerned. On the other hand, any technique rightly chosen for desirable group effect or basic attitude changes must be harmless in terms of individuals involved or "the surface behavior challenges we have to meet through reality" (10:264, 272). There will always be maladjusted students, fortunately few in number, who will not cooperate with the teacher and the class. In dealing with such students, Vredvoe has summarized the principle at stake in these words: "It is important that the three to five percent who cause the problems and lack self-discipline or willingness to cooperate should not be allowed to waste the time or opportunities of the ninety-five percent." [31]

School disciplinary practices need to be based on *sound principles of learning*. Just as students need help in learning history or science, they also need help in learning desirable personal and social behavior. Just as there are low achievers and high achievers in school subjects, there are also fast learners and slow learners in the achievement of self-control.

Good teaching procedures, based on sound learning theory, are recommended as the most effective means of developing good classroom control. By stressing motivation and student participation, rather than coercion and punishment, the teacher is able to get class cooperation. The principle of *readiness*, which is applicable to academic learning, is equally relevant to the development of self-control. In referring to an unfortunate experience of losing control of a class, a teacher said: "If I were beginning

[31] Lawrence E. Vredvoe, "Third Report on a Study of Students and School Discipline in the United States and Other Countries," *Bulletin of the National Association of Secondary School Principals*, 49 (March 1965), 226.

again with this class, I would proceed differently. I assumed that the students had a maturity they did not yet have. After they were given more freedom than they could use wisely, I found it difficult to impose the restrictions that became necessary."

Adaptation of control procedures to different school levels, to different school neighborhoods, to different cultural backgrounds, or to different levels of maturity within a given grade or age group taxes the ingenuity of the teacher in making provisions for individual differences. There is always the danger of overestimating or underestimating a student's readiness for self-direction.

Another important principle of discipline is related to the *student's understanding of the purposes and functions of discipline.* The student must first understand the need for the school to establish and maintain certain conditions for the achievement of important objectives. He must develop favorable attitudes toward these necessary conditions for effective work and cooperation with others. He must also learn to respect the authority that may need to be exercised to protect both the rights of the individual and the welfare of the group. The student also needs to understand what is expected of him in terms of the behavioral goals and limits established by the school and society. He must be made to realize the consequences of his behavior and learn to accept responsibility for his actions. Most students wish to do the right thing, but they do not always know what is expected of them nor how to achieve these expectations.

Another principle of good classroom control is related to the fact that *no one prescription is applicable to all disciplinary problems.* Methods of classroom control vary with the student, the teacher, the place (home, school, community), the weather, or even the day of the week. Oliva draws a close analogy between the courts and the schools. The law of the land is not immutable but is subject to interpretation by the courts. Punishment for a crime, stealing, for example, will vary according to intent, willingness to make amends, mitigating circumstances, or the maturity of the offender (7:86–87). When punishment is necessary, it must fit the offense, the individual or the group, and the purpose to be achieved (a change in surface behavior or a permanent change in attitude).

In helping students achieve maturity, the teacher must continuously evaluate his own behavior—his speech, courtesy, and consideration. The teacher who resorts to vulgar speech, such as profanity, or to undignified actions, such as manhandling students, soon loses the respect of his students. In order to attract students to him, the teacher must first gain their respect.

In dealing with discipline problems, a teacher has to remember constantly that *all misbehavior stems from causes.* Because of the complexity of causes and the teacher's own limitations of time, skill, and resources, the reasons for many incidents of misbehavior will remain undiscovered. As previously stated, sometimes expediency rather than delayed action for investigation of cause-and-effect relationships must govern what the teacher does to correct misbehavior. Otherwise, the welfare of either the individual or the group may be jeopardized. However, even when a teacher is unable to remove the causes of undesirable behavior, he can at least develop more sympathy and understanding for boys and girls who have adjustment problems for which they are not entirely responsible. In developing a more realistic and objective attitude toward behavior problems, the teacher can avoid sentimentality on the one hand and the assumption of a dogmatic punitive position on the other.

By way of summary, then, the teacher who would exercise wise classroom control must recognize certain basic principles: (1) Discipline is a complex concept. (2) The ultimate aim of teacher control is to help students achieve self-discipline. (3) No one solution is applicable to all discipline problems. (4) Group welfare must be given primary consideration. (5) Like other teaching procedures, control techniques must be based on sound principles of learning. (6) Students need to understand the purposes and functions of discipline. (7) Whenever possible, the teacher should seek to discover underlying causes of misbehavior. (8) It is important for the teacher to analyze his own behavior constantly. (9) Without effective discipline, much of the valuable learning experience provided by the school will be unrealized. (10) A positive approach to classroom control is more effective than negative, repressive measures (7:85–89).

"Good discipline goes beyond the maintenance of school classroom order. Its prime goal is the development of socially approved self-control with due respect for democratically constituted authority." [32]

SELECTED READINGS

1.   Addicott, Irwin O., *Constructive Classroom Discipline*. San Francisco: Chandler Publishing Company, 1958.

2.   American Educational Research Association, *Encyclopedia of Educational Research,* 3d ed., Chester W. Harris, ed. New York: The Macmillan Company, 1960, pp. 137–143, 365–369, 381–383.

3.   American Educational Research Association, *Handbook of Research on Teaching,* N. L. Gage, ed. Chicago: Rand McNally & Company, 1963, pp. 422–434.

4.   Callahan, Sterling G., *Successful Teaching in Secondary Schools.* Chicago: Scott, Foresman and Company, 1966, chap. 13.

[32] Alvin Howard, "Discipline Problems and Policies as They Relate to the Classroom Teacher." Curriculum Bulletin no. 260, vol. 21, October 1965. Eugene: School of Education, University of Oregon, p. 1.

5. Glasser, William, *Reality Therapy, a New Approach to Psychiatry.* New York: Harper & Row, Publishers, 1965.

6. McCloskey, Elinor F., *Urban Disadvantaged Pupils: A Synthesis of 99 Research Reports.* Portland, Ore.: The Northwest Regional Educational Laboratory, February 1967.

7. Oliva, Peter F., "High School Discipline in American Society: A Primer on Democratic Discipline in Social Context," *Bulletin of the National Association of Secondary School Principals,* 40 (January 1956), 1–103.

8. Oliva, Peter F., *The Secondary School Today.* Cleveland: World Publishing Company, 1967, chap. 16.

9. The Prentice-Hall Staff, *Teacher's Encyclopedia.* Englewood Cliffs, N.J.: Prentice-Hall, Inc., 1966, chap. 3.

10. Redl, Fritz, *When We Deal with Children.* New York: The Free Press, 1966, pp. 254–308.

11. Schain, Robert L., and Murray Polner, *Using Effective Discipline for Better Class Control.* Englewood Cliffs, N.J.: Teachers Practical Press, 1964.

12. Tanruther, Edgar M., *Clinical Experiences in Teaching for the Student Teacher or Intern.* New York: Dodd, Mead & Company, Inc., 1967, chap. 8.

| *Constructive Classroom Management and Control*

Teachers, especially those who have just completed their preservice education, are often apprehensive of their ability to control their students. Consequently, they hope for a formula for solving all their discipline problems. It has already been pointed out that there are so many variables in specific situations involving behavior problems that it is difficult to determine in advance what action should be taken. For that reason, skeptics contend that no one can teach someone else how to solve the behavioral problems in his classes. Actually the truth lies somewhere between these two extremes. The previous chapter suggested basic principles the teacher might follow in laying the foundation for effective classroom management and control. In the discussion that follows, specific actions to be taken for the *prevention* of behavior problems are outlined in some detail. The chapter concludes with the guidance role of the teacher, specifically in relation to discipline.

EFFECTIVE ORGANIZATION TO IMPROVE STUDENT BEHAVIOR

Effective organization is the first prerequisite to good discipline. A well-organized classroom provides a businesslike environment, one in which the students can get their work done with a minimum of confusion, tension, and frustration. Good class organization eliminates waste and conserves class time for significant learning activities. By handling routine matters efficiently, enlisting student help with management, and providing for a comfortable, attractive physical environment, the teacher demonstrates his organizational ability.

How much organization is necessary? That depends upon several factors. Large classes of immature students require a high degree of organization, whereas smaller classes of more mature students may be conducted on a more informal, self-governing basis. Specialized class-rooms, such as shops or laboratories, must be sufficiently organized to protect students from accidents and the school from loss of equipment. Beginnings and endings of class periods, as well as transitions in activities during class sessions, frequently require special attention. Many class activities need to be organized on a fairly routine basis so that valuable class time will not be used each day in giving instructions on how to carry them out. More specific suggestions are given in the discussion that immediately follows.

PROVIDING FOR GOOD BEGINNINGS

The first day, sometimes the first week, marks a critical period in the history of a class. To avoid chaos, the teacher may have to become the equivalent of a ringmaster of a three-ring circus. He must keep his students occupied as he signs program cards, organizes a class roll and seating chart, and takes care of many other details. One teacher has solved this problem by recording his orientation lecture and playing it while he takes care of administrative details. Quite soon, the teacher will wish to provide a compass for the year's work by outlining requirements and future activities. He may also wish to give a pretest and administer an interest questionnaire as a basis for future assignments. Certainly, immediate assignments must be made with special attention given to student motivation.

Every teacher hopes to make a favorable first impression on his class. As said before, dress, grooming, and demeanor are especially important. Attention getters—such as bizarre clothing or hairstyling—are to be avoided. At the very first class meeting, the teacher should set an example of punctuality. In general, he needs to be friendly but businesslike, enthusiastic but reserved, confident but not overbearing, and in good humor but not frivolous. Many preservice teachers wish to know whether or not they should hold a "tight rein" on their students during the opening days of school and then relax the pattern of control later. Lacking any supporting research on this point, the authors, using the criterion of experience, consider it advisable to *begin* with a firm, businesslike approach.

MAKING PROVISIONS FOR PHYSICAL COMFORT

Proper regulation of temperature, light, and ventilation is necessary for good health and effective learning. This also has a direct bearing on discipline. Students who are uncomfortable become inattentive and unproductive. This in turn may lead to minor disorders or unruly behavior. Unsightly and uncomfortable classrooms of yesterday are being replaced today by modern facilities that are more functional, attractive, and comfortable. Despite contemporary improvement, however, the teacher must still make day-by-day adjustments as needed: adjust window blinds to prevent glare, turn on lights on cloudy days, and regulate temperature and ventilation when the room becomes stuffy or drafty. Not only must the teacher be constantly aware of the necessity for such adjustments; he should also develop student responsibility for regulating conditions that create discomfort or endanger health. Thus the teacher conserves his time for more important activities and at the same time provides a valuable learning experience for his students.

PROVIDING FOR A TIDY AND ATTRACTIVE ROOM

The classroom should not only be comfortable, but be as neat and attractive as possible. An orderly, comfortable, and attractive environment is conducive to good work habits and attitudes. The maintenance of clean floors and desks, including that of the teacher, and provision for orderly bookcases, storage cabinets, and displays are the *joint* responsibility of a teacher and his students. Even such a relatively unimportant function as the storage of supplies or equipment has more implications for discipline than may be readily apparent. Storage centers need to be decentralized to avoid traffic jams. In shops, tools should be checked systematically to avoid lost time in attempts to trace them or to assess fines against students to cover losses. Awkward situations or unpleasant incidents are thereby reduced or eliminated.

In a well-organized classroom, it is the teacher who, first of all, sets an example of good housekeeping. Then he is in a good position to insist that students do their part in keeping the classroom neat and orderly. Clean-up periods, in such classes as art, homemaking, and industrial arts, require special attention to organization. Because secondary school teachers so frequently have to share classrooms with others, they need to show special consideration by keeping chalkboards clean and by leaving the room clean and orderly. In the clean-up period for art or shop classes, there is no better opportunity for teaching students to be good housekeepers than to have them pick up after themselves and return school materials to their proper storage spaces.

No matter how modern a classroom may be in terms of design and color scheme, the teacher and his class can always make their own contribution to its beautification. Attractive bulletin boards, pictures on the wall, exhibits on window sills and interesting chalkboard designs are a few additional touches that make the classroom an enjoyable place in which to work.

When student assumption of responsibility for clean and attractive classrooms is extended to include the campus as a whole, no one could ask for better insurance against vandalism. As students take pride in the creation and maintenance of a clean, attractive, and orderly school environment, their improved behavior is reflected in every aspect of school life.

ENSURING ORDERLY STUDENT TRAFFIC

The movement of students is always a potential source of minor disturbances, some of which may lead to major discipline problems. The teacher is advised to note students' movements at such times as the following: passing to and from the classroom; going to and from chalkboards, pencil sharpeners, and so on; securing and returning books and other supplies; and passing through the halls. By all means, students should have *planned* freedom of movement. Well-regulated traffic, with an emphasis on common courtesy, is conducive to improved behavior and more satisfaction for everyone.

ASSIGNING SEATS OR STATIONS TO STUDENTS

Some organized procedure for the assignment of students to definite seats or stations is necessary to expedite attendance check, to facilitate the learning of students' names, to take care of special needs (for example, students with defective vision or hearing), and to ensure a more orderly working atmosphere for the class as a whole. Students may be allowed to choose their own seating positions initially; however, the teacher should not hesitate to make reassignments when the needs of an individual or those of the class are better served. A number of procedures may be used for checking attendance: use of a seating chart, reports by squad leaders, or response of students by numbers. A physical education teacher made the common mistake of calling the names of students as they moved around an extended area. Such procedure obviously encouraged straggling to class, horseplay, and the temptation for students to respond to one another's names. Whatever system is used, roll check should be accurate and speedy in order to discourage absenteeism or tardiness and to conserve time for learning activities.

EXPEDITING THE DISTRIBUTION AND
COLLECTION OF MATERIALS

A systematic method of handling instructional materials or student papers has a number of values. First of all, it conserves class time. Some teachers use the wasteful procedure of returning student papers one at a time in random fashion rather than in sequence by rows. A second value is an elimination of confusion. When permanent school property, such as textbooks or tools, is involved, proper handling and storage of such materials constitute good insurance against damage or loss. In order to provide more opportunities for student movement, the teacher should use student monitors, especially in junior high school, for the distribution and collection of materials. Being a monitor should be considered a privilege, which may be denied when a student persists in discharging his duties in a careless, noisy, or disorderly manner.

KEEPING RECORDS AND MAKING REPORTS

The teacher is responsible for making accurate attendance reports, keeping complete records of student progress in scholarship and citizenship, and providing other data needed for school records. Carelessness or tardiness with respect to such records and reports is a constant source of irritation to the school principal and, in some cases, an open invitation to delinquent student behavior (for example, inaccurate or time-consuming roll checks, sketchy citizenship records, failure to warn parents of a decline in student scholarship or citizenship). A teacher must have sufficient evidence for giving marks or grades. In reporting scholarship, he should avoid either extreme of having his record book cluttered with daily grades or marks or having it almost devoid of any grades. In reporting citizenship, the teacher is advised to keep anecdotal records of significant student behavior rather than base his report on vague remembrances or impressions derived from a recent, perhaps atypical, example of student behavior. The following illustration demonstrates the point.

Mr. C. kept a complete record of each student's citizenship in his class. One boy, whose mother was PTA president, received a D grade in citizenship. When the mother came to the school very much disturbed, the teacher reviewed anecdotal records for her. On one date, when Mr. C. had told the boy he might have to call his mother, the boy had said, "If you do, she will hit you over the head with a mop." That was all the mother needed to know. She indicated she would have a heart-to-heart talk with her son.

Adequate records ensure justice for students, more likelihood of better student habits and attitudes, and improved public relations.

KEEPING EVERYONE BUSY

Idleness breeds disorder. The best antidote is keeping everyone busy at worthwhile tasks. When the teacher is lecturing or demonstrating or when one or more students are making a presentation to the class, attention of the group is required. During a study or work period, the teacher may have to exert gentle, insistent pressure on would-be disturbers of the peace. He can do this by circulating around the room, passing by or standing momentarily near those who are talking or idling, sometimes asking to see completed work, or catching the eye of those exhibiting poor work habits and frowning his disapproval. It is quite important that the students soon learn they are expected to begin work immediately when the class period begins and to continue working until dismissal time.

Sometimes there is a time lag while the teacher is taking care of administrative duties. This can be corrected in a number of ways. Student monitors may take care of routine jobs while the teacher gets the class under way. Some classes have their own officers who call the group to order and get activities for the day started, even when the teacher is out of the room. A typing teacher had his class so well organized that he seldom spoke to the class for the first five or ten minutes. The students came quietly into the room, seated themselves in an orderly manner, and began working on the warm-up assignment listed on the board. Proper organization forestalls idleness and disorder.

MAKING PROVISIONS FOR EMERGENCIES

There are times when regularly planned activities are unexpectedly interrupted or have to be deferred. If a physical education class that is dependent upon outside facilities is driven inside by rain, the teacher must be able to substitute other activities on the spur of the moment by showing an appropriate film, giving a chalk-talk on rules and strategy of play, or joining another class in coeducational dancing. When an English teacher unexpectedly finds half of his class absent, he may read and have the class discuss a poem or short story held in reserve for such an occasion. The mathematics teacher may have the class work on some interesting puzzle problems or spend the day quite profitably on remedial or make-up work. In a social studies class, for example, it is advisable to have alternate activities planned in case individual or group reports are not ready on the day assigned. The teacher should not be unduly upset by a fire drill, even in the middle of a test. By anticipating emergencies and making some preparation beforehand, the teacher can soon put his class to work with a minimum of confusion and disorder as if he had planned it that way.

INSISTING ON COMMON COURTESY

It may seem strange to include courtesy under the subject of classroom management. Manners are minor virtues learned through practice. Proper organization provides the necessary setting for the exercise of good manners. Once students develop a habitual pattern of mannerly behavior, details of management become less important. In order to achieve the ideal of courtesy and consideration in the classroom, the teacher will need to help his students improve their behavior in specific situations. When students are inadvertently discourteous in speech or actions, they can be taught the value of "I beg your pardon" or "I am sorry." Unfortunately, some teachers tolerate boorish behavior without making any attempt to correct it. Unless the teacher constantly encourages thoughtful, considerate relationships in the classroom, he is failing in his obligation to teach good citizenship.

At this point, it should be remembered that courtesy is largely taught by example. The teacher may insist on the observance of rules of courtesy, but students are more likely to follow his example than his preachments. Sarcastic remarks, lack of consideration for the personal feelings of students, and failure to give recognition for contributions to the class provoke student wisecracks and lower class morale. On the other hand, some teachers make it a point to thank students who make a special contribution to the class—such as a report, a demonstration, or the operation of a motion-picture projector. *The behavior a teacher exhibits is the kind of behavior he may expect his students to exhibit.*

ACHIEVING EFFECTIVE LEADERSHIP

All these procedures suggest many details of classroom management that are important in the maintenance of a positive learning environment. However, the teacher should not only be skillful in handling details of organization but be an organized person himself. This means that he possesses the qualities of poise, assurance, and self-control that inspire confidence in his leadership. Thus the teacher needs first to become a master of himself before he can achieve the status of a master teacher, "a teacher recognized as possessing exceptional ability in the art of teaching." [1] Such mastery, of course, is not attained in a day; neither is it achieved without continuous effort on the part of the teacher to improve his own personality and character.

As a review of the items of classroom management, the reader may wish to take a self-test on the "Classroom Organization Checklist" in order to ascertain how well he fulfills the managerial roles of the teacher.

Classroom Organization Checklist

	NEEDS IMPROVEMENT	SATISFACTORY
1. Maintenance of desirable physical conditions		
a. Controlling light (natural and artificial)	_____	
b. Regulating temperature	_____	
c. Regulating ventilation	_____	
d. Maintaining comfortable working conditions in general	_____	
2. Improvement of appearance of room		
a. Keeping desks and floors neat and clean	_____	
b. Keeping chalkboard clean	_____	
c. Keeping bulletin boards attractive and up-to-date	_____	
d. Using attractive, appropriate room decorations	_____	
3. Provision for orderly movements of students		
a. Ensuring orderly movement to and from classroom	_____	
b. Regulating traffic within the classroom	_____	
c. Supervising traffic in the halls	_____	

[1] Carter V. Good, ed., *Dictionary of Education.* New York: McGraw-Hill Book Company, Inc., 1959, p. 332.

	NEEDS IMPROVEMENT	SATISFACTORY
4. Arrangement for seating students		
a. Assigning students to definite seats or stations	_____	
b. Rearranging assignments as needed	_____	
c. Making provisions for special needs	_____	
5. Provision for effective use of materials and equipment		
a. Preparing materials in advance	_____	
b. Distributing and collecting materials systematically	_____	
c. Conserving materials by proper handling, accounting, and storing	_____	
d. Using expendable materials economically	_____	
6. Preparation of records and reports		
a. Making accurate attendance reports promptly	_____	
b. Keeping a complete record of student scholarship and citizenship	_____	
c. Collecting and reporting other data promptly	_____	
7. Provision for courtesy in the classroom		
a. Insisting on mutual respect and consideration	_____	
b. Showing special consideration for new students	_____	
c. Making visitors feel welcome	_____	
8. Organization of other procedures		
a. Learning students' names quickly	_____	
b. Beginning class promptly and ending it on time	_____	
c. Keeping everyone busy	_____	
d. Making assignments definite	_____	
e. Making individual adjustments as needed	_____	
f. Keeping a continuous check on student progress	_____	
9. Achievement of instructional leadership		
a. Developing poise, assurance, and self-control	_____	
b. Planning ahead for effective leadership	_____	

SOURCE: From *Student Teaching in Secondary Schools* by Howard T. Batchelder, Maurice McGlasson, and Raleigh Schorling. Copyright © 1964 by McGraw-Hill, Inc. Used with permission of McGraw-Hill Book Company, Inc. (1: 103–104).

EFFECTIVE ACTION FOR CONSTRUCTIVE DISCIPLINE

The fundamental reason why children do not act right is because they do not have the conditions for right action.—*Francis W. Parker* [2]

Nowhere else is the adage "An ounce of prevention is worth a pound of cure" more relevant than in discipline. Under ideal conditions the teacher is able to establish and maintain a classroom atmosphere in which discipline problems are virtually nonexistent. In reality, such a happy state of affairs is rarely achievable. Nevertheless, the teacher who consistently uses constructive control measures is likely to have few, if any, major behavior problems or crises. Just what are some of the guidelines to be observed in this constructive approach to classroom management and control? The following paragraphs include a number of pertinent suggestions.

Adequate planning (discussed in Chapter 4) and good classroom organization have already been stressed as prerequisites for effective learning and improved student behavior.

A teacher may take a number of measures to establish and maintain a wholesome learning environment in the classroom. He may observe such rules of action as the following:

1. *Keep constantly aware of classroom climate.* In establishing and maintaining a constructive classroom atmosphere, the teacher must always be sensitive to the personality of the group. He needs to be alert to early danger signals that may indicate a disturbance in group climate or individual behavior. The teacher who knows what each student is doing, or not doing, can quickly take care of individual problems before the class as a whole is affected.

An alert teacher never becomes so absorbed in helping individual students that he is oblivious to the problems or needs of the rest of the class. It is true that a teacher should approach any class with a positive attitude, believing in his students and accepting them as good citizens until they prove otherwise. But he must not be so naïve as to think that all students have achieved sufficient maturity for complete self-direction. As a general rule, however, students do try to live up to the expectations of a respected teacher.

The teacher should see his class as individual personalities. Direct eye contact with individual students, an encouraging smile, or a nod of approval by the teacher all contribute to a wholesome classroom climate.

2. *Encourage student participation in classroom control.* Not only should students assist the teacher with routine class management; they

[2] Francis W. Parker, *Talks on Pedagogics.* New York: E. L. Kellogg and Company, 1894, p. 372.

should be encouraged to cooperate in setting up necessary rules for class government. The teacher is advised, however, to recognize certain limitations that may exist. For instance, if a class has had little or no experience with such cooperative procedures, the teacher will probably need to proceed with caution. In some cases, a class may be so immature or lacking in group spirit that the teacher will have to assume almost complete responsibility for control.

The teacher should always bear in mind that standards of behavior he considers acceptable must also be acceptable to the class as a whole. The students must consider restrictions as just and reasonable. It can usually be assumed that most students wish to do what is right. If this were not so, school rules and regulations would be unenforceable.

3. *Reevaluate teaching procedures constantly.* Good discipline is a by-product of good teaching. The teacher who uses a variety of learning activities and materials effectively will probably have few discipline problems. With proper attention to motivation and adequate provision for individual differences, the teacher establishes the "conditions for right action." Bright students are challenged and slow learners taste success. When class activities are well planned, interesting, and varied, students are encouraged to be on their best behavior.

4. *Make allowances for unusual conditions.* When students are over-stimulated by a change in weather, the tide of excitement before a big game, or some other unusual factor, the teacher can well afford to be more tolerant, more liberal in his expectations of the class. He may find it wise to defer or change his assignment for the day.

5. *Communicate with students at their level.* The teacher needs to avoid either extreme: talking down to students by treating them like children or addressing them formally as adults by calling them "Mr. _____" or "Miss _____" instead of "Jim" or "Mary." If a teacher transfers from junior high school to senior high school or vice versa, he will find it necessary to make adjustments in vocabulary, teaching procedures, and expectations with respect to behavior. It might also be well to point out that some boys and girls from a particular neighborhood may be more sophisticated than those from some other community, even though they are the same age. Sometimes a new teacher who has spent four or five years as a college student may have difficulty in adjusting to his role as a teacher of adolescents. Young teachers, particularly coaches and club sponsors, mistakenly believe that by permitting students to address them on a first-name basis, closeness and the desired rapport will be guaranteed. This is unsound reasoning.

6. *Stress "do" rather than "don't."* The wise teacher uses a positive approach to the improvement of behavior. "Do" is more effective than "don't," especially with adolescents who are going through a stage of rebellion in an effort to become independent when they resist adult

restrictions imposed by teacher or parent. A further refinement of this point is the fact that *requests* are usually more effective than *commands.* Requests are less likely to arouse resentment or to place either student or teacher in a position of having to save face.

7. *Encourage more student activity.* In a positive approach to classroom management and control, the teacher strives constantly to secure more involvement, more participation, and the assumption of more responsibility on the part of every student. The net results are better motivation, more effective learning, and improved behavior.

8. *Show an interest in students' concerns.* The teacher who demonstrates an interest in the affairs of students—in their cocurricular activities, for example—often finds that student behavior improves in direct proportion to that interest. Unfortunately, some teachers regard an assignment to sponsor a cocurricular activity only as an onerous task, little realizing the potential reward in terms of better teacher-student relations.

9. *Use the voice effectively.* A low, well-modulated voice has a calming effect on an unstable, restless group. If the noise level of a class begins to rise to a point where it interferes with learning, the teacher should first gain the complete attention of his students and then address them in a quiet, positive manner.

10. *Set a good example and take appropriate action when necessary.* Nothing can supersede the personal example of the teacher. But he must be more than an exemplary person; he must also be a doer. Professional judgment has to be translated into action. As he deals with problems, the teacher has to be sympathetic without being sentimental, to be friendly and approachable without being intimate, and to satisfy student needs without being indulgent.

11. *Cultivate mutual respect and consideration.* The structure of constructive discipline rests on a foundation of mutual respect and consideration. This foundation is built on many little acts of kindness, tact, and thoughtfulness. The following vignettes from the classroom illustrate the point: The teacher encouraged student questions and salvaged everything he could from the answers of students to his questions. Even if an answer was entirely wrong, he made the correction with the utmost tact. . . . As a new student entered the class, he was assigned a student to help him with his orientation to the school. . . . When an observer entered the classroom, the class president gave him a textbook and plan for the day and explained what the class was doing. . . . The teacher attempted to learn the names of his students as quickly as possible. He would check his class roster and make a special effort to learn more about the students whose names and faces he could not associate. . . . A visitor sat in the rear of the classroom. Student traffic was heavy in front of him, yet every student would ask to be excused. . . . A teacher unjustly reprimanded a student in the presence of the class, discovered his mistake, and apolo-

gized to the class the next day. . . . A student questioned the teacher's solution to a problem. The teacher noted his error and thanked the student sincerely for the correction. These illustrations indicate the kinds of actions, both of teacher and students, that contribute to a wholesome classroom environment, an environment marked by mutual trust and consideration.

By way of summary, a psychologist has outlined the conditions for what he calls "a therapeutic environment." Briefly, they are as follows:

The first, and probably the most important, essential in a therapeutic environment is a positive attitude on the part of the teacher toward children. . . .

Another necessary condition for having a therapeutic classroom environment is that the teacher feel secure in his role as a teacher. It would perhaps be more correct to say in his "roles" as teacher, because the teacher's roles are many. . . .

A third aspect of a therapeutic environment in the school is that the work is made stimulating and interesting. . . .

In a therapeutic classroom environment, each child attains success in some important (to him) area of his schoolwork. . . .

A fifth factor contributing to a therapeutic environment in the classroom is establishing limits. One function of the teacher is to set the boundaries for behavior in the classroom. . . .

A sixth characteristic of a therapeutic environment is that there is a group feeling among the individual members of the class. . . .

Finally, no environment can promote social and emotional growth if the physical surroundings are not conducive to such growth. . . .[3]

BEHAVIOR TO FIT THE OCCASION

Teacher expectations have a direct bearing on constructive discipline. Whether the kind of behavior a teacher expects of his students is reasonable and realistic depends upon the situation: the class setting, the nature of the activities, and the purposes to be served. In the discussion that immediately follows, suggestions are made concerning appropriate behavior for specific class situations.

DISCUSSION

Courtesy is the key word. In the give-and-take of free discussion, the rights of everyone are to be respected. Each one has a right to express his point of view; each one is entitled to a respectful hearing. To reiterate, the teacher demonstrates the kind of behavior he expects of his students. By permitting students to make their contributions without interrupting or repeating their remarks, by giving considerate recognition to

[3] O. G. Johnson, "A Climate to Grow In," *NEA Journal*, 46 (April 1957), 233–236. Permission to quote has been granted by the *Journal* and the author.

student responses, commending correct responses and correcting errors tactfully, and by being tolerant of opinions that differ from his own, the teacher establishes a proper classroom atmosphere for effective discussion.

SUPERVISED STUDY

Study is often an individual matter. Consequently, under such circumstances, there should be little or no need for talking or visiting among students. If or when it is desirable for two or more students to work together, they should *work* quietly without disturbing other members of the class. The teacher who permits widespread visiting with only the caution to be quiet is neglecting his responsibility for proper supervision of study. Likewise, the teacher who sits at his desk grading papers is neglectful, for he is neither providing the help that students are likely to need nor checking on potential behavior problem cases. By circulating around the room, the teacher provides the guidance for study to which his class is entitled. An administrator once remarked that he usually found the teacher who did not circulate to be lazy and ineffective.

LABORATORY PERIODS

When a class is working on experiments in science, projects in industrial arts, or problems in art, a much more informal atmosphere is more appropriate than in some other types of class activities. As much freedom and informality as are consistent with safety and effective learning should be encouraged. But when one or more students interfere with the work of others, waste time in aimless wandering or fruitless chatter, endanger the safety of fellow students, or create an atmosphere of general disorder, the teacher must restrict their freedom. Even the noise level of the class is a factor to be considered. Although he should encourage freedom of movement and communication, the teacher need not tolerate either horseplay or loud, ribald speech. The sounds in a working atmosphere are quite different from those in a noisy, disorganized laboratory situation.

GROUP WORK

Regardless of the size of the group—a three-member committee, a five-man team, or the entire class—certain conditions need to be maintained. First of all, these should be a cooperative relationship with every member participating. When subgroups are formed, they are ultimately responsible for making a contribution to the class as a whole. The teacher is always accountable for effective operation of all groups in helping them to organize, to develop a work plan, to conduct their research, and to make a worthwhile contribution to the class as a whole. To function effectively large, informal groups (such as bands, teams, or choruses) require strong teacher leadership, effective organization, and acceptance of common goals.

FIELD TRIPS OR EXCURSIONS

Because trips or tours take students away from the school campus, thorough advance preparation and organization are necessary. Planning should be on a cooperative basis, with the teacher and his class working together, so that everyone clearly understands the purposes and problems of the particular excursion. The primary purpose of the trip, of course, is to provide a learning experience that is not available in the normal classroom setting. Problems involve protection against accidents, the maintenance of good public relations, and the prevention of discipline problems in a more or less informal, uncontrolled environment. Of course, proper administrative clearance, parental permissions (although such permissions do not excuse the teacher for negligence nor do they guarantee freedom from liability), and arrangements that will reduce the disruption of other classes to a minimum must be taken care of before the trip.

STUDENT ACTIVITIES

Because of the informality, freedom, and opportunities for self-direction provided by extraclass activities, teachers who are sponsors of such activities have to exercise reasonable judgment in knowing when and how to temper student initiative with faculty direction to ensure proper observance of school regulations and the maintenance of good public relations. Without unnecessarily restricting opportunities for student leadership and self-government, the teacher-sponsor needs to impress upon his charges the importance of good sportsmanship, good citizenship, and responsible leadership.

OTHER GROUP SITUATIONS

Other situations, such as those involving groups in study halls or assemblies in the school auditorium, pose special problems in seating and supervision. Mutual responsibility for management is often shared by students, teachers, and administrators. Level of teacher control required is determined by such factors as the size of the group, the maturity of the students, and the nature of the activity. Again the criterion for effectiveness of control is based on the extent to which the purposes of the groups are achieved.

DISCIPLINE AND EDUCATIONAL INNOVATIONS

The discussion thus far has dealt with typical classroom situations (one teacher with a permanently assigned group of students).

New developments—such as team teaching and flexible scheduling— will no doubt call for new strategies in classroom management and control. Considerably more responsibility will be placed on each student for his own learning (and self-direction). The time budget in a team teaching situation may have a student devote as much as 40 percent of his time to independent learning activities. Flexible scheduling, with its frequent changes and unfamiliar patterns, holds the student accountable for meeting his own commitments (as to time, place, activity). It is obvious that all these changes place more responsibility on students for their own *self-control*—a major goal of education in a free society. However, these changes represent such a wide departure from the status quo that both teachers and students will have to make some major adjustments during the transition period.

DEVELOPMENT OF GROUP MORALE

As an instructional leader, the teacher has a twofold responsibility: to help each individual student achieve maturity and to weld aggregations of individuals into cohesive groups for effective learning.

Any classroom observer can usually detect fairly soon the climate or atmosphere of a particular class. He may sense an atmosphere of cooperation or rebellion, enthusiasm or boredom, security or tension. Such a climate is merely a reflection of the morale of the group. Thus an aggregation of thirty-five students, for example, may become a tight little group that either accepts or rejects the educational purposes of the teacher and the school. What are some of the factors or forces that promote development of a group climate conducive to desirable behavior? There are several.

BASES OF GROUP MORALE

First of all, *a group is united by common purposes.* Just any purposes, however, will not suffice. A group may be either good or bad, depending upon the worthiness of the purposes that unite its members. Obviously, a group devoted to resistance to study and learning, united on the basis of hostility toward the teacher, or prone to engage in horseplay at the slightest provocation serves no constructive educational purpose. On the other hand, whenever the teacher is able to build a strong effective group, devoted to worthwhile purposes, class morale and productivity, as well as individual learning and satisfaction, reach a high level.[4] Whenever a cohesive group discovers that specific actions are out of harmony with its objectives, the members are willing to impose certain restrictions on themselves, to limit their own freedom if necessary, in order to preserve the integrity of the group. No group can long exist without some form of control or discipline. But such control must either be self-imposed or be accepted by the group when imposed by some external authority, such

---

[4] Leland P. Bradford, "The Pupil and the Group," *NEA Journal,* 46 (February 1957), 103–105.

as the teacher. If neither of these conditions prevails, desirable surface behavior may be achieved, but the class most likely will continue to operate as an aggregate of individuals, not as a group with common goals.

A second factor in the achievement of wholesome group morale is that opportunities must be provided for the members *to work together, to engage in cooperative action.* As suggested above, such work must be directed toward the achievement of worthy goals. Furthermore, an effective group sets for itself high standards of excellence. The precision of a drill team, the smart appearance of a band, the harmony of a chorus, the teamwork of an athletic group, the unity of effort involved in the presentation of an exhibit or an assembly program, the mutual feeling of achievement in the development of a science project—all are indicative of a high degree of group morale. The teacher may well encourage group pride—the spirit of "all for one and one for all"—and devotion to excellence in achievement. Unfortunately, in the average classroom, major emphasis is placed on the individual, competitive activities that lead to a spirit of divisiveness rather than unity.

In order to improve the quality of group living, as well as the values held by individuals, a teacher needs to do less lecturing and more guiding toward desirable behavior. As a director of learning, the teacher provides the key to group spirit. He may encourage group enterprises or stress only individual performance. He may stress cooperation or competition. Ashley Montagu, the anthropologist, has pointed out that, contrary to popular opinion, cooperation, not competition, is the first law of survival.[5] What the student learns in the classroom or on the playing field can have lifelong consequences. Learning to work harmoniously with others may mean the difference between success and failure for the student in his future relationships with his boss, his family, and his neighbors.

Closely associated with the necessity of cooperative action for the development of group morale is the need for *personal loyalty.* In the final analysis, group unity is based on loyalty to persons rather than on acceptance of some abstract principle. Studies of morale in units of American armed forces in World War II revealed that loyalty to one's friends and pride in one's outfit—not such abstract principles as "freedom" or "democracy," even though the importance of these concepts must be recognized—were the chief integrating factors.[6]

PROBLEMS IN THE DEVELOPMENT OF GROUP MORALE

In attempting to build group morale, the teacher is admittedly faced with a number of difficulties. For one thing, each student is already a member of other groups—family, friends, team—before he comes to school. These

---

[5] Ashley Montagu, *On Being Human.* New York: Abelard-Schuman Ltd., 1950.
[6] Stuart Chase, *Roads to Agreement.* New York: Harper & Row, Publishers, 1951, pp. 63–65.

groups compete with the school class for the student's time and, in some cases, sanction values in conflict with those of the school. Another problem the teacher has in developing group morale is related to school organization itself. A school day that is segmented into inflexible, fifty-minute periods provides only limited time for a class to become a cohesive group. Finally, many learning activities, especially those related to evaluation, stress individual performance with each student in sharp competition with his fellows.

GROUP LIFE VERSUS INDIVIDUAL DEVELOPMENT

In the light of certain social forces that place a premium on conformity and stifle individual thought and action, some persons feel quite strongly that group life has been emphasized at the expense of individual development. It should be pointed out that group life is not an end in itself; it is designed to improve the quality of living for the individual; *"Most human needs are satisfied through interaction with other people."* [7] When a student feels at home with his group, he is able to disagree with his peers without fear of ridicule or ostracism. When a student feels accepted by his group, he has a personal concern for the welfare of his fellows. In a class united on the basis of commonly accepted, worthwhile goals, the classroom becomes "a laboratory for learning the fundamentals of democratic behavior, for developing individual maturity, for gaining skills of leadership and membership, and for developing skills of independency and interdependency." [8]

There are psychological factors that may seriously disturb group climate. Redl identifies at least six of them (7:286–298):

1. "Dissatisfaction in the Work Process." For example, the subject matter may be too easy or too difficult; or the assignment may be too heavy, too light, or poorly planned.

2. "Emotional Unrest in Interpersonal Relations." Such unrest may involve tensions related to individual friendships, cliques, or friction between teacher and student.

3. "Disturbances in Group Climate." Redl identifies such unwholesome climates as the following: "punitive," "emotional-blackmail," "hostile-competition," and "group-pride climate."

4. "Mistakes in Organization or Group Leadership." For instance, there are certain extremes to be avoided: either autocratic adult control or mistaken self-government; standards of group behavior that are either too high or too low; or too much or too little organization.

5. "Emotional Strain and Sudden Change." Included are such factors as periods of "anxiety" (triggered by examination periods or contemporary problems, for example), "boredom," or "reaction to change" (such as a change in program

[7] Chase, p. 78.
[8] Bradford, p. 104.

or leadership). Redl makes two important observations at this point: "Boredom will always remain the greatest enemy of school discipline." . . . "Any change, even for the better, tends to upset group organization temporarily. . . ."

6. "The Composition of the Group."

THE ROLE OF GUIDANCE IN CONSTRUCTIVE DISCIPLINE

For some people, the word "guidance" may suggest a specialized function performed only by certain certified personnel. For others, the term is loosely defined in the cliché "all education is guidance." Either conception is misleading. Although the primary function of the classroom teacher is teaching, he also performs many guidance functions, one of the most important of which is counseling students.

COUNSELING FOR CONSTRUCTIVE DISCIPLINE

As school guidance services are now organized, counseling is done by full-time counselors who are specifically certified, by teacher-counselors, and by classroom teachers. Counseling is designed to assist students in making decisions concerning further schooling, future careers, employment, and personal and social problems. Teachers operate in all these areas. Obviously, the teachers who help students resolve their personal or social problems make a direct contribution to constructive discipline. Indirectly, teachers who place students in courses that fit their needs and abilities, enable students to make wise choices of further education, or help them find a suitable vocational future make a definite contribution to improved classroom morale. Satisfied, successful students are seldom discipline problems.

A personnel officer once remarked, "I am looking for teachers with a guidance point of view." In order to be a successful counselor, the teacher must have a "guidance point of view." He must be more concerned about finding and removing causes of misbehavior than with treating superficial symptoms of discipline problems. He must be more interested in improving the behavior of students than in merely punishing them.

The need for each teacher of a school to become an effective counselor is critical in a system of mass education. Every student needs a confidant, an adult friend to whom he may go with his problems. Obviously, full-time counselors cannot meet that need for everyone. They are too few. Then, too, adolescents do not confide in just anyone. Consequently, all school personnel—athletic coach, librarian, classroom teacher, nurse,—need to make themselves available as counselors and adult friends to at least a few students. If all school personnel fulfill their obligations as counselors, the dividends in terms of improved student behavior will more than repay them for the extra time and effort involved.

RECIPROCAL RELATIONSHIPS BETWEEN TEACHER AND COUNSELOR

Both teacher and counselor need to recognize their dependence upon each other. How does the classroom teacher assist the full-time counselor? First of all, he serves as the eyes and ears of the counselor's office. Counselors see most students only on specific occasions if at all, whereas teachers are in daily contact with them. Thus a classroom teacher occupies a strategic position in the detection of failure, maladjustment, or illness. By all means, he needs to detect quite early critical problems he cannot solve and refer them to the appropriate counselor. Another important guidance function performed by the teacher is helping students who have received counsel for misbehavior adjust to group living within the classroom. Students may *discuss* their problems within the privacy of the counselor's office, but they must *solve* most of them within the social framework of the classroom. Probably the greatest contribution a teacher makes to the guidance services of a school is doing a good job of teaching. Poor teaching fills the counselor's office with candidates for failure and punishment. On the other hand, the teacher who maintains a class in which his students are happy and successful definitely eases the load of the counselor.

How do counselors aid teachers? Not only do they provide teachers expert help with problem cases; they also serve as the one best source of information about students. The authors stress repeatedly the necessity for teachers to know their students. Data may be secured in many ways and from many sources (as discussed at length in Chapter 2), but there is no substitute for discussion of a problem student with an understanding counselor and a study of the records in the counselor's files.

COUNSELING WITH PARENTS

Most problems of boys and girls could be solved with dispatch if parents and teacher worked more closely together than they sometimes do. Unfortunately, parents are sometimes not consulted until a problem is far advanced. They want to know how their children are getting along in school and hope the school will keep them informed, but they may hesitate to ask (8:17–18).

Secondary school teachers, who teach 180 or more students in a five- or six-period day, may well be envious of the elementary school teacher in the self-contained classroom. The common practice of having each elementary school teacher confer periodically with every parent is obviously not feasible in the highly departmentalized secondary school. A number of ways have been tried in the secondary school to bring parent and teacher closer together—parent-teacher association meetings, open houses, invitations to special exhibits, teas honoring mothers, and an occasional home visit. None of these measures, however, has reached all parents, or perhaps even a majority of them. Then, too, group situations, as indicated above, provide no opportunity for private, personal conferences between parent and teacher.

In informing parents of the progress of their children, in citizenship as well as scholarship, secondary school teachers have limited their communication largely to report cards. Whenever scholarship or citizenship is unsatisfactory, the report card may be supplemented by a warning notice. Such a cold, impersonal approach to the reporting of unsatisfactory progress certainly contributes little to a better understanding between parent and teacher or provides little real help to the student.

Although teacher conferences with all parents are apparently not feasible at the secondary school level, there are occasions when a teacher needs to arrange for special conferences with the parents of some of his students. Whenever there is evidence that the misbehavior of a student may reach major proportions, the teacher should enlist the cooperation of the parents as soon as possible. Otherwise, a problem that might have been quickly resolved could reach a crisis resulting in the suspension or dismissal of the student. In conferring with parents, the teacher is advised to keep a few important guidelines in mind, such as the following:

1. If a parent is disturbed, the teacher needs to be *a good listener*. It is good therapy for an upset individual to relieve his tensions by verbalizing his grievances. Then, too, a rational discussion of any problem cannot take place until both parties are in a state of emotional equilibrium. When a teacher is tempted to defend his own position or argue a point, he should remember that it is better to win a parent than an argument. If the teacher has made a mistake, his best defense is an honest admission of error.

2. In every parent-teacher conference where the problems of a son or daughter are the subject of discussion, the *welfare of the student* should receive primary consideration. Good points, rather than shortcomings, need to be emphasized. At the same time, however, the teacher must be honest with parents. When a student is in error, it is the responsibility of mature adults, both teacher and parents, to help him correct his mistakes and make amends for them if necessary. It is quite natural for parents to defend their children, even to be overly protective at times. Tagore expressed this admirable parental failing in these words: "I do not love him because he is good, but because he is my child." Nevertheless, as tactfully as possible, the teacher sometimes has to help parents become more realistic in assessing both the strengths and weaknesses of their children.

3. The skillful teacher encourages parents *to ask questions and to make suggestions* in the course of the interview. He should avoid repeating

"*I* think" but should *ask* the parent, "What can we do?" Parents like to feel their assistance is needed and wanted.

4. The teacher should *speak in simple terms*. There is a professional terminology teachers should understand and use among themselves, but they must avoid the use of technical terms that might confuse parents or lead to further misunderstanding. The story is told of a lecturer who spoke to a group of parents and teachers about "the whole child." At the conclusion of the talk, one parent timidly asked, "What other kind of child is there?"

5. The teacher must play *a strong, positive role* in solving the problem. Once he has established a cooperative relationship with the parents of a child with a problem, he is obligated to share the objective evidence the school has bearing on the problem. When the conference is over, the teacher should summarize and record it, and follow it up with positive action when necessary.

6. Unscheduled conferences demanded by irate, upset parents should be routed through the principal's office. A good administrator will allow the parents an opportunity to "blow off steam" before calling the teacher to attend the conference session.

7. By conducting conferences with dignity, tact, and consideration, the teacher facilitates better student behavior and improved relations with parents.

SELECTED READINGS

1. Batchelder, Howard T., Maurice McGlasson, and Raleigh Schorling, *Student Teaching in Secondary Schools*. New York: McGraw-Hill Book Company, Inc., 1964, chaps. 5, 6.

2. Blount, Nathan S., and Herbert J. Klausmeier, *Teaching in the Secondary School*, 3d ed. New York: Harper & Row, Publishers, 1968, chap. 15.

3. Burton, William H., *The Guidance of Learning Activities*, 3d ed. New York: Appleton-Century-Crofts, Inc., Division of Meredith Corporation, 1962, chap. 23.

4. Clark, Leonard H., and Irving S. Starr, *Secondary School Teaching Methods*, 2d ed. New York: The Macmillan Company, 1967, chap. 17.

5. Emery, Richard E., "Keys to Effective Classroom Discipline," in *Teacher's Encyclopedia*. Englewood Cliffs, N.J.: Prentice-Hall, Inc., 1966, pp. 101–122.

6. Heinrich, June Sark, *Unit III: Discipline in the Classroom*. Teacher Education Extension Service (Grades K–12). Chicago: Science Research Associates, Inc., 1965.

7. Redl, Fritz, *When We Deal with Children*. New York: The Free Press, 1966, pp. 254–308.

8. Stout, Irving W., and Grace Langdon, "Parent-Teacher Relationships," *What Research Says to the Teacher*, no. 16. Washington, D.C.: National Education Association, September, 1958.

9. Walton, John, *Toward Better Teaching in the Secondary Schools*. Boston: Allyn and Bacon, Inc., 1966.

CHAPTER 14 | *Remedial Classroom Control*

The preceding chapter emphasized a constructive approach to classroom control and management. Under ideal conditions, problems of misbehavior are virtually nonexistent, or, if aberrant behavior does occur, it never assumes major proportions. However, sooner or later some students will commit offenses for which they must be corrected. Because of the imperfections in human nature, as well as the environmental problems influencing human development, personal maladjustments and conflicts with social regulations are inevitable.

Before specific suggestions are made for dealing with student misbehavior, consideration will be given to any discernible trends in the nature and extent of discipline problems in the school today.

DISCIPLINE PROBLEMS TODAY

Widespread publicity about the delinquent behavior of youth, both in fact and in fiction, might soon convince one that this is a spoiled, violent, and rebellious generation. That classroom management and control are a major concern of teachers and not to be taken lightly has already been suggested. Since this chapter deals with the correction or punishment of misbehavior, a survey of the sources, nature, and extent of behavior problems is in order at this point.

In a study made by the San Diego (California) City Schools over a decade ago, teachers agreed that "poor behavior was limited to less than one out of every twenty pupils" and that fewer than "three of every 100 junior high pupils" or "two of every 100 senior high students could not be controlled satisfactorily in the classroom by the teacher." [1]

[1] San Diego City Schools, *As You See It*, "What San Diego Parents and Teachers Think of Their Schools." San Diego: Board of Education (January 1957), p. 11. A survey based on the responses of 2653 teachers and 5342 parents.

In a letter to one of the authors, dated February 25, 1963, Dr. William H. Stegeman, assistant superintendent in charge of the curriculum, San Diego City Schools, pointed out that the findings of the study just cited were published seven years ago and concluded with this statement: "Although the picture concerning discipline and the deportment of students presented by the findings summarized in *As You See It* was not especially dark, we still are firmly convinced that the situation is much improved now." He further added that "it is our feeling that the proportion is smaller now" of pupils who cannot be controlled satisfactorily by the classroom teacher.

Periodically the Research Division of the National Education Association makes a survey of teacher opinion about the sources, nature, and extent of discipline problems. Although data are not entirely parallel, the findings of the 1956 and 1965 reports will be compared and contrasted.

In the 1956 report, about 95 percent of the teachers indicated that their pupils were "exceptionally" or "reasonably well behaved." About the same percentage stated that parents were "always" or in "a majority of cases" cooperative.[2] Teachers pointed out that the incidence of misbehavior tended to increase in urban areas, in larger school systems, and in larger classes (45 or more). In equating the teacher factor contributing to behavior problems, teachers were of the opinion that maturity which comes with age and experience "tends to reduce the pupil behavior problems with which typical classroom teachers have to contend. There appears to be a point of diminishing returns, however. Somewhere between 50 and 65 years of age and after acquiring 25 to 30 years of experience, teachers begin to take a dimmer view of the behavior of young people." [3]

Types of homes and communities from which pupils come have a tremendous impact. Positive factors include all-residential areas where family income is adequate (in contrast to slum areas where living conditions are poor) and where the community provides strong recreational and moral and spiritual guidance programs. Most important are parents who are "willing to assume responsibility for what their children do in school and who cooperate with the school in seeking solutions to problems involving behavior of their children." [4]

Both this survey and the report of the San Diego City Schools strongly support the conclusion that the major cause of behavior problems is unsatisfactory home conditions or family life. Both conclude that "in general, pupil behavior is no worse than it was five or ten years ago." [5]

In the national study nearly two thirds of the public school teachers

[2] Research Division, NEA, "Teacher Opinion on Pupil Behavior, 1955–56," *Research Bulletin*, 34 (April 1956), 104–106. A survey based on the responses of 4270 teachers.
[3] Research Division, NEA, p. 74.
[4] Research Division, NEA, p. 81.
[5] San Diego City Schools, p. 17.

reported that real troublemakers accounted for "fewer than 1 in every 100 pupils." [6] The kinds of misbehavior judged to occur more frequently than occurred ten years before were "impertinence and discourtesy to teachers, failure to do homework and other assignments, and drinking intoxicants." [7]

As for discipline in the average San Diego City Schools classroom at the secondary level over a decade ago, a junior high school teacher seemed to summarize the situation reasonably well. Surveying a large class of students at work, the teacher remarked, "I wish I could meet the parents of all these boys and girls. They are to be commended for doing such an excellent job of rearing their children."

In conclusion, the 1956 report of the Research Division of the National Education Association noted that, with other things being equal, "teachers are likely to have fewer problems among pupils if (a) they feel they have sufficient authority to maintain effective control . . . , (b) they have an important voice in the determination of policies . . . , (c) most of the pupils in school are above average intelligence . . . , and (d) no pupils in their classes need psychiatric help." [8] Of all the factors contributing to good behavior, one of the most important is the willingness of parents to help solve their children's problems.

The introduction to the 1965 report of the Research Division of the NEA on teacher opinion about the causes, extent, and nature of student behavior problems includes two observations: that mass communications media dramatize the misbehavior of secondary school students, and that "the crime rate among juveniles is increasing." [9] Student behavior in general was rated as excellent or good in seven or eight classes in ten. Nearly all classes with above-average ability were rated as "excellent or good in general behavior; less than half of the below-average ability classes were considered well-behaved." [10] Of the total sample of all students, "only 3 students in 100 were considered serious troublemakers." [11] From 32 percent to 13.3 percent of the teachers reported the following kinds of misbehavior as widespread or frequent (in descending order): lack of responsibility for assignments, duties, or commitments; cheating on tests; swearing or using vulgar language; petty theft; impertinence and discourtesy to teachers (rated first in the 1956 survey); and destruction of school property. [12]

[6] Research Division, NEA, 1956, p. 104.
[7] Research Division, NEA, 1956, p. 106.
[8] Research Division, NEA, 1956, p. 106.
[9] Research Division, NEA, "Student Behavior in Secondary Schools, 1964," *Research Report, 1965*—R–12 (August 1965), p. 5. A four-page, pretested questionnaire was sent to 1219 teachers in March 1964 to 380 school systems enrolling 50 or more students in secondary grades.
[10] Research Division, NEA, 1965, p. 8.
[11] Research Division, NEA, 1965, p. 9.
[12] Research Division, NEA, 1965, p. 12.

"One teacher in seven reported that at least one student had committed an act of physical violence against a teacher or principal during the year 1963–64, but only 14 in 1,000 reported an act of violence committed against him personally." [13] Student possession of a dangerous weapon was indicated by 8 teachers in 100; student strikes or walkouts on school time, by 3 to 4 teachers in 100.[14]

As to *causes* of misbehavior, from 43.8 percent to 15.2 percent of the teachers in the 1965 report listed the following (in descending order): irresponsible parents, unsatisfactory home conditions (low income, broken homes, and so on), increased availability of automobiles to teen-agers, lack of provision for academically retarded children, unsuitable school program or curriculum, and overcrowded classes.[15]

Although neither the 1956 nor the 1965 report of the Research Division of the NEA on student behavior suggests that the typical classroom is a "blackboard jungle," the latter includes data that are less encouraging than those in the earlier report. The 1965 report asserts that "the crime rate among juveniles is increasing." Whereas teachers in 1956 believed that real troublemakers accounted for fewer than 1 in 100 pupils, the 1965 teachers placed the number at 3 in every 100. Furthermore, the teachers in the mid-sixties reported student acts of physical violence against school personnel, possession of dangerous weapons, and strikes or walkouts on school time—none of which appeared in the 1956 report. Since 1965, news media have given evidence of expanding use of drugs and narcotics among school children.

CORRECTION OR PUNISHMENT

An earlier discussion of the definitions of discipline indicated that many people consider "discipline" synonymous with "punishment." This is unfortunate, of course, for it has already been pointed out that discipline has a much broader meaning. Nevertheless, punishment or correction is an important aspect of discipline not to be ignored. Melitta Schmideberg, a psychiatrist, stresses the importance of "negative incentives in life" when she says: "As a rule, a mixture of both positive and negative incentives is most effective, and this is also a better preparation for life . . . the effect of positive incentives is necessarily limited. We cannot get pleasure from an activity until we have learned it, and studying and working are not always fun. Everyone encounters hardship, injustice, and heartbreak in the course of life." [16]

[13] Research Division, NEA, 1965, p. 10.
[14] Research Division, NEA, 1965, p. 11.
[15] Research Division, NEA, 1965, p. 13.
[16] Melitta Schmideberg, "Training for Responsibility," *Phi Delta Kappan,* 41 (December 1959), 93.

THE ROLE OF PUNISHMENT IN DISCIPLINE

Because punishment is one of the unpleasant but educative facts of life, the chief concern of the teacher is how to administer it so as to improve student behavior. It is important for the person who administers punishment to have a clear understanding of the meaning of the word. Redl has supplied us with a sound definition of "punishment" in these words: "a planful attempt by the adult to influence either the behavior or the long-range development of a child or a group of children for its own benefit by exposing it to an unpleasant experience" (10:363). In contrast to the past, today "correction of irrational forms of behavior has shifted from imposition of the will of a stronger person to imposition of the natural results of the act." [17] In order to make natural law more operative, the teacher needs to keep a number of principles in mind.

The purpose of punishment is to correct undesirable behavior. Before assuming his role as a dispenser of punishment, the teacher must develop his own philosophy with respect to what *is* undesirable or objectionable behavior. Sheviakov and Redl make the point that "different goals are pursued differently." By way of illustration, a Boy Scout troop may practice marching, which requires precision and unity. If, however, the group is climbing a mountain, symmetry is no longer necessary and individuals may walk loosely, chase butterflies, and examine rocks as long as no one gets lost or interferes with group goals. Another example is the behavior of a student who runs through the halls of the school on a Saturday afternoon in order to get to a meeting on time in contrast with his running through the same halls at recess time on a school day, interfering with the rights of others to get to class safely and efficiently.[18]

Any student in need of correction must learn to make a better adjustment to the realities of life, both as an individual and as a member of society. Consequently, the type of punishment that undermines self-esteem or the development of effective interpersonal relationships is to be avoided. Thus the use of sarcasm, public reprimands, or forced apologies would be a highly questionable procedure.

The spirit in which punishment is administered is important. Punishment should not be administered in anger or in a retaliatory or vindictive mood. The teacher must remember that most aggressive acts of misbehavior are not directed at him personally. By considering such acts as attempts on the part of the offender to relieve personal frustrations, the teacher is in a better position to deal with such misdeeds in an objective

[17] Asahel D. Woodruff, "Discipline," *Encyclopedia of Educational Research*, 3d ed. New York: The Macmillan Company, 1960, p. 383.
[18] George V. Sheviakov and Fritz Redl, *Discipline for Today's Children and Youth*, new revision by Sybil K. Richardson. Washington, D.C.: National Education Association, 1956, pp. 4–5.

manner. Corrections are always to be made in the best interests of the class and the individual concerned. Consequently, there is no place in the classroom for the teacher who inflicts punishment to relieve personal irritations or aggressions or to satisfy a desire to assert his authority or control over others. In correcting minor infractions of school rules, the teacher who can demonstrate a sense of humor is at an advantage. Not only is he better able to maintain his own self-control; he also keeps tension from building up in the classroom.

Punishment should fit the offense. Because punishment is designed to be corrective, an offender should be encouraged to make amends for mistakes he has made and to refrain from repetition of such behavior. For example, if a student carelessly damages public property, he should either restore or replace it, or at least demonstrate a willingness to do so. If a student willfully litters the classroom, he should be required to clean it up.

Individual differences need to be considered in punishment. "Two students may commit the same offense, but for reasons that are so different that a uniform system of punishments may be unjust and ineffective for both of them." [19] Not only must different reasons for misbehavior be considered, but also the sensitivity, maturity, and background of the student involved. For instance, one student may respond to a mild reproof whereas another may require more severe treatment for correction of the same kind of misbehavior. As knowledge of the nature and causes of maladjustment has increased, "the concept of discipline has shifted steadily from uniform demands on everyone to toleration of variations in behavior by individuals, and even to toleration of variations for a single individual when he is faced with fluctuating situations." [20]

This statement may seem to violate the principle of *consistency*, stressed elsewhere in this book, but it does not. Problems of misbehavior should be consistently recognized and corrected without ignoring justice and fair treatment. If it is to be truly corrective, punishment must vary according to the situation, the offense, and the offender. The school whose policy calls for automatic suspension of students using vulgar or profane language could hardly dismiss the girl who cried "Damn" when she accidentally grasped a hot test tube in the chemistry lab.

If correction is necessary, use measures that "work." When a teacher uses a given technique to correct the behavior of an individual or a group, the first question that comes to mind is "Does it work?" Superficially, the answer is "yes" if there is immediate compliance with the teacher's demands. Appearances can be deceiving. What happens when the teacher turns his back or leaves the room momentarily? Sometimes a control technique arouses so much resentment in an individual or a group that

[19] Harry N. Rivlin, *Teaching Adolescents in Secondary Schools,* 2d ed. New York: Appleton-Century-Crofts, Inc., Division of Meredith Corporation, 1961, p. 423.
[20] Woodruff, p. 383.

overt behavior becomes worse as soon as external controls are removed. However, the teacher needs to go beyond mere changes in *surface behavior*. Whether or not a technique really "works" ultimately depends upon permanent changes in attitudes and behavior. Paul Hill, a clinical psychologist, goes beyond surface symptoms by making a thorough analysis of a problem before proposing any solution to it. Although his case studies are drawn from the elementary school level, many of his suggestions are equally relevant to higher grade levels (6:48 p.)

Schain and Polner conclude that "sound discipline is created by the teacher." In analyzing actual cases of discipline problems, they use the following pattern for action: describe the *incident* and "what the teacher did about it," analyze reasons for the occurrence of the incident and evaluate teacher effectiveness in handling it, and make suggestions to improve the teacher's actions so that a similar incident may not recur in the future.[21]

Beginning teachers especially need to be wary of accepting "It works" as a criterion of successful practice. First of all, a premium is likely to be placed on changes in *surface* behavior. Furthermore, it may lead to justification of a particular technique (sometimes a very poor one) as a solution to almost every problem. Thus the variables in situation, student (maturity, background), or ultimate goals are completely overlooked. Finally, it is easy to be misled by the scoffer who rejects any proposed solution to a problem by saying, "I've tried that and it doesn't work."

Individual correction works better than group correction. Disruption of class morale usually begins with disturbances created by one or two individuals. Group discourtesy begins with the first student who demonstrates discourteous behavior without being corrected. The physical education instructor who ignores the first profane remark or bit of disruptive horseplay may eventually find himself with an unruly mob on his hands. Even such minor distractions as application of makeup or combing hair should be discouraged, for they are not conducive to the best learning atmosphere. It is comparatively easy to correct the first evidences of disruptive behavior on an individual basis; but, once disorder or undesirable behavior has infected a group, heroic measures are sometimes required to restore order.

In line with the injunction "Commend publicly, reprimand privately," Gnagey warns of the "ripple effect" on other class members when the correction of an individual is made obvious to his peers. The total effect is influenced by such factors as the prestige of the misbehaving student, "use of nonthreatening techniques," and relating demands to the learning task rather than to teacher approval (5:48–49, 54–55).

---

[21] Robert L. Schain and Murray Polner, *Using Effective Discipline for Better Class Control.* Englewood Cliffs, N.J.: Teachers Practical Press, Inc., 1964, pp. 6–7.

Corrective measures should be varied. Even when corrective measures take into account the variables indicated above and seem to be fair and workable, they still need to be varied. It has been said that a housewife should not attempt to do all her laundry with the same cake of soap. Likewise, the teacher should avoid using a particular procedure with monotonous repetition just because it seems to work. Sometimes the element of novelty or surprise adds to the effectiveness of punishment.

Punishment should be used judiciously. Neither severity nor frequency of punishment is an effective deterrent to misbehavior. Stern measures should be reserved for treatment of major offenses, not minor ones. One new teacher began sending students out of his room to sit in the counselor's office for failure to do their homework, for forgetting to bring their books to class, and so on. As a result, he merely compounded his problems, created an atmosphere of hostility in the classroom, and left himself no control measures to be used for major offenses.

When punishment becomes necessary, it should be "swift and certain" (4:93). This statement does not mean that the teacher punishes a student on impulse or when he is angry. Sometimes further investigation is needed, a cooling-off period may be advisable, the student may profit from meditating on his own misbehavior, or more thought may need to be given to the most appropriate punishment. What it does imply is that a student who misbehaves must be sure he will have to suffer the consequences of his acts. Furthermore, if the punishment is appropriate, he will be impressed with the undesirability of continuing such behavior.

A teacher who is effective in classroom management and control does not make idle threats nor forget to follow through on corrective measures. By way of illustration, a teacher may request a student to stop after class or to return after school and then promptly forget about it. Or he may warn a persistent talker that he is going to change his seat the next time it occurs, but do nothing about it. The teacher is most effective *when he follows through.*

It should always be clear to an offender why he is being punished. Usually, objectionable behavior is the kind that interferes with the rights, the safety, or the welfare of others. If this is pointed out to the misbehaving student, perhaps he can be made to realize that from the standpoint of intelligent self-interest—acceptance by his peers—such behavior does not pay.

When the student has paid his penalty, the case should be closed. The teacher should make the erstwhile offender feel that he is fully accepted as a member of the class. It is the offense, not the offender as a person, that merits the disapproval of the teacher. The continually misbehaving student who has aroused the ire of a school faculty has little or no chance of rehabilitation.

Punishment should be just. Students have the highest respect for teachers who maintain strict discipline as long as they feel treatment has been fair and equitable. Such a practice as punishing the group for the misbehavior of an individual or making an example of an offender to impress the class is no way to win friends nor to influence students. On the other hand, the teacher who is honest, fair, and impartial in all his dealings with his students is almost sure to have the cooperation of the majority, striving to please and gain his recognition.

AN ANALYSIS OF DISCIPLINARY PRACTICES

Disciplinary practices range all the way from those that are generally approved to those that are considered questionable or objectionable by most teachers. Of course, there is still disagreement over the relative merits of a number of common practices.

APPROVED DISCIPLINARY PRACTICES

Although there is unlikely to be complete agreement on the efficacy of all the following disciplinary procedures, they have been endorsed as desirable corrective measures by sources indicated below: individual conferences with students; conferences with parents; simple control measures (catching the eye of an offender, and so on); a change in seating; use of social pressure; loss of special privilege; student participation in school discipline; rectification, restitution, and reparation; "use of rewards"; "temporary isolation under supervision"; detention for a specific, clearly stated purpose; and "referral to a school officer . . . after the teacher has exhausted all his own possibilities" (8:76–84; 1:383–384).

INDIVIDUAL CONFERENCES   An individual conference with a student is the most desirable of all the corrective measures the teacher might use. It enables the teacher to perform his guidance function, to obtain additional information, and to secure the reactions of the student. In some cases, it is advisable to have the student suggest his own punishment. Such a conference may be limited in its effectiveness, however, by a lack of knowledge, time, interest, or understanding of adolescents on the part of the teacher. Furthermore, some teachers may be inclined to harbor resentments toward offenders or be unable to establish rapport with them (8:76).

When an individual conference is held, it should be in private. There should be freedom from outside distractions or eavesdropping by other students or faculty members. It is never advisable to confer with two misbehaving students at the same time, unless they are mutually involved, for they are likely to reinforce each other in resisting the counsel of the teacher.

CONFERENCES WITH PARENTS   Conferences with parents have a number of potential values: to strengthen relationships between home and school;

to enable parents and teachers to share information and to attack the problem on a united front; and to provide the teacher with a better understanding of the student's home environment. The disadvantages of such conferences may stem from the teacher's lack of skill in interviewing and making home visits and in diagnosing and interpreting student misbehavior. Then, too, it is often difficult to arrange such conferences, either at home or at school (8:77).

Unfortunately, conferences between teachers and parents of misbehaving students often take place under unfavorable conditions. The parents may not be summoned to school until misbehavior has already reached serious proportions, perhaps to the point of expulsion. It is understandable that such parents would be on the defensive and probably in a belligerent mood. Earlier notification might forestall such a difficult situation. It should also be noted that neither a note nor a telephone call is a satisfactory substitute for the personal interview. On handling such an interview, even when parents are upset, the reader is referred to suggestions given in Chapter 13.[22]

SIMPLE CONTROL MEASURES   The use of simple control measures—quiet disapproval techniques, such as eye contact, moving near trouble spots— is not likely to disturb the class as a whole, to result in "unpleasant scenes," or to have harmful effects on personality. With difficult classes, however, such control measures are ineffective. Furthermore, the teacher "attacks surface behavior only, neglecting underlying causes" (8:76). At times no action is best. The beginning teacher is often advised to avoid nagging or making issues of trivial incidents. Admittedly this poses a problem. Lacking experience, the new teacher may not be able to judge what is significant or trivial in terms of the students' actions. A simple criterion may be applied: If persistence of a particular kind of behavior results in a gradual deterioration of the learning situation, then such behavior cannot be considered trivial.

The teacher must be able to distinguish between normal, exuberant actions of youth and danger signs of real aberrant behavior. Sometimes as teachers grow older, they should be reminded that they may create their own discipline problems by becoming fussier, more impatient, and less tolerant of the high-spirited behavior of normal adolescents.

CHANGE OF SEATING   A change of seating may correct minor disturbances, such as excessive talking. The teacher should avoid measures that create feelings of shame or resentment, perhaps making the offender even worse. For example, seating a girl among a group of boys, placing a talker

---

[22] Norma E. Cutts and Nicholas Moseley, *Teaching the Disorderly Pupil in Elementary and Secondary School.* New York: David McKay Company, Inc., 1957, pp. 86–87.

conspicuously in the front of the room or apart from the group, or placing an offender at the back of the room where it is difficult to keep him under observation are changes in seating that may do more harm than good. Some teachers have found it useful to talk with the student, to suggest a change in seating to improve his behavior, and to ask him where he would like to sit.

LOSS OF PRIVILEGE   When a student is punished by loss of privilege, he is made aware of the relationship between duty and privilege. For example, if one condition for participation in cocurricular activities is contingent on maintenance of satisfactory citizenship, the student soon learns that unsatisfactory behavior does not pay. Depriving a student of a privilege he has abused or temporarily confiscating a possession that is causing the trouble are punishments that fit the offense. The chief danger in this type of control if applied too long is that the student may be denied valuable learning experiences.

STUDENT SELF-GOVERNMENT   It has already been suggested that there are definite advantages to having students participate in setting up rules to govern their class. However, when a group begins to exhibit patterns of idleness or disorder, what action should the teacher take under those conditions? With a group of sufficient maturity, the teacher may profitably arrange for a candid discussion of the problem. Such a session permits students to air their dissatisfactions and provides a means whereby a teacher and his class may reach a mutual agreement on what is needed to promote a more effective learning situation.

Again the teacher needs to be warned of the danger of attempting to establish self-government in a group that is not yet ready for it. Sheviakov and Redl cite the case of a Miss Jones who undertook to use democratic procedures in a class with a bad reputation, including some of "the worst hoodlums in school." Several unfortunate results followed: bullies took over, showing favoritism toward their friends; rules were made and broken; and no fundamental improvements in school attendance, work habits, or overall behavior occurred.[23]

RECTIFICATION, RESTITUTION, AND REPARATION   Some forms of punishment can be justly and impartially associated with the offense. For example, if a student charges out of the room when the dismissal bell rings, endangering the safety of himself and others, he should be made to return to the room and walk from it in an orderly manner. Or until he is willing to leave the room in an acceptable way, he may be required to remain in his seat each day while all other class members leave.

Students need to develop a sense of social responsibility for making amends when they willfully destroy or take property belonging to others.

[23] Sheviakov and Redl, p. 33.

A problem arises in the application of this corrective measure, however, whenever the student is financially unable to pay for damages or parents too readily supply the money themselves, thereby "destroying the educative value of the punishment" (8:78). The common practice of shop teachers of collecting money from all students when a tool is lost may be questionable on legal grounds.

REWARDS OR PRIZES   The use of rewards or prizes is a positive approach to the promotion of desirable behavior, but there are a number of dangers in this procedure: rewards may become ends in themselves; they may not be available "to all students on an equal basis"; and prizes may encourage personal selfishness and greed. If rewards are used, they should "appeal to higher motives such as group welfare, citizenship, and service" (8:78).

"TEMPORARY ISOLATION UNDER SUPERVISION" [24]   Temporary isolation under supervision is sometimes a necessity when the behavior of an individual becomes completely objectionable in terms of group welfare. The offender may be set apart from the group within a classroom or referred to the office of a counselor or principal. It is not advisable to have a student stand or sit outside the classroom or to leave for some unspecified destination. When such punishment is exercised too frequently or for too long a period, it may rob the student of valuable educational experiences and increase his difficulty in making adjustment to the group.

USE OF SOCIAL PRESSURE   Social or peer pressure may be an effective measure for the correction of misbehavior when used judiciously. The following example illustrates the point:

Jerry was a perpetually disturbing element in the eighth-grade social studies class. Whistling, mumbling, making sound effects, heckling his neighbors, and wandering aimlessly made up his assortment of distractions. One day the class played a baseball game for a unit review. Anyone who was on the same team as the student at bat (answering a review question) and who coached his teammate received a strike against his team. Jerry's team had three men on base, two outs, and two strikes on the "batter," who had decided to try for a "home run." The teacher asked him a difficult review question. As the batter painfully concentrated on the answer, with his classmates waiting excitedly, Jerry blurted out the answer and the side was retired. The displeasure of his team, soon made evident to Jerry, served as an effective deterrent to his uninhibited behavior.

Jerry's behavior very likely indicated a desire for attention. But he needed to learn how to secure recognition in more socially accepted ways, a lesson a boy can sometimes learn most effectively from his peers. The use of social pressure is harmful if it alienates a student permanently from his group. By all means, the teacher should not himself encourage a group to

[24] Woodruff, p. 384.

reject an offender, but should arrange the situation so that the student suffers the social consequences of his own acts.

DETENTION AFTER SCHOOL   Detention after school, one of the most widely used and presumably most widely acceptable forms of punishment, is easily administered and may serve as a deterrent to further misbehavior when the student is prevented from doing something he would very much like to do. It may also be an appropriate corrective measure for the student who is persistently tardy or wastes time during school hours.

The disadvantages of this form of punishment, however, seem to outweigh its advantages. First of all, basic causes of misbehavior are not considered. Furthermore, it is often used as a blanket form of punishment for all types of misbehavior; hence correction may fit neither the offense nor the offender. In having to supervise the offender after school hours, the teacher is also punished, a fact that may be relished by the offender himself. Detention may seriously conflict with such after-school activities of the student as work, medical appointments, cocurricular activities, and school bus transportation, although some schools provide before-school detention. Finally, it is a real problem to decide what to have the student do during detention. If he just sits, nothing of value is accomplished. If he is assigned homework, he may learn to strengthen his dislike for school. If he is assigned other tasks, then the punishment is probably no longer associated with the act of misbehavior.

Detention after school cannot be justified unless it enables the teacher to give extra help or counsel to the student or enables the student to make up work. Detention during recess or noon periods is condemned; it is even illegal in some states (8:79–80).

REFERRAL TO SOME OTHER SCHOOL AUTHORITY   Exclusion from the classroom is necessary when a student becomes incorrigible in the classroom, engages in serious forms of misbehavior (committing immoral acts or assaulting others, for example), or gives evidence of being emotionally disturbed or socially maladjusted. Teachers may err in either of two extremes, by sending students to the principal for even the most minor offenses or by putting up with intolerable disruptive behavior in the classroom without seeking help.

Before resorting to referrals, a teacher needs to exhaust his own resources, by trying any or all of the following measures:

Making classwork more interesting
Seeking to discover underlying causes of misbehavior
Securing more information about his students
Conferring privately with an offender
Providing opportunity for special recognition
Conferring with homeroom teacher, counselor, or vice-principal

Conferring with parents
Ignoring minor annoyances unlikely to disturb group climate
Changing seating
Isolating an offender temporarily within the classroom
Taking away special privileges
Detaining an offender after school for reasons related to the offense

QUESTIONABLE OR OBJECTIONABLE DISCIPLINARY PROCEDURES

The preceding discussion has been concerned with corrective measures in classroom management and control generally approved in school practice. However, of the last three forms of punishment—isolation, detention, and referral—there are those who would classify them as questionable rather than acceptable procedures. Obviously, all the corrective measures listed above are not equally acceptable. Some probably can be justified only on the basis of immediate necessity. In the following discussion, an analysis will be made of control procedures that are considered questionable or objectionable.

There are a great number of corrective measures used in classroom management and control about which there is considerable difference of opinion: use of corporal punishment; use of group punishment; forcing apologies; lowering marks; use of sarcasm or ridicule; use of threats and repeated vocal correction; assignment of extra tasks unrelated to the offense; making an example of a misbehaving student; arguing with students in the presence of the total group; use of suspension; and expulsion (8:84).

CORPORAL PUNISHMENT   The use of corporal punishment is the subject of much controversy. Opinion polls have shown that parents and particularly administrators favor it. There is also evidence that the use of corporal punishment is gaining in favor again. If used at all, such a corrective measure would obviously be more appropriate at the elementary level than in high school. When corporal punishment is authorized, there are usually definite requirements outlined for its administration, such as having witnesses, using moderation, and the like to avoid legal complications.

Except in extreme cases, when the safety of a student or the teacher himself is at stake, the teacher is advised to avoid the use of physical force in dealing with a recalcitrant student. It is better to summon assistance if needed. Physical contact with a student, such as slapping or restraining him, may result in a number of complications: he may strike the teacher; the teacher may feel it necessary to defend himself; or the parents may resort to court action.[25] The teacher faces a real dilemma in

[25] Cutts and Moseley, pp. 34–35.

dealing with disadvantaged boys because they attach great value to "toughness and masculinity" (7:33). Although school personnel usually consider the use of physical force inappropriate in the correction of misbehaving students (especially adolescents), a disadvantaged boy is likely to interpret other types of correction by the teacher as a sign of weakness. Nevertheless, the teacher of high school youth is still advised to avoid physical contact with them.

GROUP PUNISHMENT   Although in some instances an entire class may seem to be deserving of punishment, the teacher has to exercise discretion in its application and a finesse that may even be appreciated by the recipients. By way of illustration, an entire student body once cut school on April Fool's Day. Upon their return, the principal called a general assembly and, without making any reference to the affair, announced in a suave manner, "Students, it seems that we are getting a little behind in our work. So the board and I have decided that it is advisable for us to lengthen the school day forty-five minutes from now until the end of the term." Sometimes a teacher punishes a class for the offense of an individual in the belief that group disapproval will be directed against the offender. More often than not, resentment is directed toward the teacher and he loses the support of the students who had previously favored him. Group punishment is also likely to be unjust, for the innocent must suffer with the guilty.

FORCED APOLOGIES   A forced apology is objectionable in the first place because such an apology is no apology at all: it is an act of hypocrisy. A true apology is a voluntary expression of sincere regret for thoughtless behavior. By all means, the teacher should encourage a student to feel responsible for his misbehavior, to regret it, and to wish to make amends to those whom he may have wronged. For instance, the teacher may say, "Don't you feel that you owe the class an apology for what you have done?" but not "You *must* apologize to the class before you return to it." In encouraging students to apologize for their misdeeds, the teacher must be willing to set a good example. When he has erred, he should admit it and ask the forgiveness of those he may have misjudged or treated unjustly.

LOWERING SCHOLARSHIP MARKS   Lowering grades as a method of correcting behavior is a misuse of the school's marking system. It is perfectly logical to lower citizenship grades for misbehavior but to lower scholarship marks as punishment is unjustifiable. Such marks represent scholastic achievement and nothing else. A closely related practice, assigning demerits for various offenses, is objectionable for a number of reasons: causes of behavior are ignored, bookkeeping becomes onerous, and good behavior is not rewarded. As is often the case in the use of questionable practices, teachers may defend them by asserting the effectiveness of a particular system. Actually the results of many procedures are difficult to evaluate. They may bring about surface changes only or the desired conformity, with no fundamental changes in attitudes or the future behavior of the student taking place.

SARCASM OR RIDICULE   The use of sarcasm or ridicule is another corrective measure often justified on the assumption that it works. The practice is objectionable, first of all, because the offender is subjected to embarrassment and loss of self-esteem. Like group punishment, it can be a dangerous weapon. The student is forced into a face-saving situation in which his status with his peers is threatened. Sooner or later, a student will respond in kind to the teacher's sarcastic remark. With the class acting as judge and jury, it is the teacher who will be laughed out of court. Whenever a teacher is tempted to resort to sarcasm, he should remember that a basic professional principle is at stake: *A teacher can expect the same respect and consideration that he shows for his students.* Furthermore, "young people learn to respect one another when they themselves have been treated with respect by understanding adults." [26]

THREATS AND VOCAL CORRECTION   Threats and repeated vocal correction have one thing in common: they are often used as ineffective substitutes for needed action. Nothing is more futile than repetitious vocal correction. A threat may serve to notify a student that his behavior is objectionable, but it may be inconvenient, if not impossible, to carry out. Sometimes a warning may be in order, especially if the offender is told why his behavior is objectionable and will need to be corrected if continued.[27] Where two students are involved, for example, in excessive talking, the teacher may suggest that if they wish to continue to sit near each other they must mend their ways or some changes will be made in seating. The use of threats has an additional disadvantage, especially with adolescents who are passing through a stage of rebellion against adult authority; it may constitute a challenge to be tested.

Under the subject of vocal correction should be mentioned the teacher who persistently scolds or nags his students. Instead of encouraging improved behavior, such a practice lowers group morale and widens the breach between the teacher and the class.

The teacher also should avoid making comments to individuals or vocal corrections across the room when the class is at work. Sometimes a noisy teacher is the most disturbing element in the classroom.

ASSIGNMENT OF EXTRA TASKS   The assignment of extra tasks has little or nothing to commend it as a corrective measure. Punishment is un-

[26] Sheviakov and Redl, p. 11.
[27] Cutts and Moseley, p. 29.

related to the act of misbehavior; dislike for schoolwork is likely to be increased; and motivation to learn is stifled.

MAKING EXAMPLES OF STUDENTS   Making an example of a misbehaving student is objectionable on several counts. First of all, the self-esteem of the student is undermined. Second, when a student is threatened with loss of face in the presence of his peers, he may defy the authority of the teacher. Furthermore, such punishment is unjust when some student is selected as a scapegoat to serve as an object lesson for the group. Finally, the procedure is ineffective: the group is usually not impressed, and, in fact, the offender may become a martyr in the eyes of his classmates, and the group itself may be encouraged to imitate his behavior.

PUBLIC ARGUMENTS WITH STUDENTS   Arguing with a student in the presence of the class is decidedly unwise. This is another face-saving situation in which the teacher is pitted against the student. The teacher must absolutely refuse to become involved in such arguments. Any differences between him and a student that involve problems of behavior must be settled privately. Two examples illustrate the right way and the wrong way to handle the problem.

The following incident illustrates how a new teacher of physical education took care of a potentially explosive situation in a wise manner:

The teacher and his class were returning to the gymnasium after a period of touch football. As was the usual procedure, the teacher began collecting all the balls. When he asked one student to toss a ball to him, the boy deliberately threw the ball as far as he could in another direction. Instead of ordering the boy to get the ball, the teacher said quietly but firmly, "I'll see you in the locker room."

Here the teacher forced neither the boy nor himself into an uncompromising face-saving situation. Neither did he provide the boy an open opportunity to further defy his authority in the presence of the class.

A second illustration demonstrates how a new teacher reached a crisis in discipline by unwise handling of a minor incident.

J. J. informed an eighth-grade speech class that it was to copy material she would dictate. When everyone seemed to be ready, Chuck announced that he had no pencil. Evidently this was a delaying tactic, a subtle sabotage of class procedures for which Chuck was noted. Irritated with his behavior, the teacher sharply demanded of Chuck his reason for having no pencil. An argument ensued in which Chuck responded with wisecracks, the class burst into gales of laughter, and the teacher became increasingly confused and angry. Finally, the class became completely disorganized and J. J. made her exit in tears.

This could have been avoided in several ways: by lending Chuck a pencil, by ignoring him and letting him get his information as best he could, or by having him come in after school and copy the material on his own time for habitual failure to bring necessary materials to class.

SUSPENSION OR EXPULSION   Drastic measures like suspension or expulsion, ordinarily administered by the principal or the superintendent, are to be used as a last resort. When all other measures have failed and the welfare of the class is threatened, suspension or expulsion becomes a necessity. No student has a right to interfere with the rights of the majority to learn. Suspension may give the student an opportunity to reflect on his own behavior and impress parents with the seriousness of the problem. Neither suspension nor expulsion, however, removes the causes of misbehavior. Expulsion enables the school "to get rid of extreme cases," but it does not solve the problem for society (8:83–84).

CORRECTION VERSUS PREVENTION OF DISCIPLINE PROBLEMS

The foundation of good discipline is good morale, marked by an emotional climate in the classroom of "warm friendliness, pride in a good reputation, and group solidarity." [28] The teacher who is able to supply the guidance teen-agers need possesses qualities of "friendliness, fairness, enthusiasm, vitality, a sense of humor, a liking for [his] work, and a liking for young people." [29]

TEACHER SENSITIVITY TO STUDENTS' FEELINGS

Of all the aspects of human development, a conscious consideration of feeling or emotional activity has probably been most neglected by schools. The first book on the subject was written during this generation. Yet of all the drives to action, sources of personal enjoyment, and keys to human values, emotions probably rank first. Pestalozzi contended that education must be of the hand, the head, and the heart.[30] Formal education has scorned the first, enshrined the second, and neglected the third. Man takes pride in being a rational animal, a claim that may be open to serious question. Acquaintance with great literature, art, and music; participation in dramatic situations of emotional significance; human relationships that stir love, sympathy, and understanding are the factors that give life meaning.

Sometimes teachers have exhibited a shameful indifference to their students' feelings. Although adolescents often try to mask their true feelings, they still stand in need of a wholesome development of their affective

[28] Cutts and Moseley, p. 6.
[29] Cutts and Moseley, p. 138.
[30] J. H. Pestalozzi, *The Swan Song.* Edited by J. A. Green in *Pestalozzi's Educational Writings.* London: Edward Arnold & Co., 1916, pp. 268–269.

natures. Not only must an emotional sensitivity be developed; students must learn to control their emotions. Discussion groups, competitive games, and recreational activities are but a few of the situations in which boys and girls may learn to develop self-control. They have to learn to take defeat without bitterness and to experience victory without arrogance.

School administrators are sometimes tempted to abolish competitive student activities because of the school rivalries and personal animosities engendered by them. However, the unlovely emotional results of such contests are not always primarily the fault of the activities nor of the contestants. Parents, coaches, and fans have often been more concerned with winning loving cups than with developing the emotional quality of good sportsmanship.

Every teacher, whether he be coach or English teacher, needs to develop emotional self-control. That is critical in ensuring his own mental health as well as important in guiding his students toward emotional maturity.

TEN COMMANDMENTS OF DISCIPLINE

Ten rules for the development of good class morale:

1. *Begin right.* Good grooming, enthusiasm, and warmth are important in making a good first impression. Students should be made to feel that the class is going to be a stimulating, enjoyable, and profitable experience.

2. *Be businesslike.* Class should begin on time and close on time. Plans should be ready and all routine well organized. You should be calm, composed, and dignified in manner. Good tempo, variety, and protection of the group from unnecessary annoyances should help keep the class interesting.

3. *Be alert.* Stopping the little disturbances—idling, scuffling, loud talking—often prevents more serious disorder. You need to be immediately aware of individual aberrations in behavior or disturbances in group climate.

4. *Be tactful.* Requests rather than commands, cooperative decisions rather than those made solely by the teacher, courtesy rather than curtness, and respect for the rights and opinions of others instead of intolerance constitute the essence of tact and consideration.

5. *Be cheerful.* Radiate good humor, an even disposition, and peace of mind in your face, your voice, and your actions. At all costs, the authoritative manner, the peevish voice, or the perpetual scowl should be avoided.

6. *Be just.* Avoid hasty judgments, partiality, or prejudicial treatment in working with students. If you make a mistake, rectify it.

7. *Be persistent.* Expect good behavior and insist on it. If you set out to settle a problem, see it through. If words are ineffective, act.

8. *Be consistent.* Consistency of behavior is indicative of maturity and self-control. Fortunate are the students who have a mature teacher who provides them with the security they need.

9. *Be decisive.* As a teacher, you are morally and legally responsible for maintaining classroom atmosphere that is conducive to effective learning. If you fail in your leadership, students become insecure and classroom conditions become chaotic.

10. *Be judicious.* Avoid scenes or crises in the classroom. Avoid uncompromising situations—public argument, sarcasm, encouragement of open defiance—in which either teacher or student is in danger of loss of face. Commend publicly, reprimand privately.

SELECTED READINGS

1. American Educational Research Association, *Encyclopedia of Educational Research,* 3d ed. Chester W. Harris, ed. New York: The Macmillan Company, 1960.

2. Batchelder, Howard T., Maurice McGlasson, and Raleigh Schorling, *Student Teaching in Secondary Schools.* New York: McGraw-Hill Book Company, Inc., 1964, chap. 5.

3. Blount, Nathan S., and Herbert J. Klausmeier, *Teaching in the Secondary School,* 3d ed. New York: Harper & Row, Publishers, 1968, chap. 15.

4. Clark, Leonard H., and Irving S. Starr, *Secondary School Teaching Methods,* 2d ed. New York: The Macmillan Company, 1967, chap. 4.

5. Gnagey, William J., *The Psychology of Discipline in the Classroom.* New York: The Macmillan Company, 1968.

6. Hill, Paul L., *Solving Behavior Problems.* Dansville, N.Y.: F. A. Owen Publishing Company, 1965.

7. McCloskey, Elinor F., *Urban Disadvantaged Pupils: A Synthesis of 99 Research Reports.* Portland, Ore.: The Northwest Regional Educational Laboratory, February 1967.

8. Oliva, Peter F., "High School Discipline in American Society," *Bulletin of the National Association of Secondary-School Principals,* 40 (January 1956), 1–103.

9. Oliva, Peter F., *The Secondary School Today.* Cleveland: World Publishing Company, 1967, chap. 18.

10. Redl, Fritz, *When We Deal with Children.* New York: The Free Press, 1966, pp. 254–308.

11. Skinner, B. F., *The Technology of Teaching.* New York: Appleton-Century-Crofts, Inc., 1968, chap. 9. Division of Meredith Corporation.

PART FIVE / *Considering the Total School Program*

CHAPTER 15 | *The Secondary School Curriculum*

"Today . . . the mechanics of curriculum survival and its adaptation in our time are the most fascinating aspects of the whole educational problem." [1]

At no time in history has the curriculum maker been confronted with a greater challenge. He is faced with the paradox of attempting to maintain cultural stability and unity in a period of revolutionary change and at the same time attempting to develop a dynamic educational program to keep pace with the needs of a changing world.

"Tradition encourages us to cling to a curriculum which seems oddly impervious to the impact of contemporary epochal discoveries, to world-shaking events, and to inexorable and profound changes in our society." [2]

"At present, all over the world the schools are faced with the necessity of adjusting their programme to the drastic change around them. Yet all over the world, nations not only cling to outmoded educational programmes but also rationalize eagerly the justification for so doing." [3]

In more precise terms a psychologist has described the worldwide technological and sociological revolutions now taking place, alleged weaknesses of educational programs everywhere, and some proposed remedies:

In the period following World War II, the technological advances in space research, the continued Hot and Cold Wars, the population explosion, and the awakening and emergence of new nations converged upon the consciousness of the world's peoples in the form of increased demands for educated leaders and

---

[1] George Z. F. Bereday, Brian Holmes, and Joseph A. Lauwerys, Editors' Introduction, *The Secondary School Curriculum: 1958 Yearbook of Education*. London: Evans Brothers Limited, 1958, p. 25.

[2] Harold J. McNally, "What Shall We Teach—and How?" *The National Elementary Principal*, May 1957, p. 6.

[3] Bereday *et al.*, p. 25.

trained personnel. Automation had progressed to a point where formerly adequate levels of training were no longer of any social or economic value in industrially advanced countries. In one way or another, the world's difficulties were
traced to alleged weaknesses and flaws in educational systems. Invidious comparisons were made between one nation's educational system and another's. In
each case, the nation involved was engaged in educational soul-searching, looking for a solution to multiple problems in educational practices. Educators found
themselves in an awkward situation. On the one hand, they were being urged to
produce more highly trained citizens; on the other, they were being charged
with incompetence. The Johnnies and Ivans of the world could not read, write,
spell, calculate, or get to the moon first. Besides that, they were delinquents,
physically unfit and maladjusted. All these faults were, of course, the results of a
poor educational system. There were not enough teachers, according to some;
according to others, those teachers who were at their posts were incompletely
trained. [*Footnote:* An example of such an attack on teacher-training is the *Miseducation of American Teachers* by James D. Koerner, 1963.] Never before had
education come under so many severe criticisms and attacks. Along with the
attacks came proposals for remedies: centralized schools; teachers' aides; team
teaching; teaching by television; and, in the modern spirit of automation, teaching by machine.[4]

These statements suggest some of the challenges and problems involved in curriculum development in the years just ahead. It is imperative
for every teacher to be aware of the issues and problems at stake and to
become an intelligent and active participant in curriculum improvement.
By the very nature of his work the classroom teacher is in danger of
developing a microscopic view of the total school program and its impact
on contemporary life. Following daily routines, working with the same
group of students day after day, and teaching the same subjects year after
year may very well limit the vision of the teacher.

ORGANIZATION AND OFFERINGS OF THE SECONDARY SCHOOL

Secondary school organization in this country has developed along two
unique lines. First, the secondary school became part of a unitary or
"ladder" system, extending from the lowest grade of the elementary
school through the university. By way of contrast, the traditional type
of organization of European educational systems has been in terms of a
dual track, with one track for an academic (or socioeconomic) elite and
another for the masses. A second unique feature of the American secondary school is that it became a *comprehensive* school, one in which all boys
and girls are educated together, regardless of differences in ability, sex,

[4] From the *Psychology of Learning Applied to Teaching* by B. R. Bugelski, p. 3. Copyright © 1964, by the Bobbs-Merrill Company, Inc. Reprinted by permission of the
publishers.

religion, race (an ideal yet to be fully achieved), socioeconomic status, or occupational goals.

Prior to 1890, the secondary school was typically a four-year school that followed eight years of elementary schooling. Since 1900, various patterns of reorganization have been developing. A common pattern that has evolved has been the six-year elementary school, followed by a six-year high school (in smaller communities) or a three-year junior high school and a three-year senior high school. Today, at least in a number of states, this twelve-year program has been capped by a two-year junior or community college (grades thirteen and fourteen).

Curricular offerings consist of subjects studied in the classroom and the student activity or cocurricular program. The curriculum varies from school to school, with larger schools providing broader and more varied offerings. A comparatively new development may be gaining momentum: school organization based on a four-year primary school, a four-year middle school, and a four-year high school (back to the traditional school of grades nine through twelve).

The *classroom program* has been, and continues to be, organized primarily on the basis of separate, discrete subjects. The number of specific titles is extensive. However, subjects are usually classified under such categories as the following:

Language arts (English, speech, foreign languages)
Social studies (basically history and geography)
Mathematics
Science
Fine arts (art and music)
Practical arts (agriculture, industrial arts, homemaking, business education)
Health and physical education

Graduation requirements have been traditionally defined in terms of Carnegie units (one unit being equivalent to one period of 40 or more minutes a day of a five-day week for a school year, or 120 class hours in a subject). In a four-year high school, sixteen units have constituted normal requirements for graduation.

The *student activity or cocurricular program* consists of a number of athletic events, innumerable clubs, musical and dramatic activities, school publications, and student government. Values and problems associated with these programs are discussed later in this chapter.

THE CURRICULUM DEFINED

Traditionally, the *curriculum* has meant a course of study or the subjects that a student takes in school, with corresponding neglect of the objectives of education defined in terms of changes in student behavior.

Today, "the curriculum is defined as all the experiences that a learner has under the guidance of the school." [5] Philosophically, the broader definition has been widely accepted by professional educators in an attempt to unify the total program of the school. This is especially true with respect to an effort to coordinate more closely the organized class program with the student activity or extracurricular program. However, the union has been more theoretical than real, for in practice, as well as in common descriptions of the curriculum, a distinction is frequently made between organized class activities and the student activity program (1:360).

When the word "curriculum" is defined in such broad terms, further clarification of definition becomes necessary. To some persons, the organized classroom phase of the curriculum means merely a body of content. But curriculum involves not only *what* is taught but *how* it is taught as well, for the two are inseparable. However, both the *what* and the *how* are only means to an end—the improved behavior of the learner.

ASPECTS OF THE CURRICULUM

Not only is the curriculum divided into two different phases, the organized class program and student activities; the organized class program is further subdivided into two categories, *general education* and *special education*. The first is designed to educate for unity; the second, to educate for diversity. General education provides the learning experiences needed by all students to become effective citizens. Special education is designed to provide for the unique interests, needs, and abilities of each student individually.

In terms of subjects or courses listed in the course of study or curriculum guide of a school, general education consists of the required subjects whereas special education includes the electives.

When the curriculum maker sets up these two categories of the curriculum, he is cautioned to avoid some faulty generalizations about them. First of all, either general education or special education is more than a subject or a series of subjects. Furthermore, neither is a predetermined, fixed body of content. Finally, a sharp line of demarcation cannot always be drawn between general or special education. For example, sometimes the best vocational education (a function of special education) is that which aids students in learning how to cooperate with others (a function of general education).

PROBLEMS IN GENERAL EDUCATION

It should be noted at this point that curriculum makers encounter in the realm of general education a persistent problem that is becoming more acute: *deciding what all students need to know.* Perhaps there was a time

[5] Nolan C. Kearney and Walter W. Cook, "Curriculum," *Encyclopedia of Educational Research,* 3d ed. New York: The Macmillan Company, 1960, p. 358.

when it was relatively simple to determine "what knowledge is of most worth," but that time is obviously gone forever, especially with the accelerating expansion of knowledge and the necessity to unlearn old "facts" because of new discoveries. The problem is compounded by the traditional organization of the secondary school curriculum in terms of discrete subjects or disciplines (which are becoming even more discrete with the current stress on the unique structure of each subject). Adding to the confusion is the fact that experts in the various disciplines are unable to agree among themselves on either the structure or the content of their subjects. Even more critical, from the standpoint of the classroom teacher, is a continuous proliferation of courses or the constant addition of new units within existing courses until the curriculum reaches a saturation point in terms of content to be covered.

What is the teacher to do in a situation where coverage of content becomes an increasing source of frustration? One possibility is for the teacher to develop a sound *philosophy* of general education that can function under any type of curricular organization, regardless of its inflexibility or a constant state of flux. Such a philosophy of general education, which seems to have considerable merit, has been proposed by Phenix under six "realms of meaning," briefly outlined as follows:

Six (6) Realms of Meaning:
(1) *Symbolics:* language, mathematics, and such "nondiscursive forms" as gesture, rituals, etc. These are the "instruments for the expression and communication of any meanings whatsoever."
(2) *Empirics:* "sciences of the physical world, of living things, and of man." They are based "upon observation and experimentation in the world of matter, life, mind, and society." (Examples: physical sciences, biology, psychology, and social sciences.)
(3) *Esthetics:* the various arts, such as music, visual arts, arts of movement, and literature.
(4) *Synoetics:* embraces "personal knowledge" or "meditative thought." It signifies "relational insights" or "direct awareness." Such knowledge is "concrete, direct, and existential."
(5) *Ethics:* "includes moral meanings that express obligation. . . . Morality has to do with personal conduct that is based on free, responsible, deliberate decision."
(6) *Synoptics:* "refers to meanings that are comprehensively integrative. It includes history, religion, and philosophy." [6]

The *symbolics* "placed at one end of the spectrum of meanings, encompass the entire range of meanings because they are the necessary means of expressing all meanings whatever." The *synoptics,* "placed at the other

---

[6] From *Realms of Meaning* by Philip H. Phenix, copyrighted 1964, pp. 6–7, by McGraw-Hill Book Company. Used by permission of McGraw-Hill Book Company. The reader is urged to secure the book for an elaboration on the "realms of meaning" and for the application to different subjects or disciplines.

end of the spectrum, also gather up the entire range of meanings by virtue of their integrative character." [7] "Every student at every stage of his learning should receive some instruction in all six of the realms of meaning." [8]

Another problem in general education relates to differences in philosophical viewpoint. Briefly stated, there are two philosophical camps: those who subscribe to *liberal* education and those who champion *general* education. Although debate over the two positions may occur more often in higher education, secondary school teachers often embrace one or the other points of view, perhaps sometimes unconsciously. Witness the relative values attributed to academic subjects in comparison with so-called practical subjects. Just what the specific points of difference are has been very well summarized by Morse as follows:

Liberal education is considered to be subject-centered, with a fairly fixed body of content material, logically organized. Its goal is also the stimulation of reflective thinking, with less emphasis on behavior, and it draws its clientele from the intellectual elite. It implies a concentration in depth with frequently a more intensive cultivation of one or two special fields of knowledge. It clings closely to tradition in the kinds of learnings it sanctions.

General education, on the other hand, is more concerned with the learner than with the content, which may be organized or reshuffled with less regard to traditional fields. Its goals are individual development in its various aspects, and it places emphasis upon behavior and social usefulness as well as upon intellectual development as an outcome of learning. It is a manifestation of the democratic spirit in higher education, for it admits a wider scope of abilities and a broader clientele. In its fullest development it is decidely not merely "old wine in new bottles." [9]

BACKGROUNDS OF AMERICAN SECONDARY EDUCATION

The story of American education is the story of a "search for freedom." In the process of development of a unique system of education, the schools have been faced with certain persistent problems. Attempts to solve those problems in an evolving democracy have made the schools what they are today. A few of these problems follow: Shall education be provided for all or for an elite only? Is a democratic school system served best by local control or by a centralized, state authority? Shall control and support of education be public or private? Shall boys and

[7] Phenix, p. 8.
[8] Phenix, p. 9.
[9] From an article, "Liberal and General Education: A Problem of Differentiation," by Horace T. Morse in the April 15, 1962, issue of the *AHE College and University Bulletin*. Used by permission of the Association for Higher Education.

girls be educated in a school common to all or shall they be segregated on the basis of sex, race, religion, social class, or intellect? Shall colleges and secondary schools offer academic or intellectual studies only or shall practical subjects be included as well in the curriculum? [10]

A superficial analysis of these questions might lead one to believe that they have already been satisfactorily answered. However, a further study of current issues and trends, to be discussed later in this chapter, results in a more sound conclusion: that some educational battles have to be fought and won by each succeeding generation.

THE LATIN GRAMMAR SCHOOL

The first type of secondary school established in America was the Latin Grammar School, founded in Boston, presumably in 1635. The curriculum was classical and traditional, patterned after the curricula of European schools. Admission was selective, limited to boys of high intellectual ability. The primary purpose was to provide leadership needed by the church and state. In 1647, a Massachusetts law required every "town" (a geographical area of about 20 to 40 square miles) of 100 or more householders to establish a grammar school. Failure to do so resulted in the assessment of a fine, but many towns paid the fine rather than maintain the schools.[11]

The chief contribution of the Latin Grammar School was the establishment of the college-preparatory function of the secondary school.

THE ACADEMY

With the rise of a strong middle class of large landowners and merchant-capitalists, the need for a new type of school became evident. An examination of the advertisements in the newspapers of Boston during the first half of the eighteenth century indicates that the practical educational needs of boys, as well as girls, of this class were being met by private teachers.[12] Consequently, when the first academy was established in Philadelphia by Benjamin Franklin at the middle of the eighteenth century, the foundations of a practical curriculum had already been laid.

Product of an emerging industrial society, flexible in its policies and practices, and offering a great variety of subjects, the academy soon became a popular school. Its legacy for secondary education was to introduce practical courses into the curriculum, to admit girls to secondary education, and to free the schools from sectarian control. It had one serious limitation, however: it was not free. Because the academy had to

[10] R. Freeman Butts, "Search for Freedom—the Story of American Education," *NEA Journal*, 49 (March 1960), 33–48.
[11] Newton Edwards and Herman G. Richey, *The School in the American Social Order*, 2d ed. Boston: Houghton Mifflin Company, 1963, pp. 41, 47–62, 90–96.
[12] Edwards and Richey, pp. 77–81, 107–111, 162–163, 174–175.

depend upon tuition for partial support, many youths could not afford to attend it.

THE HIGH SCHOOL

In 1821, the first high school was established in Boston. Because the curriculum was similar to that of the academy, it was probably an attempt to provide for more *public* support and control of education to meet the needs of boys who intended "to become merchants and mechanics." Later, high schools were established for girls, or "female departments" were added to existing schools. At that time, it was recognized that both the academy and the high school had a dual function: to prepare for life and to prepare for college.

SINCE 1890

Many educational historians classify the period since 1890 as *a period of reorganization.* The Committee of Ten of 1893 recommended "English, ancient and modern foreign languages, mathematics, natural science, history, and geography" as appropriate subjects for study by all students, ignoring differences in interests, abilities, and vocational goals. A short time later, other committees succeeded in defining a high school education in quantitative terms of units of credit. Through the activities of such committees, the high school curriculum became more or less standardized until about 1930.[13]

Prior to 1918, the primary function of the high school was regarded as preparation for college. For those students who did not plan to go to college, training of the mind provided sufficient justification for pursuit of an academic curriculum. "Objectives (for adult living, self-preservation, and so on) were neglected or regarded as secondary during the time when faculty psychology and mental discipline held sway." [14]

In 1918, the Commission on the Reorganization of Secondary Education defined the aims of the high school in terms of seven personal-social goals:

1. Good health
2. Command of fundamental processes
3. Worthy home membership
4. Vocational efficiency
5. Civic efficiency
6. Worthy use of leisure
7. Ethical character [15]

[13] Edwards and Richey, pp. 547–552.
[14] Kearney and Cook, p. 358.
[15] Department of the Interior, Bureau of Education, *Cardinal Principles of Secondary Education.* A Report of the Commission on the Reorganization of Secondary Education, Appointed by the National Education Association. Washington, D.C.: Government Printing Office, 1918, pp. 10–11.

Since 1918, educational objectives have been stated by various commissions, most of them representing refinements or elaborations of these "seven cardinal principles." [16]

According to Ralph Tyler, there is a

shift in school objectives toward a more discriminating selection, toward the kinds of learning which involve intellectual skills, which require sequential experiences to reach the necessary level of competence, which involve concepts and principles that are not apparent on the surface and for this reason are not likely to be learned through the guidance of laymen.[17]

FACTORS AND FORCES IN CURRICULUM DEVELOPMENT

What are some of the factors and forces that have affected, and continue to affect, the curriculum of the secondary school?

HISTORICAL TRADITIONS

The college-preparatory function of the secondary school, a direct legacy of the Boston Latin Grammar School, still exerts a strong influence on the curriculum of the high school. Undue preoccupation with an academic tradition can seriously hamper the efforts of the school to meet the needs of all boys and girls and to deal with the persistent problems of a dynamic society.

RESEARCH

Various studies—such as studies of needs, of individual differences, of group processes, of adolescent growth and development, and of "the social structure of our society"—have had an important bearing on curriculum development.[18]

SOCIAL AND EDUCATIONAL PHILOSOPHY

Philosophical beliefs have a pervasive influence on curriculum change. For example, many of the recurring "battles" in education have been fought over a single principle: *equality of educational opportunity*. No other country in the world has attempted to provide so much education for so many for so long a period of years. To provide education on such

[16] For a review of the changes that have taken place in objectives and learning activities during the first half of this century, see the condensation of Ralph Tyler's article in Chapter 4.

[17] Ralph W. Tyler, "The Curriculum—Then and Now," *Proceedings, 1956 Invitational Conference on Testing Problems*. Princeton, N.J.: Educational Testing Service, 1956, pp. 79–94. Also published by the American Council on Education in *Testing Problems in Perspective*, 1966.

[18] Kearney and Cook, pp. 361–362.

a massive scale has created a number of complexities: to provide mass education and still maintain quality, to educate for national unity and encourage diversity, to meet the needs of all when so many differ in so many ways. Of special concern is the problem of meeting the educational needs of disadvantaged youth in depressed rural areas and in the slums and ghettos of large cities.

SPECIAL INTEREST GROUPS

Many agencies and special-interest groups exert pressure on the schools. State and local boards of education, state departments of education, legislatures, and accrediting agencies are official groups that set up minimum standards for school programs. A great many special-interest groups— such as patriotic groups, business, labor, political, and religious organizations—influence curricula through organized programs, publicity campaigns, and lobbying.

BUSINESS AND INDUSTRY

Education has become big business. In the words of Francis Keppel, president of the General Learning Corporation, "Knocking at the door of the little red school house is the giant fist of American business—big business . . . ." [19] The reference pertains specifically to recent mergers of electronic corporations—the "hardware" people (for example, IBM, Xerox, RCA, Raytheon) with publishing houses, the "software" people (such as Random House, *Reader's Digest*, Science Research Associates, and *Newsweek*)—to revolutionize the production of educational materials and equipment. Closely related to this development is the advent of computer-assisted instruction (CAI). Patrick Suppes, a pioneer in the field, believes that CAI will greatly modify the roles of teachers, offering them greater opportunity to work with students individually.[20] Some foresee eventually a total "systems" approach or an " 'economic' approach to education in the best sense of the word" that will play a vital role in administration, research, multimedia "libraries," and more effective learning.[21]

THE FEDERAL GOVERNMENT

The role of the federal government in education has expanded significantly in recent years, both in terms of legislation affecting the schools and in expenditures. In response to Soviet success in launching Sputnik, the National Defense Education Act (NDEA) was passed in 1958 to

[19] Francis Keppel, "Interest in Education," *Phi Delta Kappan,* 48 (January 1967), 187.
[20] Patrick Suppes, "The Teacher and Computer-Assisted Instruction," *NEA Journal,* 56 (February 1967), 15–17.
[21] C. H. Springer, "The Systems Approach," *Saturday Review,* 50 (January 1967), 56, 58.

strengthen programs in science and mathematics by generous grants of federal money through the National Science Foundation (NSF).[22] In 1964, the NDEA was extended to include programs for teachers of "English, reading, history, and geography," teachers of "disadvantaged youth, librarians, and educational media specialists." [23]

Following President Johnson's proposals for education to the 89th Congress in January 1965, the House and Senate expedited the passage of the Elementary and Secondary Education Act. Five educational objectives were encompassed by the bill: assistance to *all* children of low-income families; aid to libraries (in both public and private institutions); provision for "model schools, pilot programs, and community centers"; "educational research and training"; and strengthening of state departments of education.[24]

This legislation is indicative of increasing participation in education by the federal government. It is predicted that such involvement is destined to increase. On two counts proponents of federal aid to education criticize the manner in which such aid is distributed: parochial schools are also sharing in some of the benefits, and such aid is allocated to the states on a categorical rather than on a general basis.

STATE LEGISLATURES

State legislatures may actively engage in making changes in the curriculum, either directly or indirectly. They may require all students at specific grade levels to enroll in certain subjects (for example, a foreign language) and may also specify how subjects are to be taught (for example, that English and social studies must be taught as separate subjects in junior high school). Legislatures may mandate statewide testing programs. They may set up detailed, inflexible teacher certification requirements. These are but a few of the *professional* functions sometimes assumed by unqualified legislators.

THE TEACHING PROFESSION

The profession itself, through its leaders (such as Horace Mann and John Dewey) and its professional organizations, such as the National Education Association, has continuously worked for curriculum improvement.

SUBJECT SPECIALISTS

The present curriculum reform movement, which began in the early 1950s, is national in scope, but is neither nationally nor federally controlled. It has received much of its impetus from academic scholars,

[22] Sidney W. Tiedt, *The Role of the Federal Government in Education.* New York: Oxford University Press, 1966, p. 29.
[23] Tiedt, p. 155.
[24] Tiedt, pp. 189–194.

people outside local and state school systems, whose financial support comes mostly from large foundations and federal agencies. The nature of the reforms and some problems related to them are discussed later in this chapter.

TEXTBOOK AUTHORS AND TEST MAKERS

Publishers of instructional materials have more influence on curriculum development than is sometimes realized. The textbook has even been referred to as the child's "other teacher."

The widespread use of standardized tests has a definite impact on curriculum emphasis. Some educators are apprehensive about the freezing of the curriculum by test makers, especially in states where a statewide testing program has been made mandatory. A national testing program, set up by the Carnegie Corporation and the U.S. Office of Education and labeled "National Assessment," has aroused considerable controversy. Proponents of the program stress the need to understand the "strengths and weaknesses of the American educational system." They maintain that the nature of the sampling process will make impossible the comparison of individual pupils, teachers, or schools with one another. Under the program, an attempt is being made to get a *sampling* of educational achievement at "four age levels—nine, thirteen, seventeen, and adult in four geographic regions—Northeast, South, Midwest, and Far West." Also, "individuals selected will be drawn from urban, suburban, and rural areas and from two socioeconomic levels in each community." [25] Opponents of National Assessment fear that this will be the first step toward a national testing program which would standardize the curriculum and subject students to an undesirable, competitive examination system somewhat like those in a number of European countries.

COMMUNITY INFLUENCES

Because the American school system is decentralized, with considerable control residing with local boards of education, the community is one of the most important factors in shaping the school program of a given locality. The character of the people—their occupations, educational level, and economic status—has a direct bearing on the type and quality of schools provided in the area.

THE TEACHER

In the final analysis, the classroom teacher is the most important factor in curriculum improvement. In fact, the sum total of the educational experiences boys and girls have under their teachers *is* the curriculum. Be-

[25] Paul Woodring, Editorial, "National Assessment," *Saturday Review*, 49 (September 16, 1966), 71–72. Copyright Saturday Review, Inc., 1966.

cause tradition is such a strong agent in curriculum development, lasting changes are likely to occur only on a piecemeal basis. "Among the factors responsible for such piecemeal but relentless change the teachers may be singled out as the most obvious agents." [26] Wallen and Travers cite evidence that educational reformers (or administrators) who institute curricular reforms which require significant changes in teacher behavior may expect very little change in such behavior—not because of lack of cooperation but because of a psychological factor: ". . . behavior patterns which are [as] deeply ingrained as those of teachers with many years of teaching experience cannot be changed overnight. . . ." [27]

IMPROVEMENT OF THE CURRICULUM

The approach to curriculum development today is different from what it was a generation ago. Formerly the entire staff of a school system, under the leadership of administrators and curriculum consultants, was organized into committees to develop goals, study problems, organize courses of study, and, after a year or two of intensive work and study, produce the school program to be used for the next few years. Curriculum revision is now a continuous, evolutionary process. Through staff meetings, summer workshops, experimentation and research, permanent curriculum committees (with rotating membership), interschool visits, supervisory activities, and other in-service programs, the total faculty is involved in continuous curriculum revision.

School administrators have learned that no change takes place in the curriculum unless there is a change in teachers. Teachers must persuade themselves of the need for a change and then take an active part in bringing it about.

Because teacher involvement is so important, curriculum improvement depends upon the individual school's approach to experimentation. If, for example, a school system decides to explore the possibilities of team teaching, a building principal and his staff are likely to conduct the experiment, not the system as a whole.

THE 1950s—A DECADE OF CONCERN

During the 1950s, countless proposals and counterproposals were made for improvement of the school program. Even the most superficial examination of the history of education reveals that the schools have always had their critics. However, probably in no other period of American history

[26] Bereday *et al.*, p. 26.
[27] Norman E. Wallen and Robert M. W. Travers, "Analysis and Investigation of Teaching Methods," *Handbook of Research on Teaching*, N. L. Gage, ed. A Project of the American Educational Research Association. Chicago: Rand McNally & Company, 1963.

has criticism of public education reached such volume and intensity as it did during the 1950s. Some of the more significant criticisms will be analyzed in this chapter.

When the National Citizens Council for Better Schools celebrated its tenth anniversary in a special issue of *Better Schools,* a caption at the top of the front page referred to the period of 1949 to 1959 as a "Decade of Concern." The first wave of criticism came just after World War II, and a second wave began about 1953, became more violent in the middle of the decade and culminated in the organization of such groups as the Council for Basic Education. As to why the defense of public education in newspapers and periodicals seldom has equal space with that of the criticisms, the editor of *Better Schools* expressed the belief that "any sharp attack upon a public institution is news" whereas "a reply that 'things aren't really as bad as the critics say' is not news."

Losing Sight of the Major Purpose

That the schools fail to develop the intellect has been, and continues to be, one of the most persistent criticisms of public education. In fact, many other criticisms are related directly to this one.

The supporters of intellectualism have charged that the schools have deteriorated because of their emphasis on "life adjustment education," often implying that such education stresses conformity and is devoid of intellectual content. Both implications are false and misleading. "Life adjustment education" began as a movement to meet the needs of boys and girls who were not being prepared "for either a skilled occupation or higher education." During the years 1950 to 1953, the movement spread to twenty-nine states. Special emphasis was placed on the attainment of three objectives: improvement in family life, vocational preparation, and citizenship.[28]

The Superiority of European Education

The criticism that American education is inferior to that of Europe is closely related to the charge that American schools are anti-intellectual in character.

When asked to compare the product of the English secondary school with his American high school counterpart, Sir Geoffrey Crowther, chairman of the Central Advisory Council for Education in England, said, "He has been taught different things, by different methods, with a different purpose in view, in a different sort of school. There is no fair basis for comparison." [29]

"Each nation, out of its own historical, social, and cultural background,

[28] Marvin D. Alcorn and James M. Linley, eds., *Issues in Curriculum Development: A Book of Readings.* New York: Harcourt, Brace & World, Inc., 1959, pp. 238–239.
[29] Sir Geoffrey Crowther, "English and American Education," *The Atlantic Monthly,* 205 (April 1960), 42.

attempts to find answers which will solve its problems in its own way. The development of a national system of education, like that of all other institutions, is limited and determined by such background factors in the life of the nation." [30]

After contrasting American schools with those of France, André Maurois concludes, "It would be madness to ask either nation to act or teach according to the traditions of the other." [31]

These statements illustrate that one cannot compare the incomparable. Admirers of European education today, like the comparative educators of the early nineteenth century, seem unaware of the fact "that the educational system of one country cannot be transplanted into the soil of another." [32]

There are differences between the goals and practices of American and European education that cannot be easily reconciled. Leading Swedish educators, Husén and Svensson, point out that "the pattern of schools that prevails in western Europe must be characterized as selective and dual. . . . The emotional and social consequences of this selection will not be discussed here. Suffice it to say that the arrangement causes much anxiety and frustration." [33]

European secondary schools provide an academic, classical curriculum for an intellectual elite; American high schools provide both an academic and a practical curriculum for all youth. European schools are often segregated on such bases as sex, religion, intellect, or social class; the typical American high school is a *comprehensive* school, enrolling all boys and girls on a nonsegregated basis. European schools stress early occupational choice (about ages 10 to 12 years); American schools defer specialization and choice of an occupation.

At this point, it should be pointed out that those who compare American schools unfavorably with those of Europe are confronted with an interesting paradox.

It is one of the ironies of our times that in the decade of the Fifties, while domestic critics were castigating American schools for "anti-intellectualism" and comparing them unfavorably with those of Europe, the liberal democracies were abandoning their rigid caste system, with its emphasis on advanced education for the elite only, and beginning to adopt the kind of free, universal, public, unitary comprehensive school we take so much for granted.[34]

[30] John Francis Cramer and George Stephenson Browne, *Contemporary Education.* New York: Harcourt, Brace & World, Inc., 1956, p. 3.
[31] André Maurois, "A Frenchman Appraises U. S. Schools," Education Supplement of *Saturday Review,* 44 (April 1961), 74. Copyright Saturday Review, Inc., 1961.
[32] George F. Kneller, "Comparative Education," *Encyclopedia of Educational Research,* 3d ed., Chester W. Harris, ed. New York: The Macmillan Co., 1960, 319.
[33] Thorsten Husén and Nils-Eric Svensson, "Pedagogic Milieu and Development of Intellectual Skills," *School Review,* 68 (Spring 1960), 37.
[34] Stanley Elam, Editorial, *Phi Delta Kappan,* 43 (November 1961), 49.

In conclusion, it should be said that a genuine study of comparative education is valuable for both American and European educators who may learn from one another without disparaging their respective school systems in the process.

Control of the Schools by Educators

Some critics base the blame for all shortcomings of American education, either real or imaginary, upon the charge that educators (or "educationists") have taken control of the schools from the people. Because the American school system is controlled by state legislatures and by state and local boards of education, elected by the people, this charge becomes almost an absurdity. Add to this the fact that, unlike other professions, "the agencies controlling admission to teaching consist almost exclusively of members outside the profession." [35] In addition to these official agencies many other lay groups have influenced policies in public education. For example, citizens' advisory committees numbered "over 12,000 groups in 1957." [36]

Two other criticisms—that *the schools lack discipline* and that *teachers are not prepared in their subjects because they have to take too many education courses*—are discussed elsewhere in this text.

THE 1960s—A CONSERVATIVE REVOLUTION

The criticisms of the 1950s eventually subsided in volume and intensity, with words being replaced by action. In 1956, in analyzing the sources of educational aims, Tyler noted that "primary attention is currently given to the opinions of subject specialists" [37] (a reversion to the period between 1900 and 1918). In the recommendation of Conant, that "students should be grouped according to ability, subject by subject," mastery of the subject as a major goal of education is implied.[38] A number of limitations of Conant's reports have been indicated, including his failure to give "the nature of the learner and the learning process . . . the consideration they probably deserve." [39]

By the middle 1960s, Roberts reported on a few projects and research studies that reflected such new and important emphases as the following: "the growing concern for grounding curriculum development and experi-

[35] Research Division, NEA, "Ten Criticisms of Public Education," *Research Bulletin,* 35 (December 1957), 135.
[36] Research Division, NEA, 1957, p. 137.
[37] Tyler, p. 83.
[38] James B. Conant, *The American High School Today.* New York: McGraw-Hill Book Company, Inc., 1959, p. 49.
[39] American Educational Research Association, "Curriculum Planning and Development," *Review of Educational Research,* 30 (June 1960), 234.

mentation in theory from the behavioral sciences, concern with structure of the discipline and of cognitive styles of learning as a means for directing curriculum development, a need for sequencing learning from kindergarten through twelfth grade, a need for better articulation from level to level, and a need for the continued retraining of teachers in the several curriculum areas." [40] On the other hand, Roberts also cited a number of reports on so-called curriculum innovations that reflected the following limitations: they have tended "to cram information into pupils," to move down "topics traditionally taught in the later grades," to focus on "single subjects—planned generally from the top down," to provide for "poor evaluation techniques, and experiments that were really not experimental . . . ," and to neglect "a fresh look at curriculum theory." [41]

CONSERVATIVE CURRICULUM PROPOSALS

Conservative proposals for changes in the American public schools have come from various sources. Some proposals follow:

That a statewide system of examinations be adopted

That preparation for teaching include more academic subjects and fewer courses in education and nonacademic subjects

That all students follow the same academic course of study

That the schools assign more homework, be stricter, and lengthen the school day, week, and year

That the departmentalized organization of the high school be extended into the elementary school

That academic subjects be taught at earlier levels, for instance, teaching algebra in the eighth grade and requiring foreign language in the sixth or seventh grade

That the junior high school be abolished and the "eight–four" type of organization be reinstated

That a national curriculum commission be established

That organization of subjects into broad fields (such as social science or general science) be abandoned in favor of such discrete subjects as English, history, or chemistry

That modern methods be abandoned in favor of older methods which purportedly produced better results: by using the phonics approach to reading and eliminating the "readiness" concept in reading and arithmetic

That education for social development or "life adjustment education" be eliminated from the school program

[40] Julian Roberts, "Curriculum Development and Experimentation," *Review of Educational Research*, 36 (June 1966), 359. Copyright © 1966 by the American Educational Research Association, a department of the National Education Association.
[41] Roberts, p. 353.

Each proposal represents one or more of three positions on curriculum development: a return to the past, an emphasis on intellectualism, and an adoption of European patterns of education.

During an era when criticisms of education may be particularly rife, a new teacher may be overwhelmed by what he reads and hears. In order to place these criticisms in proper perspective, the beginning teacher needs to remember several things. First of all, criticisms are not new: people have always complained about their schools. Second, while a few critics appear to be dishonest, most are probably sincere. Some are merely expressing genuine differences of opinion, a right they have in a democracy. Others, especially parents, may register dissatisfaction because of misinformation about what the schools are doing. Finally, a school in which the people have a genuine interest and concern is more fortunate than one toward which the public has an attitude of apathy.

CONCLUSIONS CONCERNING THE CONSERVATIVE REVOLUTION

Although a number of these conservative developments may be disturbing to professional educators, they are not the chief cause of concern. The major issue is *the way in which curriculum change is taking place.* Dangerous precedents are being set.

In some cases lay advisory groups, some self-appointed and others appointed by boards of education and state legislatures, are making policy recommendations related to the curriculum without sufficient consultation with professionally qualified people. Even more disturbing is the fact that some of these groups represent minority pressure groups and not the majority of the people.

It is recognized that through its elected representatives society has a right by majority vote, based on investigation of *all* the relevant facts, to make decisions about the kind of schools that are desired and needed. It should also be recognized that teachers and other educators have the right and responsibility to provide authoritative information and opinions concerning policies they must eventually put into effect. However, participation in policy making does not give professional people alone the right to dictate educational policy. That would also be a form of anarchy.

The viewpoint of the authors is very well summarized in the minority opinions of four of the twenty-seven members of a citizens' advisory commission, chosen by a joint committee of the California legislature to study the public education system. Their statement, which disagreed with the final report, reads as follows:

The undersigned disagree with the recommendations for mandatory state testing and enactment of curricular requirements by the legislature. Mandatory state testing encourages uniformity and an emphasis on educational purposes that can be measured by objective tests, and it does not provide for the wide range of differences between and within local school systems. Mandatory state testing can inhibit creativity and individual incentive and be a hindrance to the development of an educational program of high quality. A school curriculum shaped by legislative action is likely to be too rigid to utilize effectively advances in knowledge and to lack comprehensiveness and balance. Decisions as to what is taught in the schools are of vital importance. They should be made only after the most careful consideration and the utilization of the best talents available, particularly those of classroom teachers. The school curriculum should be flexible enough to meet local and individual needs and encourage continual efforts for improvement.[42]

ISSUES IN CURRICULUM DEVELOPMENT

From this discussion of criticisms of the schools and the conservative currents in education, a few critical issues in curriculum development should become obvious.

EDUCATION FOR ALL VERSUS EDUCATION OF AN ELITE

If there is one educational principle to which the citizens of this country are committed, it is this: All youth of secondary school age are entitled to *equal educational opportunity*. As this nation has developed, the people have rejected aristocracy in any form, whether it be of birth, religion, government, or intellect. Yet there are strong, insistent voices today that would create an intellectual aristocracy in the public school system. That a large number of youths in secondary school today would fail to profit from a strictly academic program is no longer debatable.

The imposition of an academic program on all boys and girls in high school would leave the school but one of two unacceptable alternatives: to fail a large number of students or to dilute the program until it would lose its value. The general public would reject the first alternative; the academic scholars, the second. Some who reluctantly admit that a large segment of the student population is lacking in both motivation and aptitude to succeed in a program that is exclusively academic suggest a third alternative: enroll such students in nonacademic courses but clearly label such courses as being inferior to academic subjects. As long as any subject can be justifiably retained in the curriculum and as long as any student is required to remain in school, *no subject should be labeled as a second-rate subject and no student should be classified as a second-class citizen*.

Related to this issue of an educational program to meet the needs of all students is the concern for *quality* in education. As a subtitle to his book *Excellence*, John Gardner, then president of the Carnegie Foundation, raises the question: "Can We Be Equal and Excellent Too?" His main thesis is that excellence is required in every line of human endeavor. Gardner condemns American confusion of values, which defines "success

---

[42] Report of the Joint Interim Committee on the Public Education System published by the senate of the state of California, 1961, p. 63.

in terms of high personal attainment," with college attendance "virtually a prerequisite of high attainment." He then climaxes his indictment with this conclusion: *"Human dignity and worth should be assessed only in terms of those qualities of mind and spirit that are within the reach of every human being"* (7:81).

BALANCE IN THE CURRICULUM

As the cold war accelerated, with its emphasis on scientific development for military survival, there was growing concern about the maintenance of balance in the curriculum. C. P. Snow, British scientist and novelist, is convinced that "western society is increasingly being split into two polar groups—literary intellectuals and scientists." [43]

Three areas of imbalance have been identified by Goodlad:

First, program development in the social sciences, humanities (especially the arts), health, and physical education . . . does not compare in intensity or accomplishment with what has already transpired in mathematics, physics, chemistry, and biology; [second] many subjects that could be part of the curriculum are not included [for example, sociology, economics, political science, and psychology in the social science area]; [and third] the piecemeal school curriculum produced by adopting several programs that have been prepared independently of each other [8:105–106].

The 1964 extension of NDEA was a partial attempt to correct the first area of imbalance cited above.

Attacking the root of the problem, Alexander and Michael stress the need "to find a content, possibly far removed from the time-honored disciplines, which makes more of a dent on the child who comes to school disinterested and unmotivated in subjects he perceives as frozen in a way of life that all too frequently is not for him." [44]

Achievement of balance in the curriculum becomes even more difficult in a period of national crisis. By appeals to fear and insecurity, alarmists can exert effective pressure for the hasty adoption of ill-advised programs, changes that are adopted without sufficient study and experimentation.

Another problem is maintaining balance between academic subjects and practical courses. As has already been suggested, this has been persistent in the history of education and is especially acute at this time.

Other problems of balance in the curriculum are:

Maintaining balance between the needs of the learner and the needs of society

[43] C. P. Snow, *The Two Cultures and the Scientific Revolution.* New York: Cambridge University Press, 1961, p. 4.
[44] William M. Alexander and Lloyd S. Michael, "Current Curriculum Developments: Problems and Prospects," in *New Curriculum Developments,* Glenys G. Unruh, ed. Washington, D.C.: Association for Supervision and Curriculum Development, 1965, p. 101.

Maintaining balance between education for unity and for diversity

Maintaining balance between education for cultural stability and education for social change

Maintaining balance in participation in curriculum change, so that all who have a contribution to make are included

Maintaining balance in achievement of the different purposes of education [45]

WHO SHALL BUILD THE CURRICULUM?

A major issue in the 1960s is whether or not curriculum change will be effected by all who have a contribution to make or by vested interests or pressure groups.

As has already been indicated, there is evidence of an increasing tendency on the part of lay boards of education and state legislatures to accept the advice of laymen, sometimes representing vested interests, in such professional matters as qualifications of teachers, curriculum content and organization, and methods of teaching. When experts are called in, quite often only those qualified in subject matter are consulted. As a result, the needs of society and the needs of the learner may be ignored.

Strangely enough, classroom teachers, who are most responsible for implementation of the curriculum, seem to be the last group to be consulted. As teachers have become better qualified professionally, prescriptive courses of study have been gradually superseded by curriculum guides that have allowed teachers much more freedom of action.

There is a movement in some parts of the country to treat teachers as hirelings rather than as professionally educated people. Sometimes they are singled out as a special group to take loyalty oaths. Self-appointed censors tell them what textbooks they may or may not use. Legislative restrictions go so far as to indicate the *what, when, how,* and *why* of teaching. Statewide testing programs may constitute a further threat to teacher initiative and creativity in curriculum development. An enlightened use of testing can, of course, result in the maintenance of high standards of achievement. On the other hand, an unintelligent and unprofessional use of tests, such as making invidious comparisons between individual school districts or even between teachers, can result in curriculum stagnation. If high test scores alone become the status symbols for a good school or a good teacher, then the test makers may well be the curriculum makers of the future.

NEW DEVELOPMENTS IN THE CURRICULUM

Although the public schools have been subjected to a barrage of criticisms during the last fifteen years or more and many proposals for change have

---

[45] Association for Supervision and Curriculum Development, "Balance in the Curriculum," *1961 Yearbook*. Washington, D.C.: The National Education Association, 1961.

been extremely conservative if not reactionary, the schools have continued to make progress toward curriculum improvement.

EFFECTS OF CRITICISM ON THE CURRICULUM

Criticism may have a good or bad effect on curriculum development. Criticism that is severe and persistent, resulting in withdrawal of public support, can stifle new developments and impede progress. On the other hand, continuous, critical evaluation of the school program destroys complacency and encourages school administrators and their staffs to evaluate their curricula continuously and to make needed improvements.

Some evidences of the overall effects of criticism on educational institutions may be deduced from the experience of the junior high school. For over a decade, the junior high school has been subjected to severe criticism. Despite proposals to abolish it and to return to the "eight–four" type of organization, "the junior high school is found in 53 percent of the urban school systems." Also during the period from 1948–1949 to 1958–1959, "junior high schools were established for the first time by 15.1 percent of the school districts, and were eliminated by 1.9 percent." [46]

DEVELOPMENTS IN TEACHING METHODS

During the last decade or so, improvements in teaching methods seem to be progressing toward more *effective mass instruction* and toward more provision for *self-instruction*. The first has been aided by developments in educational television (ETV); the second, by the use of programmed learning materials (via teaching machines and scrambled textbooks). Computer-assisted instruction (CAI) may be even more of a breakthrough in the individualization of instruction. Both mass instruction and self-instruction are featured in *team teaching*. All of these developments are discussed elsewhere; hence they will receive no further consideration here.

DEVELOPMENTS IN CURRICULUM CONTENT

International tensions, a vast store of knowledge constantly increasing and changing, and recent technological advances have accelerated developments in the content of certain subjects.

Reforms now taking place in the curriculum spring from discrete subjects or disciplines, with emphasis placed on the "structure" and "methods of inquiry" peculiar to each. Major stress is placed on an understanding of basic concepts or principles rather than on the acquisition of specific facts or information. "At the same time, the new curriculum is a response to insights recently gained into human behavior and its development. Young people, even the very young, it is now realized, can be led inductively toward the 'discovery' of principles through the intuitive grasp of

[46] Research Division, NEA, *Research Bulletin,* 39 (May 1961), pp. 47–50.

patterns" (6:xv). [47] Students are urged to think as scholars do in the various disciplines. The curriculum worker is urged to examine *"the working methods of the intellectual practitioner: the biologist, the historian, the political scientist, for the significant processes of their craft, and the use of these processes in our classroom instruction"* (12:48).

New approaches to curriculum development do have their limitations, as pointed out in the following conclusions by Sulkin:

Emphasis on specific subject fields tends to separate them from each other.

The new approach works more easily with some disciplines than others—the natural sciences, for example, as against the social sciences and the arts.

Subject matter of greater quantity and complexity is pushed lower and lower in the grades.

The new curriculum, no matter how carefully developed, is not proof against poor class instruction (such as drilling students on rules of inductive reasoning or following too religiously a package of course material complete in itself).

The new curriculum . . . may ignore whatever relationship the discipline might have to the needs of society.

Most improvements seem intended to benefit students planning to go to a four-year college.

Finally, experimentation has had little to do with the development of the new curriculums. In too many areas change has been adopted simply on the basis of assumptions about what needed to be done. . . . [48]

Widespread efforts to improve the content of science and mathematics courses have been especially noteworthy. A brief discussion of the major projects follows:

BIOLOGY The Biological Science Curriculum Study (BSCS) was begun in 1958 by the American Institute of Biological Science (AIBS). The purpose of the study was to develop and evaluate new materials for three different "versions" of the biological science course, for every grade level from kindergarten through graduate school. Laboratory experimentation was organized in terms of "blocks," each covering a six-week period. By 1961–1962, some 400 schools were participating in the project. The first textbook materials seemed too difficult for slow learners, but the laboratory programs were accepted with enthusiasm by both teachers and students. Later a fourth version for low-ability students was developed. Another AIBS project has been the development of a complete general biology course on films.

CHEMISTRY Beginning in 1957, the Chemical Bond Approach project (CBA) was organized by a team of teachers from high schools and col-

[47] Sidney Sulkin, Introduction, in *The Challenge of Curricular Change*. New York: College Entrance Examination Board, 1966, p. xv. This and the following quotation are used by permission of Sidney Sulkin, Senior Editor of *Changing Times*, and of the College Entrance Examination Board.

[48] Sulkin, pp. xv–xvii.

leges to develop a new course based on the concept of "chemical bonds." Instructional materials have been developed, tried out in the classroom, evaluated, and revised a number of times.

Participants in the Chemical Education Materials Study (CHEM) have developed a textbook, laboratory manual, and a number of films for a high school course in chemistry that uses an approach different from the one proposed by CBA. Stress is placed on laboratory work or an experimental approach to the study of chemistry. Tryouts of the new material were first conducted in 1960–1961, followed by revision of the textbook and laboratory manual and the development of a teacher's guide.

PHYSICS The Physical Science Study Committee (PSSC) was formed in 1956 at the Massachusetts Institute of Technology. The group has developed a new high school physics course, complete with syllabus, textbook, manuals, films, and teachers' guides. It was the purpose of the committee to prepare a course that would tell "a unified story" that extended from "the atom to the distant galaxies" to meet the needs of students who would pursue careers in science, as well as of those who would not.

MATHEMATICS Since 1952, the University of Illinois Committee on School Mathematics (UICSM), under the leadership of Max Beberman, has been redesigning mathematics courses for grades seven through twelve. They have been developing new materials and educating teachers in their use.

The School Mathematics Study Group (SMSG) began work in 1958 at Yale University to develop an improved program in mathematics for grades seven through twelve. The group has been working on a number of projects: the development of units and textbooks to be used on a trial basis, preparation of a series of monographs to arouse more interest in mathematics among able students, and provision for assistance to teachers.

GENERAL CHARACTERISTICS OF SCIENCE AND MATHEMATICS PROJECTS Most of the projects to develop "new" mathematics and science courses have a few features that are more or less common to all of them.

They are large-scale projects, involving nationwide study and experimentation.

They use a *team* approach, involving research specialists, college professors, and elementary and secondary school teachers.

They stress learning experiences that depend upon active inquiry or experimentation by students.

They stress more active student participation.

They stress concepts that will advance understanding. In mathematics, less emphasis is placed on computation and more on mathematical structure and concepts. In science, there is an effort to break away from laboratory exercises, passive observation of demonstrations, and memorization of classifications.

They are developing tests to evaluate understanding of concepts and principles and their application in solving problems rather than the student's ability to memorize facts and parrot them back to the teacher.

They stress problem solving and application of concepts outside the clasroom.

They are introducing concepts earlier in school.

They are engaging in continuous course revision.

They are attempting to provide more continuity in courses.

They are stressing the importance of mathematics and science for all students.

They are proposing *different* approaches to problems.

They are experimenting with grouping, using three to five groups.

They are providing assistance to teachers by means of handbooks, guides, pamphlets, films, tests, and summer institutes or workshops.

They are receiving generous financial aid from the National Science Foundation and other foundations.[49]

OTHER DEVELOPMENTS IN CONTENT   According to Goodlad, Von Stoephasius, and Klein, "The school curriculum by 1962 was seen by many to be approaching an imbalance. And two years later the writer was still unable to identify and report curriculum rejuvenation of a substantial sort in the social sciences, English, and the arts. By 1966 the social sciences were at the stage the natural sciences had been nearly a decade before. What direction school curricula in these fields will take is not clear, nor is it clear in the arts and the humanities where activity is just beginning." [50] By 1965, Harrison and Solomon reported the following trends in the development of social studies curricula for grades K–12: "(a) development of sequential curricula so that a year's course would build on the concepts and skills introduced in previous years; (b) elimination of much of the repetition in American history generally found in fifth-grade, eighth-grade, and eleventh-grade classes; (c) use of area studies and studies-in-depth of selected topics; (d) communication to students of the social scientist's methods of inquiry; (e) greater use of readings, case studies, and primary sources; (f) greater emphasis on developing skills of inductive thinking and critical analysis; and (g) greater emphasis on the affective as well as the cognitive outcomes of instruction." [51]

---

[49] Adapted from *The School Review*, 70 (Spring 1962), 1–147; "Quality Science for Secondary Schools," *Bulletin of the National Association of Secondary School Principals* (NASSP), 44 (December 1960), 3–210; "New Developments in Secondary School Mathematics," *Bulletin of the NASSP*, 43 (May 1959), 1–189; and American Educational Research Association, "Curriculum Planning and Development," *Review of Educational Research*, 30 (June 1960), 226–228, 235–237.

[50] John I. Goodlad, with Renata Von Stoephasius and M. Frances Klein, *The Changing School Curriculum*. New York: The Fund for the Advancement of Education, August, 1966, p. 21.

[51] Roberts, p. 356.

In making a 1965 progress report on Project Social Studies (launched by the USOE in 1963), Fenton and Good indicated four trends: "(a) emphasis on a study of the structure of the discipline; (b) emphasis on discovery and exploration, i.e., inductive teaching and learning; (c) attempts to integrate information from the several social sciences; and (d) emphasis on sequential learning." [52] Two years later, Girault and Cox not only noted a continuation of some of the trends cited above but also reported such problems as the following: inadequate teacher preparation in some areas; a neglect of psychology, anthropology, and cultural studies of Asia, Africa, and South America (although there is a countertendency to add courses in world cultures and in the behavioral sciences); organization of the social science curriculum around separate subjects, with a corresponding neglect of the interdisciplinary approach; and the development of curricula unrelated to the lives of the students. [53]

Hogan indicates that in the development of curricula in English an attempt is being made to define and delineate more clearly the content of English; to set up priorities in teaching language, literature, and written composition; and to establish better coordination between language arts in the elementary and the secondary schools. English departments in colleges and universities are belatedly beginning to recognize their responsibility for participation in teacher education (3:16–20). Goodlad believes that the "new" English will place more stress on inductive teaching, literature courses that are deep and analytical, and an interest in structural linguistics, generative grammar, and speech (8:76).

Some of the problems still facing curriculum workers in English, according to Hogan, are as follows: failure to relate theory and research to school programs; duplication of inferior experiments; lack of attention to sequence and articulation; failure to determine what should be read at each grade level; and inconsistent criteria for evaluating compositions (3:23–24). [54]

In summarizing trends in the development of foreign language programs, Birkmaier cites widespread acceptance of the audio-lingual approach, replacement of two-year language programs by sequences ranging from four to nine years, the development of a variety of audio-visual aids (such as the language laboratory) and materials, and the teaching of other subjects in a foreign language (for example, "world affairs in Spanish and biology in German") (3:28–32).

Despite sponsorship by the federal government of the National Foundation in the Arts and the Humanities in Washington and the Arts and Humanities Program of the Office of Education, Goodlad points out that

[52] Roberts, p. 357.
[53] Emily S. Girault and C. Benjamin Cox, "Review of Research in Social Studies, 1966," *Social Education*, 31 (May 1967), 389–391.
[54] Roberts, p. 356.

the arts still have a difficult struggle to secure a significant place in the regular school program (8:31).

EDUCATION OF ACADEMICALLY TALENTED STUDENTS

Recent years have witnessed increasing emphasis on the education of academically talented youth. Some of the provisions being made for these students include:

Acceleration—enabling students to complete their education earlier by taking more subjects each semester or by attending summer school, for example.

Segregation—placing academically gifted students in separate schools or in separate sections of courses in the same school. Homogeneous grouping, on the basis of achievement in specific subjects, is probably the most common procedure for providing for students of varying abilities.

Enrichment—providing individualized programs of greater depth and breadth for gifted students in regular classes. If several students in one class are academically talented, the teacher may use subgrouping within the classroom.

Advanced Placement—permitting students to take advanced courses in high school and, on the basis of examinations over such courses, to receive credit or advanced placement in a college or university.

Others—encouraging participation in student activities and community service projects; making arrangements for independent study; and excusing students from certain requirements on the basis of special examinations.

EDUCATION OF DISADVANTAGED YOUTH

Growing concern over the inequities in American democracy has resulted in two parallel movements—one political and the other educational. Political concern has been reflected in the war on poverty and the civil rights movement. Educational concern has culminated in a program of "compensatory education" for the "disadvantaged." Some characteristics of this group of children and youth have been identified as follows: usually retarded educationally, low in self-esteem and levels of aspiration, and controlled by external factors that are inimical to typical school programs.

According to Hunt, educational programs for the disadvantaged tend to give increasing recognition to the need for overcoming a language deficit, for providing work experience and other avenues to adulthood, for relating school to life, for using a variety of "learning styles" (because disadvantaged children differ greatly among themselves), and for placing more stress on the learning process.[55]

[55] American Educational Research Association, "Educational Programs: Adolescence," *Review of Educational Research,* 36 (October 1966), 463–473.

STUDENT ACTIVITIES

Many terms have been used to define the learning activities of the school that take place *outside* the classroom, such as *extracurricular, cocurricular, extraclass,* and *student activities.* At present, the term that seems to be gaining most widespread acceptance is *student activities.*[56]

DEVELOPMENT OF STUDENT ACTIVITIES

Student activities have a long history, dating back at least as far as the schools of ancient Greece. The idea of self-government has been an especially strong feature of the movement throughout its history. In this country, the student activity movement apparently passed "through three successive states": a period of "hostility and opposition" by the faculty, a second stage of "passive acceptance," and finally acceptance and encouragement by school authorities.[57] Indeed, a number of these activities have now been incorporated in the class program with credit given for them.

The student activity offerings today have assumed major proportions in terms of the number of activities included in the typical high school program. Almost every activity that might appeal to youth is included in such categories as athletics, publications, student government, speech and dramatics, musical activities, and clubs of every type and description.

The phenomenal growth of the student activity program has been due to various factors. The movement probably began in the form of student protests against a dull classroom program. Recognition of the needs and interests of students on the part of school faculties no doubt gave impetus to the movement. Recognition of the importance of having students assume more responsibility for their own education was probably another stimulus. Efforts to build better bridges of cooperation and understanding between school and community further strengthened the role of student activities in the curriculum until, finally, the program was given more status by scheduling many activities within the school day and giving credit for them.

VALUES OF STUDENT ACTIVITIES

A number of values of student activities have been implied—development of leadership, assumption of responsibility for self-government, greater student interest in school, and improved public relations. Such activities also build school morale or develop school pride and spirit to an extent that probably would not be possible with a classroom program alone.

[56] Roland C. Faunce, "Extracurricular Activities," *Encyclopedia of Educational Research,* 3d ed. New York: The Macmillan Company, 1960, pp. 506–507.
[57] Faunce, pp. 507–508.

They have been an important factor in encouraging students to remain in school. That participation in student activities is important in personal development is supported by the fact that permanent records now include reports of student participation. Interviewers for employment or further schooling of students often attach some significance to past participation in student activities as one criterion for success.

PROBLEMS OF STUDENT ACTIVITIES

A number of problems are related to the student activity program. There is frequently overparticipation by the few and underparticipation by the many. The first problem can be easily solved by proper restrictions, but the second is more difficult. A high proportion of those who do not participate come from low-income families. They do not participate for at least two reasons. First of all, they do not have the money, for student activities are not always free. Hidden costs—uniforms, dues, pins, letters, trips—make participation prohibitive for some. A second factor is related to the class structure of the school. School activities are usually dominated by students of privileged groups; consequently, students from less privileged socioeconomic groups are effectively barred from participation on social grounds.[58]

Another problem pertains to *sponsorship*. There are two aspects to this problem: securing faculty support and safeguarding faculty members from exploitation. Faculty attitudes toward student activities range all the way from hostility or indifference to excessive enthusiasm for a particular activity. The problem of sponsorship would be largely solved if all faculty members recognized the values of student activities and were willing to do their part in sponsoring them. In some cases, it must be determined whether or not a teacher's enthusiasm over sponsoring or coaching some activity is an adequate substitute for proficiency and experience in that area. As to exploitation of sponsors, it is now becoming clearly recognized that it is unreasonable to expect teachers to sponsor student activities as an overload. Some are being given extra pay for extra work; others are being given credit for sponsorship in their teaching schedule. The latter solution to the problem is considered preferable.[59]

Some other problems of student activities are organizations of secret societies, excessive community demands on performing groups, excessive athleticism, and interruption of class activities.

CRITERIA FOR SUCCESSFUL STUDENT ACTIVITIES

If the student activity program is to play its proper role in the total curriculum, it must meet certain criteria:

[58] Faunce, pp. 509–510.
[59] Faunce, pp. 509–510.

Student activities must contribute to the *purposes* of the school.
Student activities must be well integrated with the total curriculum.
Student activities must be carefully planned and well sponsored.
Student activities must encourage participation by *all* students (alleviating scheduling difficulties, cost barriers, and social discrimination).
Student activities must be evaluated continuously.

This chapter includes a condensed summary of the nature of the secondary school curriculum and its historical development, problems and issues affecting curriculum revision, and current trends in curricular reorganization. Because the classroom teacher is the one who ultimately determines the nature and quality of educational experiences, he is the key person in curriculum improvement. In order to be an effective, intelligent participant in this vital role, he has the difficult task of keeping up with new developments, problems, and issues that affect, not only his own special fields of interest, but also the entire school program.

SELECTED READINGS

1. American Educational Research Association, *Encyclopedia of Educational Research*, 3d ed. Chester W. Harris, ed. New York: The Macmillan Company, 1960, pp. 358–365, 506–511.

2. Association for Supervision and Curriculum Development, *Curriculum Change: Direction and Process*, Robert R. Leeper, ed. Washington, D.C.: Association for Supervision and Curriculum Development, NEA, 1966.

3. Association for Supervision and Curriculum Development, *New Curriculum Developments*, Glenys G. Unruh, ed. A Report of ASCD's Commission on Current Curriculum Developments, Robert S. Gilchrist, ch. Washington, D.C.: Association for Supervision and Curriculum Development, NEA, 1965.

4. Cay, Donald F., *Curriculum: Design for Learning*. Indianapolis: The Bobbs-Merrill Company, Inc., 1966.

5. Clark, Leonard H., Raymond L. Klein, and John B. Burks, *The American Secondary School Curriculum*. New York: The Macmillan Company, 1965.

6. College Entrance Examination Board, *The Challenge of Curricular Change*. The papers of a colloquium held under the joint auspices of the CEEB and the National Association of Secondary-School Principals. New York: College Entrance Examination Board, 1966.

7. Gardner, John W., *Excellence*. New York: Harper & Row, Publishers, 1961.

8. Goodlad, John I., with Renata Von Stoephasius and M. Frances Klein, *The Changing School Curriculum*. New York: The Fund for the Advancement of Education, August 1966.

9. Inlow, Gail, *The Emergent in Curriculum*. New York: John Wiley & Sons, Inc., 1966.

10. King, Arthur R., Jr., and John A. Brownell, *The Curriculum and the Disciplines of Knowledge*. New York: John Wiley & Sons, Inc., 1966.

11. Loughary, John W., *Man-Machine Systems in Education*. New York: Harper & Row, Publishers, 1966.

12. Parker, J. Cecil, and Louis J. Rubin, *Process as Content: Curriculum Design and the Application of Knowledge*. Chicago: Rand McNally & Company, 1966.

13. Phenix, Philip H., *Realms of Meaning: A Philosophy of the Curriculum for General Education*. New York: McGraw-Hill Book Company, Inc., 1964.

14. Saylor, J. Galen, and William M. Alexander, *Curriculum Planning for Modern Schools*. New York: Holt, Rinehart and Winston, Inc., 1966.

15. Tiedt, Sidney W., *The Role of the Federal Government in Education*. New York: Oxford University Press, 1966.

16. Trump, J. Lloyd, and Delmas F. Miller, *Secondary School Curriculum Improvement: Proposals and Procedures*. Boston: Allyn and Bacon, Inc., 1968.

The videotape recorder enables supervisors and teachers to evaluate teaching procedures. It may be stopped at any point for discussion. Probably no improvement technique is more effective than the unique experience of a teacher actually seeing himself in action. This photograph is from the Project Interaction Analysis developed by George A. Leffs, Director of Research, Clark High School, Las Vegas (Nevada). (Print furnished by Sony Corporation of America, VTR Division.)

Bigness, with its corollary of overcrowding, is responsible for many educational ills—discipline problems, ineffective learning environment, and mental health difficulties, to name a few. Despite the affluence of our nation, such a condition may be found in many schools of suburbia or the ghettoes. (Courtesy Pittsburgh [Pennsylvania] Public Schools.)

Schooling has come a long way from the "Mark Hopkins and the student on the log" image. Today, an attractive functional physical environment is assuming a more important place in the education of the nation's youth. This photo of the Covington Junior High School, Birmingham (Michigan), was supplied by American School & University, Buttenheim Publishing Corporation, New York, Linn Smith, Architect.

Teacher militancy is a contemporary phenomenon. The causes for this ferment are varied and often controversial. (Courtesy Pittsburgh [Pennsylvania] Post-Gazette.*)*

PART SIX | *Evaluation*

CHAPTER 16

Evaluation Principles and Appraisal Techniques

Each day teachers find it necessary to make many judgments of value. They seek the best possible answers to such questions as, What level of instruction would be most appropriate for this class? What instructional pace should be followed? Which students would benefit from remedial instruction? Which ones are ready for enrichment work? What student groupings might facilitate learning? How effective are the materials and methods of instruction now being employed? How far has each student progressed toward the goals of instruction? What mark has been earned by each student? Much of the success of a teacher today depends upon the quality of the judgments he makes in answer to these complex questions. Teaching was not always as complex, however.

EVALUATION IN EARLY SCHOOLS

In the typical schools at the turn of the century, teachers were little concerned with these problems. They taught small classes from a single text at a pace designed to cover the material in the comparatively short school year.

[In 1900] the schooling process consisted of following a rigid schedule of assignments and recitations based upon single textbooks. The goal was to cover the prescribed number of pages in the designated number of days. In the classroom, potential mule skinners, day laborers, and janitors sat beside embryo research physicists, surgeons, and business executives. They studied the same textbooks, heard the same recitations, pursued the same educational goals, and were marked on the same standards.[1]

In the schools of 1900, measurement of student ability and achievement was crude or nonexistent. Evaluative judgment was practically limited to a term-ending decision of "pass" or "fail."

[1] American Educational Research Association, "Improving Educational Research," *1948 Official Report,* p. 75.

EVALUATION TODAY: HOW BEST TO FACILITATE LEARNING

The task of the teacher today is exceedingly more complex. He customarily faces larger classes of students who are much more divergent in abilities and interests. The "potential mule skinners" are in schools in greater numbers and remain for a longer period of years. They prepare for a life in which there will be an absence of mules and an abundance of mechanical industrialization. American society itself is more complex. Students must be educated not only to direct effectively the forces of this industrialization but also to participate effectively in the democratic process of government, to understand it, and to appreciate it fully.

Potential research scientists are also in the schools of today in greater numbers. In many high schools such students are mastering content formerly taught only in college. Parents no longer can assist with assignments in science and mathematics because content in those fields has changed since they were in school. Science as well as technology is in a period of accelerated change. Teachers feel the sense of urgency in the nation and are receptive to the call for excellence.

Fortunately the technology of teaching also is moving forward. In addition to standardized tests of achievement, tools are being developed scientifically to measure intelligence, special aptitudes, basic skills, attitudes, and interests. Even though these instruments still are far from perfect, they are extremely useful to teachers in their study of learners. Additional innovations since 1900 include audio-visual materials, teaching machines, programmed learning, multilevel texts, teachers' guides, and supplementary curriculum materials. Many changes in teaching technique and material have taken place, and under the stimulus of research, the tempo of change is increasing. Teaching is becoming an increasingly complex process in which measurement and evaluation are playing a greater role.

The modern teacher is constantly challenged by the problem of selecting, from the multitude of available instructional techniques and materials, those best adapted to the learning peculiarities of his students and best suited to the instructional outcomes he seeks—outcomes that must be adjusted so as to command the best efforts of all his students. This is the stimulating challenge of present-day teaching.

To meet this challenge, the teacher must study his class and his techniques as well as his subject matter. If he is to use the available tools and techniques most effectively to improve student achievement, he must determine the learning characteristics of his students and keep constantly informed of the quality of learning resulting from daily instruction. In his study of student achievement, he is concerned with the attainment of a broad array of goals including knowledge, skills, attitudes, and appreciations. This very necessary part of successful teaching is broadly termed *evaluation.*

PURPOSES OF MEASUREMENT AND EVALUATION

More technically, the gathering of data through use of tests and scales is termed *measurement*, whereas the whole process of decision making involving the setting of goals and the assessment of their attainment through consideration of all obtainable evidence is termed *evaluation*. The data-gathering aspect of the evaluation process commonly includes conferences with students, parents, and colleagues; the study of records; observation of performance; and measurement through testing.

The primary purpose of both measurement and evaluation is to motivate, to direct, and to improve teaching and learning. Increasingly important specialized functions include diagnosis of learning difficulties and prediction of future performance. It should be noted that determination of achievement marks remains an important though now a secondary purpose.

EVALUATION, A CONTINUOUS PART OF TEACHING

Problems to be solved through use of the procedures of evaluation are present at all stages of instruction. As a preliminary to planning, teachers study the achievements, abilities, interests, and attitudes of their students. With this knowledge the teacher is better able to set realistic group and individual goals. Appropriate teaching materials and learning experiences can be provided to achieve these goals. Instructional groups based on interests and abilities can be organized, either by class groupings or by grouping within the class. Laggards in learning can be identified and assigned to experiences selected to remedy their deficiencies. Likewise, students of high potential for achievement can be recognized and challenged by enrichment and acceleration to work at a level better adapted to their abilities. Thus the possibility of disappointment and failure for one and boredom and mediocrity for the other can be reduced if not eliminated.

During the progress of instruction, teachers continue to study records, to confer, to observe, to measure, and to evaluate. They are anxious to determine how well their students are progressing toward their individual and group goals. Teachers seek to determine early what adjustments in planning may be necessary. They realize that when the planned methods, materials, and activities are not producing the desired results, early discovery and revision are imperative. Such discoveries must be made while there is still time for remedial action. To wait for final products and final examinations is too late. Continuous evaluation is a necessary part of good teaching.

At the conclusion of a unit of instruction, final measurement and evaluation serve to answer three related questions: How well have the unit objectives been achieved? What marks have been earned by the student?

To what extent has the instruction been effective? All three questions require the teacher's careful attention because unbiased appraisal of student achievement is an important element in good teacher-student rapport and good school-community relations. Furthermore, accurate marks are essential to effective educational and vocational guidance. Similarly, critical self-evaluation by the teacher is important because it is basic to his improvement as an instructor.

Thus it is apparent that problems of evaluation begin in the early steps of planning and continue to the final steps of reporting. Constant alertness to the principles and purposes of evaluation, combined with steady development of evaluative skills, therefore, must be recognized as essential elements in successful teaching.

EVALUATION PRINCIPLES

In the hands of the inexpert teacher, evaluation could be reduced to barren measurement and recording, whereas when used by a more proficient teacher, the process has boundless potential for the improvement of learning and instruction. Beginning teachers will find it profitable to devote much time to development of the knowledges and skills involved. The following section of this chapter is devoted to suggestions for those who desire to make full use of measurement and evaluation.

BROAD AND REALISTIC GOALS

The achievement of all important objectives of instruction should be evaluated. For example, in physical education the attainment of the objectives of good health habits, correct safety habits, good sportsmanship, and active interest in healthful recreation should be evaluated in addition to the development of game skills and knowledge of rules. When the instructor learns all he can about the interests, needs, and abilities of his students, he can set more realistic goals for the class and for individuals. The modification of objectives so that they may serve as a challenge, and at the same time be within the reach of a student, is a practice supported by research. *The Encyclopedia of Educational Research* points out the implications for teachers as follows: "the teacher needs to insure that the learner is not given tasks where he is expected to perform beyond his present capabilities . . . the student should be offered reasonable sub-goals." [2]

Teachers are rapidly recognizing the principle that goals which are unrealistic fail to motivate learning and are thus inadequate as bases for evaluation.

[2] Melvin H. Marx, "Motivation," *Encyclopedia of Educational Research,* 3d ed. New York: The Macmillan Company, 1960, p. 896.

AN INTEGRAL AND CONTINUOUS PART OF TEACHING

The major purposes of evaluation can be achieved best when the planning of evaluation becomes a regular part of instructional planning. One should not fall into the error of limiting evaluation activities to times of stress or to a few days prior to the date that final marks are due. Provisions for evaluation should be made in all daily lesson plans as well as in the plans for each unit. Because evaluation is an integral part of teaching, haphazard evaluation practices denote haphazard teaching. The importance of continuous evaluation cannot be overstressed, particularly for beginning teachers.

APPROPRIATE USE OF DATA-GATHERING TECHNIQUES

Teachers should recognize that all techniques have their strengths and their weaknesses. In order to take advantage of the strengths and avoid the weaknesses, successful teachers select techniques carefully. The following suggestions should be of value:

1. Direct observation usually provides better evidence of the attainment of skills than that provided by the indirect method of written tests. Skills in art, music, and physical education frequently can be evaluated most effectively by direct observation of both the process and the product. To appraise critically the end product alone, in many cases, would be inadequate. The boy who bats cross-handed is in need of instruction even though he occasionally hits a home run. Teachers should keep in mind that the reliability of observational data can be increased through use of rating sheets and checklists.

2. In the evaluation of knowledge, evidence of understanding based upon ability to make applications and to interpret meanings is preferable to evidence of ability merely to recall statements or facts. Newer testing techniques discussed in Chapter 17 make it possible to use objective as well as essay questions to gather evidence in this category.

3. Observation and interview provide better evidence of real attitudes than can be obtained from most written tests now available. Tests tend to indicate knowledge of preferred attitudes, but frequently fail to give valid evidence of actual attitudes. Anecdotal records based on observation of the behavior of a student should provide more accurate information in this area. Sociometric devices are also helpful.

4. Teacher-made tests should be used frequently so that both student and teacher can keep fully informed of learning status and progress. Pretests and diagnostic tests as well as tests for marks can serve their purposes best when they are built for a specific class. Skill in test building and use is a necessary part of good teaching.

5. Published tests and scales usually provide norms that enable a

teacher to compare scores of his class with those of regional and national groups. Furthermore, the technical excellence of many published tests can serve to stimulate better test building on the part of the teacher. Wise use of published tests in diagnosis and prognosis as well as in ordinary achievement testing can be a benefit to both student and teacher. Precautions to be observed are discussed in Chapter 19.

6. Tests that can be scored objectively usually provide more reliable evidence of achievement than that provided by essay tests. On the other hand, there is some evidence to indicate that essay tests encourage better study habits and greater retention. Some authorities maintain that the essay test could be eliminated without loss. However, the present tendency seems to be to use essay tests to measure abilities to organize and interpret information, particularly in the subjects of English and social studies, and to use objective tests for other testing situations. Teachers should avoid the overuse of any single technique.[3]

7. Any single test, observation, or other measurement reveals only a sample of the behavior of a student and should be interpreted with the knowledge that behaviors are subject to frequent change. Consequently, it should be recognized that any measurement may contain error attributable to variability in the behavior of the student as well as error inherent in the measurement technique employed. Teachers should avoid placing great weight upon single measurements, particularly when the results indicate large deviations from the student's general pattern of performance.[4] Fortunately, the practice of passing or failing a student on the basis of a single test is no longer a common occurrence. Important decisions are now based upon extensive accumulations of carefully collected evidence.

DIAGNOSTIC ASPECTS OF EVALUATION

It is the responsibility of the teacher not only to determine the level of achievement of his students as they enter a course of instruction and to formulate his plans and procedures to meet their needs, but also to find and remedy the weaknesses of those students who, as the instruction progresses, are not achieving up to their capacity. In the latter responsibility, diagnostic measures are invaluable.

Published diagnostic instruments are concentrated chiefly in the subjects of arithmetic and reading. When appropriate published instruments are not available, usable substitutes can be constructed by the classroom teacher. Such tests differ from ordinary achievement tests in these respects: they cover a relatively small group of objectives (for example, the use of the comma, the fielding of ground balls, or the use of gestures in public speaking); several items or chances should be provided to cover

---

[3] American Educational Research Association, *Review of Educational Research,* 29 (February 1959), 43.
[4] American Educational Research Association, p. 48.

each specific to be tested because repetition is required to reduce the effects of chance success or error; the items or situations employed should be of types that reduce chance success to a minimum; the important scores are based on single items or small groups of items designed to measure the same objective; and the results of the test are used for the purpose of guidance and not as a basis for marks.

Some information of diagnostic value, particularly with reference to the class as a whole, can be gleaned from regular instructional tests of achievement. Many teachers study the results of instructional tests to determine which items have been most difficult for the class. If the items are not faulty in themselves, this procedure will provide excellent clues to help direct succeeding lessons toward objectives that need further study. Item analysis techniques are discussed in Chapter 17.

A common teaching practice is to discuss test results with students as the papers are returned or in conferences soon afterward. This practice is recommended provided the teacher makes constructive comments and follows up with more detailed analysis and instruction. He should always keep in mind that mere admonitions to work hard coupled with threats of failure are inadequate substitutes for modern techniques emphasizing specific remedial instruction based upon accurate knowledge of student weaknesses.

Evaluative techniques other than testing are just as important in diagnosis as they are in the other aspects of a complete evaluation program. In fact, case studies (involving aptitude, personality, and interest measures, interviews, conferences, school records, and observations) frequently are necessary to diagnose the more difficult problems adequately. Because learning difficulties are at times only one aspect of a complex of adjustment problems, the classroom teacher should not hesitate to ask the help of the school counselor or principal when learning difficulties persist. A complete program of educational diagnosis would seek not only to identify and remedy deficiencies but to locate and remove their causes as well. Diagnostic and remedial procedures are time-consuming tasks, but they frequently yield results that make teaching a real pleasure.

MOTIVATIONAL ASPECTS OF EVALUATION

One of the concomitant outcomes of an effective program of evaluation is its motivating influence upon both students and teachers. Few would deny that tests encourage intensive planning and study. Some would condemn such intensive study as cramming but others encourage it. Looking to research, teachers are able to substantiate both points of view. Evaluation techniques, particularly testing, have potential for both good and bad influence upon the student and the teacher. It is extremely important that this factor be taken into account by teachers and administrators.

Some teachers remember the days when their jobs depended upon the success with which their students took tests imposed by city, county, or state administrative boards. Under those conditions teachers were motivated to cast aside all other objectives and drill incessantly upon questions that were most likely to be included in the final test. Students failed or passed on the single basis of their final test score. All their prior work, successful or unsuccessful, was ignored.

It is little wonder that some teachers still retain a dislike, if not a fear, of tests traceable to their experience as students or teachers in that type of test program. Fortunately such practices are now practically nonexistent. However, teachers today can build up the same feelings of fear and tension in their own classrooms through overemphasis upon single tests or general misuse of measurement techniques.

One of the writers recalls observing two inexperienced teachers who misused the motivational possibilities of tests. Disappointed in the level of understanding revealed in recitation, one told the class, "Unless you know your lesson better tomorrow, we will have a test." The second teacher, unable to stop the talking that was going on during a test, warned, "If you do not quiet down at once, I will add items to this test." These teachers obviously failed to understand the real purposes of evaluation.

Tests should not be used as threats, not even to enforce standards of study or discipline. According to Marx the motivational use of tests should be based upon the research-founded principle of the "desirability of continuous use of knowledge of results," [5] not upon the highly questionable principle of fear as a motivator: "It is generally recognized that the deliberate use of fear as a motivator, or the use of punishment or threat of punishment with fear as an almost unavoidable consequence, may have highly undesirable effects." [6]

Tests, as well as other measurement instruments, should furnish the teacher and student with evidence of his successes and needs. This information should be shared with the student and serve as a guide to his further study. The preponderance of evidence indicates that measurement techniques employed in this manner help to motivate better teaching and better learning by clarifying goals, designating means, and stimulating action.

Beginning teachers frequently ask whether tests should be announced or administered without announcement. Which practice results in more study and learning? The answer appears to be "Announced tests." If tests motivate prior study at all, a test that is a certainty should motivate more study than one that is only a possibility. Then any given number of announced tests should motivate more study than the same number of tests given without announcement. Furthermore, a well-known principle

[5] Marx, p. 896.
[6] Marx, p. 897.

is that "successful motivation must not only energize action, but direct it." Therefore, if a teacher wishes to stimulate the most study prior to a test he will see that his students understand the purpose of the test, the objectives to be measured, and the kinds of items to be used. Then students will be better able to plan their study.

Of course, when tests are used to their optimum in motivation, the test results will be analyzed and used by both teacher and student to energize and direct study. The study which follows a test is as important as that which precedes it.

Beginning teachers commonly ask if individual test scores or other comparable data should be posted. Does such publicity motivate students to study better? This question must be answered with a qualified "No." Posting the full results of competition in which some are invariably inferior in spite of their efforts reduces the motivational potential of tests. Regular postings should be confined to the names of those who have shown the greatest improvement and might possibly be expanded at times to include short listings of rankings within groups that have approximately equal opportunity for success. Competition serves as a motivator for those who have a fair chance to succeed. Repeated publicity of failure, particularly when such failure occurs despite honest effort, can lead only to disappointment and reduction of effort. Perhaps the most effective recording of test scores might well be the record of his own ratings that each student is encouraged to keep. Competition in self-improvement is healthy motivation.

When returning tests to students, teachers should be particularly alert to the motivation to be gained from written or quiet oral commendation to those who have improved, and also from personal encouragement and specific instructional help to those who have done less well than might be expected. Seldom should tests be returned without evaluative and motivational comment.

MORALE-BUILDING ASPECTS OF EVALUATION

Well-conducted evaluation can contribute to good classroom morale by keeping each student informed of his progress and by revealing the teacher as a sympathetic guide interested in helping him move toward the goals of instruction. Poorly conducted evaluation, on the contrary, can have a disrupting effect upon morale. Announcement of failure before the group can destroy almost any student's feeling of belonging. Consequently, teachers should make special efforts to ensure that their evaluation techniques will have positive effects upon morale.

The following suggestions should help teachers improve the morale-building potential of their evaluation.

1. Have students take part in the planning of evaluation. For example, students can help select the kinds of measurement to be used and help

schedule important tests so that they do not conflict with school activities or with tests in other classes. Students can also benefit from discussing the objectives to be measured and from constructing sample test items. Thus they can gain better understanding of the purposes and processes of evaluation.

2. Study the results of measurement with each student so as to help him recognize his needs and successes. Students welcome tests used as guides. They are eager to get accurate information about their progress. Individual attention is appreciated.

3. Avoid evaluation practices that students consider unfair. For example, students generally resent and fear surprise tests that deny them the opportunity to review. They dislike poorly timed tests which require such speed that they fail to do their best. Use of complex, "trick" questions and open posting of achievement marks also earn low ratings from students.

4. Provide practice in new measurement techniques before using them to get evidence of achievement. Students frequently lack confidence and become confused when confronted with unfamiliar techniques of measurement. This difficulty can be overcome through systematic use of practice and instructional measures.

5. Encourage students to evaluate themselves. Through the process of self-evaluation, students can gain a better understanding of their purposes in school. For many, the values of education then become more real, and their attitudes toward learning improve.

THE PUBLIC RELATIONS ASPECT OF EVALUATION

The maintenance of good public relations is an important problem in any large public enterprise, including the public schools. Much of the criticism of schools arises from lack of information (or from misinformation) concerning the purposes and processes of present-day American education. Teachers can contribute much toward improved understanding through a well-planned program of evaluation. Such a program would provide parents with more adequate written reports and supplement them with personal contacts as much as possible. Reporting practices should be flexible so as to include timely special reports and conferences. Parents have every right to be kept informed of their child's progress, particularly when problems appear to be developing. To confine reports to the regular card may be entirely inadequate. One may well imagine the reaction against teacher and school as well as the personal embarrassment of the family that arrived at school with their friends on commencement night only to find that their son was not among those granted a diploma. The regular report was still being processed in the office. Meanwhile, the teacher had wrongly assumed that the boy would inform his parents of his failure to complete graduation requirements. Even in less dramatic circumstances it is equally important that teacher and school take the responsibility for direct communication with parents.

Teachers should invite parents to share their knowledge of their child's background, interests, and needs. Conferences of this type help teachers understand individual students and help parents understand the school. It is becoming more important that teachers develop skill in teacher-parent conferences. However, it must be realized that even though conferences and visitation between home and school are increasing, many parents seldom, if ever, participate in them. Most parents still rely upon the regular report card to keep them informed. It is important that reports to parents be improved. In the secondary school there is little likelihood that report cards will ever be replaced by conferences.

As parents are being asked to give greater financial support to education, they in turn are asking for more objective information concerning instruction and learning in their public schools. Many schools are meeting this demand, in part, through use of a continuing program of standardized testing. With this information pupil gains can be determined in addition to pupil status. It means more to a parent to learn that in the ninth grade his daughter improved from sixth-grade to eighth-grade standing in reading than for him merely to learn that her final rating was one year below average. Intelligent use of standardized test results can be effective in public relations.

Teachers should be fully aware that public relations is a complex field. Practices differ from school to school. For instance, in some schools, test information is freely shared with pupils and parents, in other schools it is given out only after approval through official channels, while in still other schools such information is shared only with professional personnel. It is of particular importance, then, that teachers in training recognize the role of evaluation in public relations. They should always check their plans with their supervisors and carefully follow the policies and practices of their school. Further discussion of reporting practices is to be found in Chapter 18.

SELF-EVALUATION

Self-evaluation by the individual students, by the class, and by the instructor are all important aspects of a complete evaluation program.

Self-evaluation on the part of students can be facilitated by teaching them the necessary graphing skills and providing the basic materials and data so that they can keep an accurate record of their progress; by returning graded work promptly and requesting that samples for comparison be retained by the student in his evaluation folder; by providing class time for instruction and practice in self-evaluation techniques; by providing basic information concerning the progress of the class as a whole so that students can compare their own standing with the average or quartile points of the class; by encouraging students to compete with their own record rather than with individual classmates; and by including students in the planning as well as in other phases of evaluation. Students who participate in the selection of clearly defined goals are more likely to be interested in keeping track of their progress toward them.

Self-evaluation on the part of a class as a whole can be facilitated by scheduling class discussions for that purpose. In these evaluation sessions, care must be taken to avoid individual comparisons. Neither commendation nor censure of individual students should be permitted. Rather, emphasis should be placed upon development of group feeling. Use such questions as, How well have we progressed as a class? What have we done best? In what have we been least successful? How can we do better? What are reasonable new goals for the class? In some circumstances class evaluations can be further stimulated by centering discussions in graphical comparisons of class averages on standardized measures with local, state, or national norms for similar classes. In comparisons of this type it is important to see that the results of discussion are constructive. In essence, evaluation of group progress by the group itself should be a natural part of teacher-student planning.

Continuous self-evaluation on the part of the instructor is an essential element in successful teaching. Each day as he prepares to revise plans for the next day's teaching, he should carefully review the effectiveness of the lessons just completed. What seemed to be particularly successful? What could be improved? Could more effective methods and materials be employed? What changes might be appropriate the next time that particular content is covered? How should the next day's instruction be adapted to meet the special needs revealed? Answers to these questions should be written into daily plans. Memory alone cannot be trusted.

Periodically each teacher should also searchingly appraise himself as a professional person. He should ask such questions as, Am I improving in professional knowledge and skill? What is the quality of my rapport with students? How well do I cooperate with my colleagues? Is my response to supervision adequate? In short, how am I doing and how can I improve as a member of the teaching profession?

THE KEEPING OF RECORDS

Carefully maintained records are a necessary part of an evaluation program. No one can expect to commit to memory all the collected information pertinent to the evaluation of his students. If adequate information is to be available when needed, rather extensive records must be kept. As a minimum each teacher should maintain a class record book of test scores and other ratings of achievement that indicate the status of each student at designated points throughout the school year; a supplementary folder on selected students containing records of their abilities, interests, background, special goals, health, and adjustment, as well as anecdotal records, samples of work, and progress charts; and a folder containing similar information about the class as a whole, in addition to the teacher's self-evaluations pertaining to his instruction of that class.

In addition to these records, teachers should encourage and assist each student to maintain an evaluation folder of his own in which he can keep his returned assignments and tests, records of his test scores, statements of his personal goals, and copies of his periodic self-evaluations.

EVALUATION AND ACTION

Evaluation is of little benefit unless it leads to action. Determination of final marks is only a minor function of the entire process. To be effective in attaining its major purpose—the improvement of instruction and learning—evaluation must be followed by specific changes in the work of the student and the teacher. Tests should be analyzed to determine strengths and weaknesses of individual students and of the class as a whole. The remedial and enrichment work following should then be based on the knowledge gained. Evaluation conferences and interviews should also culminate in plans and action toward improvement. Only then will the full benefit of evaluation be realized.

TECHNIQUES OF APPRAISAL

It must be acknowledged that teachers in service differ greatly in their ability to apply the principles of evaluation. Many keep in step with the advancements of their profession; some merely teach as they were taught. Consequently, beginning teachers, observing widely different practices, sometimes find it difficult to decide what measurement and evaluation skills should be developed as part of their own professional equipment. What is a teacher expected to know about these matters? The answer should be clear. To perform at the highest levels of proficiency, today's teacher finds it essential to develop skill in:

1. The use of appraisal techniques
2. Building, administering, and scoring written tests
3. Determining marks and making reports to parents
4. Interpreting scores from standardized achievement tests and intelligence tests

The techniques of appraisal are discussed in the remainder of this chapter; each of the other topics is the subject of following chapters.

Appraisal techniques include the use of nonwritten performance tests, rating sheets, checklists, progress records, anecdotal records, and sociometry.

THE APPRAISAL OF PERFORMANCES AND PRODUCTS

In subjects such as speech, drama, physical education, industrial arts, home economics, music, art, and business education, the development of skills is a major objective. Consequently, in these subjects tests designed to measure a student's ability to perform selected skills in controlled situations are of particular importance. In such tests, correctness and speed of performance, as well as quality of the end product, are usually taken into consideration. Examples of tests of performance in varied subjects might be basketball dribbling and goal shooting, sketching an artistic figure, baking a cake, playing a musical score, or dramatic acting.

PERFORMANCE TESTS   In the selection of tasks for performance testing, teachers should consider only those that are realistic and directly related to the most important objectives of the course. Tasks of minor importance, particularly those that are time-consuming, should not be included. For example, the teacher of physical education who wished to appraise student ability to control a soccer ball soon found that it was far better to require students to dribble the ball through a 15-yard obstacle course than to have them dribble for the full 100-yard length of the field. Furthermore, problems that test a student's mental alertness or his luck rather than his skill in the subject should be avoided. For instance, the malfunctions to be used in an automobile troubleshooting test in which time is a major criterion should be selected so that their discovery will be dependent upon efficient use of regular procedures rather than upon haphazard attacks or lucky guesses.

It is generally considered that tasks for which partial scores can be assigned are more appropriate for a performance test than those which can be marked only pass or fail. Observable and significant differences in performance should be revealed in a full distribution of scores, not in just a dichotomous over-all rating. To accomplish this, a teacher can break the task into its necessary steps or elements and assign points or ratings to each. A further consideration is to keep the score assigned to perfect performance in each part in proper relation to the importance of that part in the whole task. With this type of scoring, the part scores have diagnostic value, and the total score is a valid appraisal of the total performance. For example, a published procedures checklist for a woodworking performance test designed to measure ability to square wood stock breaks the task into thirty-five check points. The final four points concerned with working the stock to thickness are shown in Table 16-1.

In the organization of a performance test including several tasks using the same basic tools, instruments, or skills, it is sometimes possible to arrange the tasks in order of increasing difficulty. Much administration time can then be saved by testing students somewhat the way a psy-

Table 16–1. Partial Rating Sheet for a Performance Test

CHECK POINT	PROCEDURE	MAXIMUM CREDIT	EARNED CREDIT
32	Takes heavy cuts to remove excess stock	2	_____
33	Reduces cut and planes to center of gauged lines	2	_____
34	Checks frequently	3	_____
35	Takes all cuts with the grain	3	_____

SOURCE: Adapted from William J. Micheels and M. Ray Karnes, *Measuring Educational Achievement.* New York: McGraw-Hill Book Company, Inc., 1950, p. 357. Used by permission of McGraw-Hill.

chologist uses a scale of intelligence or a physical education teacher conducts the pole vault or high jump at a track meet. In this kind of scaled test, no student takes the entire test. Each one starts at an optional difficulty level and proceeds only as far as his ability will take him. When a test arrangement of this type is possible, it is an extravagant waste of time to use tests that require students to attempt performances below and above their ability. It should be noted that this type of test arrangement has application possibilities in many subjects including mathematics and science as well as music, industrial arts, business, and physical education.

In the administration of performance tests, it is important to provide opportunity for retrial of simple tasks in which chance success plays a part; to provide adequate direction so that the student clearly understands what is expected; where feasible, to use squad leaders or other selected students as assistant examiners in order to permit multistation testing in a class period; to provide a carefully prepared score card, checklist, or rating sheet on which to record scores or ratings of the procedure and product of the test activity; and to plan learning activities for students not taking the test when only part of the class can be tested at one time.

Occasionally teachers find it convenient and proper to apply performance tests to groups rather than to individuals. In fact, teams in physical education, committees and panels in English and social studies, and play groups in drama are more or less natural units that might be rated on a group basis. A major pitfall in this practice must be carefully avoided, however. Each individual has the right to be rated on his own progress toward the goals of instruction for individuals, even though group ratings are important whenever improvement of group performance is also a goal of instruction. For example, a mediocre individual performance in an otherwise brilliant cast deserves a "D" rating, even though the group effect may be "A" or "B." Likewise, a star performer on a losing team in physical education may deserve an "A" rating even though the team rating is low. It is doubly bad practice in physical education to assign automatically high grades to all members of winning teams and low grades to all members of losing groups. The team grade may misrepresent the achievement of physical education objectives by the individual student and the practice teaches him that winning is more important than how well he played the game.

BETTER USE OF OBSERVATIONAL TECHNIQUES   Observation for the purpose of evaluation can also be valuable in nontesting situations. For a long time teachers have been judging student achievement to a considerable extent on the basis of observation of daily work. When used expertly, observational techniques can provide an accurate and continuous record of a student's daily progress. This use of observation has several advantages over performance testing:

1. Regular learning activity can proceed undisturbed.
2. Information gained can be used immediately to guide instruction. In fact, rating and instruction are frequently carried on in the same class period.
3. Students who tend to become tense in test situations can perform more normally because they are frequently unaware that their performance is being rated.
4. Certain objectives cannot be evaluated in any other way, by either performance or written tests (for example, an intangible such as a student's appreciation of a good book).

However, unless observation is well directed, specific, and recorded, it is of little use. Too many teachers gain only general impressions through observation. To use observation effectively as a basis for instruction and marking, teachers must be certain of what to observe. They must select appropriate sample behavior for observation and make a careful record of what they see.

Observation should be an integral part of a well-planned evaluation program. It should be planned in relation to the objectives of the course and with full knowledge of the strengths and weaknesses of other means of evaluation. Observation can be best employed to evaluate achievement that eludes evaluation by means of written tests. Such devices as checklists, rating sheets, rating scales, and progress charts serve the double purpose of directing and recording observation. These devices can be constructed rather easily by the classroom teacher.

A rating sheet designed to measure students' status in discussion and listening skills is illustrated in Table 16-2. The ratings indicate that Allan

Table 16–2. Sample Rating Sheet of Discussion and Listening Skills

STUDENT'S NAME	CONTRIBUTIONS ARE CONCISE AND CONSTRUCTIVE	SPEAKS DIS-TINCTLY	IS COUR-TEOUS	ASKS PROBING QUESTIONS	LISTENS ATTEN-TIVELY
Allan Ault	1	3	2	2	1
Bob Brown	4	2	4	4	5
Sue Smith	5	3	3	3	5

Ratings: 1 = inferior; 2 = below average; 3 = average; 4 = above average; 5 = outstanding

Ault is inferior in his contribution to discussion and in his listening attentiveness. Bob Brown is below average in the clarity of his speech, but is an outstanding listener and above average in all other ratings. Sue Smith is average in three ratings and outstanding in two. This kind of sheet is usually arranged to receive the ratings of an entire class. This arrangement facilitates recording and intraclass comparisons, but lacks the flexibility of the individual card system.

Rating devices are frequently organized so as to reveal a student's skill on a numerical, descriptive, or graphic scale or any combination of the three. The data for Bob Brown's discussion and listening skills are entered in the illustrative numerical-graphic scale in Table 16-3. This type of

Table 16–3. Sample Rating Scale of Discussion and Listening Skills

STUDENT: BOB BROWN.

	INFERIOR (1)	BELOW AVERAGE (2)	AVERAGE (3)	ABOVE AVERAGE (4)	OUT-STANDING (5)
Contributions are concise and constructive					
Speaks distinctly					
Is courteous					
Asks probing questions					
Listens attentively					

rating gives a clear picture of an individual's skills at any given time. Comparisons are facilitated by recording later ratings on the same scale in different colors or codings. It should be noted that ratings need not be restricted to the five division points, but may be placed at any position along the scale to indicate the precise judgment of the rater.

The "Rating of Student-Teaching Performance" is an instrument intended for use in periodic student teacher-supervisor conferences. The rating may be made by the supervisor, by the student teacher as a guide to self-evaluation, or completed jointly in conference. The instrument would be called a rating sheet if the appropriate numbers were inserted in the blanks preceding each factor. The device would be a true rating scale if the entire scale were repeated after each factor, with each rating marked along a line. The second arrangement would have the advantage of providing a graphic representation.

RATING OF STUDENT-TEACHING PERFORMANCE

FACTOR RATED

_____ Overall class rapport and control
_____ Effectiveness with individual problems of control
_____ Overall planning and organization
_____ Daily planning
_____ Long-term planning
_____ Effectiveness with high achievers
_____ Effectiveness with average achievers
_____ Effectiveness with low achievers
_____ Attention to motivation
_____ Use of varied methods and materials
_____ Differentiation for individuals
_____ Evaluation techniques
_____ Attention to management details
_____ Knowledge of subject taught
_____ Skills in writing and speaking (including spelling and grammar)
_____ Personal qualities (including appearance, dependability, and initiative)
_____ Professional attitude
_____ Response to supervision
_____ Overall performance rating for the period considered
_____ Overall rating of growth for the period considered

0	2	4	6	8	10	12
Failing	Very weak	Weak	Average	Strong	Very strong	Perfect

N.A.—not attempted
N.O.—not observed

Another type of rating device is the progress chart. It provides for the rating of skills developed in sequence throughout a unit or course. The sample "Progress Chart in Beginning Swimming" demonstrates an application of this technique. According to the chart, Joan Black has accomplished four steps, Mary Adams has accomplished three steps, and Suzy Cox is trailing with only two steps completed. Ratings or completion dates are frequently entered in the chart in place of the x's illustrated.

PROGRESS CHART IN BEGINNING SWIMMING

STUDENT	OPENS EYES UNDER WATER	FRONT FLOATS	FLUTTER KICKS	FRONT GLIDES	GLIDES WITH ARM STROKE
Mary Adams	x	x	x		
Joan Black	x	x	x	x	
Suzy Cox	x	x			

Below is a sample of one element in a graphic descriptive rating scale designed to measure the objective of sportsmanlike behavior. Such scales are particularly useful whenever course objectives include observable but not measurable behaviors.

SAMPLE FROM A GRAPHIC DESCRIPTIVE RATING SCALE IN PHYSICAL EDUCATION

11. Behavior when his team is losing:

Becomes surly and rough	Blames other players and complains about officiating	Eases up or clowns around	Demands to play more than his share	Courteous, fair and active player at all times

APPRAISAL OF LEARNING EXERCISES, PROJECTS, AND PRODUCTS Rating devices of all types can be of great value in objectifying the appraisal of learning projects, exercises, and products, just as they are indispensable in the evaluation of skills. However, unless teachers keep the objectives of instruction clearly in mind they may place too great weight on learning exercises and end products alone. In particular, learning exercises are weighted heavily in science, mathematics, and languages. In such areas as art, home economics, and industrial arts, product ratings often form a large part of marks earned.

The validity of these marking practices has been seriously questioned by those who maintain that completed exercises and products reveal in only a limited way the student's achievement of course objectives. The authors of this text agree to a considerable extent with that point of view. In many courses ratings of learning exercises and end products should be given only minor weight in the assignment of final marks.

The key to proper evaluation of projects lies in analysis of the purposes for which projects are carried out. The rating of end products alone is insufficient. A large share of the rating should be devoted to evaluation of students' ability to plan effectively, to employ approved techniques, to work efficiently and independently, and to generalize and apply learning. When projects are evaluated in this manner, their rating might well be a major factor in final marks.

The use of learning exercise (homework) ratings as a major part of marks is of very doubtful value. This is particularly true when there is little evidence that the completed exercises are the independent work of the student. Furthermore, rating of learning exercises at times becomes a heavy burden on the teacher. Many devote far too much time to this work. For example, research has indicated that some mathematics teachers average two or more hours a day in scoring and recording learning exercises. At the same time these teachers average less than one hour a day in lesson planning.[7]

It is recommended that whenever objective keys can be prepared, students be permitted to do their own scoring and correcting. Students can also benefit from keeping progress charts. Scoring should seldom be carried on as a group activity during class time. However, class discussions arising from that activity are frequently beneficial. Occasional spot-checking of papers by the teacher is advisable. The time saved by following these recommendations can well be devoted to careful analysis of the papers of those who are having difficulty. In general, the evaluation of learning exercises should make a major contribution to lesson planning but only a minor contribution to final marking.

THE APPRAISAL OF ATTITUDES

Checklists, rating sheets, scales, and progress charts are effective aids to the solution of a very difficult problem: the evaluation of attitudes. In addition to the help offered by the tools already discussed, much can be gained from the use of anecdotal records.

ANECDOTAL RECORDS Anecdotal records are objective descriptive accounts of significant student behavior as observed and recorded by the teacher. Their purpose is to provide cumulative evidence basic to more adequate evaluative judgments. Students frequently best reveal their true attitudes and status of social development through their actions; thus an objective record of actions often yields much more valid evidence than that obtained by means of recall or by use of written tests, scales, and inventories. To use anecdotal records to the best advantage, teachers should keep in mind that:

1. Anecdotes should be objective. Interpretations and recommendations, if any, should be distinctly separate from the factual account of what took place.

2. Anecdotes should be selective. Limitations of time will force most teachers to record only incidents that they believe to be significant in the development of the individual or in the understanding of that development (more extensive records may be required in special cases).

3. Anecdotes should be brief. Record the essential facts of the incident

[7] J. R. Schunert, "The Association of Mathematical Achievement with Certain Factors Resident in the Teacher, in the Teaching, in the Pupil, and in the School," *The Journal of Experimental Education*, 19 (March 1951), 236.

and its setting. Extensive discussion, interpretation, and recommendation should be deferred until a summary analysis of many anecdotes is made.

4. Anecdotes should record favorable as well as unfavorable incidents. It is an error to record incidents of one type only.

5. Anecdotes should be recorded on uniform blanks or cards. Filing, analysis, and summarization are facilitated by a common format.

SAMPLE ANECDOTE

Name: John Jones   *Date:* October 15, 1969
Incident: John volunteered for the first time today. He told of his recent trip to
  the desert. Classmates listened attentively.
  (John transferred to this school on September 12, 1969)
Interpretation: John is beginning to adjust to his class.
Recommendation: None at present.

SOCIOMETRY

Sociometry, the study of social relationships revealed by student choices among their classmates, was originally stimulated by Moreno's writing in 1934.[8] Since that time its use has grown steadily in American schools until today sociometric tests, sociocharts, and sociodiagrams are commonly employed by teachers who wish to obtain objective evidence of the social relationships existing in their classrooms. With these techniques teachers can identify "stars," the students who are most desired as co-workers; "isolates," the students who are not named as desired co-workers; "fringers" or "neglectees," those who have selected no one who reciprocates their desire to work together; and "rejectees," those with whom some individual would particularly dislike to work.

Likewise, teachers can identify sociometric "cliques," groups of individuals who restrict almost all their choices to members of the same group; and "cleavages," the absence of choices between two or more groups. Cleavages are commonly found between boys and girls in the upper elementary grades, between rural and urban students in consolidated high schools, and between members and nonmembers of fraternities and sororities in colleges.

Appropriate use of sociometric data facilitates guidance of the social development of individuals and enables teachers to organize sociometric groups that through working better together increase class attainment of all course objectives, including knowledge and skills as well as attitudes and appreciations. Also, by repeating sociometric tests at intervals, teachers can trace and evaluate otherwise unmeasurable effects of organization and instruction.

SOCIOMETRIC TESTS   Several principles apply to the selection of a sociometric test question to be used as the basis for class analysis:

[8] Jacob L. Moreno, *Who Shall Survive?* Washington, D.C.: Nervous and Mental Disease Publishing Company, 1934.

1. The question should relate to an action that will involve a whole class.
2. The question should not be biased to favor or disfavor anyone. All students should have an equal opportunity to be selected.
3. The action proposed in the question should be real. It should be in agreement with the interests of the age group concerned and with the goals of instruction.
4. The action proposed should be carried out. Students are more likely to give valid responses when they know that action will follow.

On the basis of these criteria the following items would be inappropriate for use in sociometric study of a class:

1. "The girls in this class will choose their girls' league representative next week. Whom do you think they should select?" (If any boys are in the class, the first and second principles are violated.)
2. "Name the persons you would like as neighbors in a new seating arrangement." (Unless it is clearly understood that their present neighbors could be selected, the second principle is violated.)
3. "If you were going on a trip to Mars tomorrow, whom would you select as companions?" (This item violates the third and fourth principles.)
4. "Name your five best friends." (This items violates the first, third, and fourth principles.)

Several additional factors must be considered in the construction and administration of sociometric tests. First, research seems to indicate that items requiring five selections yield more useful and reliable data than items which require students to make fewer choices (10:148). Second, the validity of sociometric data is improved when students are assured that their choices will be kept strictly confidential. (Test papers should be folded and turned in directly to the teacher, not passed from student to student. Furthermore, all discussion of choices should be absolutely prohibited.) Third, tests should not be administered before students have had an opportunity to know every member of the class by name. Bias due to difficulties in spelling of names can be eliminated by listing all names on each test paper so that students need only to check their own names and mark their choices. Recording of results is also facilitated by this procedure. (See the Committee Preferences Blank.) Research indicates that when these principles and considerations are satisfied, student responses to sociometric tests are informative and reliable (3:1321).

Appropriate items for sociometric use could be similar to the following:

1. "Committees will soon be organized for our next unit of instruction. Name in order of preference five persons with whom you would like to work. If there should be any persons with whom you prefer not to work, name them also."

2. "Name the five class members near whom you would most like to be seated. Present neighbors may be named if you wish."

3. "Name the five class members you would prefer to have as teammates in our next physical education activity. Your instructor will balance the teams in playing ability, so select those with whom you would most like to play." (This item probably still contains bias related to playing ability. It could be useful in the organization of teams that might play well together, but it may fail to reveal valid information basic to socioanalysis.)

A suggested format for a sociometric test is illustrated below. In the example, John Garr has selected Pete Hanson as his first choice. His second choice is Jane Nebb; his third is Phil Brown. He also has selected Jack Johns and Sam Post, but has not indicated any preference between them. His one rejection is Carl Good. Each student in the class should fill out a similar form. The data obtained should be put into a sociometric chart to facilitate interpretation.

COMMITTEE PREFERENCES BLANK (CONFIDENTIAL)

To assist in the formation of committees for our next activity, please do the following:

1. Place a check (√) in the blank before your name.
2. Place your code letter in the blanks before the five class members with whom you would prefer to work.
3. If you have distinct preferences among your choices, also number your first choice "1," your second choice "2," and so on.
4. If you would object to being on a committee with anyone, place an X through the code letter before his or her name.

CODE		NAME
_____	A.	Mary Adams
__3F__	B.	Phil Brown
_____	C.	Carol Cook
_____	D.	Della Dugan
_____	E.	Faith Farr
__√__	F.	John Garr
~~G~~.		Carl Good
__1F__	H.	Pete Hanson
__F__	I.	Jack Johns
_____	J.	Amy Jones
_____	K.	Ole Lyon
_____	L.	Marta Moe
__2F__	M.	Jane Nebb
_____	N.	Bill Nort
__F__	O.	Sam Post

Note: When you have finished marking your choices, fold your paper, place it on your desk, and continue with your work. In consideration of the feelings of your classmates, do not discuss your choices with anyone. Your teacher will also keep all choices strictly confidential. Each person will have at least one or two of his choices in the group to which he is assigned.

SOCIOCHARTS   If the format illustrated in the Committee Preferences Blank is used, it is a simple matter to transfer the responses to a socio-chart. In fact, each column of choices represents a corresponding column in the chart (Fig. 16-1). The chart can be made by cutting and pasting or by simply lining up each column and transferring its contents to the chart.

When the choices made by each student have been entered in the vertical column headed by his letter code, the total number of choices received by each can be determined by counting the entries in the horizontal row following his name. This total, known as the student's "group status," should then be entered in column I. Research reveals that little is gained by assigning different weights to choices of different rank; merely counting the number of choices is adequate (10:64). Isolates and stars can be identified on the basis of column I entries. Examination of Figure 16-1 reveals that Mary Adams has a social status score of 5, average when five selections are made. Pete Hanson and Jane Nebb, each having received eleven choices, are stars; Faith Farr and Bill Nort are neglectees; and, in addition, Bill Nort is an isolate.

The number of times a student has been rejected should be recorded in Column II. In Figure 16-1 it can be seen that Carl, Amy, Jane, and Bill each have received one rejection.

Students Chosen		Choices Made By															Totals		
		A	B	C	D	E	F	G	H	I	J	K	L	M	N	O	I	II	III
A	Mary		1BA		DA							KA		MA	NA		5	0	3
B	Phil	1AB					3FB		HB	IB			LB		NB	OB	7	0	4
C	Carol					EC							1LC				2	0	1
D	Della	AD												MD		OD	3	0	3
E	Faith								HE					ME			2	0	0
F	John		BF			EF			HF		JF					OF	5	0	3
G	Carl	AG		CG	DG		X		HG	IG	1JG	KG		1MG			8	1	5
H	Pete	AH	BH	CH	DH		1FH	GH			JH	KH	LH	MH		OH	11	0	4
I	Jack					EI	FI	GI				KI					4	0	2
J	Amy					EJ		GJ		IJ			LJ	X	NJ		5	1	2
K	Ole			CK				GK		IK	JK		LK		NK		6	0	2
L	Marta			1CL		EL					JL						3	0	2
M	Jane	AM	BM	CM	DM		2FM	GM	HM	IM	X	KM			NM	OM	11	1	4
N	Bill									X							0	1	0
O	Sam		BO		DO		FO										3	0	3

Fig. 16-1 Sociometric chart of committee preferences

Mutual choices can most simply be determined by starting in the upper left corner of the chart following down column A and across row A encircling every mutual choice. Then from the diagonal line, repeat the procedure for column B and row B. When all mutual choices have been marked, the total for each row should be recorded in Column III. For example, in Figure 16-1 Mary has received three mutual choices, and Phil has received four. The number of mutual choices received by a student gives an indication of the degree to which he is accepted as a working partner by those with whom he would like to associate.

On the basis of sociocharts, a teacher can form better working subgroups within his class and identify students who may need guidance in social development. However, the full power of sociometry is not clear until these data are graphically arranged in a sociogram.

SOCIOGRAMS   Of the various types of sociograms in common use, the target diagram is perhaps the most popular. It is built by placing symbols representing students on a target of concentric circles so that the distance of each symbol from the center of the target is inversely related to the represented student's sociometric status. Thus stars are placed in the center, and isolates on the periphery. Choice patterns can be revealed by drawing lines between symbols to represent choices given and received. When the number of students in the class exceeds ten or twelve, however, an attempt to represent more than mutual choices usually results in an uninterpretable maze of crossed lines. Therefore, it is common to restrict representations to mutual choices, or to first and second choices at most.

In the target diagram (Fig. 16-2) designed for the recording of five-choice data, the innermost circle is reserved for symbols representing individuals who received nine or more choices. The ring next to the innermost circle provides the space in which to record symbols representing students who were selected six to eight times. The next ring, number 5, contains symbols representing students selected five times.

A refinement in sociogramming designed to reveal cleavages is brought about by dividing the target into quadrants and placing the symbols representing like classifications in the same quadrant. In the illustrated sociogram (Fig. 16-3), possible cleavages between girls and boys and between students who take buses and students who live in town have been investigated. Figure 16-3 represents the data in Figure 16-1 as follows:

1. From supplementary data in the students' folders it is determined that girls A, D, and M, and boys B, F, H, and O are transported to and from school by bus.

2. Girls A, D, and M, represented by triangles, are placed in quadrant I with M in the center circle, A in ring 5, and D in ring 3 according to the social status of each as recorded in column I of Figure 16-1. (Placement

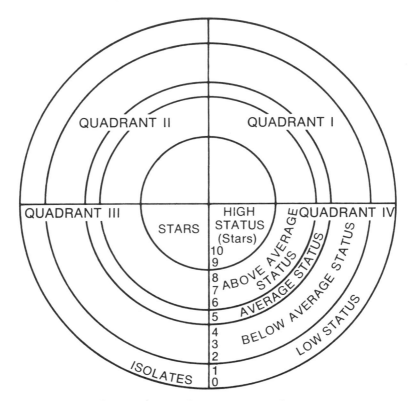

Fig. 16-2 Target on which to plot five-choice sociometric data

should be sketched lightly in pencil at this stage because minor changes in position are likely to be necessary in step seven.)

3. Circles to represent boys B, F, H, and O are placed in Quadrant IV according to the social status total of each.

4. In the same manner town girls and town boys are placed in quadrants II and III respectively.

5. Lines are drawn lightly between symbols to indicate the mutual choices recorded in Column III of Figure 16-1. For example, lines are drawn from A to B, D, and M.

6. Broken lines represent the rejections.

7. Symbols are shifted and grouped to reduce the number of crossed lines to a minimum. In this step care must be taken to maintain the correct distance of each symbol from the center of the sociogram. The sociogram is now completed. The problem of interpretation remains.

Examination of the completed sociogram reveals an absence of mutual choices between town girls and students of both sexes who travel by bus. However, restudy of the sociochart (Figure 16-1) shows that seven choices were made between town girls and boys who commute by bus, but verifies almost complete cleavage between the two groups of girls.

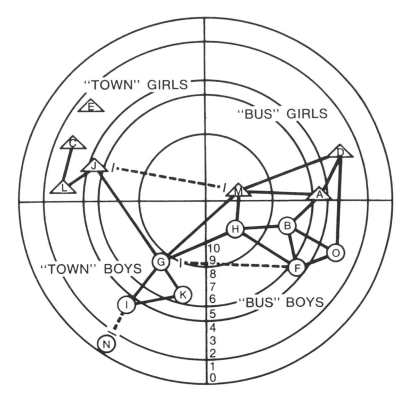

Fig. 16-3 Sociogram of committee preference
○ Boy   △ Girl   ———— Mutual choice   - - - - - - - - Rejection

Furthermore, that cleavage is magnified by the relationship of mutual rejection which has been indicated between the two girls most selected in their respective groups.

On the other hand, cleavages do not exist between students recorded in the other quadrants. In fact, the seven boys and girls who are transported by bus form a fairly close group; and at least one mutual choice and five or six single choices span the possible gaps between the other quadrants.

The sociogram reveals desired association among three of the town boys but isolation and rejection of N, the fourth. It is also clear that town girls, J, L, and C, form a chain but not a closely knit group, while E is a fringer or neglectee. Finally, stars M and H stand out clearly in the center circle, and an additional potential class leader is revealed in G, the only student having mutual choices in all four quadrants. In fact, he could be the key to improved relations among all groups of the class.

USE OF SOCIOMETRIC INFORMATION   Teachers who use sociometric data to guide the formation of groups start by placing a low-status student in each group and then add one or two persons he has selected. (Top priority should be given to his mutual choice if he shares one, and to his first and second choices if he has ranked his selections.) Additional persons selected by two or more members of the group are then added to bring the group to desired size. Care should be taken to avoid assigning rejectees and their rejectors to the same group. Also, the assignment of two isolates to the same group should be avoided if possible (10:238).

When a teacher decides to reduce or eliminate cleavages and cliques, he may find it helpful to use sociometric grouping that places members of two or more cliques on the same committee. It is considered good practice to keep at least two persons from a clique together because the basic policy is to expand groups rather than to explode them, although the latter technique may be effective in special circumstances (10:239).

Of course, teachers must take all available evidence, and not merely sociometric data into consideration whenever they form sociometric groups. For example, students known to be noisy and disruptive when together would not be assigned to the same group even though they might wish it.

It is also true that teacher action with respect to isolates, neglectees, and rejectees should not be based on sociometry alone. The sociogram serves only to draw the teacher's attention to possible problems that might be investigated more fully through use of observation and case study. Sociometry is useful but it is not a panacea. For example, many students of low social status are adequately adjusted and satisfactory in achievement. These individuals can be given minor social assistance by the classroom teacher. However, a few others may be seriously maladjusted and in need of the services of guidance personnel. Obviously, classroom teachers are not expected to handle all cases alone. Their responsibility is to learn to distinguish one type of case from another and to know when to refer students to specialists.

Finally, teachers should keep in mind that research shows that students identified as stars tend to be elected to leadership roles (10:301). It follows, then, that teachers would do well to give stars minor leadership training in the classroom. Assignments such as group chairman or class monitor, when accompanied by instruction in the responsibilities of those offices, have been found to be beneficial.

RELIABILITY AND VALIDITY OF SOCIOMETRY   Two questions sometimes asked are, Isn't sociometry intended for use only in the elementary grades? and What faith can one have in sociometric results in the high school? Research involving use of sociometry in high schools, in the military, in industry, and in hospitals shows that there is a strong tendency for groups to retain quite similar sociometric ratings over a period of several weeks or months. Individual choices may change, but the social status of an individual remains fairly constant unless planned steps are taken to bring about a change. In addition, research at all levels has shown that high-choice individuals are clearly superior to low-choice individuals in personality factors. "Only in rare instances are the low-choice individuals found to be superior to the high ones in any desirable behavior characteristics." [9]

Thus, sociometry can be used with a good deal of confidence. It has proved to be a useful and valuable addition to the evaluative techniques of the modern teacher.

SELECTED READINGS

1. Adams, Georgia Sachs, *Measurement and Evaluation.* New York: Holt, Rinehart and Winston, Inc., 1964, chaps. 1 and 8.

2. Ahmann, J. Stanley, and Marvin D. Glock, *Evaluating Pupil Growth,* 3d ed. Boston: Allyn and Bacon, Inc., 1967, chaps. 1 and 7.

3. American Educational Research Association, *Encyclopedia of Educational Research,* 3d ed., Chester W. Harris, ed. New York: The Macmillan Company, 1960, pp. 482–485, 1319–1323, 1502–1503.

4. Association for Supervision and Curriculum Development, *Evaluation as Feedback and Guide,* Fred T. Wilhelms, ch. and ed. Washington, D.C.: ASCD, NEA, 1967, chaps. 1, 2, 4.

5. Callahan, Sterling G., *Successful Teaching in Secondary Schools.* Chicago: Scott, Foresman and Company, 1966, pp. 120–128.

6. Clark, Leonard H., and Irving S. Starr, *Secondary School Teaching Methods,* 2d ed. New York: The Macmillan Company, 1967, pp. 349–357.

7. Downie, N. M., *Fundamentals of Measurement: Techniques and Practices,* 2d ed. New York: Oxford University Press, 1967, chap. 1.

8. Ebel, Robert L., *Measuring Educational Achievement.* Englewood Cliffs, N.J.: Prentice-Hall, Inc., 1965, chap. 1.

9. Gronlund, Norman E., *Measurement and Evaluation in Teaching.* New York: The Macmillan Company, 1965, chaps. 1–5, 15, 16.

10. Gronlund, Norman E., *Sociometry in the Classroom.* New York: Harper & Row, Publishers, 1959, chaps. 1–10.

11. Nordberg, H. Orville, James M. Bradfield, and William C. Odell, *Secondary School Teaching.* New York: The Macmillan Company, 1962, chap. 8.

12. Oliva, Peter F., *The Secondary School Today.* Cleveland: The World Publishing Company, 1967, chaps. 19–21.

[9] Merl E. Bonney, "Sociometric Methods," *Encyclopedia of Educational Research,* 3d ed. New York: The Macmillan Company, 1960, p. 1321.

13. Stanley, Julian C., *Measurement in Today's Schools*, 4th ed. Englewood Cliffs, N.J.: Prentice-Hall, Inc. 1964, chaps. 2 and 4.

14. Thomas, R. Murray, *Judging Student Progress*, 2d ed. New York: David McKay Company, Inc., 1960, chaps. 1, 2, 8–11.

15. Thorndike, Robert L., and Elizabeth Hagen, *Measurement and Evaluation in Psychology and Education*, 2d ed. New York: John Wiley & Sons, Inc., 1961, chaps. 1, 2, 13, 14.

CHAPTER 17 | *Teacher-Built Tests*

Every teacher needs to know how to build effective tests. Estimates based upon research indicate that, on the average, high school classes are tested approximately once each week. The frequency of test usage varies from teacher to teacher and from one subject to another. For example, one study found that in physical education and in fine arts tests were used least frequently, approximately once each month, whereas at the other extreme classes in mathematics and Latin were tested on the average of almost twice each week. Only a small proportion of the tests regularly used in the classroom are purchased; all but a few are constructed by the teacher himself. Therefore, it is apparent that teachers will find it to their advantage to develop skill in test building.

In this chapter the steps in efficient development of tests will be discussed, including: planning tests, building items, organizing tests for use, and improving the items for further use.

PLANNING TESTS

Test construction, like other important elements in the teaching process, requires careful planning. A necessary first step is to get the purpose of the contemplated test clearly in mind.

CLARIFYING THE PURPOSE

How are the results to be used? Will the test be a diagnostic and instructional device or is it to serve as a basis for determining student marks? In fact, can a test best provide the information desired, or should some other procedure be employed? Clearly identifying the purpose of a proposed test serves to determine the kind of test to be constructed and tends to eliminate test that are useless.

For example, if a test is to give direction to further instruction, items that reduce chance success to a minimum are to be preferred. It is particularly important in individual diagnosis that items having a high guessing factor be avoided. In diagnostic tests, for instance, it is better to use completion items than alternate responses. On the average, half of the students who guess on a true-false item will choose the right answer, making effective diagnosis impossible on the basis of responses to individual items. On the other hand, in tests to be used for marking purposes, the total score is important and chance response to individual items is not critical. Consequently, a greater variety of item types can be used effectively.

In addition to limiting the type of items to be employed, other factors, such as test content and test length, will also vary according to the purpose the instrument is to serve. Thus, definition of purpose sets the stage for the next steps in test planning.

It should be emphasized that no test should be given merely to satisfy an arbitrary time schedule. The beginning teacher who tests her class every Friday fails to comprehend the reasons for testing. Tests are given to serve specific purposes in teaching. To test effectively, teachers need to determine them clearly and completely before test building begins.

IDENTIFYING BEHAVIORS TO BE MEASURED

After the purpose has been clarified, the next step is to determine what to include in the test. Assuming that the test is to measure achievement at the conclusion of a unit of instruction, this step is best accomplished by examining the objectives and content of the unit. What learning outcomes are expected at the grade level taught? How are students who have achieved an objective distinguishable from students who have not? In order to reveal what students have achieved in desired knowledges, skills, and attitudes, many teachers find that at this stage test construction is facilitated by phrasing course objectives so as to describe exactly what students are expected to be able to do. Such statements are called behavioral objectives.

To be more explicit, some content topics, such as "understanding democracy," are taught at several grade levels. At each grade the topic is the same, but the behaviors sought are different. Sample behavioral objectives concerning one element of democratic understandings are listed in Table 17-1 for various grade levels. Study of this table will reveal that the behavior expected in the lower grades is "attentive listening to traditional stories." At the eleventh-grade level students are expected to be able to "identify and interpret the outstanding contributions of an extensive list of American leaders, and to give particular attention to the social, political, military, and economic circumstances from which their contributions arose." Comparable behaviors expected at the eighth grade and in college are also included in the table. Suggested evaluation techniques

*Table 17–1. Illustration of Behavioral Objectives for
One Content Topic Taught at Various School Levels*

Content: Understanding of Democracy
Specific element: Students will know about the contributions of great Americans.

SCHOOL LEVEL	BEHAVIOR EXPECTED	EVALUATION TECHNIQUE
	Most students will be able to:	
Lower grades	Listen attentively to traditional stories of American heroes	Observation
Eighth grade	Recognize the outstanding contributions of a selected list of American heroes	Objective test
Eleventh grade	Identify and interpret the outstanding contributions of an extensive list of American leaders, and relate their contributions to the social, political, military, and economic development of this nation	Objective and essay tests; ratings of group work and projects
College	Interpret and evaluate the contributions of American leaders while giving attention to the philosophical beliefs of each	Objective and essay tests; term papers
Graduate school	Evaluate the contributions to democracy of specific American leaders, and contrast and compare them with the contributions of important leaders of other ideologies on the world scene	Research papers, essay tests, and objective tests

appropriate for each objective are listed in the right-hand column of the table.

Objectives to guide testing should be stated so that the described behavior is observable. For example, rather than stating an English class objective as "The students will develop an everlasting appreciation of good literature," it would be better to say, "The voluntary reading of each student will increase in volume and quality from month to month during this school year." The first statement describes behavior that is worthy but not observable. The behavior described in the second statement can be observed, recorded, and evaluated.

Likewise, when objectives have originally been stated to describe the development of an understanding or knowledge, the objective should be restated so as to describe what the student will be able to do when he has developed that understanding or knowledge. For example, the objective "To develop an understanding of the Constitution of the United States" should be restated as "Students will be able to explain the meaning of the Constitution of the United States in their own words" or "Students will be able to identify which article of the Constitution applies to selected circumstances." The first statement does not clarify the level of behavior expected, whereas the second and third statements lead naturally to test items that can measure the behavior described.

Some experienced teachers prefer to base their tests on outlines of subject matter. However, this practice is recommended only when the teacher is thoroughly familiar with the behaviors to be expected at a given grade. Beginning teachers should always use behavioral objectives to guide both instruction and evaluation.

TEST LENGTH

A test ordinarily must be built to fit into a given instructional period. Many beginning teachers find it difficult to estimate the amount of time high school students will require to complete a test. Some overestimate the time needed and find that a test planned for thirty minutes is completed in fifteen, leaving an awkward void in the day's lesson. However, the more usual error is that of underestimating the time required. Tests planned for forty minutes or less frequently are still in progress when the bell rings for the next period. The teacher then faces the necessity of collecting the tests before the students are through (a practice that students dislike) or encroaching upon the time allocated to other classes—a practice that arouses the ire of both students and colleagues.

These situations can be avoided by more careful planning. Although the optimum time allocation for any given test can be determined accurately only after the test has been administered, a rough estimate of one minute per item requiring interpretation or application and a half minute per item concerning factual information will be a guideline suitable for many high school classes. Of course, problem items (common in mathematics and science) and essay questions (more frequently used in the social sciences) will require more testing time.

In any event, teachers must keep in mind that their students will differ greatly in the speed with which they can successfully complete a test. A test easily finished in fifteen minutes by some students may be a difficult twenty- or twenty-five-minute job for others. Therefore, estimates of testing time requirements should be flexible and take into account the needs of the class. Lesson plans for days on which tests are given should include specific suggestions for profitable use of the entire time by all students. Those who complete tests early should be advised to proceed on quiet individual projects while the slower students are finishing.

PROPORTIONATE CONTENT

After the unit objectives and content have been outlined in some detail, it will become obvious that limitations of time will not permit inclusion of test questions on everything that has been taught. It then becomes necessary to determine what topics should be tested and what proportionate share of the total test should be devoted to each. The more important topics of a unit should receive greater weight in the test than topics of lesser importance. If it is difficult to determine the relative importance of the various topics to be tested, a rough approximation may be achieved by noting the relative amount of teaching time each received. Then, because assigning different values to various items of a test greatly complicates scoring and because accurate statistical determination of weighting is beyond the skill of most beginning teachers, it is recommended that the number of items covering any given topic be in direct proportion to the relative importance of the topic. For example, four items would be allocated to a topic that is considered twice as important as a topic tested by two items. Admittedly this procedure achieves only a roughly proportionate weighting of the various topics in the test. Nevertheless, the procedure is recommended as most practical for the classroom teacher.

TYPES OF ITEMS TO BE USED

The items commonly used in teacher-constructed tests include alternate response, multiple choice, matching, completion, short answer, essay, and situation. Each type has its peculiar strengths and weaknesses, which should be taken into consideration in test planning. (Item characteristics are fully discussed in a following section of this chapter.) The first five listed are frequently classified as objective items. However, the scoring of only the first three is fully free from the scorer's personal feelings or prejudices. In truly objective items, each item will have only one correct answer, regardless of who does the scoring. Tests made up of the first three types can be scored directly from a key or by a machine. The scoring of completion questions and problems is somewhat less objective in that alternative responses may be acceptable for full or partial credit. The scoring of essay items is least objective of all. When the planned test is to be scored by someone other than the teacher, fully objective items only should be used.

The selection of item types for a test should be further governed by two factors: the purpose of the test and the conditions under which the test is to be administered. The fact that in diagnostic and instructional tests completion-type items are to be preferred to alternate-response types has been mentioned previously in this chapter. Test administration conditions should be fully considered in test planning. If his classroom is overcrowded or if more than one class section is to be tested, it may be advisable for a teacher to prepare alternate forms of the test. Teachers must be realistic and face the possibility that some students may copy answers when objective tests are used in overcrowded rooms or when information is available from students who have taken the test in an earlier period.

Table 17–2. *Plan for a Fifty-Item Test to Measure Objectives and Content of Chapter 17*

		CONTENT						
OBJECTIVES	WT. (%)	TEST PLANNING (10%)	ITEM BLDG. (44%)	TEST ORGANIZ. (20%)	ITEM ANALYSIS (10%)	TEST ADMIN. (10%)	TEST SCORING (6%)	NO. OF ITEMS
Students should remember:								
Terms	4		2					2
Facts	4					2		2
Methods	8	2		2				4
Criteria	4		1		1			2
Principles	20		6			3	1	10
Students should be able to:								
Compute indices of difficulty and discrimination	4				2			2
Differentiate between good and poor items	6		3					3
Identify weaknesses in poor items	6		3					3
Evaluate items on basis of criteria	4				2			2
Select best methods for scoring tests	4						2	2
Construct items to measure stated objectives	14		7					7
Develop test plans	6	3						3
Organize a test to fit a given test plan	16			8				8
Totals	100	5	22	10	5	5	3	50

The preparation of alternate forms of objective tests can reduce, if not eliminate, copying. Equivalent forms of matching or multiple-choice items can be constructed easily by merely changing the order of the choices. For example, the following items have different-lettered answers:

FORM I	FORM II
1. Who discovered the Pacific Ocean?	1. Who discovered the Pacific Ocean?
A. Magellan	A. Cortez
B. Balboa	B. Columbus
C. Columbus	C. Balboa
D. Cortez	D. Magellan

It has been found that essay items also discourage copying on the part of the students. Essay items, however, have the disadvantage of being easily handed on by students in an earlier section to those in a later one.

The selection of items is also affected by the availability of adequate duplication facilities. Wide adoption of the ditto process has made it much easier to prepare objective tests for use in the classroom. The older methods of writing the tests on the chalkboard or of dictating the items to the class are now outmoded. At best these older methods of test presentation were uneconomical. Too much class time was consumed in copying questions from the board or in waiting for the next question to be read aloud by the teacher. When test duplication facilities are not available, teachers are seriously limited in the kinds of tests they can use effectively. Concisely stated problems and essay items are the most efficient to use when it is necessary to dictate a test or to write it on the chalkboard. (Tests are to be presented orally to the class only as a last resort, except in the case of spelling, shorthand, or the foreign languages.)

Opinions differ concerning the advisability of using several types of items in a test or restricting the test to a single type.

Arguments favoring the use of only one type of item in a test point out that a truer score can be obtained by eliminating the confusion sometimes developed by changing the kind of response required. The use of a variety of types with clear directions and sample items for each in a test not only adds interest to the test but makes it possible to use each type to its best advantage. Table 17-3 indicates the recommended use and the relative objectivity of various types of items.

BUILDING TEST ITEMS

The building of good test items is an extremely time-consuming task. Highly trained professional test builders consider it a successful day when they have constructed one, two, or perhaps three unique items that eventually meet the rigorous requirements of a published test. Teachers cannot devote comparable time to the construction of classroom tests, but

Table 17–3. Use and Objectivity of Various Item Types

STUDENT BEHAVIOR TO BE MEASURED	MOST APPROPRIATE ITEM TYPES	OBJECTIVITY OF SCORING
Ability to exercise judgment, recognize relationships, and make associations	1. Alternate response 2. Multiple choice 3. Matching	1–3. Usually most objective
Ability to recall information and solve problems	4. Completion 5. Short answer	4–5. Usually fairly objective
Ability to organize recalled information and express judgment meaningfully	6. Essay	6. Usually least objective
Ability to interpret data, apply learning, think critically, and reason logically	7. Situation	7. Same as basic types (1–6)

they must recognize that tests built in a few hours usually are much in need of improvement. Time, however, is only one element in successful test construction. To build useful test items, a teacher must have knowledge of course objectives and course content, knowledge of item-construction principles, time to practice construction skills, and ideas for item content.

SOURCES OF IDEAS FOR ITEMS

The time to start test construction comes much earlier than most beginning teachers realize. Many of the ideas for test items should evolve in connection with lesson planning. At the time that teachers plan their lessons, the important objectives are clearly in mind. Consequently, at that time ideas for related test questions are much easier to develop than later on when the particulars of any single day's lesson have been forgotten. These ideas should be catalogued, preferably on separate cards, and filed so that they are available when needed. Item ideas in physical education might be statements like the following:

1. Matching item concerning the position of players on a softball diamond in given play situations.
2. True-false item about the infield fly rule.
3. Multiple-choice item concerning choice of plays in a given game situation.

A rich source of ideas for test items is the written work of students. An equally important source is student behavior. Common errors should be recorded for use when item ideas are needed.

Another excellent way to get item ideas is to give a pretest made up of completion items. The erroneous ideas recorded make very useful distracters in later multiple-choice or matching questions.

Some useful ideas for items may be obtained through examination of textbooks, courses of study, and tests in the subject. However, these sources are likely to yield ideas less pertinent to a particular class than the sources discussed above. Under no circumstances should the course textbook be substituted for the test plan. Teachers who use their textbook in lieu of a test plan are very likely to develop inferior tests. If items are based solely on ideas noted while paging through a text, it is almost inevitable that the resulting test will be a mere collection of questions concerning unusual facts that may have little or no relation to the real course objectives.

Item ideas, like fully developed items, should be filed so that they are readily available. Many teachers have solved the problem by recording ideas and items on separate cards and keeping them filed in boxes classified by unit objectives. A record of the effectiveness of each item, determined after its use, can also be kept on the same card.

GENERAL PRINCIPLES OF ITEM CONSTRUCTION

Before starting to build test items, teachers should become thoroughly acquainted with the general principles of item construction listed below.

STATING ITEMS CLEARLY   In order to do this:

1. Use vocabulary suitable to the students' level. Teachers sometimes fail to realize that many high school students are just beginning to develop technical vocabularies. Beginning teachers especially are likely to transfer their collegiate vocabulary almost unchanged to the high school classroom.

2. Avoid the use of figurative, ambiguous, complex, and unnecessarily qualitative expressions. Use specific and direct language in items. Eliminate unnecessary words.

3. Avoid trick questions. Place critical information in the most prominent part of the sentence. When essential information is hidden in minor clauses or complex phrases, the students' mental alertness and reading ability are measured rather than their achievement of the course objectives.

4. Be grammatically correct. Particularly avoid double negatives and inconsistent constructions.

5. Use negative statements sparingly. When they must be used, draw the students' attention to the negative element through use of special direction or underlining. If several such items are to be used, group them together, preferably at the end of the test.

6. Directions for taking the test should be clear, complete, and concise.

All directions should be included in the test so that, once the test is started, interruptions for further directions from the test administrator become unnecessary.

ELIMINATING CLUES   Items should be stated so that achievement is measured rather than student ability to draw clues from the form or language of the item. Specifically:

1. Avoid using certain words such as "no," "none," and "all" in such a manner as to determine specifically the answer desired. (See the discussion of true-false items for examples.)

2. Avoid making the longest answer consistently the best answer. (See the discussion of multiple-choice items for examples.)

ENCOURAGING GOOD STUDY HABITS   To accomplish this end:

1. Avoid asking for the mere reproduction or completion of statements taken directly from class discussions or from assigned readings. Such items can be answered on the basis of memorization without any knowledge of meaning. Tests should measure ability to understand, to apply, and to interpret rather than mere ability to memorize by rote.

2. Avoid use of stereotyped phraseology (except in distracters) for the reasons just cited.

STATING ITEMS FOR OBJECTIVE SCORING   The final score on a test should depend as little as possible on interpretations peculiar to the scorer.

1. Avoid use of recall and recognition items that unintentionally lead to debatably equivalent answers.

2. Essay questions should be carefully stated and keyed so that scoring can be as objective as possible.

BUILDING ALTERNATE-RESPONSE ITEMS

Alternate-response items are statements or questions which require that the student select one of two possible answers. The most common form is true-false, although yes-no, right-wrong, and completion forms are also widely used.

Examples:

T	F	1. Nixon was elected president in 1968.
Yes	No	2. Was Edison the inventor of the telephone?
Right	Wrong	3. The square root of 64 is 8.
_____		4. Joan (lent, borrowed) her book to me.

The cluster true-false form is an adaptation of the original true-false type.

Example:

If a painted cube 3 inches on an edge is sawed into 1-inch cubes, then of the 1-inch cubes

T F 1. four will be painted on one side.
T F 2. six will be painted on two sides.
T F 3. eight will be painted on three sides.
T F 4. none will be painted on four sides.
T F 5. none will be entirely unpainted.

Another modified true-false form requires that the student correct false statements by substituting words or phrases for underlined parts of the original statements. This form has some of the characteristics of completion items. It has been found to have higher reliability than the ordinary true-false form.

Example:

Monday 1. Labor Day comes on a Sunday.
True 2. In the United States, national elections are held on a Tuesday.

Alternate-response items are comparatively easy to construct and are economical of testing time. A wide sampling of course content is possible in minimum time through use of this type of item. However, these advantages are largely counterbalanced by several disadvantages: encouragement of memorization of unrelated factual information; negative learning effect of false statements; and unreliability due to the comparatively large possibility of guessing the correct answer. Perhaps the greatest weaknesses of this type of item are its lack of effectiveness in diagnosis and the tendency to overemphasize knowledge of unusual factual content. Nevertheless the alternate-response form remains one of the most frequently used item forms in educational testing. Specific suggestions for its construction follow.

AVOIDING HIDDEN FALSE PHRASES Many readers automatically assume that all qualifying phrases are true.

Poor: 1. California, which in area is the fifth largest state in the United States, has its capital at Sacramento.
               1. T F

Improved: 1. California is the fifth largest state in the United States.
               1. T F
     2. The capital of California is Sacramento. 2. T F

STRUCTURING THE SENTENCE In a statement of reason, the false part, if any, should follow the word "because."

Poor: A cubic foot of ice weighs more than a cubic foot of water because water increases in volume when it freezes.

Improved: A cubic foot of ice weighs less than a cubic foot of water because water decreases in volume when it freezes.

AVOIDING USAGE CLUES Avoid consistently using certain words in true statements more frequently than in false statements. It has been found that many teachers inadvertently provide clues to the truth or falsity of items by using such words as "none," "never," "all," "no," and "always" predominantly in false statements just as they use words like "may," "most," "some," "often," and "generally" predominantly in true statements. Before making the final draft of a test, teachers should check to see that these words are used about equally in both true and false items. Research has also shown that in the tests of many teachers, items including specific citations or enumerations as well as items more than twenty words in length are usually true (12:240). These clues, too, can be avoided.

AVOIDING AMBIGUOUS AND QUALITATIVE EXPRESSIONS

Poor: 1. In 1960 the population of St. Paul was quite large.

                                                           T   F

Improved: 1. In 1960 the population of St. Paul exceeded 600,000.

                                                           T   F

Poor: 2. Boys usually can run faster than girls.   T   F

Improved: 2. Ten-year-old boys usually can run faster than girls of the same age.   T   F

AVOIDING STATEMENTS TAKEN DIRECTLY FROM TEXTBOOKS   Use of textbook quotes in tests encourages students to squander their study time on educationally sterile rote memorization.

AVOIDING STATEMENTS THAT MAY BE EITHER TRUE OR FALSE   True-false statements that are not absolutely true or absolutely false pose an unreasonable problem to the student. He is forced to guess what degree of truth or falsity will be tolerated by the teacher. There is danger that the best students will miss these items merely because they know of unusual exceptions that the scorer has overlooked or considered inconsequential. The same items are answered easily by students with less information.

Poor: There are 365 days in a year.   T   F

Improved: An ordinary calendar year contains 365 days.   T   F

The first statement could be scored as true, but some students would mark it false because they possessed information concerning such exceptions as leap year, solar year, tropical year, lunar year, or astronomical year. (The period of the earth's revolution around the sun is approximately 365 days, 5 hours, 48 minutes, and 46 seconds.)

REDUCING CHANCE SUCCESS   The "50–50 guessing" weakness of ordinary alternate response items can be remedied by requiring students to change underlined words in false statements so as to make the statements true. However, this procedure reduces the guessing factor to acceptable levels only when the underlined words have at least three alternatives that could be considered plausible corrections by students who do not know the correct answer.

Poor: Eight-year-old girls usually <u>are</u> taller than boys of the same age.

Poor: Eight-year-old girls usually are taller than <u>boys</u> of the same age.

Improved: Eight-year-old girls <u>usually</u> are taller than boys of the same age.

Improved: Eight-year-old girls usually <u>are</u> taller than boys of the same age.

BUILDING MULTIPLE-CHOICE ITEMS

A multiple-choice item is composed of a question or an incomplete statement, together with at least three possible responses or completions. The student must select the one answer that is correct or best. The part of the item that precedes the responses is called the stem; the incorrect responses are known as distracters.

Examples:

(Question stem)

_____1. From what country was the Alaskan territory purchased?
    A. China
    B. Russia
    C. Japan
    D. England
    E. Canada

(Incomplete-statement stem)

_____1. The Alaskan territory was purchased from
    A. China
    B. Russia
    C. Japan
    D. England
    E. Canada

         A. to
_____2. Robert threw the ball B. two fast.
         C. too

Many experienced constructors of tests rate multiple-choice items superior to all other types. By careful organization of distracters, the builder of this type of item can measure a student's ability to make judgments of predetermined exactness; at the same time the item is easy to score and comparatively free from the factor of guessing. Some susceptibility to clues and relative difficulty of construction are the chief drawbacks of this item form. Careful attention to the following suggestions should help teachers improve the quality of their multiple-choice items.

USING AN ADEQUATE STEM   The stem should include enough to indicate clearly the kind of answer required and also eliminate unnecessary repetition in the responses.

Poor: The Mean

A. is computed by subtracting the low score from the high score and dividing by two.

B. is computed by adding the scores.

C. is computed by dividing the sum of the scores by the number of scores.

D. is computed by adding the scores and dividing by two.

Improved: How is the mean of a distribution determined?

A. Subtract the low score from the high score and divide by two.

B. Add the highest score to the lowest score and divide the sum by two.

C. Divide the sum of the scores by the number of scores.

D. Find the middlemost score by counting halfway through the distribution.

REFERRING TO ONE OBJECTIVE ONLY   The stem as well as the choices should relate to one objective only. When this principle is violated precision in measurement is lost.

Poor: Abraham Lincoln was

A. assassinated.

B. the 14th President of the United States.

C. married to Betsy Ross.

D. coauthor of the Monroe Doctrine.

Improved: The death of Abraham Lincoln was caused by

A. heart failure brought on by the strain of leading a nation at war.

B. the gunshot of an assassin.

C. cancer of the lungs.

D. natural processes of aging.

Improved: George Washington was the first President. What was Abraham Lincoln's numerical position among the Presidents?

A. 13th

B. 14th

C. 15th

D. 16th

E. none of these

AVOIDING CLUES Carelessly constructed multiple-choice items frequently include such keys as grammatical inconsistency, lack of homogeneity among the responses, systematic location of the correct answer, and unusual length of the correct response.

Poor: Francis Bacon was an
                     A. Dane
                     B. Englishman
                     C. Frenchman
                     D. German
                     E. Spaniard

Improved: What was the nationality of Francis Bacon?
                     A. Danish
                     B. English
                     C. French
                     D. German
                     E. Spanish

Poor: What Spanish explorer looked for the fountain of youth?
                     A. Cabot
                     B. Ericson
                     C. Lafayette
                     D. Ponce de León

Improved: What explorer looked for the fountain of youth?
                     A. Balboa
                     B. De Soto
                     C. Coronado
                     D. Ponce de León

It has been shown that in some tests the correct answer appears so frequently in the same position (such as the second or fourth choice) that students who discover the clue can improve their score. Another common error is to make the correct answer consistently the longest or the most smoothly worded response.

USING ONLY PLAUSIBLE CHOICES To students who lack the achievement being tested all listed responses should appear to be homogeneous and plausible.

Poor: Who discovered the continent of North America?
                     A. Washington
                     B. Edison
                     C. Cabot
                     D. Ford
                     E. Lindbergh

Improved: Who discovered the continent of North America?
A. Columbus
B. Balboa
C. Cabot
D. La Salle
E. Ponce de León

Poor: The ratio of 8 ounces to a pound is
A. 16:1
B. 1:16
C. 8:16
D. none of these

Improved: The ratio of 8 ounces to a pound is
A. 1:2
B. 2:1
C. 8:1
D. 1:8
E. none of these

BUILDING MATCHING ITEMS

A set of matching items is composed of two related groups of materials. The problem is to select for each item in one group the single best associated or matching element in the other group.

These items can be used to advantage in a wide variety of situations. For example, sets could be built using such combinations as a list of men together with a list of their works, a list of items together with a list of their definitions, a list of play situations together with a list of the rules which apply, a list of events together with a list of their causes or of their effects, a list of problems together with a list of their solutions, or a list of cities together with a chart of their geographical locations.

Matching items have characteristics similar to those of the multiple-choice type. In fact, a matching exercise could be looked upon as a group of multiple-choice stems combined with a single set of possible responses. Matching items are particularly well adapted to measure student ability to recognize relationships and to make associations. However, in the measurement of fine discrimination, understanding, and judgment, this type is inferior to the multiple-choice type. Because a group of matching items is organized into a unit, with one set of responses, the type is economical in its use of test space, and requires less construction time for each item than multiple-choice items of comparable quality. The chief limitation of matching items is the frequency of the presence of clues in exercises constructed by individuals who fail to realize the importance of employing only homogeneous materials and supplying a surplus of choices. The following example is an illustration of these common errors.

Poorly constructed matching exercise:

Directions: Match Column I with Column II

I	II
1. signal caller	goal line
2. field goal	quarterback
3. illegal use of hands	15-yard penalty
4. number of downs in a series	3 points
5. must be crossed to score a touchdown	4

Any high school student, regardless of the paucity of his knowledge of football, would be able to answer all five items above on the basis of the clues presented. For example, quarterback is the only player listed; therefore it becomes the automatic answer to item 1. In item 3 the word "illegal" is easily associated with the word "penalty" in the list of answers. The word "number" in item 4 limits the possible selections for that item to the only number in Column II. Because a "line" is the only feasible choice to be "crossed to score," choice one becomes the automatic answer to item 5. That leaves "3 points" to match effortlessly with "field goal" by the simple process of elimination.

It is obvious that these terms, all relating to the game of football, still lack the degree of homogeneity necessary to make up a usable matching exercise. The items should be revised into separate completion, alternate-response, or multiple-choice questions. They could be made usable in matching forms only by expansion into several separate exercises. These might include players and their functions; scoring plays and their point value; and illegal plays and their penalties. In addition to having relatively heterogeneous content and an undesirable balance between the number of item stems and the number of choices, the sample exercise needs revision in several other respects.

1. No space has been designated for the answers. Blanks should be placed to the left of each numbered item.
2. The terms in Column II are not labeled. Upper-case letters (A, B, C, D, and so on) are to be preferred.
3. The directions are inadequate. They might better read, "Match each football term in Column I with the best selection from Column II. Any lettered choice may be used once, several times, or not at all."

Specific suggestions for the improvement of matching items are discussed below.

LIMITING CONTENT TO HOMOGENEOUS MATERIAL To the student who lacks the achievement measured, every element among the responses should appear to be a plausible answer to every element in the column of stems. If the material to be tested cannot satisfy this condition, the exercise should be recast into items of a type other than matching.

AVOIDING PROCESS OF ELIMINATION TESTING   Provide more responses than stems in each set, and occasionally use a single response as the match to more than one stem. This will increase the number of distracters and reduce the possibility of answering items by the process of elimination.

LIMITING CONTENT TO MATERIAL THAT SATISFIES THE OVERALL PLAN OF THE TEST   Resist the temptation to append additional items to matching exercises merely because they easily fall into the pattern of the matching set. To ignore this restriction is to destroy the validity of the total test. If the content in question is not important enough to include as separate alternate-response, multiple-choice, or completion items, then it is not of sufficient importance to be tested by matching.

KEEPING MATCHING SETS RELATIVELY SHORT   The maximum number of responses to include in a single exercise should be determined by the reading difficulty and organization of the content. Ordinarily, eight to ten responses is a feasible limit. However, for extremely well-organized and concise responses the limit might be extended to twelve or fifteen without loss of efficiency. Remember, however, that to attain most effective measurement *every* choice in the response column must be a plausible response to *every* item in the column of stems.

Poor:	*Stems*	*Choices*
_____	1. Capital city of Alaska	A. Alaska
_____	2. USA state largest in area	B. Austin
_____	3. Capital city of Texas	C. Beef cattle
_____	4. A noted product of California	D. Juneau
_____	5. A noted product of Texas	E. Oranges

Improved:	*Stems*	*Choices*
_____	1. The state for which Juneau is the capital	A. Alaska
_____	2. The USA state having the largest area	B. California
_____	3. The state for which Austin is the capital	C. New York
_____	4. The state noted for its citrus fruit	D. Pennsylvania
_____	5. The state noted for its long-horn steers	E. Texas

ARRANGING FOR EASY UNDERSTANDING AND SCORING   Each item stem should be numbered, preceded by an answer blank, and placed in a column near the left margin of the page.

Each response should be clearly labeled and placed in a column at the right side of the paper, if possible. Upper-case latters (A, B, C, for example) are to be preferred to numbers or lower-case letters because they are less susceptible to confusing distortions. If the responses are to appear on a chart, diagram, map, or other figure, be sure that the choices are all clearly marked.

The responses should be put in alphabetical, chronological, or other meaningful order if possible.

The responses should be the shorter phrases and the stems the longer ones (with a possible exception of lists of terms and their definitions).

All parts of the exercise, including any necessary charts, diagrams, and figures, should be placed on the same page. It will be necessary to recheck this as the test is being typed for reproduction.

STATING DIRECTIONS CLEARLY   The directions should succinctly explain how the matching is to be done. Particular care should be taken to emphasize whether the responses are to be used only once or more than once.

Sample matching exercise:

Directions for items 1–8: Select the letter which best indicates the location of the following materials in our school library. Any choice may be used once, several times, or not at all.

	Library Materials	Choices for Items 1–8
_____	1. Dictionary	A. bibliography room
_____	2. Cumulative Book Index	B. curriculum library
_____	3. School Review	C. office
_____	4. Encyclopedia	D. periodical desk
_____	5. Education Index	E. reference desk
_____	6. School and Society	F. reserve room
_____	7. Bulletins	G. none of these
_____	8. NSSE yearbooks	

BUILDING COMPLETION ITEMS

Completion items are made up of sentences from which key words or phrases have been omitted. The student must think of the appropriate completions and write them in the blanks provided. A completion exercise may involve a single sentence, several sentences, or a paragraph. Each sentence may contain any number of blanks so long as the meaning of the exercise can be distinguished easily by students who possess the achievement being tested.

The completion item can be used in a wide variety of situations, but is most commonly used to measure recall of factual information and is particularly useful in diagnostic and instructional tests because the factor of guessing is much lower than in alternate-response, multiple-choice, and matching types. Good-quality completion items are considered relatively easy to construct, but because of the frequent necessity of considering the value of equivalent answers and the problem of reading some handwriting, their scoring is very time-consuming.

Sample completion items:

_____ 1. "The Lady of the Lake" was written by (*1*).
_____ 2. In basketball a field goal counts (*2*), and a free throw
_____ 3. counts (*3*).

1–5. In any right triangle the altitude to the hypotenuse:
_____ 1. is the mean proportional between (*1*) of
_____ 2. the (*2*),
_____ 3. forms (*3*) with the hypotenuse, and
_____ 4. forms two triangles which are (*4*) to each other
_____ 5. and to (*5*).

_____ 1. The (*1*) of the United States is made up of the House of Representatives and the Senate. Each member of the
_____ 2. House is elected for a term of (*2*) years, whereas
_____ 3. members of the Senate are elected for terms of (*3*) years.
_____ 4. All states have equal representation in the (*4*) and
_____ 5. proportionate representation in the (*5*). The presid-
_____ 6. ing officer of the Senate is the (*6*).

Specific suggestions for the improvement of completion items are illustrated in the following paragraphs.

OMITTING IMPORTANT WORDS   Avoid asking for details that you would deem unworthy of testing by other means.

Poor: Alexander _____ Bell is _____ for inventing the telephone.

Improved: Alexander Graham Bell is noted for inventing the

_____.

AVOIDING TOO MANY OMISSIONS   Enough should be left so that the meaning of the item is clear to the student being tested.

Poor: The _____ of a _____ is found by multiplying the _____ by _____.

Improved: The area of a rectangle is found by multiplying the _____ by the _____.

AVOIDING AMBIGUOUS STATEMENTS   Phrase statements so that the kind of response desired is clearly indicated. Careful attention to this factor will save much time for the scorer as well as for the examinee.

Poor:	Charles Lindbergh made his transatlantic flight in _____.
Improved:	The year in which Charles Lindbergh made his transatlantic flight was _____.
Improved:	The type of airplane in which Charles Lindbergh made his transatlantic flight was _____.
Improved:	The name of the airplane in which Charles Lindbergh made his transatlantic flight was _____.

AVOIDING UNINTENDED CLUES   Do not precede blanks with the articles "a" or "an." Make all blanks the same length. Check all items to see that the omitted words are not automatically associated with any words remaining in the statement.

Poor:	A football player is ineligible to receive a forward pass unless he is a back or an _____.
Improved:	The only football players eligible to receive forward passes are backs and _____.
Poor:	In the circle formula $A = \frac{1}{2}rc$, c and r are symbols for _____ and _____.
Improved:	In the circle formula $A = \frac{1}{2}rc$, c and r are symbols for _____ and _____.
Poor:	In Alaska the summer days are extremely long just as in the wintertime the _____ are dark and _____.
Improved:	Alaskan nights are long in the _____ season of the year.

OMITTING WORDS NEAR THE END OF THE STATEMENT   Statements are more difficult to understand when omissions are made at their beginning and clearer when they occur at the end.

Poor:	_____ is the longest side of a right triangle.
Improved:	The name of the longest side of a right triangle is _____.

AVOIDING STATEMENTS FROM ASSIGNED READING   Revise such materials so that mere rote learning will be discouraged. Test application of learning.

Poor:	For every action there is an equal and opposite _____.
Improved:	Robert can pull 90 pounds and Bill can pull 60 pounds. If they alone are pulling steadily on opposite ends of a rope, the maximum tension in the rope is _____ pounds.

BUILDING SHORT-ANSWER ITEMS

Short-answer items are direct questions or specific directions that require recalled responses. The responses usually require only a few words. Because the form is natural, the items are easy for the student to understand and comparatively easy for the teacher to construct.

This type of item can be used to measure a wide variety of objectives in a manner that reduces to a minimum success on the basis of guessing. However, since the response required is short, there is some tendency to overemphasize the measurement of factual and unorganized learning. Use of this type is further limited by the fact that scoring is frequently less objective and more time-consuming than scoring recognition items.

Sample short-answer items:

_____ 1. In what year did Columbus discover America?

_____ 2. How much annual interest is payable on a 6 percent loan of $10,000?

_____ 3. Compute the cost of burning a 100-watt light for five hours, assuming electricity sells for $.08 a kilowatt hour.

4–6. Name the capital city of each of the following states.

_____ 4. Oregon

_____ 5. Illinois

_____ 6. Maine

7–10. List the four largest cities in the United States in the order of their 1970 census population.

_____ 7.

_____ 8.

_____ 9.

_____10.

_____11. Define "adjective."

Construction of short-answer items will be improved by following the suggestions below.

USING SPECIFIC STATEMENTS   Avoid statements that will elicit a wide variety of responses.

Poor: What do you know about the United Nations?
Improved: What is the principal purpose of the United Nations?
Poor: Name the four most beautiful cities in the world.
Improved: List the four most populous cities in the world.

USING PROBLEM SITUATIONS   Avoid overemphasis on mere recall of factual information. Measure the application of learning.

| *Poor:* | Define kilowatt. |
| *Improved:* | How long will a 200-watt lamp burn in consuming one kilowatt of electricity? |

AVOIDING ALTERNATE-RESPONSE STATEMENTS   Construct questions so that the guessing factor remains at a minimum.

| *Poor:* | How does the area of Brazil compare with the area of the United States? |
| *Improved:* | What South American country, if any, contains an area greater than that of the United States? |

LIMITING ITEMS TO FIVE OR SIX LISTINGS   Do not use items that encourage students to learn long lists of miscellaneous information.

| *Poor:* | List the ten largest cities in the world. |
| *Improved:* | Name the three largest cities of the world in the order of their size. |

SPECIFYING ACCURACY IN NUMERICAL RESPONSES

| *Poor:* | What is the value of pi? |
| *Improved:* | What is the value of pi to the nearest one hundredth? |

AVOIDING UNNECESSARY COMPLEXITIES   Do not introduce unnecessarily complex computation when knowledge of a principle is the main objective to be measured.

| *Poor:* | Find the area of a trapezoid having bases of 4.06 inches and 11⁵⁄₁₂ inches and an altitude of 11.9 centimeters. |
| *Improved:* | Find the area of a trapezoid having 4-inch and 6-inch bases and an altitude of 8 inches. |

Answer: _____ square inches

BUILDING ESSAY ITEMS

Essay items are questions or statements that require the student to organize a comparatively long answer in his own words. These items differ from the short-answer type in that they permit the student to express himself freely. His response is not limited to a numerical answer nor to a few words recalled from his learning.

Essay items can be used advantageously to measure ability to organize and express ideas, to discuss issues, to evaluate trends, to interpret meanings, to explain relationships, to criticize constructively, to summarize effectively, to describe application of principles, and the like. This type can be used in all subject matter areas but seems to have greatest applicability in the social studies, in studies of literature, and in some aspects of the sciences. In mathematics, physical education, industrial arts, and other subjects that emphasize the achievement of specific skills, essay items are somewhat less useful.

A further advantage of considerable importance is the tendency of this type of item to encourage students to study better and to remember their learning longer. When studying for essay items rather than for ordinary recognition or short-answer types, students frequently devote more time to noting relationships and organizing information into larger units.

Essay items are not without their serious limitations, however. Unless they are extremely well constructed and keyed, their scoring is so subjective as to destroy their practical usefulness as diagnostic instruments. Furthermore, they ordinarily take so much time to answer and so much time to score that they seldom can be used efficiently as instructional devices.

One study (15:43–47) is typical of the many that establish an irrefutable fact: essay tests—whether scored by the same teacher, different teachers, or by specially trained experts—yield almost *unbelievably inconsistent* results. This study involved 130 teachers who scored each of five essay papers. A common model response rated at 25 points was provided each teacher. The findings revealed that every paper was given as few as 5 points by at least one teacher and as many as 18 points by other teachers. The minimum range of scores on any paper was nineteen out of twenty-six possible ratings. Furthermore, every paper was ranked poorest among the five by some teachers, and every paper was also ranked best among the five by others. If a percentage scale of 90 percent = A, 80 percent = B, 70 percent = C, 60 percent = D, and less than 60 percent = F had been used, every paper would have received C grades, D grades, and F grades, and three of the five papers would have received all grades A through F. The researchers concluded that their results illustrated ". . . the situation that commonly prevails in evaluating essay responses" (15:47).

Nevertheless, some respected scholars, expert in fields other than measurement, have become so enamored with the virtues of essay tests that they completely ignore their faults. A few of this group maintain that essay tests should be the only test form used in educational measurement. Such a conclusion is unsupported by scientific evidence. In fact, if a teacher were to adopt such a practice:

1. He would be restricting his measurement procedures to a technique that has changed little in over 100 years of use in American schools.
2. He would be rejecting the scientific developments in objective testing of the last fifty years.
3. He would be ignoring the research facts that reveal the extreme unreliability of essay testing.
4. He would be ignoring the advice of measurement experts that has been accepted by business, industry, government, and the military.

5. He might merely be unwilling to put forth the considerable effort that would be expended in learning how to build and interpret objective tests of high quality.

The proper conclusion is not to abandon the use of all essay testing as some measurement authorities have advocated, but merely to abandon the use of the poorly constructed and scored variety. When essay items are well constructed and properly keyed, they can be scored with some objectivity. However, when they are employed in the usual manner, they substitute two guessing factors for the one that is common to recognition types in that students must guess at the meaning of the questions and teachers must guess at their scoring.

Construction of essay items can be improved by following the suggestions below.

APPROPRIATE QUESTIONS Questions beginning with "why," "how," "criticize," "contrast," "evaluate," and similar words, are more appropriate to essay items than those beginning with such terms as "where," "who," "when," "what," "list," and "enumerate," which can be used in other types of testing.

Poor: Discuss basketball with respect to (1) who originated the game, (2) when and where it was originated, (3) what size court and ball are official, (4) the names of the positions, (5) what team won the national AAU championship last year, (6) what defensive style was most popular in that tournament.

Improved: In 100 to 200 words, contrast the zone and man-to-man defenses in basketball. Explain how they differ with respect to (1) basic techniques involved and (2) their appropriate use in typical game situations.

AVOIDANCE OF VAGUE GENERAL QUESTIONS Provide sufficient directions to limit the length and suggest the specific content of the response desired.

Poor: Discuss basketball.
Improved: (See example above.)

ADEQUATE SAMPLING To evaluate achievement more fully, use several questions requiring answers of approximately 50 to 100 words rather than fewer questions requiring longer responses.

Poor: In 600 to 1000 words trace the westward movement in American history.

Suggested improvement: Six or eight questions, each requiring a 50- to 100-word discussion of a clearly defined aspect of the movement.

OPTIONAL CHOICE OF ITEMS　It is poor practice to ask the student to select his own test by responding to such directions as "Answer three of the following four questions" or "Answer four of the following seven questions." Test-construction experts agree that ability to make optional choices destroys the possibility of making comparative evaluations of student achievement on the basis of the test results. When choice of content is permitted, the students take different tests.

It should be pointed out that it may be advisable for a teacher to ignore this recommendation of the experts if he is teaching in a school in which the provision of optional items is customary. Students almost without exception look upon the optional-choice arrangement as a privilege that safeguards the fairness of the test.

POINT VALUE　Provide specific information concerning the value of each item if different weights are to be assigned to the various items. It appears to be advisable to give the same point value to all essay items unless they vary greatly in length or difficulty. Research is inconclusive but seems to indicate that little or nothing is to be gained by assigning varying weights to items. However, if more than a single weight is used, the weight assigned to each item should be clearly indicated.

TIMING　Include suggestions for the amount of testing time to be given to each item. This practice is particularly helpful to students when time limits for the total test are rigid.

Examples:

1. (5 points—ten minutes) In approximately 50 words compare the
   . . . .
2. (10 points—fifteen minutes) In 100 to 150 words, discuss the
   . . . .

SCORING　Build a complete key to be used in scoring the items. An accurate and usable key will make more efficient scoring of essay items possible. Further suggestions for scoring are discussed later in this chapter.

BUILDING SITUATION ITEMS

The types discussed up to this point—alternate-response, multiple-choice, matching, completion, short-answer, and essay—constitute the basic types of test items in common use today. However, innumerable modifications and combinations of these forms are constantly being developed by the builders of educational tests. At least one of these forms, variously referred to as situation, problem solving, and interpretive testing, merits special mention.

In this kind of test, exercise material (in such form as a written description, a chart, a table, or a photograph) is presented, followed by a series of related items in ordinary form. Comprehension and analysis of the presented material, as well as recall of learning, are required to respond successfully to the questions.

This type of item can be used to advantage in the measurement of ability to interpret data, to think critically, to reason logically, and to apply principles to a new situation. Difficulty in finding suitable materials and an increase in the length of time required to take the test are its chief limitations. To construct this type and other modified types, follow the suggestions discussed under the basic item types involved. Two sample situation-type item sets follow.

Sample A: Situation-type item set

Directions for items 31–35: From the table at the right, choose the pupil who *best* answers the following descriptions. Any lettered choice may be used once, several times, or not at all.

Descriptions

_____31. Most mature intellectually.

_____32. Most mature educationally.

_____33. Brightest for his age.

_____34. Most *accelerated* educationally, from the standpoint of *chronological* age.

_____35. Most *retarded* educationally, from the standpoint of *mental* age.

Choices for items 31 through 35

Pupil	C.A.	M.A.	E.A.
A	12-10	13-8	13-9
B	11-7	13-6	13-0
C	12-11	12-6	13-8
D	12-8	13-10	13-8
E	11-10	12-6	13-7

Sample B: Situation-type item set

Directions: Study the following description of an experiment and then answer the questions as directed below.

The Situation

A teacher of science in the ninth grade of a four-year high school firmly believed that teachers of the lower grades were shamefully mishandling that subject. While at college one summer he determined to prove his point. He collected the following data on his 150 science pupils of the previous year.

1. The number of his pupils who had received previous science instruction, (60). Group A.
2. The number of his pupils who had not received previous science instruction, (60). Group B.

3. The number of his pupils for whom no data of this kind were available, (30).
4. The final science test scores for all 150 pupils.

His Procedure

With the use of a system of random numbers he assigned 15 of the "no record" pupils to the "previous science" group (A) and the remaining 15 to the other group (B). He computed the average final test scores for each group, the probable error of the difference of these averages, and a set of correlations.

His Findings

1. Group A (with previous science) averaged 77 on the final of 120 points.
2. Group B (no previous science) averaged 80 on the final of 120 points.
3. The probable error of the difference in these averages was 1 point.
4. The correlation between amount of previous science and science achievement in grade nine was minus .01.

Mark items 1–6 either S, U, or C according to whether the statement is (S) substantiated, (U) unsubstantiated, or (C) contrary, respectively, to the findings of the study.

His Conclusions

_____1. Ninth-grade pupils do better in science if they have had no previous science.

_____2. Teachers of the lower grades do more harm than good in their attempts to teach science.

_____3. The differences noted were significant at the 1 percent level.

_____4. Teachers of the lower grades should learn to teach science well or leave it alone.

_____5. Instruction in science in the lower grades in his school district reduced the science marks of his average ninth-grade pupils of the last year by 1 percent.

_____6. The problem should be given further study.

7. (14 points) Criticize this study from the viewpoint of scientific investigation. Point out specific changes that you would make if you were conducting this study (200–300 words).

ORGANIZING THE TEST

After the items have been constructed, the next step is to organize them into a test that can be administered and scored efficiently. Tests should be attractively and logically arranged. They should be easy to read and easy to score. Too many potentially excellent groups of items have been reduced to mediocrity as a result of haphazard organization. The effectiveness of tests can be enhanced by careful attention to the following principles and suggestions.

HEADINGS

Provide blanks at the top of the first page for the student's name, the class period, the date, and the final score. Also place the test title and the number of each copy at the top of page one.

Example one

Social Studies
Test One, Copy No 12

Name _____   Date _____

Score _____   Period _____

ANSWER BLANKS

Establish definite positions for the answers. Do not scatter these positions about the page. Throughout the test use a column of numbered blanks or symbols on either the left or the right margin of the paper. Some teachers prefer the right-hand margin because it is somewhat more convenient for right-handed examinees and test scorers (see example two). However, the answer column placed at the left-hand margin (see example three) is more easily associated with the proper item without extra numbering. In addition, many students, when writing, rest their left hand across the top left-hand portion of the test paper. Thus they effectively, though inadvertently, shield the filled-in answers from students who might be tempted to copy. For tests exceeding one or two pages in length, it may be advisable to prepare separate answer sheets.

Example two

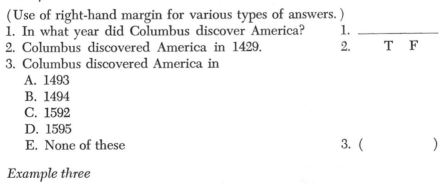

(Use of right-hand margin for various types of answers.)
1. In what year did Columbus discover America?   1. _____
2. Columbus discovered America in 1429.   2.   T   F
3. Columbus discovered America in
   A. 1493
   B. 1494
   C. 1592
   D. 1595
   E. None of these   3. (   )

Example three

(Use of column on left for various types of answers.)
_____ 1. In what year did Columbus discover America?
  T   F   2. Columbus discovered America in 1429.

(   ) 3. Columbus discovered America in
           A. 1493
           B. 1494
           C. 1592
           D. 1595
           E. None of these

READABILITY

Space items and their parts so as to achieve maximum readability. For example, in matching exercises place the column of item stems on the left side of the paper and the column of choices at the right (see example four, a sample matching exercise).

Example four

Directions for matching items 36–40: Select the day of the week upon which each listed holiday occurs. Place each selected letter in the proper blank at the left. Any lettered choice may be used once, more than once, or not at all. (The first item illustrates correct procedure.)

Holidays	*Choices for Items 36–40*
____B____(X) Labor Day	A. Sunday
_____ 36. Easter	B. Monday
_____ 37. Independence Day	C. Tuesday
_____ 38. Thanksgiving	D. Wednesday
_____ 39. Christmas	E. Thursday
_____ 40. National Election Day	F. Friday
	G. Saturday
	H. Varies from year to year

In multiple-choice items, place the choices in a column beneath the stem. This suggestion may be ignored when the choices are so short that they can all be placed effectively in a single line (see example five, a multiple-choice sample).

Example five

Directions for multiple-choice items 21–35: In the blank at the left of each numbered item write the letter of the answer you have selected for that item.

_____21. What color results when equal portions of yellow and blue pigments are mixed?
           A. Black
           B. Green
           C. Purple
           D. Yellow orange
           E. None of these

_____ 22. The sum of 6 plus 3 is

　　　　　　(A) ½　(B) 2　(C) 3　(D) 9　(E) 18

In completion exercises, the omissions should be numbered in parentheses. Correspondingly numbered blanks for the answers should be placed on the same line in the column at the left (see example six, a sample completion item).

Example six

Directions for completion items 41–46: Each of the numbered spaces in the following paragraph indicates the omission of a word. Complete the meaning of each statement by writing the correct word in the correspondingly numbered blank at the left. The first item is answered as an example.

____9____ (X) There are (X) playing positions on a baseball team.
_____ 41. The defensive player positioned about midway between
　　　　　　　　second and third base is the (41). He frequently must
_____ 42. pivot at second base in order to complete (42). If
_____ 43. he is the "clean-up" hitter, he bats in (43) position.
_____ 44. When he hits a home run with the bases full, four (44)
_____ 45. are scored. However, if the (45) calls a third strike
_____ 46. on him, he is (46).

Avoid placing part of the item on one page and the remainder of the item on another. If the bottom of the page is reached with part of an item left over, place the entire item on the next page, or rearrange the items so that they fit the page. An exception must be made for items more than a full page in length. For such items place the parts on pages that face each other. Illustrated material should be placed just ahead of the items for which it is intended.

DIRECTIONS

State directions briefly and clearly. Use vocabulary at the level of the students. Include only information essential to their understanding of the general conditions of the test and of how to proceed.

　　Place general information at the beginning of the test, clearly stating the purpose of the test, its time limits, the point value of the items, and whether or not a correction formula is to be used in scoring the test (see example seven).

Example seven

Test information: This test will tell you how well you are achieving the goals of this unit. The results will *not* be used in marking. Each item will count 1 point. Your score will be found by subtracting one third of the number of your errors from the number of items you answer correctly.

Omit those items for which you have little or no knowledge of the answer. *Do not guess wildly.* You will be allowed twenty to thirty minutes to complete the test.

Put specific directions immediately before each different group of items.

Example eight: Sample true-false items

Directions for true-false items 11–21: For items that are true, cross out the letter T. For items that are false, cross out the letter F. The first two items are marked to illustrate the proper procedure.

T̸   F   (1) The sum of 2 plus 2 is 4.
T   F̸   (2) The sum of 2 plus 2 is 5.
T   F   11. Thomas Edison invented the sewing machine.
T   F   12. The steamboat was invented by John Claremont.

Place directions at the end of the test for those who finish the test early. These directions should indicate what the student should do after he has completed the test (see example nine).

Example nine

When you have completed this test and have checked your answers, place the test face down on your desk. Do *not* bring it to the teacher's desk. After your test has been picked up, proceed *very quietly* with your assigned studies. Remain in your seat until your teacher has indicated that the testing period is over. Your complete cooperation will be appreciated by everyone.

Use simplified directions when students understand them. After students have become accustomed to a particular testing procedure, directions can be reduced in length and illustrative items eliminated. In particular, teachers who make frequent use of instructional tests find that they can keep their students alert to the requirements of the items employed. It is much better to introduce new item types in practice situations than to take up valuable testing time to give instruction. The following example of simplified directions also indicates appropriate wording when the test is to be scored with a stencil key:

Example ten

General information:
   Purpose: Marking. Approximately 5 percent of semester's mark.
   Scoring: 1 point per item. No correction for guessing.
   Time: Approximately forty to fifty minutes.
Specific directions:
   True-false items 1–30: Cross out T for true, F for false.

Multiple-choice items 31–65: In the column at the left, cross out the letter representing the best choice.

Ending directions:

Remember to work quietly on assigned studies after you have completed this test.

ARRANGEMENT OF ITEMS

Arrange the sequence of items so as to encourage the student and not confuse him. Insofar as possible:

Place items of the same type together in the test. To change frequently from one type of item to another is disconcerting to the student.

Place the easier items at the beginning of the test and the more difficult and time-consuming ones near the end.

Items on related objectives or on related content should be kept together in the test.

ELIMINATION OF CLUES

Avoid patterns of responses that might provide clues to the answers or might easily be transmitted from one class section to another.

The lettered choices should be used as the correct responses in a random order. Avoid systematic patterns of responses. Students soon become alert to clues of this type.

No particular choice should be the correct answer noticeably more frequently nor less frequently than any other choice. Keep count of the number of times each selection is used as the answer on the entire test. Revise the items if there is an unreasonable lack of balance in this respect. Many teachers unconsciously favor one letter over others.

Check the entire test to see that clues of all types are eliminated. In particular, make sure that:

Words like "no," "none," "sometimes," and "generally" are used about equally in true and in false items.

The longer choices in multiple-choice items are correct responses no more frequently than the shorter choices.

No item contains information that could be used directly to answer a different item.

DUPLICATION OF COPIES

Tests should be duplicated so that each student has a copy. It is very poor economy to write tests on the board, and even less advisable to read them aloud to the class. Reproduction of the test for class use should be as expert a job as is possible. Only one side of the paper should be used unless it is so heavy that disconcerting shadows do not show through.

For clear copies the type must be clean and the duplicating machine operating properly. More than a few tests are reduced in effectiveness through lack of attention to details at this stage. If the teacher does this work himself, as is frequently the case, he must be sure to get adequate instructions in the proper use of the machine. If clerks do this work, it should be remembered that they will do a much better job when given time to work carefully.

PROOFREADING

The master copy should be proofread carefully before it is run off. Any necessary corrections can be made most easily at that time. After the test is duplicated, it is too late to make corrections effectively. Proofreading should be done early. If it is delayed until students are taking the test, it may be found too late that typographical errors have played real tricks with some items.

For example, the following incident actually occurred:

A psychology professor, during the administration of a test, became aware of a ripple of ill-concealed amusement among his students. His reaction may well be imagined when he belatedly read his test and discovered that the letter "g" had been dropped from the word "sing" in the following item, with which he had intended to measure knowledge of the effects of heredity upon musical talent:

True-False. "A girl is more likely to be able to sin expertly if her mother is gifted with the same talent."

From that day on, at least one psychology professor has taken special care to proofread his tests.

IMPROVING TEST ITEMS

Clues leading to test items that need improvement can be found by noting items that are difficult for students to understand, by examining the responses of students to find choices that have not been selected, and by analyzing the difficulty and discrimination of all items.

OBSERVATION

While administering a test, teachers can gain many clues to needed improvements by noting items misinterpreted by students. If the questions of students repeatedly concern the same items, those items should be studied for needed revisions. It is good practice to tabulate (on a copy of the test) the number and character of questions that arise during test administration. These notations will be useful when items are revised.

In multiple-choice or matching exercises all choices should appear plausible to at least a few members of the class. If close check of the test reveals that some responses have been selected by no one, those responses should be revised.

ITEM ANALYSIS

Item analysis is an extremely fruitful technique for test builders to use. More than thirty methods of item analysis have been developed. An effective method easy to apply involves the following steps:

1. Score the tests, then select the highest-scoring quarter and the lowest-scoring quarter of the papers. That is, if 160 students took a test, put the highest-scoring forty papers in one pile and the lowest-scoring forty papers in another.

2. Tabulate the number of errors made on each item by each group. Item 1 may have been missed by eight of the high-scoring students and by thirty of the low scorers.

3. Compute the discrimination index of each item by subtracting the percentage of error of the top group from the percentage of error recorded for the bottom group. For item 1 above, the computation would be $8 \div 40 = .20$; $30 \div 40 = .75$; $.75-.20 = .55$. The discrimination index of item 1 is .55.

4. Compute the difficulty index of each item by finding the average percentage of error scored by the top and bottom groups. For item 1 above, the computation would be $(.75 + .20) \div 2 = .475$. The difficulty index of item 1 is .475.

The indices of discrimination and difficulty are important indicators of the quality of items used in tests designed to measure *differences in*

Table 17.4. Analysis of Four Items Administered to 160 Students

	TABULATION OF ERRORS				ESTI-MATED DISCRIM-INATION A − B	ESTI-MATED DIFFI-CULTY (A + B)/2	EVALU-ATION
ITEM NO.	40 LOWEST PAPERS (25%)	ERROR (A)	40 HIGHEST PAPERS (25%)	ERROR (B)			
1	//// //// //// //// //// ////	.75	//// ///	.20	.55	.475	Good
2	//// //// //// ////	.50	//// //// //// ////	.50	0	.50	Revise
3	//// ////	.25	//// //// ////	.375	−.125	.31	Replace
4	//// //// //// ///	.45	//// //// ////	.35	.10	.40	Revise

achievement among students. (In diagnostic and instructional instruments the indices are of little consequence as measures of item quality.)

For the purpose of measuring differences among students, the theoretically optimum difficulty index is .50. In practice almost the full range of indices from zero to 1.00 is usable, although the greater the deviation from .50, the less effective the item becomes. At the extremes of zero and 1.00 the item adds nothing to the measurement desired. This fact is more easily understood when it is realized that on a test made up of items each having zero difficulty, every student would have a perfect paper. On the other hand, if a test were composed of items of 1.00 difficulty, all students would miss all the items. In either event, no differences in achievement are measured.

This index of discrimination indicates the degree to which an item is more difficult for the low-scoring group on the whole test than it is for the high-scoring group. If the low group as a whole makes fewer errors on an item than are made by the high group, the index of discrimination is negative. Such items should be revised or replaced before the item is used again. A discrimination index of zero indicates that the item fails to measure differences between the high scorers and the low scorers. These items should also be revised or replaced. The best items have discrimination indices of .60 or higher. In general, a discrimination index of at least .20 is required for effective measurement.

ITEM JUDGMENT CRITERIA

Although item analysis offers dramatic objective information concerning test items, it cannot, by itself, prove that an item is of high quality. The technique is extremely useful for directing attention to weak items, but should not be taken as the sole criterion of item value. For instance, consider such items as "What is the color of the book assigned yesterday?" and "How many steps are in the stairway leading to the library reading room?" These items might be perfect when judged on the single basis of discrimination and difficulty indices but are completely unacceptable when the criterion of "measurement of valid course objectives" is applied.

Before an item can be accepted for use unconditionally, it must receive affirmative ratings on *all* the following points:

1. Does the item measure a valid objective of the course?
2. Is the item easy to understand? Is it fair?
3. Is the item's index of discrimination satisfactory (at least .20)?
4. Is the item's index of difficulty satisfactory (between .10 and .90)?
5. Does the item fit the test plan?

ADMINISTERING TESTS

After you have constructed the test items and organized them into a test, you must prepare yourself to administer the test effectively. Test administration is not just sitting at your desk while the students work. In fact, a good test administrator is too busy to sit down. The job should not be taken lightly. Unless the test is administered intelligently, all the work of construction will be ineffective. It is up to you to learn to do the job right.

RESPONSIBILITIES OF A TEST ADMINISTRATOR

It is the responsibility of the test administrator to do the following:

1. Become thoroughly familiar with the test and its directions. See that the test is ready to be administered.
2. Establish favorable physical and psychological conditions for testing.
3. See that the students have all the necessary materials and understand what to do with them.
4. Maintain proper testing conditions throughout the test period.
5. Collect the test materials and check them for completeness.

SUGGESTONS FOR TEST ADMINISTRATORS

1. Become thoroughly familiar with the test and its directions. See that the test is ready to be administered.
   a. Count the tests and number the copies as soon as they have been duplicated. Be sure that you have at least two or three extra copies. One of these extra copies should be used for a key and the others held as reserves to be used if for any reason copies become unusable. Numbering the copies enables you to keep better track of the test and also serves as a code number by which test scores can be reported confidentially.
   b. Prepare the key *before* you administer the test. The best way to prepare the key is to take the test yourself. Read each item carefully, then check your key with your answers on the original draft of the test. Correct any discrepancies. In that manner you will become thoroughly familiar with the test and be able to do a better job of administering it.
   c. At the time you prepare the key, make written notes of any suggestions or clarifications that should be announced at the time the test is administered. Also make written notes concerning any items that may prove difficult for students to understand. With this information you will be better able to answer the most likely questions of students.

d. Put the tests and keys in a safe place, and remember where you put them. Do not leave test materials or keys on your desk, in unlocked drawers or cabinets, or on open shelves about the room. Place them in a securely locked file or storage cabinet. Some teachers prefer to store these materials at home.

2. Establish favorable physical and psychological conditions for testing.

a. Make certain that conditions of light, heat, ventilation, and seating are adequate throughout the entire room. No student should be required to sit at a desk or a table that for him is too large or too small. Left-handed students should not be seated at desk-armchairs designed for right-handed individuals. It is difficult for students to do their best when they are suffering physical discomfort.

b. Determine the best seating arrangement for the test. If the test is to be used for marking purposes, students should be seated far enough apart to provide adequate working space and to discourage copying. Few high school classrooms have enough unoccupied seats to permit an alternate seat arrangement. However, many modern classrooms are furnished with movable desk-armchairs that can be easily arranged to gain full use of the entire area of the room. It is advisable to have the necessary seating arrangements completed before the arrival of the class to be tested.

c. Eliminate distracting noises. For example, window shades that flap persistently in a draft should be adjusted, and desks that creak should be tightened up, oiled, or left vacant. Clanking heating system radiators and noisy ventilator fans are other common distracters that should be reported for repair to the maintenance staff.

d. Discourage visitation in your classroom during testing periods. Testing periods are not suitable for teacher-parent, teacher-teacher, or other conferences. In some instances, it may be necessary to post a sign on the door: "Testing—no visitors, please."

e. Establish testing readiness in your students. Discuss plans for the test with your class a day or two ahead of its scheduled administration. The purposes of the test should be fully explained, the objectives and content to be measured should be outlined, and practice with unfamiliar item types should be provided. This pretest discussion and practice should encourage and direct review on the part of the student, and at the same time reinforce his confidence. Much fear of tests is based on fear of the unknown.

f. Encourage a positive attitude toward tests. A positive attitude can be developed or destroyed in students, depending upon the approach adopted by the teacher. The tone of pretest discussions and practice should not be one of urgency. Neither overlook nor deplore deficiencies. Be businesslike, but pleasant. Tests should be discussed as opportunities to learn more about oneself. Following tests with constructive conferences and using tests principally as diagnostic and instructional devices will go a long way toward establishing a favorable student attitude toward them.

g. Establish control of the class from the beginning of the test period. Do not permit unnecessary communication. Last minute trips to the water fountain or the pencil sharpener should be discouraged. Be pleasant but firm. Insist upon prompt compliance with directions.

3. See that the students receive all the necessary test materials and know what to do with them.

a. Establish an efficient procedure for distributing test materials. Supplementary materials, such as answer sheets, scratch paper, and pencils, should be passed out before the tests are distributed.

b. Read the directions aloud to the class. Speak clearly and slowly. Be sure that the test purpose, the time limits, and the method of scoring are understood. Be brief, businesslike, but not severe. You should try to reduce tensions in students, not build them up.

c. If any corrections in the test are necessary, announce them before the test is begun. Put the essential corrections on the board so that students can double-check their changes.

d. Announce that after the test has begun no one is to speak or to leave his seat without permission. Questions on procedure will be answered at the student's desk. Direct the students to raise their hands quietly when they need assistance.

e. Do not permit students to start the test before you have given the starting order. Unless you insist on compliance with this requirement, you will find that some students will fail to follow directions merely because they were reading test items when they should have been listening to directions or studying them.

f. Permit students to ask questions about the test directions after the oral directions have been completed. Keep any necessary question period to a minimum. Most students will be anxious to start the test.

4. Maintain proper conditions for testing throughout the testing period.

a. Move about the room while the test is under way. Check carefully to see that directions are being followed. A complete circuit of the class should be made for that purpose at the beginning of the test and periodically thereafter. Quietly observe the work of each student, but do not watch any one person so long or intently that he becomes aware of the observation. Under no circumstances should you remain seated at your desk.

b. While the test is under way, you should answer only the legitimate questions of students who have indicated their need with a raised hand. Do not permit students to direct questions to you from across the room. Nor should students bring questions to you. It is much less distracting to other students if you give assistance only at the desk of the individual who asks for help. Speak very quietly so as not to disturb the rest of the class. Answer questions concerning interpretation of directions or clarification of typographical errors only. If a student understands the directions but still has difficulty in understanding an item on the test, do not define words in the item or give similar assistance. Tell the student to work on the other items and return to the most difficult ones last. Give no information that indicates the answer to any problem in the test. Furthermore, avoid smiling or frowning in response to answers you read. Some students can derive clues from the facial expressions of the teacher as he observes their work.

c. Be alert to detect any copying that may be taking place. Always be in a position to observe the entire class. In particular, avoid becoming so intent upon helping one student that you ignore the needs or the transgressions of others. If you observe questionable behavior, do not create a disturbance. Most situations can be corrected with a mere glance or by standing near the possible offenders long enough to let them know you are aware of what is being attempted. If your suspicions are confirmed, do not hesitate to act quickly and firmly. Do not seize the test papers and dramatically tear them to bits as one new teacher was observed to do. Merely quietly tell the offender to report after class, at which time the problem should be discussed rationally and without rancor.

Your chief responsibility in moving about the room during the test period is to help answer necessary questions and to help students who are observed to be misinterpreting the test directions. The prevention of cheating is a secondary responsibility of the test administrator. When tests are properly motivated, evaluated, and administered, cheating seldom occurs.

d. Maintain a quiet working atmosphere throughout the test period. Do not permit students to move about the room while testing is still in progress. Carry several sharpened pencils that can be traded with students who otherwise would wish to use the pencil sharpener.

e. Urge students to work at their maximum accurate speed. Some students attempt to work too fast while others spend too much time trying to answer every item in sequence. You should become acquainted with students who make these errors and quietly guide them to the most profitable use of their time.

5. Collect the test materials and check them for completeness.

a. In the case of untimed tests, pick up the completed test and any supplementary test materials as soon as the student indicates that he has finished. If tests are collected by the teacher, much confusion is avoided. Do not permit the students to deliver the tests individually to the teacher's desk.

b. In case the entire class finishes a test together (as frequently happens with short, timed tests), the tests and test materials can be returned efficiently through use of student monitors.

c. Be certain that students who complete the test early immediately begin to work quietly on assignments.

d. When tests are completed early, it is well for students to check them carefully for unintentionally omitted items.

e. Count all returned materials and check your records to see that everything is turned in. Arrange the returned tests so that they are ready for scoring.

SCORING TESTS

The question of who should score tests is largely academic. Usually the teacher does the scoring with little or no help from clerks or students. Nevertheless, there is some evidence to indicate that learning could be enhanced by greater use of students in the scoring process. Administrators may eventually provide clerical service for the clerical parts of the job.

Students can be used to advantage in the scoring of instructional tests made up of objectively scored items. Practically all scoring of essay items and most scoring of recall items require subjective judgment that can be supplied by the teacher alone.

It is to be recommended that students score instructional tests employing items of the alternate-response, multiple-choice, and matching types. Students might also score carefully constructed completion and short-answer items. Exchange of papers has been found to increase the accuracy of scoring. Rechecking by the writers of each paper is recommended. Much learning takes place in the process of scoring.

Teachers should score all essay items and all tests to be used for purposes of diagnosis or marking. Well-trained clerks, if available, could adequately score all tests other than those composed of essay items.

ASSIGNING WEIGHTS TO ITEMS

Strict application of logic would indicate that items be assigned different weights according to their importance or their difficulty. Results of research, however, reveal that little is to be gained by that procedure.[1] Students have been found to retain very nearly the same rank in class regardless of whether unweighted or weighted scores were used. The increase in the difficulty of scoring occasioned by the use of differential weights does not seem to result in a correspondingly more accurate score. Consequently, it is recommended that the same number of points be assigned to each item.

[1] Robert L. Abel and Dora E. Damrin, "Tests and Examinations," *Encyclopedia of Educational Research*, 3d ed. New York: The Macmillan Company, 1960, p. 1512.

USE OF CORRECTION FORMULAS

Test items of the alternate-response, multiple-choice, and matching types tend to encourage students to guess. Successful guesses increase the number of correctly answered items and thereby hide the true achievement of the student. Therefore, many teachers use a correction formula to get an approximation of the score that each student would have earned had he not guessed. In the formula used $S = R - W/(C\text{-}1)$, S is the corrected score, R is the number of items answered correctly, W is the number of errors made, and C is the number of choices provided in each item. The expectation is that, on the average, guesses on alternate-response items will be correct one half of the time, guesses on three-choice items will be correct one third of the time, and so forth. For example, if a student knew the answers to eight items of a 10-point alternate-response test, and guessed at the answers to the other two items, he would get one of them correct. By the formula, he would get a score of 8, the number of answers he actually knew ($8 = 9 - 1/2\text{-}1$). The correction formula is based on the assumption that the laws of chance apply. In practice, this assumption is satisfied part of the time only. For instance, when the student is able to eliminate one or more responses of a multiple-response item, application of the formula will undercorrect. On the other hand, the formula overcorrects when students read the entire item and are drawn by purposely plausible distracters.

The authors of this text do not recommend use of the correction formula to adjust scores of individual students for several reasons: (1) The formula is based on a statistical concept, not a purely mathematical one. It can be used correctly to adjust class measures, but for individuals it will overcorrect part of the time and undercorrect at other times. (2) The resulting adjustments in score usually lead to only small changes in the ranking of individuals. These changes are hardly worth the additional scoring effort, particularly when the number of choices in the items is three or more. (3) Pupils disfavor use of the formula. It is difficult for them to understand the loss of points already earned by answering items correctly.

Use of the correction formula has the advantage of discouraging wild guessing on the part of the student. When the formula is used, students tend to give more careful consideration to their responses. Some teachers use the correction formula solely for the purpose of encouraging students to work more carefully.

In case you should want to obtain corrected scores for a test composed of alternate-response items, a recommended procedure is to award 2 points for each correct item, 1 point for each omitted item, and no points for errors. The adjustment accomplished parallels that obtained through use of the formula $S = R - W/(C\text{-}1)$. This adjustment in score is usually considered fairer by all students, including those who object to the regular correction formula.

SCORING KEYS

The scoring of tests, frequently a tedious task, can be greatly simplified through use of adequate keys. The four types most frequently used to score all items except essay items are the keyed test, the strip key, the accordion key, and the stencil key. The most common form of key is built by writing the answers in the proper blanks on a copy of the test. A strip key is made by cutting the columns of answers from a keyed test or by carefully spacing the answers for each page of items on a separate cardboard strip. An accordion key results when the answer strips are all placed on one sheet of heavy paper, which is then folded to the width of a single column of answers in the manner of an accordion. Each of these three types of keys is used in the same manner. The proper column of correct answers is placed alongside the corresponding column of responses, one test page at a time. The stencil type of key is most effective when an answer sheet has been used. A stencil can be made easily by marking the correct answers on an answer sheet and then punching holes in the key corresponding to each correct answer. When the stencil is superimposed on an answer sheet, the correct responses are visible through the punched holes. An entire test can be scored quickly by merely counting the number of marks that show through the holes.

Essay items are much more difficult to score. Keys for essay items should indicate the main points to be discussed in each response. Credit should be allowed for the substitution of equivalent points. If ability to organize and to express ideas is an objective of your course, point credit should be given for organization and expression.

Scoring of essay items has been found to be most efficient when the entire set of test papers is scored on one item before a second item is scored on any paper. In this manner the scorer can become thoroughly familiar with the application of the key. Furthermore, this procedure materially reduces the likelihood that the score on one item will affect the objectivity of scoring a following item. Finally, it is recommended that answers be placed on one side of the test paper and the student's name be placed on the reverse side. Objectivity of scoring can be improved by keeping the scorer unaware of the name of the person who wrote the paper being scored.

SELECTED READINGS

1. Adams, Georgia Sachs, *Measurement and Evaluation*. New York: Holt, Rinehart and Winston, Inc., 1964, chaps. 10–12.

2. Ahmann, J. Stanley, and Marvin D. Glock, *Evaluating Pupil Growth*, 3d ed. Boston: Allyn and Bacon, Inc., 1967, chaps. 2–6.

3. American Educational Research Association, *Encyclopedia of Educational Research*, 3d ed., Chester W. Harris, ed. New York: The Macmillan Company, 1960, pp. 1503–1514.

4. Clark, Leonard H., and Irving S. Starr, *Secondary School Teaching Methods*, 2d ed. New York: The Macmillan Company, 1967, pp. 357–373.

5. Downie, N. M., *Fundamentals of Measurement: Techniques and Practices*, 2d ed. New York: Oxford University Press, 1967, chaps. 6–10.

6. Durost, Walter N., and George A. Prescott, *Essentials of Measurement for Teachers*. New York: Harcourt, Brace & World, Inc., 1962, chap. 4.

7. Ebel, Robert L., *Measuring Educational Achievement*. Englewood Cliffs, N.J.: Prentice-Hall, Inc., 1965, chaps. 2–7, 11.

8. Garrett, Henry A., *Testing for Teachers*, 2d ed. New York: American Book Company, 1965, chaps. 8–10.

9. Gerberich, J. Raymond, *Specimen Objective Test Items: A Guide to Achievement Test Construction*. New York: David McKay Company, Inc., 1956, chaps. 2–13.

10. Gronlund, Norman E., *Measurement and Evaluation in Teaching*. New York: The Macmillan Company, 1965, chaps. 6–11.

11. Payne, David A., and Robert F. McMorris, *Educational and Psychological Measurement*. Waltham, Mass.: Blaisdell Publishing Company, 1967, pp. 123–162.

12. Remmers, H. H., N. L. Gage, and J. Francis Rummel, *A Practical Introduction to Measurement and Evaluation*. New York: Harper & Row, Publishers, 1960, chaps. 7, 8.

13. Rupiper, Omer John, *Item Writing: A Programed Text of Rules for Writing Objective-Type Test Items*. Norman, Okla.: Harlow Publishing Corporation, 1964.

14. Stanley, Julian C., *Measurement in Today's Schools*, 4th ed. Englewood Cliffs, N.J.: Prentice-Hall, Inc., 1964, chaps. 3, 6–8.

15. Thorndike, Robert L., and Elizabeth Hagen, *Measurement and Evaluation in Psychology and Education*, 2d ed. New York: John Wiley & Sons, Inc., 1961, chaps. 3 and 4.

16. U.S. Department of Health, Education, and Welfare, Office of Education, *Interpretation of Test Results*, OE–25038, Bulletin 1964, no. 7. Washington, D.C.: Government Printing Office, 1964, pp. 34–46.

17. Wood, Dorothy Adkins, *Test Construction: Development and Interpretation of Achievement Tests*. Columbus, Ohio: Charles E. Merrill Books, Inc., 1960, pp. 20–60, 81–125.

CHAPTER 18 | *Marking and Reporting*

All teachers face the important problem of how to determine and report marks. In attacking this problem, they must recognize that marking practices to a great extent are defined by the overall marking policies of each school. The format of the report, the basic standard with which individual student achievement is compared, the achievements marked, and the general distribution of marks are all matters of policy ordinarily determined by the administration of the school. No teacher should attempt to establish his own system nor should he make adaptations without the approval of his principal. Experienced teachers will avoid the error of the beginner who proudly stated that his C grades were as good as any other teacher's B's.

The teacher's first responsibility in marking is to determine and then to follow the policies set by the school. (When revisions in policy are desired by the school and its community, participation on study committees becomes a professional opportunity.) The second responsibility of the teacher is to see that his marks reflect evaluation of student progress toward all important objectives of the course. Too many teachers base their marks exclusively on the most conveniently obtainable evidence. Better marking practices require the teacher to seek and to use a wide variety of evidence concerning the attainment of course objectives.

This chapter contains a discussion of common marking practices, a discussion of questions and issues in marking, recommendations on how to combine the achievement data into a single mark, and suggestions for reporting.

PURPOSE OF MARKS

Achievement marks serve several purposes: informing parents and the student of educational progress; motivating better study; guiding the selection of course work in both high school and in college; and providing bases for grouping, promoting, and graduating. In addition, some schools employ marks to determine honors as well as eligibility for participation in extraclass activities. These purposes can be summarized as information, motivation, guidance, and administration.

To accomplish these purposes effectively, a marking system must be easy for students, counselors, and parents to understand. It must be as objective and reliable as possible. It must be not only economical of time but acceptable to the majority of students, counselors, parents, and teachers in the area where it is employed. No single system now in use fully satisfies all criteria. However, it appears that the most suitable solution would involve both letter marks based on summation of standard scores and descriptive comments to parents based on observation and standardized test interpretation.

MARKING PRACTICES

What marking systems are likely to be encountered in a modern school? Looking to research for an answer, teachers will find that many different systems of marking and reporting achievement are currently used in American schools. Letter symbols, numbers, and descriptive statements are all used either singly or in combination.[1] It is impractical to study all the variations, but every teacher should be acquainted with the methods from which the variety of systems is derived. With this knowledge he can better adjust to the particular practices of his school and more capably cooperate in their improvement.

The most common system of marking employs five letters: A for excellent, B for above average, C for average, D for below average but passing, and F for failure. This system is used by approximately 75 percent of all schools. A few schools denote fine gradations by adding letters or by attaching plus or minus signs to the passing marks. Other schools use fewer categories, such as H for honors, S for satisfactory, and U for unsatisfactory or S and U alone. The letter systems have the advantage of wide usage, but the disadvantage of grouping a wide range of achievement under a single mark. For example, a grade of C usually is earned by 35 to 50 percent of a class. Thus, many differences in achievement remain unrevealed when only two to five categories of marks are employed.

The numerical systems of marking include percentages, rank orders, percentile ranks, and standard scores. Numerical systems provide a greatly increased number of marking categories, but it should be recognized that fine discriminations in marking can be both a weakness and a strength.

[1] Ann Z. Smith and John E. Dobbin, "Marks and Marking Systems," *Encyclopedia of Educational Research,* 3d ed. New York: The Macmillan Company, 1960, pp. 783–789.

For example, to mark John 75 percent and Mary 76 percent indicates that they differ in achievement, which is quite likely to be true; but these marks also indicate that Mary exceeds John by 1 percent, which may or may not be true, considering the limitations of present evaluation techniques.

Of all numerical systems, percentage marks have been in use the longest and are still the most popular. In this system the standing of each student is computed as a percentage of a theoretically perfect performance. An arbitrary passing point is usually 60, 70, or 75 percent. Percentage marks differ from other numerical marks in that percentages are based on absolute achievement and not on the attainment of the class. Theoretically, all members of a class could pass or all could fail. However, in practice it is possible to manipulate the difficulty of tests so that "appropriate" proportions of students fall into the various categories. At one time, percentage marks were very widely used but have been largely replaced by letter marks.

In the rank order system, the student having the highest achievement is 1, the next highest is ranked 2, and so on. If there were thirty-five students in a class, the lowest in achievement would have a rank of 35. Passing may be set at any point. Ranks are difficult to interpret unless the size of the class is known. A rank of 6 in a class of sixty may represent a quite different level of achievement from that represented by the same rank in a class of only seven or eight students.

Percentile rank marks indicate the percentage of the class exceeded by any given student. That is, a student who achieved better than 75 percent of his class would receive a percentile mark of 75. The basic meaning of this system is fairly easy to understand. However, the system has the disadvantage of being subject to misinterpretation when comparisons are involved. For example, a percentile rank of 40 does not necessarily represent an achievement twice that of a percentile rank of 20. An increase in percentile rank from 10 to 15 exceeds an increase from a rank of 45 to 50 but is frequently interpreted as equivalent by those who do not understand the characteristics of percentiles.

The use of standard scores in marking is a comparatively new technique. In this system the student is marked according to the number of standard deviation units between his position in class achievement and the average achievement of the class. Students at the class average are marked 0. Those below average receive negative marks and those above average get positive marks. The most common adaptation of this system, Z-scores, eliminates algebraic signs and uses 50 as the average score. Marks range from a low around 20 to a high around 80, with a passing mark most frequently set at about 35. Standard scores overcome several of the defects of other numerical systems. For classes in which achievement is approximately normally distributed, standard scores are quite simple to interpret. Nevertheless, many parents and teachers find it difficult to orient themselves to a system that employs a statistically derived basic unit.

Looking ahead, it appears that standard scores will be used extensively to form basic distributions from which letter marks can be more accurately derived.

In recent years an increasing number of schools have been employing descriptive written reports to parents or teacher-parent conferences as a means of supplementing or replacing traditional reports. Of these practices, the most feasible at the secondary level appears to be the checklist of descriptive phrases (see Table 18-10).

QUESTIONS AND ISSUES IN MARKING

In addition to determining school policy concerning the form of marks to be used, teachers must also determine the school policy concerning the bases to be used for marking, and the school-recommended distribution of marks. In other words, teachers must find the answers to such questions as these: Should achievement, citizenship, and attendance be marked separately? How can subject matter achievement and citizenship be differentiated? How should citizenship marks be determined? Should marks be adjusted according to student ability? Should marks be based on an absolute scale, a percentage scale, or a relative scale? What proportion of a class should receive each mark? What is the school's policy toward failing marks? Are special notices to parents and conferences with counselors required when failing marks are anticipated? What systems for recording and combining marks are most feasible? The next section of this chapter will be devoted to a discussion of these questions.

MARKING ACHIEVEMENT AND CITIZENSHIP SEPARATELY

During a marking period teachers are expected to accumulate data concerning the quality of each student's homework, tests, projects, reports, study habits, attention, effort, leadership, cooperation, and the like. There is little wonder that some beginning teachers, amid this maze of information, are overwhelmed by the task of marking and reporting.

Although teachers, students, parents, and administrators generally accept that an achievement mark should represent a student's achievement of all objectives of a course, it should be obvious that a single mark cannot portray accurately the standing of a student on so many divergent items. Nevertheless, a few schools attempt to adjust a single mark to assess a student's record in all these factors. Most schools, however, follow the more satisfactory practice of reporting attendance records and citizenship ratings separately from achievement marks.

It is conceded that good habits of study, attendance, and citizenship are important school objectives, but to include them in the subject matter mark reduces the accuracy of the information conveyed by the mark and lowers its effectiveness. It is, therefore, strongly recommended that factors of attendance and citizenship be reported in marks separate from those used for achievement.

DIFFERENTIATING SUBJECT MATTER ACHIEVEMENT AND CITIZENSHIP

Some teachers have difficulty differentiating the factors that should be considered in a citizenship mark from those factors that should be part of the mark of subject matter achievement. Many schools offer specific instruction concerning this point. If such information is not provided, the following guidelines should prove helpful:

When instruction to bring about a particular behavior is regularly offered as part of a course (or an earlier course in a sequence of courses), the behavior is usually a factor to be considered in the achievement mark of the given course.

When, in addition to satisfying this point, a particular behavior is uniquely sought in a given course, the behavior is always a factor to be considered in the achievement mark for that course.

When these conditions are not met, the behavior concerned is usually a factor to be considered in the citizenship mark.

The following examples should clarify application of the guidelines:

1. A student is occasionally late in arriving at his class. This behavior belongs in the citizenship category.

2. A student fails to clean up around his desk or bench. This behavior should be reflected in the citizenship mark unless instruction in neatness is regularly and uniquely offered as part of the course.

3. A student uses equipment so as to endanger the safety of his classmates. Assuming that instruction in the safe use of equipment is offered, the behavior should affect the achievement mark. If the student willingly persists in the dangerous behavior after instruction has been offered to him specifically, his citizenship mark should also be affected.

The obvious exceptions to these guidelines are behaviors in the fundamentals of reading, writing, arithmetic, grammar, spelling, and speech. When behaviors in these fundamentals merit attention in courses not usually offering such instruction, it is likely that neither citizenship marks nor achievement marks in the course will be affected. However, in such circumstances a report under "Comments to parents" and a report to the counselor responsible for assignment of students to remedial courses might both be appropriate.

DETERMINING AND USING CITIZENSHIP MARKS

If citizenship marks are to have real significance in secondary schools, teachers must give careful attention to their preparation. The student behaviors to be observed and rated must be clearly identified, the resulting ratings must be carefully recorded and synthesized into final marks, and the final marks themselves must be given meaningful recognition by the school. Examples of the last point are found in schools that provide honor awards or special school privileges for their outstanding citizens. Other schools require students to have average or better citizenship ratings as prerequisites to graduation, or as prerequisites to participation in the cocurricular activities of the school. The supporters of this kind of requirement maintain that the privilege of participation in school activities should be denied to students whose behavior is unsatisfactory.

When they determine citizenship marks, teachers customarily follow either of two procedures. In the first procedure teachers assume that all students begin a marking period with a top rating in citizenship. Subsequent misbehaviors during the marking period lower the rating of the transgressors. Thus students who do not misbehave earn the top mark in citizenship. In the second procedure, teachers assume that all students begin with an average rating in citizenship. During the marking period, the rating is lowered for students who misbehave and raised for students who make positive contributions to the class through acts of leadership or service. Thus, in this system, top citizenship marks are earned only by students who make positive contributions to the class. The students who offer neither trouble nor leadership earn average citizenship marks. Although sound arguments can be developed to support either system, the second system appears to have greater merit.

Some school systems report student citizenship by means of descriptive rating sheets or checklists. Such communications provide parents with much more usable information than is provided by the single-mark report commonly used (see Table 18-10).

ADJUSTING MARKS ACCORDING TO STUDENT ABILITY

Some educators maintain that each student should be marked according to his ability to achieve. Advocates of this view point out that under other systems of marking high-ability students can earn top marks while working below their capacity. They also suggest that low-ability students can earn only low marks even though they work at their utmost capacity. In other words, advocates of marking according to ability believe that other systems encourage loafing on the part of high-ability students and frustration leading to ultimate reduction of effort on the part of low-ability students. Undoubtedly marking according to ability has much to be said in its favor; however, as a single system of marking it is inadequate. The resulting marks have no consistent meaning. Such marks, which can serve only the motivational purpose of marking, fail to serve the other common purposes.

Achievement marks should be kept as independent as possible of factors other than achievement. As a matter of fact, the motivational purpose of ability marking can be largely accomplished through use of appropriate supplementary written and oral comments to students, counselors, and parents. Such supplementary use of this type of reporting is strongly encouraged.

BASING MARKS ON SCALES

Should marks be based on an absolute scale, a percentage scale, or a relative scale? Teachers agree that marks should be based on the most reliable and meaningful scale available. Unfortunately, scales with known zero points and units of equal size are available in very few subjects. Typing achievement can be measured in words per minute, and some performances in physical education can be measured in equally reliable scales of time and distance. However, for most subjects, the only scales available are teacher-constructed tests that measure a limited range of achievement in units of unknown size. Furthermore, teacher-built tests over the same content vary in an uncontrolled manner from test to test whether they are built by the same teacher or by different teachers. In particular, some tests are much more difficult than others built to measure the same content. As a result, percentage scores for the same student will vary widely from test to test. Clearly, in most subjects absolute scales of achievement do not exist and percentage scales are highly unreliable. Many teachers therefore follow the practice of professional test builders and base their evaluation of a given test score upon its position in a distribution of scores for that test. Likewise, they assign marks according to the position of a student in the distribution of total scores for his class or grade. This practice is based upon the belief that in a series of measurements over the same content, a given student is more likely to maintain his relative position in his class more consistently than he would maintain a particular percentage score.

In many schools, the practice of assigning marks in approximate agreement with a student's standing in his class or in a group of similar classes has largely replaced marking according to a percentage system. It should be emphasized that this change in procedure has neither increased nor decreased the proportion of high grades earned: the procedure is only the first step in determining the letter mark earned by a given score. Whether or not the top score has earned a mark of A, B, C, D, or F depends upon several other factors.

In conclusion, because absolute scales in education are seldom available and because percentage scales are highly unreliable, the most meaningful basis for marks is the relative scale: position in a given distribution of scores. Obviously, marks determined in this manner must be interpreted in relation to the group measured. Top positions in a distribution of low-ability students are not given the same marks as comparable positions in a distribution of high-ability students.

It should be noted that classes differ in ability level under several circumstances:

1. The students may be assigned to separate sections according to their intelligence or their proficiency in the subject.

2. The course itself may attract a disproportionate enrollment of high-ability students or low-ability students. (Some electives attract students of high ability; other electives, the opposite.)

3. The class may be taught during an instructional period in which an unusual number of classes in the first two categories are also offered. The result may be an unusually high or low grouping.

4. The class may differ from average merely because of chance variation that occurs when no attention is given to grouping.

MARKING STANDARDS

What proportion of a class should receive each mark? The proportion of A, B, C, D, and F marks earned by a particular class should depend upon three factors: the marking policy of the school, the ability level of the class, and the achievement level of the class.

A beginning teacher may find that his school has no official marking policy. Actually, in some schools teachers mark completely according to their own standards. In such a situation, the beginner would do well to follow the average practice of teachers having classes like his own. In a great many schools, however, the beginner will find a statement of marking policy in the administration's handbook for teachers. Table 18-1 represents the kind of direction a principal might provide for the teachers in a school having both heterogeneous classes and classes selected according to ability.

Table 18–1. Suggested Distribution of Marks

MARKS	UNSELECTED STUDENTS (%)	SELECTED STUDENTS			
		LOW (%)	AVERAGE (%)	ADVANCED (%)	HONORS (%)
A	10	0	0	20	80
B	20	0	20	60	20
C	40	20	60	20	0
D	25	60	20	0	0
F	5	20	0	0	0

The marking distributions in Table 18-1 are recommended for the consideration of teachers at a particular high school. It is expected that minor deviations from the suggested percentages will be the rule rather than the exception. However, because the honors classes enroll only highly selected students of proven ability, it is expected that no student in those classes will be given a grade lower than B unless he has been issued a deficiency notice and given an opportunity to transfer to a group of lower classification.

In some schools marking policies are worked out in detail by joint committees of teachers and administrators. The following report, "General Philosophy for Determining Scholarship Marks at 'Y' High School," is adapted from the work of such a committee. This statement of policy includes the committee's answers to eight frequently asked questions and represents the way administration and faculty can cooperate intelligently to give greater uniformity and meaning to a marking system. It should be recognized that at present marking practices differ so greatly that a similar committee at another school might make quite different recommendations. This variability in opinion makes it all the more imperative that educators work together to bring about more uniform practice.

GENERAL PHILOSOPHY FOR DETERMINING SCHOLARSHIP MARKS AT "Y" HIGH SCHOOL [2]

Evaluation is a continuous process for guiding growth in every class. This process is carried on in many ways, such as through written work, group discussions, or individual conferences. The quarter grade is a cumulation of this process.

Periodically the teacher reports student progress to the students. This procedure becomes increasingly effective when based on a common philosophy which is understood by teachers, students, and parents.

The following statements attempt to establish a uniform policy for grading scholarship in this secondary school. Answers are proposed for questions which teachers frequently ask. This report is proposed as a basis for discussion by faculty groups.

A and B grades are recorded when student achievement is definitely above average for the grade level (not necessarily for a particular class). High quality of achievement is the criterion, rather than the quantity of work done or the effort expended. The A and B grades indicate that students receiving such marks could succeed in college or advanced work in the field.

C and D grades are recorded when student achievement is average or below average for the grade level (not necessarily for a particular class). In this category should fall marks (1) for students with superior ability who are doing only average or below average work, (2) for students with average ability who are doing average or below average work, and (3) on a counseling basis for students with inferior ability who would not benefit from repeating the course.

---

[2] Adapted from the report of a joint committee of teachers and administrators at Pacific Beach Junior High School, San Diego, Calif.

F grades are recorded when student achievement is definitely inferior, and no credit should be granted for the course. If the course is a required one, the student must repeat the course.

INTERPRETATION OF SCHOLASTIC GRADING
IN SPECIFIC SITUATIONS

1. Should teachers attempt to follow a grading curve?
   The expression "grading curve" usually refers to a symmetrical curve of distribution in which the percentages of grades, A to F, are 7, 24, 38, 24, 7; 10, 20, 40, 20, 10; 5, 20, 50, 20, 5; or the like. If the philosophy stated above is accepted, then any symmetry which results in the grading pattern is purely coincidental. In actual practice distributions like 12, 25, 38, 20, 5; or 15, 30, 35, 15, 5, are more common. *However, an individual classroom will seldom fit the typical pattern* and departmental distributions will usually vary in predictable ways. Even entire school distributions may be influenced by community factors.

   Students in elective courses, where special aptitude or interest is likely to be evident, will usually earn more high marks than students in required courses. *Students in advanced courses should receive the marks which the same effort and achievement would earn in regular classes; they should not be penalized for being in advanced courses.*

2. How should extra credit assignments be evaluated?
   Extra assignments for able students should represent superior quality and genuine student interest. The completion of average extra credit assignments, however, does not necessarily reflect superior scholarship. For example, twenty assignments representing only average workmanship do not indicate superior student achievement.

3. Should teachers grade by a point system where a certain number of points are given for each completed assignment?
   The point system frequently tends to emphasize quantity rather than quality of work. The student who reads twenty easy books or writes twenty poor compositions is neither a good reader nor a good writer.

4. Should students receive lower grades at the beginning of the year than at the end?
   Students should be graded according to the same general policy throughout the year.

5. How should grades be awarded when the teacher is using ability groups within a class of unselected students?
   The students should be graded in relation to average achievement for the grade level. If students in slower groups consistently make high grades, the work should be made more difficult. In faster groups, the difficulty of the assignment and the quality of achievement should indicate high grades for the student, but students who demonstrate only average achievement should receive average marks. If the work is too difficult for the student, he should be transferred to a group better suited to his ability.

6. How should the teacher grade students in two-track courses, such as advanced and regular mathematics?
   The students should be graded on the same comparative bases as listed above.

High marks should indicate work above the average expectancy for the grade. If students in the regular class receive a disproportionate number of high marks, the work should be made more difficult or the students should be transferred to an advanced class.

7. How should students be graded in adjustment and remedial classes?
   These students should be graded on the same basis as regular students. When the student doing remedial work is doing outstanding work in his group, the work should be made more difficult or the student should be transferred to a regular class.

8. How should students in honors courses be graded?
   These students should be graded on the basis of quality the same as students in regular classes. Since these students are selected for their high level of achievement, they would be expected to receive high marks. No student should be penalized in grades for being in an advanced or accelerated class.

After a teacher has determined the marking policy of his school and the ability level of the class to be marked, he must make a decision concerning the quality of achievement attained by his class. If the teacher has adequate evidence to conclude that his class has achieved at a level higher than might be expected for a group of its classification, he should increase the proportion of high grades assigned. On the other hand, when he has evidence that a class is not performing up to expectations for its level, the proportion of low grades should be increased. At no time should the suggested proportions be followed automatically. However, when a teacher finds that his marks regularly deviate in the same direction from the suggested pattern, he should reassess his marking practices.

Whenever an individual teacher's marks are either consistently higher or consistently lower than the pattern established for a given quality of work at a school, then that teacher has failed to act in accord with highest professional standards. Marks that must be interpreted differently for individual teachers are unfair to students, parents, and other teachers. Therefore, it is important that teachers make serious efforts to mark in as similar a manner as possible.

OLDER SYSTEMS OF DETERMINING MARKS

Three methods of recording data and determining marks are in common use: raw scores, percentages, and letter marks. Each will be discussed in the following paragraphs.

RAW SCORE MARKING

Teachers frequently use raw scores as their basic method of recording ratings of student achievement. In this system, students earn points toward marks for items answered correctly on quizzes and examinations, for completeness and accuracy of laboratory exercises and written assignments, and for success on any other factors the teacher wishes to include. The number of points assigned to each type of measurement is an arbitrary decision of the teacher, as is the apparent weighting of each factor to be used in the final distribution of raw scores.

In the use of the raw score system of recording and marking, a teacher might proceed as follows:

Step 1. The teacher decides that he will give 40 percent of the final mark to ratings of learning activities, 40 percent to quizzes, and 20 percent to the final examination. Thus he intends that the relative weight of scores concerning activities, quizzes, and the final examination will be in the order of 2:2:1.

Step 2. He decides that he will record twenty activity marks and give four quizzes of equal weight during the marking period.

Step 3. Next he decides to have a total of 100 raw score points on the final examination. Then, to achieve apparent balance, each of the four quizzes will contain a possible total of 50 points, and each of the twenty recorded activity marks will be assigned a possible 10 points.

Step 4. At the end of the marking period, the teacher merely totals the number of points earned by each student and places the totals in a frequency distribution.

Step 5. He then assigns marks A, B, C, and so on, to various portions of the distribution according to the marking policy of the school. Note: At this point he could follow the "absolute system" and give A's to totals above a set percentage, such as 90 percent (450 points); B's to totals between 80 and 90 percent (between 400 and 450 points); and so forth. However, use of this system is justified only when all the component measures are standardized.

LIMITATIONS OF RAW SCORE MARKING   The raw score system explained above appears to work precisely, but careful examination will reveal two debilitating flaws: a student's standing prior to the final computation is difficult to determine, and *the teacher's control of the effective weights of the various components of the final mark is an illusion.*

Not all teachers realize that when final marks are determined according to a student's relative position in a distribution formed by combining scores from separate measures, the effective weights of the different com-

Table 18–2. Planned Component Weights

COMPONENT MEASURED	WEIGHTS		TOTAL POINTS	POINTS EACH
	PERCENT	RATIO		
20 assignments, and so on	40	2	200	10
4 quizzes	40	2	200	50
1 final examination	20	1	100	100

*Table 18–3. Effective Weights of Component Measures Vary
According to Their Respective Standard Deviations (Example One)*

COMPONENTS	TOTAL POINTS	STANDARD DEVIATION	PLANNED WEIGHT	EFFECTIVE WEIGHT
Activity ratings	200	9	2	1
Quizzes	200	9	2	1
Final examination	100	9	1	1

ponents are directly proportional to the variability (standard deviation) of each component—not proportional to the total score possible on each.

The two examples in Tables 18-3 and 18-4 demonstrate the manner in which the effective weights of components can differ from the weighting planned when a system of raw score marking is used.

Tables 18-3 and 18-4 show that teachers who use the raw score system of determining marks have relinquished control of the relative weights of the components of the final mark. To maintain control of the relative weights of all measures used in a total, it is necessary to establish component distributions that have predetermined variability and predetermined means. This is exactly what is accomplished by use of the standard score system to be discussed later in this chapter.

PERCENTAGE MARKING

Percentages are commonly used as a basic system of recording data and determining marks. In this system a teacher proceeds as follows:

Step 1. The teacher scores and records each assignment—quiz, exam, or laboratory report—as a percentage score. When a paper is judged to be worth 30 of a possible 40 points, a score of 75 is recorded. Similarly, when another paper is judged to be worth 90 points out of a total of 120 points, a score of 75 is recorded. Thus, the number of raw score points on each measure is immaterial.

*Table 18–4. Effective Weights of Component Measures Vary
According to Their Respective Standard Deviations (Example Two)*

COMPONENTS	TOTAL POINTS	STANDARD DEVIATION	PLANNED WEIGHT	EFFECTIVE WEIGHT
Activity ratings	200	30	2	6
Quizzes	200	5	2	1
Final examination	100	10	1	2

Step 2. He decides to weight activity ratings, quizzes, and the final examination in the ratio of 3:2:1.

Step 3. At the end of the marking period, the percentage marks in each category are averaged for each student. The teacher then triples the activity average, doubles the quiz average, and adds the two totals to the final examination mark. Thus the total mark for each student is made up of six parts based on the planned component ratio of 3:2:1.

Step 4. The teacher then forms a distribution of the students' weighted percentage totals and assigns marks of A, B, and C to specified proportions of the distribution according to the policy of the school.

If the teacher in the above illustration had recorded eight activity rankings, five quizzes, and two examinations for each student, the final mark for a student having the scores listed below would be computed in five steps. In the first step of the computation the percentage scores in each category are totaled.

ACTIVITY RATINGS	QUIZZES	EXAMINATIONS
60	70	15
65	80	85
80	96	——
55	74	100
85	80	
75	——	
50	400	
90		
——		
560		

In the second step of the computation, the average for each category is found:

ACTIVITY RATINGS	QUIZZES	EXAMINATIONS
$560 \div 8 = 70$	$400 \div 5 = 80$	$100 \div 2 = 50$

In the third step of the computation, the average score for each category is multiplied by its predetermined weighting factor:

ACTIVITY RATINGS	QUIZZES	EXAMINATIONS
$70 \times 3 = 210$	$80 \times 2 = 160$	$50 \times 1 = 50$

In the fourth step of the computation, the weighted components are totaled:

$$210 + 160 + 50 = 420$$

In the fifth step the student's total of 420 is placed in the class distribution of similar totals and given a letter mark according to the school policy for that particular type of class. (*Note:* The student's average weighted percentage can be found by dividing his total of 420 by 6. The resulting score of 70 percent is sometimes reported as his mark or is assigned a letter mark, according to local practice; that is, if 70 percent is considered barely passing, the student would be given a mark of D. This practice is fairly common, but seldom justified.)

LIMITATIONS OF PERCENTAGE MARKING   Some teachers conclude that use of percentage marks will overcome the flaws existing in the raw score systems of recording and marking. This conclusion is approximately 50 percent correct. It is true that percentage marks on individual measures can be more easily interpreted, but percentages used as components of final letter marks suffer from the same flaw of weighting as that which afflicts the raw score system. The effective weights of the components vary with the standard deviations of the component distributions.

The described procedure of weighting and combining percentages would produce totals having the intended component weights of 3:2:1 only when the components have identical variability. The relationship of three components having different ranges of measurement can be described mathematically by the ratio $a:b:c$. Multiplying a by 3, b by 2, and c by 1, as was done in the preceding illustration, results in weights of $3a:2b:c$. This relationship is equal to the ratio 3:2:1 only when $a = b = c$.

Perhaps the concept of a test's effective weight will be made more clear by use of a nonmathematical explanation. Suppose that a class studying the skill of dart throwing is to be measured by two tests. Each class member is to throw one dart at each of two targets from a distance of 10 paces. Bull's-eye hits will count 100 points; hits in the first inner ring will count 90 points; hits in the next ring will count 80 points, and so forth. Each student will be given a letter mark according to his average score on the two tests. Assuming that one target covers a large tablecloth, and the other target is drawn on a small handkerchief, which target will have the greater effect in determining a student's mark? Will their effects be equal?

It should be obvious that even though both targets are scaled from zero to 100, their effective weights in determining marks are not the same. Students will undoubtedly score either 90 or 100 points on the larger target; whereas on the smaller target their scores may well range all the way from zero to 100. When the two scores for each student are combined and placed in a distribution, the relative positions of students in that distribution will be almost wholly dependent upon the small-target scores. Likewise, when the two scores of each student are averaged, the range of averages will be determined almost wholly by the small-target scores. Thus the component that provides the greater range of scores is the component that carries the greater effective weight in determining final marks.

Figure 18-1, which should further clarify the meaning of test weights, shows the range of scores on two tests of 100 points each. Scores on the first test ranged from 15 to 95, whereas on the second test the range was from 65 to 85. By following the appropriate broken line it can be seen that a student who scores at the top of Test I and at the bottom of Test II would have an average of 80 points $\left(\dfrac{95 + 65}{2} = 80\right)$. However, a stu-

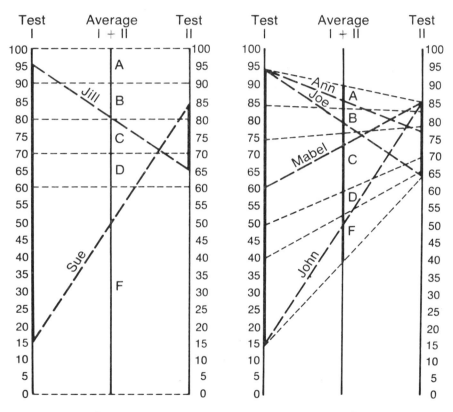

Fig. 18-1   Graphic representation of the effect of differences in the range of scores upon the average of those scores (A + C frequently does not average B)

Case 1: Letter marks are given on a percentage basis, with F covering the largest range.

Case 2: Letter marks are given on a "curve" basis, with C covering the largest range.

	I	II	I + II
Jill	A	D	B
Sue	F	B	F

	I	II	I + II
Ann	A	C	A
Joe	A	F	B
Mabel	C	A	C
John	F	A	F

dent who scores at the bottom of Test I and at the top of Test II would average only 50 points $\left(\dfrac{15+85}{2}=50\right)$. Thus, Test I carries greater effective weight than Test II.

Figure 18-1 also reveals that other letter marks assigned on the basis of the average scores would be strongly weighted in favor of Test I. A student who scores A on the first test and F on the second test would earn a mark of B on the illustrated combination. On the other hand, the lowest student on Test I would fail on the combined average regardless of his success on Test II.

It should be clear from this illustration that teachers who base marks on accumulated raw scores or accumulated percentages bias the results in favor of students who happen to score high on the measures having the greatest spread of scores.

LETTER MARKING

The most widely used systems of marking base letter marks on class distributions of numerical scores. This type of transfer is seldom automatic because recommendations for the allocation of the various marks usually are flexible. The final decisions are left to the teacher. In the exercise of their judgment, most teachers find it helpful to arrange numerical scores in a frequency distribution and determine division points between letter marks on the basis of the "breaks" in the distribution. For example, assume that a 120-point test has been given to a class of forty students. Their scores on the test were as follows:

78, 60, 84, 68, 89, 74, 81, 66, 61, 75, 87, 76, 84, 77, 74, 65, 73, 58, 86, 70, 83, 71, 90, 68, 80, 83, 66, 74, 81, 74, 76, 77, 75, 86, 78, 78, 73, 76, 84, 75

Further assume that the class is slightly better than average in a school recommending a policy of A's, 10 percent; B's, 20 percent; C's, 40 percent; D's 20 percent; and F's, 10 percent. A frequency distribution of scores should be made, having the lowest score (58) at the bottom and the highest score (90) at the top (see Table 18-5).

Then, using his knowledge of the general quality of the class together with his knowledge of the school's marking policy, a teacher will find that convenient breaks in the distribution suggest letter allocation as follows:

five A's (86–90), eight B's (80–84), seventeen C's (73–78), seven D's (65–71), and three F's (58–61).

The slight deviation from the proportions recommended by the school is justified by the character of the distribution and the quality of the class.

Teachers commonly combine letter marks into a single mark in either of two ways: averaging letters by assuming that an A and a C will

Table 18–5. Determination of Letter Marks
from a Distribution of Numerical Scores

RAW SCORE DISTRIBUTION	LETTER GRADES
90 /	
89 /	
88	A
87 /	
86 //	
85	
84 ///	
83 //	
82	B
81 //	
80 /	
79	
78 ///	
77 //	
76 ///	C
75 ///	
74 ////	
73 //	
72	
71 /	
70 /	
69	
68 //	D
67	
66 //	
65 /	
64	
63	
62	
61 /	F
60 /	
59	
58 /	

average B, or temporarily assigning numerical equivalents to letter marks and then averaging the numbers before finally changing back to a letter mark.

As an illustration of the first method, marks of C, A, F, B, D would be combined as follows: The A and the F would be changed into two grades of C, the B and the D would also average C. The result would be five C's or an average of C.

MARKS	STEP ONE	STEP TWO	STEP THREE
C	C	C	
A	C	C	
F	C	C	C
B	B	C	
D	D	C	

The same five marks would be combined by the second method (using $A = 4, B = 3, C = 2, D = 1, F = 0$), as follows:

MARKS	STEP ONE	STEP TWO	STEP THREE
C	2		
A	4		
F	0	$10 \div 5 = 2$	$2 = C$
B	3		
D	1		
	10		

The second method can be further illustrated by a problem frequently encountered at marking time. What mark should be given a student who had earned ten daily marks (A, B, F, C, D, D, C, B, D, A); four quiz marks (C, A, B, C); and a final examination mark of C?
Assumptions:

1. The daily marks are to be weighted equally.
2. The quiz of grade B is to be weighted double that of each of the other quizzes.
3. The final mark is to be made up of daily work 50 percent, quizzes 25 percent, and final examination 25 percent.
   The first step toward a solution would be to combine the daily marks.

DAILY MARKS

A	4
B	3
F	0
C	2
D	1
D	1
C	2
B	3
D	1
A	4
	21

$21 \div 10 = 2.1 = C$

The second step is to combine the quizzes, giving double weight to the one on which the student earned a mark of B.

QUIZZES
C   2
A   4
B   3 + 3 $14 \div 5 = 2.8 = B$
C   2
       ─────
    11 + 3 = 14

The third step is to combine the averages (giving double weight to the daily marks so as to preserve the recommended 50–25–25 ratio).

Daily marks   2.1
              2.1
Quizzes   2.8 $9.0 \div 4 = 2.25 = C$
Final exam   2
              ────
              9.0

The earned mark therefore would be C. (If pluses were used, the mark would be C plus.)

LIMITATIONS OF THESE COMPUTATIONS   It should be recognized that letter marks also have serious limitations as a basic system of recording and marking. Merely to substitute the letter A for 100 points and B for the score of 90 does not alter the fact that the effective weight of a component in a combination of marks is related to the spread of scores of the component.

Furthermore, neither illustrated method of combining letter marks is defensible unless the underlying assumptions are recognized and judged acceptable. Far too many teachers use marking systems without considering the rational foundations involved. For example, when a teacher combines an A and a C to equate with two grades of B, and when he combines an F and a C to equate with two grades of D, the first underlying assumption involved is that each letter mark represents an equal range of achievement. Also, when the letter marks themselves have been obtained by use of raw score or percentage scales, the tenability of the assumption of equality of resulting letter mark units depends upon acceptance of assumptions with respect to the uniformity of the basic raw score or percentage units.

That is, when letter marks have been based upon percentage scales using 90 through 100 as A, 80 through 89 as B, 70 through 79 as C, 60 through 69 as D, and 0 through 59 as F, a letter mark of F *cannot* be combined justifiably with a letter mark of A to yield two marks of C *unless* the percentage range of 90 through 100 is accepted as equivalent

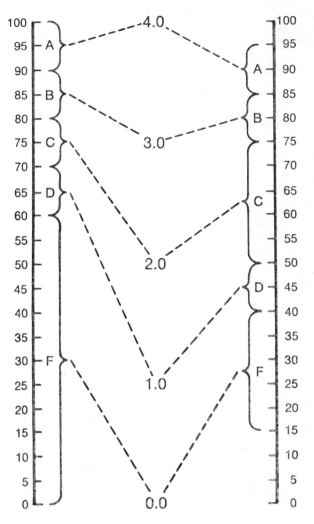

*Fig. 18-2   Transfer of marks and scores to the scale: A = 4, B = 3, C = 2, D = 1,
F = 0*

Case 1: Marks based on percentages.   *Case 2:* Marks based on a "curve."
Weaknesses

1. Differences of scores within groups are ignored.
2. The range of scores represented fails to be constant from point to point on
   the scale. For example, in case 2 the scale score 1.0 represents 10 raw score
   points (scores between 40 and 50), whereas the scale score 2.0 represents
   25 raw score points (scores between 50 and 75).

to the percentage range of 0 through 59. Similar discrepancies exist in letter mark ranges measured in raw score units (see Fig. 18-1). Consequently, it is illogical for a teacher to combine A's and F's to obtain C's in either situation.

On the other hand, transfer of letter marks to a numerical scale, such as A = 4.0, B = 3.0, reduces but does not eliminate the major problem of combining scores. Because the component letter distributions are translated to a system having a constant range, the weights of components are brought partially under control. Full control, however, is not achieved until the component distributions have been made identical by conversion to normalized standard scores.

It should also be recognized that transfer of letter grades to the discrete-point scale of A = 4.0, B = 3.0, involves the assumption that differences within the range of a component letter mark are not important, whereas even smaller differences in range at the division points between letters are critical. Figure 18-2 shows that on a particular test (case 2) all scores from 50 through 74 were transferred to the single point 2.0. No allowance was made for differences as great as 24 points in that part of the scale, whereas a difference of only 12 points in other parts of the scale (39–51, and 74–86) could raise the letter equivalent from 0.0 to 2.0 or from 2.0 to 4.0. These conditions usually are acceptable only when the frequency of scores in an interval is considered a better marking base than the raw score or percentage units involved.

In spite of its weaknesses, the transfer of letter marks to a scale having constant range is a step in the direction necessary to accomplish scientific control of weighted marks. The logical next step is to transfer the original measures to a controlled scale that represents the original measures with greater fidelity. Without question, standard score scales serve that purpose. It is to be hoped and expected that teachers will soon recognize the inadequacies of older methods and adopt the more accurate method of standard scores.

NEWER SYSTEMS OF DETERMINING MARKS

Standard scores are of two basic types: linear transformations which establish distributions having the same shape as the original distributions of raw scores or area transformations which change the shape of the original distributions to conform with a normal distribution. The second type, known as normalized standardized scores, is appropriate for use whenever it is logical to assume that valid and reliable measurement in accurate units would result in a normal distribution. That assumption usually is tenable only when the scores of hundreds of students have been placed in a single distribution. When the teacher is concerned with the measurement of only one or two relatively small classes, it is usually more appropriate for him to use standard scores based on a linear transformation. For this reason standard scores of the linear type only are discussed here.

Z-SCORE MARKING

The most commonly used standard score of the linear-transformation type is the Z-scale. On a Z-scale, the mean score is 50 and the standard deviation is 10. Thus each unit is equal to one tenth of a standard deviation: a score of 60 is always one standard deviation above average; and a score of 45 is one-half standard deviation below average. Raw scores can be transferred to Z-scores by using the four steps listed below:

Step 1. Put the raw scores into a frequency distribution of unit interval.
Step 2. Determine the mean of the raw scores by adding all the raw scores and dividing the total by the number of scores.
Step 3. Compute or estimate the standard deviation of the raw score distribution. *One* of the following methods should be used.

1. For distributions that are approximately normal and contain no more than fifty individual scores, a rough but useful estimated standard deviation can be found by dividing the range of raw scores by four. Formula: $S = R \div 4$
2. When raw score distributions deviate from the normal at the extremes, a more accurate approximation of the standard deviation is provided by either of the following formulas:
$S = .4 \, (C_{90} - C_{10}); \; S = .3 \, (average \; of \; the \; top \; 10 \; percent \; minus \; the$
$average \; of \; the \; bottom \; 10 \; percent)$
3. When a mathematically accurate standard deviation is desired, the following formula should be used:

$$S = \sqrt{\frac{\Sigma(X - \bar{X})^2}{N}}$$

In the above formulas, S represents standard deviation, R stands for range, C indicates centile point, X is any score, $\bar{X}$ is the mean, and N is the number of scores.

Step 4. Determine the Z-score for each raw score by *either* of the following techniques:

1. From Tables 18-6 or 18-7 take the Z-scores in the column headed by the raw score standard deviation and place them alongside the raw score distribution so that 50 is opposite the mean, 60 is opposite the raw score which is one standard deviation above the mean, and so on.
2. Compute each Z-score by substitution in the formula:

$$Z = \frac{10(raw \; score - raw \; score \; mean)}{standard \; deviation} + 50$$

Table 18–6. Z-Scale Equivalents for Raw Scores
Having Standard Deviations from 1 to 10.

(Each pattern repeats between Z-scale standard deviation points.)

	RAW SCORE STANDARD DEVIATION									
$X - \overline{X}$	1	2	3	4	5	6	7	8	9	10
10				75	70	67	64	63	61	60
9			80	73	68	65	63	61	60	59
8			77	70	66	63	61	60	59	58
7			73	68	64	62	60	59	58	57
6		80	70	65	62	60	59	58	57	56
5		75	67	63	60	58	57	56	56	55
4		70	63	60	58	57	56	55	54	54
3	80	65	60	58	56	55	54	54	53	53
2	70	60	57	55	54	53	53	53	52	52
1	60	55	53	53	52	52	51	51	51	51
0	50	50	50	50	50	50	50	50	50	50

Table 18–7. Z-Scale Equivalents for Raw Scores
Having Standard Deviations from 11 to 20

(Each pattern repeats between Z-scale standard deviation points.)

	RAW SCORE STANDARD DEVIATION									
$X - \overline{X}$	11	12	13	14	15	16	17	18	19	20
20										60
19									60	60
18								60	59	59
17							60	59	59	59
16						60	59	59	58	58
15					60	59	59	58	58	58
14				60	59	59	58	58	57	57
13			60	59	59	58	58	57	57	57
12		60	59	59	58	58	57	57	56	56
11	60	59	58	58	57	57	56	56	56	56
10	59	58	58	57	57	56	56	56	55	55
9	58	58	57	56	56	56	55	55	55	55
8	57	57	56	56	55	55	55	54	54	54
7	56	56	55	55	55	54	54	54	54	54
6	55	55	55	54	54	54	54	53	53	53
5	55	54	54	54	53	53	53	53	53	53
4	54	53	53	53	53	53	52	52	52	52
3	53	53	52	52	52	52	52	52	52	52
2	52	52	52	51	51	51	51	51	51	51
1	51	51	51	51	51	51	51	51	51	51
0	50	50	50	50	50	50	50	50	50	50

Tables 18-6 and 18-7 are recommended for use in Step 4 whenever repetitious use of the formula alternative would become tedious. For example, the Z-score equivalents of the raw scores in a distribution having 76 as the mean and 8 as the standard deviation could be determined quickly by placing a Z-score of 50 at the mean of 76 and placing the Z-scores of 30, 40, 60, and 70 at the appropriate standard deviation points in the distribution. The intervening Z-scores would be found by using the digits 0, 1, 3, 4, 5, 6, 8, and 9 given in Column 8 of Table 18-6. That is, the Z-score equivalents of raw scores 76 through 83 would be 50, 51, 53, 54, 55, 56, 58, and 59 respectively, and the Z-score equivalents of raw scores 60 through 67 would be respectively 30, 31, 33, 34, 35, 36, 38, and 39.

In Table 18-8, the four steps are applied to the group of forty raw scores used earlier. From this illustration it can be observed that the raw score mean of 76 has an equivalent Z-score of 50, and that every raw score is transferred to the Z-scale in a manner which maintains its relative position in relation to the mean.

When daily work, quizzes, and examinations are recorded in Z-scores, it is a simple matter to control the contribution of each to a combination mark. For example, if daily marks are to count 25 percent, quizzes 50 percent, and examinations 25 percent, marks for a student would be combined as illustrated below:

DAILY WORK	QUIZZES	EXAMINATIONS	WEIGHTED AVERAGES	
61	47	40	Daily work	55
50	61	46	Quizzes	52
55	53	$\overline{86}$	Quizzes	52
60	45		Exams	43
70	54	$86 \div 2 = 43$		$\overline{202}$
52	$\overline{260}$			
45				
48	$260 \div 5 = 52$			
57				
60				
47				
$\overline{605}$				

$605 \div 11 = 55$

The student's total of 202 points is then put into a distribution of students' totals from which letter marks are assigned according to the policy of the school.

It should be noted that the precision of the weighting of each component could be slightly increased by building a distribution of average Z-scores for the component and from it determining a new Z-score for each student. It should also be noted that teachers frequently record daily assignment marks in raw scores ranging from 0 to 3 or 4 points. At the

Table 18–8. Transformation of Raw Scores to Z-Scores

SOURCE OF DATA	RESULTANT Z-SCALE	STEP 1: BUILD THE RAW SCORE DISTRIBUTION	STEP 2: COMPUTE THE MEAN	STEP 3: ESTIMATE THE STANDARD DEVIATION
Step 3	70 +2S	92	$\bar{X} = \Sigma X \div 40$	$S = .4(C_{90} - C_{10})$
	69	91		
	68	90 /	90	$S = .4(86 - 65.5)$
	66	89 /	89	$S = .4(20.5)$
Step 4	65	88		
	64	87 /	87	$S = 8.2$
	63	86 //	172	
	61	85		Mark the standard
Step 3	60 +S	84 ///	252	deviation points in
	59	83 //	166	the distribution:
	58	82		
	56	81 //	162	$Z_{70} = \bar{X} + 2S =$
Step 4	55	80 /	80	$76 + 16 = 92$
	54	79		$Z_{60} = \bar{X} + S =$
	53	78 ///	234	$76 + 8 = 84$
	51	77 //	154	$Z_{40} = \bar{X} - S =$
Step 2	50 $\bar{X}$	76 ///	228	$76 - 8 = 68$
	49	75 ///	225	$Z_{30} = \bar{X} - 2S =$
	48	74 ////	296	$76 - 16 = 60$
	46	73 //	146	
Step 4	45	72		
	44	71 /	71	STEP 4:
	43	70 /	70	
	41	69		
Step 3	40 −S	68 //	136	Fill in the remainder
	39	67		of the Z-scale by use
	38	66 //	132	of column "8" in
	36	65 /	65	Table 18–6.
Step 4	35	64		
	34	63		or
	33	62		
	31	61 /	61	Compute each point
Step 3	30 −2S	60 /	60	by use of the for-
	29	59		mula:
	28	58 /	58	
Step 4	26	57		$Z = \dfrac{10(X - \bar{X})}{S} + 50$
	25	56	$\overline{3034}$	
			$3034 \div 40 = 76$	

Table 18–9. Difference between Combined Raw Scores (Unequally Weighted) and Combined Z-Scores (Equally Weighted)

	TEST I ($\overline{X} = 55$; $S = 20$)			TEST II ($\overline{X} = 75$; $S = 5$)			COMBINED SCORES	
STUDENT	RAW SCORE	POSI-TION	Z-SCORE	RAW SCORE	POSI-TION	Z-SCORE	RAW SCORE (I:II $= 20:5$)	Z-SCORE (I:II $= 1:1$)
Alice	95	+2S	70	85	+2S	70	180	140
Clayton	95	+2S	70	65	−2S	30	160	100
Esther	55	$\overline{X}$	50	75	$\overline{X}$	50	130	100
George	35	−S	40	85	+2S	70	120	110
Manfred	15	−2S	30	85	+2S	70	100	100
Rose	15	−2S	30	65	−2S	30	80	60

end of a marking period, these scores are totaled, placed in a distribution, and transferred to the Z-scale.

Table 18-9 shows that combining two Z-scores gives results different from those obtained by combining the raw scores from the same two tests. In the table, the ratio of the raw score standard deviations of the two tests is 20:5. Test I therefore has four times the weight of Test II in a raw score combination. This effect can be observed by noting that the two students who scored 95 on Test I rank 1 and 2 on the raw score combination. On the other hand, when the tests are weighted equally by use of Z-scores Alice remains in rank 1, but George moves from fourth to second position because his relatively low score on Test I no longer is quadrupled in weight.

ADVANTAGES AND LIMITATIONS OF STANDARD SCORE MARKING

Obviously, use of standard scores will not improve the validity of poorly constructed tests, nor will their use guarantee that teachers will assign marks in judicious agreement with school policy. *But use of standard scores will do two things that are not done by older systems of marking.*

1. Standard scores provide measurements that have *consistent meaning* with respect to an individual's standing in a group. That is, a Z-score of 40 always indicates a position 1 standard deviation below the mean of the base group.

2. Standard scores enable a teacher to give whatever weight he wishes to each component of a final mark because each element has a constant mean and a constant standard deviation.

Teachers should recognize that users of Z-scores accept the assumption that marking based upon the relative standing of students in a defined group is more meaningful and reliable than marking based upon students' attainment of arbitrary percentage scores on measures of unknown and variable difficulty. However, class-size groups also can be of "unknown and variable" quality. Consequently, use of standard scores does not obviate the desirability of developing a broad scoring base by occasionally administering tests to all classes in a given subject. When school-wide tests in a subject are not feasible, a teacher should accumulate achievement data from his own classes over several semesters. In that manner he can keep a check on his judgment of the performance level of a particular class.

In conclusion, it again should be emphasized that even the best scoring systems serve only to enable the teacher to combine measurements accurately, and thus to place students accurately in rank order according to the measurements employed. Whether or not the top-ranking students deserve a mark of A, B, or lower is entirely up to the teacher's professional interpretation of the school's marking policy. However, the fairness and accuracy of a teacher's marking will depend upon his ability to build and use valid tests, his ability to collect and record additional evidences of student achievement, his ability to judge the value of student rankings in accordance with school marking policy, *and his ability to use the most accurate scoring system available.*

REPORTING TO PARENTS

Reports to parents concerning the progress of students commonly take three forms: report cards, supplementary reports, and personal conferences. It is unlikely that any one procedure alone will do an adequate job of reporting. Teachers should become proficient in the use of all three.

REPORT CARDS AND SUPPLEMENTARY REPORTS

Report cards in their most common form include a single achievement mark in each subject, citizenship marks, comments to parents, and a record of attendance and tardiness (see "Sample Report Card"). Such cards are usually sent to the student's home every six to twelve weeks. Most reports require parental signature before they are returned to school. More elaborate reports include ratings on progress toward separate objectives and invite comment and visitation.

In addition to a regular report card, many schools employ supplementary progress reports. These reports are unstructured letters as used by some schools, but more commonly detailed checklists descriptive of student behavior are employed for this purpose (see Table 18-10).

Supplementary reports are most frequently called for when students are in danger of failing. In fact, many schools require that parents and students be notified of any deficiencies in scholarship or citizenship several weeks before the end of a marking period. (Notification of impending C

SAMPLE REPORT CARD

Student ___ Jane Doe ___ Grade 11 Counselor Jackson

Report for period ending ___ March 15 ___ Central High School

PER.	COURSE TITLE	SCHOLAR-SHIP	CITIZEN-SHIP	PERIODS ABSENT	PERIODS TARDY	TEACHER'S SIGNATURE
1	U.S. History	A	S	2	0	J. Jones
2	English	B	E	2	0	S. Smith
3	Homemaking	C	S	2	1	E. Brown
4	Physical Ed.	C	U	5	6	D. White
5	Chemistry	C	S	2	0	A. Evans
6	Algebra	D	E	2	0	F. Olson

Comments to Parents

Per. 1. *Jane is an excellent student of History*

4. *Jane needs to change her attitude towards Phys Ed.*

6. *Jane is working hard and showing some improvement*

Comments from Parents

Parent's signature___

Parents are cordially invited to comment above or to visit the school to discuss this report. Conferences with teachers, counselors, or administrators may be arranged by telephoning the school: No. 582-3993.

---

or D grades should be given to students in advanced classes just as notices of possible failure are given to students in groups of lower classification.)

Appropriately used, deficiency notices serve two distinct purposes: they direct the attention of the teacher, student, and parent to the specific needs of a particular student, and they reduce the shock of failure to both student and parent. A basic principle of marking is that unsatisfactory marks should never be a surprise to a student or his parents.

Every teacher should be fully aware of the important public relations aspect of reporting. Little can be gained, except perhaps ill will, by thoroughly negative reports. To tell a mother that her son is a complete rascal and totally ignorant of the purposes of school may be a true representation of at least part of the facts, but as a report it is completely inadequate. Nothing constructive is gained. Parents want facts, but they also have a

Table 18–10. Citizenship Report

—————I. RESPONSIBILITY RATING. Behaviors considered:
————— 1. Comes to class on time
————— 2. Hands in schoolwork on time
————— 3. Demonstrates an interest and a will to learn
————— 4. Brings necessary equipment to class
————— 5. Prepares and brings to class extra materials
————— 6. Does not waste school supplies
————— 7. Takes good care of school building, equipment, and grounds
————— 8. Works independently
————— 9. Finds his own material for reports and other activities
—————10. Accepts responsibility for developing projects helpful to the class
—————11. Accepts leadership roles
—————12. Has a positive influence on class morale

—————II. COOPERATION RATING. Behaviors considered:
————— 1. Listens when someone is talking
————— 2. Does not talk to other students unnecessarily
————— 3. Cooperates with class officers and committee chairmen
————— 4. Respects opinions of others
————— 5. Controls his voice and actions
————— 6. Abides by group decisions
————— 7. Does nothing that would bring criticism on his class or school

—————III. WORK HABITS RATING. Behaviors considered:
————— 1. Gets to work without urging by the teacher
————— 2. Does not waste time
————— 3. Does his work carefully
————— 4. Prepares written work neatly
————— 5. Prepares reports in his own words
————— 6. Is careful to follow directions
————— 7. Uses intelligently the index, table of contents, and dictionaries
————— 8. Completes assignments promptly

E = Excellent
U = Unsatisfactory (needs improvement)
no mark = satisfactory

Source: Adapted from a self-rating form used by the Los Angeles City School Districts.

right to expect competent professional analyses and constructive suggestions which give evidence that the problems are being studied with at least some prospect of successful solution. Too many reports to parents just baldly state that the student is failing. When a parent responds to such a communication, he frequently is angry or annoyed and is psychologically unable to provide the help of which he would be capable under more favorable circumstances. Such situations must be prevented. It is not without design that in many schools all communications to parents must be approved by the principal. Beginning teachers should be prepared to meet such regulations with understanding.

PARENT-TEACHER CONFERENCES

Under present teaching schedules in secondary schools, it would be practically impossible for teachers to confer with any significant number of parents during regular teaching days even if the parents were able to keep appointments at the school. Consequently, parent-teacher conferences on the secondary level remain the exceptional practice rather than the rule. Nevertheless, it would be advisable for beginning teachers to be ready to participate in parent-teacher conferences concerning student deficiency.

For that type of conference, several guidelines have been developed:

1. Prepare yourself prior to the conference. Review records of the student's ability, background, and performance. Also learn something of the parent if possible. Communication is facilitated when the teacher is aware of the parent's level of familiarity with school purposes and school terminology.

2. Prepare materials to help the parent visualize the student's learning status and progress. Charts and graphs are well understood by some parents, but all will understand a set of well-selected samples of the student's test papers, assignments, and projects. Such concrete materials often tell much more than mere words.

3. Be a good listener. A parent-teacher conference should be a discussion and an interchange of information. It is not intended to be a lecture on the part of either participant, although there may be times when it would be well for the teacher to permit the parent to present his grievances without interruption.

4. Be constructive. Listening, of course, is not sufficient. The teacher should discuss steps that he expects to take to help the student, and he should also invite the parent to suggest steps that might be taken by the student's home.

5. Keep the conference on a professional level. The discussion should seek remedies, not the assignment of blame. In particular, teachers should avoid evaluation of the contribution other teachers may possibly have made to the development of the student's problem. The matter of scheduling the conference should also be given consideration. Parent conferences with teachers should be by appointment only, scheduled far enough in advance to permit adequate preparation, and held in a school conference room which permits free discussion without overt or accidental eavesdropping. A classroom shared with students, an office shared with colleagues, or a PTA meeting are not adequate places to conduct a professional conference. When parents expect informal discussions in such

surroundings, courteously suggest making an appointment. The confidential professional nature of parent-teacher conferences deserves more widespread recognition.

REPORTING STANDARDIZED TEST RESULTS TO PARENTS

Whether or not to report standardized test scores, including IQ's, to parents has long been a perplexing problem for beginning teachers. Research conducted by the American Educational Research Association in 1961 found that roughly 90 percent of the secondary school teachers in a national sample thought that parents, in most cases, should be told the achievement test scores of their children.[3] Slightly more than half of the sample favored giving that information to all parents as standard practice. The research also found that there was almost an even division between secondary school teachers who favored and those who opposed telling parents their child's IQ, although less than 20 percent thought that it should be done as standard practice.

Authorities in the field of educational and psychological testing appear to be in agreement that schools should accept the responsibility of communicating standardized test results to parents as well as to students.[4] They stress the point, however, that the reporting of scores as single specific numbers does not constitute proper communication. In fact, they insist that unless the meaning of a score is conveyed, no effective communication has taken place. Therefore, it is recommended that teachers recognize the error present in scores, and report achievement test results only in terms of estimated bands like those in Figure 18-3. Grade placement scores have value in discussions among educators, but in communications to parents and students percentile bands are much more likely to be correctly understood. For example, a high school freshman might be told: "Jim, your test result in vocabulary is the percentile band 35 through 60. You have scored higher than about 35 percent of high school freshman and about 40 percent have made scores higher than yours." Then, if this is one of Jim's weak spots, and because standardized achievement test results serve teacher and student best as starting points, not culminations, the discussion might well be continued to outline steps toward remediation.

Intelligence test results—if they are to be communicated at all—should be explained in relation to their expected use. IQ's, in particular, should be discussed only with the greatest discretion. It is highly unlikely that a teacher should ever tell a parent, "Your son's IQ is 117," even if that score

[3] Research Division, NEA, *Research Bulletin*, 40, no. 4 (December 1962), 122.
[4] Walter N. Durost, "How to Tell Parents about Standardized Test Results," *Test Service Notebook No. 26*. New York: Harcourt, Brace & World, Inc., 1961.

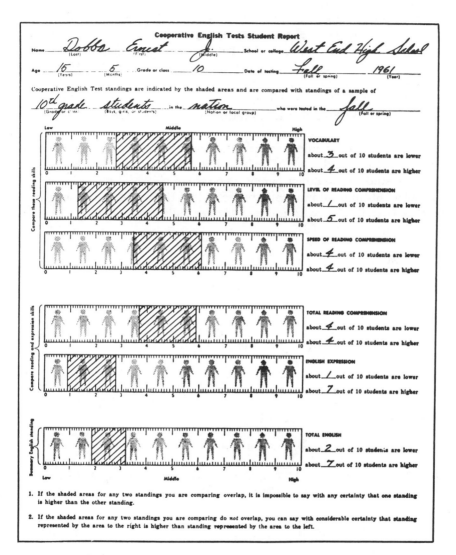

Fig. 18-3 *Student report of percentile-band results on the Cooperative English Tests*

is obtained on the best test currently available. As a matter of fact, it would be better if teachers themselves refrained from thinking of an IQ as a single number.

When school policy approves communication of intelligence test results, they should be interpreted as rough estimates of academic potential. If a parent requests his son's intelligence score for that purpose, he might be told, "John's estimated academic potential is like that of students who on the whole make average grades in that course." Or, if selection of a college is his purpose, the records of the school might permit the teacher to say, "Forty percent of our graduates having scores like John's have earned passing grades (or honors, if that is the case) at a certain university." When school records are less adequate, intelligence test results could well be referred to only in terms of the broad categories: superior, above average, average, and below average.

In conclusion, it should be emphasized that there is, as yet, no generally accepted policy with respect to the communication of intelligence test scores to students and their parents. The trend clearly is toward more free exchange of this information, but for the time being, the beginning teacher is well advised to follow very carefully the policy of the school in which he is employed.

SELECTED READINGS

1.   Adams, Georgia Sachs, *Measurement and Evaluation,* New York: Holt, Rinehart and Winston, Inc., 1964, chap. 16.

2.   Ahmann, J. Stanley, and Marvin D. Glock, *Evaluating Pupil Growth,* 3d ed. Boston: Allyn and Bacon, Inc., 1967, chap. 16.

3.   American Educational Research Association, *Encyclopedia of Educational Research,* 3d ed., Chester W. Harris, ed. New York: The Macmillan Company, 1960, pp. 783–789.

4.   Callahan, Sterling G., *Successful Teaching in Secondary Schools.* Chicago: Scott, Foresman and Company, 1966, pp. 359–373.

5.   Clark, Leonard H., and Irving S. Starr, *Secondary Teaching Methods,* 2d ed. New York: The Macmillan Company, 1967, chap. 16.

6.   Durost, Walter N., and George A. Prescott, *Essentials of Measurement for Teachers.* New York: Harcourt, Brace & World, Inc., 1962, chaps. 8 and 9.

7.   Ebel, Robert L., *Measuring Educational Achievement.* Englewood Cliffs, N.J.: Prentice-Hall, Inc., 1965, chap. 13.

8.   Gorow, Frank F., *Statistical Measures: A Programmed Text.* San Francisco: Chandler Publishing Company, 1962.

9.   Gronlund, Norman E., *Measurement and Evaluation in Teaching.* New York: The Macmillan Company, 1965, chap. 17.

10. Oliva, Peter F., *The Secondary School Today.* Cleveland: The World Publishing Company, 1967, chaps. 22 and 23.

11. Payne, David A., and Robert F. McMorris, *Educational and Psychological Measurement*. Waltham, Mass.: Blaisdell Publishing Company, 1967, pp. 299–302.

12. Stanley, Julian C., *Measurement in Today's Schools*, 4th ed. Englewood Cliffs, N.J.: Prentice-Hall, Inc., 1964, chap. 11.

13. Thorndike, Robert L., and Elizabeth Hagen, *Measurement and Evaluation in Psychology and Education*, 2d ed. New York: John Wiley & Sons, Inc., 1961, chap. 17.

14. U.S. Department of Health, Education, and Welfare, Office of Education, *Interpretation of Test Results*, OE–25038, Bulletin 1964, no. 7. Washington, D.C.: Government Printing Office, 1964, pp. 53–58.

CHAPTER 19 / *Interpretation and Use of Standardized Tests*

The use of a wide variety of standardized measurement instruments has become common practice in American schools.[1] Thousands of standardized tests have been developed to measure a student's general intelligence, specific aptitudes, achievement, and personality characteristics. The results are employed by administrators to appraise the effectiveness of their instructional program, and to enable them to classify students for programming. In addition, school counselors use standardized instruments when they study a student's adjustment status, his educational needs, and his vocational interests. And classroom teachers employ standardized tests:

1. To determine the range of ability and achievement within a class so that appropriate instructional level, goals, pacing, materials, and activities can be selected.

2. To identify individuals who are potentially fast learners and consequently most likely to benefit from special motivation, enrichment work, and acceleration.

3. To identify individuals who are slow learners and laggards in the subject matter of the particular class. For these students the teacher can plan a slower pace of instruction, more concrete illustrations, more frequent drill and review, and—if class size permits—individually adapted remediation.

4. To identify individuals who are achieving less than might reasonably

[1] A standardized instrument is a test or scale for which regularized procedures of administration and scoring have been established and for which scores of norm groups have been determined. In the standardization process, the instrument is administered to norm groups carefully selected to be representative of all those for whom it was designed. The resulting distributions of scores are then used as norms to aid interpretation of scores made in subsequent administrations of the instrument.

be expected. These students may benefit from special study by the teacher or counselor.

5. To discover, through item analysis, any broad subject matter topics which might be given greater instructional emphasis, provided that such emphasis is acceptable within the local course of study.

6. To compare the achievement of a class and its individual members with the national norms for classes and individuals of similar ability. This information can help a teacher evaluate the success of his instruction.

7. To help a student select a program of studies compatible with his needs and abilities.

8. To help motivate better teaching and better learning. Knowledge of success, or lack of it, when intelligently interpreted can be a powerful motivator for both teacher and student.

To ensure that he gets all the help possible from the standardized testing program of his school, a teacher should study the scores of his classes, using analytical lists, charts, graphs, and individual profiles, and then should supplement that information with careful, long-term observation of the students themselves, for tests alone merely give helpful indications, not final answers.

The purpose of this chapter is to acquaint beginning teachers with the general characteristics of the standardized tests and test scores they will be most likely to find in use wherever they teach. Assistance in the reading and interpretation of test scores will be the principal focus of the chapter; however, a necessary first step is an introduction to the nature of educational measurement.

THE NATURE OF SCORES
IN EDUCATIONAL MEASUREMENT

A basic problem in the science of education is the development of measuring instruments scaled so as to have a true zero point and units of equal size throughout the range of measurement. Until such instruments are in existence, teachers will be unable to use measures of a student's intelligence, his growth in knowledge of subject matter, or his changes in attitude in the same manner as they use measures of a student's height and weight. That is, when the units involved are not of the same size, measurements made in different parts of a scale cannot be compared accurately. To be more specific, tests of educational achievement yield raw scores that usually indicate the number of items correctly answered. Thus, on any educational scale the basic unit is an individual test item—but such a scale is composed of unequal units unless the items are all of equal difficulty or are individually weighted according to the amount of knowledge measured.

Gains measured in different parts of many educational scales are therefore not directly comparable. For example, a student who has changed in weight from 120 to 125 pounds has gained exactly as much weight as another student who has changed from a weight of 90 to 95 pounds. A 5-pound change is precisely the same amount in any part of the weight scale. However, when a student's score on an achievement test moves from 120 to 125 points his gain in achievement is not necessarily equal to the gain made by a student whose score changed from 90 to 95 points. The units involved may be of different size. Consequently, educational tests ordinarily do not enable a teacher to make precise comparisons of change.

Furthermore, even when units are equivalent, comparisons involving multiplication or division cannot be made unless zero on the scale represents complete absence of the quality being measured. The problem of developing scales that register zero only when there is complete absence of the quality measured is not peculiar to educational measurement. For example, the same difficulty is encountered in the measurement of temperature. When the familiar Fahrenheit and centigrade scales were developed, the absolute zero point (total absence of heat) was not firmly established. On the centigrade scale the zero point was set at the freezing point of water under certain prescribed conditions, while the zero point on the Fahrenheit scale was set 32 units below the freezing point. The size of a degree on each scale is constant, but differs from one scale to the other. Therefore, it is obvious that a reading of 75 degrees on one scale does not represent the same temperature as a reading of 75 degrees on the other. Also it should be noted that neither scale justifies the statement that a temperature of 80 degrees is twice as warm as a temperature of 40 degrees.

For the same reason, it is incorrect to say that the earth was twice as old in A.D. 1000 as it was in A.D. 500, for the zero point concerning the age of the earth has not been firmly established. In educational measurement it is inaccurate to state that a student having an IQ of 150 is twice as intelligent as a student having an IQ of 75, or that a student who scores 80 points on an arithmetic test has twice the arithmetic skill of a student who scored only 40 points on the test. Zero points in these factors and in many others have not been established.

Because the basic unit of measurement is undefined, a student who scores a certain number of points on a test constructed by one teacher is unlikely to score the same number of points on a test constructed by another teacher to cover the same subject matter. However, if the tests are sound tests of the subject, a student can be expected to hold very nearly the same position among his classmates on each of the two tests. Under these circumstances—and they are the usual circumstances in educational measurement—scores become more stable and informative measurements when they are transformed to numbers that in some manner describe positions in a distribution of scores. For this reason, the building of frequency distributions of raw scores and their transformation to derived scores is common practice in educational measurement. By definition, "a frequency distribution is a tabulation of scores from high to low, or low to high, showing the number of individuals that obtain each score or fall in each score interval." [2]

Points or positions in a frequency distribution are described by use of several variations of two basic procedures:

Procedure one: The position of a particular score in a distribution can be described according to the number or percentage of *individuals* who scored either above or below the given score.

Procedure two: The position of a particular score in a distribution can be described according to its *numerical value* in relation to selected mathematical properties of the distribution.

SCORES BASED ON COUNTING INDIVIDUALS

NUMERICAL RANK The simplest of scores derived by counting individuals (frequencies or cases) in the distribution is numerical rank. In this system, every frequency in the distribution is numbered according to its ordered position counted from the top. Whenever the frequency at any score is greater than one, all cases at that score are assigned the average of the numerical positions filled. For example, in Table 19-1, the score of 83 is said to have a numerical rank of 1 because it is the single top score. The two individuals who scored 82 take up positions two and three; hence each is assigned a rank of 2.5, the average of those positions. In the same way, every case in a distribution can be ranked. Numerical rank, however, is seriously limited in application because identical ranks in groups of different size may have extremely different meanings.

CENTILE POINTS The basis for an improved ranking scale is obtained by designating points in a distribution according to the *percentage* of the frequency falling *below* each point. In Table 19-1 it can be observed that $12/100$ of all frequencies fall below the midpoint of score 58; therefore 58 can be designated as the twelfth centile point, C_{12}, in the distribution.[3] In this manner, it is possible to designate 100 points of reference in any frequency distribution.

The most commonly used reference point of the centile type, the fiftieth centile point (C_{50}), is also known as the *median*. In Table 19-1, the me-

---

[2] Roger T. Lennon, "A Glossary of 100 Measurement Terms," *Test Service Notebook*, no. 13. New York: Harcourt, Brace & World, Inc., p. 2.

[3] One half of the frequencies at any score are assumed to fall below the midpoint of that score. In Table 19-1, the two scores of 58 are assumed to spread out evenly between 57.5 and 58.5 so that exactly one frequency falls below 58.0.

Table 19–1. A Sample Distribution of 50 Raw Scores and Their Equivalent Derived Scores

DERIVED MATHEMATICALLY			DISTRIBUTION OF RAW SCORES			DERIVED BY COUNTING FREQUENCIES				
STANDARD SCORES Z	z	DEVIATION POINTS	X	TABS	f	NUMERICAL RANK	ACCUM. f	CENTILE POINTS	%ILE RANK	T
			84							
71	2.1		83	/	1	1	49.5	C_{99}	99	73
70	2.0	← $\overline{X} + 2S$ ←	82	//	2	2.5	48		96	68
69			81							
67			80							
66			79							
64	1.4		78	/	1	4	46.5		93	65
63			77							
61			76	//	2	5.5	45	C_{90}	90	63
60	1.0	← $\overline{X} + S$ ←	75	/	1	7	43.5		87	61
59			74	//	2	8.5	42		84	60
57			73	///	3	11	39.5		79	58
56	.6		72	//	2	13.5	37		74	56
54			71	////	4	16.5	34		68	55
53			70	////	4	20.5	30		60	53
51			69	//////	6	25.5	25	median	50	50
50	0.0	← mean ($\overline{X}$) ←	68	///	3	30	20.5		41	48
49			67	//	2	32.5	18		36	47
47			66	/	1	34	16.5		33	46
46	−.4		65	//	2	35.5	15		30	45
44			64	///	3	38	12.5	C_{25}	25	43
43			63	//	2	40.5	10		20	42
41			62	/	1	42	8.5		17	41
40	−1.0	← $\overline{X} - S$ ←	61	/	1	43	7.5		15	40
39			60							
37			59							
36	−1.4		58	//	2	44.5	6	C_{12}	12	38
34			57							
33			56	/	1	46	4.5		9	37
31			55							
30	−2.0	← $\overline{X} - 2S$ ←	54	/	1	47	3.5		7	35
29			53	//	2	48.5	2		4	32
27	−2.3		52	/	1	50	.5	C_1	1	27
			51							
			50							

(marginal labels: "one standard deviation" marked at successive intervals in the deviation column; "Range" marked along the ACCUM. f column.)

Procedure

$$z = \frac{X - \overline{X}}{S} \qquad S = \sqrt{\frac{\Sigma(X - \overline{X})^2}{N}}$$

$$\overline{X} = \frac{\Sigma X}{N}$$

$$Z = 10z + 50$$

	f	NUMERICAL RANK	ACCUM. f	%ILE RANK	T
	Count tabs	Count f down	Count f up to midpoint of score	$\dfrac{\text{Accum. } f \cdot N}{100}$	Take from %ile in "normal" table

dian of the distribution of raw scores is 69. Students who score below the median are in the bottom half of the distribution, just as students who score below C_{25} are in the bottom quarter of the distribution.

PERCENTILE RANK   It is important to note that all frequencies at a given centile point are said to have a percentile rank of that particular centile number. That is, all cases at C_{10} have a percentile rank of 10, and all cases at the median have a percentile rank of 50. Likewise, a student who has a percentile rank of 25 exceeds roughly 25 percent of the individuals in the distribution, and roughly 75 percent exceed him.[4] Percentile rank within a school grade is the type of score most commonly used in standardized testing at high school and college levels. Such a score clearly indicates the percentage of the norm group that scored below any given point in the norm group distribution. For example, when 60 percent of high school juniors fall below a score of 37 in the norm group distribution established for a standardized test, a percentile rank of 60 among high school juniors is assigned to anyone scoring 37 on subsequent administrations of the test.

Percentile rank scores are more meaningful than numerical rank scores but are susceptible to unique misinterpretations discussed later in this chapter.

MATHEMATICALLY DERIVED SCORES

The mathematical properties most used in procedure two are the distribution's *arithmetic mean* and *standard deviation*. An arithmetic mean, commonly called average, is the measure of a distribution's central tendency obtained by dividing the sum of all the scores by their total number.[5] In Table 19-1, the sum of the fifty scores is 3400. The arithmetic mean of the scores, then, is 68. A standard deviation is a mathematical measure of the variability of scores in a distribution.[6] When the scores are spread out widely from the mean, the standard deviation is relatively large, but when the scores cluster closely about the mean, the standard deviation is relatively small. The full range of scores in a distribution practically never is less than twice as large as the standard deviation, nor more than six times as large as that measure. In distributions containing 100 or more

---

[4] The percentile rank of a given score is found by counting half the frequencies at the score and to that number adding all the frequencies below the score. The obtained sum is then divided by the total frequency of the distribution.

[5] The formula for the arithmetic mean $\overline{X} = \dfrac{\Sigma X}{N}$ indicates that the mean $(\overline{X})$ of a set of scores is equal to the sum of (Σ) the scores (X) divided by the number of scores (N).

[6] The formula for the standard deviation $S = \sqrt{\dfrac{\Sigma(X - \overline{X})^2}{N}}$ indicates that the standard deviation of a group of N scores is equal to the square root of the average of their squared differences from the mean.

scores, the full range is usually from four to six times as large as the standard deviation. In Table 19-1, the range of the fifty scores is 32 points (83.5–51.5), and the standard deviation is 7 points.

In the interpretation of standardized tests, the mean score of a defined age or grade group is commonly used as the basic reference point and their standard deviation is commonly used as the basic unit of measurement.

AGE NORMS   When a test is being designed to measure a characteristic that, for a school-age group, typically increases with age (such as mental ability or physical development), the test is administered to sample groups of thousands of individuals at each age level for which the test is intended. The arithmetic mean of each age group is then reported as an age norm. Thus, in the standardization of a mental test, it may be found that children 10 years and 4 months old averaged 46 points. Then any child scoring 46 points on the test would be said to have a mental age of 10 years and 4 months (10-4). Similarly, in the determination of the familiar age norms for height, measurements are made on large groups of persons at each developmental age. The average height of each age group is then tabled so that a child can measure his height, refer to the table, and determine his standing in relation to the average.

Age norms have also been developed for educational achievement. Such norms are called *achievement ages, subject ages, educational ages,* or *age equivalents.* Thus a student whose arithmetic score is average for students 11 years and 6 months old would be said to have an arithmetic age of 11-6. If his score on a battery of achievement tests is average for students 10 years and 9 months old, his educational age is said to be 10-9.

AGE QUOTIENTS   Selected age scores of individuals are sometimes compared by the mathematical process of division so as to yield quotients that help teachers answer three popular questions:

1. How does Johnny's performance on mental ability tests compare with the scores of other children of his chronological age? This question is answered by dividing Johnny's mental age score (MA) by his chronological age (CA) and moving the decimal point two places to the right. The result is Johnny's *intelligence quotient,* the formula for which is

$$IQ = \frac{MA}{CA} \times 100$$

2. How does Johnny's performance on a battery of achievement tests (his educational age) compare with the scores of other children of his chronological age? This question is answered by determining the student's *education quotient* by dividing his educational age (EA) by his chronological age (CA) and multiplying the result by 100:

$$EQ = \frac{EA}{CA} \times 100$$

3. How does Johnny's performance on a battery of achievement tests compare with the scores made by other children of his mental age? To answer this question Johnny's *accomplishment quotient* is obtained by the formula:

$$AQ = \frac{EA}{MA} \times 100 \text{ or } AQ = \frac{EQ}{IQ} \times 100$$

Quotient scores appear to be simple to interpret: scores of 100 indicate performance equal to the group average, scores below 100 indicate lower than average performance, and scores above 100 indicate better than average performance. However, quotient scores are particularly susceptible to errors of interpretation. For example, IQ, by far the most extensively used quotient score, varies so widely in meaning for different age groups that it is being replaced by the deviation IQ (discussed later in this chapter). Furthermore, the AQ (accomplishment quotient) contains such a strong tendency to overrate the accomplishment of low-ability students and underrate the accomplishment of high-ability students (because of factors associated with the reliability of measurement) that the AQ must be used with extreme caution, if, in fact, it is used at all.

GRADE NORMS   In the measurement of educational achievement, scores are commonly reported as averages for given grade levels, called *grade norms, grade placements,* or *grade equivalents*. Age norms and grade norms are very similar concepts. Each is an arithmetic mean for a given group. It should be noted that, whereas age norms are based upon a twelve-month year and expressed by two numbers separated by a dash, grade norms are based upon a ten-month school year and expressed as a decimal. An age norm half way between 10 years and no months (10-0) and 11 years and no months (11-0) is 10 years and 6 months (10-6). The grade norm midway between the beginning of the tenth and eleventh grades is 10.5. A grade equivalent of 6.7 would be interpreted to mean that the obtained score was average for a group that had completed half or more of the seventh month of the sixth grade. In actual standardization, however, tests frequently are administered in only one month of each successive grade. The grade equivalent scores of intermediate months are obtained by interpolation. Grade norms are the derived scores most commonly used at elementary school level.

LINEAR DERIVATION OF STANDARD SCORES   The position of a score in a distribution also can be described according to its raw score deviation from the mean. Thus, in Table 19-1, a score of 80 could be said to be +12 points (80–68) from the mean, and a score of 64 could be said to be

−4 points (64–68) from the mean. Such scores roughly locate positions in reference to the mean but fail to indicate whether or not a score is near one of the extremes of the distribution. In a distribution having a standard deviation of 36, a score 12 points above the mean is only a third of a standard deviation from the mean—a position relatively close to the center of the distribution. On the other hand, in a distribution having a standard deviation of 4, a score 12 points above the mean is three standard deviations above the mean—a position seldom exceeded by anyone.

To overcome this confusion in meaning, the sigma or z-score system has been evolved. In that system, a score's position is described by a number that indicates its distance from the mean in standard deviation units.[7] A raw score at the mean of a distribution always becomes a z-score of zero, a z-score of −.5 always denotes a position one-half standard deviation below the mean, and so on.

The z-score system is basic to all standard score scales. The Z-scale, for example, is obtained from z-scores by the formula $Z = 10z + 50$. By use of a mean of 50 and a standard deviation of 10, this scale avoids the negative signs and decimals that complicate the z-scale. Other linear standard scores may be obtained by application of the formula

new standard score $= z($ *new standard deviation* $) +$ *new mean*

The transformation of a distribution of raw scores to z-scores or Z-scores is known as a *linear transformation* because the graph of the relationship is a straight line. This fact is pictured in Figure 19-1, a line graph of the relationship between Z-scores and raw scores having a mean of 28 and a standard deviation of 4.

Standard scores of the linear transformation type are extremely useful to teachers when they are determining student marks as explained in Chapter 18. Furthermore, Z-scores derived from distributions of varied shapes maintain precisely consistent mathematical meanings. The mean is always denoted by a Z-score of 50, a Z of 60 is always one standard deviation above the mean, a Z of 40 is always one standard deviation below the mean, and so on. However, Z-scores fail to have consistent percentile rank equivalents unless they are derived from distributions of the same shape.

NORMALIZED STANDARD SCORES   Fortunately, when large numbers of students are measured by practically any educational or psychological test, the resulting distribution of scores has a strong tendency to resemble *a normal curve* for which percentile rank scores and standard score equivalents are well known. That is, in a normal distribution a percentile rank

---

[7] The z-score of any raw score X can be found by substitution in the formula
$$z = \frac{X - \overline{X}}{s}.$$

of 2 is always two standard deviations below the mean (at $z = -2$), a percentile rank of 16 is always one standard deviation below the mean (at the point z equals -1), a percentile rank of 50 is always at the mean

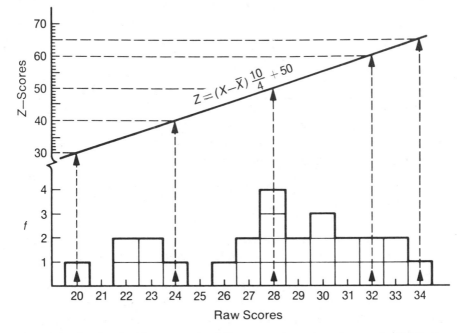

Fig. 19-1 Graphical and computational linear transformation of a sample distribution of twenty-five raw scores ($\overline{X} = 28$, $S = 4$) to their equivalent Z-scores

Sample Computations for Scores in the Above Distribution in Which $\overline{X} = 28$ and $S = 4$

Computation for a score of 20	*Computation for a score of 34*
$Z = \dfrac{(raw\ score - mean)\,10}{standard\ deviation} + 50$	$Z = \dfrac{(raw\ score - mean)\,10}{standard\ deviation} + 50$
$Z = \dfrac{(X - \overline{X})\,10}{4} + 50$	$Z = \dfrac{(X - \overline{X})\,10}{4} + 50$
$Z = \dfrac{(20 - 28)\,10}{4} + 50$	$Z = \dfrac{(34 - 28)\,10}{4} + 50$
$Z = \dfrac{(-8)\,10}{4} + 50$	$Z = \dfrac{(6)\,10}{4} + 50$
$Z = -20 + 50$	$Z = 15 + 50$
$Z = 30$	$Z = 65$

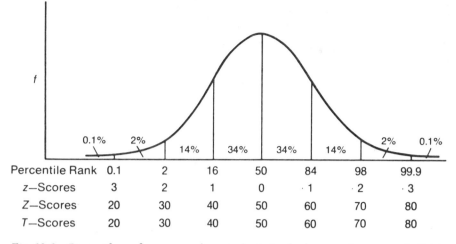

Percentile Rank	0.1	2	16	50	84	98	99.9
z–Scores	3	2	1	0	1	2	3
Z–Scores	20	30	40	50	60	70	80
T–Scores	20	30	40	50	60	70	80

Fig. 19-2   Percentile rank scores and equivalent standard scores in a normal distribution

($z = 0$), and so on. The relationship of percentile rank scores and standard scores when the raw scores are *normally distributed* is shown in Figure 19-2.

It is sometimes advantageous to transform nonnormal distributions of raw scores to percentile ranks and then assign each percentile rank the standard score it would have in a normal distribution. For example, in Figure 19-3, the frequency of cases (four) below 23.0 is represented by the shaded area. Four cases are 16 percent of the total frequency (twenty-five) in the distribution. Therefore, a raw score of 23 has a percentile rank of 16. From Figure 19-3 or from statistical tables of normal curve data, it is found that the equivalent position (percentile rank equals 16) in a normal distribution is always exactly one standard deviation below the mean, at $z = -1$. The raw score of 23 is then assigned a score that is one standard deviation below the mean on whatever standard score scale is used. Each raw score in the distribution can be transformed to a standard score in the same manner. When standard scores are derived by this transformation technique, they are classified as *normalized standard scores*.

Use of normalized standard scores is appropriate when it is logical to assume that a distribution of raw scores deviates from normal because of errors of measurement or when it is necessary to force large sets of data into similar distributions so that various segments of a battery of tests will yield comparable scores. The American Psychological Association, the American Educational Research Association, and the National Council on Measurements Used in Education all recommend that standardized test results be reported as normalized standard scores. This recommendation is followed by a great many publishers of educational and psychological

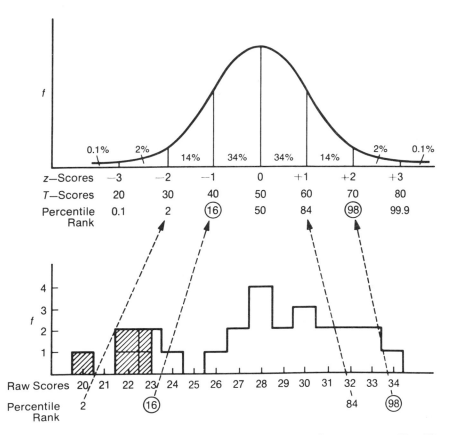

Fig. 19-3   Transformation of a sample distribution of twenty-five raw scores ($X = 28$, $S = 4$) to their equivalent normalized standard scores

Sample Computation for Scores
in the Above Distribution

	For a Raw Score of	
	23	34
Step 1: Count all frequencies below the score's mid-point.	4	24.5
Step 2: Divide the obtained accumulated frequency by the total frequency in the distribution. (This is the percentile rank of the raw score.)	$\dfrac{4}{25} = .16$	$\dfrac{24.5}{25} = .98$
Step 3: Read the standard score of the obtained percentile rank from a graph or table of a normal distribution.	$z = -1$ $T = 40$	$z = 2$ $T = 70$

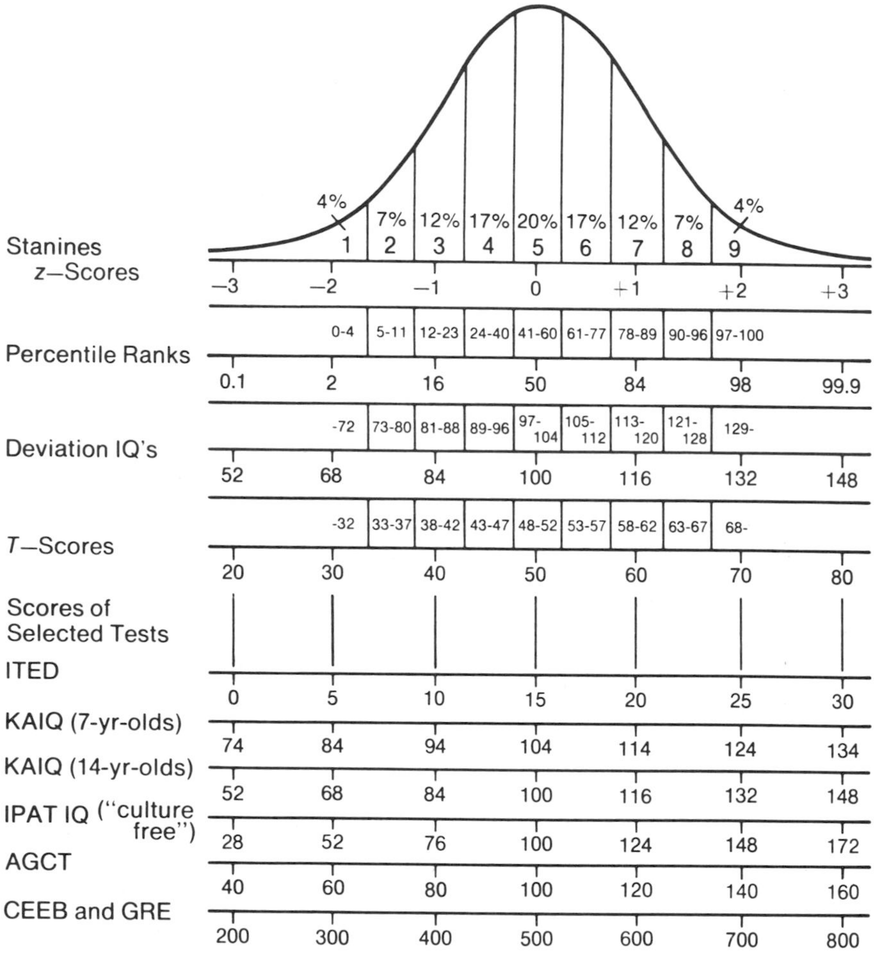

		4%							4%	
			7%	12%	17%	20%	17%	12%	7%	
Stanines			1	2	3	4	5	6	7	8	9
z–Scores	−3	−2		−1		0		+1		+2	+3

	Percentile Ranks			0-4	5-11	12-23	24-40	41-60	61-77	78-89	90-96	97-100	

Percentile Ranks — 0.1 — 2 — 16 — 50 — 84 — 98 — 99.9

Deviation IQ's: -72 | 73-80 | 81-88 | 89-96 | 97-104 | 105-112 | 113-120 | 121-128 | 129-
52 — 68 — 84 — 100 — 116 — 132 — 148

T–Scores: -32 | 33-37 | 38-42 | 43-47 | 48-52 | 53-57 | 58-62 | 63-67 | 68-
20 — 30 — 40 — 50 — 60 — 70 — 80

Scores of Selected Tests

ITED: 0 — 5 — 10 — 15 — 20 — 25 — 30

KAIQ (7-yr-olds): 74 — 84 — 94 — 104 — 114 — 124 — 134

KAIQ (14-yr-olds): 52 — 68 — 84 — 100 — 116 — 132 — 148

IPAT IQ ("culture free"): 28 — 52 — 76 — 100 — 124 — 148 — 172

AGCT: 40 — 60 — 80 — 100 — 120 — 140 — 160

CEEB and GRE: 200 — 300 — 400 — 500 — 600 — 700 — 800

Fig. 19-4   The relationship of stanines to the normal curve and to a variety of other scores

tests. Some of the most common scores of this type are shown in Figure 19-4.

T-SCORES   The most commonly used normalized scale employs 50 as a mean and 10 as a standard deviation. This derived score is called a T-score and should not be confused with the similarly numbered but differently derived Z-score. The T-score was originated as a normalized standard score by McCall, who is said to have named it in honor of the psychologists Terman and Thorndike. Because T-scores are derived from the percentile rank data of normal distributions, a T-score of 50 always indicates the median, a T-score of 40 always indicates a percentile rank of 16, a *T*-score of 60 always indicates a percentile rank of 84, and so on, as revealed in Figure 19-2. On the other hand, a Z-score will have these percentile rank equivalents only when the original raw score data are normally distributed. However, regardless of the size and shape of a distribution, its Z-scores will have precise meaning in terms of the distribution's mean and standard deviation—an advantage not possessed by the *T*-score. Consequently, Z-scores, despite restricted interpretation, may be used with distributions of any size and shape, whereas *T*-scores ordinarily are appropriate for use only with groups normally distributed.

DEVIATION IQ   A normalized standard score of special importance is the deviation IQ, a scale that has practically replaced the quotient IQ. This scale has a mean of 100 and a standard deviation of 16 (or 15 as used by some tests) for all chronological ages. Thus, regardless of the age at which a person is tested, if his resulting deviation IQ is 148, his score is three standard deviations above the mean of his age group and his percentile rank is 99.9 in that group. This was not true of the outmoded quotient IQ. That long-used intelligence score is plagued by the fact that the IQ's of different age groups frequently have different standard deviations even when measured with the same test. On that scale (quotient IQ) an IQ of 148 for a 16-year-old sometimes represents a percentile ranking inferior to that represented by an IQ of 132 for a person measured at an earlier age. The deviation IQ, like all normalized standard scores, provides consistent interpretation in terms of percentile rank.

STANINES   The stanine (standard nine) scale is a normalized standard scale of bands having a mean of 5 and a standard deviation of 2. The scale divides a normal distribution into nine segments, the middle seven of which are each one-half standard deviation wide. Figure 19-4 shows that the bottom 4 percent of the distribution is in stanine one, the next 7 percent in stanine two, and so forth. Teachers should note the unlimited width of the first and ninth stanines. For example, stanine nine contains IQ's of 129 as well as those of 148 and higher. Thus, the scale is inadequate to identify the top 1 to 2 percent of students who in many schools are classified as gifted and provided special learning opportunities. Nevertheless, the stanine scale has gained wide acceptance in education in the comparatively short time since its origination by psychologists in the U. S. Air Force of World War II.

This section concerning the nature of measurement has sought to develop a general understanding of the scores discussed. The development of computational skill has not been intended. Those beginning teachers who feel the need of computational exercises should consult the readings listed at the end of this chapter or textbooks in elementary statistics. The measurement concepts developed here are basic to the proper use of intelligence tests and standardized achievement tests, the topics that follow.

INTELLIGENCE TESTS AND THE CLASSROOM TEACHER

Some beginning teachers—and more experienced ones, as well—have the erroneous idea that intelligence tests and their resulting scores are intriguing but valueless, having meaning for guidance workers and psychologists only. These teachers do not bother to determine the intelligence ratings of their students and a few profess thereby to be fairer and less biased in their work with students. On the other hand, there are teachers who lean heavily on intelligence testing. These teachers may ignore errors of measurement and expect all students with IQ's measured at a given point to learn less than students with scores a few points higher. They may also ignore other limitations affecting IQ interpretation; for example, they frequently expect all students of low to average IQ to be low to average in all things, with the possible exception of physical stature and strength.

Fortunately, only a small proportion of teachers fall into these two extreme categories. In between these extremes is found the great majority of teachers. They regularly use IQ's in their study of the learning problems of their students, and they expect students of high intelligence to surpass others in academic achievement. However, these teachers realize that IQ differences of 5 or 10 points on a single measurement have little, if any, meaning in relation to the learning potential of individual students. The reasons are simple: single scores frequently are in error by that amount and many variables other than intelligence are involved in learning. In short, the majority of teachers recognize that intelligence tests are useful but not infallible instruments.

DEVELOPMENT OF INTELLIGENCE TESTS

Instruments for the measurement of intelligence have an interesting but not mysterious background of development. Prior to the beginning of the twentieth century, men in many countries tried to measure intelligence but all were unsuccessful. However, during the first decade of this century, two Frenchmen, Binet and Simon, developed an intelligence scale that was an outstanding contribution to the advancement of scientific measurement. Their work is basic to many tests now in worldwide use. In the United States, the Stanford-Binet Intelligence Scale, authored by Terman in 1916 and revised in 1937 and 1960 by Terman and Merrill, has been the adaptation held in highest esteem by psychologists and educators. This test, together with two scales developed by Wechsler, the Wechsler Adult Intelligence Scale (WAIS) and the Wechsler Scale for Children (WISC), is used whenever most precise measurement of intelligence is necessary. These tests are particularly important in clinical work and in the measurement of the IQ's of persons having reading difficulties. However, all tests of this type are limited in school application by the fact that they must be administered orally and to only one individual at a time.

The need for a test of intelligence that could be administered to groups was first satisfied by the Army Alpha Test authored in 1917 by Otis and other American psychologists. This test helped solve the World War I classification needs of the United States Army, just as its many successors have been successfully applied to the classification problems of schools, business, and industry.

Several outstanding group tests, including those of Otis, Terman, Cattell, Kuhlmann, and the Thurstones, were developed in the 1920s, 1930s, and 1940s. These tests have been repeatedly published in new editions modified in content, printing style, or scoring procedure. Through this process they have remained in extensive use over a long period of years. They are by no means the only intelligence tests in use, however. According to Buros' *Tests in Print*, there were more than 200 intelligence tests on the world market in 1961.[8] Approximately 150 of these were being published in the United States.

Among the forty or more "individual" tests of intelligence now available are some specially designed to measure the IQ's of children who have defective motor ability, hearing, or vision.[9] Among the group tests are some that claim to be nonverbal (unaffected by individual differences in ability to understand words), culture-free or culture-fair (unaffected by individual differences in cultural background), or multiracial (unaffected by individual differences in racial origin). In fact, if the need arose—and the test titles could be taken at face value—an intelligence test could now be found to measure almost any type of person at any time from his birth to his dotage!

Obviously the 200 or more intelligence tests of the 1960s vary greatly in quality and in popularity. No teacher could possibly be expected to be informed about all of them. However, every teacher should be able to use and interpret the tests adopted by his school.

THE INTERPRETATION OF INTELLIGENCE SCORES

Study of test manuals will reveal that intelligence test results are reported in a variety of scores including IQ's, mental ages, percentile ranks, and grade equivalents. The derivation of these scores was discussed earlier; however, a recapitulation may be helpful.

A mental age of 12 indicates that the student has made a test score equivalent to that of the average 12-year-old in the test's standardizing

[8] Oscar K. Buros, *Tests in Print*. Highland Park, N.J.: The Gryphon Press, 1961, p. xxvi.
[9] Buros, pp. 120–127.

group, whereas an IQ of 100 indicates that the student has made a score that is average for his own chronological age. Likewise, a student's percentile rank indicates roughly what percentage of the tested group scored below the student, and his grade equivalent indicates the grade level at which his score would be average. For example, an average 14-year-old would have a mental age of 14, an IQ of 100, a grade equivalent of grade nine, and a percentile rank of fifty in that grade.

Of the common methods of reporting intelligence test results, mental age alone has the advantage of indicating the level of mental ability attained. That is, in any group tested simultaneously, the student who earns the highest mental age score has demonstrated the greatest mental ability. Mental ages, however, have the disadvantage of changing from year to year. Up to the age of about 16, an average student gains one year in mental age for each year gained in chronological age, but a student with an IQ of 75 gains only three fourths of a year each year of his early life. On the other hand, IQ's remain relatively constant from year to year, but fail to denote the relative mental level of members of a group made up of individuals of varying chronological ages. It is only for persons of equal chronological age that IQ's indicate relative mental ability.

In the interpretation of intelligence quotients, teachers should not assume that students of the same IQ necessarily possess the same capacity for learning. In fact, identical IQ ratings are derived from identical intelligence test scores only when the tested students are of identical chronological age. That is, the highest IQ in the class does not necessarily possess the greatest problem-solving ability. He merely is best for his age. For example, Tom, 11 years of age, Jim, 12, and Bill, 14, are in the seventh grade. If they made identical scores on an intelligence test, giving each of them a mental age of 12 years, Tom's quotient IQ would be 109, Jim's would be 100, and Bill's would be 86. Yet Tom, Jim, and Bill, as measured by the test, would have the same ability to solve problems involving mental processes.

Teachers should keep alert also to the fact that most commonly used intelligence tests, weighted heavily with verbal factors, are adequate predictors of success in the verbal activities of the school but do not serve to predict effectively a student's potential in the nonverbal learnings. Furthermore, intelligence tests do not measure native capacity alone. The scores are affected by the kinds and quality of experience available to the student. Students from backgrounds that fail to provide experience considered common to American urban culture are likely to receive lower scores than they would if the tests were more adequate. Students of lower socioeconomic background, those having reading difficulties, and those having adjustment or health problems typically score lower than their potential. Intelligence scores, then, of a particular student are meaningful only when that student is similar to the standardizing group with respect to the nonintellectual factors that might affect test scores. For example, the mental score of a rural youth might not be valid if the standardizing group is predominantly of urban background.

Finally, because of errors of measurement (discussed later in this chapter), any single intelligence score can be interpreted safely only as an indication of the midpoint of a range of scores within which the student's true score can be expected to occur. The range of scores should be at least 10 points wide in the case of total test scores, and at least 15 points wide for all subscores, including those termed "verbal," "nonlanguage," "reasoning," and "quantitative." Thus, even when they are of the same age and background, two students must differ by at least 10 or 15 points in intelligence scores before it is reasonable to assume that one exceeds the other in true intellectual potential. And even then such a conclusion frequently would be incorrect. Obviously, all teachers must exercise extreme caution when they interpret intelligence measures.

STANDARDIZED ACHIEVEMENT TESTS AND THE CLASSROOM TEACHER

The interpretation of scores from standardized achievement tests also is a regular task of secondary school teachers. To know each student's approximate potential for learning as measured by an intelligence test is of tremendous help in instruction, but this knowledge is only one facet of the teacher's study of the learner. If the teacher is to do the best job of teaching, and if he is to know something of the extent of his teaching success, he must also find answers to such questions as: What is the level of each student's study skills? How well can he read? How does his general educational development compare with that of other students of his ability and grade level? Are each student and the class progressing as well as might be expected? How does their learning compare with local, state, and national norms? Reliable answers to questions like these are not easily determined by observation alone. Fortunately, hundreds of instruments have been produced to help supply the objective evidence needed. The development of these instruments has been the result of efforts that began more than 100 years ago.

THE DEVELOPMENT OF ACHIEVEMENT TESTING

The first step toward improved measurement of achievement in American schools was made before the Civil War by Horace Mann, who urged that written tests of the essay type replace oral examinations, the mode of measurement commonly used at that time. His recommendations were not widely adopted until late in the nineteenth century.

The next addition to testing techniques can be traced back to J. M. Rice, who in the 1890s conducted the first testing survey of educational achievement. His informal study was followed in the early 1900s by the more accurate work of Thorndike, Stone, Ayres, and others, who developed tests and scales for use in surveys of achievement in arithmetic, handwriting, and spelling.

The idea of grouping several tests of common school subjects into a single booklet or "battery" evolved about 1920. In the fifteen years immediately following that date, three outstanding and long-lived batteries were published. (The latest revisions of these tests, the Stanford Achievement Test, the Metropolitan Achievement Test, and the California Achievement Test are among the most popular tests of the present.) In addition to these batteries, many single-subject tests were published for the first time in the 1920s and 1930s. All these tests would be classified as inadequately standardized if they were judged according to present-day standards. Nevertheless, in the relatively short period between World Wars I and II significant progress in testing techniques was made. It was also in these productive years that two additional kinds of tests came into general use: diagnostic tests which identify a student's specific weaknesses in subjects such as arithmetic and reading, and practice tests which provide drill materials accompanied by performance norms.

All the tests published in this period were characterized by the use of items requiring short and specific answers that could be scored in an objective and impersonal manner. Consequently, the instruments became known as objective tests.

The teacher-built tests of the 1920s and 1930s also began to feature objectively scored items. Soon thereafter, true-false, matching, multiple-choice, and completion forms of items practically replaced the use of essay questions in many classrooms. It should be noted that the adoption of objective testing in schools was stimulated by more than mere ease of scoring. The accumulating research evidence of that day indicated that the results of essay testing were highly unreliable. In fact, studies revealed that not only would an essay test frequently be assigned widely different scores by different teachers, but the same teacher often would fail to score a paper the same way on a second reading. Faced with this evidence, classroom teachers as well as local and state officials took action to accelerate the use of objective tests.

Admittedly, objective testing as used by many teachers also had its weakness. It encouraged overemphasis upon the measurement of memorized factual information. Recognition of this fault gave impetus to the "evaluation movement" of the 1940s and 1950s. This movement correctly stressed the necessity of using evidence beyond objective measurement in the assessment of educational achievement. The residual effect upon testing in the 1960s has been that measurement instruments now give greater emphasis to the measurement of understanding, application, interpretation, and problem solving. Regular use of this type of measurement, as part of a broad program of evaluation, is now common in American schools.

SELECTION OF STANDARDIZED TESTS

A teacher wishing to select a battery subtest, a practice test, a diagnostic test, or a year-end test for use in a particular class can easily determine what tests are published in the subject by referring to *Tests in Print*.[10] His next step might well be use of the *Mental Measurements Yearbooks* to learn what experts think of each test's weaknesses and strength.[11] He then could order specimen sets of the tests that appear to be most promising. Such materials are frequently available from the publisher at nominal cost. Finally, the teacher could become thoroughly acquainted with the standardized test by actually taking the test, scoring it, and using the test manual to help him interpret the results.

In selecting a test, teachers frequently are aided by department heads or counselors. Teachers, however, shoulder the primary responsibility alone when it comes to interpretation of the results of standardized tests, including the results of test batteries.

GRAPHICAL REPRESENTATION OF TEST RESULTS

The results of testing programs involving use of batteries of standardized tests are often reported to teachers in the form of graphs or profiles that picture a student's standing in each of the tested areas. Consequently, it is highly important that teachers learn to read the various types of profiles with ease.

Profiles are two-dimensional graphs constructed so that the scale of scores is along one axis and each test is listed at an assigned position along the other. In the irregular-line type of profile, points representing the student's obtained scores are plotted and connected by straight lines. The lines themselves have no meaning in the graphical sense. They merely serve to guide the reader's eye from one test score to another.

Carol Kramer's profile of percentile scores on the Iowa Test of Educational Development (see Fig. 19-5) reveals that she has scored highest in correctness of expression and in the use of sources of information. Her lowest scores are in social studies background and in the reading of literature. This profile places the scale of scores along the vertical axis with lowest scores at the bottom and highest scores at the top.

In Figure 19-6, the individual profile chart of Mary Ashland's scores on the Metropolitan Achievement Tests, the scale of scores is on the horizontal axis. Low scores are on the left and higher scores are on the

[10] Buros, pp. 1–238.

[11] Oscar K. Buros, ed., *The Sixth Mental Measurements Yearbook*, Highland Park, N.J.: The Gryphon Press, 1965, pp. 324–870.

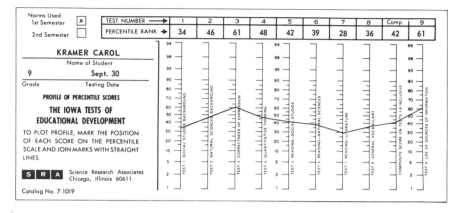

Fig. 19-5 Profile of percentile scores on the Iowa Tests of Educational Development

right. It should be noted carefully that the sample interpretation accompanying Mary Ashland's profile correctly gives little or no attention to the minor fluctuations in the line representing the scores. For example, Mary scored below her Pintner intelligence measurement in three tested skills, but in only one case (study skills in social studies) is it presumed that the discrepancy is serious. The use of dashes instead of a solid line to connect scores on the subtests measuring the mechanics of language emphasizes the fact that these scores are less reliable than the total language score.

Interpretation of Janet James's profile of scores on the California Achievement Tests (Fig. 19-7) should be equally cautious. On this battery, as well as on all batteries, only extreme differences in scores within subtests are likely to be meaningful. For example, it is quite probable that Janet's skill in solving arithmetic reasoning problems exceeds her ability to interpret arithmetic meanings. However, her relative standing in arithmetic problems and arithmetic symbols very well could be reversed upon retest.

In addition to the irregular-line graph, profiles employing either bars or bands are in common use. One style of graph uses a bar to illustrate an obtained score's deviation from a starting point of zero located either at the left edge of the graph or at the bottom as shown in Figure 19-8, the pupil profile chart of Sheila Branch's scores on the SRA Achievement Series. On this chart, the length of each bar indicates how much the represented score differs from zero on the scale used.

From Sheila's profile chart (Fig. 19-8) it should be clearly apparent that in comparison with the norm group she has scored about average in work-study skills, above average in language arts, and high above average in arithmetic. Her weak points are in reading comprehension and

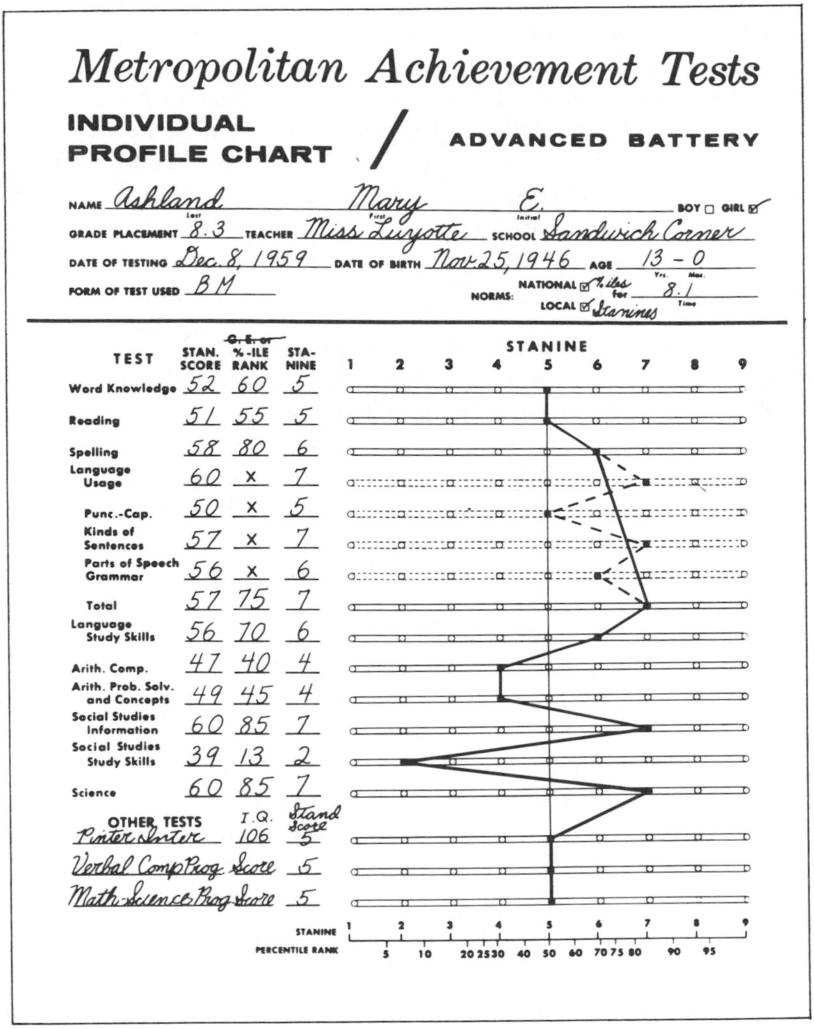

Metropolitan Achievement Tests

INDIVIDUAL PROFILE CHART / ADVANCED BATTERY

NAME Ashland (Last) Mary (First) E. (Initial) BOY ☐ GIRL ☑
GRADE PLACEMENT 8.3 TEACHER Miss Luyotte SCHOOL Sandwich Corner
DATE OF TESTING Dec. 8, 1959 DATE OF BIRTH Nov 25, 1946 AGE 13 - 0 (Yrs. Mos.)
FORM OF TEST USED BM
NORMS: NATIONAL ☑ %iles for 8.1 (Time) LOCAL ☑ Stanines

TEST	STAN. SCORE	~~G. E. or~~ %-ILE RANK	STANINE
Word Knowledge	52	60	5
Reading	51	55	5
Spelling	58	80	6
Language Usage	60	x	7
Punc.-Cap.	50	x	5
Kinds of Sentences	57	x	7
Parts of Speech Grammar	56	x	6
Total	57	75	7
Language Study Skills	56	70	6
Arith. Comp.	47	40	4
Arith. Prob. Solv. and Concepts	49	45	4
Social Studies Information	60	85	7
Social Studies Study Skills	39	13	2
Science	60	85	7

OTHER TESTS	I.Q.	Stand Score
Pinter Inter	106	5
Verbal Comp Prog. Score		5
Math-Science Prog. Score		5

Fig. 19-6 Individual profile chart of stanine scores on the Metropolitan Achievement Tests

Ashland, Mary E. Mary's age is 13 years and 0 months which makes her about 6 months younger than the median age of children in the early months of the eighth grade. Her Pintner Intermediate IQ is 106 and the mental ability stanine corresponding to the median standard score is 5. Word Knowledge and Reading, the two Metropolitan tests correlating most highly with intelligence, are average. Mary's skills in the mechanics of language seem well developed. The stanines of 4 in the arithmetic area are within the chance limits, but considering the superior performance in

(Continued next page)

vocabulary. The teacher probably would be justified in planning special reading experiences for Sheila. However, in the absence of an intelligence measurement standardized on the same norm group, it is impossible to form any sound hypotheses about whether or not Sheila's performance in any of the measured skills represents satisfactory achievement. For example, if Sheila's intelligence happened to be near the 99th percentile in comparison with the norm group used on the SRA Achievement Series, then her performance in at least three of the four skill areas might justify further study by the teacher.

Three additional points should be noted in Sheila's profile:

1. Because percentile ranks do not represent equal raw score units throughout a scale, the numbers along the vertical percentile scales at the left- and right-hand edges of the chart are not equally spaced. They have been adjusted to represent more nearly the position each percentile would have along the base line of a normal distribution of raw scores. When an adjusted scale is not used, teachers must be careful to remember that percentile differences near the middle of the range (near 50) represent much smaller differences in test score than are represented by percentile differences of equal size near either extreme of the scale. In the case of Sheila, the work-study skills scores of the 55th percentile in references and the 45th percentile in charts are correctly separated by less vertical distance than separates her percentile scores of 80 in arithmetic reasoning and 90 in arithmetic concepts. Without adjusted-normal charts these discrepancies in percentile rank scales would be difficult to visualize.

2. Percentile rank scores usually cannot be directly averaged. (When percentile ranks of composite scores are desired, each percentile should be reconverted to its raw score. The raw scores of each individual are then added and the totals are placed in a distribution from which the

---

science, lower arithmetic scores might indicate the need for some corrective work if Mary should decide to enter some occupation within the scientific area. Since these tests were given early in the year the teacher would have an opportunity to work with her. The only serious discrepancy on the Profile Chart is in the area of Social Studies Study Skills. Certainly some attention should be paid to this poor performance and some remedial work instituted unless an examination of the test booklet or other supplementary information indicates that for some reason this is not a valid result.

Mary's composite prognostic scores in both the verbal and math-science area have corresponding stanines of 5 which reinforces the rather obvious conclusion that Mary is a typical student for the eighth grade. She would be a questionable risk for a college preparatory course in high school if this presupposes subsequent attendance in a typical liberal arts institution. Generalizations of this sort, however, are risky unless they are supported by similar performance for other years. This emphasizes the need for a good cumulative testing program.

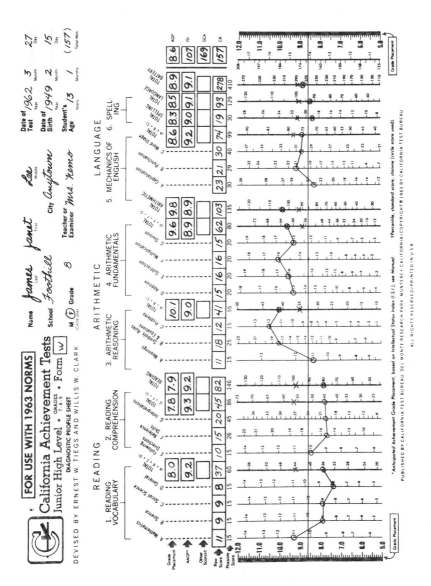

Fig. 19-7 *Diagnostic profile of grade placement scores on the California Achievement Tests*

Copyright 1963. Used by permission of the California Test Bureau, a Division of McGraw-Hill Book Company, Monterey, California.

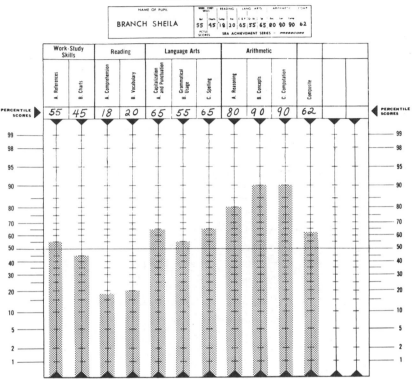

PUPIL PROFILE CHART

Fig. 19-8   Pupil profile chart of percentile scores on the SRA Achievement Series

Several weeks ago you took some interesting tests called the SRA Achieve-ment Series. These tests show how well you are doing in school by com-paring your scores with those of other boys and girls all over the country. The types of schoolwork measured by each test are described on the back of this page. When you look at your score for each test, turn this page over and read about the test.

Your teacher will help you draw a line showing how you scored on each of the tests. Look at your line. Is it straight and right next to the center line? If it is, then you have scored about the same as the average pupil in your grade in the United States. Most probably, though, it is not straight, but has some peaks and valleys. The high points show where you are doing your best work, and the low points show where you are weakest. The numbers at the side of the chart show how much above or below the average each score is. For example, if one of your scores is opposite the number 70, that means that you did better on that test than 70 percent of the boys and girls who took the tests. In other words, in every group of 100 pupils that took the tests, you scored better than 70 of them. If one of your scores is 45, then you scored better than 45 of the 100 pupils.

percentile of each composite raw score can be determined directly.) This principle can be verified in Sheila's case. Her percentile rank on the composite of all scores on the test is correctly reported as 62 even though the arithmetic average of her ten separate percentile scores would be 58.3.

3. Profiles of scores on achievement batteries are sometimes prepared by individual students under the supervision of their teacher. The directions at the bottom of Sheila's profile chart were placed there to help her prepare a broken-line graph which, of course, could be used alone or be superimposed on the bar graph illustrated.

A second style of bar graph is shown in Sherrell Murphy's individual profile of scores on the Metropolitan Achievement Test (Fig. 19.9). This graph employs a bar to reveal the extent of an obtained score's deviation from the mean score of the norm group. Each bar starts at the mean and ends at the score represented. Graphs of this type are particularly useful to portray a student's performance in comparison with the average performance of his grade or age.

Similarly, when the picture desired is a comparison of a student's performance with his measured potential, each bar is started at the level of the student's intelligence score. Furthermore, when an error allowance of at least one stanine on each side of Sherrell's intelligence stanine of 8 is made, the teacher can analyze Sherrell's profile somewhat as follows:

Except for Punctuation and Capitalization and the two arithmetic tests, deviation from expected performance is well within chance limits, if one assumes that Sherrell's capacity lies somewhere between a 7 and an 8. It would appear to be a good working hypothesis that Sherrell needs to do some additional work in the punctuation and capitalization area. Understanding the pupil's work may be facilitated by carefully examining her paper for clues as to possible reasons for the poor performance.

It would seem to be quite clear that Sherrell is a handicapped child in the area of arithmetic. The very low stanine of 2 in Arithmetic Computation suggests that the difficulty lies in her failure to master fundamentals. Her performance is just average in Arithmetic Problem Solving. Since this test involves more reasoning ability, it is logical for her stanine to be higher here than in Computation. One cannot tell from the profile alone the nature of her difficulty, but an alert teacher would consider this to be a danger signal calling for careful study.[12]

With the help of a profile, a teacher can quickly identify a student's relative strengths and weaknesses. However, the interpretation of profiles is not quite as simple as it first appears to be. Since the graphs are based on tests, each of which involves error, comparisons of the relationship between scores on any two tests must take into consideration both sources

[12] Metropolitan Achievement Tests, Directions for Completing Individual Profile Chart, All Batteries. (one page leaflet) Copyright 1960, by Harcourt, Brace & World, Inc., and used with their permission.

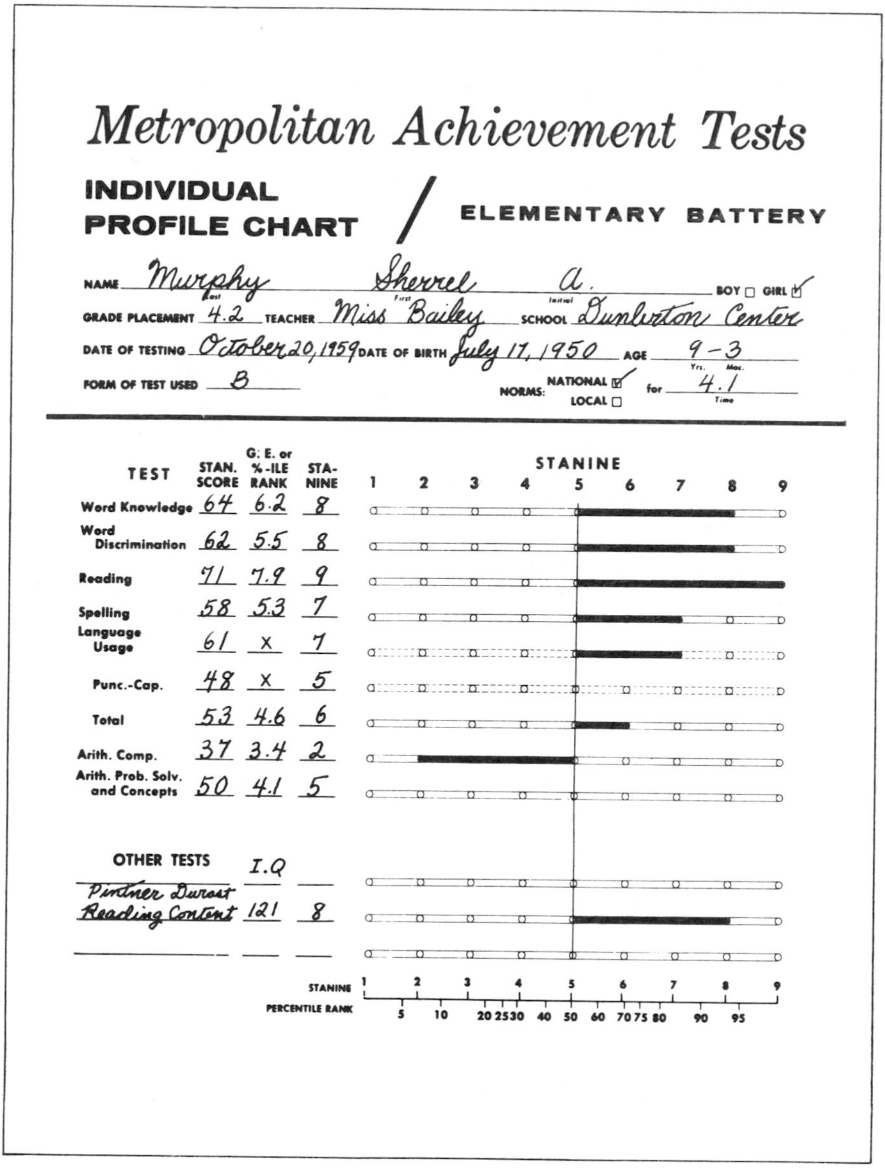

Metropolitan Achievement Tests

INDIVIDUAL PROFILE CHART / ELEMENTARY BATTERY

NAME: Murphy (Last) Sherrel (First) A. (Initial) — BOY ☐ GIRL ☑

GRADE PLACEMENT: 4.2 TEACHER: Miss Bailey SCHOOL: Dunlerton Center

DATE OF TESTING: October 20, 1959 DATE OF BIRTH: July 17, 1950 AGE: 9–3 (Yrs. Mos.)

FORM OF TEST USED: B NORMS: NATIONAL ☑ LOCAL ☐ for 4.1 (Time)

TEST	STAN. SCORE	G. E. or %-ILE RANK	STA-NINE
Word Knowledge	64	6.2	8
Word Discrimination	62	5.5	8
Reading	71	7.9	9
Spelling	58	5.3	7
Language Usage	61	x	7
Punc.-Cap.	48	x	5
Total	53	4.6	6
Arith. Comp.	37	3.4	2
Arith. Prob. Solv. and Concepts	50	4.1	5

OTHER TESTS	I.Q	
Pintner Durost		
Reading Content	121	8

Fig. 19-9 Individual profile chart of stanine scores on the Metropolitan Achievement Tests

of error. For example, is Sheila's percentile rank of 65 in spelling (Fig. 19-8) reliably superior to her grammatical-usage score of 55? How frequently do students equal in these abilities make test scores that are ten or more percentile points apart? To answer these important questions, one must have knowledge of the standard errors involved. Usually these figures must be searched for in a test manual or tediously computed. However, the band type of profile shown in Figure 19-10 portrays error information as an integral part of the profile. This practice must be highly recommended.

Band profiles, prepared by the test publisher or by the classroom teacher, reemphasize the fact that a test score is only an estimate of the range of scores within which the student's true score may be expected to fall. When two bands overlap, it is not possible to say that the tested student is better in one measured subject than in the other.

Technically described, each band is centered at the obtained score and extends one standard error on each side of that point. Consequently, the chances are only about 68 in 100 that the true score lies within the band. Therefore, it should be recognized that there remain about 16 chances in 100 that the band is too low, and 16 chances in 100 that the band is too high, to include the true score. It may be interesting to note that if the band were doubled in length, the chances that it would then encompass the true score would be increased to approximately 96 in 100.

From Figure 19-10 it can be concluded with high confidence that in comparison with the norm group the student's ability is considerably above average in listening, science, and mathematics; slightly above average in reading; and average or below in writing. More specifically, the reading percentile band indicates that the chances are about 68 in 100 that the student's true percentile rank in reading lies between 54 and 71. Comparing the various ratings among themselves, a teacher could confidently make such conclusions as these: "The student's performances in mathematics and in science exceed his performances in social studies and writing, whereas his scores in mathematics and science are not significantly different from each other." Clearly, this type of profile offers the teacher a great deal of information.

In addition to their use to portray a student's standing on a single administration of a battery of tests, profiles are also used to picture a student's growth pattern in grade equivalent scores or converted scores as measured by periodic testing. Still another use of profiles involves the graphing of class averages. This procedure enables a teacher to study the relative strengths and weaknesses of different classes and to trace class growth from one testing to another. When this is done, class norms—not norms for individuals—should be used. Furthermore, it is incorrect to use percentile scores as averages or as the basis for growth comparisons. Of course, in these uses and in all uses of profiles, teachers must keep in

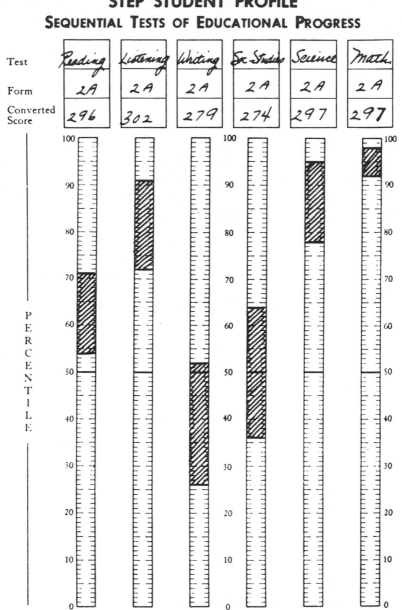

STEP STUDENT PROFILE
SEQUENTIAL TESTS OF EDUCATIONAL PROGRESS

Test	Reading	Listening	Writing	Sr. Studies	Science	Math.
Form	2A	2A	2A	2A	2A	2A
Converted Score	296	302	279	274	297	297

Fig. 19-10   *Profile of percentile-band results based on the Sequential Tests of Educational Progress*

mind that tests on the same profile must be recorded on the same scale of units, and to be strictly comparable, all tests on the same profile must be standardized on the same norm group.

From the preparation and study of profiles, teachers undoubtedly learn a great deal to help their teaching. However, this task is only part of the job that prepares them to make the best use of standardized measures.

BASIC CONSIDERATIONS IN THE INTERPRETATION OF STANDARIZED TESTS

Before teachers can adequately interpret the results of standardized tests, they must answer several key questions:

1. With respect to factors that might affect test scores, does the locally tested group differ from the sample group upon which the test was standardized? (Local norms may be necessary.)
2. To what extent does the test usually accomplish the task for which it was intended? Is it valid for your purposes?
3. How accurately does the test measure? What is its reliability and standard error of measurement?

Information pertaining to these questions usually is contained in manuals provided by test publishers.

ADEQUACY OF NORMS

In their study of the first question, teachers must realize that standardized tests are intended for use only by individuals and groups similar to those represented in the norm group. For example, achievement test results of a class or school can be expected to differ from national norms when the local group and the norm group differ with respect to such factors as:

1. Intelligence
2. Instructional facilities
3. School curriculum
4. Admission and promotion policies
5. Socioeconomic level and emotional tone of the students' homes
6. Student study habits, student health, and student attitude toward testing and toward school

Neither the adequacy of instruction nor the adequacy of student achievement can be judged fairly unless the norm group and the tested group are known to be similar. Unfortunately, very few test manuals provide sufficient detailed information concerning norm groups. Without such information, interpretation of test results should be limited to description of student status in relation to the norm group; whether or not that status is as high as it should be remains unknown. For example, teachers have little cause for elation when their superior-ability students merely exceed the norms for groups of mixed ability. Likewise, no one should be critical of a teacher merely because his students of inferior ability score below the achievement norm of higher-ability students.

TEST VALIDITY

Before they attempt to interpret the scores of a test, teachers should examine evidence concerning the validity of the test. This term has been defined as the measure of the extent to which a test does what it is intended to do. Consequently, tests that have different purposes require different kinds of validating evidence. Such evidence usually is available in test manuals.

To judge the validity of an achievement test, teachers should seek evidence that shows how well the test samples the content of the course to be measured. This type of evidence establishes a test's *content validity*. Evidence that reveals how well the results of a given test agree with other immediate measures of the same thing establishes a test's *concurrent validity*, and evidence that shows how well a test predicts later performance of those tested establishes a test's *predictive validity*.

Content validity is of primary importance for tests used to evaluate achievement and instruction, whereas concurrent validity and predictive validity are of greatest importance when tests are used for the ordinary administrative and guidance purposes.

Teachers should realize that the single most important characteristic of any test is its validity. Until evidence concerning the validity of a test is established, student scores obtained on the test can have little, if any, meaning.

STANDARD ERROR OF MEASUREMENT

Teachers will fail to interpret tests adequately unless they recognize that a single test score is merely a sample measurement that almost always contains considerable error. Experienced teachers know that when a student is tested more than once with the same test or with equivalent tests, he seldom, if ever, makes the same score twice in succession. Furthermore, it is known that if he were to be retested an unlimited number of times, the resulting scores would form a normal distribution called the *sampling distribution* of his scores. The mean of a sampling distribution is defined as a *true score*. The standard deviation of the sampling distribution is a measure of the variability of the student's scores and is defined as the *standard error* of his scores. Different individuals are likely to have somewhat different distributions. Obviously, unlimited retesting of individuals is not a feasible procedure; hence test publishers substitute appropriate statistical analyses of their standardization data to produce sound estimates of the average standard error involved in measurements made with their tests. This information, termed the *standard error of measurement* of the test, is made available in test manuals and is sometimes superimposed upon graphical reports of test results. In any event, teachers must be able to associate standard errors of measurement with normal curve data if they are to understand the predictable variability of test scores.

Study of Figure 19-11 will reveal that roughly 68 percent of measures made can be expected to fall within the range of ±1 standard error of the true score, the remaining 32 percent can be expected to fall above and below that range. Likewise, roughly 96 percent of measures made by a test can be expected to fall within a range of the true score ±2 standard errors; the remaining 4 percent can be expected to fall outside that range. When applied to the most accurate intelligence tests currently in use (S.E. equals 5 IQ points), these figures reveal that 68 percent of such IQ's are likely to be within ±5 points of the true IQ, and 32 percent will deviate more than 5 points from the true IQ; 96 percent are likely to fall within a range of ±10 points of the true IQ, and roughly 4 percent are likely to be more than 10 points in error. Recognizing these facts, teachers will not be surprised to find that a student's scores fluctuate from one administration of a test to another. Any single obtained score can be accepted only as a fairly rough estimate of the level at which the student may be expected to perform in repeated measurements by the given test.

Knowledge of the standard error of measurement is also essential whenever a teacher wishes to interpret the relationship of scores made on two administrations of the same test or of different tests. In practice this problem appears in situations like the following:

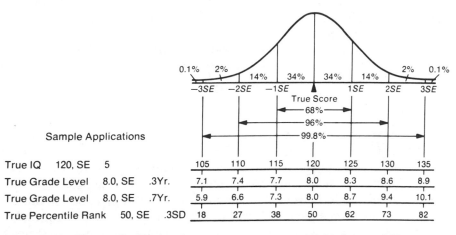

Fig. 19-11   The standard error of measurement: an estimate of the variability of test scores that would be obtained in repeated measurement of the same individual

Tommy has scored at a grade level of 8.3 on a test of arithmetic and at a grade level of 8.7 on a test of reading. Is his reading skill really better than his skill in arithmetic? What is the likelihood that a difference as large as 0.4 could represent a chance fluctuation of scores due to errors of measurement rather than a difference in true scores in arithmetic and reading?

Assuming that the two tests were standardized on the same sample so that the scaling is consistent, and further assuming that the standard error of the difference in the two test scores is 0.5, then, by applying the standards listed below, the teacher should conclude that the measured difference is too small to be accepted as proof of a difference in true scores. Tommy's score in reading would have to exceed his score in arithmetic by 2 times 0.5 (a full year) before it would be acceptable to conclude that he is really more skilled in one subject than in the other (and even then the conclusion would be incorrect about one time in twenty).

The following standards are usually followed when differences in test scores are being interpreted:

1. The difference between two measurements is assumed to be highly reliable when the difference exceeds three times the standard error involved. The chances then are more than 100 to 1 in favor of the existence of a difference in true scores.

2. The difference between two measurements is assumed to be fairly reliable when the difference exceeds twice the standard error involved. The chances then are about 19 to 1 in favor of the existence of a difference in true scores.

3. The difference between two measurements is assumed to be of questionable reliability when it is more than the standard error but less than twice that amount. The chances then are at least 2 to 1 in favor of the existence of a difference in true scores.

4. The difference between two scores is assumed to be unreliable when it is less than the standard error involved. The chances then are less than 2 to 1 in favor of the existence of a difference in true scores.

TEST RELIABILITY

The accuracy with which a test measures is also expressed as a reliability coefficient in decimal form ranging from .00 to 1.00. A reliability coefficient of 1.00 indicates perfect consistency in individuals' scores in a test-retest situation. If such a test could be constructed, its standard error of measurement would be zero. A reliability coefficient of zero, on the other hand, indicates a complete lack of consistency in measurement. An individual upon retest might score at any point within the range of scores produced by the test. Such a test would be useless.

In practice, it is generally considered that a test must have a reliability of at least .80 before it can be accepted as a satisfactory measure of individual performance—and higher reliability is much to be desired.

Coefficients of reliability must be employed with a degree of caution, however, for they can be determined by a variety of procedures, each designed to serve a particular purpose and each yielding a slightly different coefficient. The size of reliability coefficients also varies somewhat according to the ability level and variability of the groups upon which they are based. Classroom teachers should therefore recognize that the relative accuracy of measurement of two tests can be judged accurately on the basis of reliability coefficients only when the coefficients have been computed by application of the same formula to data obtained from measurement of comparable groups. Only then can one be reasonably certain that the test having the higher reliability coefficient will measure with the greater accuracy.

INTERPRETATION OF AGE AND GRADE NORMS

Age and grade norms are among the easiest norms to understand. The concept involved is simple, but when applied at the secondary school level, age and grade norms have severe limitations.

1. Many student characteristics, such as scores on mental tests, computational ability, and physical height, show variable and decreasing annual change as students progress through high school. Some characteristics show no measurable increase with age beyond the early teens, and a few reveal a decrease in average test performance. For example, in many schools United States history is offered in the eighth grade and again in the eleventh grade. American history norms, then, would be expected to increase at those grade levels and remain fairly stable or decrease for students not taking the subject.

2. Age and grade norms frequently are inadequate to indicate properly the standing of high- or low-scoring pupils. For instance, tests intended for high school use will be standardized on grades nine through twelve. In an average school, half of the twelfth graders would be expected to score higher than the twelfth-grade norm. If the twelfth-grade norm is 73 points on a particular test, what is the standing of a student who scores 80 points? Test publishers attempt to answer this question, if they answer it at all, by extrapolating their standardization data so as to estimate what groups beyond their sample would score if the assumptions accepted by the publishers were true. Thus the test publisher might assume that the annual increment beyond grade twelve would be 3.5 points and assign the score of 80 a grade norm of 14, even though no one beyond grade twelve had been tested in the standardization sample. To be specific, the Iowa Tests of Basic Skills, intended for grades three through nine, provide approximate grade equivalent scores for the range

1.0 to 12.5 by extrapolation beyond the measured sample's range of 3.1 to 8.1.

It should be noted that extrapolation upward from one school level to another is particularly subject to misinterpretation. For instance, a student, teacher, or parent might conclude that an eighth-grade student who scored at the eleventh-grade norm in reading on a junior high school test would be able to read eleventh-grade material as well as the average eleventh grader. Such a conclusion would be justified only when the standardization sample included eleventh graders and when the test was composed of content appropriate to that grade level. The eleventh-grade norm on a test designed for the seventh, eighth, and ninth graders usually is an extrapolated score and, at best, is only the average score of eleventh graders on seventh-, eighth-, and ninth-grade material. An eleventh-grade norm earned on a test intended for junior high schools does not indicate that the junior high school student could perform at average eleventh-grade level on a test designed for use in senior high school. The score merely indicates that the junior high school student has done a particularly good job in the junior high school content covered by the test.

Age norms, in particular, are quite likely to be inaccurate for ages at both extremes of an established range since age norms are frequently determined by administering tests to grade levels and then making separate distributions of scores for each age represented. For example, when a test is standardized on the seventh, eighth, and ninth grades, the modal (most common) age at each grade is 12, 13, and 14 respectively. However, some of the most brilliant 14-year-olds will have been accelerated into grades beyond the sample, and the slower 12-year-olds will not yet have reached seventh grade. Thus, the 14-year age norm would be too low and the 12-year age norm would be too high to be truly representative of all students of those ages.

3. Grade norms and age norms are an inadequate basis for comparison of the relative standing of students in schools following admission and promotion policies different from those predominant in the standardization sample. Students who are overage or underage for their grade frequently make average scores different from those made by the age group that is at age for a given grade. In recognition of this problem at least one test publisher reports separate grade norms for students who are at the age most typical for a given grade. These norms are called modal-age grade norms. When they are not available it is important to know the age composition of the grades in the standardizing sample.

4. Probably the most serious weakness in age and grade norms is their susceptibility to misinterpretation as standards to be achieved by all students of a given age or grade. Half of an average class should be expected to exceed the established norm. Likewise, in an average class, half of the

pupils can be expected to score lower than the norm for their age or grade. Ordinarily, age norms and grade norms are midpoints of distributions of typical groups. They can be used as standards only for average students seeking average goals in an average environment.

INTERPRETATION OF PERCENTILE SCORES

Percentile scores generally are considered to be an improvement over age and grade norms since they are free from errors of extrapolation and are not so likely to be misused as single standards. They provide 100 reference points for an age or grade group rather than a single point. However, percentile scores must also be interpreted with caution because they are subject to the same errors of norm group sampling that affect the validity of age and grade norms; in addition they have certain weaknesses because they are directly related to numbers of persons below given points in a distribution and are not directly related to raw scores.

1. Percentile scores tend to exaggerate differences in raw scores near the middle of the range and to reduce relative differences of raw scores near the extremes. This aberration is brought about by the fact that on most measures norm groups tend to cluster near the middle of the range of scores and scatter out near the extremes. This fact brings about a serious nonlinear relationship between raw scores and percentile rank equivalents. Consequently, comparisons of the percentile ranks of students are likely to be quite different from comparisons of their equivalent raw scores. For example, a 3-point difference in raw score in the middle of the range on the language segment of the SRA Tests of Educational Ability yields a percentile rank difference of 20 points, whereas a 3-point difference in raw score near the top of the same scale yields a percentile rank difference of only 3 or 4 points. On practically all tests, individuals who differ as much as 15 or 20 percentile points in the middle range (from about a percentile rank of 35 to a percentile rank of 65) are more alike in raw score than individuals who are only 5 or 10 percentile points apart in either the lower or upper parts of the percentile range.

2. The standard error of percentiles near the middle of the range is much larger than the standard error at the extremes. For example, the manual for the California Achievement Tests gives a standard error of nine months for the eleventh-grade spelling norms. Translated to the percentile scale, this standard error becomes about 15 percentile points for true scores near the 50th percentile, and reduces to a standard error of about 5 percentile points for true scores around the 5th and 95th percentiles. Thus obtained percentile scores on that test (and on many other tests) will be 15 or more points in error for about one third of the large group of students who in true measurement would score about average for their grade. For the smaller number of students who in true

measurement would rate either very low or very high, the California test yields percentile scores in spelling that are 15 or more points in error only about one or two times in 100. Accordingly, teachers must recognize that on all standardized tests, percentile scores near 50 frequently are in error as much as 10 or 15 points, whereas errors of that magnitude are much less frequent in high and low percentile scores.

3. Percentiles cannot be averaged directly. A student who has percentile ranks of 60 on half of the tests in a battery and percentile ranks of 80 on each of the remaining tests is not likely to have a percentile rank of 70 on the total battery. When averages or totals of several percentile scores are desired, the percentiles should first be transformed to raw scores or to other scores having an arithmetic base.

4. Percentile scores are meaningless without direct reference to the group upon which they are based. A single raw score total on a test might be described truthfully as the 50th percentile for high school seniors as well as the 90th percentile for students in a lower grade. Consequently, the base group should be named whenever percentile norms are discussed.

THE ETHICS OF STANDARDIZED
ACHIEVEMENT TESTING

Many teachers engaged in standardized achievement testing are perplexed by such questions of ethics as, What can a teacher properly do to prepare students for a standardized achievement test? Is it permissible to excuse inferior students from the tests? What legitimate use can be made of test scores and item analyses? Definitive responses to many such questions await the study of authorities. However, valuable, but tentative, answers to some of the important questions have been suggested in an article abstracted below: [13]

1. When teachers prepare students for a standardized achievement test:

It is acceptable and proper to explain to students something about the purposes and general form of the test. Such a discussion would not include any references to the specific content of the test. It might properly cover such matters as the various types of objective questions; the fact that some items will be easy and some will be very difficult; the fact that students should not worry if they cannot answer every question; the importance of working rapidly without racing; and the advisability of making intelligent guesses.

It is acceptable and proper to familiarize students with the mechanics of a standardized achievement test through the use of practice exercises. These exer-

[13] Anton Thompson, "Tentative Guidelines for Proper and Improper Practices with Standardized Achievement Tests," *California Journal of Educational Research*, 9, no. 4 (September 1958), 159–166.

cises should teach students how to mark their answers to the various types of questions but should not offer any clues as to the content of the approaching test.

It is acceptable and proper in giving a machine-scored test to pass around a sample, well-marked answer sheet before the test is begun, and to point out the possibility that the students will lower their test scores if they do not mark their answer sheets in the same way.

It is acceptable and proper to try to bring about optimum motivation of the students for the taking of a standardized test. This means encouraging students to do as well as they can. It does not mean that pupils are to be threatened or made extremely tense and anxious.

It is *not* acceptable and proper for a teacher to coach students on the subject matter of a specific standardized test. Such coaching will invalidate the scores earned by the students. Not only will such scores have no value; they may actually do the student harm if they are recorded and used for guidance or instructional purposes. Testing authorities are in complete agreement that teachers and students should take standardized tests without such preparation.

It is *not* acceptable and proper to use the report of a previous item analysis to prepare other students for that test.

It is *not* acceptable and proper to use a particular standardized test as a model for the construction of an elaborate set of drill exercises that parallel the content and format of that test.

It is *not* acceptable and proper to give one form of a standardized test a few days or weeks before a second form of the test is to be given as a district-wide or school-wide survey.

It is *not* acceptable and proper to make individual students overanxious and tense concerning the outcome of a standardized achievement test, nor to set impossible goals for a class.

It is *not* acceptable and proper to exclude a regular student from taking a district-wide survey on the grounds that his teacher thinks the student is a poor learner or because the student is said to become confused when he takes a test. Presumably the norm group also included some persons who were dull and some who hated to take tests.

It is *not* acceptable and proper to neglect in any way the instruction of any students in order to concentrate more effort on instruction to raise the scores of other students.

2. During the administration of a standardized test:

It is *not* acceptable to alter the directions or time limits. The standard conditions prescribed for the test must be followed exactly.

It is *not* acceptable and proper, after a test is under way, to give students any help beyond that allowed by the test manual. For most tests, this means that the tester cannot help a student who raises his hand to ask the meaning of a particular test question. Although the testers are usually given some leeway in answering questions not dealing with the content of the test, it is a safe rule to err on the side of explaining too little rather than too much.

It is *not* acceptable and proper for the administrator of a standardized test to give special assistance to the poor readers in a class by reading test items aloud. This holds true even though the test is an arithmetic test and a teacher is confident that certain students who could not otherwise do so could correctly solve a test exercise if it were just read aloud to them. If a test was normed without reading items aloud to the students in the standardization sample, then the test must be given the same way if students' scores are to be interpreted through use of the publisher's norms.

3. Shortly after a standardized test has been given:

It is acceptable and proper to make use of the results of an item analysis as a basis for remedial work with the students.

It is acceptable and proper for a teacher to return a student's scored test booklet or answer sheet to the student for use in class discussion or in individual conference. The booklets or answer sheets should not be taken from the classroom, since they may then fall into the hands of others who will be taking the same test. The usual purposes of returning a scored booklet or answer sheet are to inform the students concerning their individual results on the test and to call attention of the class to any group weaknesses in learning revealed by the teacher's study of the frequency of errors on each test item—weaknesses that may suggest a need for subsequent reteaching and relearning.

4. With respect to the long-term effects of a standardized test:

It is *not* acceptable and proper for a teacher to make a collection of various standardized tests for the purpose of using items from them in his own tests.

It is *not* acceptable and proper for a teacher to develop instructional materials that include specific items from a standardized test even though the materials also include other content not taken directly from a test. Once test items have been lifted out of a test and used as instructional material, the value of that test as a standardized measuring instrument has been destroyed, and the teacher responsible is subject to prosecution for violation of copyright laws.

It is *not* acceptable and proper to use a standardized achievement test as an abbreviated course of study. A standardized test is merely a sampling of many learnings that should be in a complete course of study. It is not intended that the test content influence the teaching emphasis of any teacher. For example, if a course of study in a certain district recommends that one third of an English course be given to the study of American literature, a teacher of the course should not alter his attention to that literature merely because he knows that the standardized test used does not devote one third of its items to the coverage of American literature.

It is acceptable and proper for a teacher whose course of study recommends the development of a given learning to continue to teach the recommended material even though he knows that the standardized test used contains a specific question relating to that particular learning. Knowledge of the general content of an approaching test does not require the teacher to go out of his way to avoid any reference to the learnings in the test. The real criterion of propriety is whether the teacher omits learnings because they are not in a given test, whether he includes materials not in the course of study because they cover items that are in a given test, and also whether he consciously gives undue attention to particular learnings in the course of study because he knows they are in a given test.

Teachers should note that these suggestions refer to the administration and use of achievement tests only. Tests of intelligence, special aptitude, and personality are administered according to somewhat different sets of regulations. Fortunately, these tests are usually administered under the direct supervision of a psychometrist or counselor. To prepare teachers for that service is not included among the purposes of this textbook.

A brief history of the development of intelligence and achievement tests and an introduction to selected concepts of measurement have been sketched in this chapter. The principal concern has been that of preparing beginning teachers to understand the test scores and profiles they will use in the classroom.[14] To that end examples of correct profile interpretation have been included, together with discussion of the pitfalls to avoid in the interpretation of norms. Also, it has been pointed out that among the hundreds of standardized tests published for school use, there are likely to be several specifically designed for the subjects taught by each teacher. To use these instruments intelligently and ethically in the improvement of instruction is both the responsibility and the privilege of the teacher of today.

SELECTED READINGS

1. Adams, Georgia Sachs, *Measurement and Evaluation*. New York: Holt, Rinehart and Winston, 1964, chaps. 2, 3, 5, 13.

2. Ahmann, J. Stanley, and Marvin D. Glock, *Evaluating Pupil Growth*, 3d ed. Boston: Allyn and Bacon, Inc., 1967, chaps. 8 and 11.

3. American Educational Research Association, *Encyclopedia of Educational Research*, 3d ed., Charles W. Harris, ed. New York: The Macmillan Company, 1960, pp. 807–816, 1510–1514.

4. Buros, Oscar K., ed., *The Sixth Mental Measurements Yearbook*. Highland Park, N.J.: The Gryphon Press, 1965.

5. Buros, Oscar K., ed., *Tests in Print*. Highland Park, N.J.: The Gryphon Press, 1961. Use latest available edition.

6. Clark, Leonard H., and Irving S. Starr, *Secondary School Teaching Methods*, 2d ed. New York: The Macmillan Company, 1967, pp. 373–378.

7. Downie, N. M., *Fundamentals of Measurement: Techniques and Practices*, 2d ed. New York: Oxford University Press, 1967, chaps. 2–5.

8. Durost, Walter N., and George A. Prescott, *Essentials of Measurement for Teachers*. New York: Harcourt, Brace & World, Inc., 1962, chaps. 1–3, 5, 6, 11.

---

[14] Another facet of test score interpretation—communication of scores to parents—is discussed in Chapter 18.

9. Ebel, Robert L., *Measuring Educational Achievement.* Englewood Cliffs, N.J.: Prentice-Hall, Inc., 1965, chap. 8.

10. Gronlund, Norman E., *Measurement and Evaluation in Teaching.* New York: The Macmillan Company, 1965, chaps. 12–14.

11. Payne, David A., and Robert F. McMorris, *Educational and Psychological Measurement.* Waltham, Mass.: Blaisdell Publishing Company, 1967, pp. 172–186, 199–204, 224–236.

12. Remmers, H. H., N. L. Gage, and J. Francis Rummel, *A Practical Introduction to Measurement and Evaluation.* New York: Harper & Row, Publishers, 1960, chaps. 2–6.

13. Stanley, Julian C., *Measurement in Today's Schools,* 4th ed. Englewood Cliffs, N.J.: Prentice-Hall, Inc., 1964, chaps. 4 and 5.

14. Thorndike, Robert L., and Elizabeth Hagen, *Measurement and Evaluation in Psychology and Education,* 2d ed. New York: John Wiley & Sons, Inc., 1961, chaps. 6–8, 11.

15. U.S. Department of Health, Education, and Welfare, Office of Education, *Interpretation of Test Results,* OE–25038, Bulletin 1964, no. 7. Washington, D.C.: Government Printing Office, 1964, pp. 1–53.

PART SEVEN / *Becoming a Professional Person*

CHAPTER 20 / *Advancement in the Profession*

THE TEACHER AS A MEMBER OF A PROFESSION

This is the true joy of life, the being used for a purpose recognized by yourself as a mighty one . . . *George Bernard Shaw*

Education has had a tremendous increase in stature since World War II or, for that matter, even since 1960. Many soldiers who returned home after the war were imbued with high ideals and social objectives; a large number of these men and women entered the teaching profession. Explosions in science and geopolitics hurtled education into the mainstream of public consciousness. Spectacular developments of nuclear bombs, intercontinental missiles and rockets, various satellites, and orbiting capsules alarmed the public. After decades of thinly veiled smoldering of governmental concern about education, the 1958 Congress became suddenly alerted to the lag in education and hurriedly passed the National Defense Education Act. Since that date and precedent, the federal government has given ever-increasing recognition to school matters of policy, finance, personnel, and other assistance. From top to bottom the public attitude toward education has changed. The American people are willing as never before to support their schools and to demand new programs.

Before 1940 school enrollments remained relatively constant; increases were gradual and predictable but since 1940 enrollments have risen sharply. It is estimated that they will continue to rise for the next decade at least. The 1960s have been years of high enrollments everywhere.

The birth rate has remained high—more than 80 million children have been born since World War II. This population explosion and the social phenomena accompanying it have made it impossible for schools to carry on as usual. Migrations of citizens from country to city and from central urban areas to suburban developments have enlarged the problems. A growing concern for the rights of all citizens—political, social and cultural rights—has brought new challenges. In some ways schools have been quick to react to the demand for new values; in others they have been slothful and have moved only when prodded. But nearly all agree there is now an urgency in matters of education.

About 200,000 new teachers are needed each year to serve new school enrollments and to replace teachers leaving the profession. Other factors behind this increased need for teachers are added curricular offerings, reduction in class size, and federal programs and assistance.

Currently the teaching profession includes:

2,038,821	total instructional staff—teachers, supervisors, counselors, and others
220,000	private elementary and secondary school personnel
130,000	administrative officers
350,000	professional personnel in higher education institutions
25,500	professional staff members in professional organizations, in governmental offices of education, and in private agencies
2,764,321	total for the profession [1]

Teacher shortages exist in many high school teaching fields, a condition not likely to change suddenly in the near future. Shortages are even more acute in the elementary field. Taken together, the big cities are almost without exception below their optimum needs. In 1966, Philadelphia, for example, according to newspaper reports, was 1100 short on a staff of 11,000. The state of Illinois lacked 15,000 to be able to put a fully certified teacher in every classroom; Texas, 10,000. A report by the National Education Association stated that on the basis of past experience only 81.2 percent of those qualifying for elementary school certificates and 66 percent of those ready for high school certification actually sought teaching positions when they left the colleges and universities. Currently the teacher need stands at 364,500—more than was ever needed before in any one year.[2]

In order to keep the schools open, drastic measures have been adopted in many cities and states. The two most common are to crowd more students into classrooms where there are teachers, and to issue temporary certification to persons without full qualifications. Other measures include desperate recruitment campaigns in other states (a temporary expedient that injures one community at the expense of another), the use of paraprofessionals in a variety of school tasks, and the acceptance of college graduates without certification on condition that they work simultaneously for credentials.

[1] *Estimates of School Statistics, 1967–68*, Research Report 1967–R19. Washington, D.C.: National Education Association, 1967.

[2] *Estimates of School Statistics, 1967–68;* also Research Division, *NEA, Research Bulletin,* 44 (December 1966), 117.

Many reasons lie behind the teacher shortages: prestige, salary, working conditions, opportunities in other fields, and, in the opinion of many people, unreal and artificial certification requirements. Some blame for the shortages has been placed on the federal government for siphoning off good teacher potential for the Peace Corps, the Job Corps, and civilian employment in foreign countries. Some critics feel that outside the big cities there has been a reluctance to accept minority racial personnel as teachers. Among the minor causative factors that have been mentioned are loyalty oaths, abridged academic freedom, and infringement on personal freedom.

OPPORTUNITIES IN THE PROFESSION

Most young people who think of teaching will naturally think of classroom service. The person who has prepared himself for teaching, secondary school teaching in this instance, truly has many types of educational work other than instruction open to him. Of course, about 90 percent of positions are in the classrooms of public and private schools. When a person has completed the basic preparation for the profession, numerous types of service are available. Some of these opportunities require specialized or advanced preparation and nearly all are predicated on successful classroom experience.

Some positions entail travel or living in a foreign country. Others are generally available in this country, but are limited to the larger cities where extensive educational programs are supported. Small schools do not have the diversified programs that call for specialized services.

Educational opportunities for high school teachers include:

A. Instructional service
  1. Classroom teacher
  2. Critic teacher in a laboratory or experimental school
  3. Departmental head (part-time teaching only)
  4. Athletic coach
B. Administrative service
  1. Principal
  2. Assistant principal
  3. Research director
C. Counseling service
  1. Guidance director
  2. Dean of girls or boys
  3. Vocational counselor or placement officer
  4. Visiting teacher
D. Supervisory service
  1. Departmental head
  2. Subject supervisor

       3. General supervisor
       4. Curriculum consultant
  E. Special services
       1. Director of audio-visual materials
       2. Coordinator of language laboratories
       3. TV coordinator
       4. Director of programmed learning materials
       5. Librarian
       6. Director of research and development
  F. Service outside the United States
       1. Teacher—military bases, embassies, insular territories
       2. Teacher—mission schools
       3. Teacher at corporation installations
  G. Miscellaneous
       1. Teacher—Indian schools
       2. Camp director
       3. Director of youth organizations
       4. Teacher—private or church schools
       5. Textbook and test writers
       6. Regular substitutes
       7. Paraprofessionals; aides

This outline indicates that the teacher has a host of colleagues, all of whom are members of the team and are working toward the same goal—effective and efficient instruction geared to society's needs. On the team, the teacher works with people who teach the same subject he does; people whose teaching is complementary, special teachers, and the teachers of other disciplines; counselors, supervisors, administrators, coordinators of special services, and a new group of research and development people who are also colleagues. Of course, not all the positions are found in all schools. Research and development, for example, is quite uncommon since education now spends only about one tenth of 1 percent of its funds in this manner. But in 1963 the NEA Project on Instruction recommended that "school systems should allocate an appropriate proportion of their annual operating budget—not less than 1 percent—for the support of research, experimentation, and innovation." The move to allocate funds for R&D was begun by the Ford Foundation, and has since been augmented by "pushes" from the National Science Foundation, the NEA, the ESEA, and industry.

Lately the use of paraprofessionals and teacher-aides is receiving a renewed emphasis, possibly because of the growth of technology, greater employment of special services, and a desire to release teachers from a burden of routine tasks that do not require credentialed personnel.

During the last decade many teachers have turned to such specialized assistance as textbook writing, editing, and designing. Programmed learning devices require educators with great skill and understanding to write programs. Item writing and analysis for the preparation of standardized tests is another area of recent specialization.

Has the modern school eliminated any traditional positions? It is hard to think of any that have disappeared. No longer do we have study hall keepers, as such, but if we did, this supervisory task would probably be given to an aide. The great urban movement of the population, the greater understanding of variability among students, and the proliferation of career opportunities obligate society to provide more school services.

CERTIFICATION Most of the positions listed in the immediately preceding outline require a certificate or credential. Teaching certificates are granted by the departments of education in the fifty states, upon recommendation of colleges and universities where the teachers received their education. The requirements or standards for certificates are set by the states, but the teacher education departments or schools administer them. Although all candidates presumably meet the same standards, with something like 1500 institutions handling certification, a variety of philosophies, including liberalities in substitutions and waivers, undoubtedly prevails. That this is good or bad is open to argument.

Certificate specialization is unsettled at the moment. In some states, where subject fields are designated on the certificate, the teacher may teach only those designated subjects. In other states a broader certification obtains, and a teacher may, for example, teach any subject in the junior or senior high school curriculum.

With the prevailing teacher shortage many opponents of certification and uniform standards are taking the occasion to advocate that requirements be lowered, modified, or abolished. In particular there is much criticism of the fact that the states require a certain number of teacher education courses. Some of these critics seem to feel that *any* college graduate is equipped to teach. The origin of certification standards can be traced back a hundred years, when anyone who applied for a teaching position was eligible to be hired. Obviously, some method of screening out the incompetent was needed. Teaching is not the only profession to require certification; indeed, it is a hallmark of any profession.

Unfortunately, once certain requirements are set, they change slowly. Great changes in the cultural pattern of the nation and in philosophical points of view may easily be overlooked as may be other possible roads to certification.

It is rather common for most states to issue life certification. This policy should be scrutinized. There are literally tens of thousands of teachers in service who were credentialed long ago but who have made little or no professional growth since. Too large a proportion of these people are teaching on their experience. Even the acquisition of an advanced degree somewhere along the line may not necessarily keep them up-to-date on the educational, psychological, and sociological understandings needed. Moreover, a great many women teachers drop out of the profession after a few years of teaching in order to rear a family and then return a dozen or so years later with no updating of competencies.

Certification gives security to teachers, and security is a necessary ingredient of effective work. The other side, too, needs to be scanned. Many teachers allow their professional efficiency to deteriorate. A study at Indiana University [3] of several hundred history teachers revealed what is fairly common knowledge: a great majority read practically nothing in their subject field nor any material of substance in related fields. A further look at in-service professional growth will be taken later in the chapter.

SUBJECT COMBINATIONS IN HIGH SCHOOL TEACHING   A matter of concern to high school teachers is that of subject combinations. With broad or even narrow certification regulations, teachers frequently find that they are required to teach in two or more subject fields. This is particularly true in the case of beginning teachers who frequently start in the small school districts. Although teaching combinations tend to be reasonably logical, at times one finds combinations that are utterly devoid of content relationship. The larger high schools tend to place their teachers in one teaching field only.

Most teachers will do a large part of their teaching in their major or minor fields. Combinations of English, speech, and social studies are quite common. The combination of mathematics and science is also common. Foreign language teachers may find themselves teaching two different languages, or they may have some teaching in another subject area. Teachers of such special subjects as music, art, and home economics are less likely to teach outside their major concentration than are the teachers of the more academic subjects.

In this connection, it should be noted that many college and university schools and departments of education require student teachers to complete a certain amount of their preparation in at least two teaching areas.

LOCAL PROFESSIONAL ORGANIZATIONS   Professional organizations exist at the local, state, national, and international levels. Most teachers find their greatest interest and involvement in the first three of these levels.

Local professional organizations are so numerous that no attempt has been made to count them. For example, California alone has more than 500 such local groups. They may or may not be affiliated with state or national organizations, but they are important. Usually, any district with

[3] Maurice G. Baxter, Robert H. Ferrel, and John E. Wiltz, *The Teaching of American History in High Schools.* Bloomington: Indiana University Press, 1964.

twenty-five or more teachers will have one or more local professional organizations. These are the grass roots groups who speak for teachers in matters of policy formation. Members of these local groups carry their ideas to the state organizations, where larger decisions are made. Local organizations hold a great potential for the profession, and all teachers should belong to them and make themselves heard.

It is no exaggeration to say that the increased effectiveness of present-day teachers' organizations is due to the emergence of local professional activity. These groups have been chiefly concerned with teacher welfare, personnel policies, rights, responsibilities, ethics, and public relations.

Local organizations are the training grounds for state and national professional leadership. The democratic concept finds its best expression at this level.

STATE PROFESSIONAL ORGANIZATIONS   Teachers have professional organizations in each of the fifty states, the District of Columbia, and Puerto Rico. These organizations enroll a majority of the teachers of the several states and maintain permanent headquarters with full-time staffs.

State organizations are essentially legislative and policy-making bodies. Their functions are carried out through a host of commissions and committees of members (usually unpaid service). In general their purposes are to advance the interests of the teaching profession and to promote and improve public education in the state. In California the association cites these specific purposes for teachers:

To decide, through democratic processes, what they think about the issues and problems that affect their teaching and their jobs.
To speak for themselves, effectively representing the concerns of the profession to all those interested in public education in California.
To improve their own profession by working together to raise standards of teaching service, personnel relations, teacher education, community relations, and economic security.[4]

Legal responsibility for formulating and administering major educational policies for education rests with the state departments of education. These departments are created by constitutional or statutory law, but they work closely with the voluntary self-perpetuating teacher organizations. Legislation concerning teachers originates from many sources, one of the most fertile of which is the professional group itself. School law, of course, is the prerogative of the legislature.

NATIONAL PROFESSIONAL ORGANIZATIONS   Three national organizations should be mentioned at this point—the National Education Association (NEA), the American Federation of Teachers (AFT), and the National

[4] *The California Teachers Association: What It Is—How It Works.* Burlingame. The Association [n.d.], p. 3.

Catholic Education Association (NCEA). The latest available membership figures were 1,028,000; 144,500; and less than 100,000, respectively.[5] The first two organizations will be discussed in detail because they vie for the right to represent the nation's public school teachers.

ASSOCIATION OR FEDERATION?   The question of what type of organization shall represent teachers has become a live issue. Essentially, two points of view are represented—unionism and professionalism. To some teachers the two viewpoints are incompatible; other teachers see no overriding incompatibility.

Over the past decade, the issue of unionism versus professionalism has been brewing. Sporadic teacher strikes over the country seemed to have little or no effect on the issue one way or another. Then, on November 7, 1960, the United Federation of Teachers of New York City called a strike over the issue of collective bargaining and what agency should represent the teachers at the bargaining table. The strike lasted one day, but with no clear settlement of issues.

A second strike (labeled by some as a revolt, not a strike) occurred in New York City on April 11, 1962. It was reported that 20,588 teachers, or 51 percent of the 40,000 in the system, stayed away from their classrooms. Reverberations of this strike were heard throughout the country. On the whole, the professional organizations deplored the strike as illegal, unprofessional, and belittling. There were, however, proponents who claimed that teachers are workers, albeit professional workers, and that their occupational needs and the needs of the society they serve demand forceful action. These individuals feel that youth is being sacrificed if schools are permitted to pay poor salaries, employ poorly trained teachers, and maintain policies inimical to the best interests of society. The New York City strike has been evaluated and reevaluated, but the basic issue of unionism remains.

The AFT has achieved its greatest support in the urban areas, particularly in such cities as New York, Chicago, Washington, and Boston. At the moment the NEA is strongest in the Middle and Far West. The AFT has been more militant in its activities. It has not hesitated to call strikes, and even to defy court injunctions. In the face of this militancy and the vigorous drive for memberships, the NEA has become more aggressive as both groups strive to be the sole bargaining agency for teachers. The NEA has accepted the strike tactic recently and reluctantly but it has more often resorted to a scheme called "sanctions" to assist teachers in their struggle with school boards and state legislatures. Sanctions have not been defined, but in effect they are characterized by teachers not returning their contracts, by wholesale resignations involving entire dis-

[5] *NEA Handbook*. Washington, D.C.: National Education Association, August 1967, p. 8; *American Teacher*, January 1968, p. 3.

tricts, by advising all members of the NEA not to take positions in the city or state affected, by accepting only semiannual instead of annual appointments, and by calling the time spent away from the classrooms professional conference time. These tactics suggest the tactics used in strikes. The difference between sanctions and strikes may be a semantic one. In 1963 the National Commission on Professional Rights and Responsibilities described the broad characteristics of sanctions in this way:

. . . [they] mean censure, suspension or expulsion of a member; severance of relationship with an affiliated organization, or other agency; imposing of a deterrent against a board of education or other agency controlling the welfare of the schools; bringing into play forces that will enable the community to help the board or agency to realize its responsibility; or the application of one or more steps in the withholding of services.[6]

Statewide sanctions have been called in Utah, Oklahoma, and Florida. In these instances state legislatures, according to the NEA and the state affiliates, had been remiss in voting acceptable school funds. The NEA, spearheaded by the Department of Classroom Teachers, which enrolls about 80 percent of all NEA members, worked closely with the state organizations in the several disputes.

During the summer and fall of 1967 teachers showed a renewed militancy. Focal points of action were the states of Florida and Michigan, and the cities of New York, St. Louis, Boston, and several smaller communities. In Detroit and New York the opening of schools was delayed for two weeks while negotiations took place among teachers, school boards, and municipal authorities. In several instances state law prohibits strikes by public employees, but authorities were reluctant to resort to legal action. Few, if any, teachers were fined or went to jail; however, some leaders were jailed and the union was fined. During the time the teachers were not on the job, school boards in some instances tried to keep the schools open by using supervisory personnel, retired teachers, parents, and high school students. In some cities, students protested that they were being hurt by the possible loss of credits, delay in the completion of standard curricula, and general academic weakness arising from poor instruction.

Teacher work stoppages were minimal up to 1960. In the decade 1955–1965 there were only 55, but in 1966 alone the number rose to 33, and in 1967 to approximately 100. The trend will undoubtedly continue for a time. An interesting thing about these work stoppages, sanctions, or strikes—whatever they are called—is the fact that they were not directed so much against local school administration as against state legislatures. The causes of this new militancy seem to lie in a long-standing feeling of neglect and in a lack of full sharing in an affluent economy. Sam Lambert,

[6] *Guidelines for Professional Sanctions.* Washington, D.C.: National Education Association, November 1963.

executive secretary of the NEA, says, "This new breed of teachers is younger, better educated, more active, more highly skilled, but also more demanding and more courageous than ever before." [7]

THE COLLECTIVE NEGOTIATIONS MOVEMENT   Coincidental with the power struggle between the NEA and the AFT is the growth of the professional negotiations or collective bargaining movement in education. Employee-employer relations have become so involved that teachers feel the need for a collective negotiations structure similar to the union-management bargaining apparatus. Teachers are asking for the right to negotiate on equal terms with school boards through their own exclusive bargaining agent or representative on such matters as salary, work conditions, professional codes, and a voice in determining school policy. Such matters as size of classes, methods of teaching, assignments, leaves and vacations, extra-duty compensation, length of school day, school calendar, protection of probationary teachers, curriculum, transfers, duty-free lunch periods, rest periods, and grievances are involved. In the past, these matters were regarded as solely the responsibility of boards of education and administrative officials. Today's teachers feel that they should have a voice in these matters because they fall under the umbrella of "school improvement."

In New York City the AFT, through the United Federation of Teachers, won complete bargaining rights for teachers and successfully negotiated for increased salaries and other benefits. The union also won the right to participate in the determination of school policy. Union officials meet once a month with the superintendent of schools to discuss problems of mutual concern, and also to hold similar meetings with building principals.

By 1967 ten states had passed legislation sanctioning collective bargaining for teachers. But who will represent the teachers at the bargaining table, and what machinery should be set up with which to select these representatives? In the first instance the matter is a tug-of-war between the NEA and the AFT. The ancillary problem is how to select the agent.

In most states where legal provision for such selection has been made, exclusive negotiation rights have been granted to the organization representing the majority of professional employees ("Professional employee" needs careful definition). In other states—California is an example—if more than one organization purports to represent the teachers, a council of five to nine members (exact number to be established by the school board) is set up, with membership on the council to be proportionate to the organizational membership. Thus, if organization A has 100 members and organization B has 50 members, and the school board has provided for a council of nine, then six representatives would come from A and three from B. There is no compulsion for teachers to affiliate with any organization. This procedure for proportional representation has evoked considerable dialogue. One side feels that it is the ultimate in democratic representation; the other feels that it is unrealistic and unworkable, and that an exclusive organizational body should represent all the teachers. The AFT has been waging a campaign to have the California law changed.

All authorities agree that provisions for "professional negotiation" or "collective bargaining" should be such that the scope of negotiations not be narrowly restricted, that written agreements be "finalized," that negotiations take place in an atmosphere of "good faith," that representatives not be arbitrary, that impartiality prevail so that nonorganized teachers are protected, and that machinery be set up to avoid an impasse. Mediation, fact-finding, and public recommendations should replace strikes or sanctions. The NEA Research Bureau has reported these types of agreements found in 1540 school districts: no organization recognized, 105; Level I—recognition of an organization to represent teachers and/or staff, 124; Level II—recognition plus negotiations procedures, 615; Level III—above plus "impasse" resolution procedures, 298; and Level IV— "comprehensive or substantive" agreements, 398.[8]

The whole matter of teacher representation has moved so rapidly that only temporary guidelines have been drawn. Many knowledgeable people believe that the time is not distant when all teachers will belong to a local, state, and/or national organization of some kind; possibly they will not be able to find employment until they show membership. These same people also foresee a membership dues checkoff similar to that in vogue in unions. Not only will master agreements be negotiated at local levels; larger agreements may develop to cover counties or even states. Again, many people believe that teachers, as do doctors and lawyers, will eventually authorize the licensing of members of their own profession. Teachers would then determine who enters the profession and how, and would draw up a professional code of ethics with machinery for disciplinary action.

The power struggle between the NEA and the AFT seems destined to continue for some time. Some educators who claim to hold unbiased, objective views about the controversy would like to see the organizational house put in order and plead for a merger of the NEA and the AFT. Desirable as such a move is, one must realistically face the obstacles, chief among which appear to be the fact that the NEA has no restriction on administrators becoming members, and, second, that one organization is preponderantly larger than the other. Some writers think that unless a merger is accomplished, in time, a third organization will emerge and replace both. In an editorial discussing a possible merger, Stanley Elam,

[8] Research Division, NEA, *Research Bulletin,* 45 (December 1967), 102–103.

editor of the *Phi Delta Kappan,* wrote, "Before NEA–AFT merger can be accomplished, however, the rank and file teacher and the lower eschelon leader will probably need to begin insisting on it. And before this can happen teachers must have a more sophisticated understanding of the possibilities offered by collective action." [9]

Although more militant than formerly, the NEA prefers to maintain its "professional" character, avoiding wherever possible such words as "union," "closed shop," and "strike." The NEA is an old and solidly built organization with grass roots in every state. The AFT has behind it the massive power of the AFL–CIO.[10]

Whether the strike is a proper weapon for teachers will remain an unanswered question for years to come. Other questions that stem from the same issue deal with matters of school support, public acceptance, school policies, organizational democracy, and even the objectives of education themselves. There are no definitive answers. Stinnett and his associates write:

> The basic justification for professional negotiation is the added power generated by participation as equals. With a clear and meaningful share in the formulation of policy, teachers (or any workers) are impelled toward higher levels of productivity. They are stimulated by the urge to make their own policies work. They are impelled by the sense of being personally involved in a creative enterprise. The deadly monotony of performing routine tasks, made so by unilateral planning, is transformed into an exciting, jointly planned venture.[11]

Many perceptive educators feel that state legislation is a rather wishful manner in which to deal with the teacher unrest. They hold that more can be accomplished by working through local school boards who understand their position of policy development rather than administration or negotiation, by employing school superintendents who by temperament and training can assume full administrative responsibility of management, and by recognizing that teaching is the heart of representative government.

INTERNATIONAL EDUCATION ORGANIZATIONS   Cultural relations between nations and international groups have been expanding rapidly. Only in recent years have nongovernmental international professional organizations achieved much importance. Today, the World Confederation of Organizations of the Teaching Profession (WCOTP) and the International Association of Universities (IAU) are providing leadership in better

---

[9] *Phi Delta Kappan,* 47 (February 1966), 285.

[10] Headquarters: National Education Association, 1201 Sixteenth Street, N.W., Washington, D.C. 20036; American Federation of Teachers, 1343 H Street, N.W., Washington, D.C. 20005.

[11] T. M. Stinnett, Jack H. Kleinmann, and Martha L. Ware, *Professional Negotiation in Public Education.* New York: The Macmillan Company, 1966, p. 3.

understanding among educators around the world. These and other responsible organizations are in a position to do more for international cultural relations than can random or self-organized minority groups.

PROFESSIONAL ETHICS   Standards of conduct beyond those governed by law are usually spelled out in a code of ethics. Most professions have such codes. The medical profession, for example, relies on the Hippocratic oath and the principles of medical ethics. The American Bar Association has its canons of ethics, and the architects their standards of professional practice.

A code of ethics is self-imposed and becomes effective only if the members of the profession abide by it. All the state teachers associations embrace a code of ethics that covers such areas as teacher-pupil relationships, teacher-parent relationships, teacher-administrator relationships, teacher-board of education relationships, and teacher-professional relationships.

The NEA has subscribed to a code of ethics since 1929. The 1963 revision is stated in terms of four principles:

Principle one stresses the obligations of teachers to guide learners in the pursuit of knowledge and skills so that they may become "happy, useful, self-supporting citizens."

Principle two states that teachers have an overriding commitment to the community they serve.

Principle three deals with the teacher's personal conduct both in the classroom and in the community.

Principle four defines the ethics of employment and fosters regard for mutual respect and good faith between employer and employee.[12]

PROFESSIONAL GROWTH: IN-SERVICE TEACHER EDUCATION

Many avenues to professional growth are open to teachers. One of the hallmarks of a profession is found in the demand for continuous in-service growth: "The competent teacher is a growing teacher." As a teacher grows, he contributes in increasing degree to his community. This fact is one of the basic reasons why many school boards provide part or all of the costs of in-service education for their teachers. Few professions provide the opportunities for mental and personality growth that teaching does. Both teachers and communities should be aware of the fact that in-service education is to their mutual advantage. To this extent the teacher contributes time, effort, and resources; the school district contributes encouragement and resources.

Opportunities for in-service growth are varied. Those most frequently

[12] NEA Committee on Professional Ethics, *The Code of Ethics of the Education Profession*. Washington, D.C.: NEA, 1963.

available to teachers are study programs, group study of school problems, community study or activities, school visitation, travel, workshops, exchange teaching, writing, reading, research, and a miscellany of other activities. These growth opportunities will be described in the paragraphs that follow.

CONTINUED PROFESSIONAL AND CULTURAL DEVELOPMENT   No attempt is made here to separate professional and cultural types of activities. They are treated as two sides of a coin. As a coin is spun the two sides blend; as a teacher grows and matures, cultural and professional development blend.

College and university summer sessions draw their largest enrollments from teachers. At times, school districts provide part or all of the costs of summer study. In some districts salary increments are correlated with advanced college preparation. Some states are mandating additional college study for the renewal of certificates, especially for the renewal of substandard certificates. Most American teachers start their teaching careers with the bachelor's degree. No data are available to indicate how many teachers have master's or doctor's degrees but it is safe to say that the number is substantial. It can also be safely assumed that most of these advanced degrees were earned by the teachers after they had begun their careers.

In addition to courses taken for credit, there are noncredit study opportunities offered by colleges and by the school districts themselves. Extension courses are available in practically every community.

Group study of school problems provides another in-service growth opportunity of great value. Such study is usually connected with the development of new school programs or projects or the evaluation or redesign of old ones. Other opportunities arise through surveys, census polls, catalogue construction, and the production of courses of study or curriculums. Often these studies engage sizable committees who may have the assistance of consultants and valuable resource persons. Projects may involve teachers from a single building or may bring together teachers from several buildings, or perhaps teachers from different school districts.

Workshops continue to grow in popularity. Teachers join together to study a common problem. They meet after school, during special conferences, on weekends, or during regularly scheduled summer terms. At times the workshop group goes off to an isolated spot at the seashore or in the mountains for relaxed and uninterrupted pursuit of a problem. The workshop, too, may be integrated with a travel tour at home or abroad. Chandler defines this group study device in this manner:

A workshop is a systematic program of group study which is characterized by a focus on the specific concerns and problems of those involved, as distinguished from formal courses whose content is typically determined by the subject matter organization or by the instructor. Democratic planning under the leadership of a director is an additional characteristic of workshops. Often consultants or specialists in the field of study are obtained to help.[13]

Activities at workshops are as varied as the interests of teachers. They involve previewing films, constructing courses of study, making tests, cataloguing lists of resource materials, building crafts, or doing similar useful professional tasks.

Opportunities to work with any of the several aspects of community life are also valuable. Teachers need to know their communities in as much detail as possible: the philanthropic and charitable agencies, cultural resources, economic and vocational aspects, governmental agencies and services, and other ramifications of the community.

School visitation is almost invariably helpful to teachers. This may be home visitation or, equally important, it may be interschool or intraschool visitation. This is an area for teacher growth that has not been fostered by school officials to any considerable extent. Visitation does involve problems, such as teachers being away from their classrooms, the payment of substitute teachers, and other administrative details, but the values to teachers are unquestionably there.

WRITING, READING, RESEARCH, AND TRAVEL　In one sense, reading, writing, studying, and growing in cultural and professional stature are obligations of teachers, but they are also opportunities. Few vocations offer these opportunities, at least to the same extent. Teaching constantly forces its members to clarify their thinking, to reexamine their beliefs because they deal with ideas that are never static. Someone has said that a teacher constantly renews his youth. And, in a very real sense, the teacher is paid for all this.

Teaching is a broad occupation and teachers may range far beyond their specialization in their reading, writing, and the arts. They may range over every type of literature from biography, fiction, travel, adventure, science, poetry, to journalism. Their interest in music, drama, and the fine arts may be just as catholic. Such interests tend to "elevate and liberate the human spirit."

For the teacher who has the talent and the desire, the opportunities for writing are almost endless. Coupled with writing is research. These activities cannot help but add to the stature of the teacher, and they may be financially profitable. Sir Francis Bacon wrote, "Reading maketh a full man, conference a ready man, and writing an exact man."

Travel, too, is an enriching experience. Whether travel is limited to one's own country or extends to foreign lands, it is bound to enhance teaching

[13] B. J. Chandler, *Education and the Teacher.* New York: Dodd, Mead & Company, Inc., 1961, pp. 325–326.

effectiveness because, if the traveler understands what he sees, he has a firsthand knowledge of places, events, peoples, and cultures. Not only is travel fun; it can also "soften prejudices, religious or political, and liberal-ize a man's mind."

As a group, teachers travel widely—singly or as part of a tour. Tour groups are commonplace today, and are sponsored by colleges, universi-ties, state education associations, and the National Education Association. Some school districts recognize travel to the extent of allowing credit toward salary increments.

Many teachers have an opportunity to do an occasional stint of ex-change teaching, either here or in a foreign country. This is an unusually rewarding experience. Contacts may be made through a state teachers association, the National Education Association, the Office of Cultural Affairs of the State Department, or through any of a large number of private organizations.

The use of teachers as paid consultants is new. Some of them are very knowledgeable specialists whose services are useful to industry founda-tions, the military, and foreign governments.

GROWTH OPPORTUNITIES   Most teachers agree wholeheartedly about the advantages their profession offers. These opportunities are wonderful, but are they available to *all* teachers? Undoubtedly, many in-service growth activities are open to all who wish to participate, but other activ-ities are limited and fall to those individuals who have earned a certain amount of recognition. Leadership is a maturing, developing role. It be-gins in small ways and increases with sincere and systematic effort. Certainly a school system that attempts to promote in-service growth among its teachers will bend every effort to offer opportunities to all teachers. Advanced study, travel, participation in community life, and work with teacher groups and workshops are beneficial and open to all teachers regardless of grade or departmental level. Writing or doing re-search, for those suited to this type of work, either for pay or for fun, adds another cubit to the stature of the teacher.

There are so many avenues for professional advancement that no one need feel he is limited or handicapped. Not all teachers may travel, but most will. Not all teachers may attend a workshop, but most will find an activity that makes a fair substitute for it. Such activities are found in committee work, conferences, conventions, or service on survey teams.

People who are active and do things are usually interesting people. They break the bonds of provincialism. The great English scientist, Herbert Spencer, once wrote, "That man is best educated who has touched life in most places." And, in a somewhat similar vein, the noted American literary critic, John Mason Brown, has written:

What happiness is, no person can say for another. But no one, I am convinced, can be happy who lives only to himself. The joy of living comes from immersion in something that we know to be bigger, better, more enduring and worthier than we are. People, ideas, causes—these offer the one possible escape not merely from selfishness but from the hungers of solitude and the sorrows of aimlessness. No person is as uninteresting as a person without interests.

The pitiful people are those who in their living elect to be spectators rather than participants; the tragic ones are those sight-seers who turn their backs deliberately on the procession. The only true happiness comes from squandering ourselves for a purpose.[14]

THE TEACHER AND COMMUNITY PARTICIPATION

Every beginning teacher should take a look at his community. This he can do through the pupils in his classes, his colleagues, the parents of the pupils, the organizations and institutions of the community, the occupations and businesses that are the livelihood of the community, as well as through countless other ways. A community has so many sides that it is impossible to inventory it adequately. Some of its characteristics are tangible; some are not. But all the characteristics and factors that make up a community affect the citizens who live there. And Haskew and McLendon state and restate, "The total community educates" (6:45–58).

The teacher often finds his new teaching community different from the one in which he grew up. Such a situation should offer a challenge to any sincere teacher. It is a new and a different world for the teacher from the rural interior to face problems of some urban areas. The adjustment is just as great when the situations are reversed. One community may have problems of undernourished children, another of delinquent children; some may be more privileged, with completely different problems. The true teacher accepts these students and does what he can for their educational development. Of the children of another environment, one teacher said, "I remember only the doors they have opened for me, the prejudices I have shed."

Another reason for teacher participation in community affairs is to vitalize the curriculum. It is stressed elsewhere in this book that some of the most valuable resources in teaching are found *outside* the four walls of the classroom. Students in the junior high school may, in some instances, be reading at the third grade level. The vocabulary of most of their reading is over their heads, and the content is uninteresting. Teachers who can adapt and organize some of the culture of the community for curriculum use perform a valuable service. Again it should be pointed out that a school program which fails to take into account other educational forces of the community becomes ineffective and sterile. The ivory-tower concept of the school as an institution isolated from the rest of the community is no longer tenable. The teacher who is ignorant of and

[14] William I. Nichols, ed., *Words to Live By*. New York: Simon and Schuster, Inc., 1949, pp. 79–80.

indifferent to community currents and forces is robbing the taxpayer and shortchanging his students. Other educational agencies, which are competing, conflicting, or cooperating with the school, need to be understood. Teacher participation brings about understanding. Those agencies that work with the school deserve teacher support. Those agencies that misunderstand the purposes and program of the school may be enlightened by an interpreter who is known and respected as an *active* citizen of both the school and the larger community.

By exerting the leadership his profession calls for, the teacher can promote a better social and political climate. He has a heavy responsibility to help make democracy a real, functional way of life. This begins in the classroom, and the teacher whose own life personifies democratic ideals will inevitably affect the outlook of his community. The goodwill that any teacher develops in a community comes back to the school in better school support and understanding. Without community rapport teachers may feel that the very people whom they are trying to help seem to turn against them. School districts comprise many neighborhoods and in some instances these neighborhoods are quite unlike as well as divided on school matters. With more comprehensive integration teachers may touch hands with more than one neighborhood. This brings teachers into contact with majority and minority families alike. Students from one of the latter may have a speech pattern little better than a patois. To work with these students with any degree of success teachers need an abiding rapport with the community. Peace Corps workers know the importance of cooperation between worker and community. Cooperation, in fact, is the very keystone of the program; without it, failure is the only result. The meaning of teacher-community relationship can be enhanced by reference to Chapter 1, "The Roles of Teachers."

FACTORS INVOLVED IN SECURING A TEACHING POSITION

FACTORS TO CONSIDER

In seeking a first position or in contemplating a change in positions, a teacher should investigate such matters as the general philosophy of the school, including the degree of personal freedom allowed teachers both inside and outside the school. It is unwise to accept a position that will in all likelihood be incompatible with one's philosophical and cultural ideas. Other general matters that should be investigated are those pertaining to living conditions, welfare, geography, and the teacher's ultimate professional goal.

The following paragraphs will describe briefly some of the specific factors that should be considered in analyzing the job.

SALARY The immediate salary offered in any particular teaching position, although of great importance, must be equated with several other factors before a decision is made to accept or reject a position. Is a salary schedule in operation in the school system where employment is desired? If a salary schedule is used, where will the applicant be placed if employed? Are regular increments a part of the schedule? How large are these increments, and what is their number? What is the maximum salary one can obtain, and how many years will it take to reach the maximum? Does the salary schedule reward one for study, for travel, and for other procedures by which professional improvement is made? Is the starting salary large enough to enable a person to live in the community? Will the salary be paid throughout the school year on a yearly basis, or will it be paid only during the months when school is in session? (Many school districts pay salaries throughout the calendar year in an attempt to provide an additional measure of stability for the staff.) Is a single salary schedule, based upon *training* and *experience,* in effect in the school? (Single salary schedules have no sex differentials with respect to beginning salary, advancement in salary through increments, and maximum salary obtainable.)

The beginning salary, the maximum salary, and the length of service necessary to reach the maximum are important in a choice of position. However, they must be weighed against tenure and retirement benefits before a choice can be made. Finally, what is the attitude of the board of education and the community with respect to teachers' salaries? Has the school a record of consistent attempts to maintain salaries at the highest level possible for the district, or has it been niggardly in respect to salaries?

TENURE Nearly half of the states in this country have passed legislation, either permissive or mandatory, that protects certificated employees against unjust dismissal by boards of education. Teacher tenure laws provide for a probationary period of service in a school district of from two to three years. If a teacher successfully completes the probationary period and begins to teach the following year, he has reached "permanent" status in the district. Then he may be dismissed only for cause, after a hearing is held to determine the justness of the dismissal. Such tenure laws provide a measure of security for teachers that is unavailable in most other professions. A teacher with tenure will be able to plan ahead for the years to come, to finance a home, to make and keep friends in the community, and, as long as he maintains good teaching and moral standards, to work in his teaching job secure in the knowledge that an unjust dismissal is impossible.

When one chooses a position, the tenure possibilities must be seriously considered. Is tenure available in this particular community by mandatory state legislation? If the district does not qualify under mandatory legislation, has it adopted permissive measures to provide tenure for the teaching staff? If no tenure legislation is available in the state in which a job is sought, the amount of teacher turnover from year to year (in the district in question) is an important factor to be considered. Does a large proportion of the teachers remain in this district year after year or do most of them move to other districts at the end of each school year? The percentage of teacher turnover each year in a school district is a reflection of the adequacy of salaries, the attitude of the board of education and the administration, the working conditions in each school, and the community conditions under which teachers live and work.

THE COMMUNITY   What can the teacher expect of the community, and what does the community expect of the teacher? Is a teacher able to live a normal life outside school hours? Is the community large enough to provide the recreational opportunities one desires? Is housing available at a price a teacher can afford to pay? Are teachers accepted by the community and invited to participate in churches, clubs, and other aspects of community life? These are important questions that will determine to a great extent a teacher's happiness outside the classroom.

WORKING CONDITIONS   Labor unions have fought an extended battle for the past century to improve the conditions of safety and health under which their members work. A similar movement has been in existence with much less fanfare in the teaching profession. Boards of education, school administrators, and teachers, along with the help and encouragement of state agencies, have been constantly working to improve school plants, teaching materials, and general working conditions for teachers. The new teacher should consider the following factors that will help make it possible for him to do his best work.

Teaching load. Teaching load is to a certain extent standardized, but the beginning teacher might very well inquire about how many different classes or preparations he will have. Class size is another matter of interest to the beginning teacher; class size affects the load to be carried.

Equipment and facilities. Does the school under consideration possess good equipment and facilities? Information about equipment can be obtained by asking questions of other teachers, or, if feasible, by making a tour of a school building.

Classroom space. Teachers are happier if they have their own classrooms. Shared classrooms mean shared bulletin boards, storage space, desk. Chalkboards may not be adequate for two teachers; therefore, everything must be removed before another teacher comes in.

Teaching assignment. One of the most important things to investigate concerns the teaching assignment. Is the assignment in the area of major or minor preparation? Teaching in peripheral areas in the first year of teaching can be difficult. These assignments always mean more preparation.

Extraclass load. The extraclass load can make the difference between a pleasant assignment and a vexing, time-consuming one. The teacher can expect to participate in extraclass activities, but he must guard against an overload.

Probationary conditions. In practically all instances beginning teachers, by statute or board regulation, serve a probationary period. To many teachers this probationary period, usually three years, is a difficult one. Probationary teachers may be moved about from building to building, subject assignments switched, and other conditions changed according to administrative desire. Some indication of the seriousness of this condition in some school systems is the fact that this item was listed as a grievance in some of the recent teacher strikes.

The principal. It is often possible to find out a few significant things about the principal. The important matters concern philosophy, staff morale, support in crises, status, and similar matters.

No beginning teacher should feel that he must investigate every detail before he accepts a new position, but a few inquiries about basic matters may save misunderstandings and regrets.

LEAVE OF ABSENCE   Although nearly half the states and almost every major school system make some mention of leaves of absence for teachers, there is no uniformity. Where leaves are granted without loss of pay, the time may vary from a day or two to a week or two. In some districts unused sick leave may be cumulated for as much as twenty or twenty-five days. Leaves of absence for sickness, death in the family, and maternity are of major importance. Safeguards in the area of illness, for example, are as important a consideration as retirement, and are a major factor in teacher welfare.

RETIREMENT AND PENSION ALLOWANCES   Some kind of retirement laws, in effect in every state, are being improved all the time. At one time teachers had one of the best retirement outlooks of all the professions. Today, the Federal Social Security Act has made liberal retirement allowance available to thousands of workers. Several states have integrated their state plans for retirement of teachers with those of the federal system.

Retirement is usually permissible at 60 or 62 years of age; compulsory at 65 or 70. The allowance that goes with retirement is based upon earnings and length of service. Most retirement plans are contributory. The teacher contributes a percentage of his salary, and the state or district contributes a sum based on the salary or the teacher's contribution. This is also the basis of social security.

One of the problems at present is the matter of reciprocity between states. Teachers frequently move to other states. Their retirement accounts should go with them.

EFFECTIVE APPLICATIONS

Seeking a job should follow accepted procedures for best results. The following paragraphs outline the steps that are likely to produce the most satisfactory results.

THE JOB OUTLOOK　With a long preparation nearly completed, the prospective teacher looks for a job. The labor market goes in cycles. Studies made by the NEA show that the market is reasonably good viewed from the standpoint of teacher placement. Supply is likely to be below the demand for some years to come. The National Commission on Teacher Education and Professional Standards of the National Education Association has made recommendations in connection with identification, admission, and retention of teachers, which are the first steps in successful job placement. The commission recommended "that the selective process at least be based on evaluation of emotional maturity, moral and ethical fitness, health, demonstrated ability to work with children and youth, academic aptitude and intelligence, academic achievement, demonstrated competence in speech and basic skills, and professional interest and motivation" (10:203).

For teachers with qualifications like these, placement is practically assured. Teachers of this type are readily in demand.

COLLEGE AND UNIVERSITY PLACEMENT SERVICES　More and more employing officials are seeking candidates for their positions rather than waiting for candidates to come to them. It is natural for them to turn first to the college and university placement offices. Practically all colleges have placement bureaus whose officers are eager to see their graduates successfully placed.

Chief recruitment methods used at this time are:

1. Getting in touch with placement bureaus of colleges and universities, commercial teachers' agencies, state departments of education, state teachers associations, and state employment services.
2. Selecting teachers from applications sent in voluntarily by candidates.
3. Making inquiries at conferences, conventions, and similar gatherings.
4. Making written inquiries of other school systems or officials.
5. Mounting recruitment campaigns by a traveling school official.
6. Advertising and publishing lists of vacant positions.

Here it should be mentioned that there is a growing trend toward direct recruitment by school officials on college campuses. The superintendent, the director of personnel, or a similar official visits a number of college campuses each spring expressly seeking the teachers needed by his school district. Such visits may be to colleges and universities in a local area or even to campuses in other states.

Placement offices compile recommendations, furnish personal data forms, and obtain transcripts of high school and college courses. Students planning to teach should get in touch with the local placement office long before they complete their program. Placement opportunities in various subject areas, subject combinations most sought as reflected by the records of the placement office, and other facts will be available to those making inquiry. Placement offices not only assist directly in job placement but also help protect students from making unwise choices.

Applicants should fill out placement office blanks with the utmost care and neatness. These forms will be examined by prospective employers. It is also necessary to file photographs made expressly for placement purposes. Good photographs are a solid investment. For the photograph, the person should dress neatly and conservatively. Dark clothing provides contrast and usually photographs best. Good grooming is imperative.

Students completing their education program should file placement papers even though they do not desire immediate placement. Military service, graduate study, marriage, and other conditions may delay placement, but nothing is lost by filing papers.

In connection with filling out application or placement office forms, the prospective teacher should carefully consider the matter of recommendations. The best recommendations can be made by persons who know the candidate's professional ability. Employers give greatest consideration to recommendations written by college supervisors of student teaching, supervising or critic teachers, principals, and other schoolteachers. Professors of one's major and minor subject areas are also valuable references. At times a character reference is in order. No person's name should ever be used as a reference until permission has been obtained to use it.

Placement offices assemble all the data about a candidate, including recommendations, and on request send the file to prospective employers. Placement credentials and recommendations are confidential and are not available to the candidate.

STATE TEACHERS' ASSOCIATIONS   Most state teachers' associations maintain a placement service for their members. Membership in the association is required of those who wish its help. The placement bureaus of state teachers' associations are highly reputable and perform a valuable service. They are especially valuable for the person seeking employment in a section of the state not reached by the local college placement office.

COMMERCIAL PLACEMENT AGENCIES   Private agencies also assist in the placement of teachers. They are particularly helpful during times of teacher oversupply, and they cover wide geographical areas. Some of them are national in scope. Thus, a prospective teacher can make contacts well beyond the areas covered by most college and university placement offices. Most commercial agencies are reliable. Their fees range from 5 to

10 percent of the first year's salary, a condition that may place a heavy financial drain on earnings during the first year.

SEEKING A POSITION INDEPENDENTLY   Candidates may wish to canvass likened to a barnstorming adventure, and, although it may be profitable, it can also be frustrating and expensive both in time and in money. Barnstorming is like fishing in unknown waters: there are possibilities of a catch, but generally the results are poor.

Teachers should always be on the lookout for positions if they are in the field independently in an attempt to locate a position. This may be the market for a first position, or a change of position. The placement agencies are helpful, but efforts in one's own behalf are in order. Inquiry among friends and acquaintances may furnish clues to openings.

LETTERS OF APPLICATION   Employing officials, consciously or unconsciously, evaluate candidates by their letters of application and by the manner in which application blanks are filled out. Three types of letters may be used in applying for a position: letters of inquiry, letters of application, and follow-up letters.

Although it is not ethical to apply for positions that are not known to exist, it is ethical to write a *letter of inquiry*. There are at least two occasions on which such a letter is in order. First, the candidate may desire to teach in a state or an area of his own state not served by his college placement office. Second, he may have heard rumors of a vacancy in a certain district.

A letter of inquiry should be carefully written and should be predicated upon a sincere desire to learn about a vacancy in a given district. Such letters should be accompanied by a stamped self-addressed envelope, and should be framed in such a way that a reply can be quickly and easily made.

When it is known that a vacancy exists, the candidate should write a *letter of application*. The letter may contain complete information about the candidate, or the information may be set forth in a résumé accompanied by a covering letter. Current practice tends to favor the second type.

Letters of application are usually necessary even though the college placement office has forwarded the candidate's credentials. The candidate should state in the first paragraph of his letter how he learned of the vacancy. This should be specific, not "I have learned of a vacancy in your school." If the candidate has any unusual or special reason for desiring this position, he should state it in as straightforward a manner as possible. He does not beg for the job; he offers his services.

Needless to say, letters of application should be meticulously prepared. Mistakes in grammar, spelling, and composition may cause the letter to be rejected with only passing consideration. Most school officials prefer typed letters, especially for high school positions. Good-quality paper, clean typewriter keys, and a fresh typewriter ribbon will help give a professional look to a letter of application.

Letters of application should supply the usual personal information. Major emphasis should be placed on the educational background in high school and college. The employing official wishes to know about majors and minors, degrees, honors received, teaching credential held, and other educational experience. He is also much interested in any teaching experience the candidate has had. Experience should be considered broadly, and should include paid teaching, student teaching, work experience, and volunteer experience with organizations such as the Red Cross and the Scouts. Hobbies and extracurricular interests should be included.

The information in the letter of application must be brief and concise; yet the candidate must make a favorable impression if he desires the job. Form letters are usually unsatisfactory; under no circumstances should mimeographed résumés or letters be used. This letter, like the letter of inquiry, requires a self-addressed stamped envelope.

It is customary not to mention salary in these letters. Little is to be gained by a mention of salary since public schedules govern compensation in most school districts.

Whether one should mention church or other affiliations is up to each individual. In most states, employers and placement officials are prevented by law from making inquiry into such affiliations. If the candidate has reason to believe that his affiliations will be received favorably, he is privileged to volunteer the information.

Brief, courteous, *follow-up letters* are in order after an interview. They do not reiterate qualifications; they may remind the official of some salient point in the application. The follow-up letter gives the candidate an opportunity to thank the hiring official for his interview. Most of all, the letter serves as a dignified reminder.

THE PERSONAL INTERVIEW   The importance of the first personal contact with a prospective employer cannot be overestimated. First impressions are lasting impressions. The letter of application, the personal data sheet, the photograph, and the letters of recommendation have been carefully examined and analyzed by the prospective employer. The administrator now wishes to talk to the candidate personally. An interview will give him a chance to make up his mind about how well the candidate will fit in with the rest of the faculty. It also gives him an opportunity to appraise such matters as the candidate's interest in teaching, his community interests, and some of his theories concerning the growth and development of boys and girls.

Before the interview, it is well to obtain as much information about the position as possible. If a job is offered and accepted, this community will be home. Caution, however, is in order because undue inquisitiveness and excessive prying are worse than no interest at all. One should use good judgment in seeking information.

Special care should be given to personal appearance. Extremes in dress and styles should naturally be avoided; the same is true of cosmetics and jewelry.

During the interview the ability to talk to the school administrator in professional language in a mature manner is of great importance. There will rarely be any questions of competence, unless the candidate's qualifications are unsuitable for the position. The administrator will naturally assume that the college has taken care of the matter of subject competence. There will be more questions about classroom control, the likelihood of remaining in teaching as a career, why the individual selected teaching as a vocation, and his general outlook on life. Frequently questions about extracurricular activities and guidance are discussed.

The interview helps the prospective employer to make up his mind about the candidate's general enthusiasm concerning teaching. He senses many things even in a short interview. He observes courtesy, introversion or extroversion, promptness, boastfulness, and general ability to communicate ideas.

Employing officials also learn a great deal from the questions a candidate asks. Were the questions mature and professional? Did they reflect a rich cultural background? Interviews are two-way streets. Both candidate and employer should come away from the interview with some positive opinions.

The candidate should sense the proper time for ending the interview. Nothing is gained, often something is lost, by attempting to prolong an interview after it has accomplished its purpose. A question as to when a decision will be reached is perfectly in order. And common courtesy requires the candidate to thank his interviewer for the time he has given.

THE ETHICS OF PLACEMENT

Principle four of the code of ethics of the National Education Association specifically makes recommendations concerning placement and contract. This section of the code resulted from the fact that in the past some of the interpersonal relationships of teachers, job seekers in this instance, have not been entirely satisfactory.

Candidates for teaching positions should not make application for positions that do not exist. Inquiry will determine whether a certain vacancy exists; if it does, an application is in order. In this same connection, it is considered bad taste, if not unethical, to make wholesale applications for positions. When positions are scarce, candidates are likely to feel that many applications should be circulated at one time. School superintendents have let it be known that they have had literally hundreds of applications for a single position. The wasted effort and the disappointments involved in such a situation are unfortunate. Today, however, this super-fluity of candidates rarely exists.

If a candidate has been offered two or more positions, he must not play one position against the other in the hope of gaining an unusual financial advantage. Harmful effects are almost sure to follow. They may be in the form of ill will either toward the candidate or toward the college from which he is graduating. The fortunate person with two good offers considers them carefully and makes a decision.

One of the most unethical of practices is to underbid another applicant for a position. Abuses of this sort are offset by the fact that most school districts have open salary schedules. This prevents unsavory bargaining.

When a candidate has accepted a position, he should notify all other employing officials who have him under consideration. Also, the college placement officer should be informed. This will enable the placement office to recommend another candidate for the vacancies.

It is unethical to break a contract willfully. If another position involving an unusual opportunity presents itself, the teacher should present the matter to the employing official and request mutual abrogation of the contract.

Positions involved in a school controversy should be handled with delicacy. It is better to wait until the controversy is cleared before placing an application.

LEGAL RIGHTS AND RESPONSIBILITIES OF TEACHERS

Beginning teachers are seldom adequately informed concerning their legal rights and responsibilities. As a result, some through inappropriate action or inaction unknowingly expose themselves to loss of employment or to a suit for damages. The following brief introduction to the essentials of school law will acquaint the beginning teacher with selected legal aspects of employment, dismissal, and liability. Additional topics of law are treated in books listed in this chapter's recommended readings.

LEGAL ASPECTS OF TEACHING CONTRACTS

All certificated teachers have the right of contract. That is, when certificated, they are qualified to enter into a contractual relationship with a board of education. Teachers should be aware that in most school districts the school board is the only body legally authorized to contract for teaching services. Agreements, verbal or written, made by a super-intendent of schools or a member of his staff usually are not legally valid until officially approved by the board. A decision of the Supreme Court of Colorado illustrates this point: "Although it is common practice for superintendents of schools to select and 'employ' teachers, they may not actually enter into formal contract with a teacher in the absence of express legislative authorization to do so." [15]

A contract, once legally signed, assures the teacher of employment and compensation for the length of the contract or for the length of time that the teacher is able to perform the contracted duties. On the other hand, the contract also legally binds the teacher to perform the duties required by the board for the life of the contract. Although teachers customarily are granted release from contracts when they resign prior to a date that permits the board to find a satisfactory replacement, contracts are legally binding agreements. In some states teachers are subject to fines for breaking contracts and in others they can be penalized by loss of their teaching certification. In addition, professional ethics support the sanctity of contracts. Teachers should, therefore, sign only those contracts they intend to fulfill. Evidence of the widespread lack of understanding of teaching contracts is the fact that nearly one third of court litigation involving teachers is on the problem of contracts.

TYPES OF CONTRACTS   The specific requirements of teaching contracts differ from state to state and sometimes from district to district within a state. Nevertheless, most contracts are of two general types: annual and continuing. The life of an annual contract is only one year. At the end of that time, either the board or the teacher may refuse to renew the contract without being bound to give a statement of reasons or to provide a hearing. Continuing contracts, on the other hand, are automatically renewed each year provided that neither the board nor the teacher prior to a set date gives notice of intent to terminate the agreement.

In addition to the two basic types of contracts, many states have tenure laws which provide that after a specified number of years of service, usually three or four, the teacher under contract achieves tenure. In some states tenured status merely signifies the existence of a continuing contract but in other states the board of education can legally terminate the contract of a tenured teacher only for specified reasons subject to official hearings and court review. The latter condition provides the greatest job security to teachers and also gives the students and the community a more stable and professional teaching force.

It should be noted that tenure laws frequently protect teachers from "unjust demotion or reduction in salary as well as dismissal. They do not, however, interfere with the school board's right to transfer teachers, since tenure does not guarantee continuance in the same position." [16]

---

[15] *The National School Law Reporter*, R. R. Hamilton, ed., 18, no. 12 (August 1, 1968), 1. Reprinted by permission of the publisher, Croft Educational Services, New London, Conn.

[16] Madeline K. Remmlein, *School Law*, 2d ed. Danville, Ill.: The Interstate Printers & Publishers, Inc., 1962, p. 29.

A court case in Ohio illustrates this principle. A teacher had been a school counselor for a number of years prior to 1966, when she was reassigned to a straight teaching position. She petitioned the courts for reinstatement in her former position but the Court of Appeals ruled that a teacher does not acquire a vested right to perform specific duties.[17] In a similar case, the court ruled that a "tenured teacher may be transferred to another position but his salary cannot be reduced thereby unless such reduction is part of a broad-based plan." [18]

A 1967 decision of a district Court of Appeals in California indicates that transfer of tenured teachers must be based on justifiable reasons. In that case a teacher had been reassigned to a less desirable position because he insisted upon wearing a beard. The court upheld his petition to be restored to his original job.[19]

LOYALTY OATH REQUIREMENTS Beginning teachers should know that the majority of states require the signing of a loyalty oath as a prerequisite of certification or employment as a teacher. In addition to promising support of the state and national constitutions, these oaths in some states require teachers to swear to teach patriotism and not to advocate overthrow of the United States government by violent methods. Objectors to loyalty oaths—and there have been many—do not claim that disloyal persons should be permitted to teach, but allege violation of certain amendments to the Constitution. The courts in general have supported the legality of the oaths although decisions from state to state have differed. For example, in 1967, the United States District Court in New York upheld the constitutionality of the oath required in that state, but in the same year the teacher loyalty oath in Oregon was declared unconstitutional.

In general, recent decisions seem to indicate that

1. The courts will refuse to countenance guilt by association.
2. The courts will hold invalid those loyalty oaths that penalize teachers for innocent affiliation with organizations listed as subversive.
3. The courts will uphold those loyalty oaths that penalize teachers knowingly affiliated with such organizations.[20]

[17] *The National School Law Reporter*, R. R. Hamilton, ed., 18, no. 8, June 15, 1968. Reprinted by permission of the publisher, Croft Educational Services, New London, Conn.

[18] *The National School Law Reporter*, R. R. Hamilton, ed., 17, no. 14 (September 15, 1967), 3. Reprinted by permission of the publisher, Croft Educational Services, New London, Conn.

[19] *The National School Law Reporter*, R. R. Hamilton, ed., 17, no. 21 (January 1, 1968), 3. Reprinted by permission of the publisher, Croft Educational Services, New London, Conn.

[20] Robert L. Drury and Kenneth C. Ray, *Essentials of School Law*. New York: Appleton-Century-Crofts, Inc., Division of Meredith Corporation, 1967, p. 151.

LEGAL BASES FOR DISMISSAL OF TEACHERS

The word "dismissal" means board action that terminates a teaching contract before the contracted date of expiration. "Incompetence," "neglect of duty," "immorality," "unprofessional conduct," and "other good and just causes" are frequently found among the statutory grounds for dismissal.

Legal interpretations of incompetence have included inability to discipline students, lack of knowledge of subject matter, failure to cooperate with teaching colleagues, as well as physical inability to perform the duties regularly required by the teaching position. When a board of education charges a certificated teacher with incompetence as a basis for dismissal, the teacher has the right to a hearing. Should the case be taken to court, the burden of proof of incompetency falls upon the board. The fact of certification is usually considered basic evidence of competency before the law. Courts have held that one or two instances of deficiency are not sufficient grounds for dismissal. The law requires only that the teacher reveal average competency, not that possessed by those most proficient in the profession.

Neglect of duty at times has included excessive tardiness, absence from duty, inadequate preparation, and various other acts, both willful and unintentional, that result in a teacher's inferior performance or failure to perform assigned duties. Under the charge of "neglect of duty," courts have upheld boards of education that dismissed teachers who had chronic illnesses that frequently prevented them from teaching. In their interpretation of this aspect of neglect, courts have been somewhat inconsistent, but their rulings seem to have been based on their judgment of the extent to which the school district was deprived of contracted services and not the extent to which the teacher willfully failed to provide those services.

The interpretation of immorality and unprofessional conduct as bases for legal dismissal changes as the mores of the community and the profession change. One hundred years ago, some school boards prohibited teachers from loitering in barber shops, and it is quite possible that a woman teacher dressed in the skirt style acceptable in the late 1960s would have been dismissed if she had been seen in public in that style in the 1950s. Perhaps because communities tend to expect teachers to set good examples for their children, courts seem to be more strict in their judgment of teachers than they are in their judgment of the general public. For example, a teacher in 1966 was legally dismissed in California for the charge of living with a woman to whom he was not legally married. The teacher, a widower of a few months, had traveled to Mexico with one of his former students who obtained a divorce in that country and married him there. The couple was aware that the Mexican divorce was not accepted as legal in California. Thus, behavior that is not strictly illegal but deviates from the mores of a community has been upheld as a legal basis for dismissal.[21]

In another case the Supreme Court of Wyoming upheld the dismissal of a teacher who had been charged with drinking alcoholic beverages at the school and offering them to students. The court said, "Even charges of or reputation for immorality, although not supported by full proof, might in some cases be sufficient ground for removal. Not merely good character but good reputation is essential." [22]

A further example of unprofessional conduct was ruled upon by the Supreme Court of Wisconsin in 1961. The court concluded that a teacher could be discharged for discussion of sex matters in class in a manner violating the contemporary standards of propriety. The testimony brought out that the teacher in his speech class had spent several hours discussing such topics as houses of prostitution, including their price schedules, and had given each member of his class, all males ranging in age from 17 to 19 years, his estimate of whether or not the student would be admitted to a house. In addition, he was shown to have discussed premarital sexual relations in such a way as to give the impression that he favored the practice.

The majority opinion of the court said that the topics of themselves were not unprofessional, only the manner in which they were handled. A strongly worded minority report of the court maintained that sex education should be taught only in specific classes under the direction of teachers adequately prepared to handle the subject.[23]

The catchall expression "other good and just causes" for dismissal has been used in the absence of more specific laws to legally support board action to dismiss teachers who join subversive organizations, refuse to testify before an official investigative body, show insubordination to school officials, fail to take or pass physical examinations, and the like. A related example is the case of the teacher in Illinois who was dismissed for publishing statements judged to be misleading and detrimental to the schools. He gave the newspapers a number of inaccurate statements including his allegation that the school board had spent $200,000 on varsity sports while the needs of teachers were neglected.[24]

From the foregoing it is evident that the person who signs a contract to teach assumes a position of responsibility in his community and at the

[21] *The National School Law Reporter,* R. R. Hamilton, ed., 17, no. 15, October 1, 1967. Reprinted by permission of the publisher, Croft Educational Services, New London, Conn.
[22] Chester Nolte and John Phillip Linn, *School Law For Teachers.* Danville, Ill.: The Interstate Printers & Publishers, Inc., 1963, p. 281.
[23] *Hamilton School Law Service,* 4 (1965), 6163.5–2.
[24] *The National School Law Reporter,* R. R. Hamilton, ed., 17, no. 20, December 15, 1967. Reprinted by permission of the publisher, Croft Educational Services, New London, Conn.

same time gives up his "right" to act irresponsibly. Court decisions have also limited the power of boards of education to act according to whim or with prejudice. Illustrative of this point are the actions of the Supreme Court of New York, which ruled that in New York State a teacher may not be "denied certification to teach merely because she is overweight"; the ruling of the Supreme Court of Wisconsin which held that a teacher could not be dismissed if "one of the reasons was that he was active in the teachers' union"; and the action of the Colorado Supreme Court which ruled that a teacher could not be discharged for using corporal punishment if the board had not officially adopted a policy forbidding that punishment.[25]

The Court of Appeal of California stated,

A governmental agency seeking to impose restrictions on the exercise of an individual's constitutional right must demonstrate that (1) the government's restraint rationally relates to the enhancement of the public service; (2) the benefits that the public gains by the restraint outweigh the resulting impairment of the constitutional right; and (3) no alternatives less subversive of the constitutional right are available.[26]

THE LIABILITY OF TEACHERS

In addition to being responsible for handling specific instructional duties in fulfillment of their contracts, teachers are also responsible for supervisory duties related to the education, morals, health, and safety of students. In most states teachers stand *in loco parentis* to students while the students are at school or engaged in school-directed activities. In that role teachers are expected to act more prudently than average parents because teachers are professionally trained individuals. To be specific, teachers are expected to be sufficiently alert to foresee and, if possible, forestall potentially dangerous conditions and situations. Teachers may be judged legally liable if a student is injured in a situation that would have been avoided or corrected by a teacher of average knowledge and foresight.

TEACHERS CAN BE SUED   School districts as agencies of the state cannot be sued for damages unless the state legislature passes a law that permits such action; however, teachers are subject to suit and, if judged negligent, must pay the assessed damages unless they are teaching in one of the relatively few states that permit school districts to assume the liability of their employees.

[25] *The National School Law Reporter*, R. R. Hamilton, ed., 18, no. 9, July 1, 1968; 18, no. 2, March 15, 1968; 18, no. 9, July 1, 1968. Reprinted by permission of the publisher, Croft Educational Services, New London, Conn.
[26] Research Division, NEA, "Teacher's Day in Court: Review of 1966," *Research Report*, 1967–R-6, p. 1.

There are a number of school situations and activities in which problems of liability are most likely to arise. Some of these will be discussed in the following paragraphs.

LIABILITY DANGERS IN DISCIPLINE As "substitute parents" teachers may legally discipline students and, unless specifically prohibited by state law or by school board regulations, may, without fear of liability, apply corporal punishment that is reasonable, causes no permanent injury, and is not administered in anger. Nevertheless, much litigation arises over parents' objection to teachers' use of corporal punishment. A fairly typical case was taken to the Louisiana Court of Appeals. Testimony in the case revealed that a 230-pound male teacher lifted a disobedient 110-pound boy, shook him in anger, and dropped him. In the fall an arm of the boy was broken. The court ruled that "the teacher's actions were clearly in excess of the physical force necessary to either discipline the pupil or to protect himself." [27] The board and the teacher were held liable for excessive punishment of the pupil.

Even though in some school districts, moderate physical force may be applied legally to students in need of discipline, the authors of this text strongly recommend that beginning teachers refrain from the use of physical force in any manner.

LIABILITY DANGERS IN SPECIAL COURSES AND ACTIVITIES Students enrolled in science laboratories, industrial arts, physical education, and interscholastic athletics are exposed to an unusual number of opportunities for accidents. To reduce the likelihood of accidents and to avoid suits for damage, teachers of science laboratories should:

1. Make certain that the pupils know and understand beforehand the nature of the experiment to be performed and the dangers that may arise if proper procedures are not followed.
2. Give careful and adequate instruction on the use of the equipment and materials available for experiments.
3. Maintain proper supervision of the classroom tests and experiments.
4. See that chemicals and other substances used in the laboratory are properly packaged, labeled, and stored.
5. Keep potentially dangerous chemicals under lock and key.
6. Control access to the supply room so that pupils cannot take chemicals for private use without permission.[28]

Accidents in industrial arts classrooms and laboratories can be reduced and the likelihood of suit for negligence can be avoided if the teacher:

[27] *The National School Reporter*, R. R. Hamilton, ed., 17, no. 14, September 15, 1967. Reprinted by permission of the publisher, Croft Educational Services, New London, Conn.
[28] Research Division, NEA, *Who Is Liable for Pupil Injuries?* Washington, D.C.: National Commission on Safety Education, February 1963, p. 55.

1. Reports knowledge of hazardous conditions and defects relating to the shop, the machinery, and equipment to the proper school authorities.
2. Regularly inspects machinery, equipment, and environmental factors for safety.
3. Posts in his shop conspicuous notices of regulations, possible hazards, safeguards, and precautions.
4. Makes certain that appropriate safety devices and guards are available and used by students.
5. Makes sure that students know and understand pertinent safe practices relating to the activities in which they are engaged.
6. Requires students to wear appropriate personal protective equipment, such as goggles, aprons, helmets, and gloves, during hazardous activities.
7. Adequately instructs and demonstrates the use of power tools or other hazardous equipment before initially permitting such use by a pupil; permits initial use only under direct supervision of the teacher.
8. Shuts off power tools if he must leave the shop.
9. Exercises continuous supervision to see that shop safety practices are observed.
10. Makes himself a model for pupils to follow by personally obeying all safety rules and practices.[29]

In physical education and athletics, the instructor should take extraordinary precautions to see that students are assigned to activities within their abilities, and when physical contact is contemplated, students should not be overmatched.

The courts in Washington State held a teacher liable for a student's injury incurred in a tumbling exercise in a physical education class. The court upheld the claim that the teacher should have known that the student was unable to perform the exercise safely.[30]

In a similar case in New York State, the Court of Appeals ruled negligent supervision in an injury case based on an incident in a physical education class in which, at the call of a number, two boys on opposite sides of the room ran out and kicked a ball. The boys were mismatched physically and injury resulted.[31]

Full instruction on proper and safe execution of skills, careful maintenance of equipment and grounds, and constant supervision are prerequisites to avoidance of injury as well as litigation. Should injury occur, medical treatment should be given only by a licensed doctor. Coaches and instructors invite liability suits when they give medical aid beyond their authority.

[29] Research Division, NEA, 1963, p. 53.
[30] Research Division, NEA, "The Teacher's Day in Court: Review of 1965," *Research Report*, 1966–R-8.
[31] *Hamilton School Law Service*, 4 (1965), 6163.5–2.

THE CHARACTERISTICS OF A PROFESSION

A profession is not easily defined except in a very narrow sense. The concept "teaching profession" is best generalized through its characteristics. It is a way of making a living, yet it is not a business: it has no profit motive. It is therefore a form of public service. Individuals who engage in teaching must acquire a large body of general and special knowledge along with specialized professional education. Teachers have been given great freedom to pursue their work with a minimum of outside interference. In the main, those individuals who qualify are accorded prestige and esteem, but they must constantly merit this esteem.

Another characteristic of a profession is *spirit*. It cannot be taught but it crystallizes through professional courses, observation of teachers at work, working with other professionals in workshops and on committees, and through the unpaid services that teachers render their organizations. In the past, too many teachers never seemed to acquire this spirit. Frequently teaching was just a job, but today the situation is different. Greater professional knowledge and maturity, together with a genuine desire to serve, have helped to weld a profession.

Throughout this text strong support has been given to the idea that teaching is a profession, and as such it faces up squarely to the criteria posed above. From the very beginning of his career a teacher should be a "professional teacher," one who thinks and acts in a professional manner. He possesses and exemplifies the characteristics already described. Although many of these characteristics continue to grow as long as one teaches, the teacher concept is present even in the student teacher.

Centuries ago Sir Francis Bacon wrote a phrase that every professional person should heed: "I hold every man a debtor to his profession." To teachers this phrase is particularly cogent. Teachers belong to a great profession they have made by their energies and actions; yet the profession is greater than the sum of its parts. Teachers can and should be proud of their profession.

Education as a profession exhibits all the characteristics of any profession. These characteristics, as indicated, are numerous, although they may change as the demands of society dictate. In summary, the principal characteristics of the profession include a broad general education plus specialized knowledge; respect for a generally accepted professional code of ethics; provision for some form of control over the membership; elevation of personal service above personal welfare; view of employment as a lifework; high standards of conduct; responsibility for the development of their clients (pupils); assumption of leadership in the community and in their professional organizations; and acceptance of the fact that much of their status is defined by specific law—national, state, and local.

Finally, the professional person has regard for his appearance, and has pride in his speech. The professional person is one who seeks to bring dignity and respect to the profession and feels a debt to it. The professional person is circumspect about his activities inside and outside the classroom, and is proud to say, "I am a teacher."

SELECTED READINGS

1. Betchkal, James, "NEA and Teachers Unions Bicker and Battle for Recognition," *Nation's Schools*, 74 (August 1964), 35–41.

2. Drury, Robert L., and Kenneth C. Ray, *Essentials of School Law*. New York: Appleton-Century-Crofts, Inc., Division of Meredith Corporation, 1967, pp. 40–76.

3. Elam, Stanley, "Who's Ahead and Why: The NEA–AFT Rivalry," *Phi Delta Kappan*, 46 (September 1964), 12–16.

4. Flowers, Anne, and Edward C. Bolmeier, *Law and Pupil Control*. Cincinnati: The W. H. Anderson Company, 1964, chaps. 1, 4, 6.

5. Hamilton, R. R., ed., *The National School Law Reporter*. (Issues published every two weeks.)

6. Haskew, Lawrence D., and Jonathan C. McLendon, *This Is Teaching*, 3d ed. Chicago: Scott, Foresman and Company, 1968.

7. Lieberman, Myron, "Teachers' Strikes: Acceptable Strategy?" *Phi Delta Kappan*, 46 (January 1965), 237–240.

8. Maskow, Michael H., "Recent Legislation Affecting Collective Negotiations for Teachers," *Phi Delta Kappan*, 47 (November 1965), 136–141.

9. NEA, National Commission on Safety Education, *Who Is Liable for Pupil Injuries?* Washington, D.C.: 1963, chaps. 1, 4, 5, 6.

10. *Phi Delta Kappan*, "The Politics of Education," Vol. 49, February 1968. The entire issue is devoted to this topic; numerous contributors. Also see the entire issue of June 1968.

11. Research Division, *Negotiation Research Digest*. Washington, D.C.: The Association. (Published ten times a year.)

12. Research Division, NEA, "Salary Schedules for Teachers, 1967–68," *Research Report*, 1967–R-16. (Published annually.)

13. Research Division, NEA, "Teacher Supply and Demand in Public Schools, 1966," *Research Report*, 1966–R-16. (Published annually.)

14. Research Division, NEA, "The Teacher's Day in Court." (Published annually.)

15. Stinnett, T. M., "Professional Negotiations, Collective Bargaining, Sanctions, and Strikes," *Bulletin of the National Association of Secondary School Principals*, 48 (April 1964), 93–105.

16. Stinnett, T. M., Jack H. Kleinman, and Martha L. Ware, *Professional Negotiations in Public Education*. New York: The Macmillan Company, 1966.

17. United States Department of Labor, *Occupational Outlook Handbook 1966–67*, Bulletin no. 1450. Washington, D.C.: The Department, 1967. (Revised every two years.)

18. Wilson, Thurlow R., "The Disruptive Student," *Youth Service News*, 19 (Winter 1967–1968), 8–13.

19. Woodring, Paul, "On the Causes of Teacher Discontent," *Saturday Review*, 50 (October 21, 1967), 6–62.

INDEX